OPERATIONS MANAGEMENT

DAVID BARNES

OPERATIONS MANAGEMENT

AN INTERNATIONAL PERSPECTIVE

THOMSON

Australia   Brazil   Canada   Mexico   Singapore   Spain   United Kingdom   United States

THOMSON

Operations Management: An international perspective
David Barnes

Publishing Director John Yates	**Publisher** Jennifer Pegg	**Development Editor** Alice Rodgers Rachel Sturgeon
Content Project Editor Leonora Dawson-Bowling	**Manufacturing Manager** Helen Mason	**Senior Marketing Manager** Angela Lewis
Typesetter ICC Macmillan Inc., India	**Production Controller** Maeve Healy	**Cover Design** Nick Welsh
Text Design Design Deluxe, Bath, UK	**Printer** G. Canale & C., Italy	

ISBN: 978–1–84480–534–1

British Library Cataloguing-in-Publication Data
A catalogue record for this book is available from the British Library

This book is dedicated to my father, Lawrence James Barnes (1927–2005). For him 'abroad' was always a far away country, full of 'foreigners' – people of whom we could know very little. As, in one sense, we are all foreigners, my aim in writing this book is, in some small way, to help us all know a little more about each other.

BRIEF CONTENTS

CONTENTS

PART TWO THE INTERNATIONALIZATION OF OPERATIONS MANAGEMENT 45

3 The internationalization processes: drivers, challenges and benefits 47

4 International operations strategies 74

PART THREE STRUCTURAL ISSUES 105

5 Facilities 107

6 Capacity 137

7 Process technology 163

8 The supply network 208

PART FOUR INFRASTRUCTURAL ISSUES 233

9 Planning and control 235

PART FIVE THE FUTURE OF OPERATIONS MANAGEMENT 429

15 Current trends and emerging issues 431

LIST OF FIGURES

LIST OF TABLES

ABOUT THE AUTHOR

DAVID BARNES is Senior Lecturer in Operations Management and Strategic Management at the School of Management, Royal Holloway, University of London, where he teaches on undergraduate programmes and the MBA in International Management. He has held lecturing posts with the Open University and Thames Valley University, and was a visiting Research Fellow at the University of Cambridge. He holds a BSc (Eng) degree from Imperial College London, an MBA from the Open University and a PhD from Staffordshire University.

Prior to his academic career he worked for over 15 years in the process plant contracting and building products industries, in engineering and line management positions for a number of organizations ranging from blue chip to small family owned businesses.

His research interests encompass the strategic management of operations, performance management and the impact of e-business on operations. He has written extensively in these fields, including over 50 journal articles, conference papers and chapters in books. He has written a number of teaching texts for the Open University and edited their reader, *Understanding Business Processes*.

ACKNOWLEDGEMENTS

There are many people that I should acknowledge and thank for their contributions to the production of this book.

First, my thanks to all those at Thomson Learning who contributed so much throughout the preparation and production of this book. My special thanks to Jennifer Pegg for persuading me that I could, and indeed, should write this book, to Rachel Sturgeon for helping and guiding me throughout the writing process and to Alice Rodgers for steering the book through production. I would also like to thank the reviewers for their comments and helpful suggestions.

My special thanks to the case writers, Marianna Sigala (who wrote no fewer than ten cases) and Riccardo Spinelli.

To the innumerable academic colleagues at various universities who provided me, often unknowingly, with many of the ideas, suggestions and inspirations, not to mention books and papers that helped shape this book.

To my employers, Royal Holloway, University of London, for affording me that most precious commodity, the time to write.

To those whose contributions to operations management have inspired me, especially Wickham Skinner, Bob Hayes and Nigel Slack.

Finally, my appreciation and thanks goes to my family; to James and Georgina, and especially my wife, Veronica, for their tolerance, help and support throughout the time it took to produce the book.

Publisher's Acknowledgements

The author and publisher would like to thank the following people for their help in reviewing the book

Andrew Lyons, *University of Liverpool*
Louis Brennan, *Trinity College*
Desmond Doran, *Kingston Business School*
Herbert Kotzab, *Copenhagen Business School*
Birger Rapp, *Linkoping Institute of Technology*
Marianna Sigala, *University of the Aegean*

For the contribution of case studies:

Marianna Sigala, *University of the Aegean*
Riccardo Spinelli, *University of Genoa*

For the reproduction of copyrighted material:

ALUMIL
Biz/ed
Elsevier
Fast Company
Gallup
ICFAI Center for Management Research
John Wiley & Sons Limited

McDonald's
South-Western
The Financial Times
Thomson Learning Asia
Toyota

For the reproduction of photographs:

A.P. Moller – Maersk
ALUMIL
B&B Italia
Baleno
Dell Inc.
Giordino
ICICI One Source
INCAT
Infosys
Jessops
Marks and Spencer PLC
The W. Deming Institute®
Toyota
TUI
Unilever
Wal-Mart
Wolseley

Every effort has been made to trace and acknowledge ownership of copyright. The publisher will be glad to hear from any copyright holders whom it has not been possible to contact.

FOREWORD

The world is changing to one in which goods, people and information all move across the world with greater speed and frequency than ever before. Organizations of all kinds now rarely conduct all aspects of their business within the confines of their own national borders. The forces of globalization are making business operations increasingly international rather than national in scope. Operations managers have to learn how to adapt to the requirements of managing across many different borders, time-zones, cultures and languages. These changes are reflected even within what some perceive to be the rarefied atmosphere of higher education. The students that I teach in London are as likely to come here from Beijing or Bangalore as Birmingham. The fact that I also teach students who reside in places as far away as Hong Kong studying for a University of London degree by distance learning further illustrates how industries of all kinds are touched by internationalization. Furthermore, the fact that I can support the learning of some of these students without ever physically meeting them, illustrates the power and impact of one of the drivers of globalization, namely the Internet.

I was therefore excited when I was asked to teach a course entitled 'International Operations Management' as an introductory course for students on my university's MBA and MSc degrees in international management. It seemed obvious to me that in such an increasing international world, operations management needed to be taught from an international perspective. However, when I came to look for a suitable textbook to support the course, I was disappointed. Whilst there are many fine English language textbooks for operations management, from the USA as well as the UK, if they consider international issues at all they do so in a limited and often a very peripheral fashion. It seemed to me that the teaching of operations management was failing to match the progress made by other business subjects in incorporating an international perspective into the teaching of the subject. What was required was a book that placed international issues at the heart of operations management, rather than treating them as a bolt-on extra. Expressions of my disappointment to various book publishers brought the obvious retort – why don't you write it yourself. This book represents my response to that challenge.

PREFACE

Operations management is concerned with those activities that produce the goods and/or deliver the services required by customers. These activities are at the core of any organization and typically involve the management of the vast majority of its assets, employees and expenditure. Operations management is often not as well recognized an area of study as the other functional disciplines of marketing, human resource management and finance and accounting. And yet, operations management is every bit as important as those other functions. No organization can hope to be successful unless its operations are well managed. Like the other business functions, operations management has developed as a distinct academic discipline.

The world in which operations management is practised is changing rapidly. The forces of globalization, underpinned by Internet-based technologies, the lowering of trade barriers and a reduction in transport costs, have prompted firms of all sizes to source their supplies, outsource their activities, set up production facilities and serve markets well away from their home countries. Most developed economies have seen a significant growth in their knowledge- and service-based industries as many basic manufacturing operations have moved to lower cost locations. Many back office service operations have also witnessed similar moves off-shore. Studying operations management now requires an international perspective.

The changes taking place present a significant challenge to those involved with the management of an organization's operations. They can represent major shifts in the strategic configuration of the resources and competences that underpin an organization's competitive capabilities. Once an organization engages in international activities, the role of its operations managers becomes increasingly important because the strategic significance of their decisions and actions multiplies. More and more organizations are faced with the challenge of how to manage a combination of supply and demand across many countries. The greater the number of countries that are involved, the more complex operations management decision-making becomes. The consequences will be felt not merely in the operations function but throughout the whole organization. These decisions usually involve significant sums of money and affect the competitive position of the organization for many years. By any definition these are truly strategic decisions.

The prime aim of the book is to provide an international perspective on the most important topics of operations management. It does this by:

- Explaining the importance of operations management to the success of an organization operating internationally.
- Identifying the challenges posed for the management of an organization's operations from operating internationally.
- Presenting conceptual frameworks for analyzing the strategic impact of key operations management decision areas in international operations.
- Exploring the likely challenges posed for international operations by potential future changes in the business environment.

The book will take a truly global perspective, illustrating its key points with examples from around the world. In particular it will acknowledge the growing importance of Asia beyond Japan and Korea, recognizing the role of China and India not only as producers of manufactured goods and providers of many service operations but also as important consumer markets.

In addition to an international perspective, the book also provides:

- A focus on the key concepts of operations management rather than emphasizing the many quantitative techniques associated with the subject. As such, the book takes an avowedly qualitative approach to the teaching of operations management.

- A balanced treatment of services and manufacturing operations. The book aims to be accessible and relevant to those familiar with services as well as those more used to manufacturing environments.

- A strategic context for the study of operations management. The book highlights the strategic consequences for the long term competitiveness of an organization of the many decisions and actions taken within the remit of operations management.

The international perspective adopted by the book provides an operations management text that is relevant to the needs of the twenty-first century. It is suitable for all introductory courses in operations management at both undergraduate and postgraduate level. Its strategic and conceptual perspective makes it particularly suitable for many MBA courses.

WALK THROUGH TOUR

Learning objectives appear at the start of every chapter to help you monitor your understanding and progress through the chapter. Each chapter also ends with a summary section that recaps the key content for revision purposes.

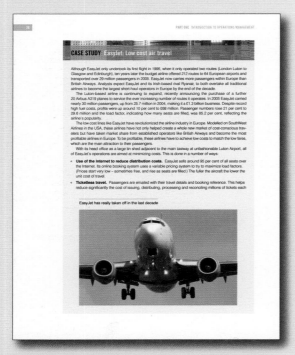

Case studies appear in every chapter to show how real organizations deal with operations management issues. Each case is accompanied by questions to help test your understanding of the issues (visit www.thomsonlearning.co.uk/barnes for suggested answers to questions).

Key terms are highlighted in colour throughout and explained in full in the margin. A full glossary of all key terms can be found at the end of the book.

When things go wrong case studies appear in every chapter and describe how operations management failures created major problems for real organizations. Each case is accompanied by questions to help test your understanding of the issues.

Summaries close each chapter. These comprehensive summaries provide a thorough re-cap of the key issues in each chapter, helping you to assess your understanding and revise key content.

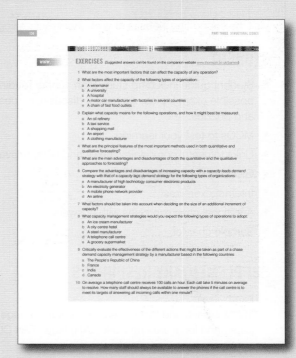

Exercises are provided at the end of each chapter to help reinforce and test your knowledge and understanding. Answers are provided for lecturers on the website.

Case exercises from real organizations are found at the end of every chapter. These longer length case studies provide an in-depth look at the issues dealt with in the chapter. Each case is accompanied by questions to help test your understanding.

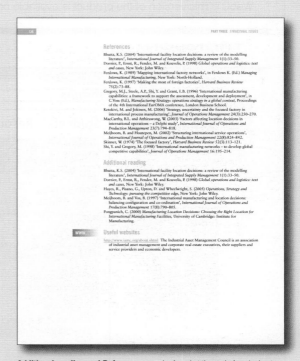

Additional reading and References can be found at the end of each chapter to allow you to explore the subject further, and act as a starting point for projects and assignments.

Useful websites are a good starting point to begin exploring operations management issues on the Internet.

About the website

Visit the supporting website at www.thomsonlearning.co.uk/barnes to find further teaching and learning material, including:

STUDENT

- Student guide including study plan, further reading, possible exam topics, exercises, discussion questions and puzzles.
- MCQs to test your learning.
- Links to useful companies, news and other relevant sites.
- Glossary explaining key terms.
- Internet exercises.
- Additional case exercises with answers.
- Sample chapter.

LECTURERS

- Instructor's manual including
  - answers to end of chapter exercises
  - case study teaching notes
  - additional case studies
  - discussion questions
  - sample course outline
  - book transition guide.
- PowerPoint lecture slides.

SUPPLEMENTARY RESOURCES

Examview®

This testbank and test generator provides a huge amount of different types of questions, allowing lecturers to create online, paper and local area network (LAN) tests. This CD-based product is available only from your Thomson sales representative.

VIRTUAL LEARNING ENVIRONMENT

All of the web material is available in a format that is compatible with virtual learning environments such as Blackboard and WebCT. This version of the product is available only from your Thomson sales representative.

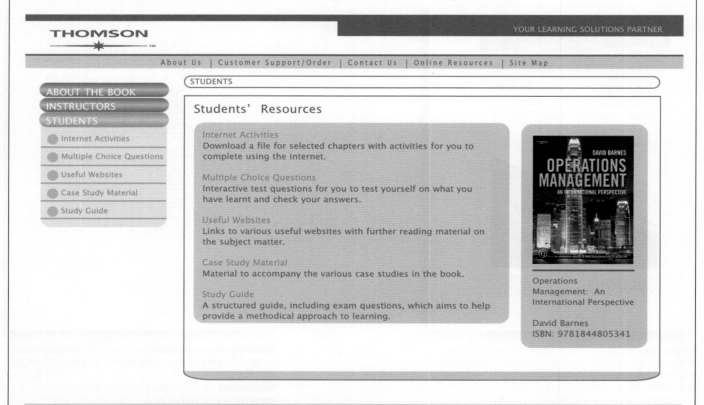

OPERATIONS MANAGEMENT

PART ONE

INTRODUCTION TO OPERATIONS MANAGEMENT

PART ONE

Part One introduces the academic discipline of operations management. Operations management is concerned with those activities that produce the goods and/or deliver the services required by customers. These activities are at the core of any organization and typically involve the management of the vast majority of its assets, employees and expenditure. A commonly held misconception is that operations management is only concerned with manufacturing activities. However, services are increasingly important and the contribution of services to most national economies far outstrips that of manufacturing. Similarly, the overwhelming majority of employment is provided by services industries. Although there are some important differences between manufacturing and service operations, the operations management curriculum contains areas of interest to both. Chapter 1 introduces some of the basic concepts of operations management. Another common misconception held about operations management is that it is only concerned with short-term, day-to-day, tactical issues. Chapter 2 seeks to correct this view by considering the strategic importance of operations. An organization's operations contain most of the key resources and competences that are likely to provide the distinctive capabilities on which its source of competitive advantage will depend. As such the myriad of decisions and actions taken within an organization's operations can have significant strategic consequences for long-term competitiveness. This chapter introduces frameworks that enable an organization's operations to be understood from a strategic perspective.

CHAPTER 1

OPERATIONS MANAGEMENT

INTRODUCTION

It would be disappointing but not surprising if you had not previously encountered the academic discipline known as operations management. Disappointing, because operations management is vitally important to the success of any organization. Unsurprising, because operations management is often not as well recognized as an academic discipline as the other functional areas of marketing, human resource management and finance and accounting. And yet, operations management is every bit as important as those other functions. The operations function is the 'doing' part of the organization. It is that part of the organization where the goods and services required by customers are produced. No organization can hope to be successful unless its operations are well managed. The importance of operations to an organization is emphasized by Hill (2005), who points out that it is the 'function responsible for 60–70 per cent of costs, assets and people'.

Operations management is important because of its impact on an organization's costs. No organization can be successful unless it is able to manage its operations efficiently, making best use of the resources at its disposal. A high level of efficiency helps ensure that the organization can achieve low operating costs. But achieving low costs is rarely enough to ensure success. Organizations must also ensure that their customers are satisfied with the goods and services they provide for them. Operations management is also important because of its impact on the quality, availability, timeliness and reliability of the goods and services produced by an organization. All customers judge the value of what they receive by some combination of those factors. No organization can be successful unless it is able to manage its operations effectively, ensuring that its customers receive what they consider to be a high level of value. To be successful all organizations must aim to manage their operations to achieve both a high level of efficiency and effectiveness. The activities of the operations function are central to achieving these aims. However, achieving efficiency and effectiveness simultaneously can often

operations management
This is concerned with the management of the resources and processes required by an organization to produce goods or services for customers.

operations function
That part of the organization that has the responsibility for operations management.

efficiency
A measure of the success of an operation in converting inputs to outputs.

effectiveness
A measure of the success of an operation in producing outputs that satisfy customers.

create conflict. That is what makes operations management such a challenging, as well as such an important, task in any organization. The case example 'Toyota: On target to become number one' demonstrates the vital role played by operations in the success of the Japanese motor car manufacturer.

CASE STUDY Toyota: On target to become number one

If it meets its sales targets of 9.06 million vehicles for 2006, Toyota will overtake General Motors (GM) to become the world's biggest motor car manufacturer. The American giant has been the top carmaker in the world for 74 years. The Japanese company moved into the number two spot back in 2003 when it overtook Ford. 2005 saw sales by both the US carmakers fall; GM by 10.2 per cent and Ford by 8.7 per cent.

By contrast, Toyota said its US sales increased by 8.2 per cent. Furthermore, in an industry in which most carmakers are struggling to turn a profit, Toyota is due to increase its profits to well over $10 billion for the year to March 2006. By contrast, GM and Ford's combined losses are likely to be around $10 billion for the same period. Both companies plan factory closures to stem their losses. Both have announced further price cuts to stimulate flagging sales. Nonetheless, many analysts believe it will be many years before either company returns to profit. In contrast, Toyota is expanding its manufacturing capacity both in established markets like the US and in the fast developing market of China. Toyota's technologically advanced and environmentally-friendly hybrid cars, that combine petrol and electric power to reduce fuel consumption, are enjoying strong demand. Its Lexus subsidiary is the best selling luxury brand in the US.

Although established before the Second World War, Toyota did not become a major car manufacturer until the 1950s. Over the next two decades, under the guidance of Taiichi Ohno, it developed its renowned

Toyota RAV4 Sports Concept

Issued 03/2006

'Toyota Production System' (TPS). The TPS is based on principles of the elimination of waste (*muda*), continuous improvement (*kaizen*), automation with a human face (*jidoka*) and the involvement of all employees. These manifest themselves in the practices of just-in-time, total quality management, team-working and cellular layouts. TPS also involves the closest collaboration with suppliers. It has enabled Toyota to achieve high volumes and high flexibility but with low levels of inventory and minimal defects. The application of these principles to its design operations also typically enables Toyota to get new products to market faster than its rivals, and with fewer design glitches.

The TPS has been extensively studied and copied by carmakers across the globe. It forms the basis of what is now widely regarded as manufacturing best practice, so-called world class manufacturing, for many products, not just motor cars. More recently, these ideas have been popularized under the banner of 'lean' production. Its principles have been successfully applied in many service environments.

The TPS has ensured that Toyota's factories consistently achieve higher levels of productivity and greater flexibility that produce cars with fewer defects than most rivals. Consequently, Toyota has more satisfied customers who are willing to buy their products without recourse to the kind of price discounting prevalent in the industry.

Questions (Suggested answers can be found on the companion website www.thomsonlearning.co.uk/barnes)

1 What aspects of Toyota's operations contribute to efficiency?

2 What aspects of Toyota's operations contribute to effectiveness?

WWW.

All organizations have operations functions, although many are given other names. These often reflect the specific activities that they carry out, for example, catering, distribution or nursing. There is a misconception that operations management is only concerned with manufacturing activities. Although many of the concepts on which the academic study of operations management is based have their origins in the manufacturing industries, many are equally applicable to services. Conversely, recent advances in the study of service operations have yielded valuable insights into the management of manufacturing operations. The distinction between manufacturing and services is in many respects artificial and increasingly irrelevant because even the most basic product will have some element of service accompanying it. Equally, most services have some tangible product as an integral part of what is delivered to the customer.

THE TRANSFORMATION MODEL

Any operation can be depicted as a **transformation process** which converts inputs of resources (e.g. people, equipment, materials, energy, information) to outputs of goods and services. Slack *et al.* (2004) usefully developed this model by distinguishing between *transformed* and *transforming* resources (see Figure 1.1).

Transformed resources are those resources that are themselves transformed to become part of the output of the operation. Typically these are materials and/or information and/or and customers.

Transforming resources are those that are necessary to carry out the transformation but do not themselves form part of the output. Transforming resources can be classified as:

- Facilities: These are the resources that are necessary to undertake the operation but are not used up in the operation. Typically these include the land, buildings, plant, equipment and vehicles used by the organization to perform the operation. These resources are usually intended to be used over several years. Consequently they are normally designated as fixed assets by

transformation process
The system by which inputs of resources (e.g. people, equipment, materials, energy and information) are converted into outputs of goods and services.

FIGURE 1.1 The input–output transformation model for operations

Inputs
Transformed resources:
- Materials
- Information
- Customers

Transforming resources:
- Facilities
- Consumables
- People

The transformation process

Outputs
- Goods
- Services

accountants and their value appears in the fixed assets column of the balance sheet.

- Consumables: These are the resources that are used up as part of operation. Examples include the energy necessary to power buildings, plant and machinery, and the materials necessary to maintain, repair and operate them (often referred to as MRO supplies).

- People: The human resources necessary to undertake the operation. These will usually include the staff of the organization. However, employees of other organizations might also be involved in the transformation process, for example those belonging to the suppliers or subcontractors of the organization undertaking the operation.

DIFFERENT TYPES OF OPERATIONS

Operations can be classified into three different types depending upon which type of resource is predominantly being transformed by the operation:

- Materials processing operations, in which materials are transformed either from one form to another, and/or from one place to another. Manufacturing operations in which raw materials and components are transformed into finished products fall into this category. Other material processing operations include mining, and the transport, storage and distribution of goods in warehousing and retailing operations.

A materials processing operation

An information processing operation

- Information processing operations, in which information is transformed, from one form to another and/or from one place to another. There are many examples of information processing including accountancy, banking, financial services, telecommunications, and research of all kinds. Nowadays it is difficult to think of information processing operations that do not involve the use of computers.

- Customer processing operations, in which the customer is transformed by the operation. There are many examples of this type of operation including hospitals, hairdressers, education, hotels, travel and entertainment.

A customer processing operation

Whilst one of these types of processing often predominates in any particular operation, many operations also typically involve two or even all three types. For example, a restaurant processes both materials (food) and customers; a book publisher processes both information (the text for the book) and materials (the paper, ink, etc.); an airline processes customers (passengers) and materials (their baggage).

SERVICE OPERATIONS

services
The intangible outputs from an operation.

Operations can be classified more simply in terms of their outputs, as either goods or services. The factors which distinguish them are:

- Tangibility – Goods are physical products which can be touched, seen, tasted, or smelled. As physical entities, goods can be stored and transported. The ownership of goods can be transferred from the supplier to the customer. Services on the other hand are intangible, and therefore unlikely to possess any of these properties.
- Simultaneity – Services are distinguishable from goods in that their production and consumption usually take place simultaneously. As such, it is usually not possible to store a service that has just been produced for consumption at some time in the future. Normally customers have to be present to receive the service when it is produced. On the other hand, goods can usually be stored ready for future consumption by a customer.
- Customer contact – Because of their intangibility and simultaneity, services normally require some degree of contact with the customer, although the degree of that contact can vary. Similarly, some services are much more labour intensive than others, and might involve the customer coming into contact with large numbers of employees of the service delivery organization.
- Quality – Because of the nature of the output of a service operation, it is much more difficult to define and measure the quality of a service. The quality of a product can be defined and measured in terms of its functionality (i.e. its fitness for the purpose for which it is intended). The quality of a service on the other hand, can often only be judged by its recipient. Service quality is dependent on the perception of a customer. Such perceptions may vary between one customer and another, and between the customer and the service deliverer. As such, service quality often depends upon the psychological state of a customer at the time of consumption. Indeed some services are intended to change a customer's psychological state.

It is possible to think of examples that equate to the extremes of pure goods (coal mining) and pure services (psychotherapy). However, a closer consideration of the outputs of most operations reveals that it is rare to find such extremes. Usually there are elements of service in most goods producing operations. For example, even extractors of commodity goods like coal or oil typically provide their customers with information about their chemical composition or offer technical advice on their use. Similarly, even producers of a highly customized service like management consultancy will usually produce some tangible output, such as a written report of some kind. It is usually more helpful to think of the outputs of operations as being located somewhere on a continuum between pure services and pure goods (see Figure 1.2).

As services have grown in importance in most of the world's major economies, service operations management has emerged as an increasingly important field of study.

Services normally account for the overwhelming majority of the value of a country's output, its gross domestic product (GDP). Although the USA remains the world's biggest manufacturer, its manufacturing output makes up only 13 per cent of its GDP (*The Economist* 1 October 2005). Services also provide most sources of employment (see Table 1.1).

gross domestic product (GDP)
A measure of the size of a country's economy. It is defined as the market value of all final goods and services produced within the country.

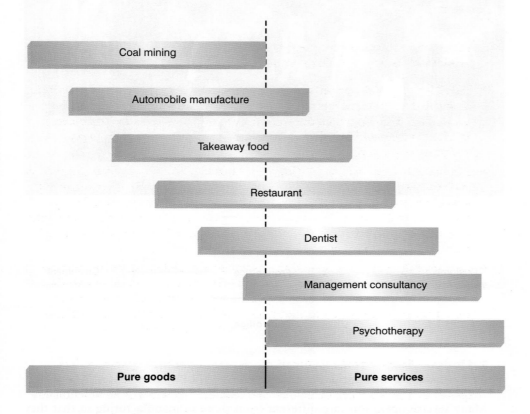

FIGURE 1.2 The goods–services continuum

	MANUFACTURING AS PERCENTAGE OF TOTAL EMPLOYMENT	
COUNTRY	1970	2005
Germany	40	22
Italy	28	22
Japan	27	18
France	28	16
UK	35	14
Canada	22	14
USA	25	10

SOURCE: *THE ECONOMIST* 1ST OCTOBER 2005

TABLE 1.1 Manufacturing as percentage of total employment in major economies

Unlike materials, customers do
mind being made to wait

(BY IAN MILES-FLASHPOINT PICTURES/ALAMY)

FIGURE 1.3 Front office/Back
office operations

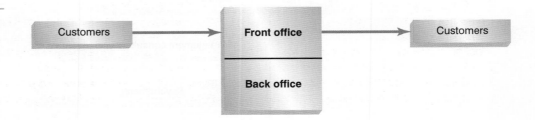

front office
The area of an operation in which contact
with customers normally takes place.

back office
The area of an operation in which there is
normally no contact with customers.

Many service operations are different from those in manufacturing in that they usually require the operation to have some degree of contact with the customer. Organizations that treat their customers in the same way that they treat the inanimate objects that are materials are neither likely to retain existing customers nor attract new ones.

The study of service operations has led to the development of some useful concepts in addition to those that have emerged from the study of manufacturing. One such concept is that of the difference between the front office and the back office. The area in which contact with customers occurs is termed the front office. This primarily involves customer processing operations. The area where there is normally no contact with customers is termed the back office. This may involve information and/or materials processing operations (see Figure 1.3).

The transforming resources required in the front office are likely to be significantly different from those needed in the back offices. In particular, operations in the front office need to revolve around the customer. The people that work in the front office are likely to require quite different skills from those in the back office. Front office staff need high levels of interpersonal skills if they are to interact successfully with customers. The physical resources used in the front office, buildings, machinery and equipment, may also need to be quite different from those in the back office. Indeed, the front and back offices may well be physically located in quite different places. However, the relationship and interaction between front and back office operations is often a key part of the management of operations.

WHEN THINGS GO WRONG   Hong Kong Disneyland: The not-so-grand opening

Disney's newest theme park, Hong Kong Disneyland, opened to its first paying guests on 12th September 2005. The $1.8 billion joint venture with the Hong Kong government was expecting to attract more than five-and-a-half million visitors in its first year. The park, Disney's second in Asia (the first is in Tokyo), is hoping to attract visitors from all over SE Asia, but is mainly targeting China's vast and increasingly wealthy population.

The park had already attracted criticism before its opening. Environmentalists had complained of damage to breeding grounds for fish and rare white dolphins. The company had already been forced to remove shark fin soup, a local delicacy, from its menus after campaigners condemned the dish as cruel and ecologically destructive. Animal welfare groups had also complained about the destruction of 40 dogs that were roaming the site. Human rights activists have also pointed to the employment conditions of workers in a Chinese firm supplying merchandise to the park, claiming that workers had to work 13-hour days in unsafe conditions for less than the minimum wage.

Once completed, a number of operations problems soon became apparent. The park had set its daily capacity limit at 30,000 visitors. However, it was clear that this was an overestimate, when 29,000 locals flocked to the theme park at a test day prior to the official opening. They found they had to queue for over 45 minutes at the 'fast' food outlets and over two hours for rides. The local media described the day as 'chaotic'. The park plans to extend opening times and increase discounts on ticket prices during weekdays.

On the grand opening day itself, some 16,000 entered the gates; about a third from mainland China. The presence of the mainlanders upset some locals. Complaints included queue-jumping, smoking in restaurants and other non-smoking areas, children urinating in a flower bed, people being barefoot and putting their feet on chairs and spitting in public. Many Hongkongers blamed Disney for allowing such behaviour in the park. However, there were reports of some staff being unhelpful or even rude to visitors.

Some mainland Chinese have complained about the lack of the use of Mandarin, the principle language in China in Hong Kong Disneyland. Although both English and Chinese are its official languages, Cantonese

Not everyone enjoyed their first visit to Hong Kong Disneyland

predominates as the spoken Chinese language in the park. (Cantonese is the language of southern China including Hong Kong.) None of the characters in any of the three live shows speaks Mandarin and the props and voice-overs on all but one of the rides are in English. Mandarin is used only by the Jungle Cruise tour guides and for safety announcements on all rides. While the majority of the 500 Disney performers are from Hong Kong, eight nationalities are represented in its performing ranks, including mainland Chinese.

In the days after the opening, there have been a number of disruptions to the park's rides. In the first month, there were 50 reports of rides being brought to a halt due to technical reasons which triggered the safety protection system. No-one was seriously injured but there were six reports of visitors complaining of feeling sick or sustaining minor injuries caused by the sudden suspension of the rides.

Local labour leaders have reported signs of worker disquiet at the park. They cited 40 complaints from Disneyland staff, who said they were forced to work shifts of between 10 and 13 hours a day. This was compounded by long travel times to and from the park. Another problem involved a supposedly chaotic shift system the management had designed. Some staff also complained about disciplinary procedures and an alleged lack of communication with Hong Kong Disneyland's local management. The staff, some of whom trained with Disney in the United States, said the Hong Kong management does not have the same level of industrial relations awareness and conflict resolution skills as their US counterparts.

Some Disney enthusiasts have complained that Hong Kong Disneyland has opened with fewer attractions than its other theme parks. Hong Kong has 22 major attractions, compared to 44 in Paris, 45 in Tokyo and Florida, and 65 in California. Despite its lower priced entry ticket, Hong Kong works out as the highest cost per ride among all Disney theme parks.

Disney does not normally release visitor figures for their parks. However to counter local media reports of lower than expected numbers, a company press release on 24th November 2005 said it had welcomed over one million guests to Hong Kong Disneyland during its first two months of operation.

(Source material www.thestandard.com.hk and www.bbc.co.uk)

Questions (Suggested answers can be found on the companion website www.thomsonlearning.co.uk/barnes)

1   What were the main problems experienced by Hong Kong Disneyland in its 'front office' operations?

2   What seem to be the main causes of these problems?

3   What more could be done to overcome these problems?

SUPPLY NETWORKS

outsourcing
One of the terms used to describe the process of obtaining inputs of goods or services from a source outside of the organization.

No operation whether service or manufacturing can exist in isolation. All operations have suppliers from whom they acquire their resource inputs, and customers to whom they supply their outputs. Those suppliers may be from sources within the same organization or from outside. In recent years, many organizations have increased their reliance on external sources of supply, using outsourcing as a means of reducing costs and of concentrating on their core competencies. Some organizations have even gone as far as splitting off parts of their organizations that used to be internal suppliers to create quite separate businesses. Indeed organizational boundaries of all kinds have typically become more blurred. Whatever the status of the suppliers to an operation, they too may well have suppliers, who also have suppliers and so on. It is helpful to think of the suppliers as lying in a series of tiers, with Tier 1 suppliers supplying direct, Tier 2 supplying to Tier 1, Tier 3 to Tier 2 and so on.

Similarly, there are often similar tiers of customers on the demand side acting as intermediaries between the producer and the end consumer. These intermediaries receive outputs from the operation and pass them on to their customers and so on until an ultimate end consumer is reached. For example, goods from a factory may be transported via a warehouse, to a distributor, to a wholesaler, to a retailer's shop where they are purchased by a consumer (see Figure 1.4). There can be similar routes to market for services. For example, the travel insurance product of an insurance company may be

CASE STUDY Li & Fung: A global supply network

Li & Fung is Hong Kong's largest trading group. Founded in Guangzhou in 1906, the company is now a multi-billion dollar global multi-national employing over 12,000 people in nearly 40 countries worldwide.

Li & Fung specializes in managing the supply chain for its clients, which include many leading multi-national brands such as Levi Strauss, The Limited, Warner Brothers, Avon, Hema, M&S Mode and Ben Sherman. Although it can offer a wide range of consumer goods (e.g. fashion accessories, furnishings, gifts, toys, sporting and travel goods), the vast majority of its business is in garments. Li & Fung does not own any production facilities itself, but has a global network of over 7,000 suppliers. This enables it to be flexible and adaptable. It has the ability to offer a complete supply package, which can include product design, production management, customs clearance and delivery. The company is constantly on the look-out for new suppliers who can meet its requirement for quality and low cost and an ability to deliver to tight deadlines. Li & Fung has been a pioneer in quick response manufacturing out of Asia since the 1970s. While cost considerations have resulted in the concentration of manufacturing activities in Asia, recent years have seen an expansion of Li & Fung's supply networks in areas like the Mediterranean, Eastern Europe and Central America that are closer to customers in Europe and the US.

With a Hong Kong base and long history of conducting business in China, Li & Fung was ideally placed to take advantage of the opening up of the People's Republic's economy to foreign participation. Although its ability to manufacture at low cost has made China the world's workshop, it seems clear that in the future, its consumer markets will become increasingly attractive.

Speaking to the *Asia Wall Street Journal* in July, 2005, Dr Victor Fung, Chairman of Li & Fung, pointed out that China's rise has coincided with, and reinforced, a revolution in production. In the past, the manufacture of a product was usually done under one roof and in one country prior to export for consumption in another country. Nowadays production has become increasingly spread across different countries. Dr Fung describes the company's approach to processing an order for shirts:

Li & Fung sources products from throughout China

'First, we consider the best place to source the yarn. If we decide that, say, Korea is best for this particular type of yarn, we then identify a factory to produce it. Next, where do we do the weaving and dyeing? It depends on the client's need, the timing, the capacity and the technology requirements. Let us say we decide that Taiwan is the best place. We ship the yarn to, say, two factories in Taiwan. The next thing is to identify the best place to put the shirt together, the cut, make and trim. For labour capacity and skill reasons, we may want to do it in Thailand. To save time, we may use three different factories in Thailand. In the end, the final product that arrives on the retailer's shelf should look as if it has been made in one single factory, but in fact we have done it in six factories in three different countries. What makes that all possible is the development of information technology and modern logistics. We have dissected the entire manufacturing process into different components at different stages. At each stage we consider the best place to produce a component. The end-product is the result of a truly globalized manufacturing process.'

Dr Fung argues that China may not be cost-efficient in every stage of the manufacturing process. There may be a comparative advantage in countries that produce or have access to the raw materials. As such, supply chains may originate in those countries who can undertake the first two or three stages of production. However, the final stages are likely to be done by China, whose abundant labour resources and cost efficient production capabilities make it a formidable competitor upstream. Thus, many supply chains originate in South East Asia, moving through China to the United States or Western Europe. Li & Fung's success relies on an ability to put these supply chains in place, manage them and synchronize them effectively and efficiently.

(Source material http://www.lifung.com)

Questions (Suggested answers can be found on the companion website www.thomsonlearning.co.uk/barnes)

1   Draw Li & Fung's supply network for the example of the shirt manufacture described in the case study.
2   What are the biggest challenges for Li & Fung in managing supply networks?

purchased by a holiday company to become part of a package holiday deal, sold through a travel shop to the person making the trip.

All operations typically have such a complex set of supply relationships, involving the interaction of many linked transformation processes. The totality of those relationships from the supplier's suppliers to the customers' customers is often referred to as a supply chain. The growing recognition of the importance of the management of operations that cross organizational boundaries has seen the development of the subject of supply chain management. This is particularly concerned with the management of operations that involve continuing relationships across organizational boundaries. Although it is a widely used term, the description of these relationships as a chain, is often a gross oversimplification. Many people prefer the term supply network as a better depiction of the complexity of most operations (see Figure 1.5).

The successful management of any supply network depends on there being a flow of information to match that of the flow of goods and/or services. Managers can not make decisions about the management of any single operation, however simple, without information. When a large number of operations are interconnected, as is the case in a supply network, the requirement for adequate, sufficient and timely information is even more vital. In essence, information is the lifeblood of any supply network. The increasing complexity of supply networks within and especially between organizations, and their increasing geographic spread has only been possible with the development of ever more powerful and extensive computer networks. The seemingly inexorable increase in the power and availability of information and communication technologies (ICT), networked through the Internet has enabled supply networks in industries of all kinds to become truly global. Operations managers need to know not just about their immediate work area of their factory, shop or office, but about where their operation fits into the supply network as a whole. Increasingly that means taking a global and international perspective on operations management.

supply network
The set of interconnected relationships between all the parties that supply inputs to, and receive outputs from, an operation (including the suppliers' suppliers and their suppliers etc. And the customers' customers and their customers etc.).

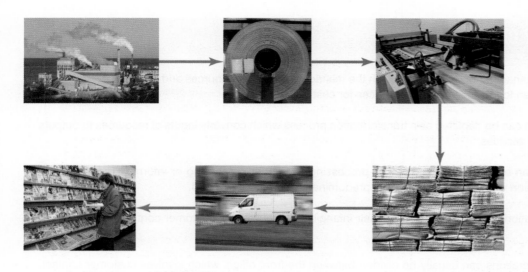

FIGURE 1.4 The stages in the newspaper printing supply chain

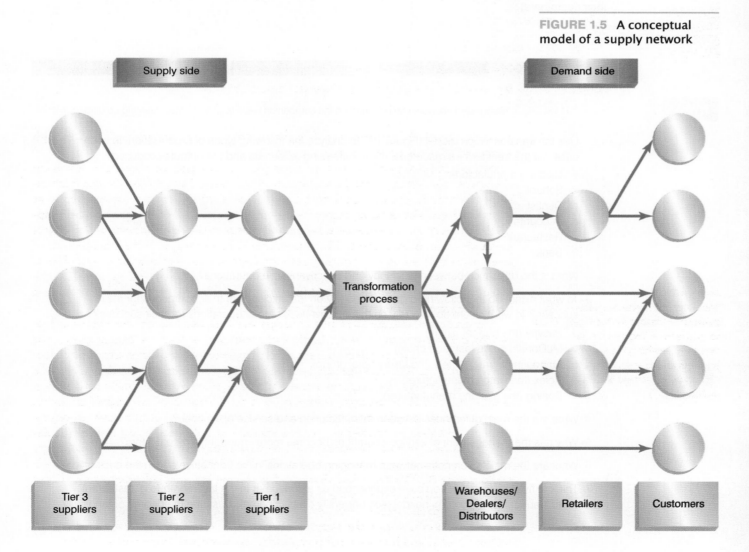

FIGURE 1.5 A conceptual model of a supply network

SUMMARY OF KEY POINTS

Operations management is concerned with the management of the resources and processes required by an organization to produce goods or services for customers.

Any operation can be depicted as a transformation process which converts inputs of resources to outputs of goods and services.

Operations can be classified as materials processing, customer processing or information processing, depending upon which type of resource is predominantly being transformed.

Service operations are distinguished by their intangibility, simultaneity, customer contact and subjective quality.

In-service operations can usually be divided between the front office, which involves customer contact, and a back office, which customers do not normally visit.

Most operations take place within a supply network, which comprises all the suppliers to the operation (plus their suppliers and their suppliers) and the customers of the operation (plus all their customers and their customers).

WWW.

EXERCISES (Suggested answers can be found on the companion website www.thomsonlearning.co.uk/barnes)

1 Use the transformation model (Figure 1.1) to analyze the following types of organization. In each case, list the transformed resources, the transforming resources and the outputs produced.
   a   Clothing manufacturer
   b   School
   c   Dentist
   d   Accountancy
   e   Restaurant
   f   Bank

2 What is the difference between efficiency and effectiveness in operations?

3 To what extent do the following organizations rely on the efficiency of their operations for their success? To what extent do they rely on the effectiveness of their operations for their success?
   a   Easyjet (the budget airline)
   b   McDonald's (the fast food chain)
   c   Mandarin Oriental Hotels (the luxury hotel group)
   d   Rolex (the watch manufacturer)
   e   Boeing (the airplane manufacturer)

4 What are the main differences between manufacturing and service operations?

5 Why has the management of service operations become more important in recent years?

6 What are the main differences between managing operations in the front office and in the back office?

7 Think of five services that you have experienced as a consumer in the last month (e.g. restaurant meal, transportation system, hairdresser, university class, cinema). Describe the degree of tangibility,

simultaneity and customer contact you experienced with the service in each case. How did these affect your perception of the quality of the experience?

8 Explain for the benefit of a friend who is not studying the subject, why operations management is vitally important for any organization.

9 Why has the supply chain network perspective of operations management become more important in recent years?

10 Draw the supply network for:
   a A dairy (producing milk for consumers)
   b A motor car manufacturer (producing cars for drivers)
   c An oil company (supplying petrol to car drivers)

CASE STUDY EXERCISE Hotel Matina

Hotel Matina is a family owned three star resort hotel located on a Greek holiday island. Although the hotel is medium sized, having 40 rooms and one suite, managing its operations is still a rather complex business. The hotel's operations can be both varied and complex, involving customer, material and information processing. They encompass front office operations, that have direct contact with the hotel's guests (e.g. reception, swimming pool, bar services) and back office operations, that take place out of sight of the guests (e.g. housekeeping, procurement, laundry). However, it is the hotel's reception and housekeeping departments that are fundamental to ensuring that the guests are provided with a reliable and quality overnight experience.

The hotel reception

The hotel's reception is the focal point for the customers; it is their first and major contact point during their stay at the hotel. It also provides the customers' last impression of their entire hotel experience. Reception is involved with reservations, check-in, customer service and check-out. Hence, its location within the hotel is at the most important and visible entry and exit point of the hotel. Its physical layout aims to not only convey a warm first impression to the guests, but also to provide enough functional space to make it convenient and pleasant for guests who are waiting to be served. Whilst background music plays, arriving guests who have prepared their registration cards online can utilize the express check-in service. Similarly, departing guests who have checked their bill via their room TV set can use the express check-out services.

Reception's main role is to provide guests with personal contact that can satisfy their request for information about the hotel and the surrounding area and meet their needs for a range of individual services such as taxi bookings, Internet connections, restaurant bookings and so on. Given the personal nature of their encounter with customers, all reception staff are trained to have good communication and presentation skills. They need to show empathy and demonstrate a desire to serve guests' needs immediately and in a pleasant way. The emotional demands on reception staff can be very great, as they need to always be smiling and to speak to customers in a warm and friendly way, irrespective of their own physical, mental and psychological situation. Being at the focal point of the hotel, reception staff also have an important role to play in promoting and selling the hotel's other services, such as the swimming pool, the bar and the restaurant.

The reception also acts as a communication hub for other hotel employees, since it provides information about events taking place at the hotel, vacated rooms that are ready to be cleaned, electrical faults reported by guests that need to be transferred to the maintenance department, and so on.

The back office

The work of reception is supported by a back office, located in the basement of the hotel. This is responsible for collecting and processing a vast amount of customer information during all stages of the guest cycle, from initial contact before arrival, during their stay and after their departure. Unlike those at the reception, back office staff do not need any special knowledge of languages or communication skills. Instead, a great emphasis is placed on their analytical and computer skills. The major activities in the back office include:

- Reservations: take reservations, check information about room rates and inventory availability, accept and/or decline reservation, take customer information and details and/or check with the marketing database to see if customer details already exist, and confirm reservation with the client.

- Room status and allocation: upon arrival guests need to be allocated to a room depending on their reservation requests (e.g. double bed) and the current status of the hotel's room stock. The maintenance of the status of the hotel's stock of rooms is a process that involves staff from different departments (e.g. housekeeping, reception, maintenance); its management is crucial since it can significantly affect guest service and satisfaction. For example, they need to avoid any delays in providing guests with their required room, whilst ensuring that rooms that are still dirty are not released.

- Billing: all charges that guests incur within the hotel (at the bar, restaurant, room service, etc.) need to be charged on a daily basis to the guest's folio. Information on guests' folios needs to be timely and accurate in order to avoid any faults (e.g. charging customers for items they have not purchased, and/or avoiding the loss of any payments). Co-operation and communication with all hotel departments is required. On the day of departure, the department prints the bill, which is passed to reception, so that guests can check it and settle their bill.

- Night audit: at the end of every day, all information recorded during the day needs to be checked for accuracy and reports generated for the next day's activities. Specifically, the status of all rooms has to be checked, arrival and departure reports have to be printed and disseminated to reception and housekeeping.

- Reporting: the back office should be able to provide reports of the hotel performance at any stage that the hotel manager may require such information (e.g. level of reservations, occupancy rates and average room rates).

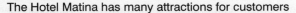

The Hotel Matina has many attractions for customers

- Guest history: after their departure, guests' details and any information generated from their activities (e.g. a request for a second pillow, a specific newspaper, preference for a particular wine) has to be typed and transferred to the hotel's marketing database. This information is important in establishing relations with guests (e.g. posting birthday and Christmas cards) and for personalizing their future stays. The marketing department is also responsible for accumulating and analyzing such customer information in order to develop appropriate marketing activities.

Housekeeping

The work of a housekeeper is physically demanding, repetitive, unskilled and of low status. However, it is equally as important for the provision of an excellent hotel stay as any of the hotel's other jobs. Moreover, the scale and complexity of maintaining the cleanliness of the hotel should also be highlighted. Apart from cleaning bedrooms, housekeeping staff also need to clean the public areas (reception, lobbies, corridors, etc.). The traffic volume in public areas can be quite large, with more than 200 people walking through these areas of the hotel on a typical day, sometimes more than once.

Room cleaning is a very standardized process. Check lists are provided to staff, so that they know what to clean, in what order, and what to check before finishing the maintenance of each room. The hotel housekeeper makes random controls on a daily basis to ensure that rooms have been prepared to the required standard. Housekeeping tasks are very suitable for the application of time and motion studies. This has enabled, for example, the room cleaning trolley used by housekeeping staff to be designed to carry around all necessary cleaning and maintenance materials. Similarly, bedroom furniture is fixed to the walls thereby preventing its re-arrangement by guests, which might slow down floor cleaning. Also, the time needed to clean a bedroom has been accurately calculated (20 minutes on average). This greatly simplifies the task of scheduling the work of housekeeping staff each day, as staffing levels and tasks can be based on the number of guests and reservations.

The cleaning of the public areas is divided into a number of tasks with different frequency and timings, devised according to their importance and the risk of their becoming dirty. For example, floors are scheduled to be cleaned at least three times per day (early morning, afternoon and evening), window cleaning is planned for every other day, while surfaces are scheduled for cleaning once a day. Curtains are cleaned once a month to remove wind-blown dust accumulations. Public toilets need regular attention to ensure that they are clean and re-stocked with toiletries. Consequently, they are normally checked at least three times per day; more on days when there are large numbers of check-ins and check-outs. A checklist is displayed prominently in the toilet areas so that guests can see a record of the timing of cleaning and re-stocking that has taken place.

Overall, the hotel housekeeper maintains a complete schedule of cleaning activities, ranging from day-to-day cleaning tasks, through regular but less frequent cleaning of particular items, to deep cleaning or 'seasonal cleaning'. Moreover, the range of different floor surfaces, linen and furniture items in the hotel, which in turn requires different treatments, detergents and cleaning regimes, serves to demonstrate the complexity of housekeeping activities. The wrong use of a cleaning material and chemical may have a harmful effect on the item, the person using it and the environment. Chemicals can be dangerous in their use and so staff also have to comply with any relevant legislation.

—*Marianna Sigala*

Questions (Suggested answers can be found on the companion website www.thomsonlearning.co.uk/barnes)

1 List as many of the operations taking place in the hotel as you can. For each of these identify their inputs, transformation processes and outputs.

2 Classify each of these operations according to the dominant transformed resource (materials, customers, information).

3 Which are front office and which are back office operations?

4 What are the main challenges for those managing the hotel's operations?

5 What types of skills are required by the staff working in each of the hotel's operations?

WWW.

References

The Economist (1st October 2005) 'Industrial metamorphosis', 81–82.

Hill, T. (2005) *Operations Management* 2nd Edition, Basingstoke: Palgrave Macmillan.

Slack, N., Chambers, S. and Johnston, R. (2004) *Operations Management* (4th Edition), Harlow: Pearson Education.

Additional reading

Clark, G. and Johnston, R. (2005) *Service Operations Management: Improving Service Delivery,* Harlow: Pearson Education.

Ohno, T. (1995) *Toyota Production System: Beyond Large-scale Production,* New York: Productivity Press.

Slack, N., Chambers, S. and Johnston, R. (2004) *Operations Management* (4th Edition), Harlow: Pearson Education.

Chase, R., Jacobs, R. and Aquilano, N. (2005) *Operations Management for Competitive Advantage* (11th Edition) New York: McGraw-Hill.

www. Useful websites

http://www.euroma-online.org The European Operations Management Association (EurOMA). A European-based network of academics and managers from around the world interested in developing Operations Management.

http://www.poms.org The Production Operations Management Society (POMS). A US-based international academic organization representing the interests of POM professionals from around the world.

http://www.iomnet.org.uk The Institute of Operations Management is the professional body for those involved in operations and production management in manufacturing and service industries in the UK.

http://www.apics.org The Association for Operations Management. APICS is a US-based professional organization that provides information and services in production and inventory management and related areas.

http://www.mhhe.com/omc OM Center is sponsored by Irwin/McGraw-Hill to provide a focal point for finding operations management resources that are valuable to students and faculty. It was conceived, designed, constructed and is maintained by Byron Finch, Professor of Management and Director of Faculty Development for Information Technologies for the Richard T. Farmer School of Business Administration, Miami University (Ohio).

www.sussex.ac.uk/Users/dt31/TOMI/ The Technology and Operations Management Index (TOMI) is a portal for discovering operations management resources on the Internet. TOMI is maintained by Dr David Twigg of the University of Sussex, UK.

CHAPTER 2

OPERATIONS, STRATEGY AND OPERATIONS STRATEGY

INTRODUCTION

An organization's operations function is concerned with getting things done; producing goods and/or services for customers. Chapter 1 pointed out that operations management is important because it is responsible for managing most of the organization's resources. However, many people think that operations management is only concerned with short-term, day-to-day, tactical issues. This chapter will seek to correct that view by considering the strategic importance of operations.

All business organizations are concerned with how they will survive and prosper in the future. A business strategy is often thought of as a plan or set of intentions that will set the long-term direction of the actions that are needed to ensure future organizational success. However, no matter how grand the plan, or how noble the intention, an organization's strategy can only become a meaningful reality, in practice, if it is operationally enacted. An organization's operations are strategically important precisely because most organizational activity comprises the day-to-day activities within the operations function. It is the myriad of daily actions of operations, when considered in their totality that constitute the organization's long-term strategic direction. The relationship between an organization's strategy and its operations is a key determinant of its ability to achieve long-term success or even survival. Organizational success is only likely to result if short-term operations activities are consistent with long-term strategic intentions and make a contribution to competitive advantage.

The relationship between operations and the other business functions is similarly important. The objective of the operations function is to produce the goods and services required by customers whilst managing resources as efficiently as possible. This can lead to conflicts within an organization. Conflicts between the operations and the marketing functions are likely to centre on the desire of marketing to ensure that operations concentrate on satisfying customers. Whilst this may seem desirable, marketing will usually want operations to be able to meet customer needs under any circumstances. This is likely to lead to demands to produce greater volumes, more variety, higher quality, a faster response, and so on, all of which are likely to lead to less efficient operations. Conflicts between the operations and the accounting and finance functions, on the other hand, are likely to centre on the desire of accounting and finance to want operations to manage resources as efficiently as possible. This will tend to pull operations in exactly the opposite direction of that desired by marketing. Conflicts between operations and the human resource management function are likely to centre on issues of recruitment, selection, training, management and the reward of those employed within operations. For example, operations managers may want to vary organization-wide policies in order to meet local needs; a move likely to be resisted by human resource managers. The operations function lies at the heart of any organization and interacts with all the other functions. As such, achieving agreement about what decision areas lie within the remit of operations, and what should be the basis of decision-making within operations is an essential part of ensuring the consistency of action over time necessary for a successful organizational strategy.

THE NATURE OF STRATEGY

Strategy is one of the most over-used words in the business dictionary. Yet, surprisingly, there is no agreement on what the term actually means. No-one challenges its military origin, used with regard to how a commander might deploy his resources (i.e. armed forces) throughout a campaign aimed at achieving a particular objective (e.g. conquering territory or thwarting an invasion). The idea that a business organization could have a strategy seems to have first emerged in the 1960s, when the techniques of long-term business planning were first popularized. Since then many different interpretations of the concept and practice of strategic management have been developed. Indeed, entire books have been given over to contemplating the nature of strategy. For example, Mintzberg *et al.* (1998) characterize ten 'schools of thought' in their consideration of what constitutes strategy. A widely accepted definition is offered by Johnson *et al.* (2005), who define strategy as 'the direction and scope of an organization over the long-term, which achieves advantage in a changing environment through its configuration of resources with the aim of fulfilling stakeholder expectations'. In its determination of the long-term direction of an organization, strategy involves the interplay of three elements: the organization's external environment, its resources and its objectives (in meeting the expectations of its stakeholders). Operations management is principally concerned with the organizational resources. However, the way that the operations function manages resources will impact both the way that the organization interacts with its external environment and its ability to meet the needs of its stakeholders. Thus, operations management is an integral part of an organization's strategy.

Strategy can be considered to exist at three levels in an organization (see Table 2.1):

- *Corporate level strategy:* Corporate level strategy is the highest level of strategy. It sets the long-term direction and scope for the whole organization. If the organization comprises more than one business unit, corporate level strategy will be concerned with what those businesses should be, how resources (e.g. cash) will be allocated between them, and how relationships between the various business units and between the corporate centre and the business units should be managed. Organizations often express their strategy in the form of a corporate mission or vision statement.

strategy
The direction and scope of an organization over the long-term, which achieves advantage in a changing environment through its configuration of resources with the aim of fulfilling stakeholder expectations (Johnson *et al.*, 2005).

(ADAPTED FROM HAYES *ET AL.*, 2005 P. 71)

TABLE 2.1 **Levels of strategy**

STRATEGY LEVEL	KEY ISSUES
Corporate	• What businesses shall we be in? • What businesses shall we acquire or divest? • How do we allocate resources between businesses? • What is the relationship between businesses? • What is the relationship between the centre and the businesses?
Business	• How do we compete in this business? • What is the mission of this business? • What are the strategic objectives of this business?
Function	• How does the function contribute to the business strategy? • What are the strategic objectives of the function? • How are resources managed in the function? • What technology do we use in the function? • What skills are required by workers in the function?

TABLE 2.2 **Criteria for evaluating an operations strategy**

Consistency (Is the strategy consistent . . .?)	• Between the operations strategy and business strategy • Between operations strategy and the other functional strategies • Between the different decision areas of operations strategy
Contribution to competitive advantage (Does the strategy . . . ?)	• Enable operations to set priorities that enhance competitive advantage • Highlight opportunities for operations to complement the business strategy • Make operations strategy clear to the rest of the organization • Provide the operating capabilities that will be required in the future

- *Business level strategy:* Business level strategy is primarily concerned with how a particular business unit should compete within its industry, and what its strategic aims and objectives should be. Depending upon the organization's corporate strategy and the relationship between the corporate centre and its business units, a business unit's strategy may be constrained by a lack of resources or strategic limitations placed upon it by the centre. In single business organizations, business level strategy is synonymous with corporate level strategy.

- *Functional level strategy:* The bottom level of strategy is that of the individual function (operations, marketing, finance, etc.) These strategies are concerned with how each function contributes to the business strategy, what their strategic objectives should be and how they should manage their resources in pursuit of those objectives.

The remainder of this chapter will consider in more detail what constitutes an operations strategy and what its relationship is with the other constituents of organizational strategy. As Hayes *et al.* (2005) point out, effective operations strategies need to be consistent and contribute to competitive advantage (see Table 2.2).

Details of the constituents of an operations strategy are explored in more detail in Chapters 5 through 14.

OPERATIONS AND STRATEGY

Strategy in a business organization is essentially about how the organization seeks to survive and prosper within its environment over the long-term. The decisions and actions taken within its operations have a direct impact on the basis on which an organization is able to do this. The way in which an organization secures, deploys and utilizes its resources will determine the extent to which it can successfully pursue specific performance objectives.

operations performance objectives
A criterion against which to evaluate the performance of operations. There are considered to be five possible operations performance objectives: cost, quality, speed, dependability and flexibility.

Slack *et al.* (2004) argue that there are five operations performance objectives:

1   **Cost:** The ability to produce at low cost.
2   **Quality:** The ability to produce in accordance with specification and without error.
3   **Speed:** The ability to do things quickly in response to customer demands and thereby offer short lead times between when a customer orders a product or service and when they receive it.
4   **Dependability:** The ability to deliver products and services in accordance with promises made to customers (e.g. in a quotation or other published information).
5   **Flexibility:** The ability to change operations. Flexibility can comprise up to four aspects:

   i.   The ability to change the volume of production.
   ii. The ability to change the time taken to produce.
   iii. The ability to change the mix of different products or services produced.
   iv. The ability to innovate and introduce new products and services.

Excelling at one or more of these operations performance objectives can enable an organization to pursue a business strategy based on a corresponding competitive factor. These relationships are outlined in Table 2.3. However, it is important to note that the success of any particular business strategy depends not only on the ability of operations to achieve excellence in the appropriate performance objectives, but crucially on customers valuing the chosen competitive factors on which the business strategy is based. Matching operations excellence to customer requirements lies at the heart of any operations based strategy. How this might be done is discussed later in the chapter.

It is unlikely that any single organization can excel simultaneously at all of the five operations performance objectives. Trying to do so is likely to lead to confusion if operations mangers pursue different objectives at different times. This lack of clarity

TABLE 2.3 Operations excellence and competitive factors

EXCELLENT OPERATIONS PERFORMANCE IN . . .	GIVES THE ABILITY TO COMPETE ON . . .
Cost	Low price
Quality	High quality
Speed	Fast delivery
Dependability	Reliable delivery
Flexibility	Frequent new products/services Wide range of products/services Changing the volume of product/service deliveries Changing the timing of product/service deliveries

is likely to lead to suboptimal performance and result in a failure to excel in any of the operations performance objectives. Consequently, organizations need to choose which performance objectives they will give priority to. This may result in having to 'trade-off' less than excellent performance in one aspect of operations in order to achieve excellence in another. The concept of trade-off in operations objectives was first proposed many years ago by Skinner (1969). He argued that operations could not be 'all things to all people'. What was needed was to identify a single goal or 'task' for operations; a clear set of competitive priorities to act as the objective. The task would then act as the criterion against which all decisions and actions in operations could be judged. The airline EasyJet offers an example of a company that has a clearly defined task for its operations, namely achieving the lowest possible operating costs.

It is worth noting, that some operations management scholars reject the concept of the trade-off. They point to the ability of some organizations to outperform their competitors on multiple dimensions. They appear to have better quality, greater dependability and a faster response to changing market conditions and lower costs. Ferdows and de Meyer (1990) argue that certain operational capabilities enhance one another, enabling operations excellence to be built in a cumulative fashion. In their 'sandcone' model of operations excellence (see Figure 2.1), they maintain that there is an ideal sequence in which operational capabilities should be developed. The starting point, the base of the sandcone is excellence in quality. On this should be built excellence in dependability, then flexibility (which they take to include speed), then cost. They emphasize that efforts to further enhance quality should continue whilst commencing efforts to build dependability. Similarly, actions on quality and dependability need to continue whilst building flexibility. Finally efforts to reduce costs take place alongside continuing efforts to improve quality, dependability and flexibility. They claim that operational capabilities developed in this way are more likely to endure than individual capabilities developed at the expense of others.

Skinner (1985) argued that operations could become a 'Formidable Competitive Weapon' if the function was allowed to play a full strategic role in the organization. That this was not the case in some organizations, was due to there being inappropriate expectations of and attitudes towards operations.

In their four-stage model, Hayes and Wheelwright (1984) categorize different types of organizations based on their attitude towards their operations (see Table 2.4).

Hayes and Wheelwright's four stage model is underpinned by their belief that an organization's operations can provide a source of competitive advantage. It can

trade-off

The concept based on the premise that it is impossible to excel simultaneously at all aspects of operations. This means that an operations strategy can be successful only if it is based upon a single clear goal, determined by a prioritization of operations performance objectives (e.g. cost, quality, speed, dependability and flexibility).

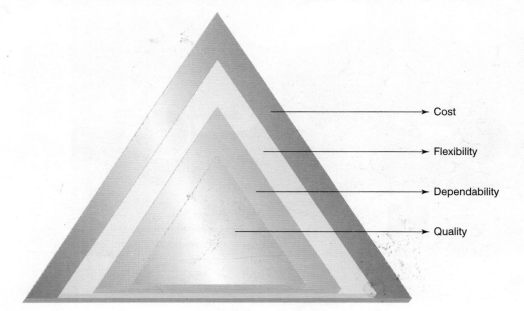

FIGURE 2.1 The 'sandcone' model of operations excellence

SOURCE: THE JOURNAL OF OPERATIONS MANAGEMENT, FERDOWS, K. AND DE MEYER, A. 'LASTING IMPROVEMENTS IN MANUFACTURING PERFORMANCE', PAGES 168–184, © ELSEVIER, 1990. REPRODUCED WITH PERMISSION.

CASE STUDY EasyJet: Low cost air travel

Although EasyJet only undertook its first flight in 1995, when it only operated two routes (London Luton to Glasgow and Edinburgh), ten years later the budget airline offered 212 routes to 64 European airports and transported over 29 million passengers in 2005. EasyJet now carries more passengers within Europe than British Airways. Analysts expect EasyJet and its Irish-based rival Ryanair, to both overtake all traditional airlines to become the largest short-haul operators in Europe by the end of the decade.

The Luton-based airline is continuing to expand, recently announcing the purchase of a further 20 Airbus A319 planes to service the ever increasing number of routes it operates. In 2005 EasyJet carried nearly 30 million passengers, up from 25.7 million in 2004, making it a £1.3 billion business. Despite record high fuel costs, profits were up around 10 per cent to £68 million. Passenger numbers rose 21 per cent to 29.6 million and the load factor, indicating how many seats are filled, was 85.2 per cent, reflecting the airline's popularity.

The low cost lines like EasyJet have revolutionized the airline industry in Europe. Modelled on SouthWest Airlines in the USA, these airlines have not only helped create a whole new market of cost-conscious travelers but have taken market share from established operators like British Airways and become the most profitable airlines in Europe. To be profitable, these airlines have to achieve low costs to match the low fares, which are the main attraction to their passengers.

With its head office as a large tin shed adjacent to the main taxiway at unfashionable Luton Airport, all of EasyJet's operations are aimed at minimizing costs. This is done in a number of ways:

- **Use of the Internet to reduce distribution costs.** EasyJet sells around 95 per cent of all seats over the Internet. Its online booking system uses a variable pricing system to try to maximize load factors. (Prices start very low – sometimes free, and rise as seats are filled.) The fuller the aircraft the lower the unit cost of travel.

- **Ticketless travel.** Passengers are emailed with their travel details and booking reference. This helps reduce significantly the cost of issuing, distributing, processing and reconciling millions of tickets each

EasyJet has really taken off in the last decade

year. Neither does EasyJet pre-assign seats on-board. Passengers sit where they like. This eliminates an unnecessary complexity and speeds up passenger boarding.

- **No free on-board catering.** Eliminating free catering on-board reduces cost and unnecessary bureaucracy. Passengers can purchase food and refreshments on-board.

- **Efficient use of airports.** EasyJet flies to the less crowded airports of smaller European cities and prefers the secondary airports in the major cities. These also have lower landing charges and normally offer faster turnarounds as there are fewer air movements. EasyJet's efficient ground operations enable it to achieve turnarounds of less than 30 minutes. This means EasyJet can achieve extra rotations on the high-frequency routes, maximizing the utilization of aircraft. EasyJet's ability to offer point-to point travel means that it does not have to worry about onward connections for passengers and their baggage, further simplifying its operations.

- **Paperless operations.** EasyJet has embraced the concept of the paperless office, with all its management and administration undertaken entirely on IT systems. These can be accessed through secure servers from anywhere in the world thereby enhancing flexibility in the running of the airline.

(Source material www.EasyJet.com and www.bbc.co.uk)

WWW.

WWW.

Questions (Suggested answers can be found on the companion website www.thomsonlearning.co.uk/barnes)

1 List all the ways in which EasyJet achieves low cost operations.

2 Evaluate EasyJet's operations strategy against Hayes *et al.*'s criteria of consistency and contribution to competitive advantage (see Figure 2.2).

3 To what extent does EasyJet's concentration on low costs limit its ability to perform well against the other operations performance objectives?

4 What are the risks associated with EasyJet's strategy?

TABLE 2.4 The four-stage model of the strategic role of operations

Stage 1	Internally Neutral	The operations function is internally focused and reactive. They are viewed as a 'necessary evil'. The best that the organization hopes for is that operations 'don't screw up'.
Stage 2	Externally Neutral	The operations function tries to be as good as the competition, or to achieve parity with industry norms. Such an organization is likely to benchmark its operations against its competitors, and adopt best practice in its industry so that it does not hold the organization back.
Stage 3	Internally Supportive	The operations function seeks to provide credible support for the organization's business strategy. An operations strategy will be developed which will be derived from, and support, the business strategy. The organization's operations are likely to be amongst the best in its industry.
Stage 4	Externally Supportive	The operations function provides the basis of competitive advantage for the organization, by setting the standard in their industry. The operations function is likely to aim to be world class by seeking to emulate best practice wherever it is to be found. Operations will be seen as the means of exceeding customer expectations by delighting the customer. Operations will be managed proactively to drive the business strategy of the organization.

(HAYES AND WHEELWRIGHT, 1984)

only do this if the operations function is managed strategically. As such, they argue, all organizations should aspire to reach the highest level possible, ultimately reaching stage 4.

A stage 1 organization finds it impossible to manage its operations strategically, as its operations performance objectives are continually changing between low cost, increased flexibility, improved quality, etc. Because operations managers never have the time to focus on a consistent set of objectives, a stage 1 organization is characterized by a reactive approach to operations management. In such an organization, operations can never provide a source of competitive advantage.

A stage 2 organization manages its operations by seeking to emulate those of its competitors. It is likely to copy the prevailing best practices of its industry, such as JIT (just-in-time), TQM (total quality management), BPO (business process outsourcing) etc. However, as they always adopt these techniques in the wake of industry leaders, they are never likely to have developed the same level of expertise in their application. The best that such an approach can achieve is to match the operations performance of its competitors. Although the combination of operations practices adopted by a stage 2 organization may be considered by some as amounting to an operations strategy in that they are consistent, they will not be overtly linked to business strategy. Indeed, it may be that such an operations strategy is inappropriate for the organization's business strategy. In any event, a stage 2 organization's operations can not provide the basis for competitive advantage.

A stage 3 organization has an operations strategy that is linked to and derived from its business strategy. This means that its operations performance objectives are aligned with, and supportive of, its business objectives, offering the possibility that operations can provide the means of achieving a competitive advantage. The chances of achieving competitive advantage will be considerably increased if the organization has adopted industry best practice in its operations.

A stage 4 organization is radically different to one at any of the other stages. A stage 4 organization uses its operations excellence as the basis for its business strategy – an operations-based strategy. The operations of a stage 4 organization are at the forefront of developments in best practice in that they set industry standards in ways that delight customers. Thus, the organization's operations enable it to retain its existing customers and attract new ones. For an operations-based competitive advantage to be sustainable, the organization must continually develop its operations, as any source of advantage is liable to be imitated by competitors. To remain at stage 4, an organization needs to learn how to make the most of its existing resources and competences to learn how to develop new capabilities. Recent advances in the understanding of organizational performance have emphasized the importance of path dependency (i.e. how organizations got to their present position), the dynamic nature of the capabilities on which organizational success ultimately depends and the role of organizational learning. (See for example Teece and Pisano, 1994; Cohen and Levinthal, 1990.)

OPERATIONS STRATEGY

The foregoing discussion has highlighted the strategic importance of operations to organizational performance. An appropriate operations strategy is essential to an organization not only as this will determine the extent to which its business strategy can be implemented, but also as its operations can be a source of competitive advantage. But what exactly is meant by the term operations strategy?

Slack *et al.* (2004: p.67) argue that an 'operations strategy concerns the pattern of strategic decisions and actions which set the role, objectives and activities of operations'. Their use of the term 'pattern' implies a consistency in strategic decisions and actions over time. This concept is consistent with management guru Henry

operations strategy
This concerns the pattern of strategic decisions and actions which set the role, objectives and activities of operations (Slack *et al.*, 2004).

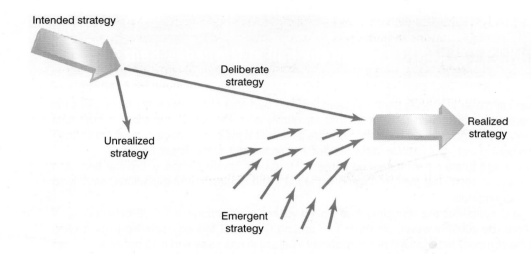

FIGURE 2.2 The strategy formation process
SOURCE: STRATEGIC MANAGEMENT JOURNAL, MINTZBERG, H. AND WATERS, J. 'OF STRATEGIES, DELIBERATE AND EMERGENT', 1985. © JOHN WILEY & SONS LTD. REPRODUCED WITH PERMISSION.

Mintzberg's view of strategy as being a 'pattern in a stream of actions' (Mintzberg and Waters, 1985). Mintzberg sees strategy as being realized through a combination of deliberate and emergent actions (see Figure 2.2). An organization can have an intended strategy, perhaps as a set of strategic plans. However, only some of this intended strategy may be realized through deliberate strategy. Some of the intentions may be unrealized. Strategies which take no regard of operational feasibility are likely to become unrealized, remaining merely as a set of intentions. Strategy may also emerge from actions taken within the organization, which over time form a consistent pattern. Actions of this kind will, almost inevitably, arise from within the operations of the organization. So, whether planned or otherwise, the organization's operations are bound to have a major impact on the formation of organizational strategy.

It is often believed that strategy is an issue that is somehow separate from day-to-day organizational activities. Taken to extremes this can result in strategy being regarded as some kind of cerebral activity performed by superior beings who need to be removed from day-to-day operational pressures. Mintzberg is amongst those who point to the dangers of managers becoming detached from the basics of the enterprise. Mintzberg and Quinn (1991) call this the 'don't bore me with the operating details; I'm here to tackle the big issues' syndrome. They caution that, 'the big issues are rooted in little details'.

The remainder of this chapter will address two related issues concerning operations strategy, namely its process and content:

a Operations strategy process: How an organization sets about developing an appropriate operations strategy

b Operations strategy content: What the key decision areas that need to be addressed in developing an operations strategy are.

OPERATIONS STRATEGY – PROCESS

As discussed above, operations strategy has a vertical relationship in the corporate hierarchy with business and corporate strategies, and horizontally with the other functional strategies, most notably with marketing strategy. Operations strategy might come about in a top-down or a bottom-up process with regard to business and corporate strategies. Similarly, an operations strategy might be developed in response to market requirements (i.e. market-led) or be based on the capabilities of its operations

WHEN THINGS GO WRONG   Eyes off the ball at Mercedes-Benz?

Luxury German car maker Mercedes Benz has been having a bad time of it recently. For many years the company's cars were considered to be a byword for quality and reliability but in the last few years Mercedes' famous three pointed star has become a little tarnished in the eyes of many buyers. These days Mercedes lags behind arch-rival BMW in terms of sales and profits and, some argue, image.

Its problems seem to stem from the tie-up between Mercedes' parent company, Daimler-Benz and America's Chrysler in 1998. The merger created the world's fifth biggest car manufacturer, employing 385,000 workers worldwide.

At that stage Chrysler was the struggling third placed volume manufacturer in the US behind General Motors and Ford. By 2005, however, efforts to turn around Chrysler's fortunes seemed to be paying dividends as the company reported a 5 per cent annual increase in unit sales and a 10 per cent increase in revenues in its results for 2004.

Meanwhile Mercedes Benz's operating profits fell in 2004 on the back of poor sales of the luxury brand and restructuring costs at its Smart car division; the ultra-small 'citycar' division had failed to perform as expected since its launch in 1998.

Mercedes itself has been struggling with quality control problems on many of its vehicles and increasing numbers of its previously loyal customers have been moving to competitors such as Audi or BMW. In 2005, the company even had the embarrassment of having to issue the biggest product recall in its history. Problems with batteries, alternators and brakes on a number of models made since 2001 necessitated 1.3 million cars having to be returned to dealers to be fixed. The move is likely to cost many millions of euros, hampering efforts to improve its product image, and hitting profits.

Many analysts believe that the many initiatives being undertaken at DaimlerChrysler have distracted from the management of its previously highly profitable Mercedes business. Some accuse the company's

Another happy customer for Mercedes-Benz?

managers of 'taking their eye off the Ball' as far as Mercedes operations are concerned. Some question whether the highly technologically sophisticated gadgetry on its latest top of the range S-class cars can be trusted to perform. They fear that any electronic gremlins could further damage the entire marque's image and further alienate its customers.

In an effort to improve performance and financial results, Mercedes is cutting more than 8,500 jobs at its Sindelfingen plant in Germany. DaimlerChrysler's newly appointed Chief Executive, Dieter Zetsche said the firm is determined to retain Mercedes' position as the world's most successful luxury brand. He said efforts to improve productivity, which is well behind rivals such as BMW and Toyota's Lexus, would not be allowed to compromise efforts to tackle Mercedes' recent quality problems.

(Source material www.bbc.co.uk)

Questions (Suggested answers can be found on the companion website www.thomsonlearning.co.uk/barnes)

1 What has been the source of Mercedes' competitive advantage?

2 What seems to be the cause of its recent problems in operations?

3 Is it possible for the firm to simultaneously improve its performance in both productivity and quality?

4 Where would you position Mercedes Benz on the Hayes and Wheelwright four-stage model? Give your reasons.

WWW.

WWW.

resources (i.e. operations-led). As illustrated in Figure 2.3, this gives rise to four perspectives on operation strategy (Slack and Lewis, 2002). Each perspective places a different emphasis on the nature of the operations strategy process.

Top-down

The top-down perspective is one in which the operations strategy is derived from, and is supportive of the organization's business strategy; an operations strategy that

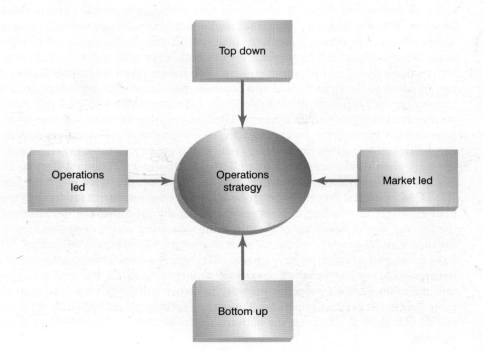

FIGURE 2.3 The four perspectives on operations strategy
SOURCE: OPERATIONS STRATEGY, SLACK AND LEWIS, PEARSON EDUCATION LTD. REPRODUCED WITH PERMISSION.

the organization uses to realize its business strategy. This concept is in line with that of the Hayes and Wheelwright stage 3 organization. According to this perspective, the process of developing an operations strategy would follow Skinner's approach of identifying an operation's 'task' (Skinner, 1969). The task for operations would be determined logically from the business strategy. Using Slack *et al.*'s (2004) five operations performance objectives is one way of articulating the operations task. For example, if the organization's business strategy is one of offering low prices, then the operation's task should be one of achieving low costs in operations. If the business strategy is based on offering customers fast delivery, the operations task should be one of achieving speed in operations, and so on.

In a multi-business organization, the top-down perspective envisages operations strategy being linked to corporate strategy via the business strategy of each business unit. This then raises the question of whether it is possible to talk of a 'corporate' operations strategy. If a corporate operations strategy means commonality in all aspects of operations, then this would only be possible if each business unit had similar business strategies and similar operations tasks. However, some authors (e.g. Hayes *et al.*, 2005) argue that a corporate operations strategy does not mean that every facet of operations must be the same in each business unit. Rather, operations decisions are considered holistically at the corporate level with a view to meeting corporate strategic objectives. A failure to do this means that operations decisions are taken only at the level of the business unit, with a view to meeting the immediate needs of that business unit. The dangers of doing this have been pointed out by Prahalad and Hamel (1990), who caution against letting the needs of the business unit dominate strategic thinking. This can lead to operational competences being confined within individual business units, thereby restricting their future development, preventing their spread to other business units and limiting opportunities for synergistic developments across the corporation. This can be particularly important in multi-site, multi-national enterprises.

Bottom-up

The bottom-up perspective is one which sees operations strategy emerging through a series of actions and decisions taken over time within operations. These actions and decisions might at first sight appear somewhat haphazard, as operations managers respond to customer demands, seek to solve specific problems, copy good practices in other organizations, etc. However, they can build over time to form a coherent pattern recognizable as an operations strategy. The actions taken within this kind of strategy are likely to be characterized by a continuous series of incremental improvements rather than the large one-off technologically led changes that require large capital investments in new plant and machinery. The bottom-up perspective is one in which the organization learns from its experiences, developing and enhancing its operational capabilities as operations managers try new things out in an almost experimental fashion using their workplaces as a kind of 'learning laboratory' (Leonard-Barton, 1992). Many of the manufacturing practices that are now considered leading edge (such as JIT, TQM, Statistical Process Control) were developed in just such a fashion by Japanese manufacturers responding to the constraints placed upon them in the aftermath of the Second World War. One of the problems associated with this perspective is that the organization may not recognize what its operations strategy is. Mills *et al.* (1998) have developed a technique that aims to overcome this by enabling managers to construct a visual representation of operations strategy as realized. It does this by tapping into the organization's collective memory (whether written or verbal) to map all the most significant events in operations over the previous number of years. This should enable managers to recognize the patterns that now make up the existing operations strategy.

Market-led

The market-led perspective is one in which the operations strategy is developed in response to the market environment in which the organization operates. There are a number of approaches in the operations strategy literature that suggest how this might be done.

The best known of these is that of Terry Hill (1985). He suggests that an organization's operations strategy should be linked to its marketing strategy by considering how its products and services win orders in the market place. He believes it is possible to identify two types of competitive criteria in any market. Market qualifying criteria are those factors that must be satisfied before customers will consider making a purchase in the first place. Order winning criteria, on the other hand, are the factors on which customers ultimately make their purchasing decision. For example, for many airline passengers, the order winning criteria is price, with criteria such as destination city, time of flights and convenience of travel to and from airports being market qualifying criteria. For others, notably business travellers, the order winning criteria may be factors such as in-flight service or total travel time. Consequently, an operations strategy should be developed which will satisfy market qualifying criteria, but excel at order winning criteria for the market segment that the operation wishes to serve.

Platts and Gregory (1990) use an approach that audits the products or groups of products that the organization offers to its markets. The aim is to identify any gaps between market requirements for particular products and services and the performance of the organization's operations in delivering those products and services. First the market requirements for the product or service are analyzed in terms of various competitive factors (such as cost, quality, reliability). The performance of the organization's operations against those factors are then assessed. An operations strategy should be developed which will enable operations to match the level of performance required by customers in each of the competitive criteria.

Operations-led

The operations-led perspective is one in which its excellence in operations is used to drive the organization's strategy. This is in line with the Hayes and Wheelwright stage 4 organization and fits with the resource-based view (RBV) of strategy that currently dominates the strategic management literature. The premise of the RBV is that superior performance comes from the way that an organization acquires, develops and deploys its resources and builds its capabilities rather than the way it positions itself in the market place (Barney, 1991; Wernerfelt, 1984). Thus, the process of strategy development should be based on a sound understanding of current operational capabilities and an analysis of how these could be developed in the future. This can then provide the basis for decisions about which markets are likely to be the best in which to deploy current and future capabilities, which competitors are likely to be most vulnerable and how attacks from competitors might best be countered (Hayes et al., 2005). Mills et al. (2002) have developed methods through which organizations can apply these ideas in practice. This involves undertaking an analysis of the resources that have underpinned the activities of a business unit over an extended period of time (at least the previous three to five years). Six resource categories, which are not mutually exclusive, are used: tangible resources, knowledge resources skills and experience, systems and procedural resources, cultural resources and values, network resources and resources important for change. The resources are evaluated against three criteria: value, sustainability and versatility. Resources that individually or collectively score highly in these criteria are considered to be important resources. They are sources of existing or potential competitive advantage to the organization.

CASE STUDY   Operations strategy development at Askeys

Askeys has been manufacturing ice cream cones, wafers and other biscuits normally eaten with ice cream since 1910. The ice cream cone was first introduced in 1904 at the St Louis World Fair in America. Six years later, Askeys brought the ice cream cone to the UK when founder, Italian Laurens Tedeschi, set up business in Kensal Road, London. The company moved to Aylesbury, a small town some 35 miles north-west of London, in the 1960s.

The business was sold to Kellogg's, the American food manufacturing giant, most famous for its breakfast cereal in the 1970s. Under their ownership, Askeys was used solely as a manufacturing site, with all marketing, sales and distribution, together with all support services such as purchasing and personnel being run from Kellogg's UK head office in Manchester. During this period, the factory concentrated on the mass production of a limited range of standard cones and wafers. These were mostly sold to ice cream parlours and kiosks, ice cream vans and other outside caterers. Sales to this market were highly seasonal, and also weather dependent, and so such stocks were considered essential if peak summer demand was to be met. Indeed, the storage area for finished products was built to be as large as the manufacturing facility itself. However, through the 1980s, the market was changing and sales through supermarkets became much more important. By the 1990s, the vast majority of Askeys products were sold via

Some of Askeys' products

the major national supermarkets. Although most of these sales were still under the Askeys brand, some products were provided under supermarket own labels. A large, but diminishing quantity of business remained destined for the catering trade and ice cream vendors. During this time production processes were labour intensive, particularly in the packaging areas. The handling and packing of such large numbers of low value extremely brittle products like ice cream wafers and cones was considered best entrusted to human dexterity. Production continued uninterrupted around the clock Monday to Friday with a shift system. Extra hours including weekends were worked if required in the summer. During this time, Askey's profitability declined under the relentless downward price pressure exerted by the supermarkets. Nonetheless, Askeys retained its position as the largest British manufacturer of ice-cream accompaniments, producing literally millions of wafers and cones of all shapes and sizes every year. Very little effort was put into developing new products.

In 1995, Askeys was acquired from Kellogg's in a management buy-in led by two experienced food industry executives, financed by venture capitalists. The new owners set about extending the product range. Over the next decade other ice cream biscuits were added to the Askeys range, including the waffle cone, supplied to ice cream manufacturers for the production of 'cornetto' type ices, and a wide range of fans, curls and dessert baskets aimed at the catering trade (including fast food outlets and restaurants) and home sales via supermarkets. A range of crumb products, used by caterers and food manufacturers as toppings, or as ingredients for cakes and biscuits was also developed. They also experimented with the manufacture of non-related products with the installation of a 'dry mix' plant. This was intended to be used for the production of powdered soups and desserts.

Askeys now has a wide range of products aimed at home consumers, the catering trade and other food manufacturers. To meet the demand for these, the factory has had to learn to cope with a vastly increased product range. Many of these products have a very variable demand and are often made in relatively small batch sizes. Alongside this, they have had to continue to meet large-scale demand for the traditional cone and wafer products. Although this has not been without its problems, Askey's manufacturing operations have gradually developed the new competencies required.

In 2004 Askeys was sold to The Silver Spoon Company, Britain's largest sugar and sweetener producer. The company says it intends to continue expanding the business through exploring new markets, expanding existing ones and new product development.

(Source material www.askeys.co.uk and interviews with company managers)

Questions (Suggested answers can be found on the companion website www.thomsonlearning.co.uk/barnes)

1 How has Askeys' operations strategy changed over the years?

2 In which aspects of performance has Askeys' operations had to excel in order to compete in its chosen markets?

3 Which of the four perspectives of operations strategy best describes the operations strategy process at Askeys at the different stages of its history? Give your reasons.

WWW.

WWW.

OPERATIONS STRATEGY – CONTENT

What then are the key decision areas of operations management that need to be considered when an organization is developing an operations strategy? Although there are a number of classifications in use, operations management scholars generally agree (e.g. Leong *et al.*, 1990) that the major strategic decision areas in operations can be conveniently divided into ten categories under two broad headings: structure (the physical attributes of operations; the hardware) and infrastructure (the people and systems of operations; the software).

The structural decision areas comprise:

- Facilities: the location, size and focus of operational resources. These decisions are concerned with where to locate production facilities, how large each facility should be, what goods or services should be produced at each location, what markets each facility should serve, etc.
- Capacity: the capacity of operations and their ability to respond to changes in customer demand. These decisions are concerned with the use of facilities, for example through shift patterns, working hours and staffing levels. Decisions about capacity will affect the organization's ability to serve particular markets from a given location.
- Process technology: the technology of the equipment used in operations processes. For example, the degree of automation used, the configuration of equipment, and so on.
- Supply network: the extent to which operations are conducted in-house or are outsourced. Decisions about vertical integration are also concerned with the choice of suppliers, their location, the extent of dependence on particular suppliers, and how relationships with suppliers are managed.

Structural decisions often involve major capital investment decisions, which once made will set the direction of operations for many years to come. They invariably impact the resources and capabilities of an organization, determining its potential future output. It may be prohibitively expensive to change such decisions once implemented, and hence these must be considered to be truly strategic decisions for the organization. It may be much easier to change the organization's marketing strategy (e.g. its target markets, or its promotional activities) than it is to change its operations strategy with respect to the structural decision areas.

Infrastructure decision areas comprise:

- Planning and Control: the systems used for planning and controlling operations.
- Quality: quality management policies and practices.
- Work Organization: organizational structures, responsibilities and accountabilities in operations.
- Human Resources: recruitment and selection, training and development, management style.
- New Product Development: the systems and procedures used to develop and design new products and services.
- Performance Measurement: financial and non-financial performance management and its linkage to recognition and reward systems.

These issues are also important to an organization, involving the use made of the operating hardware discussed above. It is possible to change aspects of operations infrastructure more quickly and easily than is the case for operations structure. Nonetheless the difficulty of so doing should not be underestimated, neither should the impact of making inappropriate infrastructural decisions.

The key decision area of operations management will be considered in greater detail in Part Three – Structural Issues and Part Four – Infrastructural issues. First however, Part Two will consider the challenges for operations posed by the growing internationalization of business created by the forces of globalization and the new economy.

SUMMARY OF KEY POINTS

Strategy is concerned with the actions an organization takes in order to survive and prosper in its environment over the long-term. Strategy can exist at three levels in an organization: corporate, business and functional.

An organization's operations strategy comprises the totality of the actions and decisions taken within the operations function. The decisions and actions taken have a direct impact on an organization's business and corporate strategy.

An organization's operations can be a source of competitive advantage if they are managed strategically in pursuit of a clear goal for operations.

There are five possible operations objectives (cost, quality, speed, dependability and flexibility). It is unlikely that any operation can excel at all of these simultaneously, so competitive priorities must be determined on which to base the operations strategy.

The process of operations strategy concerns the way in which an organization develops its operations strategy. This might be top-down (i.e. formed in pursuit of its business and corporate strategy), bottom-up (i.e. formed from the actions and decisions taken with operations), market-led (i.e. formed in response to market requirements) or operations-led (based on the resources and capabilities within its operations).

The content of operation strategy consists of the key decision areas concerned with the structure (i.e. the physical attributes of facilities, capacity, process technology and supply network) and infrastructure (i.e. planning and control, quality, organization, human resources, new product development and performance measurement) of operations.

EXERCISES (Suggested answers can be found on the companion website www.thomsonlearning.co.uk/barnes)

WWW.

1 Why are an organization's operations crucial to its strategic success?

2 What is operations strategy? Explain its relationship within the model that depicts organizational strategy as existing at three different levels.

3 Explain how excelling at each of the five operations performance objectives (cost, quality, speed, dependability and flexibility) could provide an organization with a competitive advantage.

4 How can an organization use its operations as a 'formidable competitive weapon'?

5 Explain how the following types of organization might use their operations to gain a competitive advantage (i.e. like a Hayes and Wheelwright stage 4 organization):

   a an airline
   b a hospital
   c a university
   d a domestic appliances manufacturer

6 Toyota seems to perform well in all five operations performance objectives. Do you think the sandcone or the trade-off model of operations offers the better explanation for this?

7 What are the four perspectives on operations strategy? Which of these do you find most convincing in explaining operations strategy process in practice?

8 What are the key decision areas that organizations need to take into account when determining their operations strategy?

9 What advice would you give to an organization that wanted to ensure that it had an operations strategy that was consistent with its business strategy and made a contribution to competitive advantage?

10 Choose a well-known organization (or an organization for which you can easily access relevant information).
   a Identify its business objectives and strategy (perhaps as stated in its mission statement).
   b Identify its operations strategy by analyzing its actions in the key decision areas of structure and infrastructure.
   c Identify its operations performance objectives. (You may need to infer these by assessing its performance in the five operations performance objectives (e.g. cost, quality, speed, dependability and flexibility).)
   d Compare its business objectives and strategy with its operations objectives and strategy using Hayes *et al.*'s (2005) criteria of consistency and contribution.
   e Classify the organization in terms of the Hayes and Wheelwright four-stage model of strategic role of operations.

CASE STUDY EXERCISE Giordano

Company background

From small beginnings in Hong Kong in 1981, Giordano International Limited expanded throughout the Asia Pacific region to become one of its most well-known and established apparel retailers. By 2005, it employed over 11,000 staff in over 1,700 shops operating in 30 territories in Greater China, Japan, Korea, South East Asia, Australia, India and the Middle East. Giordano specializes in casual clothing for both men and women, and operates under the brand names 'Giordano', 'Giordano Ladies', 'Giordano Junior' and 'Bluestar Exchange'. In 2005, sales of HK$4,413 million (up from HK$4,003m in 2004), delivered after tax profits of HK$431m (HK$418m in 2004).

As early as the 1980s, Giordano realized that it was difficult to achieve substantial growth and economies of scale if it operated solely in Hong Kong. The key was to expand, both in the region and beyond. Moreover, after surviving the Asian economic crisis of 1997–1999, Giordano has also been endeavoring to move up-market to avoid the fierce price competition prevalent in the discount sector. However, as it moved into new segments and territories, Giordano had to consider how to adapt its marketing and operations strategies to suit these different markets.

Giordano was originally founded as a wholesaler for Hong Kong-based manufactured clothing going to the USA. However, in 1983 it scaled back its wholesale operation and set up its own retail shops in Hong Kong. It soon expanded into Taiwan through a joint venture and in 1985 opened its first retail outlet in Singapore. Until 1987, Giordano sold exclusively men's casual apparel. When it realized that an increasing number of women customers were attracted to its stores, Giordano started selling unisex casual apparel.

It began to re-position itself as a retailer of discounted casual unisex apparel with great success; its sales more than quadrupled from HK$712 million in 1989 to HK$3,479 million in 2001. A willingness to try new ways of doing things and learning from past errors was an integral part of management at Giordano. The occasional failure represented a current limitation and indirectly pointed to the right decision for the future.

Operations

Besides the willingness to accept mistakes, Giordano's success is also firmly grounded on its dedicated, well-trained and ever smiling sales force. Its front-line customer service workers are its heroes. Stringent selection procedures ensure that only candidates matching its strict requirement are employed. Training workshops further test the service orientation and character of new employees before they make it into the shops. Giordano has extended its philosophy of quality service to its overseas outlets. Its Singapore operations, for example, have achieved ISO 9002 certification. This obsession with providing excellent customer service is exemplified by an insistence that even office employees work in a store for at least one week as part of their training. For Giordano, investment in service meant investment in people. The company also offers one of the most attractive salary packages in the industry, which helps to ensure low staff turnover and an eager-to-please sales force. Managing its human resources has become an even greater challenge to Giordano as it expands into global markets. For example, its recruitment, selection and training practices may require modifications in countries with different cultures, education and labour regulations. Also, policies for expatriate staff helping to run Giordano outside of their home country need to be considered.

Giordano believes that its flat organizational structure and relaxed management style help it to react speedily to market changes on a day-to-day basis. There are no separate offices for higher and top management in Giordano; rather their desks are located alongside their staff, separated only by shoulder-high

Giordano: One of Asia's most successful fashion retailers

GIORDANO

panels. This closeness allows easy communication and speedy decision-making. Speed also enables Giordano to keep its product development cycle short. Similar demands for speed are also expected of its suppliers.

Giordano's home base, Hong Kong, is flooded with retailers, both large and small. Although many retail outlets in Hong Kong compete almost exclusively on price, Giordano has long believed that there are other key factors for success to beat the dog-eat-dog competition prevalent in Asia. Giordano has looked to Western retailers to benchmark key aspects of its activities: (1) computerization (from The Limited), (2) a tightly-controlled menu (from McDonald's), (3) frugality (from Wal-Mart), and (4) value pricing (from Marks & Spencer).

Giordano has achieved great success with a distinctive competitive advantage based on value-for-money and service. Its commitment to excellent service has been reflected in a long list of service-related awards. Giordano was ranked number one by the *Far Eastern Economic Review,* for being innovative in responding to customers' needs, for eight consecutive years from 1994 to 2001. Its stores and employees in Hong Kong and Singapore have been frequent winners of customer service awards in those cities. To ensure that every store and individual employee provides excellent customer service, performance evaluations are conducted at each store twice a month, while individual employees are evaluated once every two mouths. Shoppers can nominate individual employees for the monthly 'Service Star' in each store. In addition, every store is evaluated by mystery shoppers. Based on the combined results of these evaluations, the 'Best Service Shop' award is given to the top store. Customer feedback cards, available at each store, are posted at the office for further action.

Giordano is able to provide value-for-money merchandise through the careful selection of suppliers, strict cost control and by resisting the temptation to increase retail prices unnecessarily. For example, in markets with expensive retail space, Giordano maximizes sales from the square foot of the store by not having a storeroom, but replenishing stock from a central distribution centre. Giordano uses IT to skillfully manage its inventory and forecast demand. When an item is sold, the barcode information, identifying size, colour, style and price is recorded by the point-of-sale cash register and transmitted to the company's main computer. This information is used to compile the store's order for the following day. Orders are filled during the night ensuring new inventory is on the shelves before the store is opened for business. Another advantage of its IT system is that information is disseminated to production facilities in real time. This allows customers' purchase patterns to be understood and this provides valuable input to its manufacturing operations. This close integration enables Giordano to minimize the retailer's twin nightmare of slow-selling items being stuck in the warehouse and fast-selling popular items that are out of stock. Savings from more efficient inventory holding can then be passed to customers, thus reinforcing Giordano's value-for-money philosophy.

When a business becomes successful, there is always a temptation to expand into more products and services to meet customer needs. However, Giordano has retained its belief in keeping stores simple, managing inventory carefully and getting the best out of limited resources. Whilst its stores typically have no more than 100 items, with approximately 17 core items, other retailers typically have 200–300 items. Giordano believes that merchandizing a wider range of products makes these retailers much slower to react to market changes.

The Asia apparel industry

The apparel industry was severely hit by the Asian economic crisis from 1997 to 1999, resulting in dramatic restructuring and consolidation. Many retailers reduced the number of shops in their chains, or closed down completely. Almost everyone in the industry implemented cost-cutting measures while at the same time cajoling reluctant customers with promotional strategies. Yet, there was a silver lining, as the more competitive firms were able to take advantage of lower rentals and the departure of weaker companies. Some firms, including Giordano, worked towards strengthening their positioning and brand image to compete better in the long run. Some retailers also explored opportunities, or accelerated their presence in markets that were less affected by the Asian crisis – mostly in markets outside Asia.

Until recently, Giordano's main competitors for low-priced apparel were Hang Ten, Bossini, U2 and Baleno. United States-based Hang Ten and Italian-based Bossini were generally positioned as low-price retailers offering reasonable quality and service. While Hang Ten and Baleno were more popular among teenagers and young adults, Bossini had a more general appeal. These companies also focused on different markets. For instance, while Hang Ten was only strong in Taiwan, Baleno was increasingly strong in China and Taiwan. On the other hand, Bossini was very strong in Hong Kong and relatively strong in Singapore but had little presence in Taiwan and China.

The squeeze of the retailing sector caused by the crisis, had pushed formerly more upmarket firms such as Esprit and Theme to compete for Giordano's value-for-money segment. Esprit is an international fashion lifestyle brand, selling a wide range of women's, men's and children's apparel, footwear accessories and other products. Esprit's good quality and value-for-money offering placed it in direct competition with Giordano. Theme originally served a niche in the Hong Kong market, for high-quality, fashionable ladies business wear, although it subsequently expanded into casual wear. Theme had expanded from a single store in 1986 to a chain comprising over 200 outlets throughout Asia Pacific, competing directly with Giordano Ladies. A threat from US-based The Gap was also looming. The Gap was already operating in Japan, and was expected to expand into the rest of Asia.

In general, although these firms had slightly different positioning strategies and targeted dissimilar but overlapping segments, they all competed in a number of similar areas. In the years after the crisis, industry analysts predicted that opportunities would continue to be driven by value. However, the retailing environment was becoming more dynamic, a change that was perhaps led by growing sophistication of tastes and rapid advances in the media, communications and logistics environment. Giordano's response to these trends would be the key to its ability to compete in the future, especially as these trends seem to commoditize its current competitive edge in IT, stock control and logistics.

Marketing

Giordano has been able to distinguish itself from its competitors with its high-quality service and cost leadership that together provided great customer value that none of its competitors have been able to match. In a study by *Interbrand* on top Asian brands, Giordano was Asia's highest-ranking general apparel retailer. However, Giordano was still far off being a world label. As a spokesman on consumer insights for advertising agency, McCann-Erickson said, 'It is a good brand, but not a great one. Compared to other international brands, it doesn't shape opinion'.

In the past four to five years, Giordano has begun to reposition its brand, shifting slowly away from its low pricing strategy to one of margin enhancement. Giordano's relatively mid-priced positioning worked well during the Asian economic crisis, when its inexpensive yet contemporary looking outfits appealed to Asia's frugal customers.

However, this position has become inconsistent with Giordano's attempts to gradually re-market its core brand into a trendier label. In order to continue to cater to the needs of customers who favored its value-for-money positioning, in 1999 Giordano launched a new product line Bluestar Exchange (BSE), to cater to the needs of its budget-conscious customers (similar to The Gap's Blue Navy). The good market responses to this new line triggered plans to expand to up to 20 Bluestar stores in Hong Kong, 15 in Taiwan, 2 in Singapore and 100 in Mainland China.

Giordano's willingness to experiment with new ideas could also be seen in its introduction of the sister brands, Giordano Ladies and Giordano Junior. Giordano Ladies with its line of smart blouses, dress pants and skirts is a venture into mid-priced women's fashion. Aiming at the executive woman, the company was hoping to target the fatter profit margins enjoyed in the more upscale niches of women's clothing. This, however, brought them into direct competition with more than a dozen established brands, including Theme and Esprit. Initial market feedback was that whilst there were no complaints about the look or quality of the line, Giordano failed initially to differentiate its new clothing line from its mainstream product line. Nevertheless, it persisted in its efforts and has since made a success of Giordano Ladies, which now has outlets in Hong Kong, Taiwan, China, Indonesia and the Middle East. Giordano Ladies offers a highly personalized service with, for example, staff being trained to memorize names of regular customers and recall past purchases.

Giordano has now cast its sights on markets beyond Asia, driven partially by its desire for growth and partially by its desire to reduce its dependence on Asia in the wake of the 1998 economic meltdown. As part of its globalization process, Giordano already has outlets in Australia in Brisbane, Melbourne and Sydney. It plans to add new outlets to existing stores in Germany and Japan.

While the crisis had made Giordano rethink its regional strategy, it was still determined to enter and further penetrate new Asian markets. This led to the successful expansion into mainland China. Since entering in 1992, China had become particularly important to Giordano. By 2001 it had overtaken Hong Kong to become Giordano's main market, its 680 outlets accounting for about 45 per cent of its total operations. China is also the main manufacturing base for Giordano; it produces 80 per cent of all its clothes there. This helps it to achieve higher than industry average gross margins. China's consumer market is expected to grow rapidly as incomes rise. Some analysts estimate that China's leisurewear retail sector will nearly double between 2004 and 2010, to be worth US$58 billion. However, this is a crowded market, with more than 2,000 brands of casual clothes according to some estimates, with newcomers like Spain's Zara and Japan's Uniqlo also joining in. Giordano has enjoyed a good level of growth in China. In 2005, for example, sales grew by 6 per cent, although this was less than the company's overall 10 per cent sales gain. Giordano has continued to open new stores, particularly in China's second and third tier cities. However, this has been at the expense of sales per square foot, which has been falling since 2000. Analysts project retail growth for Giordano ranging from 3 per cent to 6 per cent per year through 2008. Giordano has also been rolling out its brand segmentation strategy across China. For example, Giordano Ladies is targeted at more affluent working women in big cities like Shanghai and Beijing and BlueStar Exchange for more price-sensitive consumers. Giordano had also opened up more stores in Indonesia in Jakarta, Surabaya and Bali. It would also increase its presence in Malaysia, refurnishing its outlets and converting some of its franchized stores into self-managed stores to improve their profitability.

Giordano's success in these markets would depend on its understanding of them, and consumer tastes and preferences for fabrics, colours and advertising. In the past, Giordano had relied on a consistent strategy across different countries, with common marketing and operations strategies, with local managers only allowed limited tactical discretion (e.g. promotional campaigns) in their respective countries. Each country's performance (e.g. sales, contribution, service levels and customer feedback) was monitored by regional headquarters (e.g. Singapore for South East Asia) and at the head office in Hong Kong. Weekly performance reports were made accessible to all managers.

Future issues

Giordano was confronted with some important issues as it prepared for the next five years. Although it had been extremely successful, the question was how it could maintain this success. In the past it seemed to have a clear understanding of the core competencies that formed the basis of its competitive advantages. However, as it moved into new market segments and territories it needed to consider whether these would be sustainable, or whether strategic adaptations to its operations and marketing strategies would be required.

—Adapted from a case by Jochen Wirtz in 'Business Strategy in Asia',
Singh, Pangarkar and Heracleous (Thomson Learning Asia)

WWW.

Questions (Suggested answers can be found on the companion website www.thomsonlearning.co.uk/barnes)

1   Describe Giordano's operations strategy. Assess its internal consistency and its contribution to the company's competitive success.

2   How consistent is Giordano's operations strategy with its marketing strategy?

3   What are the biggest operations management challenges for Giordano as it expands into new market segments and territories?

4   What advice would you give to Giordano regarding its operations strategy in the future?

References

Barney, J. (1991) 'Firm resources and sustained competitive advantage', *Journal of Management* 17:99–120.

Cohen, W. and Levinthal, D. (1990) 'Absorptive Capacity: A New Perspective on Learning and Innovation', *Administrative Science Quarterly* 35(1):128–152.

Ferdows, K. and de Meyer, A. (1990) 'Lasting improvement in manufacturing', *Journal of Operations Management* 9(2):168–184.

Hayes, R.H. and Wheelwright, S.C. (1984) *Restoring our competitive edge: competing through manufacturing*, New York: John Wiley.

Hayes, R., Pisano, G., Upton, D. and Wheelwright, S. (2005) *Operations, Strategy and Technology: Pursuing the Competitive Edge*, New York: John Wiley.

Hill, T. (1985) *Manufacturing Strategy*, Basingstoke: Macmillan.

Johnson, G., Scholes, K. and Whittington, R. (2005) *Exploring Corporate Strategy* (7th Edition), Harlow: Prentice Hall.

Leonard-Barton, D. (1992) 'The Factory as a Learning Laboratory', *Sloan Management Review* 34(1):23–38.

Leong, G.K., Snyder, D.L. and Ward, P.T. (1990) 'Research in the Process and Content of Manufacturing Strategy', *Omega* 18(2):109–122.

Mills, J.F., Neely, A.D., Platts, K.W. and Gregory, M.J. (1998) 'Manufacturing Strategy: A Pictorial Representation', *International journal of Operations and Production Management* 18(11):1067–1085.

Mills, J.F., Platts, K.W., Bourne, M.C.S.B and Richards, H. (2002) *Competing through Competences*, Cambridge: Cambridge University Press.

Mintzberg, H., Ahlstrand, B. and Lampel, J. (1998) *Strategy Safari*, Hemel Hempstead: Prentice Hall.

Mintzberg, H. and Quinn, J.B. (1991) *The Strategy Process* (2nd Edition), Hemel Hempstead: Prentice Hall.

Mintzberg, H. and Waters, J.A. (1985) 'Of strategies, deliberate and emergent', *Strategic Management Journal* 6:257–72.

Platts, K. and Gregory, M. (1990) 'Manufacturing audit in the process of strategy formulation', *International Journal of Operations and Production Journal* 10(9):5–26.

Prahalad, C.K. and Hamel, G. (1990) 'The core competence of the corporation', *Harvard Business Review* 68(3):79–91.

Skinner, W. (1969) 'Manufacturing: The missing link in corporate strategy', *Harvard Business Review* 47(3):136–145.

Skinner, W. (1985) *Manufacturing: The Formidable Competitive Weapon*, New York: John Wiley.

Slack, N., Chambers, S. and Johnston R. (2004) *Operations Management* (4th Edition), Harlow: Pearson Education.

Slack, N. and Lewis, M. (2002) *Operations Strategy*, Harlow: Pearson Education.

Teece, D.J. and Pisano, G. (1994) 'The dynamics capabilities of firms: an introduction', *Industrial and Corporate Change* 3(3):537–556.

Wernerfelt, B. (1984) 'A resource based view of the firm', *Strategic Management Journal* 5:171–180.

Additional reading

Hayes, R., Pisano, G., Upton, D. and Wheelwright, S. (2005) *Operations, Strategy and Technology: Pursuing the Competitive Edge*, New York: John Wiley.

Slack, N. and Lewis, M. (2002) *Operations Strategy*, Harlow: Pearson Education.

www.   ## Useful websites

http://www.smsweb.org The Strategic Management Society is a US-based association that brings together the worlds of reflective practice and thoughtful scholarship. It aims to focus attention on the development and dissemination of insights on the strategic management process. It has a membership of academics, business practitioners and consultants in 50 different countries.

http://www.sps.org.uk The Strategic Planning Society is a UK-based organization that fosters and promotes research and best practice in strategic thought and action. It aims to create a link between the academic and practitioner worlds of strategy by keeping strategists up-to-date with developments in strategy-related research and practice.

PART TWO

THE INTERNATIONALIZATION OF OPERATIONS MANAGEMENT

PART TWO

Except for a relatively few large multi-national corporations, until comparatively recently, the production processes of most organizations were organized and took place within national boundaries. Now, more and more organizations of all sizes are confronted with decisions about whether, and to what extent, they should:

- Purchase raw materials and components abroad.
- Outsource primary production operations abroad.
- Outsource support activities abroad.
- Sell their products and services to other countries.
- Supply, export and meet demand from their home base.
- Set up their own primary production facilities in other countries.
- Set up their own support activities in other countries.

Service providers, as much as manufacturing, increasingly operate on an international scale.

The two chapters of Part two consider this internationalization of operations management. Chapter 3 identifies the technological, political, economic and socio-cultural forces driving the internationalization process. It presents models that help explain the internationalization process and discusses the specific challenges posed by, and the benefits available from managing operations internationally. Chapter 4 considers the implications for the management of an organization's operations once an organization engages in international business. It identifies the different types of strategies that are available for international operations and discusses their implications and benefits.

CHAPTER 3

THE INTERNATIONALIZATION PROCESSES: DRIVERS, CHALLENGES AND BENEFITS

INTRODUCTION

Until comparatively recently, operations management was a local, or at most a national, matter. Most production processes in most organizations were organized and took place within national boundaries. This was particularly true of services. It was rare to find any service which was not produced and consumed locally. Although many manufacturers imported raw materials (which was often necessary in industrialized countries), the processes that produced the finished goods typically took place within a single country. Although many manufacturers exported their goods, most produced primarily, if not exclusively, for local consumption. Consequently, most operations managers rarely had to concern themselves with processes that crossed national boundaries.

This has been changing for some time. For many organizations, the last decade has seen an acceleration of the trend towards the fragmentation of production processes. Today, many production processes involve a series of interlinked stages that take place at different geographic locations, often in different countries. Improvements in transport systems have made the movement of materials much easier and cheaper, thereby facilitating the internationalization of manufacturing processes. New centres of manufacture have emerged in newly industrialized economies (NIEs) that offer resources, particularly labour, at a fraction of the cost available in traditional manufacturing locations. Other resources vital to the operations of many organizations can move more freely and more quickly across most international borders than ever before. Workers, especially those with the most sought after expertise, can move between countries with much greater speed and ease than was the case

LEARNING OBJECTIVES

On completion of this chapter, you should be able to:

Outline the forces driving the internationalization of operations.

Understand the internationalization process.

Discuss the main challenges of operating internationally.

Understand the benefits to an organization in operating internationally.

internationalization

The process of expanding business operations across international boundaries. At first this might only involve exporting or importing goods and/or services. But it might go on to involve the establishment of production facilities in other countries, as well as facilities to support sales, research and development, and other activities in foreign countries.

newly industrialized economy (NIE)

Sometimes also termed a newly industrialized country (NIC), this is a country which has undergone a considerable level of

(continued on next page)

industrialization in the recent past, switching its primary economic activity from agriculture to manufacturing, and possibly services. NIEs are not quite yet at the status of the industrialized nations of the West, but are more advanced than the countries of the third world.

in the past. Today's financial systems and markets enable virtually unlimited amounts of capital to be transferred across the world instantaneously. And, perhaps most importantly, unlimited quantities of information, including new ideas and innovations can be communicated and shared across the globe between anyone with a PC and Internet access. These factors are important not only in manufacturing industries but also in many service industries, and particularly in information and knowledge-based industries. Many operations processes now cross international boundaries in ways that were simply not possible less than 20 years ago. Most operations now have an international dimension to at least some extent. The case of Mittal Steel offers an example of a company with truly global operations. By 2005, the company had become the world's largest steel maker with production facilities in 14 countries, sales and marketing offices in a further 11, research and development facilities in the USA and France and customers in 120 countries.

CASE STUDY Mittal Steel – A truly global operator

By the end of 2005, Lakshmi Mittal could look back on the thirty years of achievement growth of the company of which he was Chairman and Chief Executive. Mittal Steel was now the world's largest steelmaker and was a truly global operator. It owned steel-making facilities in 14 countries (USA, Canada, Mexico, Trinidad, France, Germany, Czech Republic, Poland, Romania, Bosnia, Macedonia, Kazakhstan, Algeria and South Africa). It had sales and marketing offices in a further 11 countries and research and development facilities in Chicago, USA and Gandrange, France. It employed 175,000 people of 45 different nationalities. Its 5,000 strong customer base spanned 120 countries. The company, registered in the Netherlands, with headquarters in London and Rotterdam, was 87 per cent owned by the Mittal family. The remaining shares were traded on both the New York and Amsterdam's EuroNext stock exchanges. Lakshmi Mittal, an Indian living in London, was one of the UK's richest men and had topped *Asiana* magazine's 'Asian rich list' for a number of years. His personal fortune was estimated to be worth more than £15 billion.

Lakshmi Mittal founded Mittal Steel in 1976 and had since actively pursued a policy of growth. A series of mergers and acquisitions and the purchase of former state owned assets, meant that he had made Mittal Steel the world's biggest steelmaker by 2004. Mittal Steel's growth had been accompanied by high levels of capital investment. It was one of the most technologically advanced steel companies in the world, operating a range of modern steel making technologies. It adoption of best practice and modern production techniques throughout its plants, had placed it among the most efficient steel producers in the world. In 2005 Mittal Steel made shipments of over 49 million tons and had revenues of over US$28 billion.

However, Mr Mittal was not content to rest on his laurels, and in January 2006, Mittal Steel launched an audacious 18.6 billion euros (£12.7 billion) take-over bid for one of its rivals, Arcelor. Registered in Luxembourg, Arcelor had extensive facilities in Western Europe especially France and Belgium. If successful, the take-over would create a giant steel firm with over 250,000 employees and revenues in excess of US$50 billion, producing approximately 10 per cent of the world's total steel output.

The steel industry was once regarded as a sick industry. It was dominated by poorly managed and inefficient state-run firms that were protected by trade barriers. Governments regularly gave aid to their steelmakers for a mixture of social and strategic reasons. However, in recent years the industry had reshaped, largely through cross-border consolidation. A smaller number of globally integrated firms had emerged that were now highly profitable businesses. Their performance had been aided since 2003 by a

One of Mittal's steel mills

strong demand for steel from China's fast-expanding economy. However, Chinese domestic steelmaking capacity had been increasing rapidly and seemed set to rise further.

Arcelor's board immediately rejected the offer. The governments of Luxembourg and Belgium, which both own a slice of Arcelor, expressed doubts about the approach. Although it did not have a stake in Arcelor, the French government joined the country's media and trade unionists in knocking Mittal's plans. Thierry Breton, France's finance minister expressed 'profound concerns' over the offer. Mittal sought to allay fears about job losses by vowing there would be none and offering to move the new company's head office to Luxembourg.

Arcelor's Chief Executive Guy Dollé, claimed that Mittal Steel lacked 'European' values. Although Mittal Steel had been subject to some criticisms for the environmental, safety and employment standards of some of its plants in developing countries, many commentators thought Guy Dollé's claim strange, given that Mittal Steel was based in Rotterdam and London. They saw it as a thinly veiled attack on Mr Mittal's own origins. It was also difficult for Arcelor to claim disdain for overseas hostile takeovers given its own recent success in acquiring Dofasco of Canada in such a bid. Mittal Steel said it would sell Dofasco if it was successful in its bid for Arcelor. Mittal claimed that there was clear strategic logic for the deal as Arcelor's strengths in Western Europe complemented its own in Eastern Europe.

The emergence of Mittal Steel as one of the world's major steelmakers can be viewed as being due largely to its ability to take advantage of the forces of globalization. However, it was now perhaps for the first time experiencing the impact of those seeking to limit the effects of unfettered globalization. Although it took over five months for Mittal Steel to persuade shareholders and the European competition authorities of the merits of the bid, Arcelor was eventually captured by June 2006.

(Sources http://www.mittalsteel.com/, http://bbc.co.uk/ and http://www.economist.com/)

WWW.

WWW.

Questions (Suggested answers can be found on the companion website www.thomsonlearning.co.uk/barnes)

1 Identify the forces of globalization that Mittal Steel had been able to capitalize on.

2 Was Guy Dollé justified in his claim that Mittal Steel lacks 'European' values?

globalization

This refers to the increasing integration of economic activity around the world, evidenced by the growth in international trade and the increasing interdependence of national economies. An increase in cross-border social, cultural and technological exchange is also a feature of globalization. Critics of globalization claim it gives too much power to free market economics and multi-national enterprises and has detrimental effects on less developed countries and the environment.

multi-national enterprise (MNE)

Sometimes also termed a multi-national company (MNC), this is a business organization that has operations in a number of different countries.

less developed country (LDC)

A country whose economy is under developed, relying mostly on agriculture (and possibly extractive industries), and whose population has a low standard of living.

This chapter will examine the internationalization of operations. It will identify the forces driving the internationalization process. Although these are dominated by advances in technology, particularly the power of the Internet, they also encompass political, economic and socio-cultural factors. The chapter will go on to discuss the specific challenges posed by, and benefits available from, managing operations internationally.

DRIVERS OF INTERNATIONALIZATION

It is generally accepted that in the latter years of the twentieth century and the early years of the twenty-first century a number of powerful technological, political, economic and socio-cultural factors have combined to produce strong drivers for the globalization of business. There is no agreed definition of the term globalization. At its most basic, it is the increasing integration of economic activity around the world, evidenced in the growth in international trade and the increasing interdependence of national economies. Many commentators also emphasize the increase in cross-border social, cultural and technological exchange as essential concomitant elements of globalization. Globalization has proved to be a contentious issue. Its critics point to the dominance of Westernized free market economics, the growing power and influence of multi-national enterprises (MNEs), and the detrimental impact on less developed countries (LDCs) and the natural environment. This book will studiously avoid considering the rights and wrongs of globalization. There are many other forums in which to do so. Our concern is rather to understand the phenomenon and its resultant impact on the internationalization of operations management.

The underlying drivers of internationalization in operations management can be classified as technological, political, economic, and socio-cultural.

Technological

e-commerce

The undertaking of business transactions through the medium of Internet-based information and communication technologies (or other computer networks). Sometimes the term electronic business or e-business is used as an alternative to e-commerce. Occasionally the term e-business is used to emphasize the use of ICTs in an organization's own business processes and throughout its entire supply network.

There can be little doubt that the Internet and its associated information and communication technologies (ICTs) constitute a truly significant technological advance. Many analysts argue that these ICTs and their supporting infrastructure of cables and satellites have created a new techno-economic paradigm that is underpinning a fifth Kondratiev long-wave[1] of economic growth (Dicken, 2003). There can be no doubting the growing importance of the Internet for businesses and individuals. In advanced economies, business use of the Internet is virtually 100 per cent in all but the smallest firms. In the UK, e-commerce accounts for 14 per cent of business turnover. In South Korea, 52 per cent of businesses allow customers to place orders online. In Sweden, 72 per cent of companies place orders online (E-business watch, 2005). At its commercial beginnings in the mid-1990s, less than one million people, mostly in the USA, were using the Internet. By the end of 2006, this had grown to around one thousand million, over 16 per cent of the world's population. However, with penetration rates varying widely between countries, the 'information society' (Castells, 1996) does not yet encompass all parts of the globe (see Table 3.1).

The main benefit of the Internet is that it facilitates cheap and easy direct personal access irrespective of distance. Whether there is justification for the claim that it amounts to the 'death of distance' (Cairncross, 1997) is probably questionable, but its ability to reduce the effects of distance can be significant. The use of email enables individuals and organizations to communicate virtually instantaneously almost anywhere on the planet. Almost limitless quantities of data can be transferred within seconds. More sophisticated applications can support synchronous working on documents between people thousands of miles apart. Low cost PC video-conferencing though the Internet can enhance the often impersonal medium of the computer keyboard and screen.

NO.	COUNTRY OR REGION	PENETRATION (% POPULATION)	INTERNET USERS (000)
Top 20 in Penetration			
1	Iceland	86.3	258
2	New Zealand	74.9	3 200
3	Sweden	74.7	6 800
4	Portugal	73.8	7 783
5	Australia	70.2	14 729
6	United States	69.6	210 080
7	Falkland Islands	69.4	2
8	Denmark	69.2	3 762
9	Hong Kong (China)	68.2	4 879
10	Luxembourg	68.0	315
11	Switzerland	67.8	5 098
12	Canada	67.5	21 900
12	Norway	67.4	3 140
13	Japan	67.1	86 300
14	Singapore	66.3	2 422
15	Greenland	66.3	38
17	Faroe Islands	66.3	33
18	South Korea	66.1	33 900
19	Netherlands	65.7	10 806
20	United Kingdom	62.3	37 600
Top 20 in Penetration		68.1	453 045
Selected others:			
Latin America/Caribbean		16	88 779
China		10	132 000
India		3.6	40 000
Africa		3.5	32 766
World Total Users		16.6	1 093 530

TABLE 3.1 Internet penetration in 2006

B2B (business to business)
In e-commerce this refers to a transaction that takes place between one business organization and another.

B2C (business to consumer)
In e-commerce this refers to a transaction that takes place between a business organization and an individual consumer (i.e. individual citizens).

disintermediation
The removal of one or more intermediaries (such as a distributor, wholesaler, broker or agent) in a supply chain. (Known colloquially as 'cutting out the middleman'.) This is a common feature of e-commerce, especially B2C e-commerce.

re-intermediation
The reintroduction of an intermediary in a supply chain. The growth of e-commerce has prompted the emergence of new kinds of intermediary in many industries.

EDI (electronic data interchange)
The computer-to-computer exchange of structured information via a telecommunication link. EDI has been used by business since the 1970s and there are agreed international standards covering its use. It is still used by many MNEs to automate their purchase of goods and services.

Within a few short years, online trading between businesses (**B2B**) and between businesses and consumer (**B2C**), has become commonplace. Traditional business supply chains have been disrupted, with both **disintermediation** and **re-intermediation** in evidence. In some cases, suppliers have chosen to bypass the traditional distributors of their industry and trade directly with customers (e.g. Amazon, Dell). In other cases, new intermediaries have emerged in reconfigured supply. For example, Expedia for travel and Kelkoo for shopping. If products can be digitized (e.g. music, movies, the written word), they can be delivered directly to consumers via the Internet, thereby removing the need for the traditional distribution channels. The Internet can facilitate access to new customers at a fraction of the cost of more traditional means. For example, online banking makes it possible to offer customers the ability to undertake almost all traditional transactions without the need for traditional banking halls.

The Internet is also being used by organizations in their dealings with suppliers. For example, the use of online auctions can enable companies to attract bids from many more potential suppliers than would be economically viable using more traditional means. For many years, many large organizations have conducted much of their business with their suppliers through **electronic data interchange (EDI)**. This improves information flows between the companies, for example to enable exact order requirements and stock positions to be updated instantaneously. The objective is to replace inventory with information. More recent technological advances, using global positioning satellites, have enabled the exact location of goods in transit to be tracked. ICTs are also used by organizations to enable workers in different locations to work together effectively. This has been particularly pronounced in the separation of front and back office operations in some service organizations. In all cases the impact of technology is to shrink distance, reducing the importance of proximity between supplier and customer.

It is also worth noting the impact that improvements in technology in the latter half of the twentieth century have had on the speed and cost of transportation of both goods and people. Advances in air travel mean that virtually any part of the inhabited world can be reached from any other in less than a day. Improvements in transport infrastructures on both land and sea, and in transportation systems (particularly the near universal adoption of containers) have led to dramatic reductions in the total time taken to transport goods. Taken together with the impact of Internet-based ICTs, the world can truly be said to have shrunk.

Political

For almost half a century after the Second World War, the world was essentially divided into three groupings. The industrialized countries of the 'west' (North America, Western Europe and Japan) manufactured most of the world's goods and accounted for most international trade. The USA was the most dominant political and economic force as the European powers and Japan recovered from the devastation of war. The 'communist block' of the Soviet Union and Eastern Europe sought to create its own economic system quite separate from that of the capitalist West. The rest of the world outside of these two groupings was the 'third world'. This comprised the mostly poor and under-developed countries that were often the sources of the world's raw materials and food. Many countries were emerging from colonialism during this period and some became battlegrounds (usually metaphorically, but sometimes literally) between the competing interests of the West and communism.

An increasingly important political development since the Second World War has been the emergence of international agencies to promote international trade and development, such as the World Trade Organization (WTO), the IMF and the World Bank. Most countries belong to such agencies. The WTO negotiates agreements between governments that govern the rules of trade between nations. It has promoted trade liberalization by brokering deals that have progressively lowered trade barriers and tariffs between countries. The International Monetary Fund (IMF) promotes international monetary co-operation and provides temporary financial assistance to countries in financial difficulty. The World Bank provides low cost finance to developing countries for education, health and infrastructure projects. Although the economic development of many third world countries has been disappointing, some have advanced significantly and are now considered as newly industrialized economies (NIEs). These include countries such as South Korea, Taiwan, China and Brazil.

As well as co-operating globally to promote increased international trade, countries have also done so regionally to create formal trading groups. The first of these was the European Union (EU). Originally formed by six countries in 1957 as the European Common Market, by 2005 the EU had expanded to encompass 25 countries, with the prospect of additional members over the following years. The EU has also expanded its activities politically, well beyond a concern only for trade alone. The countries of ASEAN (the Association of Southeast Asian Nations) agreed to move towards a free trade zone across their territories after negotiating the AFTA (ASEAN Free Trade Agreement) in 1992. A similar free trade agreement, the North American Free Trade Agreement (NAFTA) was set up between the USA, Canada and Mexico in 1994.

The fall of communism in Europe in 1990 represented a major shift in the world order. It saw the extension of capitalism into East Europe, the reunification of Germany and the gradual incorporation of many former communist countries into the political institutions of the west (including the EU and NATO). This even included some of the new countries created by the break-up of the Soviet Union. These events would have been unimaginable even a few years earlier. They open the way for massively increased trade across the whole of Europe including Russia.

The other major political change worthy of note is the process of change in the world's most populous country, China. It has been a one-party communist state since the revolution of 1948 and the power of the party remains absolute. However, China has been gradually changing from a centrally planned to a market orientated economy since the late-1970s. China has progressively allowed increased foreign direct investment and increased access to its markets. It joined the WTO in 2001 to become a fully-fledged member of the international trading system. China seems set to become an ever more powerful political and economic force in the world.

Economic

In the period since the end of the Second World War the world has experienced the most sustained period of economic growth in its history. Despite disruptions in commodity markets, most notably the quadrupling of oil prices in the 1970s, financial market upheavals such as the bursting of the dotcom bubble in 2000 and acts of violence such as the attacks of September 11, 2001, volumes of world trade and GDP have continued to grow. In particular, the world's largest economy, the USA, has experienced financial stability and continuous growth through the 1990s and early years of the twenty-first century (World Trade Organization, 2006). This has offset the economic problems experienced by some industrialized countries most notably Japan, and Germany after its reunification.

Major stimuli to the world economy have also been given by the emergence of new manufacturing centres in the NIEs of the 'Tiger' economies of Asia (e.g. South Korea, Taiwan, Singapore, Hong Kong, Malaysia, Thailand, Philippines, Indonesia) and of

Latin America (e.g. Brazil, Mexico). More recently China has emerged as the 'workshop of the world' with a reported trade surplus of over US$100 billion in 2005. With reported economic output at US$2.25 trillion China was reckoned to be the world's fourth-largest economy in 2005 (BBC, 2006). The growth in the international trade in services has become a notable feature of the world economy in recent years, far outstripping the growth in manufactured goods (World Trade Organization, 2006). Advances in technology have enabled more services to be traded internationally, especially in financial services and ICT. Of the developing countries, India has been particularly successful in benefiting from this trend.

Finally in discussing the economic drivers of globalization, the role of MNEs should be noted. These are amongst the world's largest businesses and they operate in countries outside of their homeland. Indeed their activities often span the globe and their products can be found in virtually every country. Companies such as McDonald's, Coca-Cola, Toyota and BP readily come to mind. The financial value of the activities of such businesses can exceed that of many nation states. The decisions taken by their executives can have a greater impact than that of many government ministers. Unlike governments, their decisions are taken not in pursuit of national interest but rather in pursuit of growth and profits for their shareholders. Their decisions, about where to locate their operations and where to source their suppliers, can have significant impacts on the economies of the countries involved. In most countries, MNEs can take advantage of the freedoms afforded by banking and financial systems that operate electronically on a 24-hour basis to transfer funds unhindered from government restrictions. Thus, many MNEs are powerful economic forces in their own right, that often act independent of national governments.

Socio-cultural factors

The closing years of the last century and the early years of this one have seen an increase in the movement of people around the world. More open borders and cheaper travel costs have contributed to the numbers migrating, both legally and illegally, to seek work and improved economic circumstances, or to escape war and persecution. More people travel greater distances to take holidays. Many young people now often undertake extended periods of travel, sometimes including short periods of work, typically before going to university or taking a permanent job. Many students now choose to study in universities outside of their homelands. Satellite television and the Internet make it possible to learn about life in other countries very quickly. People all over the world now aspire to access the same products and services which might previously only have been available in the more advanced economies. This has fuelled the trend for global products that have the same level of quality wherever in the world they are produced and consumed. The world may not yet be a global village, but many people now feel themselves to be citizens of the world as much as citizens of their country of origin or current residence.

THE PROCESS OF INTERNATIONALIZATION

In the wake of these powerful forces, organizations have increasingly sought to internationalize their business operations, developing international and global business strategies. Although some businesses have always operated internationally, until recently, they tended to be few in number and large in size. This is now changing, with more and more organizations of all types and sizes becoming involved in cross-border trade.

There are a number of theories concerning the internationalization of organizations:[2]

Vernon's product cycle theory

Vernon (1966) offered an analysis of the internationalization process based on the product lifecycle. He identified five phases:

- *Phase 1*: All export markets are served from production in the home country.
- *Phase 2*: Production facilities set up in high income markets to serve local markets. Low income markets in less developed countries (LDCs) continue to be served from production in the home country.
- *Phase 3*: The newer lower cost facilities in the high income markets export to LDCs displacing exports from the home country.
- *Phase 4*: The newer lower cost facilities in the high income markets export to the home country.
- *Phase 5*: Newer lower cost production facilities set up in LDC, which export back to the home country.

Vernon's theory was based on his analysis of the overseas investments of US corporations and his prediction of likely future events. Modern critics argue that his theory does not explain more recent patterns of internationalization. They maintain that his model is too simplistic in today's much more complex world.

Dunning's eclectic theory

Dunning (1976) argued that a firm will engage in international production at a particular location when all of the following three conditions are present:

- *Ownership-specific advantages*: The firm must have access to assets not possessed by competing firms. Such assets might be tangible (e.g. raw materials, plant and machinery, skilled labour) or intangible (technological or marketing know-how, patents, brand-names, management expertise). Large firms tend to be better placed to internationalize as they usually have access to greater amounts of finance at lower cost.
- *Location-specific factors*: There must be factors at the foreign location that make it more advantageous for the firm to locate its operations there rather than at home. These factors might include access to markets, the availability of resources, lower production costs, favorable political conditions and cultural/linguistic affinities. The importance of each will vary depending on the type of activity taking place.
- *Internalization*: The firm must internalize the use of its ownership-specific advantages at the location, exploiting them itself, rather than selling them or leasing them to other firms.

Dunning's theory is sometimes known as OLI in reference to the three factors. Although some critics argue that it is more a list of factors rather than a theory, it offers a useful framework to examine specific cases of internationalization of operations.

Stage theories

Various authors have argued that firms internationalize in a series of incremental sequential stages. A number of different models describing the various stages have been put forward.

The best known of these is the Uppsala model (Johanson and Wiederscheim-Paul, 1975) which identifies four stages:

- *Stage 1*: No regular export activity.
- *Stage 2*: Export via agents.

- *Stage 3*: Establishment of a sales subsidiary.
- *Stage 4*: Establishment of foreign production.

Ohmae (1994) adds two further stages beyond the Uppsala model. Ohmae's stage 4 (his Stage 1 equates to Uppsala's stage 2, as he omits Uppsala's stage 1), is *complete insiderization*. At this stage, the firm becomes an 'insider' in the markets it services with all the resources necessary for that including R & D, production and marketing. This requires the diffusion of organizational activities to different locations around the world, to meet the needs of the various markets. The fact that various functional activities have become replicated around the world is likely to lead to tensions within the organization, with national managers attempting to meet the specific requirements of local markets clashing with those at headquarters trying to co-ordinate and control disparate efforts around the globe.

Ohmae's stage 5 is *true globalization*. This requires all members of the organization to make a mental adjustment and adopt a truly global mindset. This is one where the loyalty of each employee is to the firm as a global entity not to the headquarters or the country where they work, and the focus is on meeting the needs of customers irrespective of where they are located in the world. Overcoming the problems caused by the dispersion of operations and functional activities around the world leads to a new role for senior managers at corporate head office. Their role becomes one of guarding corporate identity. As such, they will focus their efforts on controlling branding and ensuring that corporate policies can meet the needs of all stakeholders across the globe. Thus, Ohmae's stage model has the following stages:

- *Stage 1*: Export via agents.
- *Stage 2*: Establishment of a sales subsidiary.
- *Stage 3*: Establishment of foreign production.
- *Stage 4*: Complete insiderization.
- *Stage 5*: True globalization.

Stage model theories of internationalization have been criticized in a number of ways. First, they are based on an analysis of how a relatively small number of companies have behaved in the past. They do not adequately describe how all companies have internationalized. Some empirical studies have shown that some companies have followed a number of different paths to the establishment of foreign production facilities, skipping one or more of the stages (e.g. Turnbull, 1987; Clark *et al.*, 1997). Indeed some companies can be 'born global' (Rennie, 1993), operating in international markets on a substantial scale from their earliest days. Furthermore, some companies have behaved differently when entering different overseas markets. Second, the models do not mean that all companies must or will follow these stages in the future. The stage models do not necessarily represent best practice and organizational strategists may well be able to devise other ways to internationalize. Finally, all stage model theories seem to assume that internationalization is market-led, with organizations entering particular countries to meet an identified market need in that country. However, as was discussed in Chapter 2, strategy can be operations-led. Establishing operations in one foreign market may be part of a process of building knowledge and expertise that can subsequently be used, not only to expand further into that market, but also as a springboard for entry into other markets. Lessons learnt from experiences in one market can be used to inform and shape actions in others.

Internationalization of services

As was discussed in Chapter 1, services have become increasingly important and represent the overwhelming majority of economic activity in industrialized countries. Chapter 1 also noted the differences between manufacturing and service operations. Although the distinctions between them are not always clear cut, it is possible to think of many examples of what are self-evidently service providers that do operate internationally (e.g. the banking and financial services, media, telecommunications, business service industries). However, most theories about internationalization are implicitly, if not explicitly, based only on a consideration of manufacturing organizations. The assumption seems to be being made that service organizations internationalize in exactly the same way as manufacturers. So, is this fair? Should services be considered as a special case?

One of the most important distinctions made between services and manufacturing is that of customer contact. Manufacturing does not usually require any direct customer contact. However, back office services do not require direct customer contact either. A great deal of the internationalization of services in recent years has taken place in back office services. This practice of off-shoring has often been driven by a desire to move labour intensive support services to low labour cost locations. India has especially become a favored destination for the off-shoring of back office services. Some companies have chosen to set up their own back office operations in foreign countries. Others have outsourced these operations to locally owned external providers. Back office operations can be viewed as another form of manufacturing, and so in many respects it seems quite legitimate to consider their internationalization as being akin to that of manufacturing operations.

Front office operations, however, appear to be different, as these require some degree of customer contact. So where and how that contact takes place is a key element in these operations. The facilitation of contact between service provider and service user may necessitate one or other of them to move. The service provider may need to move to meet the service user. The service user may need to move to meet the service provider. Front office services can be categorized on the basis of a 2×2 matrix formed by considering these movements (see Figure 3.1).

Separated services

These are services where there is no need for face-to-face physical contact between service provider and user. Contact in these services is typically technology mediated in some way, as is the case for TV, radio, telephone and Internet services. Technological advances have seen an increase in cross-border separated services. Satellite TV is an obvious example. Reductions in the cost of telecommunications have fuelled the vast increase in the off-shoring of call centres, especially to India and other low labour cost countries with an abundance of well-educated English speakers. The widespread availability of the Internet has made it possible for business and consumers alike to conduct most commercial transactions online. Increasing band width is making it possible to deliver many services online for the first time. This is especially so for entertainment. It is now possible to download music, videos and movies from the Internet. Internet technology may well still be in its infancy and the possibilities seem unlimited. Technologically speaking, the location of an online service provider has become irrelevant. This is opening up new approaches to the internationalization of any service that can be digitized, and our understanding of the internationalization process seems certain to be challenged.

Demander-located services

Some face-to-face services need to be provided at the user's location, with the provider needing to move to deliver the service. Management consultancy is one example of such a demander-located service. Some industrial services such as the repair and commissioning of equipment also fall into this category. The internationalization of this type of service requires the provider to have the capability of delivering the service in the user's country. This clearly has implications for the skills required by the service delivery personnel, the provision of any necessary equipment they require, the cost of delivery, and so on.

FIGURE 3.1 Customer contact service location matrix

Provider

Does not move　　　　　　　　　　　　　　　Moves

Does not move

Separated services
(e.g. media, advertising)

Demander-located services
(e.g. management consultancy)

User

Moves

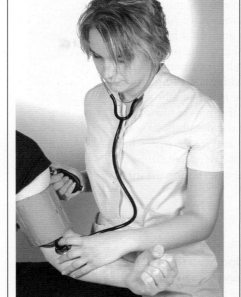

Provider-located services
(e.g. medical services, hotels)

Peripatetic services
(e.g. trade shows, conferences)

WHEN THINGS GO WRONG   Marks and Spencer in Hong Kong

Opening its first store in Hong Kong in 1988 seemed like a natural step to Marks and Spencer (M & S), the UK's leading retailer. At that time the company was in the midst of what seemed like an unbroken run of success, with increasing sales and profits the norm for its home operations. M & S had taken its first steps outside of the UK in the 1970s when it opened stores in France and Belgium. But 1988 saw it reinvigorate its plans for international expansion when it acquired Brooks Brothers, an American clothing company and Kings Super Markets, a US food chain. Moving into the then British colony of Hong Kong seemed like a low risk way of entering the increasingly attractive markets of the Far East.

Hong Kong was prosperous and home to a large expatriate community who were likely to have been M & S customers back in the UK. M & S also took confidence in the knowledge that its goods had been sold in Hong Kong for over 40 years by Dodwells, a well-known department store. However, M & S knew that to be successful in Hong Kong it would need to attract custom from the local Chinese population, who made up over 90 per cent of the colony's inhabitants. Furthermore, retailing in Hong Kong was fiercely competitive. M & S knew that it would be difficult for it to command the price premium it enjoyed at home due to its strong brand name and reputation for quality goods and customer service.

Initial trading in Hong Kong proved problematic for M & S. The intention was that around 90 per cent of the goods in its Hong Kong stores would be identical to those sold in Britain. However, this approach seemed to ignore the very different weather conditions of south China and took no account of different local tastes. Furthermore, the initial inventory made available in the stores seemed to take no regard of the much slimmer physique of most Chinese women and the shorter height of most Chinese men compared to their European counterparts.

There are also different attitudes to shopping in Hong Kong compared to the UK. In Hong Kong shopping is more of a leisure experience likely to involve the whole family. People like to shop in large family groups,

Marks and Spencer's Hong Kong Store

(PAT BEHNKE/ALAMY)

taking considerable time to inspect and talk about the merchandise on offer, before deciding whether to buy. They also expect much more attentive service from sales assistants than would be the case in the UK, where store workers often do little more than operate the cash tills. In Hong Kong retail shopping space is in short supply and expensive. Shop layout is critical to success. Operators have to balance the need to offer shoppers space to move around in against the need to display their wares. Having the right goods on display in the right environment supported by appropriate customer service is crucial to making a sale. In the UK, M & S could rely on the loyalty of their customers built up over many years. In Hong Kong, that loyalty had to be created.

However, over time, M & S was able to overcome these difficulties, being able to learn from its very direct exposure to its customers and adjust to the very different trading conditions in Hong Kong. By the mid-1990s it was operating six stores profitably and was able to successfully navigate the changes in its trading environment that followed the handover of the colony to the People's Republic in 1997. However, trading difficulties at home saw the company pull back from its internationalization strategy. In 2001 it announced it would be closing all its international stores. The Hong Kong business would be franchised.

Questions (Suggested answers can be found on the companion website www.thomsonlearning.co.uk/barnes)

1 Can any of the models of internationalization adequately describe Marks and Spencer's move into Hong Kong?

2 To what extent is M & S a service operation?

3 Which of the service types (as shown in Figure 3.1) best describes M & S operations?

4 What were the biggest operations management problems encountered by Marks and Spencer in Hong Kong?

Provider-located services

The provision of some face-to-face services requires the user to move to the provider's location. This is often the case where the service needs specialist equipment or staff, as is often the case for medical services. Some services are provided specifically for users who are themselves travelling, whether for business or pleasure (e.g. in the hotels and hospitality industries). Some times the user travels to the provider's home country to receive the service, as is the case for some specialist medical treatments. However, more normally, this category of service requires the provider to establish service provision locations to suit the user. This clearly has implications for internationalization.

Peripatetic services

Although they are more unusual, there are services where the provider and the user both move in order to facilitate the service encounter. Trade shows, conferences and some live entertainments fall into this category. The encounter needs to take place at a location suitable for the event, so the service provider needs to have the ability to access such venues.

Internationalization normally creates a conflict between the pressure to standardize provision globally in order to maximize economies of scale and scope and the pressure to customize in order to meet the different requirements of customers in each locality. Services have traditionally been seen as being more difficult to globalize because of the imperative to tailor the service offering to meet different local needs. This is particularly true for front office services where the requirement of customer contact makes them fundamentally different to manufacturing. This ought to prompt a somewhat different consideration of the internationalization process for at least some types of services. However, with some exceptions (e.g. Segal-Horn, 2005), the development of theory of the internationalization of services has lagged that for manufacturing.

CHALLENGES OF OPERATING INTERNATIONALLY

Once an organization is involved in international activities, it falls to its operations managers to rise to the challenges posed in managing what can often appear as disparate activities in far-flung locations. The most significant challenge is perhaps that of overcoming the dilemma that is inherent in most international operations, namely that of attempting to reconcile the competing demands of managing on both a global and a local scale. On the one hand, hard-won knowledge and expertise gained from past operational experience needs to be exploited on a worldwide basis in order to produce and deliver goods and services as efficiently as possible. This creates a pressure to harmonize operations across the globe, using standardized systems and technologies, for easier co-ordination and control. On the other hand there are pressures to respond to the specific circumstances in each location. The quality and quantity of input resources (e.g. labour, raw materials) may vary at each location. Legislation may differ from country to country. There may be significant cultural differences between people (employees, customers, suppliers, etc.) in different countries. Products and services may need to be customized to meet local requirements. This tends to fragment operations. Organizations who successfully manage international operations are able to balance these conflicting pressures. They neither seek to impose standard solutions irrespective of location, nor permit individual locations to operate entirely independently of one another. Recent advances in ICT are increasingly offering the means to achieve the intensity of interaction required to facilitate the management of operations across the globe.

Managing international operations is likely to pose considerable challenges in many areas of operational activity both structural and infrastructural, making managerial decision-making more difficult and complex. Operations managers may be faced with trying to serve differing and possibly unfamiliar markets, with operating systems in different locations, possibly using differing technology with workforces of varying levels of skills, in very different societal contexts. There will inevitably be conflicts of what activities to undertake at what location and with what priority.

BENEFITS FROM OPERATING INTERNATIONALLY

However, there are also significant benefits to be gained by operating internationally (other than the obvious financial ones being sought through increasing sales and lowering costs). Organizations with successful international business strategies typically tend not to view the challenge of managing international operations as a problem to be overcome. Rather, they treat their exposure to new and different ways of operating and to the differing demands of customers across the globe as a series of learning opportunities. Organizations that operate in more than one country have many opportunities to learn from their exposure to different international environments. Also, the increased internationalization of business provides organizations with many opportunities for learning from the good operations practice of other organizations they encounter across the world. Successful international organizations actively seek to feed back this new knowledge and diffuse it throughout the organization. They use their learning from their international operations as a source of competitive advantage to drive their business strategy.

Kogut and Zander (1993) have argued that multi-national organizations are much better placed to learn than organizations that only undertake international transactions at arms-length. This is because they are more efficient at transferring knowledge gained about operating in different countries between their subsidiaries. They attribute this to their use of the same internal evaluation and accounting systems, which also makes them more likely to invest quickly if they see opportunities. Flaherty (1996) points out that truly global operations (in the sense intended by Ohmae (1994) as

CASE STUDY Golden Arches bridge local tastes

Diners at the approximately 800 McDonald's restaurants in China will notice something different on the menu this year: rice burgers. Launched last year in Taiwan, the rice burger consists of crispy chicken – or sliced beef – with a mixture of cabbage and lettuce, served between two lightly toasted and flavoured 'rice patties'. Its success in Taiwan, where it accounted for 6 per cent of sales growth in 2005, has inspired McDonald's to expand the concept to Hong Kong, Singapore, the Philippines and Malaysia.

For a fast food chain that operates in 118 countries, offering locally appealing food beyond its core menu of burgers and fries is not new. When the US-based company opened its first European outlet in the Netherlands in 1971, the menu included breaded meatball *krokets*. In Australia, a McOz Burger arrives with a slice of beetroot (the New Zealand version used to include a fried egg). Pork teriyaki burgers have been on the menu in Japan for a few years.

But the current drive is about more than one-off alterations to the menu. It is a systematic approach to localization that is prompting changes ranging from the design of kitchens to how the company manages its regional businesses. 'McDonald's was built on a strong foundation of a core menu that we took around the world, but taste profiles and desires are changing', says Ken Koziol, Vice-President of worldwide restaurant innovation. Dan Coudreaut, head chef at McDonald's, says: 'The world is getting smaller. We're going to be working increasingly with the individual tastes of a region'. Faith Popcorn, Chief Executive of BrainReserve, a brand specialist, says the days of hero worship of American cuisine are over: 'A brand had better start to make friends with the culture it's in'.

Others argue that the attempt to show more of a local face around the world poses a challenge to the way McDonald's manages its brand, long perceived as a global icon whose survival has depended on maintaining trust with a mass of consumers interested in a familiar core menu. Lovers – and haters – of fast

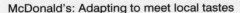

McDonald's: Adapting to meet local tastes

food have for decades known the Golden Arches as the global flag carrier for convenience eating, US-style. Simon Anholt, a British author and founder of Nations Brand Index, a quarterly global survey of countries as brands, says the increasing localization of McDonald's menus may end up being counter-productive. While the anti-American mood in many parts of the world appears to be punishing sales of US-branded goods, he says, McDonald's brand identity means, paradoxically, it cannot stray too far from its core menu. He says

'By putting local food on the menu all you are doing is removing the logic of the brand, because this is an American brand. If McDonald's serves a poor imitation of your local cuisine, it's going to be an insult'.

Such dilemmas may have prompted the company to do some soul-searching of its own. In its first European Corporate Responsibility Report, issued in November, McDonald's says: 'Ask people a simple question: 'Do you trust McDonald's?' and you will get a huge variety of answers'. It continues: 'Many of those answers reflect the fact that people's opinions about McDonald's are shaped by factors that go way beyond what we actually do as a company. Attitudes towards the USA. Perceptions of 'fast food'. Views about globalization itself'.

Yet the company believes it is possible to be global and local at the same time. Mary Dillon, chief marketing manager, says: 'The business at McDonald's is much more about local relevance than a global archetype. Globally we think of ourselves as the custodian of the brand but it's all about relevance to the local markets'. McDonald's current advertising drive – which uses the slogan 'I'm lovin' it' – is the company's first unified global marketing campaign. Yet 'I'm lovin' it' is also translated into the local language of the country wherever it runs.

Asia is where the localization strategy faces arguably its biggest test. Tim Fenton, McDonald's head of Asia-Pacific, Middle East and Africa, manages a business spanning 15 time zones and embracing a region that includes people speaking 800 different languages and dialects. A new 'food studio' will open in Hong Kong in May, where chefs will devise meals aimed at specific local markets in the region. The studio is similar to one already open in Paris, which is doing a similar job for European palates. Mr Fenton acknowledges that McDonald's competition in Asia – where the most popular menu item is not a burger, but the Filet-O-Fish – will be tough. 'Most consumers frequent market stalls, food courts, hawker stands and convenience stores for fast meals. This is our competition, it's non-traditional and at times very random', he says. 'McDonald's is already meeting the needs of our consumers' local tastes in ways that are different from the corner noodle shop'.

By 2007, McDonald's will also be ready to roll out a 'flexible operating platform' – a modular kitchen that can cook more than one type of meal in the same restaurant. This involves a 'combi oven' – still at the prototype stage – that can cook several varieties of dishes at once. These include as yet undeveloped offerings such as a tilapia sandwich, McRoasters (a type of roast potato), salmon with lemon and dill sauce and 'Flautas', a Mexican dish consisting of tightly rolled corn tortillas with a variety of fillings.

Robert Goldin, Executive Vice-President at Technomic, a Chicago-based food service consultancy, says this will inevitably add complexity to McDonald's business. 'I'm not sure that the return is there to support it'. Mr Koziol says the company is 'very aware' of the extra investment needed but says: 'It's a migration, to be done in a staged manner'. Such concerns are unlikely to stop McDonald's for now. Jim Skinner, Chief Executive, says: 'We're a local business with a local face in each country we operate in'.

(Excerpted from the article by Jeremy Grant, *Financial Times,* London 9th February 2006)

Questions (Suggested answers can be found on the companion website www.thomsonlearning.co.uk/barnes)

WWW.

1 What are the most significant factors that have driven McDonald's to change the basis of its international operations?

2 What problems will McDonald's face in trying to strike a balance between a desire to maximize efficiency by standardizing operations globally and the pressure to customize its operations to meet local requirements?

discussed previously), rely on a network rather than a hierarchy for co-ordination. A network is better at promoting joint learning between its members. It can enable them to more easily share the different solutions they may have developed to solving specific problems in their own operating environments. Lessons from these experiences can prove useful to other members faced with similar problems in their own environments. This can be especially helpful if one operation has had to learn to satisfy particularly demanding customers in one part of the world.

The increased internationalization of operations means that there is now more likelihood of organizations being directly exposed to the practices of others in similar industries or operating similar processes in different industries. This can offer tremendous opportunities for learning from their best practice. There have been particular opportunities in recent years for Western manufacturers to learn from the world class operations of many Japanese companies, particularly with regard to lean manufacturing practices such as JIT, TQM, *kaizen* and so on. Neither has it been necessary to go to Japan to do this as many Japanese firms have set up manufacturing facilities in various parts of the world. This was particularly so in the UK in the late-1980s and early-1990s. This provided local British firms with an opportunity to benchmark their operations against high performing Japanese companies who were facing the same operating environment as themselves. In their study of UK manufacturing firms during this period, Hanson and Voss (1993) showed the benefit of this, finding that high performing British companies were five times more likely to use benchmarking as an improvement tool than low performance companies. Companies that won contracts to supply the new arrivals were especially able to benefit. The report was also able to show that these companies had significantly better practices than suppliers to other longer established larger firms. This they attributed to the use of the vendor's supplier development programmes.

SUMMARY OF KEY POINTS

Many operations, both in services and manufacturing organizations, have become internationalized in recent years. Most operations now have an international dimension to some extent.

The internationalization of operations is being driven by powerful forces of globalization. These forces are a combination of political, economic, socio-cultural and especially technological factors.

There are a number of theories concerning the internationalization of organizations including Vernon's product cycle theory, Dunning's eclectic theory and various stage theories (e.g. the Uppsala model and Ohmae's). None of these offer entirely satisfactory explanations of the internationalization process.

Services, especially customer contact services may be a special case of the internationalization process.

Operating internationally presents many challenges to operations managers. The most significant of these is probably reconciling the conflicting demands globally and locally. Globally there is a pressure to maximize efficiency by standardizing operations for easier co-ordination and control. Locally there is a pressure to customize operations to meet the specific requirements of each location, which can lead to a fragmentation of operations. Successful international operations management requires that these conflicting pressures be balanced.

Organizations can benefit from operating internationally if they can share the learning from their own experiences and also learn from the practices of other organizations that they come into contact with in other countries.

EXERCISES (Suggested answers can be found on the companion website www.thomsonlearning.co.uk/barnes)

WWW.

1 What are the most important forces of globalization?

2 What are the main theories covering the internationalization of organizations?

3 What is the most significant challenge in international operations management?

4 What are the main benefits to be gained by operating internationally?

5 Why have some but not all service providers been able to internationalize their operations in recent years?

6 To what extent do you think that the internationalization of services should be treated as a special case from that of manufacturing?

7 Choose one of the major MNEs and identify the most significant forces of globalization that have impacted on the international operations of the company in the last few years. What has been the organization response to those forces?

8 Choose two companies that have internationalized in recent years; one manufacturer and one service provider. Which of the theories of internationalization best describes the way that each company underwent internationalization?

9 Is the increased globalization of operations inevitable?

10 What are the risks associated with an organization increasing the internationalization of its operations?

CASE STUDY EXERCISE IPC Corporation

Introduction

IPC Corporation was started in 1976 under the name Essex Electric by Patrick Ngiam and his brothers, with financial help from the Local Enterprise Finance Scheme of the Singapore government. Leaving the safe and familiar path of his family's seafood business, Ngiam decided to put his engineering background to good use, launching himself into the personal computer (PC) business – a product that was at best a luxury with an uncertain future. The Ngiam brothers propelled their brainchild IPC into a massive growth spurt over the next 15 years. By 1995, IPC had sales of $1.5 billion globally and had rapidly grown to become one of the leading Asian firms in the PC industry. However, a sudden slide starting in 1996 reduced IPC to barely half of its former self, leading it to refocus activities in the Asia Pacific region. This reorientation caused the firm to lose 48 per cent of its sales, its stock to plummet, and total assets to shrink from over $1 billion to less than $25 million in 2002.

The PC Industry

The introduction of the first personal computer in the mid-1970s quickly led to the emergence of one of the largest, most dynamic, economically important and rapidly growing industries in history. Table 3.2 provides summary information on the PC industry.

The PC industry was also characterized by a high degree of fragmentation, intense levels of competition and high rates of technological change. As the PC approached commodity status, a high degree of standardization, widely available components and easy assembly, allowed relatively easy entry into the market. Many firms with limited technological abilities continued to enter the market. On the other hand, there was an

TABLE 3.2 Global PC shipments

WORLDWIDE SHIPMENT TRENDS																
	1990	1991	1992	1993	1994	1995	1996	1997	1998	1999	2000	2001	2002	2003	2004	2005	2006
PC's	23.99	25.98	30.46	37.12	44.18	55.67	30.65	36.56	41.41	51.64	56.75	60.08	63.38	68.30	73.95	80.80	87.37
% Growth	8.3%	17.2%	21.9%	19%	26%	21.3%	−45%	19.3%	13.2%	24.7%	9.9%	5.9%	5.5%	7.7%	8.3%	9.3%	8.1%
Laptops	–	–	–	–	–	–	2.48	2.63	4.01	4.98	5.63	5.93	6.13	6.49	6.96	7.52	8.09
% Growth	–	–	–	–	–	–	–	6.2%	52.3%	24.3%	13.0%	5.3%	3.4%	5.9%	7.3%	7.9%	7.7%

ASIA PACIFIC PC UNIT SHIPMENTS											
	1996	1997	1998	1999	2000	2001	2002	2003	2004	2005	2006
PC's											
China	2,101.00	3,501.00	4,080.00	4,729.00	5,578.00	5,767.40	6,135.70	7,071.40	8,392.30	9,977.00	11,467.40
Hong Kong	27	27.5	26.1	27.6	29.5	30.1	30.8	31.7	33.6	35.5	37.6
India	40.9	53.2	79.8	150.9	301.8	397.6	467.1	544.6	600.9	674.6	741.4
Indonesia	318.4	347.4	307.1	340.3	405.6	434	460.7	508.4	585.1	671	763.4
Japan	1,405.90	1,771.00	1,677.00	2,228.00	1,974.70	1,991.00	1,991.90	2,000.80	2,079.40	2,284.20	2,548.40
Malaysia	47.2	41.8	34.3	37.4	38.8	39.3	40.6	43.3	47.7	53.3	60.4
Philippines	94.2	108	112.4	123.5	239.4	249.3	264.1	296.6	333.4	380.9	437.9
Singapore	27.4	27	24.1	27.7	29.2	29.5	30.3	31.6	33.4	35.8	38.7
South Korea	1,866.00	1,921.00	1,500.00	1,432.50	1,935.30	1,974.30	2,041.10	2,171.40	2,350.50	2,617.30	2,911.40
Taiwan	786.1	931.1	1,060.60	1,163.70	1,256.30	1,256.40	1,271.10	1,346.10	1,434.40	1,559.90	1,730.00
Thailand	226.2	238	185.8	202.6	223.2	224.8	228.5	242.8	266.3	302.6	348.8
Australia	549.7	608	680	788.4	869.3	957.2	1,042.60	1,111.80	1,174.90	1,229.30	1,290.80
New Zealand	224	196.3	208.3	220.3	221.7	234.3	246.2	256.7	275.3	292.8	310.9
Total	7,714	9,771.3	9,975.5	11,471.9	13,102.8	13,585.2	14,250.7	15,657.2	17,607.2	20,114.2	22,687.1
Laptops											
China	93.6	146.9	205	303	463	532.8	574.8	685	846.2	930.2	1,024.00
India	–	1.7	2	2.5	3.3	3.9	4.7	5.7	6.4	7.1	7.7
Japan	1,375.20	1,341.80	1,378.40	1,499.80	1,524.80	1,540.70	1,541.40	1,550.00	1,589.10	1,684.90	1,818.80
Philippines	–	–	–	–	34	37.4	40	43.8	47.7	52.5	57.6
Singapore	17.4	18.9	21.6	25.4	26.6	26.8	27.7	28.9	31.1	33.8	37.3
Vietnam	–	–	–	–	5	5.7	6.5	7.1	7.9	8.9	9.6
Australia	118.6	123.7	132.3	156.7	160.2	169	187.8	203	216.9	232.2	249.3
New Zealand	47	41.2	43.7	46.3	46.5	47.3	50.3	52.9	57.2	61.8	66.6
Total	1651.8	1674.2	1783	2033.7	2263.4	2363.6	2433.2	2576.4	2802.5	3011.4	3270.9

SOURCE: IDC (FOR 1990 TO 1995) AND GLOBAL MARKET INFORMATION DATABASE, EUROMONITOR INTERNATIONAL.

emerging trend for greater concentration, as firms such as Dell, IBM, Gateway and HP captured an increasing share of sales. However, even the five largest players, had only between 8 per cent and 15 per cent of world market share in 2004. PC manufacturers focused their efforts on manufacturing, assembly and logistics improvements. The rapid changes and the differing skills required for different parts of the PC industry encouraged specialization. Efforts to reduce costs drove some PC firms to outsource manufacturing to specialist contractors. Others, such as Dell and Gateway, resorted to direct sales to gain significant cost and flexibility advantages by dealing directly with customers. Product cycles were very short, often being less than one year, and prices declined rapidly and steeply within weeks of introduction. As much as 80 per cent of the total industry profits made on a particular product would be earned within the first three to six months of its introduction. Customers were increasingly resistant to paying premiums for brand names. Only products that led in performance or were customized for specific needs, were able to command temporary price premiums.

Growth

Essex Electric began to manufacture printed circuit boards for multi-national corporations in 1981. Realizing that their deal with the multi-nationals could not be permanent or secure, the Ngiam brothers decided that their company needed to manufacture, distribute and market under its own brand name. This led them to purchase machines and equipment for the manufacture of PCs. However, the company did not immediately attack the domestic computer market or even other regional markets of South East Asia. Instead, IPC introduced its first personal computer, an IBM PC/XT clone, into the European markets. Distributors for Sweden and the Netherlands were appointed in 1986.

IPC's products attracted the attention of a small French electronics distributor, Systec, in 1987. Being new to the PC business, Systec decided to sell IPC's products by mail order, which was a novel approach for France. The lower delivery costs and Systec's reliability allowed sales to increase rapidly. Systec spearheaded a marketing push that saw the company's market share surge from zero to 2.9 per cent over the next six years. IPC achieved consistently high ratings in France and in 1993, briefly had the largest sales of any PC manufacturer in the country. By 1993, France accounted for just over a quarter of IPC sales worldwide, counting among its customers giant French companies like Thomson and Matra.

IPC's German subsidiary, IPC Europa, was set up in 1990 and achieved a fair degree of success, establishing IPC as a strong niche brand. Competitive pricing combined with excellent after-sales service was the key to IPC's success in the face of such strong rivals as IBM, Compaq, Bull and Olivetti. It was a strategy that was to serve the company in good stead all over Europe, including Spain, Germany, the Netherlands and the United Kingdom, all of which saw rapid establishment of IPC's presence in the late-1980s and early-1990s.

In 1991, on the wings of a five-year tax-free holiday granted by the Singapore government, the Ngiam's company took to the expansion trail. First, they capitalized on the IPC brand name by renaming the company IPC Corporation (Pte) Ltd. They then made capacity expansion a priority by constructing the $12 million IPC Building, to house their production and headquarters. Importantly, the company also invested in the construction of an R & D department. Next, the company expanded into network hardware manufacturing, producing by late-1991, a line of RISC multi-processor server computers, large office systems that connect to other nearby terminals and allow multiple users simultaneously. Another product, the IPC Point of Sale (POS) terminal, a computer terminal used as a cash register in a retail store or supermarket, caught on rapidly in Europe. Finally, to ensure full control over its successful European efforts, Patrick Ngiam expanded his control over the distribution by establishing a series of retail outlets. For example, IPC purchased Systec, renaming it IPC France.

By end 1991, international giants such as IBM had signed contracts with IPC for the manufacture of personal computers, a clear testament to the quality and efficiency with which IPC was producing PCs. IPC also became a moderately successful brand at home, occupying a niche as a relatively high-end local brand in Singapore. Recognition for IPC's achievements was widespread, with major awards including the Singapore Businessman of the Year for Patrick Ngiam in 1993.

Rapid Expansion

IPC's expansion continued in 1992 with investments in overseas production and a joint venture with a Mexican firm Plus Sistemas to manufacture for the North American market, which was about to be liberalized by the North American Free Trade Agreement (NAFFA). In 1993, IPC entered the US market directly, acquiring Texas-based Austin Computer Systems, a small mail-order computer firm with its own manufacturing plant. As Bernard Ngiam explained, 'We also bought the company to use it to generate global advertising – American PC magazines are read all over the world and the name will spin off from there'. IPC also established subsidiaries in Australia and Korea and proposed further acquisitions in China and India.

The rapidly-growing PC market had attracted thousands of entrants from around the world and competition was severe. In order to differentiate itself, the company began to emphasize its brand name, target new customers, expand its retail channel, broaden its product range and build its R & D capabilities. IPC placed particular emphasis in Asia on the small business segment. By the end of 1994, within three years of opening its first store, IPC had 120 retail outlets in South East Asia and Europe. The firm planned to have 300 outlets by 1997. With the exception of IPC France and its Austin subsidiary, IPC sold its products through its own distribution channels and retail outlets. Patrick Ngiam argued that the expansion into retail outlets was an essential element of IPC's strategy.

IPC placed high priority on research and development. It entered into three R & D contracts in 1994. The first of these was with AT&T to develop sound and telephony products (such as answering machines) for PCs. The second was with the Information Technology Institute for the development of a series of multimedia products, including video and CD-ROM storage. The third was the Singapore Digital Media Consortium, a forum for local companies to collaborate on R & D ideas.

Next, the company turned its attention to finding a joint venture partner for its entry into manufacturing in China. IPC acquired a 51 per cent stake on a consumer electronics manufacturer, the Zhuhai Torita Group in May 1994. While the new acquisition was initially expected to act as a cheap manufacturing centre for low-end components, the long-term objective was to use Torita as a beachhead into the potentially vast and lucrative Chinese market. IPC also acquired and operated 24 wholesale and distribution hubs as part of this deal. These stores would form the base for a rapid expansion of IPC's electronics and electrical outlets, of which 100 would be set up throughout China by 1997. The drive into China was further reinforced in 1995 with a $6-million joint venture with SCATDC that would provide value-added data-processing services such as credit/debit card transactions electronic data interchange and database and network communications in China.

By the mid-1990s, IPC products were available in at least 66 countries in North and South America, Western and Central Europe, the Middle East and the Asia Pacific. Its core businesses are described in Table 3.3.

While IPC was expanding geographically, its R & D investment allowed it to tap into new markets in terms of product innovation. In 1995, it established a new vision – to be a 'total IT solution provider'. This meant furnishing all of the client's computer needs, from basic PC manufacturing to video-on-demand service to value-added network services like electronic mail.

Ngiam noted 'the only way to create a bigger market share is through new products'. To further these interests, IPC acquired shares in two Israeli firms, Optibase and VCON, in order to access the technology for video-conferencing products. This technology enabled IPC to introduce Singapore's first video and

---

TABLE 3.3 IPC's product and service range (1990s)

IT Products:
- *General Purpose Computers (GPC)*
  Entry-level desktop PCs to servers created for the home and corporations.
- *Consumer Computing Products (CCP)*
  Mobile computing products such as notebooks, subnotebooks and personal interactive organizers.
- *Application Specific Products (ASP)*
  Point-of-sale terminals to cater to all major segments of the retail automation industry.
- *Multimedia Products*
  A range of audio and video boards, simultaneous communication add-on peripheral boards and complete multimedia upgrade kits for PC multimedia applications.
- *Peripherals*
  Computer-related peripherals such as PCMCIA cards and motherboards.

IT Services:
- *Interactive Media Services*
  IT-based services such as video-on-demand, karaoke-on-demand and home-shopping.
- *Commercial VAN Operators*
  Operation of value-added networks such as Electronic Funds Transfer authorization, Electronic Data Interchange and Internet in China.

Consumer Electronics:
- Consumer Electronics (under IPC's subsidiary Torita in Zhuhai China) comprises television sets, tape recorders, video camera, fax machines, cordless handphones, pagers, video CDs and karaoke players.

Distribution:
- Distribution of computer parts and peripherals to OEMs and System Assemblers in the Asia-Pacific (via the Corex Group).

SOURCE: ANNUAL REPORTS.

karaoke-on-demand systems in a condominium. IPC also achieved some success in other areas, developing in-room TV services for hotels (including the world's first global hotel TV network, an interactive credit card authorization system, a lottery gaming system, and a shopping system) and a big commerce network system in China. It also ventured into the manufacture of flat panel displays and batteries for its notebook PCs.

As IPC celebrated the tenth anniversary of its incorporation, it looked to be in a healthy position. It was a market leader in several markets in Asia. It was the second largest PC supplier in Singapore and the third largest in the corporate PC market. It had a 23 per cent market share in the Korean POS market. It was expanding aggressively into a wide variety of IT areas, and appeared to be well on its way to becoming a total IT solutions provider. Overall revenue grew by 135 per cent; those from the Asia-Pacific regions by 140 per cent. IPC appeared to be poised for growth and success.

Crisis

By 1995, IPC had grown into a mid-sized firm with sales of $1.5 billion (see Tables 3.2 and 3.6 for a summary of IPC's financial performance). Yet this was not enough for the ambitious firm. It established sales targets of $2.3 billion for 1998 and $5 billion for 2005. The announcement of these targets marked what proved to be IPC's high point.

IPC's problems with Austin heralded a change of fortunes. Unexpectedly, IPC aborted its retail operations in the US in 1996 at the cost of US$100 million in lost annual revenues. Patrick Ngiam explained, 'We want to concentrate in the Asia-Pacific, and that itself will require a lot of cash'.

IPC's Australian operations also suffered a severe blow in 1996. Aggressive expansion in 1994 led to the establishment of 54 retail stores within 13 months. However, these proved to be costly and unprofitable. So

TABLE 3.4 IPC financial summary

($M)	89	90	91	92	93	94	95	96	97	98	99	2000	2001	2002	2003
Turnover	54.9	67.7	183.6	274.5	579.5	1,359.4	1,542.4	801.9	410.4	57.3	24.6	20.5	7.0	17.2	28.0
Gross Profit	–	–	–	–	–	–	–	–	–	–	9.8	7.0	3.2	4.4	3.8
Other revenue	–	–	–	–	–	–	–	–	–	–	0.4	9.0	2.1	0.5	1.0
R&D Costs	–	–	–	–	–	–	–	–	–	–	0.1	–8.1	–3.3	–1.3	–1.7
Selling & Operating costs	–	–	–	–	–	–	–	–	–	–	–11.9	–15.8	–7.6	–6.7	–8.5
Operating Profit	0.9	6.4	14.4	43.9	55.0	83.9	64.8	21.6	17.0	–27.6	–2.7	–8.0	–5.7	–3.1	–5.4
Finance Costs	–	–	–	–1.3	–1.4	–3.8	–10.5	–7.9	–13.3	–15.8	–19.6	0.4	–	0	0
Share from Associated Companies	–	–	–	–	–1.2	0.4	1.2	–2.0	–0.2	–	–0.4	–0.1	–	0	0
Exceptional Items	–	–	–	–	–	–	–	–	–2.2	2.0	10.8	2.9	–	2.9	4.7
Tax	–0.6	–0.02	–0.1	–1.0	–0.9	–3.6	–0.8	–0.3	–0.1	–0.7	–0.9	0.1	0.5	0.1	0.6
Profit after tax	–	–	–	41.5	51.6	76.9	54.7	11.5	3.4	–44.1	–25.7	–10.4	4.7	–1.7	0.1
Minority Interest	–	–	–	–0.5	–	–4.6	–2.1	–2.0	–0.6	–1.3	2.5	2.0	0.4	0.3	0.6
Extraordinary Items	–	–	–0.9	–	2	–	–	–37.4	–113.3	–250.1	–26.7	20.1	–	–	4.7
Net Profit	0.9	6.4	13	41.1	53.6	72.3	52.7	–23.9	–109.4	–295.4	–49.9	7.7	5.1	–1.4	0.5
Non-current Assets															
Fixed Assets	0.9	1.2	3.5	11.1	18.9	147.5	193.3	49.6	46.5	53.6	53.6	17.5	17.8	14.6	13.6
Investments & Property	–	–	–	–8.4	69.6	158.0	160.0	195.2	242.5	161.2	137.4	92.4	96.4	66.9	77.2
Intangible Assets	–	–	–	–	7.2	22.6	21.9	4.6	3.9	1.3	1.1	5.4	1.0	4.7	2.2
Current Assets															
Debtors	–	–	–	57.5	86.6	186.1	320.4	265.2	169.6	44.9	34.1	4.1	3.6	8.4	12.2
Stocks	–	–	–	32.4	86.0	210.8	243.6	119.6	93.8	1.3	1.3	0.4	0.1	0.1	0.5
Cash & Bank	–	–	–	9.9	96.1	88.4	61.9	41.9	6.3	6.1	36.5	26.1	19.8	14.9	16.8
Other current Assets/non classified	9.6	15.7	25.6	–	–	–	–	–	–	23.1	17.84	17.3	24.9	59.2	62.3
Current Liabilities (Creditors)	9.1	9.1	13.9	53.1	117.8	359.9	504.7	238.9	246.2	291.5	77.1	30.2	17.4	24.4	23.5
Non Current Liabilities															
Long Term Creditors	0.2	0.2	0.2	0.1	0.1	98.0	105.4	118.7	84.1	0.1	9.6	–	–	–	20.8
Other Liabilities	–	–	–	–	0.1	–	0.1	0.1	0.1	–	–	–	–	–	–
Equity (Capital + Reserves)	–	–	–	49.4	246.5	355.5	390.8	318.4	298.0	12.9	–44.3	132.9	146.3	143.7	141.8
Convertible Loan	–	–	–	–	–	–	–	–	–	–	8.3	–	–	–	–
Scheme of Arrangement	–	–	–	–	–	–	–	–	–	–	231.0	–	–	–	–
Gross Dividends	–	–	–0.5	–20	–10	–12	–16	–5.2	–	–	–	–	–	–	–

SOURCE: ANNUAL REPORTS.

TABLE 3.5 IPC sales by region (5 million)

REGION	1992	1993	1994	1995	1996	1997	1998	1999	2000	2001
America	8.79	145.82	408.69	443.7	59.64	42.18	5.63	5.06	0.42	0.89
Europe	121.88	213.83	386.27	329.99	127.51	102.93	4.81	3.35	1.86	1.58
Asia Pacific	136.15	202.58	491.28	720.6	608.81	260.10	41.83	14.53	17.35	3.92
Others	7.69	17.22	73.16	48.08	5.94	5.21	4.99	1.66	0.89	0.61
Total	274.51	579.45	1,359.40	1,542.35	801.90	410.43	57.26	24.60	20.51	7.00

SOURCE: ANNUAL REPORTS.

after initially closing 28 stores in July 1995, the remaining 25 stores were sold in January 1996 for $15 million. However the sudden closure of the stores resulted in some consumers not receiving warranted technical assistance, which harmed IPC's reputation in the country.

These closures and limited returns from its diversification into multimedia and value-added network services were reflected in poor 1996 results. First-half profits in 1996 fell an astounding 85 per cent, ending any further plans to finance diversification ventures. Poor second-half sales caused the annual sales tally to be 48 per cent lower than the year before, when IPC sales had crossed the $1.5 billion mark.

Worse news arrived shortly thereafter. In January 1997, IPC Corporation (Korea) Ltd defaulted on $923,400 worth of promissory notes. After its Korean CEO absconded, investigations revealed massive mismanagement and fraud. This ultimately resulted in total losses of $45.5 million for 1996 and the closure of operations in Korea, one of Asia's most promising PC markets. To raise additional capital IPC disposed of its Hong Kong and Netherlands operations, and reduced its holdings in Corex Technology from 100 per cent to l8.87 per cent and in Essex Electric from 100 per cent to 19 per cent.

It also became clear in 1997 that IPC's major product launch of the last few years, a highly integrated computer for the home, had failed. Launched with an expensive advertising campaign, the MY.G.E.N.I.E computer was intended to drive IPC's entire home PC product line for several years. This PC served multiple functions, receiving television and radio broadcasts, and serving as a telephone answering machine and a games machine in addition to performing standard PC tasks. However, sales were disappointing, reaching only 25 per cent of the expected 200,000 and 300,000 units a year. Observers pointed to a poor concept, poor product quality, and unresponsive service as reasons for the failure of this line.

These difficulties, increasing competition, and rapid technological change in the PC industry encouraged IPC Corp to search for more stable industries. As a result, IPC chose to expand into telecommunications, entering the mobile telecommunications industry in 1996 by acquiring a 37 per cent stake in German firm Hagenuk Telecom. Already significant in 1996, the mobile telecommunications industry was rapidly growing into one of the largest industries in the world. Competition was severe, and the industry was fragmented (see Table 3.6). IPC, however, felt it had selected the right partner. Describing Hagenuk as a leading telecommunications giant and a thoroughbred, IPC indicated that telecommunications and computers would now represent its two core businesses. Patrick Ngiam indicated that IPC's future would largely be in telecommunications, which would account for between 60 per cent and 80 per cent of profits: 'We have decided to be a niche player in the computer world, and we are putting major efforts in telecommunications'.

Despite the range of products and technologies it had ventured into, Ngiam dismissed suggestions that IPC had diversified too broadly and indicated that IPC had a new vision: 'It's not a question of diversification, but a question of participation in the digital business area because it will become a digital world. We want to provide a total market solution integrating computers, communications and services on demand'.

During the first half of 1997, the new enterprise seemed to be successful, and Hagenuk earned profits of $9.2 million. Encouraged, IPC took a 49 per cent stake in a US$10 million venture with state-owned Guangzhou Post & Telecommunications Equipment in China to produce 800,000 hand-phones a year for the Chinese market. As part of the joint venture Guangzhou Post & Telecommunications Equipment signed a deal to buy US$50 million worth of handphones from IPC over 12 months.

TABLE 3.6 Mobile phone handset market shares (1997)

	GLOBAL %	EUROPE %
Motorola	24.5	21.3
Nokia	19.9	23.1
Ericsson	15.5	21.4
Matsushita	7.3	5.0
NEC	5.0	2.3
Siemens	3.6	8.0
Samsung	3.0	0.0
Mitsubishi	3.0	1.7
Sony	2.6	0.8
Alcatel	2.5	5.5
Philips-Lucent	2.0	4.5
Northern Telecom	0.6	1.6
Others	10.5	4.8

SOURCE: AUTHOR, FROM VARIOUS PUBLISHED SOURCES.

However, in August 1997 problems arose. Much to IPC's surprise, Hagenuk was discovered to be in severe financial difficulties, forcing the beleaguered firm to file for bankruptcy protection. Hagenuk's actions eventually cost IPC a $79.6 million charge against its 1998 profits.

In August 1997, IPC was hit with lawsuits for $32 million in Korea and the USA. These were in addition to an on-going case in Australia and three others in Singapore. Most of these suits were for 'breached component orders', the failure to supply promised computer parts. IPC however explained that these cases were common in the PC industry.

A new strategy

IPC's computer sales declined drastically between 1997 and 1999, capturing less than 1 per cent market share in Asia Pacific. This performance seemed to drive major change in IPC's strategy in 1999 – an exit from the PC industry. Write-offs related to this withdrawal essentially eliminated IPC's entire asset base.

Patrick Ngiam announced that IPC would concentrate on three businesses: thin clients, telecommunications, and services. A thin client is essentially a PC without certain components thought to be unnecessary for office usage, or which were for functions best performed by servers over networks. Thin clients cost as little as 50 per cent of many PCs. Their introduction was a radical shift for IPC. The firm subsequently introduced a related product, the Buddy, which allowed up to five users to share one PC. IPC also forged an alliance with Boundless Technologies, a US based computer vendor catering to a thin-base clientele. Under this agreement Boundless would market IPC's computers in Asia, Australasia, India and the Middle East.

In March 2000, IPC announced the purchase of a US-based business-to-business Internet infrastructure services firm, brokerserver.com, for $84 million. IPC explained this acquisition was part of its shift towards providing e-services for businesses. Another effort was a joint venture with leading Chinese firm TCL Holdings, to provide Internet payment services for Chinese households.

IPC also announced a major shift in its business, into residential and commercial property development in China. Its landmark project was the development of a 170,000 square metre residential-commercial project in Zuhai, China. IPC had acquired the land for $113 million through a share swap with a Chinese firm. The first phase of the project was to be launched in early-2002.

By mid-2001, the restructuring had achieved some success, as all debt was repaid, and net tangible assets moved back into a low positive state. IPC also achieved profits in 2000, after five years of losses.

By April 2001, IPC had identified a new vision, 'Vision C' – the provision of *Convenience* for users in a digitally-based global interactive information technology and communications application environment. IPC listed its three main businesses as:

- Full Service Providers of e-Services System Development Centre
- Thin Computing
- Wireless Telecommunications/Broadband Systems Integration

The situation in 2005

IPC's performance continued to improve, and in March 2003, IPC announced a third year of operating profits and improved turnover. Patrick Ngiam was confident enough to predict that IPC's market capitalization and net profits would surpass their all time highs of $2 billion and $72 million respectively by 2007, explaining that:

'We are in good shape now, generating positive cash flow. Going forward, it can only be better. We aim high but from lessons that we've learnt, we need to be more careful in the way we execute our business plan'.

In mid-2004, IPC appeared to be well on the road to a bright future. Its resilience was perhaps best captured by its surprise acquisition of the Nanyang Institute of Management (NIM) in July 2004 for $1.3 million. NIM, a private firm focusing on education in Singapore, had run into difficulties. Patrick Ngiam indicated that IPC's rescue of NIM represented an extension of the firm's core businesses of e-services and e-training, and had good prospects: 'The market potential is there. It already has a base of students. It is not like we are starting from scratch'.

In early-2005 Patrick Ngiam announced that revenues for 2004 had increased by 18.5 per cent to $33.3 million, and gross profits by 53 per cent to $5.9 million. IPC appeared to have put its troubles behind it, and to be ready for bold action again.

—Adapted from a case co-authored by Ishtiaq Mahmood in 'Business Strategy in Asia',
Singh, Pangarkar and Heracleous (Thomson Learning Asia)

WWW.

Questions (Suggested answers can be found on the companion website www.thomsonlearning.co.uk/barnes)

1 What were the main drivers of the internationalization of IPC's business up to the mid-1990s?

2 Which theory best describes IPC's internationalization?

3 What operations management problems did IPC experience in the mid-1990s? To what extent did these contribute to the company's crisis?

4 What major challenges does IPC's new corporate strategy give to the firm's operations management?

Notes

1 Kondratiev theorized in the 1920s that economic growth occurs in 'waves' of about 50 years duration, each ushered in by technological advances. The first wave corresponded with the mechanization of the industrial revolution (ca.1770–1830), the second with the coming of the steam engine and the railways (ca.1830–1880), the third with the introduction of electricity (ca.1880–1930) and the fourth with mass production systems (ca.1930–1980).

2 This review of internationalization process theories is based on material in the Open University Business School pioneering MBA course *B890: International Enterprise*.

References

WWW.

BBC (2006) 'China's economy continues to soar', 25 January 2006 available at http://news.bbc.co.uk/2/hi/business/4645874.stm, downloaded 1st February 2006.

Cairncross, F. (1997) 'The Death of Distance: How the communications revolution will change our lives', *Harvard Business School Press,* Massachusetts: Harvard.

Castells, M. (1996) *The Rise of the Networked Society*, Oxford: Blackwell.

Clark, T., Pugh, D. and Mallory, G. (1997) 'The process of internationalization in the operating firm', *International Business Review* 6(6):605–623.

Dicken, P. (2003) *Global Shift* (4th Edition), London: Sage.

Dunning, J.H. (1976) *US Industry in Britain*, Aldershot: Gower.

E-business watch (2005) 'Overview of e-business developments – July 2005', European Commission Enterprise and Industry Directorate General available at http://www.ebusiness-watch.org downloaded 31st January 2006.

Flaherty, M.T. (1996) *Global Operations Management*, New York: McGraw-Hill.

Hanson, P. and Voss, C. (1993) *Made in Britain*, Dublin: IBM Consulting.

Johanson, J. and Wiederscheim-Paul, F. (1975) 'The Internationalization of the Firm: Four Swedish cases', *Journal of Management Studies* October, 305–322.

Kogut, B. and Zander, U. (1993) 'Knowledge of the firm and evolutionary theory of the multinational corporation', *Journal of International Business Studies* 24(4):625–645.

Ohmae, K. (1994) *The Borderless World: Power and Strategy in the Global Marketplace*, London: Harper Collins.

Rennie, M.W. (1993) 'Global competitiveness: born global', *McKinsey Quarterly* 4(4):45–52.

Segal-Horn, S (2005) 'Globalization of service industries', in McGee, J. (ed.) *The Blackwell Encyclopedia of Management: Strategic Management*, Oxford: Blackwell Publishing, 147–154.

Turnbull, P.W. (1987) 'A challenge to the stages theory of the internationalization process', in Rosson, P.J. and Reid, S.D. (Eds) *Managing Export Entry and Expansion*, New York: Praeger.

Vernon, R. (1966) 'International investment and international trade in the product cycle', *Quarterly Journal of Economics* 80:190–207.

World Trade Organization (2006) 'International trade statistics 2005' available at http://www.wto.org/english/res_e/statis_e/its2005_e/its05_toc_e.htm, downloaded 1st February 2006.

Additional reading

Castells, M. (1996) *The Rise of the Networked Society*, Oxford: Blackwell.

Dicken, P. (2003) *Global Shift* (4th Edition), London: Sage.

Dunning, J.H. (1993) *Multinational Enterprises and the Global Economy*, Reading, Mass: Addison-Wesley.

Friedman, T.L. (2006) *The World Is Flat: A Brief History of the Twenty-first Century*, London: Penguin Books.

Useful websites

http://www1.worldbank.org/economicpolicy/globalization/index.html The World Bank's Globalization homepage. Provides access to some recent presentations on globalization and some of the leading research on the subject.

http://www.wto.org/ The World Trade Organization (WTO). Provides information on the latest development in trade and access to reports and statistics.

http://www.unctad.org/ The United Nations Conference on Trade and Development (UNCTAD). Provides information on the latest development in trade and development and access to reports and statistics.

http://www.imf.org/ The International Monetary Fund (IMF). Provides information on IMF's work and access to reports and statistics. A good source of information on individual countries.

http://www.ifg.org/index.htm The International Forum on Globalization. One of the organizations that has concerns about the impact of economic globalization.

http://www.dti.gov.uk/europeandtrade/index.html The Europe and World Trade webpages of the UK government's Department of Trade and Industry (DTI). A wealth of information for companies operating internationally.

CHAPTER 4

INTERNATIONAL OPERATIONS STRATEGIES

INTRODUCTION

As discussed in Chapter 3, more and more organizations of all kinds have been internationalizing in recent years, in response to the powerful forces of globalization. Once an organization starts to pursue an international business strategy there will inevitably be an impact on its operations. Organizations can internationalize for many different reasons. There are a number of different routes that they can take on the path to internationalization. As such, there is a need for an organization to develop an international operations strategy appropriate to its international business strategy. Its international operations strategy will profoundly affect its ability to rise to the challenges of, and to realize the benefits available from, internationalization.

As was pointed out in Chapter 2, to be effective an operations strategy needs to be consistent, and make a contribution to competitive advantage. Most theorists agree that having a clear set of objectives for operations is an essential first step if this is to be achieved. However, this may not be straight forward for organizations that operate internationally. They may have different business objectives in different countries because of the nature of markets, the state of competition, or the organization's own longer-term goals in a particular country. This might lead to different and possibly multiple objectives for the operations that served those markets. Customer expectations and perceptions of levels of quality, service and cost may well differ from country to country, making it more difficult to satisfy customers with standardized products and processes. The cost, quality and availability of necessary resources may vary from country to country making some locations more attractive than others. Having operations in more than one country, makes the task of setting clear operations objectives much more complex and difficult than would be the case for an organization operating only in a single country.

LEARNING OBJECTIVES

On completion of this chapter, you should be able to:

Assess the implications of international business strategy for an organization's operations.

Identify the principal objectives that organizations can have in internationalizing their operations.

Describe the different ways in which an organization can enter and serve foreign markets.

Discuss the relationship between business strategy and operations strategy in an organization operating internationally.

Highlight the benefits available from an appropriate international operations strategy.

This chapter will consider the relationship between business strategy and operations strategy in organizations operating in an international context. It will identify the different types of international operations strategy that are available and discuss their implications.

THE IMPLICATIONS FOR OPERATIONS MANAGEMENT

Once an organization adopts an international business strategy, there will inevitably be an impact on its operations. The transformation process model, introduced in Chapter 1, can provide a helpful framework to consider the likely implications of internationalization on an organization's operations (see Figure 4.1.). This chapter will now look at each part of the transformation process in turn.

Outputs

Despite trends towards greater homogeneity of customer tastes, very few products and services can be offered outside of their home markets without some adaptation to cater for variations in customer tastes in different countries. Even McDonald's, the American fast food chain, whose business grew on the basis of offering the same basic burger-and-fries-based menu in all its outlets, has had to vary its offering in some parts of the world to cater for local eating habits (see Chapter 3). The need for products and services to be adapted to local conditions presents a significant challenge for operations management. On the one hand there is likely to be a pull towards standardization in order to achieve low costs through the **economies of scale** of mass production. On the other hand there will be a pull towards specialization, in order to meet specific local demands. A failure to tailor products to local markets risks a loss of business. However, increasing product variety makes operations complex, difficult and potentially more costly.

Resolving the standardization *vs* specialization dilemma can be especially problematic for organizations that provide customer service operations via the telephone. Using

economies of scale
Reductions in unit cost of output due to increasing production volumes. Unit cost savings are achieved by spreading the fixed costs of production over an increased volume and from the increased efficiency available from the division of labour and from using large-scale machinery.

FIGURE 4.1 Implications of internationalization on operations

Inputs	Transformation process	Outputs
Greater flexibility from suppliers	Increased complexity	Pressure to tailor products and services for local markets
New suppliers	Multiple and conflicting performance objectives	vs.
Pressure for: • Low cost sourcing • Lower cost labor • Business process outsourcing	Pressure to standardize: • Economies of scale • Economies of scope vs. Pressure to specialize: • Mass customization • Dedicated operations Extended supply chains Foreign facilities • Expatriate vs. local staff • Increased risks	Risks of alienation of customers with standardized products and services

a centralized call centre to provide telephone services, such as after sales support, has long been seen as the best means of achieving economies of scale by many service providers. In recent years, many organizations have outsourced their call centre operations to specialist providers, who by serving a number of different clients can achieve economies of scope in addition to economies of scale. Initially this work tended to be done domestically. However, many call centres serving English speaking customers have now moved to lower labour cost countries. India, with its wealth of well-educated English speakers has proved especially popular. Some organizations have relocated all their English language telephone services to single call centres in India. However, the nature of this type of service means that customer's judge their experience of the organization on the basis of the individual interaction they have with whichever call centre operative handles their telephone call. Providing a standardized service from a single location in a foreign country has proved less than satisfactory for many customers due to many operators' inability to offer the kind of specialized individualized service that customers expect. There have also been many complaints from customers who say they cannot understand operatives' English pronunciation. The case of Dell's Mumbai helpdesk illustrates some of the problems that have arisen.

The Process

Serving diverse international markets has significant implications for operations processes. Operations typically have multiple performance objectives e.g. cost, quality, speed, flexibility or dependability (Slack *et al.*, 2004). It can be problematic enough trying to achieve those performance objectives that are appropriate for markets inside an individual country. However, the task for operations becomes that much more challenging when a multiplicity of markets, each requiring operations to achieve different performance objectives, are involved. It is very difficult for any single operations facility to simultaneously satisfy demands to achieve the lowest possible cost in order to compete on the basis of price, and to offer the additional features or special adaptations needed for the customization required to compete in a number of very different markets. The conflict between standardization and specialization becomes even more difficult to resolve when a number of operating facilities located in a number of different countries are expected to serve markets in many different countries.

There are essentially two approaches to tackling this problem. One is mass customization (Pine 1993). This aims to achieve economies of scope by using a single process to produce a wide variety of products (or services) in the same way that mass manufacturing aims at achieving economies of scale. This requires a high degree of 'flexible specialization' (Hirst and Zeitlin, 1988) from the organization's operations to enable production to be switched easily from one product to another. This can be achieved through the use of general purpose rather than specialist machinery and by multi-skilling workers to enable them to perform as many tasks as possible. Probably the best known example of mass customization is computer manufacturer Dell. Dell enables its customers to choose the exact computer that they want by ordering directly from them online or by phone. Once they have chosen the model that they want, customers are guided through a range of options which enables them to order the exact specification and configuration that they want. That computer is then built to order for them in one of its seven factories across the world (Austin, Texas; Nashville, Tennessee; Winston-Salem, North Carolina; Eldorado do Sul, Brazil; Limerick, Ireland; Penang, Malaysia; and Xiamen, China) and shipped directly to them.

The second approach is to create a number of separate focused operations each aimed at achieving specific performance objectives. This usually involves dedicating the facilities at any particular location to serving certain specified market or markets

---

Reductions ... available from increasing the number of products produced. Unit cost savings are achieved by spreading certain overhead costs (such as administration, distribution, marketing, etc.) over an increased volume of output, assuming that these costs do not increase as a result of increasing the number of products.

mass customization
The use of a single process to produce a wide variety of products (or services). It aims to realize unit cost reductions through economies of scope in the same way that mass manufacturing aims to achieve economies of scale.

focused operations
Based on Skinner's (1974) idea of a 'focused factory', this is the notion that a facility that concentrates on a single or very narrow range of tasks will outperform one trying to achieve a broader range of tasks. Focus might be achieved by limiting the markets served, the products produced or processes used at a particular facility.

WHEN THINGS GO WRONG Does Michael Dell know? A tale of unhappiness at Dell's Mumbai helpdesk

In January 2006, Dell, the world's largest computer maker, announced plans to set up its fourth call centre in India. The company already employs over 10,000 people in its Indian call centres, which provided a telephone help desk service to its many thousands of customers around the world. Like many other Western companies, Dell was attracted to India by the abundance of low cost English-speaking workers, many of whom are well qualified and highly IT literate. Locating call centres in India sounds like a good deal all round. Customers get access 24 hours a day, 7 days a week wherever they are in the world, companies are able to reduce costs, and workers in a developing country get jobs.

However, not everyone is happy. Niels Kjellerup, Publisher and Editor of The Call Centre Managers Forum, an online chatroom for call centre managers, argues that the rush to outsource customer contact operations to cheaper locations has resulted in the worst of management practices in US and UK call centres being exported as 'World Class Call Centre Practice' in countries like India. He says that too often what is seen in India is bad customer service delivered cheaply. He claims that many Indian call centres are run as sweatshops with intelligent people being treated like cattle. Call Centre Managers with little or no previous experience adopt 'idiotic vendor measures' such as 'how many calls' and 'how short', which simply result in the delivery of poor levels of customer service.

An informant of Kjellerup's, employed as a Technical Support Agent at Dell's Mumbai Call Center gives an insight into the pressures faced by workers who are facing increased volumes of calls. His team leader told workers to: 'Get your average handling times down. Try anything to get rid of the customer. Lie. Just get rid of those customers who take up too much call time'. Agents are required to work nine and a half hours a day, but typically work anywhere from 12 to 16 hours. Processing 28 calls an hour is mandatory. Another target is to ensure that no customer calls back within seven days. The informant

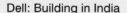

Dell: Building in India

claimed that there are few, if any allowances for time off, even for doctor visits, sick days or handling family emergencies.

'You get "leave without pay" for the day you're sick and you are rostered for an extra sixth day the next week for which you work with no pay. Lateness is counted by the minute. Everything is logged. We must account for every second of the workday, including time for scheduled breaks and restroom breaks. A reason must be given if a restroom break takes more than the allowed three minutes. Typically, a combination of about six absences or incidents of lateness in a year is grounds for termination.'

Call centre workers can also face a tough time from customers. One *Washington Post* headline claimed that 'India Call Centers Suffer Storm of 4-Letter Words' (27 February 2005). Call centre executives and industry experts say abusive hate calls are commonplace. One call centre agent said 'When some callers are unhappy with the service, their frustration often turns racist. They say, 'You should not handle our work. Indians are not good enough'. Another said,

'Many callers refuse to speak to Indians and ask for an American right away. So I tell them, "I am an Indian but I live in America." They ask, "Where in America?" I tell them I cannot disclose my location. But they are still suspicious and start asking about the weather.'

A survey by Indian information technology magazine, *Dataquest,* found that about 25 per cent of Call Centre Agents identified such calls as the main reason for workplace stress. The survey said the calls were often psychologically disturbing for workers. An executive at one call centre said,

'This is a high-stress business, and most of our agents are between 22 and 25 working the graveyard shift. I have noticed a sudden plunge in their confidence level after an irate, abusive or racist caller. They begin to fumble with words and get nervous. I counsel them not to take it personally.'

Kjellerup notes that there is a growing backlash against bad call centre management practices. Average staff turnover can be 60 per cent p.a. with even highly experienced managers leaving. This makes training and educating staff very expensive indeed, if you lose them within six months of the investment. He argues that performance measures should focus on the outcome of the call and whether the customer was satisfied. But since Indian outsourcers are not paid for such niceties it goes unnoticed.

However, companies are now facing an ever increasing number of customer complaints and dissatisfaction is growing. Kjellerup says,

'Outsourcing customer interaction has the inherent weakness that it wrongly assumes customers are either in "complaint" mode, "help me" mode or "I want to buy" mode. In fact customers shift between these modes depending on the reception they get and in most outsourced Call Centers buying signals are lost along with the revenue stream. What happened to the idea that customer service is an integral part of future revenue creation?'

Dell was founded by Michael Dell, whilst still a student at the University of Texas. By 1992, he had become the youngest Chief Executive Officer (CEO) ever to earn a ranking on the *Fortune* 500. Dell pioneered the direct sales of PCs to customers. Although its success has arguably been based on low prices, Dell had to overcome initial customer concerns about customer service, particularly after sales service, from a remote supplier. Niels Kjellerup points out that Michael Dell knew instinctively that helping a customer make a PC work was the first step in the next sale. Throughout his initial tenure as CEO (he stood down as CEO in 2004, but returned in February 2007), Michael Dell was renowned for his close personal interest in how his customers were treated.

Kjellerup argues Dell's Mumbai Call Center is an example of how bad practice can result in the delivery of very poor service to customers. He notes that responsibility for customer interaction has been delegated to the domain of the company's Chief Information Officer rather than its CEO. He claims that Dell now displays little understanding of the importance of the sales process and how the customer experience is enhanced by good customer service. Kjellerup says:

'Maybe they now think that, "It's only a Help Desk function". Soon the Help Desk will be seen as a cost on par with office cleaning and garbage removal rather than an investment in future sales. Then Dell will be confronted with a serious flaw in their business model.'

Kjellerup sighs, 'If only Michael Dell knew'.

(Based on source material from www.dell.com, www.eweek.com, www.callcentres.com.au and *The Washington Post*)

WWW.

WWW.

Questions (Suggested answers can be found on the companion website www.thomsonlearning.co.uk/barnes)

1 What business objectives does Dell appear to have for its Indian call centres?
2 To what extent are these objectives consistent with the company's business objectives?
3 What contribution do its Indian call centres make to Dell's competitive advantage?
4 How might Dell improve its customer service operations?

with a limited range of products or services (Skinner, 1974). In this way the organization assigns each of its facilities to a single task. Alternatively, the operations at a single site could be split into a number of autonomous units, or 'plants within a plant'. Each of these is then dedicated to a separate single task, with different production areas within the same site each producing different products, perhaps using different technologies, or catering for different customer demands. The principle of focused operations enables a number of different production systems at the same site to operate independently whilst sharing site overheads such as common facilities and resident support staff (e.g. technical experts). This should enable unit costs to be lowered for all products.

However, whatever approach is used, meeting the variable demand for different products from different markets raises significant challenges for scheduling operations in order to meet competing customer priorities and potentially different quality requirements, whilst always being under pressure to control costs. Additionally, in international operations supply chains may be long, making it yet more difficult to meet customer delivery requirements and putting increased pressure on costs.

Meeting customer requirements can be especially problematic in the face of growing demand for the organization's products and services. If capacity is insufficient to meet demand there may be difficult choices as to which market or customer is to get priority. If capacity is to be increased, a decision has to be made about whether the capacity of existing facilities should be increased, or whether new facilities should be established and, if so, where. Deciding to increase the size of existing operations may lead to greater complexity, making planning and control more difficult. This can put the effectiveness and efficiency of the operation at risk. Setting up additional operations at another location is likely to require a significant capital investment and also carries the risk inherent in moving to a new country. Employing staff in new and unfamiliar environments is especially challenging, and organizations must consider the extent to which they will rely on locally hired staff and the extent to which they will bring in expatriate staff from the home country. Once serving international markets, organizations usually feel they have to internationalize their operations. For service operations requiring face-to-face customer contact, especially demander-located services, there may be no choice but to internationalize by moving the service delivery system to customers in other countries.

Inputs

Internationalization is likely to have significant implications in respect to resource inputs. If increased demand from new export markets is to be met from existing facilities, the production volumes are likely to have to increase. If products for

business process outsourcing (BPO)
This involves moving certain operations that were previously carried out within an organization to an external supplier. Recently, there has been a trend to outsource support operations as well as core processing operations.

off-shoring
This involves moving certain operations to another county. This could be done either by relocating the affected operations to the organization's own facilities in another country, or by outsourcing the operations to a foreign supplier. The motivation for this is often, but not exclusively, cost saving.

market access strategy
A strategy in which operations are internationalized in order to access and serve markets outside of the home country.

resource seeking strategy
A strategy in which operations are internationalized in order to access and serve markets outside of the home country.

international markets have to be adapted in some way, then product variety will also increase, leading to increased complexity for operations. This is likely to require increased flexibility from suppliers if disruptions to operations are to be avoided.

It may be that new and additional suppliers will be required to avoid potential shortages of input resources. Increases in volume and variety may expose capacity constraints within existing facilities, whether due to labour, equipment or other input resources. Any shortage of such input resources is likely to put upwards pressure on costs.

If international demand for the organization's products and services is sustained, then the organization may consider setting up new facilities at a different location, possibly in a new country. Moving operations away from the safety of existing supply markets and supporting infrastructure involves a degree of risk as trading relations will need to be established with new suppliers in those locations. However, if operations are confined to home soil the organization may well miss out on the potential advantages available from the resources and capabilities available in other countries. In recent years, many organizations in developed economies have sought to take advantage of the lower costs available, particularly for labour, in less developed and newly industrialized countries, either by setting up their own operations in those countries or by sourcing input resources abroad. The LDCs have often been the source of raw materials. However, an increasing number of organizations have moved some or all of the stages of their production processes to LDCs and NIEs. This can involve the phenomenon referred to as business process outsourcing and off-shoring. Business process outsourcing (BPO) involves transferring processes that were previously carried out within an organization to an external supplier. Off-shoring is the term used to describe transferring processes that were previously carried out within an organization to another country. These might still be done within the organization or might be outsourced. Although the motivation for such action is often cost reduction, it may also be done to take advantage of specific skills or capabilities available at a particular location. As well as manufacturing operations, many service operations have also been subject to off-shoring and BPO. Examples of this have included software development, accountancy, customer service and support (via the Internet and telephone) and some R & D activities.

GENERIC INTERNATIONAL OPERATIONS STRATEGIES

There are two principal reasons why organizations choose to internationalize their operations (Flaherty, 1996; Ferdows, 1989). These form the basis of two generic international operations strategies:

- **Market access strategy**: A strategy in which operations are internationalized in order to access and serve markets outside of the home country.
- **Resource seeking strategy**: A strategy in which operations are internationalized in order to access and utilize specific resources outside of the home country.

These two strategies are not mutually exclusive, and indeed might be used simultaneously.

Market access strategy

A market access strategy can be thought of as being based on the market-led perspective of operations strategy (see Chapter 2). This perspective is one in which operations strategy is derived in response to conditions in the market environment. If attractive markets can be identified in other countries that the organization believes it can successfully serve, then it will wish to develop an international operations strategy to enable it to do so. Markets that have significant growth potential for the organization's products or services will be especially attractive, and may well lead to a decision to establish a presence in the country. Proximity to market offers two main potential advantages. First, it can enable the organization to better serve the immediate needs of customers, by being able to offer higher levels of service, with faster and more reliable delivery. For suppliers of goods, holding stocks may be the only way of offering customers acceptable levels of service. In many service industries, establishing local facilities is normally a prerequisite for having any kind of market presence. Second, it can help in developing the products and services which will better meet the needs of customers in the future. Being 'close to the customer' has long been advocated by management gurus (e.g. Peters and Waterman, 1982), although this may have been intended to be more figurative than literal. Nonetheless, there can be no better way of understanding customers than being physically close enough to engage in regular personal contact. This can be particularly important where there may be barriers of culture and language not easily recognized from the distance of another country. A better understanding of customers can enable the organization to adapt its products and services to local tastes. This can be important not only in consumer markets, but also in business-to-business markets, when a local presence can enable an organization to work more closely with important customers operating in that country.

An organization may also adopt a market access strategy for competitive reasons. They may wish to establish a market presence in a particular country in response to the actions of competitors. They may fear loss of market share if a competitor has a presence and they do not. As well as countering the actions of a competitor, a local presence also enables the organization to observe a competitor's operations at first hand.

A market access strategy may also be pursued as a means of circumventing trade barriers. As discussed in Chapter 3, there has been a widespread lowering of such barriers. However, regulatory barriers, import tariffs, quotas, unfavorable currency exchange rates, etc., still inhibit free trade in many parts of the world. The emergence of regional trading blocks (e.g. the EU, NAFTA) has to some extent merely moved trade barriers from national to regional frontiers. Thus, establishing an operating presence within one country inside the trading block enables an externally-based MNE to access the markets of all the block's countries. This seems to have been the motivation for many of the Japanese manufacturers who established factories in the UK immediately prior to the creation of the EU's single market in 1992. This prompted Jacques Calvet, the then head of French motor car manufacturer Peugeot, to famously liken Britain to a Japanese aircraft carrier off the shores of continental Europe.

Resource seeking

A resource seeking strategy can be thought of as being based on the operations-led perspective of operations strategy (see Chapter 2). This perspective is one in which operations strategy is derived from a desire to create superior operational capability. This might involve achieving lower operating costs or superior performance in quality, speed, dependability or flexibility.

An organization following a resource seeking strategy may enter a particular country to set up operations in order to take advantage of low cost input resources, such as raw materials, labour and energy. Much of the recent years have seen the widespread relocation of labour intensive manufacturing operations to lower wage locations. For example, much of the world's clothing is now manufactured in China and other East Asian countries.

Alternatively, a resource seeking strategy may lead an organization to set up operations in another country in order to tap into local technological resources and know-how. They may do this by employing suitably qualified staff directly or indirectly using suppliers or other collaborators. Although most front office service operations require

CASE STUDY Hornby — steaming ahead

Hornby is one of the great historic names in British toys, especially famous for its model railways beloved by generations of children and hobbyists alike. Frank Hornby founded a company in 1907 to market Meccano, the construction kit toy that he had patented six years earlier. Meccano was to become one of the classic toys of all time. Hornby's company prospered and he introduced toy trains in 1920. Hornby trains were an instant success and the company was quick to introduce more engines and accessories. In 1925 the first Hornby electric train was produced. In 1938 the famous Hornby Dublo ('00') series, featuring a range of models of famous British steam engines and rolling stock, all with cast metal bodies was launched.

In 1964, Hornby merged with its great rival Tri-ang Railways, who had developed plastic bodied trains. Although the Tri-ang Group was disbanded in 1971, Hornby was able to continue production at its Margate factory. Through the 1970s the company was able to introduce a steady flow of new locomotives. During this time it was able to upgrade the specification of its products to make them more attractive to adult enthusiasts. It provided finer scale wheels, wire handrails on locomotives, better paint finish on plastic bodies and a high definition printing of logos. The ensuing years were something of a struggle for Hornby. It endured various changes of ownership, but continued to offer products reflecting the changes on Britain's railways.

However what seems to have turned Hornby's fortunes around was a decision to move its manufacturing to China in 1995. This was originally spurred by a need to overcome the burden imposed by the high cost of operating its UK factory. However, by outsourcing all of its production to Chinese subcontractors, Hornby has been able to achieve significant advances in quality as well. In particular, Hornby claim that the attention to detail that has been achieved on its new models heralds a new era in modern image modelling. They believe the move has rejuvenated its product range, setting new benchmarks of quality for future locomotives and rolling stock. This has been reflected in Hornby's financial performance, with a doubling of sales and a quadrupling of profits since 2000.

As the *Financial Times* reported on 30 January 2005, the company's next stage of development was planned to be led by the launch of a new range of models aimed at continental European markets at the Nuremberg Toy Fair in February. Hornby is currently heavily reliant on the UK, which accounts for around 85 per cent of sales. Hornby acquired fellow model railway manufacturers Electrotren and Lima (which also includes the Rivarossi, Jouef and Arnold brands) from the receivers in Italy in 2004. The sale included more than 10,000 moulds for engines and rolling stock. Hornby hopes to revive these brands in a similar fashion to its own renewal by outsourcing manufacturing to its Chinese partners. Approximately 2,000 of the moulds have so far been sent to China, which have to date resulted in a range of 100 European locomotives and associated rolling stock being made available for sale. By the end of 2006, this is expected to have grown to around 200 items.

(Source material www.hornby.com and www.ft.com)

Questions (Suggested answers can be found on the companion website www.thomsonlearning.co.uk/barnes)

1 How has Hornby's outsourcing to China enabled it to achieve a competitive advantage?

2 To what extent is Hornby's internationalization strategy one of market access and to what extent resource seeking?

WWW.

WWW.

a local presence for reasons of market access, many back office services can be physically remote from the front office. Thus, back office operations can often be located in another country. Like their manufacturing counterparts, many labour intensive back office operations like data entry and processing are now located in low wage countries, such as India. However, many support services in manufacturing organizations, such as R & D, design, finance and accounts can also operate at locations remote from the factory. In such cases, locations may be chosen because of the expertise of the local workforce as much as its low cost. Again, India is increasingly a favoured location for such activities.

ENTERING FOREIGN MARKETS

Chapter 3 outlined a number of models that seek to explain the internationalization process. Although these models are all different in some way, they all identify four different ways that an organization might enter a foreign market:

- By direct export to the country
- Via a joint venture involving a local partner
- By establishing a sales subsidiary
- By establishing a production facility

Each of these modes of entry has different implications for operations and each needs the organization to be able to excel at different aspects of operations. These will now be considered in turn.

Direct export

In this case, the producer exports directly to customers in the new country. This is often from a production facility in the producer's home country, but might be from a third country. The main issue for operations is the arm's length nature of the relationship with customers. This increases the likelihood of communications problems between the producer and the customer. Although modern communications technologies may provide the means of limiting this, a significant risk will always remain. Considerable effort is likely to be required to ensure an adequate flow of information to avoid misunderstandings. There may be particular problems with respect to quality, especially where standards are difficult to define or subjective in nature. It may be especially important to ensure that customer expectations are fully appreciated and, if necessary, corrected.

For manufacturers, the issue of delivery is likely to be significant, especially if goods have to be transported long distances. Delays at international borders, perhaps whilst obtaining customs clearance, are always a risk. This raises a number of important questions regarding logistics and especially stockholding that need to be addressed. What level of stocks are to be held and at what point in the supply chain? Are customers to be supplied directly, or can stock be held at a warehouse or other point in the supply chain between producer and customer? Will third party logistics be used? What mode of transport will be used? Answering these questions calls for a high level of expertise in supply chain management, as there are significant implications for delivery speed and reliability, and also cost.

Some services (e.g. back office and separated services) can be delivered remotely, in effect via export from a facility in the home country or a third country. The issue of delivering a physical good does not usually arise in service provision. If the service output can be digitized then it can be delivered via the Internet or other telecommunications link, providing the necessary infrastructure exists. However, there are still risks of communication problems which may be exacerbated if the service deliverer and consumer have different languages, cultures and time zones.

Finally, serving additional markets from the same production facility inevitably adds complexity to the task of managing that facility. In times of heavy demand there are likely to be issues of prioritizing conflicting demands from the different markets. If outputs have to be tailored for different markets, this will lead to an increase in product variety, which will add to operational complexity, increasing the need for flexibility and putting pressure on costs. If stockholding is not desirable or is perhaps not possible (as in the case of perishable products and for most services) then excess capacity is likely to be required if customer demand is to be satisfied on request. Similarly, the greater the complexity required in the organization's own operations, then the greater the flexibility required from the organization's suppliers. All this calls for expertise in the planning and control of operations in any facility that is called upon to supply different countries.

Joint venture

In this case, the organization sets up some kind of joint venture with a local partner to try to overcome the problems inherent in direct export operations. Producers seeking to enter a new country often seek a partner with local sales and marketing expertise, perhaps a sales agent of some kind. Joint ventures may involve the local partner contributing to any one of a number of other different activities, including distribution, design, full or partial manufacture of goods or delivery of services. Similarly, the degree of ownership that the organization entering the country may have in a joint venture can vary enormously. Some joint ventures are based purely on contractual arrangements such as franchising, licensing or management contract arrangements, whereby the organization enables the local partner to make use of its brand name, operating systems, technology, etc. within that country for a fee (often based on the sales turnover of the local partner). Such arrangements seek to limit the organization's commitment of resources to that country. Greater levels of commitments are required when the organization establishes shared ownership of the venture through some kind of joint equity arrangement. This might involve setting up a local jointly owned or affiliated company. Sometimes a number of organizations can be involved in establishing a consortium of some kind. Obviously, a higher level of ownership confers a higher level of control but requires a greater financial commitment from the organization. Clearly the nature of any joint venture will determine which aspects of operations need particular attention. In any case, any organization entering a new country via a joint venture will come to rely on the partner for much of the provision and interpretation of information from the country, and especially that concerning its customers and markets. Consequently, the choice of partner is crucial as considerable power rests in their hands. Any new market entrant will need to be able to build and foster good working relations with the partner on the basis of mutual trust. There are always likely to be plenty of opportunities for misunderstandings, especially where the partners come from different cultural backgrounds.

Establish a sales subsidiary

Setting up a sales subsidiary is often the first real stage of foreign direct investment. It usually involves the direct employment of staff in that country. This raises the issue of whether to employ expatriates or local staff, or a mixture of both. In any event it requires the organization to fully engage directly with the economy of another country. Employing people directly raises many human resource management issues for the operation. The aim of setting up a sales subsidiary is to put the control of sales in the hands of the organization itself, thereby overcoming some of the communication problems inherent in direct exporting and the problems of joint working with a joint venture partner. However, it does place a considerable burden on local organizational members to be able to correctly interpret customer requirements. This requires a level of understanding of local working practices and culture which expatriates in particular may not immediately possess. On the other hand, employees engaged locally may not have a full understanding of the parent organization and the working practices and culture of the home country.

Establish a production facility

This is a major step for any organization and is likely to involve significant foreign direct investment. Setting up and subsequently managing a foreign production facility requires a wide range of operations management expertise. Because local staff as well as expatriates will almost certainly need to be employed, expertise in managing human resources in that country will be required. There will also undoubtedly be a requirement to establish supply arrangements for all other resource inputs. This raises the issue of the extent to which such resources should be purchased locally or be imported perhaps from existing tried and tested suppliers. Expertise in purchasing and supply management will be required. Local logistics arrangements will also need to be put in place to ensure that products reach the local customers in such a way as to satisfy their needs. There may also be a requirement to modify products and services to meet local requirements. This may require the establishment of design and development expertise at the facility. Similarly there may be a need to establish after sales service operations for local customers. Output from such a production facility may, of course, ultimately itself be exported, perhaps enabling the facility to become part of the organization's global supply network. In this case, a full range of global operations management skills will be required.

Some organizations seek to overcome the problems of setting up their own production facilities from scratch by acquiring existing facilities in that country. This may involve the purchase of specific operating assets (buildings, equipment, etc.) or the acquisition of part, or even the entirety, of an existing fully trading organization. In such circumstances, the acquiring organization will usually take over the employment contacts of employees, together with the trading relationship with and commitments to existing customers, suppliers and other supply network partners. These will almost certainly need to be reviewed to determine whether they are likely to continue to be advantageous. However, changing or withdrawing from these arrangements may be difficult in the short-term. The other significant challenge that confronts the organization is that of integrating its acquisition into its existing business systems and practices. There may be problems due to differences with employment contracts in the acquisition and those that already exist in other parts of the organization. Arrangements with customers, suppliers and other supply network partners may be similarly incompatible. There may be problems due to differences in process equipment and technology, and working practices and procedures. Incompatible information systems and technology may cause problems in the processing and communication of information between the acquisition and the existing business. Changing these is likely to be both costly and time-consuming.

CONFIGURATIONS FOR INTERNATIONAL OPERATIONS

Once an organization has production facilities and/or markets in more than one country it is faced with decisions about how to configure its operations to supply its customers in various different markets. This involves determining what products and service to produce at any particular location and what markets to serve from each location.

Bartlett and Ghosal (1987) identify four generic strategic approaches to configuring international operations:

- *Global*: which emphasizes the achievement of operational efficiency through economies of scale. Global markets are served through the mass production at centralized facilities with little or no differentiation.

- *Multi-national*: in which responsiveness to local needs is emphasized. National markets are served through local facilities (these may be national or regional) producing highly differentiated goods and services tailored to local demand.

- *International*: in which innovation in both products and processes are developed domestically and subsequently transferred to international subsidiary facilities. The success of this strategy lies in an ability to continually innovate and transfer and adapt to different international markets.

- *Transnational*: this they see as the organization of the future. One which must simultaneously achieve low costs, be responsive to national markets and achieve worldwide learning. They argue that to achieve this, what is required is a highly flexible organization made up of 'an integrated network of distributed and interdependent resources and capabilities, . . . (with) . . . large flows of components, products, resources, people, and information'.

There are likely to be a number of different approaches to configuring international operations, which might give rise to several possible configurations in practice. It is possible to identify four possible generic configuration types (see Figure 4.2a–d).

Home operations

In this configuration all production takes place at facilities within the home country. The home market is supplied from these facilities. Demand from other countries is supplied via a strategy of direct export. This approach has the advantage of keeping production under direct control in a familiar environment. It also enables the organization's facilities to take full advantage of any economies of scale and scope available

FIGURE 4.2A Home country operations with exports

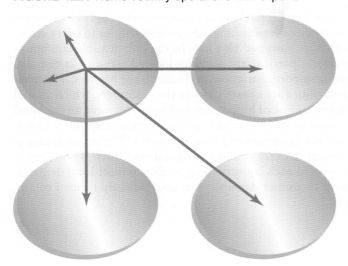

FIGURE 4.2B Multi-domestic operations

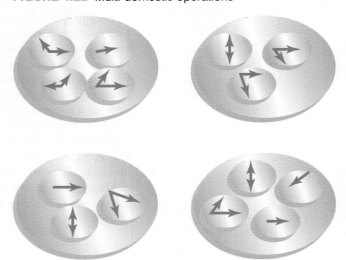

FIGURE 4.2C Regional operations

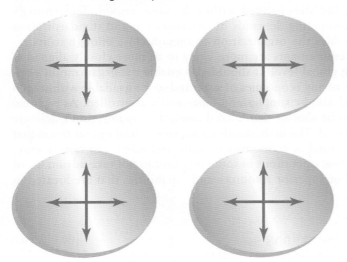

FIGURE 4.2D Global co-ordinated operations

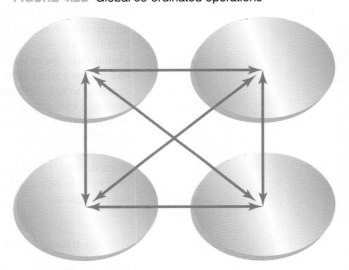

from increased production volumes. However, as discussed above there are disadvantages that arise from having no direct exposure to customers in their own country and in trying to ensure prompt and reliable delivery with an extended supply chain. Whilst some back office and separated services can be delivered remotely from home-based facilities, this is not possible in face-to-face demander-located services. Also, trying to supply a large number of markets from home-based facilities increases the complexity of the task faced by those facilities. There are likely to be requirements for products to be tailored to individual country market requirements, making scheduling and quality control more difficult. The more product variations there are, the greater the difficulty in meeting customer delivery requirements and the more difficult it is to control operating costs. Finally, confining operations to home soil may mean that the organization misses out on potential advantages available from the resources and capabilities located in other countries.

Multi-domestic operations

This approach is based upon meeting demand in each country with supply from within that country. It relies on a strategy of establishing operations facilities in every country in which the organization does business. This may be the only feasible configuration for some service operations, particularly provider-located services. It can also provide a means of overcoming import restrictions and other trade barriers. The main advantage is that the supply facilities are always close to the customers, which should provide a more intimate understanding of local tastes and help overcome any cultural barriers. It should also be easier to tailor products and services to meet local tastes. Operations should also be relatively simple and easy to control. The disadvantage is that it requires direct investment in every country of operation, which is both costly and risky. It means that facilities in each country must be able to meet local demand, risking either excess capacity or unmet demand. It is also unlikely to lead to any economies of scale or scope.

Regional operations

An alternative approach often adopted by organizations that operate on a global scale, is to divide international operations into a small number of regions. For example, there might be a European region, a Pacific region, an Americas region and so on. With this strategy, each region is self-contained with all markets in each region being supplied by facilities located within the same region. This strategy attempts to balance the competing demands of specialization and standardization within each region. It enables the organization to remain close enough to its regional customers whose requirements are more likely to be more closely aligned at the region rather than the global level. It should also enable the organization's operations to take advantage of any economies of scale and scope available within each region. Operations should also be simpler and more easily controlled. As regional supply chains are likely to be shorter than global ones, the organization's delivery capability should be improved. The main disadvantage of regional operations is that costs may be higher than usual as economies of scale and scope can not be maximized. Also it may mean that operations in some regions can not take advantage of potential lower costs and/or superior resources and capabilities that are located in other regions.

Global co-ordinated operations

Some organizations that operate internationally configure their operations on a global basis. This makes it possible for each production facility to specialize on a narrow range of tasks and supply markets anywhere in the world. This should simplify the task of operations management at each facility. The organization can maximize economies of scale and scope across its network of facilities, and take full advantage of low cost and/or superior resources and capabilities wherever they are located. However, there are some disadvantages arising from long and potentially costly supply chains and the likely separation of any given production facility from many of its customers.

It is possible to combine one or more of these generic types. For example, an organization might supply some countries by exporting from home operations, whilst having production facilities in others. It is important to recognize that most real business situations are dynamic. The configuration of any organization's network of operations is likely to evolve over time as managers respond to changes in its demand and supply markets in different parts of the world.

CASE STUDY: Globalized manufacturing at Toyota: The IMV project

By 2005 Toyota had grown to become the world's second largest car maker – only General Motors made more vehicles. Toyota employs well over a quarter of a million people worldwide and markets vehicles in more than 140 countries. In its home country of Japan, its manufacturing facilities encompass 12 of its own plants and 11 manufacturing subsidiaries and affiliates. Across the rest of the world Toyota has 51 manufacturing companies in 26 countries. The expansion of Toyota's manufacturing operations across the world was achieved in two distinct stages. In the first stage, Toyota made vehicles only in Japan and exported them across the world. This was followed by a second stage of local manufacturing in key market areas, most notably the USA and Europe. However, the summer of 2004 saw Toyota embark on a third stage, that of globalized manufacturing.

The Innovative International Multi-purpose Vehicle (IMV) project will see the creation of an interconnected multi-national production and supply system that will operate on a truly global scale. The IMV project involves the manufacture of five new models – three variants of the Hilux Vigo pickup truck, the Kijang Innova minivan and the Fortuner SUV. The project is unprecedented for Toyota, as it is being conducted almost entirely outside Japan, including purchasing, manufacturing and logistics. Toyota's Senior Managing Director Akio Toyoda called it 'a new chapter in the history of Toyota . . . and in the history of the world automobile industry'.

Diesel engines will be made in Thailand, gasoline engines in Indonesia and manual transmissions in the Philippines and India. Toyota will use plants in Thailand, Indonesia, Argentina and South Africa for vehicle assembly. These four main IMV production bases will supply Asia, Europe, Africa, Oceania, Latin America and the Middle East with the five all-new IMV vehicles. IMV-series vehicle production was projected to exceed 500,000 units in 2006.

FIGURE 4.3 Stages of global production

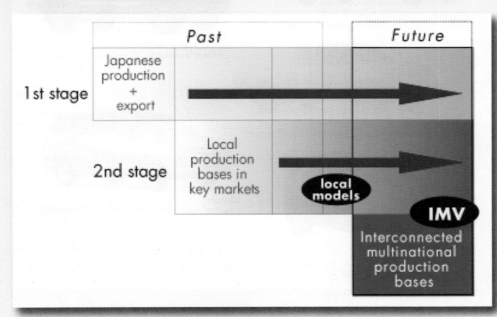

FIGURE 4.4 Vehicle supply network

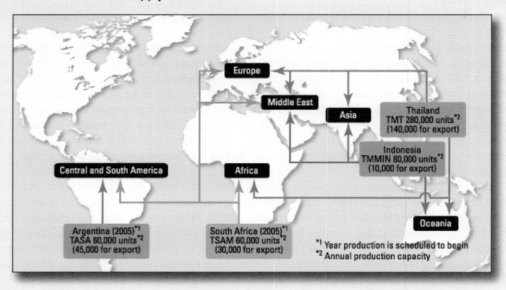

FIGURE 4.5 IMV project global standard models

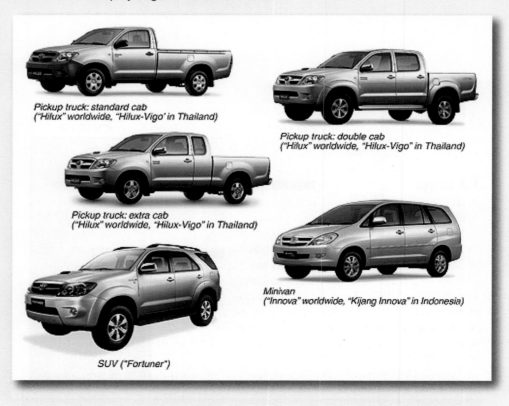

Pickup truck: standard cab
("Hilux" worldwide, "Hilux-Vigo" in Thailand)

Pickup truck: double cab
("Hilux" worldwide, "Hilux-Vigo" in Thailand)

Pickup truck: extra cab
("Hilux" worldwide, "Hilux-Vigo" in Thailand)

Minivan
("Innova" worldwide, "Kijang Innova" in Indonesia)

SUV ("Fortuner")

One of Toyota's ultimate goals in the production of IMV models is to procure nearly 100 per cent of vehicle components from sources outside Japan. At the time of the initial Thai and Indonesian launches in 2004, non-Japanese sources accounted for approximately 95 per cent of vehicle content. Toyota's IMV lines in Argentina and South Africa will also be aiming to maximize non-Japanese procurement.

Toyota is confident that it can maintain high quality standards because of its long manufacturing experience in all of the areas where it is establishing IMV production bases. Thailand, for example, was one of the first nations where Toyota produced vehicles outside Japan. Toyota's manufacturing history there goes back more than forty years.

The IMV project aims to enable Toyota to offer more attractive and more affordable products to all of its customers wherever they are in the world at the same time. Executive Chief Engineer Kaoru Hosokawa calls this the challenge of making the 'Global Best'. Toyota realized that to satisfy the needs of particular locations, the IMV vehicles had to go beyond 'Global Best' to achieve 'Local Best'. In the planning and development stages this meant listening to dealers and customers in Asia, Africa and South America and repeatedly debating the issues among members of the design and engineering teams. Hosokawa says,

> The initial customer response to the IMV series has been gratifying. However, the real test will be in the months and years ahead. We look forward to extensive owner feedback so that we can continue to improve performance and better satisfy customer needs at the local level.

(Source material www.toyota.co.jp)

Questions (Suggested answers can be found on the companion website www.thomsonlearning.co.uk/barnes)

1 Which of the four possible generic configuration types best describes Toyota's manufacturing operations for the IMV project?

2 What advantages does Toyota hope to gain from the configuration chosen for the manufacturing operations for the IMV project?

3 What are the potential disadvantages for Toyota associated with this configuration?

WWW.

WWW.

INTERNATIONAL OPERATIONS AND BUSINESS STRATEGY

As discussed in Chapter 2, it is possible to take two different views on the process of operations strategy: market-led or operations-led. The market-led perspective sees operations strategy being derived in response to conditions in the market environment. Thus, the market-led perspective sees an international operations strategy as one that seeks to access attractive markets in other countries. To be successful, an international operations strategy needs to be one that best enables operations to satisfy the specific market conditions in each country in which the organization operates. If markets are different in each country, then the more likely it is that the organization may need to develop different operations strategies in each country. This can lead to the fragmentation of its international operations. Indeed, if its operations need to be different in every country, it is questionable if the organization can be said to have an international operations strategy at all. Indeed there may be no particular advantages to be gained from taking an international view of operations. Taking a market-led perspective seems to cast operations in a rather reactive role, consigning the function to act best at stage 3 of Hayes and Wheelwright's model (see Chapter 2).

On the other hand, the operation-led perspective sees an organization's strategy being driven by excellence in operations. This view is in line with Hayes and Wheelwright's stage 4, in which operations provide the basis for competitive advantage. From this perspective an international operations strategy is one which seeks to exploit the collective resources and capabilities available to the organization across all the countries in which it operates. It takes a holistic rather then a fragmentary view of operations. One in which the totality of its operations can provide a source of competitive advantage.

What then are the potential benefits available from international operations? What strategic actions could an organization take as part of an international operations strategy that could provide a source of competitive advantage? Flaherty (1996) argues that sources of potential competitive advantage can be developed by strategic actions in international operations in the following.

Global Sourcing

1 Sourcing basic input resources (e.g. commodities, components and unsophisticated products and services) from the lowest cost location can provide a cost advantage.

2 Sourcing sophisticated products and services from the best suppliers wherever they are located can provide a technological advantage not only directly from the products and services themselves, but also from the organizational learning gained from engaging with such suppliers. Accessing the most advanced products and services should provide a quality advantage.

Location

1 Locating operations facilities near to customers can enable the organization to provide a more responsive and possibly customized offering to local customers. This could enable the organization to gain an advantage from superior customer service.

2 Locating operations facilities at concentrated locations can enable the organization to gain economies of scale and scope. This could provide an advantage from lower costs.

Network Effects

1 Configuring the supply network in ways that maximize synergies between supply network partners (with the aim of minimizing costs, maximizing speed, dependability, etc.) can enable the organization to better serve the needs of specific customers.

2 Managing the supply network to maximize organizational learning about, and for, customers can provide an advantage based on superior knowledge.

Competition

1 Exposure to competition in international markets can act as a spur to improve operations, leading to innovations in products and processes. These might provide advantages in cost, quality, etc.

2 Exposure to competition in international markets should also prompt a strategic consideration of how and where to compete. This ought to provide the stimulus for consideration of what markets to enter and what should be the basis of competition in those countries, and in particular how goods and services should be priced.

Flaherty (1996) also argues that the advent of globalization has changed the environment in which organizations operate. As such, organizations now:

- Need to compete on several dimensions, not just one. It is unlikely that competitive advantage can be sustained simply, for example, by having low costs. It is likely that low cost will need to be combined with high quality, speed of response, reliability of operations performance, etc.

- Have more opportunities for international operations, and more competitive pressures to operate in more countries.

- Can adapt and integrate their networks of international operations to create greater value than they can with independently run subsidiaries.

Viewed from the operations-led perspective, the operations of an international organization provide the basis for a sustainable competitive advantage. An appropriate international operations strategy will enable an organization to compete effectively on the basis of the existing resources and skills which comprise its core competencies (Prahalad and Hamel, 1990), also sometimes referred to as distinctive capabilities, (Kay, 1993). The basis of such competencies almost certainly resides within the operations of the organization. As Prahalad and Hamel (1990) point out, core competencies are 'the collective learning in the organization, especially how to co-ordinate diverse production skills and integrate multiple streams of technologies'. They go on to note that 'core competence does not diminish with use . . . competencies are enhanced as they are applied'. Deploying and developing operations competencies internationally can ensure that a competitive advantage can be built and sustained. In international environments an organization's operations are constantly challenged in further new and different ways than would be the case in a single country. As such, organizations have the opportunity not only to apply their existing core competencies but also to develop and build new ones, thus increasing organizational learning. Successful international organizations use their operational competencies to drive their business strategies.

SUMMARY OF KEY POINTS

Operating internationally is more complex and difficult than operating in only a single country. The impact of an international business strategy on international operations can be assessed using the transformation model, as internationalization affects all three parts of the transformation process: inputs, the process and outputs.

There are two generic international operations strategies; market access strategy or resource seeking strategy. Each is based on different motivations for the internationalization of operations.

Each of the four different modes of entry into foreign markets (direct export, joint venture, establishing a sales subsidiary and establishing a production facility) has different implications for operations.

There are four possible generic configurations of production facilities for an organization's operating internationally; home operations, multi-domestic operations, regional operations and global co-ordinated operations.

Operating internationally can provide sources of competitive advantages from global sourcing, location advantages, network effects and competition.

WWW.

EXERCISES (Suggested answers can be found on the companion website www.thomsonlearning.co.uk/barnes)

1 Use the transformation model to identify the most important implications of the internationalization of operations.

2 What are the main differences between mass customization and focused operations as approaches to standardization and specialization?

3 What are the advantages and disadvantages of off-shoring operations to less developed countries?

4 Should an organization always seek to outsource or off-shore to low labour cost destinations?

5 What are the two generic international operations strategies? Explain how each strategy can be a source of competitive advantage?

6 Outline the main implications for operations for each of the four different modes of entry into foreign markets (direct export, joint venture, establishing a sales subsidiary and establishing a production facility).

7 What are the advantages and disadvantages of each of the four generic configurations for international operations (home operations, multi-domestic operations, regional operations and global co-ordinated operations)?

8 How can operating internationally provide a competitive advantage?

9 Assess the operations management implications of internationalization for the following types of organization:
   a A motor car manufacturer
   b A manufacturer of fashionable clothing
   c An insurance company
   d A chain of fast food outlets

10 What are the advantages and disadvantages for a US company in off-shoring:
   a Its manufacturing operations to China
   b Its customer service telephone helpline to India

CASE STUDY EXERCISE TUI AG

TUI AG's restructuring and expansion

TUI AG developed from the German company Preussag AG (an industrial conglomerate) when during the middle of the 1990s, the latter decided to enter the expanding services sector by specifically focusing on the tourism and containers shipping industry. TUI AG's market transformation and company metamorphosis involved a rapid process of change characterized by restructuring, disinvestment of former assets and re-investment in others more complementary to the tourism product and which have been gradually consolidated and repositioned into a TUI umbrella masterbrand (Table 4.1). Over the last few years the Group has systematically divested itself of its industrial holdings and has clearly structured its business portfolio with brands serving diverse companies within the tourism supply chain, e.g. tour operators, travel agencies,

distribution channels (e.g. call centres, TV channels and online travel businesses), hotels and airlines. The European tour operators in the World of TUI reach more than 80 per cent of holidaymakers in Europe. In 2006 this represented some 21 million customers. In addition, under its wholly-owned subsidiary Hapag-Lloyd, TUI operates one of the world's five largest container shipping companies with more than 140 vessels.

TUI AG's tourism products and services: an integrated tourism supply chain

TUI AG manages an integrated (horizontally and vertically) tourism supply chain by owning numerous tourism companies each one performing different key functions throughout the tourism distribution chain (Table 4.2). Thus, integration includes tourism companies operating in both the tourism destinations and source markets ensuring that TUI customers can enjoy a seamless tourism quality experience from booking in a travel agency, flights with the Group's own aircraft, to accommodation in the Group's own hotels. Tourism chain integration facilitates the group to create synergies amongst its companies and to establish and control quality levels across all elements of the tourism products (i.e. from purchasing, transportation, incoming tour handling, destination excursions, accommodation, and ground handling). An integrated tourism supply chain also enables the group to achieve high utilization and occupancy rates within its tourism supplier companies. So, by owning less hotel bed capacity than air transportation, TUI AG achieves high occupancy in its own hotels and signs contracts with other hotels for serving the remaining demand.

Sales – distribution

TUI AG follows a multi-channel distribution strategy. TUI AG's sales network includes:

- Some 3,200 travel agents in 17 countries.
- Direct sales activities on the German source market are bundled in EVS Holding (Fox-Tours and Berge & Meer).
- More than 50 different homepages for Group tour operators and airlines can be accessed for information and booking.

TABLE 4.1 TUI AG's milestones in restructuring, (dis)/(re)-investments and brands' consolidation

1998
- Preussag sells its stake in steel company Preussag Stahl AG.
- Hapag-Lloyd acquires the shares in TUI held by Schickedanz.
- Preussag amalgamates the tourism businesses of Hapag-Lloyd and TUI into Hapag Touristik Union (HTU).
- Hapag-Lloyd acquires a majority stake (50.1 per cent) in TUI.
- HTU purchases 24.9 per cent of Thomas Cook, the British tourism and financial services group.
- HTU takes minority stake in First Reisebüro Management GmbH & Co. KG.

1999
- Preussag disposes of all its interest in the coal mining sector.
- HTU acquires all remaining shares in First Reisebüro Management GmbH & Co. KG to create Germany's largest chain of travel agents.
- The European Commission approves the merger of Thomas Cook and Carlson UK, and the acquisition of a majority stake by Preussag.
- For the first time Preussag AG's annual report also includes tourism activities, grouped under Hapag Touristik Union (HTU).
- Preussag reorganization sees HTU tourism holding managed directly by Preussag AG with all transport and logistics activities concentrated in Hapag-Lloyd AG.
- Preussag acquires all remaining shares of TUI from WestLB.
- Preussag sells Preussag Noell GmbH and Preussag Wasser und Rohrtechnik GmbH to Babcock Borsig.
- Preussag raises its stakeholding in Thomas Cook to a 50.1 per cent majority.
- HTU renamed 'TUI Group', incorporating all of the Preussag Group's tourism activities. Operating brand names (distributors, operators, carriers and hotels) remain unchanged.

2000
- Preussag AG joins the Swedish Celsius Group and Babcock Borsig AG to create a European shipyard alliance.
- TUI Group acquires a 75 per cent stake in GTT Holding GmbH, Vienna, which holds 100 per cent of Gulet Touropa Touristik GmbH (GTT), a leading Austria tour operator.
- Preussag forms a strategic alliance with Nouvelles Frontières, the French market leader for package tours, acquiring an initial 6 per cent stake, which is planned to be built up to 34.4 per cent by 2002.
- Preussag AG announces its intention to become a tourism management holding company and to disinvest from most of its industrial holdings.

2001
- Preussag acquires a further 7 per cent in Nouvelles Frontières
- Preussag sells its bathroom and heating company, Kermi Group.
- Preussag enters the southern European market by acquiring a 10 per cent stake in Alpitour, the Italian market leader in the organized travel market.
- Preussag sells its holdings in the heating technology sector.
- Preussag announces it will run its tourism brand worldwide under the masterbrand 'World of TUI'.

TABLE 4.1 *(Continued)*

- Preussag acquires a 50 per cent stake in Magic Life International Hotelbetriebsgesellschaft mbH, Vienna, which owns a Nile cruise liner, 22 club complexes (mainly located in Turkey, Greece, Tunisia, Bulgaria, Egypt and Austria), to complement its club range of ROBINSON and 1-2-FLY Fun Club.
- Preussag acquires a shareholding of 29.3 per cent in White Eagle Aviation, a Polish carrier.
- Thomson Travel Group is integrated into the TUI group as TUI UK, TUI Ireland and TUI Nordic.
- Preussag acquires a 40 per cent holding in EuroVacances System Beteiligungsgesellschaft mbH (EVS), a direct seller of tourism products in Germany, to open up new distribution channels.

2002

- Preussag acquires a 50 per cent holding in the new Italian charter airline Neos.
- Preussag sells its remaining holding in Howaldtswerke-Deutsche Werft AG (HDW), Kiel, concluding its withdrawal from shipbuilding.
- Preussag reorganizes its distribution, incoming and local tour operating activities in Spain as TUI España.
- Preussag bundles the main central shared functions (fleet management and planning, aircraft purchasing, flight operations and maintenance and servicing) of the 88 aircraft of its six airlines (Hapag-Lloyd Flug, Britannia Airways UK, Britannia Airways SE, Neos, Corsair and White Eagle Aviation) into TUI Airline Management.
- Preussag AG sells Fels Group, its construction materials company.
- Preussag acquires all of the remaining shares in Hapag-Lloyd AG.
- TUI enters the low-cost airline sector under the new brand name 'Hapag-Lloyd Express'.
- TUI AG completes the 100 per cent takeover of Nouvelles Frontières.
- TUI AG becomes the first European tourism group to establish itself in China by setting up a joint venture company, TUI China, with China Travel Service (CTS) and a third shareholder Martin Buese.
- TUI AG sells all the German activities of Preussag Energie GmbH to Gaz de France.

2003

- TUI AG raises its shareholding in EVS to 75 per cent.
- TUI AG sells the international operations of Preussag Energie GmbH to conclude its withdrawal from the energy sector.
- TUI China Incoming Europe is established to organize tours for Chinese tourists visiting Germany and to look after them as they tour the country.
- The TUI Group restructures under a Central Executive Board of four directors (instead of seven). The market-related management functions are largely decentralized to country organizations.
- Following the complete takeover of Nouvelle Frontières, TUI France, the new tour operator brand, is launched in France.
- TUI expands its seat-only business in the UK airline market, by using the existing Britannia fleet and adding extra capacity.
- The tourism activities in Austria are bundled into TUI Austria Holding AG, creating Austria's largest tourism company and the market leader in air-inclusive package tours and non-flight holiday products. TUI Austria Holding continues to expand into Eastern Europe, e.g. offering departures from airports in Bratislava and Ljubljana.
- TUI sells its 99.4 per cent stake in Amalgamated Metal Corporation plc.

▶

TABLE 4.1 *(Continued)*

2004
- The Group bundles its logistics activities into Hapag-Lloyd AG.
- TUI sells its 10 per cent stake in the Italian Alpitour group.
- TUI launches a new Internet booking service (www.tui-hotels.com) offering several thousand beach, city and classic holiday hotels to individual travellers.
- TUI takes a 49 per cent share in TUI Suisse from Kuoni Reisen Holding AG.
- TUI opens its first low-cost travel agency in Hamburg with Touristik Express.
- TUI Belgium launches its own airline TUI Airlines Belgium.
- TUI sells its 67 per cent interest in Algeco S.A., a European leader in the rental and sales of modular buildings.
- TUI enters the Russian market to establish TMR (TUI Mostravel Russia) a joint venture with Russian tour operator Mostravel.
- TUI integrates its two low-cost airline operating companies in Germany, Hapag-Lloyd Flug and Hapag-Lloyd Express.
- TUI increases its holding in the Austrian club holiday provider Magic Life to 100 per cent.
- TUI AG completely takes over TV Travel Shop Germany GmbH and subsequently sells a 50 percent stake to the virtual travel operator Touropa.

2005
- TUI launches Touropa.com with the virtual tour operator of Georg Eisenreich, not only to sell travel online, but also via other channels such as travel agencies, travel television and call centres.
- TUI Nederland forms its own airline TUI Airlines Nederland, branded as Arkefly.
- The holiday airline Hapag-Lloyd Flug is renamed Hapagfly.
- TUI AG enters the Indian market, taking a 50 per cent stake in the incoming agency Le Passage to India Ltd.
- TUI takes a 51 per cent stake in the incoming agency Acampora Travel S.r.l., Sorrent, Italy.
- TUI divests its rail logistics business to a wholly owned subsidiary VTG AG.
- TUI starts up the new travel portal TUI.com offering access to all its World of TUI products one website.
- TUI AG and CP Ships, the leading Canadian container shipping line, announce a merger with Ship Acquisition Inc., an indirect subsidiary of TUI AG. TUI will own 100 per cent of the new company.
- TUI takes a 49 per cent holding in the Thai company Turismo Asia Ltd bringing together the World of TUI tour operator activities in Thailand.

2006
- TUI AG announces the sale of its TQ3 business travel division to a business travel specialist in order to focus its activities on leisure tourism activities.

For TUI CEO, Dr Michael Frenzel, this is proof of the soundness of the strategy, 'to offer our products everywhere where the customer books his holiday travel'.

A sales volume of 3.2 billion euros makes TUI the European leader in the direct sale of travel products. From these, 1.0 billion euros correspond to sales generated via call centres and TV stations, while 2.2 billion euros refer to online sales. Online sales have multiplied almost 20 times over the last four years – representing

TABLE 4.2 TUI AG supply chain

TOUR OPERATORS	HOTELS & RESORTS
SM Central 1-2-Fly (Germany) GeBeCo (Germany) TUI Deutschland Gulet Touropa Touristik (Austria) TUI Austria TUI Mostravel Russia TUI Poland TUI Suisse Holding (Switzerland) **SM Western** Jetair (Belgium) Nouvelles Frontières (France) Oft Reisen (Netherlands) TUI Nederland **SM Northern** TUI Nordic (Sweden) TUI UK	**Hotel management** TUI Hotels&Resorts TUI Hotels&Resorts London Office **Hotel companies** Atlantica Hotels & Resorts Dorfhotel Gran Resort Hotels Grecotel Grupotel Iberotel Magic Life Nordotel Paladien Hotels RIU Hotels Robinson

AIRLINES	TRAVEL AGENCIES
Airline management TUI Airline Management **SM Central** Hapag Lloyd Express (Germany) Hapagfly (Germany) **SM Northern** Thomsonfly (UK) Britannia (Scandinavia) **SM Western** Arkefly (Netherlands) Corsairfly (France) Jetairfly (Belgium)	Acampora Travel (Italy) Aeolos Malta Aeolos Travel (Lebanon) African Travel Concept Aitken Spence Travels (Sri Lanka) Danubius Travel (Romania) Gulliver Travel (Croatia) Holiday Services (Morocco) Le Passage to India Mex-Atlantica Tours (Mexico) Pollman's Tours and Safaris (Kenya) Serenade Tours (Italy) SummerTime (Maritus) Travco Group Holding (Egypt) TUI Bulgaria TUI China TUI Dominicana TUI Espana TUI Hellas TUI Portugal TUI Service Tunisie Voyages Turismo Asia World of TUI Cars

SHIPPING	
Liner Shipping Hapag Lloyd Container Line **Cruises** Hapag Lloyd Cruises	

about 17 per cent of total sales in TUI's tourism division. Dr Frenzel regards this strategic approach as an opportunity for profitable growth and stresses that this need not occur at the expense of the travel agencies, as online sales represent a new market that otherwise would have booked their travel components directly with the providers or would not have travelled at all.

Tour operators

TUI has penetrated all major European source markets by owning 75 tour operators operating in 18 countries (as well as currently in China, Thailand and India). Tour operators are grouped according to the following regions clearly reflecting the major outbound markets: Central Europe, Northern Europe and Western Europe.

Flight

TUI AG encompasses both charter (TUIfly, Thomsonfly, TUIfly Nordic, Jetairfly, Corsairfly and Arkefly) and low cost airlines (TUIfly.comand Thomsonfly.com). The international TUI Airline Management operations are centralised in Hanover, whereby the team controls the strategic central functions for the more than 120 aircraft in the fleet: management, planning, IT, buying, flight operation, maintenance and repair. This policy produces synergy effects and lowers prices, as well as airlines' independence to react faster to customer changing requirements and with associated responsibility for results at a local level.

Destination

TUI Group fully owns or has stakes in 37 incoming agencies operating in more than 70 countries and on all continents in order to carry out and secure the TUI guest care and attention at the destination (Table 4.3). This service supports the core business of the tour operators and represents an important contribution in terms of product quality assurance. All travel representation activities at the destinations are bundled in the incoming agencies, which are responsible for the following: a friendly welcome at the airport, a smooth transfer to the booked hotel, a competent travel representative on site, a good offering of interesting excursions and sightseeing trips as well as the organization of rental cars and other services. Incoming agencies are involved also in other business activities, such as organizing congresses, incentives and events, assisting cruise guests and arranging travel agency services. TUI AG's network of incoming agencies reflects and enables the implementation of its strategic focus 'Think globally – act locally' for providing quality tourism experiences. Local incoming agencies have established excellent contacts to hoteliers, local government offices and airport authorities, enabling them to act effectively should any

TABLE 4.3 TUI AG incoming agency network

01 **Spain** TUI España	22 **Senegal** Nouvelles Frontières
02 **Portugal** TUI Portugal	23 **South Africa/Namibia**
03 **Italy** Serenade Tours/Acampora Travel	ATC African Travel Concept
04 **Netherlands** Holland International	24 **Tanzania** ARP Group/Ranger Safaris
Destination Management	25 **Kenya** ARP Group/Pollman's Tours and Safaris
05 **France/Corsica** Nouvelles Frontières	26 **Mauritius** Summer Times
06 **Austria** TUI Incoming Austria	27 **Réunion** Nouvelles Frontières
07 **Hungary** TUI Magyarország	28 **Mexico** Mex-Atlántica Tours
08 **Romania** Danubius Travel	29 **Dominican Republic** TUI Dominicana
09 **Bulgaria** TUI Bulgaria	30 **Guadeloupe** Nouvelles Frontières
10 **Croatia** Gulliver Travel	31 **Martinique** Nouvelles Frontières
11 **Turkey** TUI Tûrkiye	32 **Thailand** Turismo Asia
12 **Greece** TUI Hellas	33 **India** Le Passage to India
13 **Cyprus** Aeolos Travel	34 **Sri Lanka** Aitken Spence Travels
14 **Malta** Aeolos Malta	35 **China** TUI China
15 **Lebanon** Aeolos Liban	36 **Australia/Fiji** APTC
16 **Tunisia** Tunisie Voyages	
17 **Morocco** Holidays Services	
18 **Israel** Holiday Travel	■ Companies held directly by TUI AG and
19 **Egypt** Travco Travel Company of Egypt	linked to Portfolio Management Incoming &
20 **Dubai** Travco Dubai	Guest Service
21 **Oman/Abu Dhabi**	■ Incoming departments or subsidiaries of tour
Travco Oman/Travco Abu Dhabi	operators

unforeseeable, difficult situations arise. In particular, international service standards are maintained and controlled at holiday destinations because incoming agencies present the following core competencies and services:

- Worldwide TUI quality standards on site
- Many years of qualified experience in the tourism sector
- Qualified, motivated and multilingual staff
- A wide range of tourism services (including: transfer, excursions, sightseeing tours, tour representative service, group travel, incentives, cruise handling and ticketing)
- Attractive and up-to-date excursion programmes
- Competitive price-performance ratio
- Modern bus fleets and up-to-date computer equipment
- Best contacts on site to hoteliers, officials and airport authorities
- International orientation
- Mutual success through the promotion of an international exchange and sharing of experience and use of synergies

Incoming agencies are centrally co-ordinated and controlled by the Destination Management based in Hanover.

World of TUI customers are also looked after by around 5,000 of the company's own tour representatives in over 70 countries. TUI Service AG in Switzerland is the central tour representative and entertainment organization for World of TUI, managing around 1,500 tour guides and entertainers located in destinations.

Hotels

The accommodation product represents one of the most crucial parts of a holiday experience and so, quality standards have to be secured in order to guarantee customer loyalty. TUI Hotels & Resorts manages the World of TUI hotel companies and is the largest holiday hotelier in Europe. The Group has 12 hotel brands (e.g. Riu, Grecotel, Grupotel, Iberotel, Dorfhotel, Robinson, Magic Life) in 30 countries with a total of around 279 affiliated hotels and 165,000 beds. In this way, TUI can secure high quality and service levels as well as environmental standards in its accommodation products. All TUI Hotels & Resorts operate an environmental scheme and quality programmes, while when contracting with other hotels is used TUI AG overlooks their environmental and quality practices through different mechanisms, e.g. customers' and representatives' feedback.

Hapag-Lloyd Cruises

Hapag-Lloyd Cruises is the leading operator in the German-speaking countries in the premium and luxury cruise segment. The fleet includes cruise liners 'MS Europa' (5-star plus), 'MS Hanseatic' (5-star), 'MS Bremen' (4-star) and the 'MS Columbus' (3-star), and its holiday programme covers all the high seas.

TUI AG's repositioning and masterbranding: innovation of the tour operators' business model

Preussag's restructuring and focusing on the tourism sector had to be clearly communicated to its internal and external markets. Thus, from autumn 2001, Preussag runs its tourism brand world under the uniform quality masterbrand 'World of TUI'. The new logo and masterbrand name highlight Preussag's clear concentration on its Tourism Division, and aim to further enhance the integration of the various tourism companies within the Group. As illustrated in Table 4.1, the new masterbrand and the associated changes were introduced in a step-by-step approach depending on the domestic and international adaptations required for individual brands and countries. For example, it was only in 2003 when all tourism activities in Austria were bundled under the brand TUI Austria. Moreover, all TUI airlines already incorporate the logic of brand suffix 'fly'.

However, the 'World of TUI' has been growing so much and rapidly that further consolidation and rebundling of its similar brands are required under one overall masterbrand in order to: reduce the confusion created in the tourism market; link different brands with TUI quality standards and communicate these features to tourists; and provide tourists with a one-stop-shop sales' portal that consolidates several TUI offerings and provides tourists with the possibility to easily find, compare and select a travel proposal. 'World of TUI' companies that were rebundled and repositioned under a TUI masterbrand include:

- In 2005, TUI starts up the new travel portal TUI.com by combining brands and offers of World of TUI on the Internet. www.tui.com offers more than 150,000 holiday trips to more than 80 countries at more than 35,000 hotels around the world, a total of 15,000 holiday homes and more than three million flight rates with more than 150 scheduled, charter and low-fares airlines. Internet bookers can now find offers from Robinson, 1-2-FLY, Discount Travel, Wolters and, of course, from TUI all on one website. TUI intends to continue the expansion of this masterbrand portal in the future.

- In 2006, the two German TUI airlines (Hapagfly and HLX) are consolidated and rebranded under the common masterbrand of TUIfly.com. Their aircrafts fly to some 75 destinations in 17 countries. The future intention is to also include all other European TUI airlines into the TUIFly brand.

- The TUI Hotel Portal (www.tui-hotels.com) which has a selection of several thousand beach, city and classic holiday hotels for individual travellers. The comprehensive range of hotels is also integrated within existing websites and can, for instance, be combined with TUIfly flights.

This restructuring and rebranding of 'World of TUI' companies around similar groups of companies representing the different components of tour packages as well as the subsequent possibility to offer to tourists the possibility to buy tour packages' components independently and/or by bundling in personalized tour packages highlight TUI AG's strategic decision to reengineer its business model, reinvent its role and services in the tourism distribution chain in order to face the increased competition and address the needs of the new types of tourists. Current advances in Internet technology are creating a new type of sophisticated and information empowered tourist (the modular traveller) who is looking for individuality and personalization in tour planning, direct sales with suppliers, combination options and late bookings. More and more travel cyberintermediaries (e.g. expedia.com, ebookers.com) are gaining popularity and take a major market share from the traditional tour operators by enabling tourists to select and bundle their own preferred travel components into personalized tour packages.

New product and market development

New product development by TUI AG is reflected in its online portals developments that aim to cater for the modular travel market by offering dynamic packaging possibilities. Simultaneously, TUI AG aims to increase the offer to 'flight only' and 'hotel only' products in order to target the modular travel market that is also increasing due to the boom of the low cost carriers.

Product innovation by TUI AG is also evident in the off line world.

In November 2001, Preussag opened up a representative office in Berlin, the 'World of TUI Travel Mall', which covers 500 square metres. This travel retailer makes full use of state-of-the-art multimedia and virtual reality presentation technology enabling the customers to 'taste' the holiday product as a sensory experience. This innovation can substantially boost sales of a product that cannot be experienced before the client is transferred to the destination.

Following the low cost trends in the tourism market (e.g. easyJet, easyCruises, easyRent-a-car), TUI opened its first low-cost travel agency in Hamburg/Germany with Touristik Express. Touristik Express sells low-cost holidays for people who can make their minds up quickly. There are no brochures, no decorations and no seats. Customers can obtain information themselves about the latest holiday offers 'in passing' and book on the spot. TUI in Belgium launched its own airline TUI Airlines Belgium in April 2004.

In the globally expanding tourism industry, TUI AG has never hesitated to form joint ventures for developing new markets. Joint ventures is the strategy that TUI AG prefers when penetrating a new market as it reduces its initial risks, while it provides it with rich and important local knowledge and expertise that is difficult to easily and quickly acquire.

For instance, the setting up of a joint venture in China created a new platform for expanding opportunities in this country as a destination as well as developing operations on the domestic travel market for all companies in the TUI Group. Moreover, the joint venture provided additional structures for tapping the growing Chinese source market, as TUI China Travel Co. Ltd organizes and delivers the customer care and attention for travel programs designed for Chinese tourists; however, so far, it has focused only on travel within China.

In January 2006, TUI acquired a 49 per cent holding in Turismo Asia Ltd, Bangkok, Thailand and, in doing so, it also rounded off its agency portfolio in the long-haul sector. Turismo Asia Ltd emerged from the Turismo Thai Group, a family enterprise concentrating on the incoming business. However, this acquisition has enabled TUI AG to exploit the local retail network of Turismo Asia Ltd for both its incoming and outbound tourism. The latter operates central offices in Bangkok and owns a retail network of nine branch offices in the most important tourist zones as well as more than 19 offices in various hotels in Bangkok and on Koh Samui.

For penetrating the lucrative and ever expanding Russian market, TUI AG set up TUI Mostravel Russia (TMR), a joint venture with the Russian tour operator Mostravel.

India also represents a growth market with considerable potential. According to the World Tourism Organisation (WTO), the number of Indian tourists will increase by 10 per cent per year, while the number of Indians in the growing middle class that can afford foreign travel is estimated to be 45 to 70 million. Market penetration and development in India is pushed through the 50 per cent stake acquisition of the incoming agency Le Passage to India Ltd. The main thrust of the joint activities is the formation of a tour operator, while TUI customer care and attention for European holidaymakers in India is also provided by the retail network of the Indian partner.

TUI AG's representative offices in Berlin, Moscow and Beijing are the nerve centres for the development of new markets, as they are permanently in contact with government and political institutions.

—*Marianna Sigala*

Questions (Suggested answers can be found on the companion website www.thomsonlearning.co.uk/barnes)

WWW.

1 How would you characterize TUI's business strategy? Asses the role and contribution of TUI's operations in this business strategy.

2 What benefits does TUI AG achieve through its integrated tourism supply chain? Are there any disadvantages to this?

3 How has TUI configured its operations internationally in order to serve its various markets? What benefits does this provide? Are there any disadvantages?

4 What is the preferred strategy used by TUI to penetrate new international markets? What are the benefits of this strategy? Are there any disadvantages?

5 What are likely to be the most significant future challenges for the management of TUI's operations arising from its entry into the Chinese, Russian and Indian tourism markets?

References

Bartlett, C.A. and Ghosal, S. (1987) 'Managing across borders', *Sloan Management Review,* 28(4):7–17.

Flaherty, M.T. (1996) *Global Operations Management,* New York: McGraw-Hill.

Ferdows, K. (1989) 'Mapping international factory networks' in Ferdows, K. (Ed.) *Managing International Manufacturing,* Amsterdam: Elsevier.

Hirst, P. and Zeitlin, J. (1988) *Reversing Industrial Decline?* Oxford: Berg.

Kay, J. (1993) *Foundations of Corporate Success,* Oxford: Oxford University Press.

Peters, T.J. and Waterman, R.H. (1982) *In Search of Excellence,* New York: Harper & Row.

Pine, B.J. (1993) *Mass Customization,* Harvard, Massachusets: Harvard Business School Press.

Prahalad, C.K. and Hamel, G. (1990) 'The core competence of the corporation', *Harvard Business Review,* 68(3):71–91.

Skinner, W. (1974) 'The focused factory', *Harvard Business Review*, 52(3):13–121.
Slack, N., Chambers, S. and Johnston, R. (2004) *Operations Management* (4th Edition), Harlow: Pearson Education.

Additional reading

Flaherty, M.T. (1996) *Global Operations Management,* New York: McGraw-Hill.
Dornier, P., Ernst. R., Fender, M. and Kouvelis, P. (1998) *Global operations and logistics,* New York: John Wiley.
Segal-Horn, S. and Faulkner, D. (1999) *The dynamics of international strategy,* London: International Thomson Business.

Useful websites

WWW.

http://www.ifm.eng.cam.ac.uk/cim/ The Centre for International Manufacturing at the University of Cambridge. One of the leading academic research centres. It acts as a focal point for industrial managers and the wider community concerned with International Manufacturing issues and problems. In addition to its wide-ranging research activities in the International Manufacturing field, it offers a range of Industry-Academic workshops and related industrial and professional advisory service.

PART THREE

STRUCTURAL ISSUES

PART THREE

The major strategic decisions in operations can be conveniently divided into the two categories of structure and infrastructure. Structural decisions are concerned with the physical assets necessary for operations. They can be thought of as the hardware of operations.

Part Three considers the structural decision areas of operations management. (Infrastructural decisions are considered in Part Four.) Structural decisions often involve major capital investment decisions, which once made will set the direction of operations for many years to come. They invariably impact the resources and capabilities of an organization, determining its potential future output. It may be prohibitively expensive to change such decisions once implemented, and hence these must be considered to be truly strategic decisions for the organization. It may be much easier to change the organization's marketing strategy (e.g. its target markets, or its promotional activities) than it is to change its operations strategy with respect to the structural decision areas. For international organizations, structural decisions are also likely to be very complex decisions, requiring a detailed consideration of how to configure operations across a number of different countries in order to serve customers who may also be located in many other, possibly different, countries.

The four chapters of Part Three consider the structural decision areas under four broad headings:

- Chapter 5: Facilities considers the location, size and focus of operational resources. These decisions are concerned with where to locate production facilities, how large each should be, what goods or services should be produced at each location, what markets each facility should serve, etc.

- Chapter 6: Capacity management considers the capacity of operations and their ability to respond to changes in customer demand. These decisions are concerned with the use of facilities, for example through shift patterns, working hours and staffing levels. Decisions about capacity will affect the organization's ability to serve particular markets from a given location.

- Chapter 7: Process technology considers the technology of the equipment used in operations processes. For example, the degree of automation used, the configuration and layout of equipment, and so on.

- Chapter 8: Supply network considers the relationship between the organization's own resources and those of its supply network partners. These include decisions about the extent to which operations are conducted in-house or are sub-contracted; the choice of suppliers; their location; the extent of dependence on particular suppliers; and how relationships with suppliers are managed.

CHAPTER 5

FACILITIES

INTRODUCTION

This chapter will concentrate on facilities decisions. An **operations facility** comprises the physical resources (land, buildings, plant, machinery, equipment, etc.) necessary to produce the required goods and/or services at a particular location. Facilities decisions are concerned with where to locate the organization's production facilities, how large each should be, what goods or services should be produced at each location, what markets each facility should serve, etc. Facilities decisions are important because they typically involve large capital investments. Once made, these decisions are not easily or cheaply undone, as they typically determine the organization's resources and capabilities for many years to come. By any measure, these are truly strategic decisions. In recent years, more and more organizations (service providers as much as manufacturers) seem to feel that there are advantages to be gained by locating some of their facilities outside of their home country. It often seems as if they have almost unlimited choice about where in the world some of their operations could be based. However, once an organization starts to operate internationally, facilities decisions can become very complex. As well as deciding where to locate particular facilities, the organization will also have to determine the relationships between operations at different locations. In particular, consideration will need to be given about which facilities in which countries will be used to produce what products or services for which customers in which countries.

LEARNING OBJECTIVES

On completion of this chapter, you should be able to:

Describe the factors that are most important to an organization making facilities location decisions.

Discuss the issues that affect the scale and scope of operations facilities at particular locations.

Appreciate the strategic role and importance of decisions about facilities in international operations management.

Identify the factors that organizations need to consider when determining the configuration of their operations.

operations facility

A collection of resources brought together at one geographic location for the purpose of producing particular goods and/or services.

LOCATION DECISIONS

There are two principal factors influencing an organization's choice of location for its operations, namely access to markets and access to resources. Organizations may opt to locate their operations in a particular country or region in order to access an attractive market. On the other hand, location decisions may be driven by a desire to access resources, such as scarce raw materials, low cost labour, or specialist skills and capabilities.

Manufacturers often take both these factors into account when making a decision about the location of their facilities. However, for many service providers, there may be little choice about the location of their operations if they wish to access customers in a specific location. This is particularly the case in front office services that require face-to-face contact with customers. However, as already discussed in Chapter 3, appropriate use of ICT can enable front and back office operations to be physically separate. This can give organizations the same degree of freedom about the location of their back office operations as that of any manufacturing operations. Increasingly, organizations of all kinds are more willing to locate their operations in countries outside of their homeland. This can require managers to consider many different factors. Recent research has increased our understanding of international location decision-making.

MacCarthy and Atthirawong (2003) list 13 categories of factors that researchers have found to affect international location decisions. The constituents of these are listed in Table 5.1.

They went on to identify the most important motivations for firms to manufacture outside of their home country by interviewing a panel of worldwide experts. In order of decreasing importance, these are:

1 Ability to gain access to low labour costs and labour skills.

2 Ability to gain access to markets.

3 Tax incentives and other privileges from the host government.

4 Ability to gain access to host raw materials and technology.

5 Counteract competitors.

The top five major factors identified as strongly influencing international location decisions were:

- Costs
- Infrastructure
- Labour characteristics
- Government and political factors
- Economic factors

The top ten sub-factors influencing international location decisions were:

- Quality of labour force
- Existence of modes of transport
- Quality and reliability of modes of transport
- Availability of labour force
- Quality and reliability of utilities
- Wage rates
- Motivation of workers
- Telecommunications systems
- Record of government stability
- Industrial relations laws

It should be stressed that motivations for international manufacture and factors affecting location decisions will vary depending upon the type of business that the organization is in and the geographic region being considered for the location. For some operations, especially those based on agriculture or extractive industries, there is often little choice but to locate close to the source of the raw materials on which

TABLE 5.1 Factors affecting international location decisions

MAJOR FACTOR	SUB-FACTOR
Costs	Fixed costs; transport costs; wage rates; energy costs; other manufacturing costs; land costs; construction costs; others costs (e.g. R & D costs, transaction and management costs).
Labour characteristics	Quality of labour force; availability of labour force; unemployment rate; labour unions; attitudes towards work and labour turnover; motivation of workers and workforce management.
Infrastructure	Existence of modes of transport (airports, railroads, roads, seaports); quality and reliability of modes of transport; quality and reliability of utilities (e.g. water supply, waste treatment, power supply, etc.) and telecommunications systems.
Proximity to suppliers	Quality of suppliers; alternative suppliers; competition for suppliers; nature of supply process (reliability of system) and speed and responsiveness of suppliers.
Proximity to markets/customers	Proximity to demand; size of market that can be served/potential customer expenditure; responsiveness and delivery time to markets; population trends and nature of variance of demand.
Proximity to parent company facilities	Close to parent company.
Proximity to competition	Location of competitors.
Quality of life	Quality of environment; community attitudes towards business and industry; climate, schools, churches, hospitals, recreational opportunities (for staff and children); education system; crime rate and standard of living.
Legal and regulatory framework	Compensation laws; insurance laws; environmental regulations; industrial relations laws; legal system; bureaucratic red tape; requirement for setting up local corporations; regulations concerning joint ventures and mergers and regulations on transfer of earnings out of country.
Economic factors	Tax structure and tax incentives; financial incentives; custom duties; tariffs; inflation; strength of currency against the US dollar; business climate; country's debts; interest rates/exchange controls and GDP/GNP growth; income per capita.
Government and political factors	Record of government stability; government structure; consistency of government policy; attitude of government to inward investment.
Social and cultural factors	Different norms and customs; culture; language and customer characteristics.
Characteristics of a specific location	Availability of space for future expansion; attitude of local community to a location; physical conditions (e.g. weather, close to other businesses, parking; appearance, accessibility by customers, etc.); proximity to raw materials/ resources; quality of raw materials/resources and location of suppliers.

(BASED ON MACCARTHY AND ATTHIRAWONG, 2003 P. 797)

CASE STUDY India comes of age as a manufacturing hub for Smiths

John Crane's new factory in Bangalore could become a prime example of the type of manufacturing operation that may soon become the main driver of the country's economy. That, at least, is the hope of Keith Butler-Wheelhouse, Chief Executive of Smiths, a $5 billion British engineering services group of which John Crane, the world's leading manufacturer of mechanical seals, is a division. 'We've built a facility here that is better than many we have elsewhere. With India's skills and opportunities, I've no compunction in believing we can achieve our targets', he said.

After years of under-achievement in a market where its rivals, such as Flowserve of the US, are already established, John Crane is aiming to triple domestic sales by 2011. Currently its annual revenue is 240m Rupees ($5.4m), or 10 per cent of the market, way below its share in its 47 other markets. The company aims to improve this by targeting the booming petroleum products sector and expanding into beverages, where seals are used in the cappuccino machines that are attracting thousands of India's teenagers to the country's Starbucks lookalikes.

Mr Butler-Wheelhouse says these opportunities show that India is coming of age as a domestic market, extending its appeal beyond merely acting as an offshore resource for talent. India's status as a manufacturing hub, with clusters based around the textiles, vehicles components and petroleum products sectors, would only strengthen. However, this vision is hostage to the country's creaking infrastructure. 'We have come in the belief that India's infrastructure problem has to be addressed', says Mr Butler-Wheelhouse. He said this was a key concern of many CEOs when weighing up the promise of what is being touted as the next mass market after China.

Smiths is already present in China, where it manufactures aerospace components for General Electric. China was chosen because the project did not involve design work – striking at the heart of the

Smiths: High technology manufacturing in India

generic gap between the economic rivals. 'We talk about the Indian-China comparison but there is no comparison', he says, citing India's edge in education and engineering. That edge is evident in Smiths' decision not only to boost its manufacturing in India, but also to add a £1.5m ($2.6m) 'knowledge support services unit'. For instance, India's English-speaking and lower-cost graduate engineers are a compelling business and technology proposition. 'If we'd been patient enough to learn Mandarin, we'd have gone to China. But I can't tell you how much the lack of English slows down the transfer of knowledge', he says.

The upshot is that John Crane has been able to focus more closely on processes and manufacturing practices at the new Indian factory. Systems, such as the 'computer numerically controlled' machines that manage manufacturing, which Ashok Vasudevan, who heads the Bangalore unit says 'are seven times more efficient than anything else around', mean John Crane no longer has to subcontract out three quarters of its work, as it did during the past decade. The company is planning to shift more manufacturing in expensive and less efficient Europe to Bangalore to achieve cost competitiveness. Initially, about half of the Bangalore unit's output will be exported, eventually rising to 70–80 per cent. But the company says the savings it expects to feed into the bottom line from the 'knowledge centre' are potentially even greater than those in the manufacturing arm. This centre, staffed by about 80 young engineering graduates, will back up the company's divisions, such as aerospace, producing technical drawings and managing product lifecycles. Not only can this work be done while the US sleeps, cutting weeks off processing times for project proposals, it will for the first time standardize work along a seamless supply chain.

As Mike Mansell, who heads John Crane, says: 'The logic of India is wider than John Crane, it's group-wide. It is all about efficiency in a very competitive market. You have to analyze what our customers are willing to pay for', says Mr Mansell.

(Excerpted from the article by Khozem Merchant, *Financial Times,* London, 8 March 2006)

Questions   (Suggested answers can be found on the companion website www.thomsonlearning.co.uk/barnes)

WWW.

1 What motivated Smiths to set up its John Crane manufacturing facility in India?

2 What were the main factors that influenced its decision to locate in India?

3 Why did it reject China as a location for this facility?

4 To what extent do the motivations and influencing factors you identified in your answer to questions 1 and 2 reflect the results of MacCarthy and Atthirawong's (2003) research?

their processes are based. In labour intensive industries, like clothing manufacture or electronic assembly, low wage economies are particularly attractive. MacCarthy and Atthirawong stress the need to link decision-making about international location to overall business strategy. Although cost saving is often an important driver in international location decisions, it is not the only factor that needs to be considered. If the organization's business strategy is based on being able to offer superior quality or flexibility and speed of response, then making a location decision on the basis of achieving the lowest possible cost may be detrimental to those ends. Even if low cost is the main objective, even the most plentiful supply of low cost labour may not result on low overall costs if labour productivity and quality are poor.

If it is to be thorough, the location decision-making process is bound to be very complex, as there is a need to consider many different factors. As well as determining which factors to consider, the decision-makers must also determine the level of importance to attach to each factor. Many of the factors involved are essentially qualitative in nature and are hence very difficult to quantify. This is likely to limit the usefulness of many of the location decision techniques that can be found in the operations research and management science literature (for example, see Bhutta, 2004).

Additionally, many of these techniques, and the models on which they are based, often only consider a small number of factors (often precisely because they can be quantified), further limiting their usefulness.

Service operations location decisions can be yet more complex, because of the diverse nature of services (as discussed in Chapters 1 and 3). One of the key issues for service organizations is deciding whether they should centralize service provision at one (or very few) locations, or whether they should have localized service delivery. Opting for a centralized facility might enable it to be located to take advantage of low input costs (of land, labour, energy, etc.), and achieve potential economies of scale and scope. Such an approach, however, implies that many customers might have to travel long distances to reach the facility if face-to-face contact is required. Alternatively, it might be possible to provide the service remotely, thereby avoiding the need for customers to travel. Recent advances in ICTs especially those associated with the Internet (as discussed in Chapter 3), have provided opportunities to deliver many more services remotely. A strategy of providing localized service facilities will provide the opportunity for more customers to experience the service face-to-face. However, offering this higher level of service involves capital investment in buildings and equipment and employing an adequate number of people. It also makes for a much more complex operation, involving as it may well do the management of a very large number of facilities at many geographically dispersed locations.

Meijboom and Houtepen (2002) list six factors to consider when making decisions about service facility locations:

1 *The nature of the service delivery process:* If the service is delivered via a capital or resource intensive mass production process, then a centralized facility will be favoured. If the service is delivered by a labour intensive flexible process, then localized facilities will be favoured.

2 *The nature of the service product:* A standardized service is best delivered from a centralized facility, whereas a customized service can be best delivered locally.

3 *Whether customers can specify their needs:* Centralized facilities are best suited to circumstances when customers know what they want and can specify their requirements. On the other hand, localized facilities are more suited to circumstances under which customers do not know exactly what they want or can not specify what they want.

4 *Whether personal contact is required to specify customer needs:* Some services require direct contact with the customer in order to determine and specify their exact requirements. This is often the case in health and other professional services. Localized facilities are usually best suited to these cases.

5 *Whether some physical object is required for the service encounter:* Some service delivery encounters require the presence of certain physical objects. This might be the case in the delivery of certain personal services (e.g. hair dressing) or where the object itself is being transformed (e.g. car repair). Again, localized facilities tend to favour such cases.

6 *Whether the service is, in essence, an exchange of information:* Centralized facilities can be used if the service can be delivered entirely remotely. This is especially the case if the service is entirely informational in nature and can be digitized or vocalized, enabling it to be delivered via telecommunications networks.

This is summarized in Table 5.2.

scale
Decisions about the scale of operations are concerned with what quantities of goods and services should be produced at any given facility.

scope
Decisions about the scope of operations are concerned with what types of goods and services should be produced at any given facility.

(BASED ON MEIJBOOM AND HOUTEPEN, 2002)

	CENTRALIZED FACILITY	LOCALIZED FACILITIES
Service delivery processes	Capital/resource intensive mass production processes	Labour intensive flexible processes
Service product	Standardized	Customized
Can customers specify their needs?	Yes	No
Personal contact needed for customers to specify their needs?	No	Yes
Service involves a physical object?	No	Yes
Is service only an exchange of information?	Yes. Service can be vocalized or digitized.	No

TABLE 5.2 Factors influencing service operations location decisions

CASE STUDY Raja Fashion: A Hong Kong tailor comes to your town

Hong Kong is rightly famed for its bespoke tailors. Their shops abound in the innumerable shopping malls and streets of the former British colony. They are particularly numerous in the Tsim Sha Tsui area of Kowloon, where anyone of European appearance is invariably harangued by the many hawkers who throng its main streets extolling the virtues of the particular tailor's shop they represent.

Hong Kong tailors can reputedly produce a made-to-measure suit in as little as 24 hours; and for a price equivalent to what would typically be paid for an off-the-peg suit in Europe or North America, and a fraction of what might have to be paid for the equivalent of a bespoke suit in London's Saville Row.

Raja Fashion, run by Raja Daswani, is now Hong Kong's biggest made-to-measure tailoring business. Yet, before 1997, the year the colony was handed back to China and became a Special Administrative Region of the People's Republic, the company was indistinguishable from the hundreds of Hong Kong's other tailors. The customers for Raja Fashion and the other tailors were amongst the large European expatriate community as well as visitors to Hong Kong, who would typically stay for only a couple of days, often whilst en route to Australia or other parts of South East Asia. However, after 1997, many of his clients started leaving. To make matters worse, the handover coincided with a financial crisis in the region, resulting in decreased visitor numbers.

So Mr Daswani decided that if the customers would not come to him he would have to go to them. His firm had always paid an annual visit to London, but after 1997 these became more and more frequent. He now spends as much as eight months a year travelling between the major cities of Great Britain, Ireland and the USA. Recently, he has also taken in cities in continental Europe. Mr Daswani's team set up shop in a hotel suite, thereby avoiding the expense and hassle of having permanent business premises 6,000 miles from home. Customers can book an appointment in response to the full-page advert he places in local newspapers or via the Raja Fashion website. As his reputation grows, he also gets many word of mouth recommendations and is often invited in by executives of big companies. Mr Daswani also has many celebrity clients (reputedly including Tony Blair, David Beckham and Lashmi Mittal). Raja Fashion always sets up a special room for people who do not want to be seen.

Raja Fashions: Bringing the front office to the customer

(DBIMAGES/ALAMY)

Mr Daswani's strategy of taking his shop to his customers works as follows. First, he meets with a customer to discuss his requirements. Many customers bring in a favourite suit to be copied, or point out a style that they like in magazines and advertisements. Second, Mr Daswani's team takes detailed measurements and digitally photographs the customer to give extra information about his body shape and stance. These are then emailed to Hong Kong, where the suits are made. Third, the customer chooses the fabric. There are over 25,000 swatches to choose from, including cashmeres and silk mohair. The choice affects the price with prices starting from under £200. Finally, around three weeks later, the suit arrives in the post at the customer's address. If there are any problems, Raja Fashion has arrangements with local tailors who can make minor changes at no extra charge.

This approach has certainly been successful. Orders are up 100 per cent in the past five years, with Raja Fashion's workshops turning out more than 1,000 suits a week. They have 500 tailors making suits in Hong Kong and mainland China, where a skilled tailor can be employed for about £100 a month; something like 5 per cent of the equivalent cost in London.

Changing fashions have certainly also contributed to the company's success. A few years ago office wear was becoming more casual. However, smart business clothing is enjoying a revival. Mr Daswani also feels that he has helped bring made-to-measure tailoring to a wider audience. 'Although people want to look smart, they are more conscious of their budgets than they used to be', he claims. Professionals such as bankers, brokers, financiers, lawyers and the like still make up the bulk of his clientele, but a growing percentage are twentysomethings on more moderate incomes.

(Source material: http://www.raja-fashions.com)

WWW.

WWW.

Questions   (Suggested answers can be found on the companion website www.thomsonlearning.co.uk/barnes)

1   What are the most important factors influencing Raja Fashion's approach to its facilities location decisions?

2   Use Meijboom and Houtepen's six factors to explain the success of Raja Fashion.

3   Mr Daswani is considering setting up a shop in London. Do you think this is a good idea?

THE SCALE AND SCOPE OF OPERATIONS FACILITIES

As well as its location, the consideration of any particular facility must also include a determination of the scope and scale of its operations. This involves deciding exactly what goods and services should be produced at that location (i.e. the variety of its output) and what quantities of those goods and services should be produced (i.e. the volume of its output).

Increasing the volume of goods and services produced at any given location usually leads to lower unit costs in operations due to economies of scale. In the extreme case an organization could conceivably choose to produce all its output of a particular product at one location, serving all its customers in the world from one facility. This would certainly be possible for a manufacturer and also for some services (e.g. for separated services and provider-located services – as described in Chapter 3). Even for demander-located services, a single back office could be used to support any number of remote front office operations. Centering all production at one facility also has the advantage of making full use of the capabilities that may have been developed there over time, capabilities that may be difficult to replicate quickly at other locations. There may also be advantages from the proximity to suppliers to the location, thereby shortening supply chains and promoting close working relations with suppliers.

The main disadvantage of concentrating production at a single location would be the exposure of the entire organization to the risk of disruption or even catastrophic failure at such a facility. There might also be problems arising from the operation being remote from many of its markets. Despite the distance-shrinking impact of the Internet, there is still much to be said for an organization being close to its customers. This not only makes delivery of physical goods quicker, easier and cheaper but should also provide a better understanding of customer needs. Furthermore, whilst a large facility may, in theory, have adequate capacity to cope with any potential demand, that demand might be so variable as to create large peaks and troughs, leading either to unfulfilled orders or under-utilization of capacity. (The issue of capacity management is discussed further in Chapter 6.) A single large facility also increases the likelihood of diseconomies of scale being encountered.

Increasing the number of facilities can offset some of these problems, enabling the organization to overcome problems occurring at any one location and offering the ability to balance production volumes across a number of sites. However, increasing the number of locations is bound not only to lead to the loss of some economies of scale but also to the introduction of greater management complexity in operations management due to the problems of coordinating activities across the various sites.

These issues are further complicated by the fact that most organizations are involved in the production of more than one product or service. Consequently, they must also consider which facilities will be used to produce each kind of product and service, how many different types of products or services to produce at any one location, and what markets to serve from each location.

This then raises the issue of the scope of operations. Increasing the range of goods and services capable of being produced at any one location is bound to increase the complexity of operations at that site. If the operations at the site are to be able to respond to changes in demand to both the volume and variety of product demand, then a high degree of flexibility will be required. This is likely to require flexibility from the process technology being used, a multi-skilled workforce and responsive supplier base. All this increases the difficulties of planning and controlling operations at the site. (These issues are discussed in more depth in Chapters 7, 8, 9 and 10.) However, it should be possible to offset some of the losses of economies of scale due to lower volumes of individual products and services against the economies of scope which should be available from increasing the number of products and services produced.

diseconomies of scale
Increases in the unit cost of output that occur when production volumes increase too much. Diseconomies of scale may result from the complexity of managing a very large facility, from rising cost of inputs (e.g. due to having to transport raw materials increased distances or from increased labour rates necessary to attract sufficient workers), or from disruptions in production due to operating at very high levels of capacity utilization (e.g. from increased incidents of machine breakdown).

Most organizations that produce many different types of products and services for geographically dispersed customers opt for a facilities strategy involving multiple locations. Organizations often have certain facilities at some locations for historic reasons. This may have been due to their proximity to sources of vital raw material sources, their access to transportation links, or their closeness to important markets. They may also have been inherited through earlier merger and acquisition activities. However, over time most production networks have been rationalized in some way as organizations seek to reduce the complexity of their operations. The underpinning logic for most attempts to reduce complexity was first articulated over 30 years ago by Skinner (1974). He argued that the performance of individual facilities could be improved if they focused on a narrow range of tasks. Thus, a network of facilities could improve its overall performance if each location was assigned its own specific activity. This idea has been subject to much debate over the intervening years, and it has both its advocates and detractors. The premise on which Skinner's argument is based is that focusing on a single task makes the management of a facility much simpler as everyone concerned knows precisely what their objectives are. Operations management decisions and actions can then be undertaken with a view to achieving one clear goal. However, it should be noted that whilst the task of managing a single focused site is simpler than managing one with a multitude of tasks, having a network of focused facilities itself poses a significant management challenge, due to the size and complexity of the network. The greater the number of facilities, the greater the number of products, the greater the number of customer locations, then the greater the complexity. Neither does the notion of focus of itself determine what the optimum size of a single facility should be, how many facilities there should be or where each facility should be located.

One of the problems with Skinner's idea is that there is no single understanding of what is meant by focused operations. There are three ways in which a facility can be focused (Ketokivi and Jokinen, 2005):

- *Market focus:* The facility serves a carefully and narrowly defined market segment or niche. Such a niche might be based on the characteristics of its customers or could be geographic. Many service facilities, particularly for front office demander-located services are located for their ease of access to customers in specific geographic areas. MacDonald's, for example, aims to provide one of its outlets for every 25,000 people. Market focus should certainly increase the ability of the facility to respond to local market needs.

- *Product focus:* The facility focuses on a narrow range of products or services, which can be produced with the equipment and expertise available at the location. This can help maximize economies of scale. This is normally the strategy adopted by motor car manufacturers, who typically produce just one model at any plant. A variant of this approach is for particular facilities to focus on different production volumes. For example, one facility might concentrate on high volume products whilst another might focus on low volume requirements.

- *Process focus:* The facility focuses on a certain type of production technology. This allows them to produce different types of products and services, subject to the limitations of the chosen process focus. This can enable them to achieve economies of both scope and scale, and exploit the expertise of workers skilled in the specific processes in use at the facility. An example of this might be the production of computer software.

However, it should be noted that these three different types of focus are not mutually exclusive and it is possible that two or even all three could be combined. Doing this would, of course, increase the focus of the facility. In practice, organizations often have a mixture of the different types of focus. They also often have facilities with

focused operations

The concept that a facility that concentrates on a single or very narrow range of tasks will outperform one trying to achieve a broader range of tasks. Focus might be achieved by limiting the markets served, the products produced or processes used at a particular facility.

(ADAPTED FROM DORNIER *ET AL*, 1998: 264)

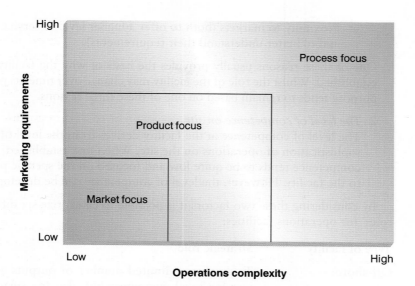

FIGURE 5.1 Orientation of operations facilities

different degrees of focus, as they respond to changing market conditions, actions of competitors, and factors in their operating environment (technologies, economic conditions, etc.).

Each of the three different types of focus approach has its own particular advantages and disadvantages. Dornier *et al.* (1998) argue that selecting the most appropriate one involves a trade-off between two dimensions:

- *Operations complexity:* The degree of difficulty of the operations process, for example the number of steps in the process, the characteristics of the goods or services being produced, the environmental requirements.

- *Marketing requirements:* The degree of difficulty and complexities involved in marketing the product, for example the amount of advertising and sales effort required, the extent to which the product must be customized or frequency with which it must be updated.

Market focus is favoured by low levels of operations complexity and marketing requirements. Product focus is favoured by medium levels of operations complexity and marketing requirements. Process focus is favoured by high levels of operations complexity and/or marketing requirements. Figure 5.1 illustrates this.

THE STRATEGIC ROLE AND PURPOSE OF OPERATIONS FACILITIES

Decisions about operations facilities often have strategic significance because of their financial impact and their long-term consequences. However, the strategic impact of the facilities of organizations that operate internationally also relates to the strategic role and purpose that each has. This can be assessed by examining two important factors (Ferdows, 1989, 1997):

1 *The primary strategic reason for the facility*
   There can be three possible primary strategic reasons for the facility.

   i Access to low cost inputs (often this is low cost labour, but it might be land, materials, energy, etc.).

   ii Access to specialist expertise (from the local labour pool, suppliers, competitors, customers, research laboratories and other knowledge centres).

iii Proximity to markets (both to offer a higher level of service to customers and to better understand their requirements).

One of these reasons usually provides the basis of why the facility was originally established. Whilst the role of the facility may change over time, its primary strategic purpose tends to remain based on one of these three reasons.

2 *The level of competence on site*
The level of competence at the facility derives from the level of technological sophistication of operations on the site. When first established, the level of competence tends to be quite low and focused on the specific purpose given to the facility. However, the level of competence can be developed over time.

By considering these two factors it is possible to categorize six different 'strategic roles' for operations facilities:

Type of facility	Strategic role
Off-shore:	To produce a limited number of outputs at low cost, not just for local customers but also for customers in other parts of the world. It is established to access sources of low cost resources, such as labour. Investments in technology and competences are kept to the minimum required for production. All key decisions about technology, suppliers, logistics and finance are taken at headquarters rather than locally.
Source:	Like the off-shore facility, its role is to produce a limited number of outputs at low cost, but it also acts as a focal point for specific components, products or processes. Local managers can take decisions about sourcing and supplier selection. They also have more autonomy about production planning, process development, product customization and logistics.
Server:	To serve specific national or regional markets. It is established to overcome import tariffs and taxes, reduce logistics costs, overcome currency fluctuations and other trade barriers. Local managers have limited autonomy to make minor changes to products and processes to suit local conditions.
Contributor:	To serve specific national or regional markets, but also to be a focal point for testing and developing certain new products and processes. It has its own product and process development competences and has autonomy over supplier selection and development.
Outpost:	To collect information from technologically advanced local suppliers, competitors, customers and research laboratories. Its location is chosen for its proximity to these sources of information. Its production role is of secondary importance but it may also act as a server or off-shore facility.
Lead:	To create and develop new products and processes for the whole organization. It taps into local expertise and resources, not only to collect information for headquarters, but also to exploit locally for its own purposes. It has full autonomy over supplier selection and development, and may enter into joint ventures. It initiates innovations and works closely with customers, suppliers, research laboratories and other knowledge centres.

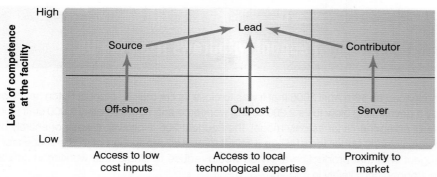

FIGURE 5.2 The strategic roles of international operations facilities

Facilities usually start out as off-shore, outpost or server facilities but often progress to undertake more technically complex tasks. However, such progress is not automatic and there is a danger that the facility may stagnate due to managerial neglect or complacency. In order to perform more technically complex tasks requires the facility to have an appropriately higher level of competence. Figure 5.2 illustrates the potential progressions possible. These are:

Off-shore to source: A source facility has responsibility for a limited number of products or processes. To become a source facility, an offshore facility must develop the specific expertise required to master the production of these products or the operation of these processes itself. This particularly requires it to develop competences in dealing with the suppliers on whom it relies for those products or processes. It takes responsibility for selecting and developing those suppliers and it must also learn how to respond to customer requirements in the markets that it serves.

Server to contributor: A contributor facility takes responsibility for product development and customization for the market that it serves. Consequently, to develop into a contributor, a server facility must be able to assess the needs of the customers that it serves and modify its products and processes accordingly. Thus it must enhance its marketing and technological competences.

Outpost to lead: A lead facility is responsible for innovation in products, processes and technologies for the whole organization. To become a lead facility, an outpost facility must develop competences in the application of the information that it has previously existed to collect.

Source to lead: To become a lead facility, a source facility must enhance its existing competences product and process development beyond that of low cost, to encompass a wider range of objectives (e.g. to improve quality, speed, dependability or flexibility). This will almost certainly require it to access a broader range of skills and knowledge than was previously the case.

Contributor to lead: To become a lead facility, a contributor facility must enhance its existing competences in product development and customization to address the requirements of customers beyond the markets that it has previously served.

It can take time to develop the necessary competences to advance from one strategic role to another. However, there is a strong imperative to progress. The future of any off-shore, outpost or server facility is bound to be open to question in the longer-term. It is possible for facilities to have more than one strategic role. However, unless a facility has a clear understanding of its strategic role and purpose, the decisions and actions taken by its managers may be confused, leading to sub-optimal performance.

WHEN THINGS GO WRONG Peugeot withdraws from the UK

When Peugeot announced on 18th April 2006 that it was to close its car making plant at Ryton near Coventry it was obviously a devastating blow to its 2,300 strong workforce and approximately 1,000 staff working at British suppliers of components for its only model, the Peugeot 206. However, it was not entirely unexpected. The plant was clearly under threat when it failed to secure production of 206's successor, the Peugeot 207. Peugeot said that production at Ryton would reduce to single shift working in July 2006 before production stopped completely in mid-2007.

The Ryton plant has been making cars since its construction by the Rootes company in the 1940s. Rootes teamed up with Chrysler of America in the 1960s, but when Chrysler Europe collapsed in 1977, Ryton was taken over by French giant PSA Peugeot Citroën. Since then the plant has made the Peugeot 309 and 405, and then the 309's successor, the 306. The 206 has been made at Ryton since 1998, with over one million being produced at the company's only UK factory.

Peugeot's UK Communications Director John Goodman said he realized it was a difficult time for staff and that employees had brought about tremendous productivity improvements. 'Unfortunately that just doesn't change the economics of the situation. Ryton is the group's most expensive manufacturing plant in Europe. Every car produced there cost 415 euros (£286) more than anywhere else in Europe', Mr Goodman said. An analysis of the group's industrial facilities during the first quarter of 2006 'clearly confirmed the

A Peugeot production line

weaknesses for the Ryton plant – high production and logistical costs – which meant that the group was unable to justify the investment needed for the production of future vehicles after the Peugeot 206'. Jean-Martin Folz, Peugeot's Chief Executive, also blamed falling demand and intense competition in Europe for small cars. The company had already reduced production at a number of other European sites at the end of 2005.

Analysts said Ryton's closure came as little surprise after the company indicated last year that it intended to move more production to lower cost factories in Eastern Europe. 'In a way, it is surprising it has lasted so long', observed Jay Nagley, automotive analyst with the Spyder Automotive consultancy. Jag Nagley also observed that 'there was no justification for the UK factory'. In 2005, PSA Peugeot Citroën's operating income fell to below 2 billion euros (£1.4 billion) from 2.5 billion euros a year earlier. Net profits fell to 1 billion euros from 1.65 billion euros in 2004. The company needed to cut costs urgently, which might have pushed forward the closure of the Ryton factory, though strained industrial relations may also have played a part. Last year, 60 per cent of Ryton's workers rejected plans for a fifth weekday shift on Fridays. Unions have condemned Peugeot's closure decision, with some officials arguing that lay-offs on this scale would be inconceivable in France where workers enjoy stronger labour laws. However, the harsh reality is that even Peugeot's French workers face an uncertain future. Production of the 206 model is set to continue in Eastern European factories, where labour costs are lower than in Britain and the rest of Western Europe. Mr Nagley noted that

'European mass market carmakers, like Peugeot, are in deep trouble. They are assembling small cars in Europe for 30 euros an hour when the Japanese and others can do it for far less. Moving production to Slovakia, where costs are about a fifth of the UK, is an entirely rational step'.

The successor to the Peugeot 206 model, the 207, was unveiled at the Geneva motor show in February 2006 and is due to hit the road in the spring. However, the 206 model will not be withdrawn immediately. Peugeot is expected to cut the price of the model sharply and market it as a cheap car for Eastern European drivers. The high cost of making the old 206 in the UK relative to the low price the car will be sold for outside Western Europe means it makes more sense to produce it in factories in Eastern Europe. Although the 207 will be targeted at drivers in Western Europe, it is still advantageous for Peugeot to make it where wages and other costs are lower. The 207 model is already being produced in Slovakia.

Professor Garel Rees, director of the Centre for Automotive Industry Research at Cardiff Business School, said the demise of Peugeot in Coventry was not down to the cars themselves. He said, 'Ryton was very much an assembly operation. They almost just received kits from the continent and then put them together in the UK. There's very little actual British content other than the labor and a few components'. Only 12.5 per cent of components, measured by cars' retail values, are produced in the UK. 'The reality is that Ryton had become self-evidently a marginal plant'.

(Source material from http://www.bbc.co.uk and http://www.ft.com)

WWW.

Questions (Suggested answers can be found on the companion website www.thomsonlearning.co.uk/barnes)

WWW.

1 Which of Ferdows' six strategic roles best describes Peugeot's Ryton facility?

2 Use this model to explain Peugeot's decision to close the factory.

THE CONFIGURATION OF OPERATIONS FACILITIES

Most organizations operate a number of different facilities at different locations. These organizations must address the issue of the **configuration** of their operations facilities. Such decisions are concerned with the relationship between operations facilities at different locations. They are concerned with determining what markets to serve with what products and services from which facilities. These decisions are often very complex and involve a consideration of a multiplicity of many inter-related

configuration

Decisions about the configuration of operations are concerned with the relationship between operations facilities at different locations.

A generic process for international manufacturing strategy

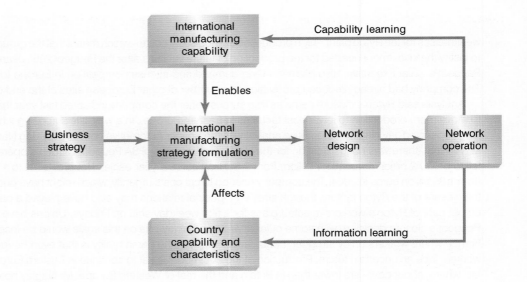

(GREGORY ET AL., 1996)

issues. The situation can be even more complex when considering the configurations across a number of different countries. This issue was discussed in Chapter 4, where four generic configurations were identified: home operations, multi-domestic operations, regional operations and global co-ordinated operations.

Gregory *et al.* (1996) have developed a framework to help determine the configuration for international manufacturing operations facilities (see Figure 5.3). They argue that the design of an appropriate configuration depends on the business strategy being pursued by the organization, the organization's international manufacturing capability and the capability and characteristics of the particular countries in which facilities could be located. The framework emphasizes the need to link the configuration adopted to whichever combination of the competitive priorities (cost, quality, speed, dependability and flexibility) that are inherent in pursuing the organization's chosen business strategies. The framework also highlights the importance of learning from operating international facilities. This learning can then be used to inform future strategic operations decision-making. Strategy-making is not a once and forever occurrence, but rather it is a dynamic process in which decisions and actions need to be reviewed constantly in the light of new knowledge.

Operations strategy has traditionally been considered in terms of the decisions made about individual facilities. At most, strategic decisions might have been made at the level of an individual country or region, a key issue being how to configure the operations facilities that serve the market at national or regional level. This is, however, limiting the consideration of operations configurations to home operations, multi-domestic operations and regional operations. It ignores the case of global co-ordinated operations, in which a worldwide perspective is taken. From this perspective, the aim is to determine how best to configure all the organization's operations facilities to best serve its customers wherever they are in the world. Shi and Gregory (1998) argue that this can only be done effectively if all of an organization's facilities are considered in their totality – as a network. Only by taking such a **network perspective** can the full potential of an organization's operations facilities be realized. They draw the parallel with developments in computing. Networks of computers are far more powerful than any stand-alone machine. They argue that the strategic

network perspective

This perspective argues that it is necessary to consider all of an organization's facilities collectively in order to realize their full potential to serve all their customers irrespective of their geographic location.

capabilities of an international network of operations facilities derive from four factors:

1 *Strategic targets accessibility*
   A widely dispersed network enables the organization to access:

   – Different markets (overcoming trade barriers, closeness to customers, speedy response)

   – Low cost resources (labour, materials, energy, technology)

   – Managerial skills

   – Specialist knowledge and understanding (of global changes in technology, customer requirements, the business environment, actions of competitors, etc.)

   – Connections to business and social networks

2 *Thriftiness ability*
   An effectively co-ordinated network enables the organization to achieve cost savings from:

   – economies of scale

   – economies of scope

   – reduced duplication of activities

3 *Operations mobility*
   A widely dispersed network enables the organization to be more flexible by being better able to:

   – move its products and process between locations (in response to changing market conditions)

   – move its managers (to promote knowledge transfer)

4 *Learning ability*
   An effectively co-ordinated network enables the organization to learn from:

   – internal and external performance and practice comparisons (e.g. benchmarking)

   – tapping into specific national strengths in different countries

   – exposure to different demands in different markets

Analyzing these factors will provide an assessment of a network's ability to achieve the operational performance objectives required for the organization's business strategy.

CASE STUDY Hoya's European move with global vision

For a Japanese company to move the head office of one of its biggest subsidiaries outside Japan is highly unusual. It is rarer still to find that the transition involves a shift to Europe, rather than China or the US. But that was the change that Hiroshi Suzuki, Chief Executive of Tokyo-based Hoya, one of the world's top three producers of spectacle lenses, pushed through last year, when he moved the headquarters of Hoya's vision care business to the Netherlands.

Mr Suzuki was prompted to make the move by Europe's technological prowess and market lead in the sector. In the $30 billion-a-year (£17 billion) business of providing people with spectacles, the continent is poised to drive much of the sector's growth over the coming decade. Hoya's decision represents a rare vote

Hoya: One of the world's leading lens manufacturers

of confidence in Europe, which is more often considered a laggard when it comes to fast-expanding technology sectors and which many believe is becoming eclipsed by rivals in fast-growing Asia, as well as by the US, with its vast market and deep reserves of business know-how.

The job of making the transition work was handed to Gerry Bottero, a Hoya executive from the US. A small office on the outskirts of Amsterdam became the new global headquarters of Hoya's spectacle lens activities. With sales of about $1 billion a year, the business accounts for roughly a third of total sales. Hoya's other activities include areas of optics technology and production equipment for the semiconductor industry, together with laser systems and tiny lenses used in cameras.

Mr Bottero says a mixture of factors makes Europe the right place to base a global lens production and sales business, particularly in the fast-expanding area of 'progressive' lenses or 'no-line' bifocals. Normally users must either own more than one pair of spectacles, or wear conventional 'lined' bifocals that adjust the eyes for short and long distances but not for those in between. Relatively expensive and novel, progressive lenses correct vision all the way from near to far vision.

'Europe is home to the key players in the technologies for more sophisticated lenses, while the consumer market for advanced types of spectacles is also far better developed than elsewhere, particularly in the US', says Mr Bottero.

'In Europe, people in general don't mind paying higher prices for premium products and this certainly helps us in the more sophisticated end of the lens business. Also I feel we have an advantage in Europe through the greater ability of employees to speak languages that are relevant for global sales. For instance, Hoya has people in Spain who are highly enthusiastic about selling lenses in Spanish-speaking South America'.

Many observers view Europe as being the focal point in the world lens industry, which is worth about $10 billion a year. According to Mr Bottero, only about 20m of the 800m lenses made each year worldwide use progressive technology, which requires ultra-accurate production machinery to match each lens to the precise defects in a person's eyes. 'However, of this 20m, about 70 per cent are made and sold in Europe, and the figure is expanding at 35 per cent a year, well ahead of the growth for the spectacle lens industry as a whole', he says.

Much of Mr Bottero's time is spent liaising with the 1,800 Hoya employees in Europe who work in the vision care part of the company, out of 7,000 in this division globally. Most work in either sales or marketing, or in the 20 or so small plants that Hoya has throughout Europe. These plants customize individual lenses from the lens blanks that are made using low-cost labour in two factories in Thailand and one in China.

A big part of Mr Bottero's job is to get the best possible flow of ideas in technology and production between the European arm and Hoya's centres in Japan and the US.

'We're particularly keen to expand in Asia outside Japan – a region that is likely to see a tremendous amount of growth in eyecare generally in the next few years – and we think we have a better chance of doing this if we can use some of the best ideas from Europe to help'.

(Excerpted from article by Peter Marsh, *Financial Times,* London, 12 January 2006)

Questions (Suggested answers can be found on the companion website www.thomsonlearning.co.uk/barnes)

1 Describe the main features of the configuration of Hoya's global network of facilities.
2 Assess the effectiveness of the network using Shi and Gregory's four factors.

SUMMARY OF KEY POINTS

Facilities decisions involve the consideration of location, scope (i.e. what goods and services should be produced at any given location), scale (i.e. what quantities of goods and services should be produced at any given location), configuration (i.e. the relationship between operations facilities at different locations) and strategic role and purpose.

Two principal factors influence facilities location decisions: access to markets and access to resources. Facilities location decisions are complex and can involve a consideration of many factors, which will vary depending upon the nature of the organization's business and the geographic region being considered for the location.

Consideration of scale and scope requires determining whether to concentrate operations at one (or very few) facilities or whether to opt for a greater number of more geographically dispersed facilities. A limited number of sites should simplify operations and lead to lower unit costs due to economies of scale and scope. More dispersed operations should provide more flexibility and provide benefits from being closer to customers.

The concept of focus argues that superior operations performance can be achieved if a facility dedicated itself to achieving a narrow range of tasks. Such a task can be based on market focus, product focus or process focus.

The strategic role and purpose of a facility can be based on one of three possible primary strategic reasons: access to low cost inputs, access to specialist expertise or proximity to market. In international operations it is possible to categorize six types of facility, depending upon their strategic role: off-shore, source, server, contributor, outpost or lead.

An organization's facilities should be configured with a view to achieving the operation's competitive priorities implied by its business strategy. In global co-ordinated operations, a network perspective is required in order to realize the full collective potential of all the organization's facilities. The strategic capabilities of an international network of facilities derive from four factors: strategic targets accessibility, thriftiness ability, operations mobility and learning ability.

WWW.

EXERCISES (Suggested answers can be found on the companion website www.thomsonlearning.co.uk/barnes)

1 Why are decisions about operations facilities so important?

2 What are likely to be the most important factors in deciding where to locate the facilities for the following types of businesses:

   a A car manufacturer
   b A fast food restaurant
   c A designer of fashion clothing
   d A research laboratory

3 What are the main factors likely to influence international location decisions?

4 A manufacturer seeking economies of scale might be tempted to locate all its operations on a single site to supply all its global customers. Why might this not always be a good idea?

5 Use Meijboom and Houtepen's six factors to assess whether the following types of service organizations would be best advised to use a single centralized facility or a series of localized facilities for their operations:

   a A book seller
   b A consumer advice service
   c A DVD rental company
   d An insurance company

6 If so many services can now be delivered remotely using ICTs, has the issue of location now become irrelevant in service operations?

7 What type of focus (market, product or process) would be best suited to the facilities of an organization that manufactures:

   a Computer hardware
   b Domestic whitegoods (washing machines, fridges, freezers, etc.)
   c Specialty foodstuffs

8 Explain what is meant by the term 'strategic focus' when applied to an operations facility.

9 Outline the main differences between an off-shore facility, a source facility and a server facility. In each case, explain how they could enhance their respective strategic roles.

10 How should a firm set about designing an international network? What factors should it take into account?

CASE STUDY EXERCISE ALUMIL

Background

Since it was founded in its present form in 1988, ALUMIL has grown rapidly. By 2000 it had become Greece's largest producer of integrated aluminium systems and one of the top European groups in its industry (based on production capacity). The company has benefited from the huge amount of construction activity in South East Europe and the Middle East as well as the economic boom and opportunities that arise from the accession of the former communist countries of Eastern Europe to the EU. (The geographic spread of the company's facilities is shown in Figure 5.4.) ALUMIL sees further expansion and penetration in these international markets as a strategic imperative. This is reinforced by the fact that many of ALUMIL's major clients in Greece are aluminium traders that operate almost exclusively within international markets. Domestic and international sales have continued to grow substantially (see Table 5.3) because of:

1   The company's success in achieving value-added-product sales (e.g. processed profiles and profiles with thermal brakes) in rather demanding markets both domestically and internationally, and

2   The on-going investments being made by the company to further boost its production capacity and improve its delivery performance.

A cross-section of one of ALUMIL's window frame systems

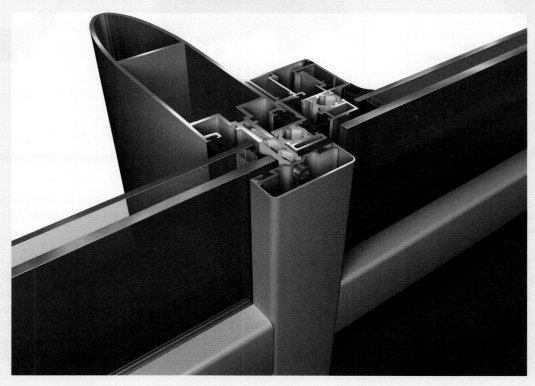

FIGURE 5.4 Map showing ALUMIL's facilities

● Production unit

▪ Distribution centre

▲ Local sales centre

ALUMIL's strategic intention of further market penetration is based on the expansion of its networks by the formation of numerous subsidiaries (see Figure 5.5) and by carefully focusing their roles and operations within their respective markets.

Products

ALUMIL designs, produces and sells integrated architectural systems for every construction type, including basic use (such as sliding, folding and opening frames, curtain walls, shop windows, roofs, etc.) and for more specialist applications (such as blowers, glass roofs, greenhouses, etc.). For each new application, an integrated system is designed which comprises the specific aluminium profile as well as all the accessories necessary to enable its subsequent assembly. Part of the production of a profile is allocated to the group's local subsidiaries. This enables time-to-market efficiency to be increased and helps ensure local trends and preferences can be better addressed. (Table 5.4 lists some of ALUMIL's products.)

Production capacity and process

Aluminium profiles are produced through an extrusion process. ALUMIL takes aluminium rods as its raw materials, which are pre-heated to temperatures of between 400°C and 500°C before being extruded in the desired shapes by forcing them into specially shaped dies. The technical characteristics and quality (e.g. without malformations, inbuilt stresses) of the profiles that are produced depend, to a great extent, on the quality

TABLE 5.3 Breakdown analysis of group sales by activity and location

		(IN TONS)	2002	2003	2004
	FOUNDRY		18 000	18 000	28 000
	Extrusion	1 600 MT (1990)	6 000	6 000	6 000
	Extrusion	1 800 MT (2000)	8 000	8 000	8 000
	Extrusion	2 500 MT (1996)	12 000	12 000	12 000
	Extrusion	3 750 MT (2003)	—	20 000	20 000
KILKIS	EXTRUSION	TOTAL	26 000	46 000	46 000
	Powder Coating	VERTICAL (1998)	12 000	12 000	12 000
	Powder Coating	HORIZONTAL (2001)	6 000	6 000	6 000
	Powder Coating	HORIZONTAL (2002)	6 000	6 000	6 000
	POWDER COATING	TOTAL	24 000	24 000	24 000
	Extrusion	1 800 MT (2000)	6 000	6 000	6 000
	Extrusion	1 350 MT (2003)	—	5 000	5 000
KOMOTINI	EXTRUSION	TOTAL	6 000	11 000	11 000
	Extrusion	1 600 MT (1998)	6 000	6 000	
	Extrusion	1 800 MT (2002)	8 000	8 000	8 000
XANTHI	EXTRUSION	TOTAL	14 000	14 000	8 000
	Powder Coating	HORIZONTAL (2001)	6 000	6 000	6 000
BULGARIA – SOFIA	Powder Coating	HORIZONTAL (2002)	6 000	6 000	6 000
ROMANIA – BUCHAREST	Powder Coating	HORIZONTAL (2002)	6 000	6 000	6 000
SERBIA – CACAK	Extrusion	1 870 MT (new line, 2004)	—	—	8 000
	Powder Coating	HORIZONTAL (2004)	—	—	8 000 (in 2005–6)
	Extrusion	1 600 MT (upgraded, 2004)			6 000
ALBANIA – TIRANA	Powder Coating	HORIZONTAL (2004)			6 000
	Foundry				2 500 (in 2005–6)
BOSNIA – VLASENITSA	Extrusion	2 800 MT (upgraded)	—	—	6 000
	Powder Coating	HORIZONTAL	—	—	1 500

FIGURE 5.5 ALUMIL production network and capacity design

ALOUSYS S.A.
It operates in the sector of machinery, accessories and aluminium systems trading – with the option to participate in similar activity companies – offering technical support to ALUMIL customers in Southern Greece.

Alukom
(Industrial Site offices: Komotini Industrial Area). It operates in the sector of building and exploiting aluminium systems production site. Despite the common operational field of ALUMIL and ALUKOM, the target client groups of the two companies vary significantly. In particular, ALUKOM produces architectural profiles and mainly unique-specifications-industrial profiles.
    Operations began within 2000, producing for ALUMIL and for third parties, i.e. industrial clients.

ALUNEF
Kilkis Prefecture. It operates in the sector of acquiring, building and exploiting aluminium systems production site. ALUNEF produces, processes and trades aluminium profiles and roll-forming profiles; additionally ALUNEF acquired (in auction) in 1999 I.AL.N.G.'s site (in Xanthi, Greece), including a 1,600 MT extrusion line, two horizontal powder-coating production lines and offices. ALUNEF operates independently, having completed the €10.27 million investment plan, including extrusion line and powder-coating line replacement.

ALUFIL
Kilkis Prefecture. It operates in the sector of building, expanding and exploiting aluminium composite panels production site.

G.A. Plastics (Kilkis Industrial Area) it operates in the sector of building, expanding and exploiting polycarbonate sheets, accessories and plastics production site.

METRON Charter
It operates in the sector of doors automations (i.e. elevator systems), machinery, automated and manually-operated control devices. (Serres Industrial Area)

ALUMIL ROM operates in trading and distributing aluminium and metallic parts, accessories and profiles. It holds 75,518 m^2 land plots and 15,000 m^2 industrial sites and offices. Additionally, it exploits 14 warehouses – three of them owned – in fourteen (14) Romanian cities, distributing through them Group products.

ALUMIL EXTRUSION operates in producing, trading and distributing aluminium accessories and profiles in Romania. Industrial site is established in Filippesti industrial zone offering motives (subsidies and tax incentives)

ALUMIL BULGARIA S.R.L.
The company produces and trades aluminium profiles and accessories for the wider area of Sofia (Bulgarian capital), covering half of the Bulgarian market. ALUMIL BULGARIA holds 10,566 m^2 land properties and 4,454 m^2 for industrial sites and offices (horizontal powder-coating plan). It also holds a 5,500 m^2 plot in Sofia, a 4,700 m^2 plot in Varna and a 4,500 m^2 plot in Filippoupoli (Plovdiv) for warehouses.

VARNA ALUMINIUM S.R.L. trades aluminium profiles and accessories, mainly for the wider area of Varna, covering the other half of the Bulgarian market.

ALUMIL HUNGARY. It deals with aluminium profiles and accessories trading activity commenced. The company holds a 25,000 m^2 plot and a leased warehouse for direct sales to wholesalers.

FIGURE 5.5 *(Continued)*

ALUMIL POLSKA. Its operations involve trading of aluminium profiles and accessories throughout Poland.

ALUMIL SRB Its operations involve trading of aluminium profiles and accessories in Serbia and Montenegro.

ALUMIL UKRAINE Its operations involve trading of aluminium profiles and accessories in the Ukrainian market.

ALUMIL MILONAS CYPRUS LTD for trading aluminium profiles and accessories.

ALUMIL CY LTD. Its operations involve trading of aluminium profiles and accessories covering the rest of the Cypriot market.

ALUMIL MISR for Aluminium and MISR for Accessories (Cairo, Egypt) for accessories production (powder coating), trading and profiles processing and trading in the Arab markets. In 2000, a 50,000 m^2 plot was bought in Ismailia industrial area, close to the capital Cairo.

ALUMIL DEUTSCHLAND GmbH for trading aluminium accessories, profiles and metal parts. The company holds a 6,000 m^2 land plot within Frankfurt's suburbs, with warehouses and exhibition centres totalling 3,400 m^2; this serves primarily as the group's Western Europe logistics centre to strategically promote sales of architectural and industrial profiles.

ALUMIL ITALIA s.r.l. for trading aluminium accessories, profiles and various metal parts.

ALUMIL ALBANIA SH.P.K. production and trading of aluminum accessories, profiles and various metal parts, covering the Albanian market. During 2003 and 2004, a total of €9 million investment was realized, for an integrated industrial site, that is, extrusion line, powder-coating and foundry installations. The company holds a 21,465 m^2 land plot on which 8,633 m^2 production sites and warehouses and 1,200 m^2 offices were built. Its warehouses promote its products in Tirana and in Ag. Saranta and later to Argyrokastro, Koritsa, Skodra, ElBasan and Fier.

ALUMIL COATING was established in 2003.

ALUMIL INDUSTRY S.R.L. trade of aluminum accessories, profiles and various metal parts in Moldavian.

ALUMIL SKOPJE D.O.O. trade of aluminum accessories, profiles, as well as various metal parts in

F.Y.R.O.M. the company is the owner of a €370,000 land plot in the wider Skopia area.

---

of the dies and their continuous maintenance. At the next production stage, profiles are processed to take on the final shape. First, they are cooled using water or air. Then they are strained and cut to the desired length. Artificial ageing in special furnaces follows. Finally, depending on the desired technical characteristics, profiles are subjected to further processes, such as powder coating, sublimation, covering with special protection and insulating materials. If no further processing is required, they simply go directly for final packaging. Any resulting scrap is re-used by repeating the whole production process at ALUMIL's foundry.

A vertically integrated production site (e.g. in Kilkis, Greece) includes an aluminium extrusion line, a powder-coating unit and a foundry. In addition to those in Greece, the company also has vertically integrated units in Serbia, Bosnia and Albania, which it recently acquired from local aluminium extraction companies

TABLE 5.4 ALUMIL's products

- Aluminium profile systems for architectural use

- Industrial profiles

- Composite panels (J-Bond)

- Polycarbonate sheets (Special plastic material)

- Automation systems

- Interiors (safety doors, internal doors, etc.)

- Aluminium and plastic accessories and supplementary products

following their privatisation (see Table 5.3 and Figure 5.5). The remaining group subsidiaries focus mainly on the latter stages of production, as well as acting as sales offices and providing customer support locally.

Key success factors in the aluminium systems industry are: prompt availability of systems and accessories; and adoption of an integrated aluminium system. However, the latter requires a commitment by the client (the profiles traders), who must be familiar with a great variety of profile products, and accessories (which typically have hundreds of barcodes). This also holds true for the manufacturer, who must invest in the proper equipment for the specific systems assembling. To achieve the above and to differentiate itself from competition, ALUMIL produces its own integrated systems and accessories. Second, to achieve optimal systems application and client satisfaction, ALUMIL also trains its manufacturers in the correct aluminium systems installation techniques. To do this, the company maintains its own state-of-the-art training centres in Athens, Thessaloniki and other cities. ALUMIL provides all parties in the aluminium construction business (architects, engineers, construction firms and manufacturers) with updates, information and promotions about its own products (and with news about the industry more generally) through its Large Projects department.

Finally, ALUMIL has also established subsidiaries in local international markets responsible for the last production stages (i.e. profiling and accessories). Acquisition of local market knowledge and trends assists in providing an enhanced ability for better production and sales forecasting, which coupled with the provision of systems support, provides ALUMIL with substantial credibility and reliability. In this way, ALUMIL has been winning significant market share from its competitors. With the evolving complexity of the international commercial network, which already involves 45 markets, ALUMIL has formed two sales departments in its organizational structure: Profiles and Accessories (see Figure 5.6).

Configuring the distribution network

ALUMIL aims to further boost its international orientation and expansion (mainly to Europe, Africa, the Middle East and the USA) by:

1 Participating in international aluminium exhibitions.

2 Cooperating with special consulting groups and institutions.

3 Integrating branded products, certified by international organizations, into its product portfolio.

The company's products are currently distributed through an extensive sales workforce consisting of the Domestic Sales Network and the International Sales Network.

Domestic Sales Network

The Domestic Sales Department supports a network of exclusive representatives within the domestic Greek market. ALUMIL offers them full customer support by providing informational bulletins and catalogues,

FIGURE 5.6 Organizational structure

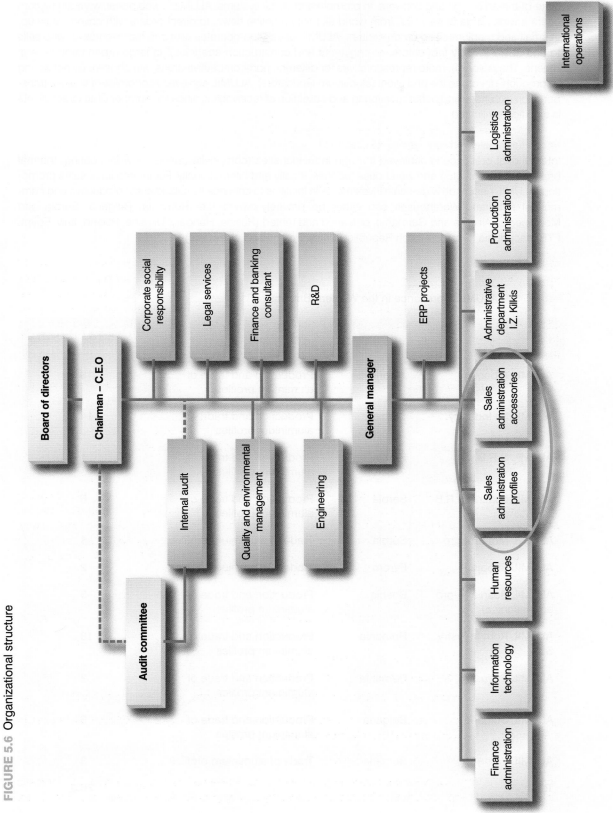

WWW.

state-of-the-art design and software, to promote and install systems. ALUMIL's web portal, www.alumil.com offers a wide range of services, from world aluminium online news, to direct orders with online follow up. In small and medium-sized urban centres, ALUMIL usually co-operates with one representative, who sells to end users (mainly fabricators, or engineers and construction agencies). In large urban centres (e.g. Athens, Thessaloniki), more representatives for different, non-competitive areas, are chosen. By not selling its products directly to the end client (aluminium fabricators), ALUMIL achieves economies of scale in transportation expenses and better monitoring and collection of receivables, since the number of its direct clients is significantly limited.

International Sales Network (in over 45 countries)

International presence is achieved through industrial sites (composite panels, powder-coating, thermal brake profile units, etc.) and warehouse facilities, locally and internationally. For international sales promotion, ALUMIL has made wide-scale investments in facilities to enhance its subsidiaries' productive and commercial activities. Warehouses can either be privately-owned (i.e. Romania, Bulgaria, Serbia and Montenegro, Albania and Germany), or leased and rented (Russia, Hungary, Ukraine, Poland, Italy, Egypt, FYR Macedonia, Cyprus, Czech Republic, Turkey, Poland and elsewhere).

TABLE 5.5 ALUMIL's presence in the Western Balkans

SUBSIDIARY	COUNTRY	ACTIVITY	INVESTMENTS (IN € MILLIONS)
ALUMIL Albania	Albania	Production and trade of aluminium profiles	18
ALUMIL Yu Industry	Serbia	Production and trade of aluminium profiles	14
ALUMIL S.R.B.	Serbia	Production and trade of aluminium profiles	1.5
ALUMIL coating S.R.B	Serbia	Production and trade of aluminium profiles	6
ALUMIL Montenegro	Serbia	Trade of aluminium profiles	1
ALUMIL Skopje	Fyrom	Trade of aluminium profiles	2
ALUMIL Bosnia (Alpro ad Vlasenica)	Bosnia	Production and trade of aluminium profiles	5
ALUMIL Rom Indystry S.A.	Romania	Production and trade of aluminium profiles	18
ALUMIL Extrusion	Romania	Production and trade of aluminium profiles	2
ALUMIL Bulgaria	Bulgaria	Production and trade of aluminium profiles	6
ALUMIL Varna	Bulgaria	Trade of aluminium profiles	3
Total			76.5

Selecting the locations of production units

Where its sales centres can demonstrate increased product demand, ALUMIL has a policy of rewarding them by establishing an independent integrated production facility in their locality to provide them with extrusion, powder-coating and foundry capabilities. This strategic model has been already applied in Xanthi (Greece), Romania, Bulgaria, Albania and Serbia, where new integrated production units were established by the end of 2004 (see Table 5.5).

ALUMIL expanded into the countries of the Western Balkans to benefit from their low labour cost, their proximity to markets that are growing rapidly and the tax relief and special tariffs available from governments anxious to boost their national economies. Entering these countries should enable the company to spread and differentiate its production base and leave it well-placed to exploit the future growth that should result from their expected accession to the EU. Based on these factors, the strategic targets that ALUMIL has set for its investments in the Western Balkans are to:

● Maintain its leadership in the area.

● Create a platform to support its subsidiaries in Eastern and Western Europe.

● Enforce its commercial presence and expand its commercial alliances.

● Expand in new product areas in special profiles, composite panels and complementary products and accessories.

However, achievements of these goals will not be easy as production units in the countries of the Western Balkans have to face a number of difficulties. These include:

● Unstable monetary and tax policy which makes production costs unpredictable.

● The increased economic risks due to the fragile banking system and the political instability in these countries.

● The political and societal corruption as well as the inefficient judicial system in these countries, which frequently translates into unequal treatment between local and international enterprises.

● The lack of both proper infrastructure (e.g. transport and warehousing) and qualified personnel, which leads to high transportation and insurance premiums and which, in turn, affects production, logistics and staff training costs.

Domestically, ALUMIL selected the prefecture of Kilkis in Greece as the location for its investment in an industrial site. This was in order to benefit from a 40 per cent grant of the invested amount provided by the Greek Ministry of Development. Its investments in Balkan countries have also benefited from a 30 per cent grant from the Ministry of Development as part of the Greek government's Balkans Economic Reconstruction Plan.

—Marianna Sigala

Questions (Suggested answers can be found on the companion website www.thomsonlearning.co.uk/barnes)

WWW.

1 What factors seem to most influence ALUMIL's decisions about the location of its foreign facilities?

2 To what extent does ALUMIL follow a strategy of focus for the operations of its various facilities, domestically in Greece and internationally?

3 Assess the strategic role of ALUMIL's foreign factories.

4 Critically assess ALUMIL's operations facilities from a network perspective. Do you think they are making the most of their facilities?

References

Bhutta, K.S. (2004) 'International facility location decisions: a review of the modelling literature', *International Journal of Integrated Supply Management* 1(1):33–50.

Dornier, P., Ernst, R., Fender, M. and Kouvelis, P. (1998) *Global operations and logistics: text and cases,* New York: John Wiley.

Ferdows, K. (1989) 'Mapping international factory networks', in Ferdows K. (Ed.) *Managing International Manufacturing,* New York: North-Holland.

Ferdows, K. (1997) 'Making the most of foreign factories', *Harvard Business Review* 75(2):73–88.

Gregory, M.J., Steele, A.P., Shi, Y. and Grant, E.B. (1996) 'International manufacturing capabilities: a framework to support the assessment, development and deployment', in C.Voss (Ed.), *Manufacturing Strategy: operations strategy in a global context,* Proceedings of the 4th International EurOMA conference, London Business School.

Ketokivi, M. and Jokinen, M. (2006) 'Strategy, uncertainty and the focused factory in international process manufacturing', *Journal of Operations Management* 24(3):250–270.

MacCarthy, B.L. and Atthirawong, W. (2003) 'Factors affecting location decisions in international operations – a Delphi study', *International Journal of Operations and Production Management* 23(7):794–818.

Meijboom, B. and Houtepen, M. (2002) 'Structuring international service operations', *International Journal of Operations and Production Management* 22(8):824–842.

Skinner, W. (1974) 'The focused factory', *Harvard Business Review* 52(3):113–121.

Shi, Y. and Gregory, M. (1998) 'International manufacturing networks – to develop global competitive capabilities', *Journal of Operations Management* 16:195–214.

Additional reading

Bhutta, K.S. (2004) 'International facility location decisions: a review of the modelling literature', *International Journal of Integrated Supply Management* 1(1):33–50.

Dornier, P., Ernst, R., Fender, M. and Kouvelis, P. (1998) *Global operations and logistics: text and cases,* New York: John Wiley.

Hayes, R., Pisano, G., Upton, D. and Wheelwright, S. (2005) *Operations, Strategy and Technology: pursuing the competitive edge,* New York: John Wiley.

Meijboom, B. and Vos, B. (1997) 'International manufacturing and location decisions: balancing configuration and co-ordination', *International Journal of Operations and Production Management* 17(8):790–805.

Pongpanich, C. (2000) *Manufacturing Location Decisions: Choosing the Right Location for International Manufacturing Facilities,* University of Cambridge: Institute for Manufacturing.

WWW. Useful websites

http://www.iamc.org/about.shtml The Industrial Asset Management Council is an association of industrial asset management and corporate real estate executives, their suppliers and service providers and economic developers.

CHAPTER 6

CAPACITY

INTRODUCTION

Capacity decisions are concerned with the ability of an operation to meet customer demand and to respond to changes in that demand over time. As such, they lie at the heart of operations management, as one of the main objectives of operations management is to satisfy customer demand. Not having sufficient capacity to meet customer demand means dissatisfied customers and lost sales opportunities. Having more capacity than required, implies under-utilized resources, which normally means higher costs than necessary and particularly higher unit costs.

The concept of capacity can be a complex one, as it can involve decisions about the size and location of each of an organization's facilities, and the size, type and mix of equipment and the working practices (e.g. shift patterns, working hours and staffing levels) at a single facility. Once made, decisions about facilities and equipment can not be changed easily or cheaply; and certainly not in the short-term. However, there can often be more flexibility in deciding how to manage those facilities. Additionally, decisions about capacity inevitably affect an organization's ability to serve particular markets from any given location. For organizations operating internationally, the issue of capacity is closely intertwined with that of facilities. On the one hand, productive capacity depends on the location, scale and scope of individual facilities, and how they are collectively configured. On the other hand, future capacity requirements for particular products and markets will strongly influence investment and operating decisions about facility requirements. This chapter will consider the nature of capacity and how it can be managed to meet customer demand.

THE MEANING OF CAPACITY

capacity
The level of activity or output that an operation (facility or organization) can achieve in a given period of time under normal working conditions.

Capacity can be defined as the level of activity or output that can be achieved (by an operation, facility, or organization) in a given period of time under normal working conditions. However, this is a rather simplistic view of capacity. To be meaningful, any understanding of what is meant by the term capacity needs to be related to an organization's ability to supply output in order to meet customer demand. In most industries, capacity is typically discussed in ways that assume it is easy to define. For example, airlines talk about the number of seats on an aircraft, retailers talk about their floorspace, hoteliers talk about the number of rooms and manufacturers talk about the processing outputs of their machines. Yet, things are rarely that simple. The number of passengers an airline can fly will also depend on other factors, such as the number of take-off and landing slots available to it at the airports it uses, the turnaround time on the ground, the length of its flights, the availability of pilots, etc. Retail capacity may also depend on the availability of car parking space or public transport to enable customers to access a store. Hotel capacity also depends on how many guests occupy each bedroom. Manufacturing capacity also depends on the availability of suitably qualified operatives and an uninterrupted supply of raw materials and components. In short, capacity is not simple to define in a meaningful way. It is affected by many interrelated factors. As Hayes *et al.* (2005: 77) put it, capacity is 'a complex interaction of physical space, equipment, operating rates, human resources, systems capabilities, company policies, and the rate and dependability of suppliers'.

They identify eight important factors that can affect capacity (Hayes *et al.*, 2005: 77):

1 *Technology* – The process technology used affects the overall capacity and the efficiency with which resources are consumed. However, the level of capacity achieved does not just depend on the technological sophistication of the equipment, but also on how well it is operated and maintained.

2 *Resources constraints* – There can be many potential constraints in any operation (e.g. equipment and labour availability, storage space, transport facilities). Resource constraints tend to cause bottlenecks in the production process. As real operations processes are dynamic in nature, the source of such bottlenecks can change over time. Consequently, capacity can fluctuate as one bottleneck is replaced by another.

3 *Capacity is mix dependent* – Different products and services consume different amounts of resources during their production. Consequently, the mix of products being produced will affect the total capacity, especially if capacity is measured as an aggregate figure (the number of units produced, customers served, sales value, etc.).

4 *Capacity can sometimes be stored* – This is typically in the form of work-in-progress inventories, which may be stored for long periods. Capacity can also be stored in the form of excess equipment and labour. If capacity is measured in terms of output achieved over a short time period when stored capacity is being drawn on, it may not accurately reflect the true level of capacity that can be sustained over a longer period.

5 *Capacity depends on management policy* – Capacity is particularly affected by management policies with regard to the number of hours worked each week. But it will also be affected by policies about what levels of work-in-progress inventory and other capacity cushions, such as excess equipment and labour, to allow. Capacity may also be affected by managerial responses to performance measurement systems. For example, the costs of investments in plant and machinery will normally be amortized over a long period, whereas expenditure on labour and materials will normally be charged in the period in the month that they occur.

6 *Capacity is dynamic* – Learning curve effects tend to mean that the longer a facility operates a particular process, the more it can increase its capacity, for example by the elimination of bottlenecks and other capacity constraints. Thus, the capacity of a process at a new location is likely to be lower than that of the same process operating at an established site, at least initially. The capacity ought to rise after workers have learnt more about the process. However, any learning depends on their willingness to learn, as well as their ability to learn and to put that learning into effect.

7 *Capacity is location specific* – It is not sensible to calculate an organization's capacity by aggregating the capacity of all its facilities, as it is not normally possible to direct excess demand from one location to another to take advantage of under-utilized capacity. The cost of so doing may be prohibitive (e.g. transport costs) or it may be necessary that production is located near to customers (e.g. front office services).

8 *Capacity is affected by the degree of variability of demand and processing time* – The capacity of an operation depends on there being a match between the rate at which work arrives and the rate at which it can be processed. If the rate at which work arrives is less than the time taken to process it, then idle time will result. Time spent waiting for work to arrive can not be stored and so that capacity will be lost forever. Customer service operations can be particularly vulnerable to this effect. This issue is discussed in more detail later in this chapter.

Capacity will be determined by these factors individually and by the way they interact with one another, both at a single location and between all the locations in an organization's operations network. Organizations that operate internationally are likely to feel the effects of these factors more acutely than those that only have domestic operations. The capacity of any particular operation will be affected by the way the organization chooses to manage that facility. For example, the level of technology provided, the mix of different products or services, the number of operating hours and the level of staffing. The capacity of a single operation is likely to be affected by its location. The proximity to customers may affect the mix of products or services it offers and the variability of demand. Remoteness from suppliers may constrain its ability to produce, requiring inventory to be stored. Also, many of the above factors can be affected by contextual factors that apply in a particular location in a particular country. For example, legislation may restrict working hours, or a lack of skilled workers may restrict a facility's ability to operate advanced technology.

THE MEASUREMENT OF CAPACITY

In the same way that capacity is difficult to define, it is also difficult to measure. Only in operations producing standardized products using a repetitive process is the measurement of capacity likely to be straightforward. There are essentially two approaches to measuring capacity. One is to measure units of input of a process, the other to measure units of output. Some examples are given in Table 6.1.

Any operation will have a theoretical capacity. This is normally referred to as the design capacity, the level of output that can be achieved by operating continuously at maximum rate. However, this level of capacity is not likely to be achievable in reality, especially over an extended period of time. Even a plant intended for 24 hours a day, 7 days a week operation will need some down time to allow for repair and maintenance to machinery. There may also be unavoidable operating time losses due to machine changeovers, or to allow time for operators to change shifts. Effective capacity is the term used to describe the capacity after deduction of planned stoppages. Actual output is

design capacity

The theoretical output that could be achieved by operating continuously throughout a given period at maximum rate.

effective capacity

The output achievable in a given period after the deduction of output lost due to planned stoppages.

TABLE 6.1 Measures of capacity in different operations

OPERATION	INPUT MEASURE	OUTPUT MEASURE
Airline	Number of seats available	Number of passengers flown
Printing press	Machine hours available	Number of items printed
Hotel	Number of rooms	Number of guests
Retail store	Floor area	Number of items sold
Hospital	Number of beds available	Number of patients treated
Telephone call centre	Operator's hours available	Number of calls answered

FIGURE 6.1 Measuring capacity

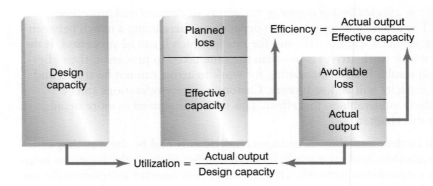

that achieved operating under normal working conditions which is likely to be less than effective capacity due to unplanned or avoidable stoppages such as machine breakdowns, absenteeism, quality problems, material shortages and so on. Actual output can be compared to design and effective capacity by calculating the ratios:

$$\text{Utilization} = \frac{\text{actual output}}{\text{design capacity}}$$

$$\text{Efficiency} = \frac{\text{actual output}}{\text{effective capacity}}$$

The measures of capacity are illustrated in Figure 6.1:

The calculation of capacity and its use in the calculation of performance figures is often a topic of debate inside an organization. Even if agreement can be reached within a single organization on how to do this, there is typically no agreed or standard approach within its industry, let alone across industry sectors. This makes comparisons very difficult. Any discussion of capacity needs to be approached with extreme caution and a clear understanding of definitions and terminology established before any progress is likely to be made.

Whilst achieving a high level of utilization may seem desirable, low figures may not always be indicative of poor performance. This might, for example, be caused by a lack of demand, rather than machine breakdowns, labour unrest or materials shortages. Neither is it always sensible to seek to operate at high levels of utilization. This might, for example, lead to necessary equipment maintenance being ignored. It can also create pressure to carry excess inventory, especially in the form of raw materials and excess labour to avoid having to stop operations due to input shortages. As discussed later in this chapter, in customer service, operations having insufficient excess capacity can lead to unacceptably long waiting times for customers.

FORECASTING DEMAND

The challenge of managing capacity is one of matching supply and demand. It would obviously be easier to arrange for appropriate capacity if future demand was known. However, as this is usually not the case, organizations have to try to make some kind of forecast of likely future demand. Forecasting future demand is important both in the longer-term and the shorter-term. Longer-term forecasts are needed when considering the design of new products and services and when planning future levels of capacity, for example by investing in new facilities and equipment. Shorter-term forecasting is needed in order to manage existing capacity in the most effective and efficient manner. There are many different forecasting techniques, the detailed consideration of which is beyond the scope of this book. There are two basic approaches to forecasting. One relies on quantitative methods, the other on qualitative methods.

Quantitative methods are based on either *time series analysis* or *causal analysis*.

forecasting
The act of predicting the future likely level of demand for products and services. Forecasting methods can be either quantitative or qualitative.

Time series analysis essentially involves extrapolating past data into the future. Analysts use mathematical techniques to look for patterns in the data over time. At its simplest, this might involve merely smoothing out random fluctuations in the data by averaging the data over a longer time period using moving average calculations (e.g. for a month, a quarter, or even a year) or by using exponential smoothing techniques. Sometimes no patterns can be found in the data using such approaches. In which case it might be possible to decompose the data into up to four components: trend, cyclical, seasonal and random. A trend is a gradual change in the data over time. Cyclical movements are recurring patterns in the data occurring over a period of more than one year. Seasonal movements are recurring patterns in the data occurring over a period of less than one year. Random movements are irregular deviations in the data which can not be predicted. The idea behind decomposition analysis is that if cyclical and seasonal effects can be isolated and understood, then the trend can more easily be separated from random movements. Decomposition analysis relies on more sophisticated mathematical techniques for which there are a number of software packages available. (These are often to be found in standard spreadsheet programs.) The advantage of time series analysis methods is that they are relatively easy and cheap to use. However, they are based on the premise that the past can be used to predict the future, which may not prove to be the case.

Causal analysis seeks to identify and model any cause and effect relationship between demand data and some other variable. For example, sales might be related to spending on advertising. Sales of some products are weather dependent; specifically sales of ice cream and beer are temperature dependent. Causal forecasting uses techniques like linear regression, curvilinear regression and multiple regression to establish relationships between demand and one or more variables and derive a model for their behaviour. The science of econometrics tries to model the behaviour of entire national economies. Like decomposition analysis, causal analysis relies on computer software packages (also often to be found in standard spreadsheet programs). Causal analysis methods are based on the premise that past relationships will hold up in the future. They are more complex and hence more costly to use than simple time series analysis. However, increasing levels of complexity and sophistication do not always make for more accurate forecasts.

Qualitative methods use subjective techniques based on estimates and judgement to try to predict future demand. There are a number of techniques, including:

Market surveys: Data are collected from customers about their future buying intentions. In mass consumer markets, this is likely to involve conducting a survey of a sample of customers. The accuracy of any survey depends on many factors, including the design of the questionnaire, the use of an appropriate sampling method, and the extent to which customers' replies can be trusted. Surveys can be costly and time-consuming.

Delphi studies: involve canvassing the opinions of a panel of experts, questioning them independently about future trends. Their initial views are then collated and circulated anonymously to all group members, who are then each invited to refine their opinions. The process continues until a group consensus is reached. This can then be used to provide a guide to future demand.

Scenario planning: gives a structure to managers' thinking about the future. The idea is that a team of experts meet to construct a small number of likely future 'scenarios' that the organization might face. Each scenario is based on different combinations of likely future situations. Future demand is then assessed for each of the scenarios. The strength of this technique is that it requires managers to think about how they would respond to a number of different possible futures.

In reality, organizations often use a number of different forecasting methods. Unfortunately, none of them have a particularly good record of accurately predicting future demand. The longer the time horizon of the forecast, the less accurate it is likely to turn out to be. Similarly, it is more difficult to forecast in some business contexts and some markets are much more volatile than others. For example, at the moment some parts of the world have been experiencing very rapid rates of growth. It is very difficult to know whether these rates can be sustained over longer periods of time. Thus, organizations seeking to serve new and unfamiliar markets are faced with high levels of risk and uncertainty. Nonetheless, any forecast is almost certainly better than none. Arguably, the mere act of thinking about the future forces managers to consider how they might best respond to changes in demand, no matter how volatile and rapid those changes might be. Although practising operations mangers will invariably call for better and more accurate forecasting, in an increasingly unstable business environment this is easier said than done. It might therefore be better for mangers to concentrate more effort on devising ways of increasing flexibility in order to increase their operations' responsiveness.

CASE STUDY Fenner: Expanding capacity to meet global demand

Fenner is the world's largest manufacturer of industrial conveyor belts. In 2005 it produced over five million metres of conveyor belting in its twelve manufacturing facilities on five continents. Its belts are used in material handling operations in a vast range of industries, including underground and hardrock mining, aggregates, power generation, grain, forestry, package handling, food processing, baggage handling, moving walkways, paper handling, computer peripherals, copiers, electrical/mechanical equipment, agricultural machinery, heating, ventilating and air conditioning, truck/bus, pharmaceuticals, machine tools, mobile hydraulics, off-highway machines, mechanical handling, construction equipment, process industries, oil, gas and aerospace.

Currently business is booming for the company which is headquartered in Yorkshire, England. Announcing its half-year results to 28 February 2006, the company announced a more than doubling of its pre-tax profits, up to £11.9 million from £4.2 million a year earlier. As the *Financial Times* (FT) reported on 11 May 2006, 'buoyant energy markets helped the company to produce a very strong set of interim results'. Revenues jumped 33 per cent to £182 million from £137 million and earnings per share rose to 5.34p from 2.58p.

Fenner conveyor belts in use in a quarry

The FT commented:

'Demand for conveyor belts, which account for about two-thirds of (Fenner's) turnover, is booming with the order flow more than double that of two to three years ago. These results clearly demonstrate the operational gearing of Fenner's business and, with the coal sector seemingly entering a super-cycle with oil prices so high, the prospects look very good'.

The FT went on to note that Fenner was the latest supplier to benefit from the booming oil and mining sectors. This was particularly the case in China, where coal consumption to feed its power stations had doubled in the past few years to about 2 billion tonnes of coal a year - twice that of the USA. The high oil price was also driving more coal mining projects elsewhere in Asia and North America. The company was also supplying the large oil-sands projects in Canada.

Mark Abrahams, Fenners' Chief Executive said, 'I have been with the group for 16 years now and this is the best [trading] I have seen.' Mr Abrahams announced that Fenner planned to expand its manufacturing capacity by as much as a third over the next three years. The company would be making capital investments of about £18 million a year on expanding its factories and building at least one new factory in China. He said a third of the investment would be targeted at China, the world's fastest growing economy. The company already has one plant near Shanghai with a second due to come on stream towards the end of 2006. It was now planning a third factory for China.

(Source material www.ft.com and http://www.fenner.com)

Questions (Suggested answers can be found on the companion website www.thomsonlearning.co.uk/barnes)

1 What are the most important factors influencing Fenner's growth?

2 How might Fenner set about forecasting demand for its products over the next 5 years?

WWW.

WWW.

CAPACITY TIMING DECISIONS

One of the most important capacity decisions is that of when to make capital investments in additional sites, plant and equipment in order to meet increasing demand for the organization's products and services. There is typically a long timelag between a decision to make a capital investment and when its productive capacity will be usable. This might be only a few months but in some cases can be years. As such, organizations have to base their capital investment decisions on forecasts of future demand.

There are three possible strategies:

Capacity leads demand

capacity cushion
The amount of excess capacity that an operation has above what is required to meet expected demand.

This strategy is one of always having more capacity than is likely to be required for the market. The intention is have a capacity cushion to enable the organization to meet unexpected surges in demand. The greater the capacity cushion the easier it is to meet extra demand from existing customers and to be able to meet demand from new customers. In an expanding market, a capacity cushion can enable the operation to cope more easily with extra demand without the deterioration in service, delivery lead times or quality often associated with attempts to increase output when there is little or no spare capacity. Without a capacity cushion, an operation might have to resort to tactics such as overtime working, rescheduling existing work and sub-contracting, which can cause disruption and increase costs. In growth markets, excess capacity can enable an organization to readily meet the needs of new customers. It might also be possible to take market share away from competitors who are unable to meet increased demand from their existing customers. A lead capacity strategy carries the extra risk that demand may not increase as expected and so the organization will incur higher costs. Also, building capacity well ahead of market demand might leave the organization with outdated process technology when compared to competitors who increase their capacity later using the latest technology. However, a lead capacity strategy does have many advantages. It can be used as part of an attacking business strategy of building market share. Utilizing spare capacity to meet increased demand should lead to an incremental lowering of unit costs due to economies of scale. This means that the organization should be well placed to use lower prices as a means of creating extra demand. This could then set up a virtuous circle of lower prices leading to higher volumes which leads to lower costs which enables lower prices and so on. Competitors operating at full or near full levels of capacity can only match price cuts by sacrificing short-term profitability. A lead capacity strategy can also be used as part of a defensive business strategy. An organization that adds capacity ahead of its competitors may deter the competitors from adding additional capacity themselves. This is particularly likely in capital intensive industries, where investment cost may be high and no producer will want to risk having under-utilized capacity. This might lead to them having to reduce prices in order to attract sales, perhaps triggering a price war. This would then reduce the new capacity's ability to achieve the desired return on investment. A lead capacity strategy might appear to be risky as it threatens short-term profitability, due to the required capital investment costs and the possibility of initially high unit costs. However, it can offer many advantages particularly where the organization has the long-term aim of building market share or establishing a market presence. This strategy has often been used as part of a market entry strategy into a new country. For some products, investments in the additional capacity can be made in the home country or in a third country well-placed to export into the target market. However, for many service organizations it might be necessary to invest in facilities in the target country. Some manufacturers may also wish to establish production facilities in the target country due to other considerations (e.g. to avoid trade barriers, or to promote the company's brandname).

Capacity matches demand

This strategy is one that aims to match capacity as much as possible with anticipated demand. The organization is attempting to balance the risk of having too much capacity against that of not having enough. Such a strategy places much reliance on forecasts for future demand. Also, capital investment decisions must be made within the lead time necessary to create the capacity required. In some cases, it may take years to build and commission the necessary plant and equipment. So the timing of investment decisions with this strategy is crucial. Invest too soon and the organization will have to bear the extra costs of under-utilized capacity. Invest too late and the organization risks lost sales opportunities and the disruption and higher costs associated with operating near to the limits of capacity (due to higher stock levels, increased changeovers, etc.).

Capacity lags demand

This strategy is based on a policy of only adding capacity once there is an established demand. Most of the time, demand will exceed capacity. The advantage of this is three-fold. First, the organization delays making capital investments thereby conserving its cash and keeping its investment options open for as long as possible. Second, it increases the likelihood that the output from its investments will be sold, thereby maximizing its return on those investments. Third, the capacity it does have will always be operating at high rates of utilization thereby achieving low unit costs through economies of scale. This strategy is sometimes said to be conservative, but it is not necessarily without risk. It leaves the organization vulnerable to any unexpected upturn in demand. If customer demand cannot be met, then the way is open for competitors to step in and steal market share. Also it will be difficult to respond to aggressive competitors who offer price cuts to tempt once loyal customers, without loss of profitability. Furthermore, as has been discussed earlier, at very high rates of utilization, operating performance may deteriorate with excess inventory, increased changeovers and longer processing times due to the disruption and confusion. This can lead to increased costs, longer lead times, inferior quality and less responsiveness to customers, all of which increases the likelihood of losing business to competitors over the longer-term.

Which of these three strategies is best will depend upon the specific situation of the organization. An organization needs to address such questions as: Is it serving markets which are expanding, mature or declining? Does it intend to pursue a growth strategy market penetration or new market entry, or does it merely want to defend its current market position? What is its attitude to risk? What level of investment capital does it have access to and what rate of return does it expect from its capital investments? For organizations expanding internationally these matters are closely related to facilities decisions. For example, what approach does the organization take to establishing a facility in a new country in order to provide the capacity to serve customers in that country? Can demand be served from existing capacity from home or a third country? At what point does it become necessary or desirable to provide additional capacity by establishing a new facility in that country? The timing of investment decisions can be crucial, especially as the construction and commissioning of new facilities can typically involve lead times of many months or even years. Invest too soon and the organization may be left with costly underutilized excess capacity. Invest too late and the organization may miss out on sales opportunities that its competitors will be only too keen to seize.

Another factor that needs to be considered is whether the operation is capital or labour intensive. In capital intensive processes, the cost of underutilized resources (especially of plant and equipment but also labour) is likely to be high; much higher than the cost of not having enough capacity, reflected in such costs as overtime working, subcontracting, and lost profits. Thus, in capital intensive industries, organizations will typically want to delay investing in new capacity until they are convinced that there will be adequate demand. On the other hand, in labour intensive industries the cost penalty for excess capacity is much less, especially if staff can be engaged on very flexible conditions. Again, this can be an important issue for organizations operating internationally and may be closely linked to facilities decisions. Organizations often feel more comfortable in investing in capital intensive facilities in their home or another technologically advanced country because of ready access to technological support. They will naturally seek to operate such plant at high rates of capacity utilization to achieve economies of scale. However, developing countries with low labour cost will be the preferred destination for labour intensive investments. Such facilities can typically offer capacity that can be used more flexibility as they can be operated economically at lower rates of utilization.

Our discussion so far has focused on the challenge of expanding capacity to meet increasing demand. However, there are situations in which an organization is faced with declining demand. It is then faced with a decision about whether to cut capacity, and if so, by how much. Having excess capacity in a declining market carries two penalties. Low utilization rates, particularly in capital intensive industries, means increasing unit costs, which is likely to lead to lower profitability. This provides a powerful disincentive to invest in the latest technology. This in turn leaves the organization exposed to competitors who do make such investments, which typically give them a performance advantage in terms of cost, quality, flexibility, etc. For organizations operating in a number of countries, the closure of facilities throws up some challenging dilemmas (apart from the obvious public relations considerations). On the one hand, there will be a desire to achieve high levels of utilization in facilities that are retained, especially in capital intensive operations. However, this would limit the organization's ability to meet any unexpected upturns in demand. Whilst more labour intensive facilities might offer more flexibility, they might be less efficient at all levels of utilization.

CAPACITY INCREMENTS

Whichever of the three generic strategies for increasing capacity is followed, decisions still have to be made about how large any additional increments of capacity should be. The organization will want to be sure that it adds sufficient capacity to meet customer demand and does so profitably. The concept of economies of scale (discussed in Chapters 4 and 5) is often placed at the heart of such considerations. This argues that unit costs will fall with increasing volumes. However, actual costs are usually very difficult to calculate with any accuracy in practice. Also, if additional capacity is underutilized, unit costs may rise, at least initially. Thus, organizations need to be confident that any additional capacity will be able to be utilized effectively. This tends to the view that capacity should be added in as small an increment as possible. However, the available process technology may mean that there is a minimum size limit for the equipment required. Also, smaller pieces of equipment may be disproportionately expensive to purchase compared to larger units. Additionally, there are likely to be economies of scale in construction, making it more disproportionately expensive to undertake smaller scale building works. There is also an argument for adding a single large chunk of extra capacity as this can provide the opportunity to upgrade processing equipment technologically and possibly replace outdated equipment. Finally, the organization will also want to consider whether expanding capacity at an existing site will lead to any diseconomies of scale. The issue of location, including the impact of economies and diseconomies of scale, was discussed in Chapter 5.

WHEN THINGS GO WRONG The Baby Jag: Over-capacity or over-ambition?

Launched in 2001, the Jaguar X-type represented an ambitious venture into the more crowded and highly competitive mid-range car market for the luxury carmaker. The X-type, nicknamed the 'Baby Jag' in reference to its small (for Jaguar) size, was aimed at drawing in buyers from a younger age range than Jaguar's more usual middle-aged customers. 'Customers for the X-type will typically be young professionals, perhaps starting a family, whose cars have to fulfil a multitude of different roles including lengthy trips on business and energetic leisure activities with friends', claimed Jaguar at the model's launch. The idea was that the X-type would act as an entry-level purchase for buyers who would progress to Jaguar's more expensive models.

Jaguar, an iconic British manufacturer, was acquired by Ford of America in 1989. Ford decided to convert its factory at Halewood, near Liverpool, into a Jaguar plant for the X-type with the capacity to manufacture the hoped-for sales of 200,000 vehicles a year. Despite being designed to share its basic engineering structure with Ford's own, more humble Mondeo, in order to keep costs down, the company was aware that sales of well in excess of 100,000 cars a year would be needed if the X-type was to be profitable at its £22,000 price tag. However, initial sales were disappointing, and had fallen to around only 66,000 for 2004. This signalled significant problems for Jaguar, threatening the finances of Ford's Premier Automotive Group (PAG), the division that houses all its upmarket brands (including Land Rover, Aston Martin, Volvo as well as Jaguar).

One reason for the declining sales was the weakness of the US dollar, making UK-made Jaguars particularly pricey in the US market which accounts for almost half of Jaguar's sales. However, it was also clear that the X-type had something of an image problem and had failed to penetrate its target market of young US executives in a big way. Its Mondeo connections and the fact that it could also be delivered as an estate with a diesel engine, hardly provide a brand booster, critics said. Some observers even suggested that the car had evolved into a popular set of wheels for the retired! This despite the very real quality improvements achieved at Halewood. When producing the Ford Escort, Halewood had been among Ford's worst factories. But after a complete revamp and a shake-up of working practices for X-type production, the plant now had dramatically better industrial relations and had become one of the Ford group's best plants.

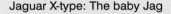

Jaguar X-type: The baby Jag

In 2005 Jaguar announced plans aimed at stemming its financial losses, estimated to be over £1 billion during the previous three years. It had decided to abandon its growth strategy and was dropping its ambition of making 200,000 X-types a year. As such, it was introducing production cutbacks and reducing working hours at Halewood. It also decided to close its historic Browns Lane factory in Coventry, the place where large-scale production of Jaguar cars started in the 1950s, and still home for the production of its most prestigious XJ range.

'We do not want to flood the marketplace with cars', a spokesman for the company said. 'We want a lower volume, higher revenue business and to concentrate on the higher series cars – the more profitable vehicle lines'. Jaguar's sales fell 21 per cent in the first three months of 2005, as a result of refocusing its car range in the US towards top-of-the-range models, the company said. Sales of the X-type dropped sharply after the company withdrew several versions from sale in the US and cut back supplies to certain states in an attempt to boost the brand image. The car had been heavily discounted, along with other models, to boost sales, but Jaguar is now trying to raise prices and protect second-hand values. 'We stopped going hell bent for volume', Lewis Booth, head of PAG, told the FT in March 2006. 'We are going for a sustainable sales level instead'.

PAG also announced that it had abandoned plans to create the 1,000 new jobs at Halewood envisaged for the building of its updated small Land Rover. Manufacturing of the new Land Rover Freelander would still be moved from Land Rover's Solihull plant to Halewood, with the loss of 1,000 jobs at Solihull. Although the award of the Freelander should ensure that there would be no job losses at Halewood, the lack of any new jobs would be seen as scant reward for the factory's success in improving its quality and productivity.

WWW.

(Sources www.bbc.co.uk and www.ft.com)

WWW.

Questions (Suggested answers can be found on the companion website www.thomsonlearning.co.uk/barnes)

1 What was Jaguar's capacity timing strategy for the X-type?

2 Do you think this strategy was appropriate?

3 What else could Jaguar have done to reduce the risk of the levels of financial losses that resulted from its X-type operations?

CAPACITY MANAGEMENT

The term capacity management refers to the various actions that managers can take in order to match supply with demand. Having laid down the capacity that it thinks it will require in the longer-term, the organization must manage that capacity to best effect. The more detailed approaches and techniques that can be used to manage capacity in the shorter term (generally referred to as production planning and control), will be discussed in Chapter 9. However, in this section we will consider the generic strategies that can be used to manage capacity over the longer term.

There are three generic capacity management strategies for matching supply and demand as illustrated in Figure 6.2.

FIGURE 6.2 Generic capacity management strategies

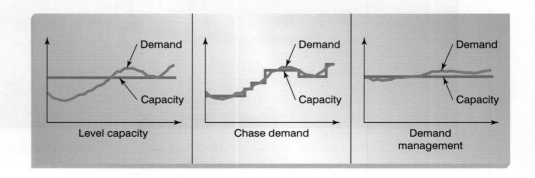

Level capacity

This strategy is based on keeping capacity at the same level irrespective of demand. This makes life much easier and simpler for operations, as the same working patterns and staffing levels can be maintained. Also, if processes can be operated at a high utilization rate, high levels of efficiency and hence low unit costs should be achieved. In manufacturing operations, excess production can be put to stock at times of low demand, ready to meet any upturn in demand. This strategy is often pursued by manufacturers supplying goods to highly seasonal markets (e.g. for New Year or religious festivals) or weather dependent products (e.g. ice cream). However, there may be limits to how long goods can be stored, if they are perishable (e.g. many foods). Also, with some goods there can be high risk of obsolescence due to rapid advances in technology (e.g. computers) or changing tastes in fashion (e.g. clothing, music). Holding inventory of any goods always attracts storage and financing costs, which must be offset against lower production costs achieved from the level capacity strategy. For manufacturers who cannot store inventory and those who make items to order, and for most service providers, a level capacity strategy is likely to mean that customers may have to wait at times of peak demand. This deterioration in service levels not only threatens relationships with customers, but may mean loss of sales to competitors who do have the capacity to meet customer demand. In services, the only way to minimize this risk is to constantly maintain a high level of capacity, often in the form of excess staff. This will inevitably be underutilized during periods of lower demand, leading to higher costs.

Chase demand

This strategy is one of flexing capacity to meet variations in customer demand. This is much more difficult to organize than a level capacity strategy, as different numbers of staff, perhaps even different types of staff, will be required at different times. This is likely to require very flexible working arrangements with employees. In many countries, particularly Western Europe, labour legislation and high levels of employer social security taxes can militate against this. If different amounts of plant and equipment are needed at different times, this means that some physical capacity will be underutilized during periods of low demand, leading to higher than necessary operating costs. Where an operation depends on external inputs of goods or services, a chase demand strategy requires suppliers to have similar levels of flexibility. Many service providers have little choice but to pursue this strategy if they want to attract, satisfy and, hence, retain customers. Manufacturers can militate against some of the worst implications of a chase demand strategy by drawing on stocks of finished or part-finished goods during periods of high demand.

Actions that can be taken to provide the flexible response required for a chase capacity strategy include:

Over-time or short-time working: Asking staff to work longer hours is commonly used as a means of increasing output at times of high demand. However, this often requires extra payments to staff often at enhanced rates of pay. In some countries, legislation or union agreements may limit the amount of overtime that can be worked. Working high levels of overtime for extended periods typically leads to reduced levels of productivity due to staff fatigue or boredom. Also, if extended working hours means that maintenance is neglected, higher rates of equipment failure may result. In some situations it may be possible to ask staff to work fewer hours than normal. However, this is not likely to be popular with staff if it means a reduction in their pay. Where reductions in pay are not possible due to legislation or contractual guarantees, staff may be asked to perform tasks not directly associated with producing saleable outputs (e.g. cleaning or maintenance). A development of this approach has been the introduction of annualized hours contracts in some industries in some countries. Instead of working a fixed number of hours each week, staff agree to work a fixed number of hours each year. However, they vary their working hours in response to customer demand, working longer hours in times of peak demand and less when demand falls.

Hire and fire staff: Varying the number of people directly employed by the organization over time by hiring extra staff when demand is high and laying them off when demand falls. In many countries, laying off staff is subject to legal restrictions and so can be a costly and slow process. Such legislation can also act as a disincentive to employ more people in the first place. In most circumstances, hiring staff can be costly and time-consuming. Even if suitable staff can be recruited, they may need to be trained if they do not possess the required skills. Thus a strategy of hiring and firing staff may in practice not provide the level of flexibility required to respond to changes in demand. In any case, such a strategy is likely to be disruptive and not conducive to harmonious working relationships within the organizations.

Temporary staff: A more practical and less disruptive approach to hiring extra staff is provided by the use of temporary (often fixed term) employment contracts. Temporary workers might be employed directly or via an employment agency. Such arrangements are often designed to circumvent employment legislation. Temporary workers might be hired for their specific specialist skills. Alternatively, they might be employed for relatively unskilled jobs, supporting the more skilled permanent employees.

Part-time staff: Staff can be employed on part-time contracts, that is, with less working hours than full-time employees. The nature of part-time contracts can vary tremendously. They might involve working regular hours each week, perhaps to provide extra staff at times of known peak demand. Alternatively part-time workers might contract to work more flexible hours in response to variations in demand or to cover for staff holidays, sickness or other absences. The main advantage with part-time workers is that they provide continuity and their skills are retained within the organization.

Subcontract at peak demand: Some aspects of work normally carried out within the organization can be subcontracted to an external supplier in periods of peak demand. This has the advantage of ensuring that customer demand can be satisfied. However, it requires that suitable subcontractors are available and prepared to undertake the work at an appropriate price. Also, managing subcontractors requires very different skills than managing an in-house operation. In particular, the contacting organization must ensure that the subcontractor meets the quality and delivery requirements of the customer. There is also the danger that subcontracts might gain valuable product and/or process knowledge. They might also be tempted to enter the market themselves and so become a competitor.

Multi-skilling the workforce: Training workers to be able to undertake a broad range of tasks increases flexibility in a number of ways. It enables workers to be moved between the different tasks necessary to produce different products or services. It enables managers to more easily arrange cover for workers absent because of holidays, sickness, etc. It can also enable part-time or temporary staff to be more easily integrated into the workforce. For example, it is likely to be easier to recruit unskilled temporary workers to perform very basic tasks, if permanent employees are capable of undertaking tasks requiring higher levels of skill.

Customer participation: In many customer service operations, greater flexibility can be provided if customers are enabled to undertake a higher degree of participation in the process at peak times. This is, in effect, replacing the organization's labour with that of its customers, enabling more customers to be served with the same number of staff. Examples of this include self-service buffets or carveries in restaurants, express check-outs at hotels, and automated (and increasingly online) checking in for flights.

Demand management

This strategy involves the organization taking actions to smooth out demand by shifting customer demand away from peak times. Although this is often thought of as being more the domain of the marketing department, it in fact requires co-ordinated action between the marketing and operations departments if it is to be successful. Demand management actions can include:

Pricing: Using the price mechanism to attract customers to off-peak periods. For example, offering lower train fares during the day, and lower priced holidays outside of school holiday periods.

Promotions: Advertising to stimulate demand outside periods of known demand. Examples include promoting ice cream in winter or turkey in summer.

Reservations: Many customer service operations reserve limited capacity by enabling customers to book appointments at specified times (e.g. doctors, hairdressers).

Waiting: Although customer service providers will generally want to avoid making customers wait to be served, queuing is an effective means of managing demand. Whilst most customers do not usually want to stand in line, they may be prepared to accept a wait under some circumstances (e.g. for emergency hospital treatment or for a ride in a theme park). The way that a queue of people is managed can have significant impact on their levels of satisfaction (see p. 201).

Alternative goods/services: Spare capacity can often be put to use to produce alternative products or services. Examples of this include a lawnmower manufacturer making snow clearing equipment in the winter, and universities letting out rooms in otherwise empty student residences during the summer vacation periods (for conferences, tour parties, etc.).

In reality many organizations use a combination of these three strategies in order to achieve the best possible compromise between the conflicting objectives of meeting customer demand and optimizing resource usage. The aim of any capacity management strategy will be to meet customer demand over time. When the output from an operation can be stored, then an exact instantaneous match between supply and demand is not required as excess inventory can be used to balance supply and demand over time. Producers will usually want to devise a longer-term plan, often termed an aggregate capacity plan, showing how output and demand will be balanced over time. This may well involve adjustments in supply (i.e. part of a chase demand strategy) as well as actions to affect demand (i.e. part of a demand management strategy).

aggregate capacity plan
A production plan aimed at meeting the totality of customer demand over the longer-term (i.e. over a period of, say, one to three years).

MANAGING CAPACITY IN CUSTOMER SERVICE OPERATIONS

Managing capacity in most customer service operations is particularly difficult because output can not be stored. The challenge is to ensure that resources are utilized as efficiently as possible to ensure that as many customers as possible are satisfied. Operations managers will want to maximize income from customers. However, they will also want to minimize the operation's capacity cushion, which becomes a costly wasted resource when not being fully utilized to serve customers.

Operations management has developed two techniques to help achieve this objective.

CASE STUDY   Capacity hits the buffers for US railways

Surging freight volumes have been causing serious congestion across the US rail network in the last few years. The country's ageing system has been struggling to cope with surging freight volumes generated by robust economic growth and has been operating close to full capacity.

Railroads remain the backbone of North America's freight transportation network. In the US, railroads account for more than 40 per cent of all freight transportation, more than from any other single mode of transportation. The country's vast distances mean that any bulky cargoes (cars, steel, coal, grain, lumber, cement, etc.) are moved most cost effectively by rail. US freight railroads are the world's busiest, moving more freight than any rail system in any other country. US railroads move more than four times as much freight as do all of Western Europe's freight railroads combined.

The four years between 2002 and 2006 have seen explosive growth for US railway companies. Industry executives say they see no signs of a slowdown, with all the big operators predicting continuing volume growth. As the US economy has rebounded from recession, a range of factors have pushed more freight on to the rails. Rail companies have been benefiting from surging energy prices because freight trains are three times more fuel-efficient than trucks. A nationwide shortage of truck drivers and worsening road congestion have also spurred the shift in freight from road to rail. The resurgence of coal as a source of electricity means that railroads are carrying record amounts of coal.

Rising volumes and limited capacity have also enabled the railroads to up their prices to reinforce their profit margins. Union Pacific, the biggest operator more than doubled its net profits during 2005 to $311 million. Norfolk Southern revealed a 57 per cent increase in net earnings to $305 million and BNSF increased its net profits by 28 per cent to $410 million during the same period. Underlying profits at CSX rose 56 per cent.

In response to the capacity constraints, rail companies have sharply increased their investments in infrastructure. According to industry body the Association of American Railroads, the biggest US freight

railroads plan to spend more than $8.2 billion in 2006 laying new track, buying new equipment and improving infrastructure. This would raise the industry's capital expenditure 21 per cent from the previous year and shatter the previous record for infrastructure spending in one year. Freight railroads are capital intensive businesses. Between 1995 and 2004, they put an average of 17.8 per cent of their revenues into capital expenditures. This compares with an average of 3.5 per cent for manufacturing. In addition, railroads spend $10 billion to $12 billion each year to repair and maintain their infrastructure and equipment, a total spending of nearly $360 billion since 1980. The $15 billion to $17 billion railroads typically spend each year on their infrastructure and equipment is equal, on average, to approximately 45 per cent of their operating revenue.

However, many customers believe the industry is still not doing enough to tackle congestion on the railroads. Entergy, a large electricity generator, is suing Union Pacific for coal supply disruptions. Others see the railroads' record profits as proof that capacity shortages are being used to inflate prices. Pointing to the near-monopoly enjoyed over entire regions of North America by the biggest six operators (Union Pacific, CSX, Norfolk Southern, BNSF, Canadian Pacific and Canadian National), many have been lobbying Congress for legislation to force the industry to behave more competitively.

Rail industry executives argue that the only way to expand capacity is to make sure the companies are making enough money to invest. Investment has been held back in the past by the industry's traditionally low return on capital. Improvements promised include double tracking of bottleneck sections of the line and investments in new technology like satellite tracking to allow trains to travel closer together safely, thereby increasing track utilization by up to 20 per cent.

Unclogging US railways will be a slow process say railroad executives. They promise that services will eventually improve but customers must accept the days of unlimited rail capacity are gone. One said, 'This industry used to be like a light switch. If you needed more railroad cars you just flipped a switch and they were available. That switch is no longer working'.

(Based on articles by Andrew Ward on 26 April, 10 May and 16 June 2006 at www.ft.com, and Association of American Railroads at www.aar.org/)

WWW.

Questions (Suggested answers can be found on the companion website www.thomsonlearning.co.uk/barnes)

WWW.

1 What capacity management strategy do US freight railroads use, and why?

2 What other actions are open to the railroads to manage capacity?

Yield management

Yield management is the term used to describe a set of techniques that have been developed aimed at maximizing income in customer service operations. Yield management is particularly useful in customer service operations where:

yield management
A set of techniques aimed at maximizing income from customer service operations.

- Capacity is relatively fixed
- The market can be segmented
- The service cannot be stored
- The service is sold in advance
- Demand fluctuates over time
- The marginal cost of making a sale is relatively low, but the marginal cost of providing addition capacity is high

Yield management was first developed in the passenger airline industry, where these conditions particularly apply (Kines, 1989). However, it is also commonly used by other providers of travel services (e.g. coaches, cruises, car hire) and accommodation (e.g. hotels). Actions include:

1 *Price discounting:* The service provider uses the price mechanism to provide incentives to customers to book for less busy periods in order to reserve

available capacity. Conversely surcharges might be applied to deter customers when demand is high and to maximize income from customers.

2 *Overbooking:* This is based on the assumption that not all passengers who have booked will turn up. The idea is to study past behaviour to identify the numbers of customers who typically fail to show at different times of the week. Overbooking by this amount maximizes the chance of utilizing all available capacity thereby maximizing sales revenue. However, the service providers need to have strategies available for dealing with any overbooked passengers who do show up. This might include financial recompense, alternative arrangements (e.g. a guaranteed seat on the next flight), and upgrading to a superior service.

3 *Varying the service type:* Most practitioners of yield management (e.g. airlines or hotels) offer different grades of service. Typically customer behaviour varies between the purchasers of these grades. For example, business travellers are usually prepared to pay a premium for a higher level of comfort but often want the flexibility to change their travel plans at the last minute. Service providers are therefore likely to use different tactics for different customer segments (for example not discounting in business class). Where possible, they may also vary capacity within each grade of service to better match demand.

However, yield management does have its risks. Customers who fall foul of its practices may become very dissatisfied with the service provider – often vowing never to use them again. Customers with such grievances do not generally prove to be good ambassadors for the service provider.

Queuing theory

queuing theory
The mathematical study of waiting lines.

In many customer service operations, demand varies over time, even minute by minute, in ways that are very difficult to predict. Operations managers will not want to keep customers waiting and so they will want to ensure that the operation always has sufficient resources available to it. However, meeting demand as it arises implies that capacity must always exceed demand. So the question is how much excess capacity should the operation have? The science of queuing theory can help operations managers tackle this issue. Queuing theory draws on often complex mathematics, which is beyond the scope of this book. However, we can make use of some of its more simple techniques to illustrate the impact of reducing the excess capacity within an operating system.

It might seem apparent that if the average processing rate is in excess of average demand rate, then capacity will be sufficient to avoid long queues of customers waiting to be served. However, queuing theory shows that this is not likely to be the case even when capacity seems to be well in excess of average. Let us take the simple example of a single server (e.g. a teller at a bank counter) processing a single line of customers. Let us further assume that customers arrive independently and that both the rate of customer arrivals and the rate at which the teller processes customers are governed by the exponential distribution. (This is reckoned to be a good approximation for most situations.)

If a = the average number of customers arriving per hour, and
        c = the average number of customers that the teller can serve per hour

the queuing theory tells us that,

the average number of people in the queue,

$$N = \frac{a}{(c-a)}$$

and the average time each person will spend waiting to be served,

$$W = \frac{a}{c\,(c-a)} \text{ hours}$$

If we take a situation in which c, the average number of customers that the teller can serve per hour is 30, then the average processing time is two minutes. When the arrival rate is 15 an hour, on average there will be one person in the line waiting on average for two minutes. With 20 people an hour arriving, this doubles to two people in line, with each person waiting four minutes for their turn to be served. With 25 people an hour arriving, this further increases to 5 people in line, with each person waiting ten minutes. Beyond this, the situation deteriorates rapidly. So that by the time the arrival rate is 28 people an hour, the line is 14 people each waiting 28 minutes, well beyond most people's understanding of an acceptable level of service. Table 6.2 shows these figures. The point is that at capacity utilization rates at much above 70 per cent, waiting times increase to unacceptable levels. In fact, this holds for most situations where demand is variable, so that planning for higher capacity utilization rates is risking a high level of customer dissatisfaction. It strikes most people as surprising that in order to avoid risking long waits, queuing needs to be designed in ways that can leave servers with as much as 30 per cent in-built idle time.

In practice, most queuing situations are far more complex than the example given above. For example, customers may arrive in groups; there may be peaks and troughs of demand at different times during the day; service times may vary more than exponentially, if the server has to perform unusual and complex transactions; there may also be constraints on the availability of staff at certain times during the day (e.g. during their lunch breaks). In such circumstances, queues may reach unacceptable lengths with capacity utilization rates as low as 50 per cent.

It is also worth remembering that customers may not behave as expected when being asked to queue. They may decide not to join the line if they perceive it as too long (this is termed 'baulking'). They may join the line, only to leave it (this is known as 'reneging') if they become impatient with their progress. In some situations they may not be able to join the line in the first place (being 'rejected'). Examples of this can be found when telephone systems or websites become overloaded. All these cases represent customer dissatisfaction and potential lost business.

Designers of queuing systems have tried many different ways of limiting queuing problems. An approach favoured for many years, has been the use of several single lines each with a single server. A variation of this is for particular servers to perform a limited range of specific tasks. Recent years have seen an increase in popularity of

TABLE 6.2 The impact of arrival rates on a queue with a processing rate (c) of 30 customers an hour

ARRIVAL RATE PER HOUR (A)	CAPACITY UTILIZATION (%)	NUMBER IN LINE (N)	WAITING TIME (W) (MINUTES)
15	50	1	2
20	67	2	4
25	83	5	10
27	90	9	18
28	93	14	28
29	97	29	58

systems that have a single queue from which customers are directed in turn to a number of different servers as they become available. Other approaches involve giving priority to specific groups of customers, dependent upon their needs (e.g. in hospitals) or their importance (e.g. in the case of business class and other higher fare paying passengers on aircraft). The queuing theory mathematics becomes ever more complex when modelling these situations, but it can offer valuable insights into their impact on customer waiting times. It is also worth noting that it may be possible to speed up processing times for a single server by introducing more modern technology. In such circumstances, queuing theory mathematics can be used to compare the impact of adding an additional server with that of an investment in new technology.

Different queuing systems and layouts are discussed in more detail in Chapter 7.

There are many types of queue

THE DYNAMICS OF CAPACITY MANAGEMENT

The aim of capacity management is to match supply and demand. However, in most situations this is a never ending task that involves balancing both short-term and long-term decisions and actions. Customer demand usually varies over time, both in the long-term (over periods of one or more years) and the short-term (over periods of days, weeks and months). Whilst it may be possible to forecast future demand on the basis of the past, this is a very inexact science. The further one looks into the future, the more uncertain any forecast becomes. Nonetheless, organizations need to form a view about the likely level of demand both in the short-term and the long-term, so that operations managers can plan how they will meet that demand both in the short-term and the long-term. The point is that some adjustments to levels of output can be made relatively easily in the short-term (e.g. by overtime or making for stock). However, other actions may take much longer before they can start to impact. For example, making changes to the level of permanent staff, whether hiring or firing, may take many months to effect. Investments in new plant and machinery can take months or even years. Building a completely new facility may take many years. Also, once taken, many decisions affecting changes to capacity may take a long time to reverse once taken. Thus, organizations must endeavour to match the timescales of their forecasts for demand with the length of time needed to put their decisions about capacity into action.

SUMMARY OF KEY POINTS

Capacity decisions are concerned with the ability of an operation to meet customer demand and to respond to changes in that demand over time.

The productive capacity of an organization is not easy to define or measure as it is affected by many inter-related factors, including the size and location of each of an organization's facilities, and the size, type and mix of equipment and the working practices at a single facility (e.g. shift patterns, working hours and staffing levels).

Forecasting involves trying to predict likely future demand on the basis of existing information. There are two basic approaches to forecasting; one relies on quantitative methods, the other on qualitative methods.

There are three approaches in deciding how to increase capacity in line with market demand: *capacity leads demand* – always trying to maintain excess capacity so that any unexpected surges in demand can be met; *capacity matches demand* – trying to match capacity with demand as much as possible; *capacity lags demand* – only add capacity when there is approved demand.

There are three generic capacity management strategies: *level capacity* – keeping capacity at the same level irrespective of demand; *chase demand* – flexing capacity to meet variations in customer demand; *demand management* – trying to smooth out demand by shifting customer demand away from peak times to periods of lower demand.

Yield management seeks to maximize income from customer service operations by maximizing capacity utilization and prices paid by customers.

In operations with variable arrival and processing rates, queuing theory shows that excess capacity of the order of at least 30 per cent is often required if excessive queues are to be avoided. This is particularly the case in customer service operations, where long queues can lead to dissatisfied customers and lost sales.

WWW.

EXERCISES (Suggested answers can be found on the companion website www.thomsonlearning.co.uk/barnes)

1 What are the most important factors that can affect the capacity of any operation?

2 What factors affect the capacity of the following types of organization:
   a A winemaker
   b A university
   c A hospital
   d A motor car manufacturer with factories in several countries
   e A chain of fast food outlets

3 Explain what capacity means for the following operations, and how it might best be measured:
   a An oil refinery
   b A taxi service
   c A shopping mall
   d An airport
   e A clothing manufacturer

4 What are the principal features of the most important methods used in both quantitative and qualitative forecasting?

5 What are the main advantages and disadvantages of both the quantitative and the qualitative approaches to forecasting?

6 Compare the advantages and disadvantages of increasing capacity with a *capacity leads demand* strategy with that of a *capacity lags demand* strategy for the following types of organizations:
   a A manufacturer of high technology consumer electronic products
   b An electricity generator
   c A mobile phone network provider
   d An airline

7 What factors should be taken into account when deciding on the size of an additional increment of capacity?

8 What capacity management strategies would you expect the following types of operations to adopt:
   a An ice cream manufacturer
   b A city centre hotel
   c A steel manufacturer
   d A telephone call centre
   e A grocery supermarket

9 Critically evaluate the effectiveness of the different actions that might be taken as part of a chase demand capacity management strategy by a manufacturer based in the following countries:
   a The People's Republic of China
   b France
   c India
   d Canada

10 On average a telephone call centre receives 100 calls an hour. Each call take 5 minutes on average to resolve. How many staff should always be available to answer the phones if the call centre is to meet its targets of answering all incoming calls within one minute?

CASE STUDY EXERCISE Aldemar Hotels and Spa

Introduction

The Aldemar Group is one of the leading hotel chains in Greece. It is owned and managed by its founder Dr Nikolaos Angelopoulos and his family. The group has a total of 5,500 beds and 1,800 employees in its eight deluxe hotel properties, located in the strategic tourism destinations of Crete, Rhodes and the Western Peloponnese. Three of the hotels feature state-of-the-art conference centres. Two of these also have sophisticated Thalasso Spa Centers. The major sources of business for the hotel chain are: a) the tour operators; b) conference guests (for properties possessing a conference centre) and c) independent travellers. However, the mix of guests at each of Aldemar's hotels depends heavily on the hotel's facilities and its geographical proximity and accessibility to potential markets. So, for example in 2006, the market segment mix at the Knossos Royal Village in Crete, which operates a conference centre, consisted of 80 per cent room-nights from tour operators' guests, 13 per cent from conference guests and a small percentage (5.5 per cent) of individual travellers. On the other hand, the Olympian Village and the Royal Olympian hotels, which are both located in the Peloponnese on mainland Greece (and so are easily accessible by car) and include a renowned Thalasso Spa and a conference centre, had a much more balanced mix of guests: 45 per cent tour operators, 31.5 per cent conference groups, and 21 per cent individuals.

However, demand for Aldemar's properties is not only characterized by high mix variability but also by great volume variability. During the hotel's main operating season (generally from April to October), demand fluctuations are high, sometimes unpredictable, and also differ depending on the market segment. For example, conference guests and holidaymakers have different price sensitivities and time preferences. On the other hand, hotel capacity is fixed and perishable. In other words, the number of rooms cannot be adjusted to match demand levels, while rooms cannot be stored for future sales. Consequently, in periods of high demand, hotels can miss the opportunity to sell more rooms or to sell at higher prices; whilst in periods of low

Relax at an Aldemar Spa

demand, empty rooms represent lost sales for ever and the hotel has to pay for unused capacity and resources (e.g. receptionists, lighting, etc.). Therefore, managing demand and capacity simultaneously in the hotel business (as in all service firms) is critically important for increasing business performance. Thus, service firms aim to ensure that their capacity is fully utilized and that revenue from it is maximized.

To achieve this, Aldemar has introduced sophisticated Yield Management (YM) practices with the assistance of a computerized reservation system. In general, Aldemar aims to set prices according to predicted demand levels; so that price sensitive guests who want to purchase at off-peak times can do so at favourable prices, whilst sales from price insensitive customers who are willing to buy at peak periods will not be lost. The application of YM necessitates the continuous collection and analysis of demand and reservation information in order to make appropriate decisions regarding pricing, booking levels and room allocations. It also requires that Aldemar has appropriate organizational structures and procedures in place for collecting demand information and applying YM practices.

Pricing and room allocation

Aldemar's approach to YM involves three levels of decision-making about pricing:

- *Strategic pricing:* This involves setting room rates and allocating capacity for each of Aldemar's targeted market segments over the longer-term, usually for an entire operating season. Contracts are signed with tour operators for a specific number of rooms at predetermined rates. Similarly, block-bookings are made with conference organizers for an agreed number of rooms at special rates for conference guests.

- *Tactical pricing:* This involves setting room rates in order to seize shorter-term sales opportunities.

- *Operational pricing:* This involves making decisions on an *ad hoc* or daily basis about whether to accept one-off reservations. This is based on setting a price range within which a hotel Reservations Manager can sell a room on a daily basis.

At a strategic level, prices are fixed based on financial targets set by the company owners aimed at achieving certain percentage increases on the previous year's performance. The company's Sales Managers provide information and assistance on pricing. The corporate YM system provides information about last year's sales performance, including occupancy and room prices achieved per guest in each of the market segments, and about annual performance variances. This enables rate tiers to be proposed. The final decisions about room rates, allocations amongst market segments and contracts with tour operators are taken by Aldemar's owners after considering information about the strength of the market segments, the country buying power of each tour operator, the general economic situation (e.g. economic growth or inflation) and what profit margin can be achieved. A great deal of information regarding the socio-economic profile and changes of each market segment are collected through market research studies. The room rates set for an operating season vary according to room type (standard room, suites, etc.) and the time of the year (low, middle, high, and super high demand periods). Competitors' rates are also monitored. However, these are not used to influence price setting directly at the strategic level, as Aldemar's core values are to maintain a good price/quality ratio. In other words, because Aldemar's vision is to be recognized for its superior service, it wants to avoid using YM to compete solely on price.

Tactical pricing decisions are delegated to each individual hotel. However, every hotel has to adhere to the room allocations contracted to it with tour operators by the hotel owners, as well as with the room rates ranges set at the strategic level for the whole operating season. Each hotel General Manager (GM) is empowered to take YM decisions with the assistance of the hotel's Rooms Division Manager and the Reservations Manager (wherever there is one). However, any final YM decision needs the approval of Aldemar's Managing Directors and the Revenue Manager at the corporate level. As there are not any Revenue Managers located at individual Aldemar hotels, the daily monitoring of booking patterns and levels, that in turn determines operational YM decisions, is done mainly by the Rooms Division Manager at each hotel. The decisions taken at an operational level need to take account of the constraints placed by higher level decision-making processes. For example, a Reservations Manager is allowed to provide a discount on the best available rate to a repeating guest, or make a reservation with a travel agency based on the contracted rates. Reservations Managers are also given flexibility to provide priority for the waiting list and booking requests to guests asking for more expensive room types (suites or villas).

Thus, on a daily basis, it is the responsibility of the hotel's Rooms Division Manager to inform the hotel's GM about changes in occupancy levels and then co-decide on corrective actions. Such decisions may refer to suggestions provided by the hotel chain Executive Management such as reducing the number of allocated rooms when release periods have passed, or even blocking sales when occupancy is getting close to 100 per cent. On the other hand, when occupancy levels are low, the hotel GM can launch special offers (e.g. room upgrades, extra services and amenities during low season) and reduce rates to entice demand. Special offers during the low periods are also developed and promoted by the sales teams located at the headquarters of the company. But such promotions are mainly programmed at a tactical and strategic level rather than an operational one. This is because the corporate sales team is in constant communication with the reservation departments of tour operators and they can easily foresee low periods and plan sales promotions well in advance.

Performance monitoring

Occupancy levels are regularly monitored by each hotel's reservations team as well by the revenue management department at the company's headquarters. This is done as a minimum on a weekly basis during the low season, but more frequently during the high and super high seasons, when it can be on a daily basis. However, if it is easy to track low occupancy levels, it is more difficult to adjust sales targets, since the majority of room-nights are contracted to tour operators at agreed rates and room allocations. Thus, a hotel only has sales flexibility when the release period for allocated rooms has passed. Price adjustments on a tactical level can take place only for the small proportion of rooms that are on a free sale basis (i.e. not-contracted). A hotel's reservations department has much greater flexibility in adjusting prices when selling via the telephone or the Internet. Furthermore, as such direct sales are increasing from year to year and these reflect more profitable businesses (with less and lower commissions, higher room rates and immediate payment to the hotel), the company's strategy is to transfer room sales towards these channels rather than tour operators.

The data required for monitoring YM performance and decision-making is collected from the company's Property Management System (MICROS-Fidelio's Opera), as well as directly from tour operators, who provide the company with estimates about the forecasted business usually at the beginning of the season. Occupancy levels are monitored on a daily basis and are calculated on a 45 'days out' window, allowing tactical decisions to take place regularly. At each hotel, the reservations team is responsible for analyzing the information collected by the Property Management System and presenting it to the hotel's management team's weekly meetings and to the executive management team via weekly reports. The hotel's weekly reports include data regarding booked room-nights and achieved room occupancies for the whole of the season (seven–eight months). These are always compared to last year's equivalent data in order to take tactical decisions. Various analyses are then performed on a regular basis by the head office revenue management team and required corrective actions forwarded to relevant hotels.

Aldemar has a policy of not overbooking rooms. This is because overbookings are costly. As the average stay for guests is 7 days, placing an overbooked guest into another property is too expensive. However, when there is another Aldemar property nearby that might be able to accept a displaced overbooking, then a hotel might overbook at a minimum level, but definitely not during the high season.

The major metrics that the company uses for measuring and monitoring YM performance are Room Revenues, the ADR (Average Daily Rate) and the Revenue per Available Room (RevPAR). These figures along with comments regarding variances from last year's performance are included in the monthly reports produced by each hotel. Evidence and data regarding the effectiveness of any YM decision during that month are also included in these reports. In addition, reports are produced by the sales teams that track the effectiveness of promotions initiated and operated by them. These reports are prepared at the end of each operating season and their results are then used to inform YM practices for next season. Weekly reports on sales promotion effectiveness are also produced. Although these contain less sophisticated information and analysis, they are critical for continuous improvement and the management of sales promotions.

To motivate staff and encourage the correct implementation of YM, the company operates a bonus system that rewards staff based on a hotel's overall performance. This is crucial since YM should be seen as a team effort and requires the sharing of information and common decision-taking (e.g. marketing department informs reservations about the profitability and loyalty of potential guests and market segments). However, as the company aims to increase room sales from direct channels (especially the Internet) at the expense of channels controlled by the group's owners (especially tour operators) the company is planning to introduce an incentive scheme that would reward operational level staff on room sales and ADR achieved.

—*Marianna Sigala*

Questions (Suggested answers can be found on the companion website www.thomsonlearning.co.uk/barnes)

1 Why is yield management so important for Aldemar?

2 What other approaches to capacity management could Aldemar use?

3 Critically assess Aldemar's current yield management practices (e.g. the organizational structures, procedures, performance monitoring).

4 If Aldemar is successful in making more direct sales (e.g. via the Internet), should it change the way it manages YM in its hotels?

This case is based on interviews with Mr George Anastasakos (Revenue Manager) and Mr Alexandros Aggelopoulos (Executive Director) of Aldemar Hotels (http://www.aldemarhotels.com/).

References

Hayes, R., Pisano, G., Upton, D. and Wheelwright, S. (2005) *Operations, Strategy and Technology: pursuing the competitive edge,* New York: John Wiley.

Kines, S.E. (1989) 'Yield Management: A tool for capacity constrained service firms', *Journal of Operations Management* 8(4):348–363.

Additional reading

Gross, D. and Harris, C.M. (1998) *Fundamentals of Queueing Theory,* New York: John Wiley.

Hayes, R., Pisano, G., Upton, D. and Wheelwright, S. (2005) *Operations, Strategy and Technology: pursuing the competitive edge,* New York: John Wiley.

Hopp, W.J. and Spearman, M.L. (2000) *Factory Physics,* New York: McGraw Hill.

Makridakis, S., Wheelwright, S.C. and Hyndman, R. (1998) *Forecasting: Methods and Applications* (3rd Ed.), London: John Wiley and Sons.

Useful websites

http://www.ibf.org/ The Institute of Business Forecasting is a membership organization that provides education and training about forecasting. The website also hosts various discussion groups.

http://www.downtimecentral.com/ Downtime Central. A site aimed at maintenance professionals with useful information about the costs of downtime.

http://www.forecasters.org/ The International Institute of Forecasters is an academic organization for the research and practice of forecasting. It aims to stimulate the generation, distribution and use of knowledge on forecasting.

http://www.forecastingprinciples.com/ The Forecasting Principles site is maintained by the Marketing Department of the Wharton School of Business at the University of Pennsylvania. It contains a wealth of information about forecasting useful to researchers, practitioners and educators.

http://www2.uwindsor.ca/~hlynka/queue.html Myron Hlynka's Queueing Theory page is maintained by the eponymous academic at University of Windsor, Ontario, Canada. The website contains a wealth of information and reference sources on queuing.

CHAPTER 7

PROCESS TECHNOLOGY

INTRODUCTION

We humans have been using technology to help us perform work ever since our ancestors fashioned rudimentary tools from pieces of wood and stone. Since then, both the complexity and capability of technology in all its forms, has increased, seemingly, at an inexorable pace. Organizations, as much as individuals, have always sought to make best use of technology. In particular, a major concern of operations management is how to make best use of available technology in the management of business processes. Technology can be used in all process types (materials processing, customer processing and information processing) to improve both efficiency and effectiveness. The challenge for operations managers is how to choose what technology to use and, equally as important, how to use it. Accordingly, this chapter is between those two broad themes; namely choosing and using technology in operations.

The first part of the chapter opens by tackling the issue of technology choice. First, it provides an overview of the types of process technologies that are available. It then considers how organizations set about determining what type of technology to use in their processes. In particular it considers what scale of technology to adopt, the extent to which that technology should be automated and the degree to which the technology should be integrated within and between processes. The role of information and communication technology (ICT) in operations is then considered. Over the last decade, ICT has become increasingly important, both in its ability to process data, but also in its ability to facilitate communications both within and between organizations. ICT has had a tremendous impact on operations management, particularly in services, freeing many activities from the previous constraints of location. The different strategies available to an organization with regard to technology adoption are then discussed, together with the factors that need to be taken into account when transferring technology between facilities at different geographic locations. Transferring technology into a new location requires an assessment both of the transferability of the technology, particularly its level of maturity, and the appropriateness of the context in which it will be operated,

LEARNING OBJECTIVES

On completion of this chapter, you should be able to:

Understand the criteria on which process technology choice decisions are made.

Appreciate the crucial role that ICT plays in modern operations management.

Explain the strategies available for technology adoption.

Understand the issues involved in transferring technologies between different geographic locations.

Outline the characteristics of generic process types in the context of the volume-variety model.

Describe the basic layout types and their relationship with the generic process types.

Appreciate the challenges of determining an appropriate configuration for process equipment.

scale of technology
The processing capacity of a type of technology (rather than its physical size).

particularly the existing technology in use at that location. The issue of technology transfer has become increasingly important as organizations have shown ever more willingness to relocate individual operations particularly to lower cost countries. This has led to an increasing incidence of processes that are global in their span.

The second part of the chapter then moves on to consider the use of technology. This is framed in terms of the relationships between volume and variety in operations. It involves the determination of how technology can be used to determine what process type is best suited to any particular operation and how the chosen process equipment should be physically able to achieve the operation's objectives. The chapter closes by returning to the issue of queuing, which was first discussed in Chapter 6. Various options for the configuration of waiting lines will be discussed and actions that can be taken to reduce the dissatisfaction of customers asked to wait in line outlined.

Early twentieth century technology

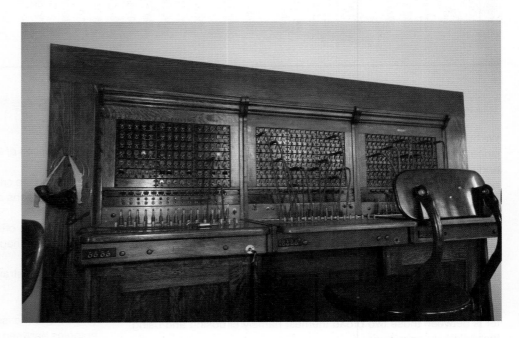

Late twentieth century technology

Early twenty-first century technology

DIFFERENT PROCESS TECHNOLOGIES

Process technologies are the tools (equipment, machines, devices, etc.) used in operations. All operations use technology to some extent. As discussed in Chapter 1, operations can be classified according to which type of resource is predominantly being transformed; materials, customers or information. Process technologies can be similarly distinguished, and examples of some of the process technologies currently in widespread use are given below. However, it is worth noting that it is not always easy to apply such a classification in practice. In particular, the greater information processing capabilities afforded by modern information and communication technologies mean that many technologies can now process materials and customers as well as information. For example, by logging on to the website of some airlines, customers can search for a flight, book it, pay for it by credit card, and even print off their boarding card.

process technologies
The tools (equipment, machines and other devices) used in operations that transform materials, information or customers.

Materials processing technologies

These can broadly be divided into four categories:

1 *Designing technologies:* Which are used to aid the design process.
2 *Forming technologies:* Which are used in processes undertaking some kind of forming operation on materials (e.g. cutting, bending, drilling, shaping, etc.).
3 *Moving technologies:* Which are used to move materials within the production process, usually between two stages of manufacturing.
4 *Integrating technologies:* Which are technologies used to integrate technologies from two or more of the previous categories.

Examples of each of these are given in Box 7.1.

BOX 7.1

Examples of materials processing technologies

Design technologies

Computer Aided Design (CAD) is a computer system that allows designers to create drawings which can also be viewed, displayed and manipulated in three dimensions from any angle on a computer screen. Once created, such drawings can be stored for future use, enabling a library of standard designs to be built up. It is also easy to transmit the drawings to other designers and engineers. CAD systems can also create a list of parts required to make the product (known as a Bill of Materials), which can then be used to purchase the necessary materials.

Computer Aided Process Planning (CAPP) extends CAD by creating a process plan that specifies how the item will be manufactured.

Computer Aided Engineering (CAE) enables simulated tests to be carried out on the design from the CAD system. This can be particularly useful when comparing a number of alternative designs.

Forming technologies

Computer Numerically Controlled (CNC) machines are machine tools that can be controlled by computer. They can operate with greater speed, repeatability and accuracy for longer than any human operator. They may also be equipped with a number of different tools that can be programmed to be automatically changed in accordance with the requirements of each job.

Industrial robots are available for some forming tasks, such as welding or assembling. These are particularly useful for simple repetitive tasks where a high degree of precision and repeatability are required and which would be very dull for humans to carry out. Robots are also often used in dirty or dangerous conditions.

Moving technologies

Automatic Materials Handling (AMH) is a term used to describe a wide range of automated materials moving technologies. These can incorporate various industrial robots (typically used to pick, hold and place items), as well as driverless vehicles, known as Automated Guided Vehicles (AGV), whose movements can be programmed, and Automated Storage and Retrieval Systems (AS/RS) that are typically used to place and subsequently pick materials in storage facilities.

A robotic arm: A material processing technology

Integrating technologies

Computer Aided Manufacturing (CAM) systems extend the use of CAD by enabling its designs to be transmitted to CNC machines, enabling them to be automatically programmed for manufacture. Such integrated systems that link designing and forming technologies in this way are sometimes referred to as CADCAM.

A Flexible Manufacturing System (FMS) is a collection of CNC machines (forming technology) that are linked by AMH technologies (moving technology). (When such systems are fairly limited in scope, they are often termed Flexible Manufacturing Centers (FMC).) The AMH technologies enable each CNC machine to be automatically loaded and unloaded, and for material to be moved from one machine to another in accordance with the manufacturing process plan for each item. The FMS is controlled by computer, and can be programmed to produce whatever combination of different items, in whatever numbers and sequence are required, provided it is within the system's capability. The advantage of an FMS, when compared to an equivalent number of similar free standing machines, is that it can produce at much higher volumes with much lower direct labour costs, and yet still offer a high degree of flexibility, as the product type and mix can be readily changed by reprogramming the controller. In practice, the limitations of the machines within a FMS often mean that very detailed planning is required in order to achieve the desired production schedules. Also, the high capital cost of such systems mean that hoped for cost savings may take some time to achieve.

Computer Integrated Manufacturing (CIM) systems integrate all aspects of the manufacturing, by linking CADCAM with all FMSs to create a fully integrated manufacturing operation, controlled by a single computer system. Whilst such systems hold out the hope of easily controllable operations with minimum labour costs, the dynamism and complexity that most manufacturers have to cope with, typically makes it difficult to realize such ambitions in practice. And it is often difficult to justify the capital costs of CIM systems.

Customer processing technologies

Many customer service operations involve an interaction of customers with the service provider's technology. There are essentially three types of customer-technology interaction (see Figure 7.1):

Passive interactions

This is where the technology controls the interaction with the customer. Examples of this include mass transit systems, moving walkways, air travel and theme parks. As the customer is guided through the service encounter by the technology, clear signage that provides simple easy to follow instructions for the customer are especially important. Where customers speak different languages, signs may need to be written in more than one language, or pictorial representations provided as well.

Active interactions

This is where the customer controls the interaction with the technology. In effect, the service encounter is one of self-service where the technology enables customers to fulfil their requirements without the help of a human server. In most cases, the technology replaces work that would previously have been carried out by an employee of the service provider. Examples of this include bank ATMs, airline check-in kiosks, rail passenger ticket machines and some automated telephone information services. The obvious advantage for the service provider in replacing increasingly costly labour with technology is one of cost saving. This is a case of the service operations following the trends of manufacturing and agriculture in previous decades. However, self-service can have other advantages, both to the service provider and the customer. In many service encounters, self-service can be quicker and, for simple services, more

FIGURE 7.1 The role of technology in the service encounter

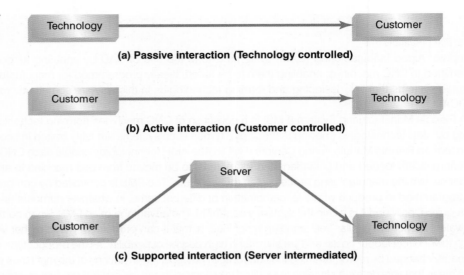

(a) Passive interaction (Technology controlled)

(b) Active interaction (Customer controlled)

(c) Supported interaction (Server intermediated)

dependable than that of a human server. Also, many customers seem to prefer the sense of control and choice afforded by technology-driven self-service. This is particularly the case where use of the technology can enable customers to by-pass a queue of customers that is waiting to be served by a human server and where the provision of technology enables the service to be offered at times when human service would not normally be available (for example, ATMs outside of normal banking hours).

The use of the Internet is dramatically increasing the use and scope of self-service. As well as ordering most kinds of goods from online retailers (books, apparel computers, etc.), it is now possible to buy more complex customized services over the web. For example, you can pre-book all your travel arrangements for a business trip, including flights, hotels, car hire, etc. without ever interacting with another human being. Professional services are also starting to be offered online, for example educational courses, share trading, some legal services and even some health services. Thus, the Internet is being used to increase sales and improve service offerings to customers, as well as reducing operating costs.

If self-service is to be successful, customers need to understand how to operate the technology they are expected to use. In a sense, customers need 'training'. Whilst training in a formal sense may be possible in business to business markets (i.e. a business customer's employees can be trained by the service provider), this is not usually possible in mass consumer markets. Customer training normally relies on providing clear operating instructions and on novice users learning from more experienced customers, either by observing their use of the technology or in conversation with family or friends. Successful training is helped if the service is simple (rather than complex) and the variety of the tasks required of the customer is low. It is also helpful if the principle on which the technology is based is familiar to users, for example making use of the type of menu-driven choices used in mobile phones.

Supported interactions

This is where a human server acts as an intermediary between the customer and the technology. The server and customer may have access to the same technology, but control of the technology normally remains with the server. Examples of this include airline check-in desks, financial transactions in a bank and most medical interventions. Although many supported interactions take place face-to-face, some can be carried out remotely via the telephone, or even online. Many customers prefer to be served by a fellow human being, valuing the human interaction. In cases where the service is complex or the technology limited, the flexibility of a human server can offer a better service than that available by self-service. It may be that the customer lacks information about the service and what advice to take from the server (e.g. when choosing a holiday). There are cases when self-service is not possible because the server is required to have specialist skills (as is the case with most medical technologies) or where customer operation of the technology would be dangerous (as with most transportation).

Servers need to be competent both in the use of the technology they use and also in their behaviour towards the customer. Thus, successful supported service encounters need servers who have not only received training in the operation of the technology, but also in using interpersonal skills appropriate to their customers.

A mass transit system: A customer processing technology

In passive interactions with customer processing technologies, customers may need clear instructions

Self service ticket machines: An
active interaction with a customer
processing technology

Information processing technologies

There can be few organizations that do not make use of computers for information
processing these days, to the extent that the terms information processing and information technology (IT) have become synonymous. Since the advent of free-standing
computers there has been a desire to interconnect them in order to communicate and
share information. Local Area Networks (LANs) connect computers within the same
building or site. Wide Area Networks (WANs) facilitate connectedness between a
number of often remote sites. LANs and WANs have been used for many years and
usually only network computers within the same organization. Electronic Data
Interchange (EDI) is a technology that has also existed for many years. EDI networks
were typically established between large purchasers (e.g. motor car manufacturers)
and their supplier, in order to automate and speed up the routine business transactions
(placing orders, sending orders, making payments, etc.). These were originally set up
over dedicated telecommunication lines, but have now increasingly migrated to
Internet connections.

It is the advent of the Internet and the World Wide Web (www) that has revolutionized so much of business practice, to the extent that the term ICT (information and
communication technology) has become virtually synonymous, and interchangeable,
with the term IT. The Internet enables any computer anywhere in the world to be connected to any other using a telephone line. Extranets use Internet technologies to link
chosen business partners (e.g. within a supply chain) using a secure network. Most EDI
(Electronic Data Interchange) is now conducted via such networks. Intranets are private networks, usually established with Internet technologies within a single organization, but not normally limited to a single site. The increasing capacity of wireless
technologies are enabling laptop computers and handheld devices (such as palmtops
and PDAs) to participate in this interconnected world via the Internet.

The Internet has enabled most aspects of business to be conducted electronically.
The term e-business is often used to describe the 'sharing of business information,

e-business

The sharing of business information,
maintaining business relationships and
conducting business transactions by
means of Internet-based technology.

BOX 7.2

Examples of information processing technologies

Office Automation Systems (OASs), which are used to manage the administrative functions, especially document electronic production and communication. Groupware is typically incorporated to help teams of people working together.

Workflow Management Systems (WFMSs) automate business processes by providing structured frameworks that control the flow of documents, information or tasks from one worker to another. They can assign work tasks to individuals or groups, facilitate collaboration, and provide records of all activities.

Management Information Systems (MISs) is the term used to describe a wide range of systems that are used to support managerial decision-making. At its basic level this includes information reporting systems (IRSs) that provide regular performance reports. Decision Support Systems (DSSs) use models to present information in such a way that managers can view the consequences of their decisions before going ahead. They typically allow for 'what if' analysis so that a number of different courses of action can be compared. Expert systems (ESs), also sometimes referred to as knowledge-based systems (KBSs), take DSSs a stage further, by offering an optimum solution. They do this by applying their programmed logic to the data they have collected. It is, of course, up to managers to decide whether to accept the decision.

Electronic Data Interchange (EDI) systems link an organization's information systems with those of its suppliers, usually via the Internet. They are typically used by large MNEs to automate the purchase of goods and services, enabling documents for orders, shipping, invoices, etc. to be placed electronically. EDI is discussed in Chapter 3.

Enterprise Resource Planning (ERP) systems are used for resource planning and control throughout an entire organization. They operate by integrating all the information systems for all the different departments and functions of an organization. As they typically use the Internet to connect between different locations, they are particularly useful for large and complex organizations, especially those that operate internationally. Recent versions of Internet-enabled ERP systems also enable the organization information systems to connect to those of its supply chain partners (suppliers, intermediaries, customers, etc.). ERP is discussed in more detail in Chapter 9.

---

maintaining business relationships and conducting business transactions by means of Internet-based technology' (Poon and Swatman, 1999). The term e-commerce is usually used to mean buying and selling over the Internet. Many, if not most, organizations have incorporated the use of the Internet within their business operations, either using this medium as an additional channel, or in some cases embracing it as their main or sole way of conducting business. The Internet has also spawned completely new businesses such as eBay and Amazon.com that only trade in an online environment. There can be few organizations that have not had to reconfigure their business operations as a result of the Internet.

Examples of some of the many different information processing technologies that are available for use within and between organizations are given in Box 7.2.

A more recent development is that of Radio Frequency Identification Devices (RFID). These devices are a development of bar codes that are used to label items of all kinds, including parts and finished products. When read by a scanner, bar codes provide sufficient information that enables each part or product to be identified as a particular type. RFID take this idea forward in two ways. First, the barcodes contain sufficient data to give each item a unique identity. Second, they can be read by a wireless radio frequency reader, so that their exact location can be determined. So, RFIDs enable individual items to be traced wherever they are. This opens up many different possibilities for their use. For example, they could enable suppliers to trace the progress of a delivery along the supply chain. They could also be used to identify the

e-commerce
The undertaking of business transactions through the medium of Internet-based information and communication technologies (or other computer networks). Sometimes the term electronic business or e-business is used as an alternative to e-commerce. Occasionally the term e-business is used to emphasize the use of ICTs in an organization's own business processes and throughout its entire supply network.

Bar codes: The basis of some information processing technologies

location of products that need to be recalled, for example for health or safety reasons. More controversially, some companies are using them to track the whereabouts of mobile workers, by requiring them to carry RFIDs on their person.

DECISION-MAKING ABOUT TECHNOLOGY

The key consideration for operations managers is what type of technology should be used in any given process. Technological choices seem to be increasing in most industries. In considering what technology to use within their operations, managers need to understand the capabilities of any particular technology and the benefits that ensue from its use. They also need to understand the associated costs and limitations of operating that technology. Although every technology choice decision must inevitably be specific to the context for its intended use, amongst the general issues to consider are:

- *The volume and variety of output* that the technology can achieve. As will be discussed in more detail on pp. 182–192 in most operations, volume and variety are inversely related. This relationship normally also holds with technology. The larger the volume that a particular technology can process, then the more limited the variety of resulting product or service. Being able to process high volumes generally lowers the unit cost of production due to economies of scale. High volume usually makes it possible to justify the large financial investments often associated with such technology. However, it is usually difficult to achieve high variety with high volume technology due to the difficulties associated with changing from one product to another. Conversely, it is usually difficult to achieve high volumes with technology that is flexible enough to facilitate a high level of variety.

- *The fit with existing technology* used within the organization. Operating new technology alongside existing technology may limit organizational flexibility and increase operating costs. In particular, those workers responsible for the operation and maintenance of the new technology are likely to have to learn new skills. It may well be difficult for them to achieve a high level of proficiency with the new technology and retain their proficiency in the old

CASE STUDY The INCAT-AFAI Joint Venture

INCAT (International Catamarans Pty. Ltd) of Australia is a world leader in the manufacture of high-speed ferries. Its innovative design and production have allowed INCAT to grow from 31 employees in 1978 to 1,000 employees in 2000. It has built approximately 50 per cent of the high-speed ferries currently in operation worldwide. INCAT's success is based on cutting-edge R & D that have set world standards for ocean-based transport for cars and passengers. The company has an enviable reputation for its customer service and the safety of its vessels. It is particularly known for two successful high-speed ferry designs. The first is a large, wave-piercing catamaran and the second is a small 'k class' catamaran, for sheltered ferry trips.

Unable to fill orders due to the limitations of its single Tasmanian shipyard, INCAT had previously licensed shipyards to build vessels in Australia, New Zealand, Hong Kong, Singapore, the United States, and the United Kingdom. However, increasing global demand led it to form a joint venture (JV) in 1996 with AFAI High Performance Ships Ltd, one of its former licensees in Hong Kong. The JV (INCAT held 49 per cent of the equity and AFAI 51 per cent), would enable INCAT's 'k class' catamaran to be built at AFAI's shipyard in Panyu, southern China. AFAI had constructed boats for INCAT from 1982 to 1989 and the trust that was built through this relationship was a major reason why INCAT chose AFAI. Having had other JVs in addition to that with INCAT, AFAI was well-versed in Western business and culture. AFAI's shipyard in Panyu in the Pearl River Delta had made it ideally located to capitalize on the rapid growth of high-speed ferry transport in southern China and had enabled it to gain valuable skills in the repair, maintenance, and development of high-speed ferries.

As part of the JV, INCAT was responsible for the design of the vessels as well as supplying the Chinese shipyard with the machinery and prefabricated components. INCAT had lower component costs than

---

An INCAT-AFAI catamaran under construction

AFAI, due to its significant buying power. Production in China further strengthened buying power. AFAI's responsibilities were to supply the labour and management to build the vessels as well as technical assistance. Through this arrangement, INCAT has been able to achieve economies of scale by specializing in its large wave-piercing catamarans in Tasmania, while the Chinese shipyard concentrated on the smaller, 'k class' vessels.

Different from the previous licensing relationship that INCAT had with AFAI, INCAT had much more control in the JV arrangement. All vessels had to be made according to INCAT's instruction. However, while control increased, so did the associated risk levels and commitment of resources from INCAT. As part of the agreement, INCAT agreed to bear all costs related to the supply of equipment and components to AFAI until the vessel was sold. In addition, INCAT was to receive no payment for the knowledge and technology that it supplied to AFAI. Therefore, INCAT had the potential to suffer financially if the construction or sale of its product was delayed, unlike the previous arrangement. Each 'k class' vessel was worth US$17 million, whereas the vessels constructed in the previous arrangement were worth US$1.3 to $2 million.

Unlike most international licensing and JV agreements, the joint production arrangement between these two companies was unusual in that it did not specify exactly what each partner would contribute in technological expertise. Both parties agreed to do whatever was necessary (within reason) to construct 'k class' vessels for the world market. The agreement requires a great deal of flexibility and it can only succeed if a relationship based on trust exists between the parties. In their agreement, both INCAT and AFAI explicitly stated that they trusted the other partner to get their half of the bargain accomplished. This fits well with the Chinese business culture of *guanxi*, which is based on trust, reciprocity and obligation, and has enabled the partnership to succeed.

Given the concern for intellectual property protection, often voiced by Western companies operating in China, why did INCAT choose such a loose contract in its JV arrangement with AFAI? This is primarily because INCAT does not see legal recourse as an effective way of protecting its intellectual property. In fact, INCAT has no registered patents or designs and has not even registered a trademark to protect its name and logo. INCAT appears unconcerned over the possibility of AFAI taking away its designs and/or processes. This is despite the fact that the Chinese government-operated company, Guangzhou Maritime Shipping Bureau, was affiliated with the shipyard. Although the JV agreement did include confidentiality clauses designed to prevent AFAI from disclosing INCAT's proprietary information to third parties, INCAT recognized the limited extent of protection that they provide.

INCAT believes that its competitive advantage is based on a relentless emphasis on innovation, sustaining its technological superiority with intense R & D activity. This is not easily protected by intellectual property laws. Although INCAT provides each of its customers with detailed plans of their vessels, it argues that these are not as valuable as they may seem. Competitors would need all the background information and research that went into the process if they wanted to build or adapt one of INCAT's designs. A vast array of essential knowledge is not embodied in the plans. The essential knowledge underlying the design is not codified. Rather it is tacit knowledge, built up over years of experience, and cannot be easily taken away. INCAT's stance is summed up by their Managing Director, who says, 'What we do is mostly in our heads. This is the kind of intellectual property which is far more valuable than being on paper'.

(Based on the case study 'The INCAT-AFAI Joint Venture: Technology transfer with a loose contract' by Sara L. McGaughey (Copenhagen Business School), Peter W. Liesch (University of Queensland) and Duncan Poulson (University of Tasmania), in Peng, M.W. (2005) *Global Strategy*, South Western, pp. 348–351).

WWW.

Questions (Suggested answers can be found on the companion website www.thomsonlearning.co.uk/barnes)

1 Why did INCAT want to establish a JV as opposed to relying on licensing agreements as before?

2 Why is INCAT comfortable with a loose JV agreement which does not delineate the details of technological expertise each party is to contribute to?

3 What are the drawbacks and advantages of INCAT's approach?

Projects can be large and complex

to coping with demands for a high level of variety within those outputs, whether they are products or services.

For manufactured goods it is possible to characterize five generic process types, according to the volume and variety that they are suited to producing.

Project

A project is a process suitable for producing a single product of almost limitless variety. Every project is unique with the product being customized to exact requirements. Projects are often characterized by their complexity and scale. They can often take a long time to complete. They should have definable start and finish times with clear time, quality and cost objectives. Managing a project involves the co-ordination of workers with many different skills and many different physical resources that must all be scheduled to arrive at the site where the work is being carried out at the appropriate time. Projects often use general purpose equipment that can be re-used on a number of different projects. Examples of projects include building construction, movie-making and installing a computer system.

Jobbing

Jobbing is a process suited to the production of very small quantities, or even one-offs. Like projects, the products can be very high in variety and made to exact customer specification. Unlike a project, jobbing usually takes place at the premises of the producer, using highly skilled workers and specialist equipment that can be used to produce many different products, often for different customers. As every product may require different types and amounts of work in different sequences, coordinating the timing and routing of products through the various production areas is a major challenge. Examples of jobbing include bespoke tailors, precision engineers and built-to-order furniture.

Building a customized laptop:
A jobbing process

Batch processing involves
processing a quantity of items
(such as catalogues) together
through each stage of
production

Batch

Batch production is a process similar to jobbing except that it involves higher volumes and lower variety. There are likely to be many standard products, which are made to satisfy repeat demand, but the operation will also be able to cope with requirements for special items. A key feature of batch production is that the production process is broken down into a number of stages. Each stage of the process is likely to involve specialist machinery operated by workers with very specific skills. At each stage, the desired quantity of components (the 'batch') are processed at the same time, so that the required quantity of finished products are completed together. At any one time, a number of different batches of different components, possibly for different finished products, are likely to be moving through the factory, with probably each requiring different work in a different sequence. This makes routing and scheduling a major challenge. Also, machines will need to be set up specifically for each different batch, leading to lost time at the change-over. Batch production is prone to the build up of work-in-progress as batches wait to be processed at different stages. Examples of batch production include components for automobiles, most clothing and printing of books, magazines and leaflets.

Mass

Mass production is a process for the production of high volumes, normally greater than that achievable by batch manufacture, but product variety is low, normally involving standard, repeat products. A key feature of mass production is that there is a fixed sequence of tasks, normally arranged in a line. Each point on the line carries out the same task repeatedly. Equipment dedicated to each single task is

Mass production is suitable for processing high volumes of similar products

used and consequently equipment utilization rates are high. As variety is low, little time is needed to set up or changeover the equipment. Each task is carried out by workers who perform only that single task. Consequently, workers require only a very narrow set of skills. The best known example of mass production is the car assembly line. Car assembly lines typically manufacture only one model of car. Whilst there can be variants of that model (e.g. with a different engine, different colours or different equipment), the line is in essence producing only one product. Other examples of mass production include domestic appliances and bottling and canning plants.

Continuous

Continuous production is a process for the production of extremely high volumes and very low variety, often a single product, typically a fluid. Typically the product is inseparable like a fluid or mineral, so the product flows along conveyors or pipework. Production is often literally continuous, 24 hours a days, 7 days a week and utilizes highly capital-intensive and automated equipment, with few if any changeovers required. Interruptions to production are usually difficult and it can be expensive to start and stop the process. Examples include oil refining, electricity generation and steel-making.

It is possible to argue that this classification can also be applied to service operations, and treat the five manufacturing types as generic descriptions for all operations processes. Service examples would be:

- Project – A management consultancy assignment or planning for a wedding
- Jobbing – Hairdressing or a hospital casualty ward
- Batch – A banquet or payroll administration
- Mass – A fast food restaurant or theme park rides

However, many people working in service operations prefer to use the following classification:

A chemical plant: An example of continuous production

Two examples of professional services

Professional services

Professional services are service processes with low volume and high variety. They are usually a front office operation involving a high degree of customer contact and the service can be tailored to meet the needs of individual customers. As such, professional services tend to be people- rather than technology-based. Examples include lawyers, doctors, auditors and management consultants.

Mass services

Mass services operate at the other extreme of service process type to professional services. They are designed to process large quantities with low variety. They typically have a low degree of customer contact with little customization. Examples include mass transit systems, supermarkets and fast food outlets. Many back office services operate as mass services, for example those that involve financial and other

A banquet: Batch processing in a mass service process

A fast food restaurant is also a mass service but it operates as a mass production process

data processing and telephone call centres. Some service operations academics (e.g. Schmenner, 1986) use the term 'service factory' to describe mass services that have low labour intensity as well as low customer interaction and customization. These encompass many back office operations. They are quasi-manufacturing in nature and typically rely heavily on technology. It is often these services that can be most easily off-shored to low cost locations.

Service shop

A service shop is a compromise between the two extremes of professional and mass services. They tend to use a mixture of equipment and people to meet customer needs. Within the service shop a mixture of processes may be utilized. A retail bank branch is a good example. Mass service processes are used for customers wishing to conduct simple transactions (e.g. withdrawing cash, make a deposit, currency exchange). Professional service processes are used for customers wanting more complex transactions (e.g. applying for mortgages or personal insurance) or advice (e.g. savings and investments). Other examples include health clubs, restaurants and universities.

Figure 7.5 illustrates these process types on a volume-variety matrix. Both of these classifications, the five manufacturing (see Figure 7.5a) and three service types (see Figure 7.5b) describe a continuum of processes and it may not always be possible to characterize any given process neatly as one single type. In practice, many processes can blur the distinctions and have features of more than one process type. It is also possible to find more than one type of process operating at a single facility. For example, a manufacturer may use mass production to produce its best selling products but use a jobbing process to make specialist products for particular customers.

The volume-variety matrices illustrated in Figure 7.5a and b highlight the fundamental impact of process choice on the performance of an operation. Processes that facilitate increased volumes should lead to lower unit costs. But they also tend to reduce flexibility and so reduce product variety. This emphasizes the need to match process type to the product characteristics. The product-process matrix shown in Figure 7.6 illustrates this. The diagonal line from top left to bottom right is a line of

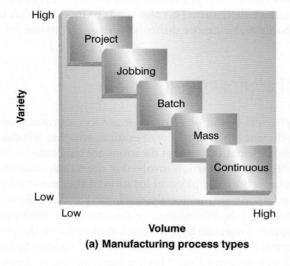

(a) Manufacturing process types

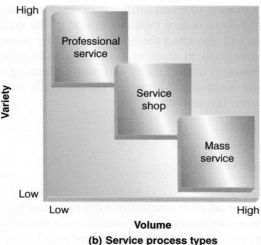

(b) Service process types

FIGURE 7.5 Generic process types

FIGURE 7.6 The product-process matrix

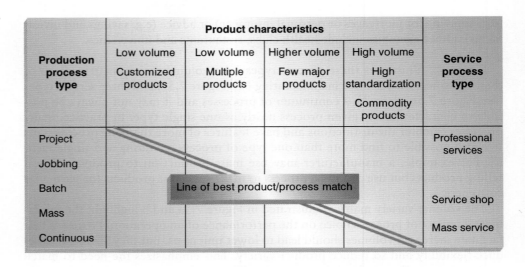

(ADAPTED FROM HAYES AND WHEELWRIGHT, 1984)

best match between process and product. Trying to increase the flexibility of the process by moving away from the diagonal towards the top right, tends to increase costs. This is probably because opportunities to standardize are being missed, leading to increased unit costs. Trying to reduce costs by moving away from the diagonal towards the bottom left, tends to reduce flexibility. This also tends to increase costs because a lack of flexibility will probably make it more difficult to change from one product to another.

THE LAYOUT OF PROCESS EQUIPMENT

Determining the physical layout of equipment used in an operation is important as layout affects the efficient function of any operation, whether it is designed to process materials, people or information. Layout decisions are concerned with the interaction of the equipment, people and materials involved in the transformation process. Choice of layout will determine both the physical location of the resources used to carry out the transformation (equipment, materials, staff, etc.) and the flow of the resources being transformed (materials, information or customers) by the operations process.

Inappropriate layout design can have a significant impact on the performance of the operation. Unnecessary movement of resources will reduce operating efficiency, adding costs while not adding value. Moving materials more times or over greater distances than necessary increases the risk of damage, thereby jeopardizing quality. Similarly, requiring customers to travel further than absolutely necessary in the transformation process is likely to reduce their perception of the quality of their experience. Choice of layout will also affect the operation's ability to respond to changes in customer demand, particularly in terms of the volume and variety of goods or services. As moving equipment is often a costly and time-consuming business, the design or re-design of a layout is important because it happens only infrequently.

There are four generic layout types:

1 Fixed position layout
2 Process layout
3 Group (or cellular) layout
4 Product layout

These are listed in order of their suitability for processing increasing volumes of product or service. However, increasing volume can only normally be achieved at the expense of decreasing variety. The relative position of each layout type with regard to volume and variety is shown in Figure 7.7.

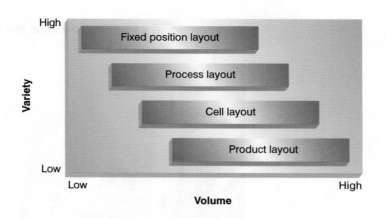

FIGURE 7.7 Generic layout types

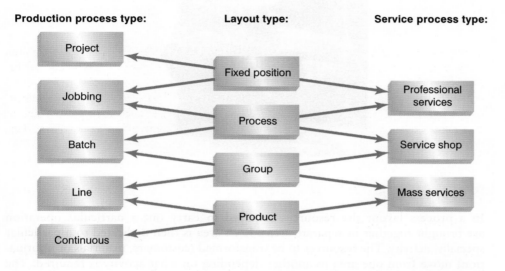

FIGURE 7.8 Generic process and layout types

Process type is an important influence on layout because each process type tends to be associated with a particular type of layout. This relationship is illustrated in Figure 7.8.

Fixed position layout

In this case there is no flow of materials, customers or information through the operation. Rather, the resources required to carry out the transformation process are brought to the position where the operation is to be carried out. This is usually because it is physically impossible, inappropriate or inconvenient to move the resources which are to be transformed by the operation. Most projects are characterized by a fixed layout (e.g. constructing a new office block or shipbuilding). Service examples would include on site mainframe computer maintenance or a roadside vehicle breakdown rescue service. Many professional services use a fixed layout (e.g. dentists or legal consultations).

The main advantage of fixed position layouts is their great flexibility. Any resources required for any task in the operation can be brought to the position as and when required, with minimal disruption for the product or customer. The disadvantage is that unit costs can be high due to very low volumes. Also, scheduling of activities can be very complex, requiring tight control and accurate sequencing of the various activities. Physical constraints of the location only add to the complexity. For example, restricting the quantity of material that can be stored.

Computer repair: A fixed position layout. The resources move to the job

Process layout

In a process layout the resources required to carry out a particular operation are brought together in separate areas. Each area is then dedicated to a particular specialist activity. The resources to be transformed (customers, materials or information) move from one area to another depending on what activity is required. The sequencing of activities can be varied to suit the requirements of the product. A manufacturing example would be an engineering factory with a machining shop, a drill shop, a welding shop, a paint shop, etc. The materials being processed to manufacture any one product can be sequenced to move from any one shop to any other in turn as required. In the same way, hospital patients may be moved to specialist areas (operating theatre, radiography, intensive care, recovery ward, etc.) depending upon their medical treatment. Also, in retail shops and supermarkets customers are largely free to move between specialist areas or departments to make their purchases.

A process layout brings together staff and equipment for specialized tasks and so facilitates the development of expertise in particular activities that are frequently required to produce different goods and services. This allows the operations facility as a whole to respond with great flexibility to differing customer orders. The disadvantage of this arrangement is that flows of materials or customers can be complex, making control difficult. For materials, this can increase transportation costs and lead to the build up of work-in-progress. For customers, this can lead to queuing and, hence, dissatisfaction.

The main task for the designer of a process layout is to minimize the distances that the material or customer is required to travel. This requires a detailed study of the frequency of movement between the various specialist areas in an actual or simulated situation. The desirability (or otherwise) of different areas being close to one another is also assessed. From this information a preferred layout can be developed. This will inevitably be complex, and a number of proprietary computer programs are available to aid these considerations.

Factories with areas dedicated to specific activities (like this grinding area) have process layouts

A car assembly line like this an example of a product layout

Product layout

In a product layout the resources being transformed (customers, materials, information) move in a predetermined sequence from one area to the next. Each of these areas contains the necessary resources (staff, equipment, materials, etc.) to carry out only a very narrow range of activities. A manufacturing example would be a motor car assembly line where each work station on the line repeats the same activity for each car that passes (e.g. mounting the engine, bolting on the wheels, inserting the windscreen). Similarly, in many self-service cafeterias each customer must pass each service point (soup, meat, vegetables, drinks, etc.) in turn to reach the cash desk. However, in this case the customer has the option of not using any particular service point.

This type of layout is suitable for the production of large volumes of similar (possibly identical) goods and services. It ensures high utilization of specialist (and often expensive) equipment and hence ensures low unit costs. The movement of materials or customers is also minimized. The disadvantages are its relative inflexibility and vulnerability to disruption. A problem at any point in the line will cause delays at all points behind. Another price to pay for the efficient utilization of resources can be the repetitive and restrictive nature of the work at each work station. This can be a particular problem for operating staff performing tasks where cycle times are very short. Staff boredom and frustration can lead to quality problems and worse.

The main task for designers of product layout is to ensure that each work station has a similar capacity so that a smooth flow can be achieved without any bottle-necks (i.e. constraints at one particular point). This task is termed line-balancing and requires that the activities at each work station be designed to take approximately the same time. This can be difficult if times vary due to the complexity or difficulty of a task. Where this is likely, designers often build in potential additional capacity (e.g. allowing a second operator to work at a work station or having a parallel work station available). An example of the latter would be where a second cash desk is opened at busy times in a self-service cafeteria.

Group (or cellular) layout

This arrangement is really an attempt to gain the advantages both of variety and flexibility of a process layout and of smooth flow, high volume and low unit cost of a product layout. A group layout is based on the concept of providing dedicated specialist areas containing all the necessary equipment, staff and other resources required to produce a range of similar goods or services.

In manufacturing this is often referred to as 'group technology'. 'Families' of products are identified on the basis of similar processing requirements. Each family is produced by a dedicated group of equipment and staff. Such groups are formed into 'cells', with individual cells often arranged in product layout for line processing. Cells often use U-shaped layouts to facilitate easy movement of staff between machines, potentially improving labour efficiency. Service examples of group layout

A cellular layout in a retail store

CASE STUDY Baleno: Natural but maybe not so simple

In the ten years since its launch in 1996, Baleno has established itself as one of Asia's leading apparel retailers. Baleno has become one of the biggest and fastest growing brands in the casual wear market. It has approximately 3,000 shops throughout mainland China, Hong Kong, Taiwan, Singapore, South East Asia and the Middle East. The brand offers a wide range of casual wear with the emphasis on 'value for money' for the mass market. Baleno aims to become one of the largest fashion retail enterprises in Asia. Its shops are bright and clean and the company strives to offer excellent in-store customer service.

Yet visiting Baleno stores in different cities does not guarantee the same customer experience. Whilst a similar layout using almost identical equipment may be used, the operation of different stores can be very different.

Let us take the example of a store in a city within a more advanced economy, such as Hong Kong. A typical layout with staffing levels is shown in Figure 7.9.

In advanced economies, wage rates tend to be high and so there is pressure on retailers to minimize the number of staff employed in their stores. Therefore, staff numbers are strictly controlled. Also, employees are expected to exhibit a high degree of multi-tasking, with everyone being able to undertake every role (greeting, selling, cashier and fitting).

In contrast, the shops with similar physical size in cities within less developed economies, such as much of mainland China, more staff are in evidence (see Figure 7.10). Typically there might be two workers acting as sellers, and two employed as cashiers. One of the cashiers would be the shop-manager, enabling a high level of supervision over the other workers in the shop to be achieved. This close supervision is in part

FIGURE 7.9 Shop layout and staffing in an advanced economy

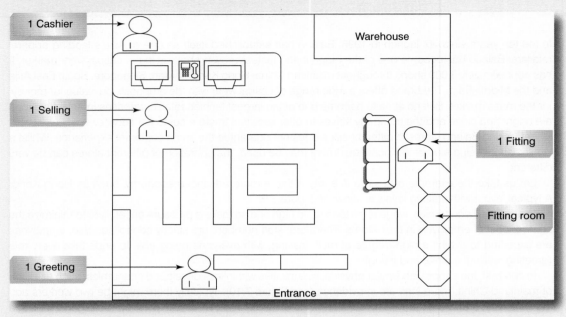

FIGURE 7.10 Shop layout and staffing in a less developed economy

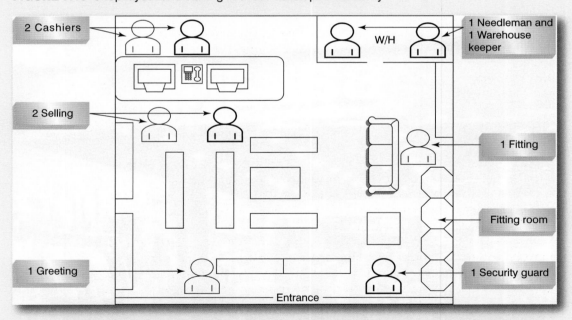

to deter and detect any dishonest behaviour amongst the staff. Two workers would be employed in the back office; one as a stock-keeper, the other as a 'needleman' to make any necessary alterations to garments for customers. The shop would also employ one or more security guards to deter shoplifting and pickpocketing, which can be a major problem in some cities.

These staffing arrangements support a much greater degree of labour specialization, with workers sticking to their designated roles. The advantage of this is that workers can very quickly be trained in a single task, and hence the quality of service to customers can be more easily assured.

Pay rates are much lower in mainland China. For example, junior sales staff might earn the equivalent of US$200 per month in Guangzhou, compared to nearly US$800 in Hong Kong. Staffing arrangements also reflect cultural attitudes towards shopping. Mainland Chinese customers, especially in Northern China, prefer attentive personal service from shop staff, whereas customers in Hong Kong display a more Westernized attitude, preferring a higher degree of self-help.

Baleno is by no means unique in its approach to retail operations. Other casual wear retailers operating in the same markets, such as Esprit, Giordano, Bossini and U2, also make similar adaptations in their staffing arrangements to suit local conditions.

(Source material Melody Mok Pui Ling and Baleno Holdings website http://www.baleno.com.hk)

WWW.

Questions (Suggested answers can be found on the companion website www.thomsonlearning.co.uk/barnes)

1   What type of layout is evidenced in Baleno stores?

2   What type of process is evidenced in Baleno stores?

3   Assess the way that external factors influence the staffing arrangements in different Baleno stores.

WWW.

would include the 'shop-within-a-shop' concept in retailing, which seeks to provide customers with a full range of goods for particular specialist requirements (e.g. all sports goods, clothing and equipment). In the same way, a hospital maternity unit is a grouping of resources dedicated to providing a service to a clearly identified group of 'customers' (i.e. women giving birth).

The advantages of group layouts are their high throughput and greater flexibility. Staff motivation is likely to be high as the arrangement offers the advantages of specialization without the disadvantages of a limited range of short-cycle repetitive job tasks. The disadvantages are the costs of setting up such an arrangement and the higher capital investment required for additional equipment. Equipment utilization may also be low.

QUEUING SYSTEMS

As discussed in Chapter 6, queues arise whenever an operation fails to meet demand instantaneously, even if average capacity is greater than average demand. Waiting times are caused by fluctuations in arrival rates and variability in processing times. Thus, unless arrival rates and processing times are known and constant, queuing is virtually inevitable and can occur in any process and with any layout type. The physical layout of a queuing system can have an impact on both the efficiency and effectiveness of a customer processing operation. The configuration adopted will determine the quantity of transforming resources required and influence the processing rates achievable. It will also impact on the behaviour and perceptions of those waiting in line and thereby influence the level of customer satisfaction achieved. There are a number of commonly used queuing systems. Three of these are described below and illustrated in Figure 7.11.

Single line single server

This is the simplest queuing system. As it relies on a single server, both its processing capability and capacity are limited to that of the technology and its operator. The advantage from the service provider's point of view is that capital investment is limited to a single piece of equipment. However, if processing times are long and processing tasks variable, queues may soon become unacceptably long, as the system has little flexibility.

FIGURE 7.11 Three common simple queuing systems

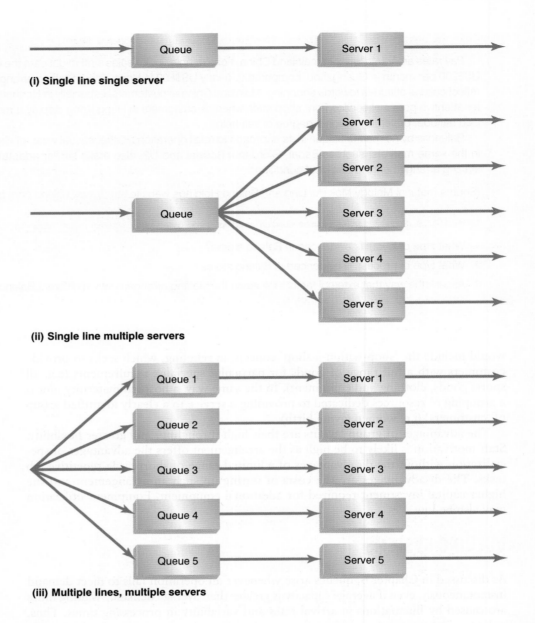

(i) Single line single server

(ii) Single line multiple servers

(iii) Multiple lines, multiple servers

Single line multiple servers

In this system, all customers are directed to a single waiting line. When they reach the head of the queue, they then go to the first available server. The advantages are that the wait is seen to be fair by customers and the line moves quickly. However, it increases the chance of customers baulking as they may see a very long line on arrival. This system requires higher levels of capital expenditure and staffing. It also needs each serving point to have the flexibility to deal with every task.

Multiple lines, multiple servers

In this system, customers must choose a line. This can cause frustration and customers jumping from queue to queue, or even reneging if they choose a slow moving line. One advantage with this system is that it does enable particular servers to offer specialist services or cater for specific types of customers.

There are mathematical models that describe the behaviour of most queuing systems, and simulation techniques can be used to model the performance of unique queuing situations. Both these approaches are beyond the scope of this book.

The psychology of queuing

Queues can arise in any process whether for materials, information or customers. However, unlike materials and information, people have feelings. It therefore makes sense to take their psychological needs into account when considering what type of queuing system to use. Surprisingly little research has been conducted into the psychology of queuing. In what is probably the best known piece of work on the subject, Maister (1985) argues that people's perception about the length of their wait is more important than the actual time spent waiting. He offers the following eight principles of the psychology of queuing, which can be used by service providers to increase satisfaction amongst queuing customers.

1 *Unoccupied time feels longer than occupied times.* Thus, it is important to keep waiting customers occupied in some way to take their mind off the wait. Maister recommends that the waiting activity should be perceived to be of value by the waiters and to relate to the service they are waiting for. For example, some theme parks show videos of the ride that customers are waiting to board.

2 *Pre-process time feels longer than in-process waits.* This is because waiting customers are anxious to know that they will soon gain admittance to the service delivery system. Thus, they like to have their presence acknowledged in a way that recognizes that the service has started in some way. For example, a restaurant might usher waiting customers into a bar area, offering them a drink and handing them the menu.

3 *Anxiety makes the wait seem longer.* This can be anxiety about when, and even if, the waiter will be served and/or about what the service itself will be like. Thus, it is important to provide information about the queue and the service. The issue of anxiety can also explain why some people are unhappy about multiple queue systems – it usually seems that you have chosen the slowest moving queue.

4 *Uncertainty makes the wait seem longer.* This is related to the issue of anxiety. It is always better to let people know how long their wait is likely to be. This also explains why most people are happier with appointment systems.

5 *Unexplained waits seem longer than explained ones.* Again, people will be less anxious and more tolerant if they know why they are being kept waiting.

6 *Unfair waits seem longer than fair ones.* People normally accept the principle of first come first served, so any perceived queue jumping is generally not well received. Thus, single queues are preferable in most circumstances.

7 *The more valuable the service, the longer people will wait.* People are more tolerant of long waits if the service is valuable to them. Conversely, there is little tolerance of waits for services that are of little value.

8 *Solo waits seem longer than waiting in a group.* This is because group interactions make the time go quicker. Servers might consider giving priority to solo customers. They might also take actions that encourage interaction between waiters, making them seem less alone.

Whilst few people actually like waiting in line, designing queuing systems with these principles in mind can help reduce the dissatisfaction felt by customers who cannot be served immediately.

SUMMARY OF KEY POINTS

Materials processing technologies can be classified as designing, forming, moving or integrating technologies.

Customer processing technologies involve the interaction of customers with the service provider's technology. These interactions can be passive, active or supported.

Information processing technologies are in essence synonymous with the use of computers, which are increasingly connected via the Internet. Most organizations have incorporated the use of the Internet within their business operations.

There are five ways (five levels) in which IT can be used to transform business operations: localized exploitation, internal integration, business process redesign, business network redesign and business scope redefinition.

Decisions about what type of process technology to use need to consider the volume and variety of the intended output, the fit with existing technology and the level of maturity of the technology.

There are three dimensions to process technology: its scale, its degree of automation and its degree of integration.

Organizations can be broadly classified as either technology leaders or technology laggards with regard to their approach to new technology adoption. Either stance can constitute a viable strategy.

Deciding whether to transfer process technology to a particular location requires an assessment of both the transferability of the technology and the appropriateness of the context where the technology will be operated.

Processes can be categorized according to the volume and variety that they are suited to producing. For manufactured goods, there are five generic process types: project, jobbing, batch, mass and continuous. For services there are three: professional services, service shops and mass services.

There are four generic layout types for process equipment: fixed position, process layout, group (or cell) layout and product layout. Choice of layout depends on process type, and output volume and variety.

Queuing is probably inevitable in any process, whether for materials, customers or information. There are many different queuing configurations which can be used to try to minimize queuing times and make effective use of resources. When queues involve customers waiting in line, consideration needs to be given to the psychology of waiting.

WWW.

EXERCISES (Suggested answers can be found on the companion website www.thomsonlearning.co.uk/barnes)

1 What are the main factors that need to be taken into account when deciding what type of process technology to use in an operation?

2 What types of materials processing technologies are likely to be used in highly automated factories? What types of products are likely to be most easy to manufacture using highly automated technology?

3   Visit a large service organization (e.g. a retailer, a theme park, a mass transit system) as a customer. What customer processing technologies do you encounter? What type of customer-technology encounters are these? How effective are the technologies that you encountered?

4   How have some organizations used Internet ICT to transform their business operations in the following industries:

   a   Air travel
   b   Book publishing
   c   Recorded music
   d   Grocery retailing

5   Use the volume-variety model to explain the difficulties inherent in designing a process to achieve high volume and high variety.

6   Visit a large branch of a retail bank. Which of the generic process types can you see in operation? How appropriate do these processes seem to be for the volume and variety of output you observe?

7   What type of layout would you expect to see in the following operations:

   a   TV manufacture
   b   The kitchen of a large luxury hotel
   c   A telephone call centre
   d   An aircraft manufacturer

8   Think of an example of queuing that you have recently experienced as a customer. To what extent did the service delivery system utilize Maister's principles of the psychology of queuing to improve your wait?

9   What factors should an organization take into account in determining whether it should be a technology leader or technology laggard with regard to its adoption of new process technology?

10 What are likely to be the most significant factors that a company will need to take into account when considering transferring some of its manufacturing process technology from an advanced Western country (e.g. Europe or North America) to:

   a   A rapidly developing country, such as China or Brazil
   b   A less developed country, such as Nigeria or Indonesia

CASE STUDY EXERCISE Nuovo Pignone

Nuovo Pignone SpA (NP) was founded as a cast iron foundry in Florence in 1842. More recently it has focused its activities within the mechanical engineering industry, especially the provision of power-generating plants. After enduring several changes of ownership, Nuovo Pignone was acquired in 1994 by the US-based conglomerate General Electric (GE), becoming part of its Energy division, one of the world's leading suppliers of power generation and energy delivery technology. Today, NP is part of GE's Oil & Gas business unit, and is one of the world's major suppliers of products (turbo machinery, compressors, pumps, static equipment, metering systems, etc.) and service solutions (including full turnkey plant) to the oil and gas industry. NP's main customers are the big players in the oil and gas industry, both in production, transportation and processing.

   NP's headquarters are still in Florence and are also the headquarters of the whole Oil & Gas business unit, which employs 5,600 people in over 60 sites worldwide and has an installed base of over 40,000 units.

ICT like this CAD system enables designers to work together anywhere in the world

Although NP's activities do result in the production of physical goods, its business is based on service provision as its key operations consist of engineering and design. All the products that NP designs belong to one of a number of pre-defined families of products. However, every order is designed to meet the unique needs of the customer for a plant with specific characteristics based on meeting strict qualitative and financial requirements. Therefore, the competitive advantage of NP, like every other engineering company, lies in its ability to adapt a portfolio of standardized solutions to the specific requirements of the purchaser. To achieve this result, NP needs to have excellent engineering competences in the design and production of individual components and of whole systems and plants.

Nevertheless, these engineering activities also include many routine and low-value tasks, which are repeated in spite of the peculiarities of the project and do not require a particularly high level of competences. These include the production and correction of the detailed design drawings. These tasks were obvious candidates for outsourcing; initially to other Italian subcontractors and then to foreign companies. By taking advantage of the lower hourly rates of pay offered by these firms, NP can obtain a significant cost savings. Outsourcing also enables NP's engineers to focus their efforts on more valuable activities. NP uses its Italian subcontracting partners as a way of flexing the capacity of its design operations, adjusting the flow of outsourced activities according to the dynamic of the orders. It has fairly loose arrangements with these firms, who continue to make themselves available for work from NP despite the absence of any formal long-term agreement or predetermined obligation for the amount of work that they might receive.

NP does, however, have long-term contracts with its foreign subcontractors. After its acquisition by GE, NP inherited GE's affiliation with two engineering companies, one Mexican, one Indian, which were already global partners of the US conglomerate. GE had a long-standing policy of outsourcing. Consequently, outsourcing levels in NP rose considerably after the acquisition. Today, NP outsources more than 50 per cent of its engineering-hours.

It is worth emphasizing that subcontract partners have been able to improve their capabilities over time. The improvement in their performances has enabled NP to outsource increasingly valuable activities, moving them from merely the correction of drawings to, for example, the design of specific components. This has been possible thanks to NP's constant efforts to facilitate the professional development of its partners. This has included enabling NP engineers to join Italian subcontractors and seconding NP staff to foreign partners to ensure that they benefit from their experience thereby gaining competences. Managing these types of relationships is generally acknowledged to be particularly challenging in knowledge-intensive companies. It is invariably difficult to transfer knowledge when it is only partially codified. In engineering design, knowledge is based not only on the specific knowledge of individuals, but also on the experiences they have developed during their working-life. In other words, it takes more than knowing how CAD software works to be an engineer. Partnering with foreign companies is even more problematic than that with domestic firms. Due to physical distance, it is much more complicated to transfer knowledge through personal contact between individuals. It is particularly difficult to obtain homogeneous behaviour and performances from the partners and to control the results of the outsourced activities.

With a foreign partner, even the apparently simple task of transferring documents and drawings is not easy. If performed in a traditional (i.e. non-digital) way, it takes a lot of time and has very high costs. That explains why international co-operation has been strongly enhanced by the application of ICT to business processes and by the development of specific software tools and applications.

One ICT application concerns the communication systems between NP's Italian offices and its foreign partners. This enables documents to be transmitted and provides communication between people, who seldom, if ever, meet and get to know each other. With respect to documents, external partners are granted access to specific sections of NP's Intranet, including archives of past projects. In this way they can download very large and complex documents in real-time at no cost – a great advantage compared to relying on traditional approaches. Previously, an Indian engineer, who needed to refer to a past project, would have had to ask an Italian colleague to look for it in the physical archive. The Italian collaborator would have then searched for the drawings, made a paper-copy and mailed them to India. This was clearly costly and time-consuming. Today, however, once digitized, this knowledge can be easily and rapidly accessed and shared from anywhere in the world.

Another important ICT application is interpersonal communication between employees. Here the tools are based on those in common use, such as e-mailing clients and messenger-like software, but enhanced with specific functions. For example, in NP's software environment it is possible to not only share files, servers or printers but also to see the screen displays of a colleague. This means that two colleagues, say one in Italy and one in India, can see the same images on their screens and interact with each other, supported by a textual or even a video chat-room. This way, the 'expert' (usually the Italian engineer) guides and corrects the 'beginner' (usually the Indian) in the execution of his tasks, pointing to those portions of the drawing on the screen which are incorrect, and commenting on them by chat or word of mouth. If only in a virtual fashion, the two colleagues are 'together' and their shared work is thus both more efficient and effective.

Another very interesting application is the CAD software, Unigraphic. This 3-D evolution of the well-known AutoCAD is characterized by a very high potential of customization. In NP, all staff involved in a project work on a shared centralized server and operators have different individual access rights, according to their role in the project. By giving wider or narrower rights, the project manager can strictly guide each person's work. For example, the project manager can select, from amongst different Unigraphic libraries, those items (e.g. basic components such as pipes, gaskets, bolts, etc.) that each operator is allowed to use, choosing those which meet the specific requirements for the project in terms of dimensions, materials or technical characteristics. Those requirements are usually set by the customer (who, for example, only wants stainless steel), by NP itself or by national or international standards. By limiting the tool-kit of the designer engineer, the project manager can minimize the risk of error from a colleague who may be working very far away. The project manager does not have to check that the right components have been used in the drawing; the software simply does not allow wrong components to be included.

By combining 2-D and 3-D rendering effects, Unigraphic also supports NP's partners' learning processes in new and original ways. A typical problem of NP's Indian partners is that their engineers usually work on the design of production plants they have only seen on screen. Therefore, they only have very partial knowledge of the practical problems related to the plant assembly or the management of space in the facility. As a consequence of this lack of direct experience, trivial mistakes are possible, such as making a pipe run in a corner where it will be very hard to assemble. The software helps overcome such problems because it shows the assembly process in 3-D, one piece at a time. This is so realistic that the virtual experience is typically sufficient to suggest a satisfactory solution for the designer.

The use of the same software by NP and its partners on a global scale also makes a decisive contribution to the simplification of international teamworking as it imposes common standards in data format, tools and routines. The last link of the chain, in this sense, is the interface between Unigraphic and CAM (computer aided management) software. This makes it possible to manage the whole production process of components, from design to manufacturing, in digital space. This also helps NP address the problem of control of foreign partners. The Internet-based software is fully integrated with NP's internal information system, and so enables the Italian project manager to check the progress of the subcontractor, including their cost and quality, and to monitor information flows, revision processes, and so on.

NP is currently extending its use of ICT. First, it is building new software, which will be able to automatically design the assembly of a plant or component, according to the items selected by the operator. Second, it is developing checklist software, to verify that the Bill of Materials includes all items and sub-items (screws, gaskets, bolts, etc.) required for the project. This is aimed at minimizing the risk that the designer forgets some minor, but decisive, items that should have been included. For example, if a flange coupling is requested, the software will ensure that the specific gaskets are included in the Bill of Materials, thereby avoiding the ensuing problems during assembly.

Finally, NP is continuing to develop the internationalization of its operations. So far, this has been confined to the international outsourcing of low value-added activities. NP is now considering about the next phase. This would involve what might be termed 'localized insourcing'. GE has created a new engineering centre in Bangalore, India. This has all the expertise necessary to perform a full range of engineering design tasks, including high value activities. This centre will, in turn, outsource low-value activities to external Indian partners. Some of these could possibly be the same companies that now work with NP and whose relationship with the Italian company could progressively fade away. With such a configuration, the Indian engineers are in all respects GE employees. This should safeguard the company's precious know-how but at a lower cost than that of their Italian colleagues. If the first step was a typical example of outsourcing of simple and recurring tasks, the second represents a new challenge for international activities. It is a move ahead towards a more complete global structure, where emerging markets, such as India, are no longer treated as a supply of 'low-cost low-level' labour force, but as a local platform for high-value activities. To achieve this result, a key factor is undoubtedly the knowledge transfer from the headquarters (in this case, Italy) to the local units (India), and the role of ICT in this process will be, again, crucial.

—*Riccardo Spinelli*

Questions (Suggested answers can be found on the companion website www.thomsonlearning.co.uk/barnes)

1 What are the main features of the technology used by Nuovo Pignone in its engineering and design operations?

2 What factors led NP to adopt this type of technology for these operations?

3 Categorize NP's use of ICT using Venkatraman's five levels of IT enabled business transformation model.

4 Critically assess the role of ICT in the relationships between NP and its Indian partners.

5 What are the advantages and disadvantages for NP in outsourcing to India?

References

Dussauge, P., Hart, S. and Ramanantsoa, B. (1992) *Strategic Technology Management,* New York: Wiley.

Froehle, C.M. and Roth, A.V. (2004) 'New measurement scales for evaluating perceptions of technology mediated customer service experience', *Journal of Operations Management* 22(1):1–21.

Grant, E.B. (1999) *Fitness for Transfer,* Cambridge: Institute for Manufacturing.

Grant, E.B. and Gregory, M. (1997) 'Adapting manufacturing processes for international transfer', *International Journal of Operations and Production Management* 17(10):994–1005.

Hayes, R.H. and Wheelwright, S.C. (1984) *Restoring our Competitive Edge: Competing through Manufacturing,* New York: Wiley.

Johnston, R., Chambers, S., Harland, C., Harrison, A. and Slack, N. (1993) *Cases in Operations Management,* London: Pitman.

Maister, D.H. (1985) 'The psychology of waiting lines', in J.A. Czepiel, M.R. Solomom and C.F. Surprenant (Eds), *The Service Encounter,* Lexington, Ma.: Lexington Press, 113–123.

Poon, S. and Swatman, P. (1999) 'An exploratory study of small business Internet commerce issues', *Information and Management* 35:9–18.

Schmenner, R. (1986) 'How can service business survive and prosper?', *Sloan Management Review,* Spring, 21–32.

Venkatraman, N. (1994) 'IT-enabled business transformation: from automation to business scope redefinition', *Sloan Management Review,* Winter, 73–87.

Additional reading

Anupindi, R., Chopra, S., Deshmukh, S.D., van Mieghem, J.A. and Zemel, E. (1999) *Managing Business Process Flows,* Upper Saddle River, NJ: Prentice Hall.

Evans, P. and Wurster, T. (2000) *Blown to Bits: How the New Economics of Information Transforms Strategy,* Boston: Harvard Business School Press.

Hammer, M. (1997) *Beyond Reengineering: How the Process-Centered Organization Is Changing Our Work and Our Lives,* New York: Harper Business.

Useful websites

www.mas.dti.gov.uk The website of the Manufacturing Advisory Service of the UK government's Department of Trade and Industry. Practical advice and case studies from UK manufacturing companies.

http://www.bptrends.com The website of Business Process Trends, an organization that aims to provide news and information relating to all aspects of business process change, focused on trends, directions and best practices.

http://bmi.omg.org The website of The Business Modeling & Integration Domain Task Force, which promotes the development and use of inter- and intra-enterprise computer integration systems.

WWW.

CHAPTER 8

THE SUPPLY NETWORK

INTRODUCTION

In Chapter 1, the concept of the supply network was introduced. This seeks to place an organization's operations in the context of the relationship with those organizations that supply its resource inputs and those that receive its outputs (whether goods or services). Organizations have always purchased some of their resource inputs from external suppliers. However, in recent years their relationships with suppliers have become increasingly important to many organizations due to the increasing use of outsourcing and off-shoring. More organizations have been increasing the proportion of inputs that they purchase from suppliers as compared to those they generate themselves. Also, supply networks have become more global in nature. More and more organizations are sourcing their supplies from outside of their own countries. Similarly, many organizations have been setting up their own facilities in other countries. These factors have tended to create extended and more complex supply networks, making them much more difficult to manage. Managing supply networks involves managing relationships with suppliers both individually and collectively across the supply network as a whole. Thus, managing the supply network has never been so challenging and yet so important for operations managers.

This chapter will examine some of these most important issues.

LEARNING OBJECTIVES

On completion of this chapter, you should be able to:

Describe the key issues in the configuration and co-ordination of supply networks.

Explain the basis and importance of outsourcing decisions.

Discuss the implications of global sourcing.

Outline the different approaches to managing supplier relationships.

CASE STUDY: Dell's supply chain symphony

In his best selling book *The World is Flat: A Brief History of the Twenty-first Century*, Thomas Friedman describes the manufacture of his notebook computer by Dell (an Inspiron 600m) as an example of a global supply network in action. From his home in Maryland, USA, he phoned his order to one of Dell's sales representatives, who then emailed the details to Dell's notebook factory in Malaysia (one of six Dell factories around the globe). Friedman then lists the sources of the main components used in the assembly of his order.

The Intel microprocessor came from an Intel factory either in the Philippines, Costa Rica, Malaysia, or China. The memory came from a Korean-owned factory in Korea (Samsung), a Taiwanese-owned factory in Taiwan (Nanya), a German-owned factory in Germany (Infineon), or a Japanese-owned factory in Japan (Elpida). My graphics card was shipped from either a Taiwanese-owned factory in China (MSI) or a Chinese-run factory in China (Foxconn). The cooling fan came from a Taiwanese owned factory in Taiwan (CCI or Auras). The motherboard came from either a Korean-owned factory in Shanghai (Samsung), a Taiwanese-owned factory in Shanghai (Quanta), or a Taiwanese-owned factory in Taiwan (Compal or Wistron). The keyboard came from either a Japanese-owned company in Tianjin, China (Alps), a Taiwanese-owned factory in Shenzhen, China (Sunrex), or a Taiwanese-owned factory in Suzhou, China (Darfon). The LCD was made in either South Korea (Samsung or LG.Philips LCD), Japan (Toshiba or Sharp), or Taiwan (Chi Mei Optoelectronics, Hannstar Display, or AU Optronics). The wireless card came from either an American-owned factory in China (Agere) or Malaysia (Arrow), or a Taiwanese-owned factory in Taiwan (Askey or Gemtek) or China (USI). The modem was made by either a Taiwanese owned company in China (Asustek or Liteon) or a Chinese-run company in China (Foxconn). The battery came from an American-owned factory in Malaysia (Motorola), a Japanese-owned factory in Mexico or Malaysia or China (Sanyo), or a South Korean or Taiwanese factory in either of those two countries (SDI or Simplo). The hard disk drive was made by an American-owned factory in Singapore (Seagate), a Japanese-owned company in Thailand (Hitachi or Fujitsu), or a Japanese-owned factory in the Philippines (Toshiba). The CD/DVD drive came

from a South Korean-owned company with factories in Indonesia and the Philippines (Samsung); a Japanese-owned factory in China or Malaysia (NEC); a Japanese-owned factory in Indonesia, China, or Malaysia (Teac); or a Japanese-owned factory in China (Sony), The notebook carrying bag was made by either an Irish-owned company in China (Tenba) or an American-owned company in China (Targus, Samsonite, or Pacific Design). The power adapter was made by either a Thai-owned factory in Thailand (Delta) or a Taiwanese-, Korean-, or American-owned factory in China (Liteon, Samsung, or Mobility). The power cord was made by a British-owned company with factories in China, Malaysia, and India (Volex). The removable memory stick was made by either an Israeli-owned company in Israel (M-System) or an American-owned company with a factory in Malaysia (Smart Modular).

(Friedman, 2006, pp. 517–518)

His computer duly arrives at his house some 13 days later. It would have arrived in 4 days but for a delay in the availability of a wireless card for the machine, due to a quality control problem. Nonetheless Friedman still marvels at what he terms Dell's 'supply chain symphony', considering it to be one of the wonders of the modern world. All the more so as Dell make over 140,000 computers every day.

WWW.

Questions (Suggested answers can be found on the companion website www.thomsonlearning.co.uk/barnes)

1 What are the biggest challenges for Dell in managing its global supply network?

2 Why does Dell have more than one source for some of its components?

3 What advantages does Dell gain from having its suppliers located in several different countries? Are there any disadvantages?

THE CONFIGURATION OF THE SUPPLY NETWORK

A supply network is the set of interconnected relationships between all the parties that supply inputs to, and receive outputs from an operation. Operations managers often focus on the activities within their own local operation or, at best, on the links with their immediate suppliers and immediate customers. However, in order to gain maximum benefits, they need to take a holistic perspective of the entire supply network. The success of any supply network depends on its ability to satisfy the needs of the ultimate customer, the end consumer of its products and services. Therefore, the network as a whole needs to be designed and managed in a way that enables it to do so as efficiently and effectively as possible. It is not just the organization's own operations that need to be managed strategically to meet customer needs, but also all the elements of the supply chain, individually and collectively. This requires an analysis not only of each part of the network but also of the linkages between them.

Quite often organizations allow their supply networks to evolve over time, giving little thought to their configuration. This can result in some fairly unordered networks. Organizations may have hundreds or even thousands of immediate suppliers. They may deliver their products and service outputs to similarly large numbers of customers. If these are not the end consumers, they may reach them through a whole raft of different kinds of intermediaries. Figure 8.1 shows a very simplified diagrammatic representation of one such supply network.

Real life examples are inevitably much more complex and messy. The problem with such networks is that they require the management of a large number of relationships with many different organizations on both the supply and demand sides. Organizational managers typically find it difficult to give enough time to each of

supply network
The set of interconnected relationships between all the parties that supply inputs to and receive outputs from an operation (including the suppliers' suppliers and their suppliers etc. and the customers' customers and their customers etc.).

supply chain
An alternative term for a supply network.

FIGURE 8.1 A supply network

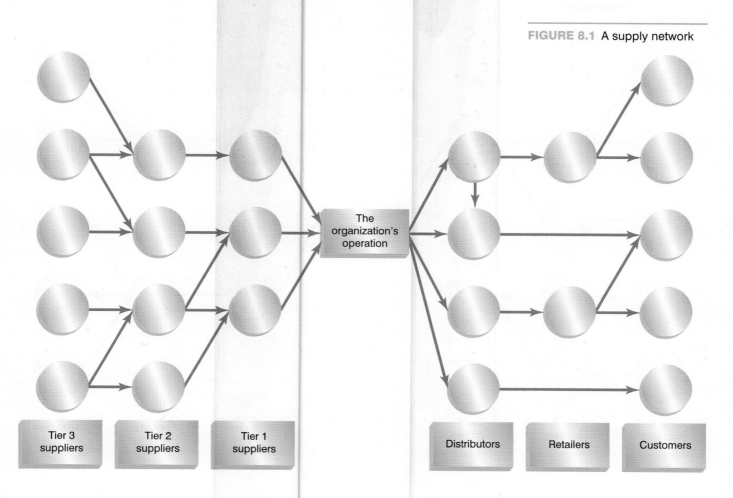

| Tier 3 suppliers | Tier 2 suppliers | Tier 1 suppliers | Distributors | Retailers | Customers |

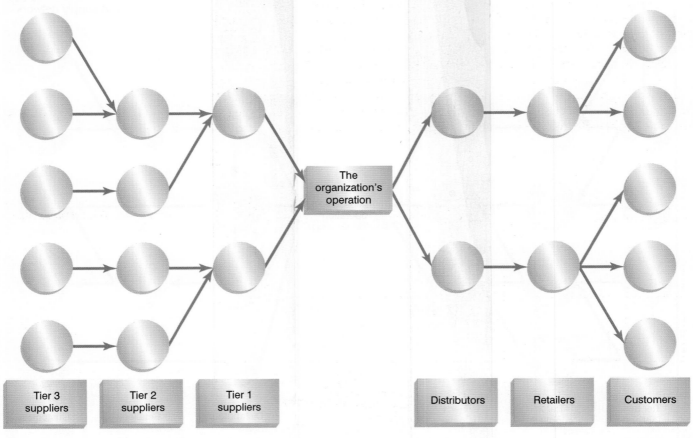

these relationships. Also, it can be difficult to get all parties to give due attention to the performance objectives required to meet the organization's strategic goals for the network. In short, managerial effort tends to be dissipated and focus is lost. In recent years there has been a growing realization that the first stage to tackling this issue is to rationalize both the supplier and customer bases.

On the supply side, the idea is to have fewer suppliers, with each one dedicated to supplying specific input resources. In manufacturing operations this might be a key raw material, component or sub-assembly. In service operations this might be a specific service, such as processing back office transactions or customer support. Some organizations go as far as reducing their supply base to a single supplier for any one input. With so many fewer suppliers, the buying organization is able to work much more closely with each immediate supplier. Relationships with these tier 1 suppliers can then be strengthened and deepened. Tier 1 suppliers assume the responsibility for managing the relationships with tier 2 suppliers and so on throughout the network.

On the demand side, the idea of reducing the customer base is not to reduce sales, but to carefully select those customers that offer the best growth prospects in the longer-term. The organization can then work closely with those customers to develop its sales-offering (i.e. its product/service package) in a way that best meets their needs and through them the needs of their customers and so on throughout the network. Sales to smaller and less important customers can be channelled indirectly through an intermediary further down the supply network.

Rationalizing the supply network, should also lead to lower transaction costs, as many fewer transactions should result (even though the value of each transaction is likely to increase). Figure 8.2 shows what the supply network in Figure 8.1 might look like once rationalized. The supply base has been reduced in number, enabling

tier 1 supplier

An immediate supplier to an organization, one that supplies directly to the organization. A tier 2 supplier supplies to a tier 1 supplier, and so on. The concept of tiers can also be applied to customers in the supply network. A tier 1 customer is one that is supplied directly from the organization's operations.

FIGURE 8.2 A rationalized supply network

Tier 3 suppliers

Tier 2 suppliers

Tier 1 suppliers

The organization's operation

Distributors

Retailers

Customers

the organization to strengthen its relationships with the remaining suppliers. The customer base has been rationalized so that the organization now sells exclusively through distributors, rather than the previous mixture of distributors, retailers and direct to end consumers. This not only reduces the number of relationships that need to be managed but also simplifies the basis of those relationships.

Rationalizing the supply network is not just a case of reducing the numbers of suppliers and customers. It also involves selecting who should be part of the supply network. This means selecting suppliers who have distinctive competencies in the production of the required resource input that support the organization's operations strategy. Whilst this might be the ability to achieve low costs, it might also be the ability to achieve high quality, fast delivery, dependable performance, flexibility, etc. Selecting suppliers also requires taking a future orientation as the world of business does not stand still. Organizations need to consider both how their own requirements of their suppliers might change in the future and how the competencies of the supplier might change over time. Selecting customers is to some extent a marketing issue, based on an assessment of their likely future purchasing requirements. However, the selection of customers should also take into account the ability of the supplying organization to meet their existing and future needs. This needs to be based on an assessment of the organization's existing distinctive competencies and how these will need to be developed in the future. In turn, these competencies will also depend upon the distinctive capabilities of the organization's suppliers.

THE CO-ORDINATION OF THE SUPPLY NETWORK

Maximizing the performance of the supply network also depends upon its effective co-ordination. The longer and more complex the network, the more difficult this is. A particular (and well known) problem experienced by those networks that supply physical goods is the so called 'bullwhip effect', first noted by Forrester (1961). This is the tendency for fluctuations in demand to be amplified as orders are placed successively back up a supply chain. This is due to the lags which occur between organization's recognizing the need for more resource inputs, placing an order and receiving the goods. Each stage in the chain tends to oscillate between over-ordering to compensate for the lag and avoid the risk of a stock-out and then ceasing to order as stocks build up. The invariable outcome of this (as illustrated in Figure 8.3)

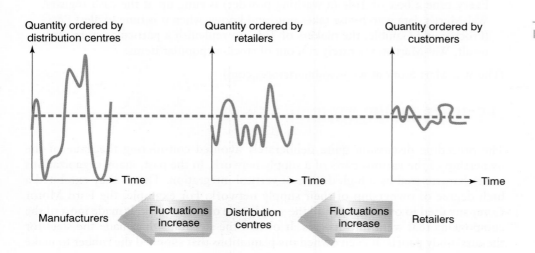

FIGURE 8.3 The bullwhip effect

is that factories are faced with either feast or famine, making scheduling difficult or impossible.

Steps which can be taken to reduce the impact of the bullwhip effect include:

- *Reducing the number of stages in the supply chain.* This might be done by eliminating intermediate warehouses or delivering directly from factory to retailer. Many B2C e-businesses deliver directly to customers, cutting out all intermediate stages.

- *Communicating end consumer demand directly to all stages of the supply chain.* This will help each stage in the network plan in the light of the full knowledge of known demand and existing orders and stock.

- *Reducing order sizes and increasing their frequency.* Reducing minimum order and delivery quantities will smooth out flows along the supply chain. Potential higher transport costs due to smaller batch sizes can be offset by consolidating orders for different products into each delivery.

- *Reducing delivery times.* Delays in ordering can be dramatically reduced by the use of ICT systems. Improving the efficiency of transportation systems can also speed delivery, as can the increased use of air freight for higher value items.

- *Reducing manufacturing lead times.* Improving the efficiency of manufacturing operations and decreasing batch sizes would help increase throughput.

- *Avoiding creating surges in demand due to price cutting and promotional campaigns.* Such campaigns often merely serve to bring forward demand rather than create new sales. Where such campaigns are deemed necessary there should be careful co-ordination between marketing and operations to try to mitigate the worst effects.

The basis of the successful co-ordination of a supply network is the integration of the activities of its various components to construct a seamless end to end process. This in turn depends upon accurate and up-to-date information being available throughout the network. This is probably the single most important factor in the operation of successful supply networks. Consequently, modern ICT networks that parallel the physical network are essential. Major retailers make use of electronic point of sale (EPOS) technology to trigger orders from their suppliers. Each time an item's barcode is swiped for payment at the checkout, the EPOS system notes the sale on a central database, so that the stock position for each item in each store is known in real time. The relevant part of the database is accessible to suppliers so that they can arrange to make and deliver replacement stock. As Wal-Mart's website explains:

> Every time a box of Tide (a washing powder) is rung up at the cash register, Wal-Mart's data warehouse takes note and knows when it is time to alert P&G (Proctor and Gamble, the makers of Tide) to replenish a particular store. As a result, Wal-Mart stores rarely run out of stock of popular items.

WWW.

(The Wal-Mart Story at www.walmartstores.com)

THE OUTSOURCING DECISION

The preceding discussion quite deliberately avoided considering the issue of the ownership of the various parts of a supply network. In the past, many organizations were characterized by a high degree of vertical integration. That is they exhibited a high degree of ownership of their supply network. For example, the Ford Motor Company used to own virtually all the supply side of its network. It made most of the components that went into its cars. It owned the steelmills that made the steel for the cars' body panels. It even owned the plantations that supplied the rubber to make the cars' tyres. Even today, some garment manufacturers own their own retail shops (e.g. Zara, Benetton, Laura Ashley). In recent years, however, there has been a trend for more organizations to outsource a greater proportion of their requirements. Much of this trend emerged from a desire to copy the sourcing practices of successful Japanese manufacturers, who typically outsource far greater proportions of their resource inputs than their Western counterparts. The trend has been further fuelled by the increased purchasing opportunities to source on a global rather than merely on a national scale. Increased outsourcing has also been driven by a belief that ownership is not a necessary pre-requisite for control, and that organizations might be better advised to concentrate their resources and efforts on their core activities. Furthermore, in today's business environment ownership of organizations and the business units of which they comprise is often not straightforward (e.g. alliances or joint ventures) and can change over time (e.g. through acquisitions or divestments). In many cases business units with a shared ownership are managed quite independently of each other even if they operate in the same industrial sector. As such, it is normally sensible to focus on the business unit as the unit of analysis of a supply network rather than the whole organization. The aim of taking a supply network perspective is to achieve integration across the supply network irrespective of the ownership of its constituents. This can be thought of as replacing vertical integration with virtual integration.

vertical integration
The extent to which an organization owns the operations of the suppliers and customers within its supply network.

Thus, the decision about exactly what goods and services should be outsourced and what should be produced in-house has assumed a much greater importance. The extent to which outsourcing should be used remains a hotly debated issue.

The advantages claimed for outsourcing include:

- *Reduced costs*. Assuming that a suitable supplier can be identified who is charging lower prices than the organization's own internal costs for the outsourced activity.

- *Use of the expertise of the supplier*. Outsourcing enables the organization to draw on expertise that it may not itself possess.

- *Better inventory control*. If the outsourced item is a physical good, then exact required quantities can be ordered as and when required, thereby reducing stockholding costs and facilitating improved inventory control.

- *Reduced capital employed*. The need to hold any raw material, component or work-in-progress stock for the outsourced item is eliminated. It may also be possible to reduce or eliminate the need for fixed assets required for its production, such as plant or machinery.

- *Reduced headcount*. Ceasing production of the outsourced item may well facilitate a reduction in headcount, which is often deemed desirable by many organizations.

- *More accurate operating costs*. Identifying the true cost of a single product or service is notoriously difficult, depending as it does on internal accounting conventions. Purchasing from an external source gives an unambiguous cost, namely the purchase price.

- *Concentrating on core business and activities*. Outsourcing non-core activities frees up internal resources to concentrate on more important activities. However, as discussed below, this assumes it is possible to identify what is core to the business.

The disadvantages claimed for outsourcing include:

- *Loss of control*. This is the argument on which vertical integration is based. It assumes that an organization can only truly control an activity if it is performed internally.

- *Quality control*. More specifically, proponents of keeping an activity in-house would argue that this is the only way that quality standards can be maintained.

- *Reliance on the supplier can lead to price rises and/or threaten continuity of supply*. The argument here is that once supply is moved externally, the supplier immediately gains a position of power. Even if the price is initially low, there is no guarantee that it will remain so. For example, the supplier might be attracted to more lucrative work with another purchaser. Similarly, future supplies may be threatened by events affecting the supplier. For example, there might be disruptions at the supplier's facilities or their suppliers. The supplier might be subject to a change of ownership, leading to amalgamation of facilities or even closure.

- *Managing the supplier*. Outsourcing is not cost free. There are management and administration costs associated with the purchasing process. Also the managerial skills required to manage an external supplier are very different from those required to manage an internal operation. Such skills may need to be developed or bought-in if the purchaser is to avoid being at a disadvantage to the supplier.

- *Under utilization of in-house resources*. Outsourcing may leave those in-house resources that were previously used to make the outsourced item underutilized. This will then negate economies of scale and have a perverse impact on unit costs, which can then create more pressure to outsource other activities. Any outsourcing needs to be done in such a way that remaining activities are not burdened with undue overheads.

- *Commercial secrecy at risk*. Allowing an external party to undertake work that allows them access to proprietary technology, knowledge or expertise is inherently risky. They may be tempted to use this directly themselves, or the knowledge may leak out to existing potential competitors or customers, putting the basis of the organization's competitive advantage at risk. This can be a particular problem if the supplier is based in a country with weak legal protection for intellectual property.

An additional and, in the longer-term, even greater danger is that outsourcing an activity previously performed internally will lead to the loss of in-house expertise, almost certainly irretrievably. The key issue here is not so much whether the loss may lead to a diminishing of competitive advantage immediately. It ought to be able to assess that. The greater danger is whether that expertise amounts to a core competence, which if developed and exploited could have led to future sources of competitive advantages for the organization. The originators of the term core competence, Prahalad and Hamel (1990) argue that an organization's core competences are those capabilities on which competitive advantage is or can be built. They are the collective learning of an organization and derive from an ability to co-ordinate diverse production skills and integrate multiple streams of technology. People are critical to core competences, and so they should be treated as corporate assets. However, unlike physical assets they do not deteriorate with use, rather they grow. Core competences are a mixture of skills, resources and processes, unique to the organization, which provide a capability that can be sustained over time. They amount to more than the skill of any single individual. They are invisible to competitors, difficult to imitate and few in number. Core competences are essential to the development of future products and services. As such, they need to be identified in order to discard any poorly thought through outsourcing decisions. Unfortunately, many of these 'make or buy' decisions (perhaps a better term is 'do or buy') have often been based on rather simplistic considerations of cost. The core competences perspective points to the need to take a broader, more strategic approach to the outsourcing decision.

Another approach aimed at gaining a greater understanding of the implications of an outsourcing decision, is that proposed by Dornier *et al.* (1998). It does this by assessing the *strategic value* and the *criticality* of any goods and services being considered for outsourcing. Its strategic value is the extent to which it provides the basis of

core competence

Something that an organization can do uniquely well. It is a capability that does or can form the basis of a competitive advantage. Core competences are the collective learning of an organization and derive from an ability to co-ordinate diverse production skills and integrate multiple streams of technology.

(ADAPTED FROM DORNIER *ET AL.*, 1998, P. 152)

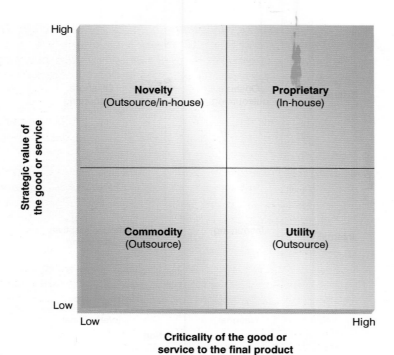

FIGURE 8.4 The outsourcing decision matrix

a competitive advantage in the market place. This is likely to be dependent upon its technical complexity, the extent to which it is based on proprietary technology. Its criticality is an indication of the contribution that it makes to the performance of the final product or service to which it contributes. This depends on its cost relative to the total cost of the final product and the extent to which the quality and reliability of the final product depends upon it. These two dimensions can be used to construct a 2 × 2 matrix (see Figure 8.4), which can be used to help inform the outsourcing decisions. The matrix identifies four types of goods and services as follows.

- *Proprietary:* Such goods and services are core products, likely to be based on the core competencies of the organization. As such, they should be kept in-house.
- *Commodity:* These are likely to be based on standardized and commonly available technology, and make a minimal contribution to the functionality of the final product. As such they are likely to be available at a low cost from a number of suppliers and so are best outsourced.
- *Novelty:* These are likely to be based on specialized and possibly restricted technology, but are not essential to the functioning of the final product. As such, these items are likely to operate in price insensitive markets where functionality and convenience are vital. The make or buy decision may be finely balanced. If suitable in-house expertise exists then it may be cheaper to produce in-house.
- *Utility:* These are critical to the final product but are based on readily available technology. They should be outsourced but only to a supplier who offers an adequate level of co-operation and service to ensure their availability.

GLOBAL SOURCING

For a number of years, researchers have been reporting that more and more organizations are sourcing more and more of their resource inputs from other countries (Babbar and Prasad, 1998; Trent and Monczka, 2005). This trend looks set to continue. As discussed in Chapter 4, off-shoring is the term used to describe the action

FIGURE 8.5 A typology of
outsourcing and off-shoring

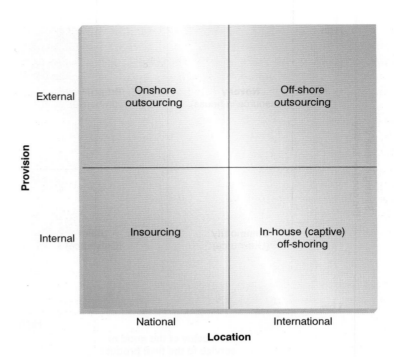

of moving some business operations to another country. This may or may not involve
outsourcing to another organization. When off-shoring is conducted within an operation owned by the organization it is sometimes termed 'in-house' or 'captive' off-
shoring, as compared to outsourced off-shoring. Figure 8.5 provides a framework to
clarify the terminology used in connection with outsourcing and off-shoring.

In one sense, deciding whether to source internationally is just an extension of the
decision about whether to outsource at all. However, an organization faces distinctive
challenges in managing a supply network that extends outside of its own country.

Monczka and Trent (1992) argue that the growth of global sourcing in an organization goes through four stages of development:

- *Stage 1: Domestic sourcing only.* The organization does not actively source
  from abroad, so it has little or no need for information on international
  sourcing. Any non-domestic goods that are purchased are sourced through
  domestic intermediaries.

- *Stage 2: Reactive international sourcing.* Direct international sourcing is
  undertaken because of some deficiency in the domestic supply market. This
  may be due to non-availability, poor quality, prohibitive prices, etc. As such
  the organization feels compelled to source internationally.

- *Stage 3: Proactive international sourcing.* International sourcing is undertaken
  as a matter of choice, driven by a desire to tap into global purchasing markets.
  This is often done as part of an organization's wider globalization strategy,
  underpinned by the belief that competing internationally requires international
  sourcing to gain the benefits of lower prices, improved quality, better service,
  etc.

- *Stage 4: Global sourcing networks.* Organizations that reach this stage are
  likely to be operating on a global basis with facilities in a number of different
  countries. This stage requires the organization to adopt a truly global mindset,
  rather than merely buying from suppliers in other countries. Consequently, it
  creates global sourcing networks based on worldwide purchasing systems.
  Purchasing requirements are integrated and co-ordinated across the whole
  organization and strategic relationships are developed with global suppliers.

Many organizations are initially attracted to purchase internationally on cost grounds. This has certainly been the case with much of the recent off-shoring of manufacturing to China and of IT and financial services to India. However, this may be a shortsighted view as there can be no guarantee that purchase prices will remain low. For example, there are already signs of inflationary pressure in China and India, with skills shortages leading to increased wage rates and higher labour turnover. Such conditions can also lead to quality problems, whether in manufacturing or service industries. However, there can be other benefits to be gained from global sourcing, including improved quality, increased capacity (to enable customer requirements for volume and delivery schedules to be satisfied), access to technological expertise and a broadening of the supply base. Global sourcing can enable the purchaser to tap into technological expertise that is not available domestically, or perhaps only at a much higher cost.

Some commentators maintain that the full benefits of off-shoring will only be realized by working jointly with overseas suppliers over the longer-term to build new capabilities. For example, Hagel and Brown (2005) point to the benefits that might be available from:

- *Different management techniques:* Organizations in newly industrialized and developing countries have lower wage rates that enable them to employ different management techniques that are too costly to deploy in more advanced economies. For example, higher supervision ratios enable managers to devote much more time to coaching workers and improving business processes.

- *Specialized ecosystems:* Overseas suppliers are supported by their own local business ecosystems (e.g. suppliers, customers, competitors, peers, bankers and knowledge networks). These comprise both formal and informal relationships that can provide a rich source of complimentary skills and resources that they can draw upon to develop and enhance their offerings to their customers.

- *Process networks:* By sourcing globally, the purchasing organization can create a global process network amongst its suppliers. Making connections between often far-flung enterprises has the potential to bring together what may at first appear to be a rather disparate collection of specialist capabilities. However, this can create opportunities for synergies with the potential to increase flexibility and enhance the potential for the creation of new products and services.

Despite the potential benefits, there can be problems with global sourcing. The initial challenge faced by purchasers seeking to source outside of their own country is in finding suitably qualified suppliers. Their knowledge of the supply market in other countries may well be limited. Research may be difficult in countries with limited disclosure requirements. Any language differences will also make this more complex. Also, once established, global supply networks are inherently more difficult to manage than domestic ones. The geographic distances involved can mean that transportation costs are increased where physical goods are involved. Also, because delivery lead times are likely to be much longer and less reliable, inventory levels will need to be increased to avoid the dangers of stock-outs. This might mean having to increase stocks of incoming raw materials and components. It might also mean the creation of new intermediate stocking points between the supplier and the purchaser's facility, for example a portside warehouse. This is bound to lead to increased costs. Despite the benefits of modern telecommunications including the Internet, geographical separation between purchaser and suppliers can lead to communication problems. Misunderstandings can still arise because of differences in language, culture or local working practices. Differences in time zones can exacerbate this. Suppliers based in less developed, and even newly industrialized countries, can experience problems due to shortcomings in transport infrastructure and telecommunications networks. They may also face labour skills shortages, inadequacies in their supplier base and lack technological support services for operating equipment. Global supply networks are also inherently more risky, as they may involve variability and uncertainty in currency exchange rates, economic and political instability, and changes in regulatory environments in different countries. These factors can amount to significant disincentives to sourcing from unfamiliar suppliers in other countries. Consequently, many organizations prefer to avoid such risks by dealing with tried and tested suppliers inside their own country, with whom they may have built up strong business relationships over many years.

The advent of improved ICTs, especially those allied to the Internet have enabled many service operations, as well as those in manufacturing, to be outsourced to off-shore locations. Off-shoring can be considered for separated services (see Chapter 3), as there is no need for face-to-face physical contact between the service provider and user. Many back office business processes are well-suited to outsourcing with suppliers in other countries. Like all outsourced operations, outsourcing service operations raises the concern about how the purchasing organization can maintain control. However, this can be particularly acute owing to the intangible nature of services. Many organizations have also been off-shoring front office services, especially call centre operations, where service operatives must speak directly with customers. Here the issue of control is even more problematic. Despite attempts to script interactions with customers, including the use of menu-driven computer programmed prompts for operatives, it is almost impossible to predetermine the course of a telephone interaction. Clearly, fluency in the appropriate language is a pre-requisite for operatives. However, there can be problems due to unfamiliar accents, colloquialisms and slang. In particular, the lack of a common cultural context in which to interpret certain words and phrases can lead to significant misunderstandings, or even complete incomprehension, between the two parties to the interaction. Without everyday familiarity with nuances of language created by local mass media, it is almost impossible for people situated remotely to keep pace with the dynamics of most languages. It might be possible to overcome such problems where relationships between individuals can be developed over time, as could be the case in the provision of business to business services. However, this is virtually impossible when servicing mass consumer markets.

Whether for manufacturing or services, international sourcing contains an inherent dilemma for purchasers. Whilst using a distant supplier may be able to offer the prospect of reduced purchasing prices and other possible benefits (access to increased capacity, additional technological expertise, etc.), they may not be able to offer the level of service and responsiveness available from a more local supplier. This could put the gains at risk if they are achieved at the expense of customer satisfaction.

RELATIONSHIPS WITH SUPPLIERS

A key facet of the supply network is the nature of the relationship between purchaser and supplier. Prompted by a desire to emulate the success of many Japanese companies, a profound shift in attitude towards this relationship has been occurring in many Western organizations over the last 20 years. This has seen a paradigm shift from what might be termed the *traditional* model of purchasing, largely based on an adversarial arm's length relationship between buyer and supplier, to a *partnership* model, based on a close and co-operative relationship between buyer and supplier.

The traditional model is characterized by a purchasing process in which a number of suppliers are invited to bid on a contract by contract basis for specified quantities of goods or services. The purchaser supplies a detailed specification of the goods or services required. The contract is generally awarded to the bidder with the lowest price, assuming that delivery schedules can be achieved. Once the contract is awarded, the purchaser is responsible for checking the quality of the goods or service received.

CASE STUDY India's ICICI OneSource goes near-shoring in Ulster

An Indian call centre company is to create 1,000 jobs in Belfast, reversing the trend of UK companies' off-shoring back office financial services tasks such as transaction processing to low-wage locations in the developing world. The announcement by ICICI OneSource, the business process outsourcing provider, is the latest in a series of investments in Northern Ireland by Indian companies.

Industry experts say it is a clear sign that banks and financial services companies that use outsourced labour in remote locations to reduce costs are starting to rethink the business model. The rethink comes at a time of growing concerns about the security of financial information and the incidence of computer-based fraud and other crime.

A recent survey on the impact of off-shoring by the Financial Services Authority (FSA) warned that off-shoring could contribute 'a material risk to the FSA objectives of market confidence, reduction of financial crime and consumer protection'. It identified as the main risk the complexity of achieving suitable manage-ment oversight and the difficulty of maintaining control from a distance. However, it concluded that with appropriate governance frameworks, risk management systems and controls, companies could mitigate the problems arising from off-shoring.

Peter Hain, Northern Ireland secretary, described the latest announcement as an example of 'near-shoring'. He said: 'Northern Ireland is clearly the most competitive near-shore option for companies seek-ing a base to service western European markets'.

Matthew Vallance, ICICI OneSource's managing director for Europe, said: 'We no longer see our business as being located all in India or all in the UK'. ICICI OneSource, based in Mumbai, has 7,500 staff in India, but half its global revenues derive from services provided for UK clients.

Experts say companies need to be nearer their clients – the computer groups and financial services companies – to offer quicker response times. India, with its good IT skills base, cheap wages and English-based business culture, has traditionally been a leading provider of this specialist business activity. According to Nasscom, India's main software trading body, India accounts for 44 per cent of the global outsourcing market, earning £9 billion a year.

The ICICI OneSource investment is the first greenfield call centre set up by an Indian call centre company in Northern Ireland, although last year HCL Technologies, another Indian company, acquired an existing business in the province. The ICICI centre is due to open next month. The company said it would generate £28 million for the local economy in terms of wages and salaries.

(Source: John Murray Brown, *Financial Times*, 14 June 2006)

WWW.

Questions (Suggested answers can be found on the companion website www.thomsonlearning.co.uk/barnes)

1 What are the main reasons listed for ICICI OneSource's decision to set up its Northern Ireland operations? Can you think of any other reasons?

2 What difficulties might ICICI OneSource face in managing its Northern Ireland call centre?

However, if any problems arise, it is the responsibility of the supplier to resolve them. On the other hand, the supplier would not seek to make improvements unless these were demanded by the purchaser. The financial benefits arising from such improvements would be the subject of negotiation between the two parties. As in this relationship, information is considered to be a source of power, and deemed to be proprietary. On the other hand, an organization adopting the partnership model is likely to adopt a very different approach to purchasing. In this case the purchaser is looking to build a long-term relationship with a supplier. Contracts will be placed using multiple criteria, with special emphasis being placed on the supplier's capabilities. If a bidding process is used at all, it will be with very few predetermined suppliers. In some cases only one supplier will be approached. The purchaser will set a performance-based specification, with the supplier expected to design a solution. Once the contract is in place, the supplier is expected to monitor the quality of the goods or services supplied. Any problems that arise are treated as a joint responsibility. Similarly, both parties are expected to work together continuously in seeking improvements, whose resulting benefits are shared equitably. Information is seen as a basis of improvement and so shared between the parties. Table 8.1 illustrates the main differences in these two approaches.

These characterize extreme forms of the two relationships. Many different intermediary positions can be observed in reality, with various mixtures of the practices described above in evidence.

An organization's approach to purchasing brings into sharp focus its attitude towards its suppliers. At the heart of the relationship between purchaser and supplier is the issue of whether both parties trust each other. This is encapsulated in the well-known management training exercise known as the 'Prisoner's dilemma'. In this a scenario is described in which you must imagine that you and a colleague are arrested and accused of a serious crime (e.g. a robbery). The police place you in separate rooms for questioning so that you and your colleague cannot communicate with each other. If you are both found guilty you will both go to jail for five years. However, you can only be convicted if one of you agrees to confess to the crime. The police decide to tempt both of you to cut a deal. They make the same offer to each of you, although neither of you know the offer made to the other. They offer to ensure

TRADITIONAL APPROACH	PARTNERSHIP APPROACH
Adversarial relationship	Co-operative relationship
Arm's length formal relationship	Close working relationship
Many suppliers	Few suppliers, often single sourcing for some items
Price the main purchasing criterion	Multiple purchasing criteria
Short-term contracts	Long-term contracts
Evaluation on bid by bid basis	Evaluation of supplier capability
Purchaser sets detailed specification of goods/services; supplier has little or no freedom in design specification	Purchaser sets performance specification; supplier designs goods/service to achieve the required performance
Purchaser responsible for quality inspection of goods/service received	Supplier responsible for quality
Problems are the suppliers' responsibility to solve	Problems are jointly solved
Improvements when demanded by buyer	Continuous improvements mutually sought
Improvement benefits shared by negotiation	Improvement benefits shared equitably
Information is proprietary	Information shared

TABLE 8.1 Traditional *vs* partnership approaches to purchasing

that if you confess, your sentence will be reduced to one year. Thus, there are four possible outcomes.

1 *You confess but your colleague does not:* You get one year and your colleague gets five years.

2 *Your colleague confesses but you do not:* You get five years and your colleague gets one year.

3 *You both confess:* You both get one year.

4 *Neither of you confesses:* You both go free.

A most successful outcome (from the prisoners' perspective) can only be achieved if both prisoners have complete trust that neither will confess. This is also the case in supply relationships. The partnership approach aims to achieve successful outcomes for both parties. But this depends on there being complete trust between purchaser and supplier. The extent to which such trust exists between real organizations in practice is difficult to determine. The best known and frequently cited examples of partnership supply relationships tend to be within supply networks centred on a single large (and hence powerful) purchasing organization such as a car manufacturer (e.g. Toyota) or supermarket (e.g. Wal-Mart), which has a large number of much smaller (and hence much weaker) suppliers. In these situations, it is usually the case that the purchaser is in an extremely powerful position in relation to the supplier. As such, it may be questionable whether their relationship can ever be a true partnership; and certainly not of equals.

CASE STUDY The Wal-Mart you don't know

Wal-Mart is not just the world's largest retailer. It's the world's largest company: bigger than ExxonMobil, General Motors and General Electric. The scale can be hard to absorb. Wal-Mart sold $244.5 billion worth of goods last year. It sells in three months what number two US retailer Home Depot sells in a year. And in its own category of general merchandise and groceries, Wal-Mart no longer has any real rivals. It does more business than Target, Sears, Kmart, J.C. Penney, Safeway and Kroger combined.

Wal-Mart wields its power for just one purpose: to bring the lowest possible prices to its customers. At Wal-Mart, that goal is never reached. The retailer has a clear policy for suppliers: on basic products that don't change, the price Wal-Mart will pay, and will charge shoppers, must drop year after year. Wal-Mart has the power to squeeze profit-killing concessions from vendors.

Wal-Mart makes the companies it does business with more efficient and focused, leaner and faster. Wal-Mart itself is known for continuous improvement in its ability to handle, move and track merchandise. It expects the same of its suppliers. But the ability to operate at peak efficiency only gets you in the door at Wal-Mart. Then the real demands start. The public image Wal-Mart projects may be as cheery as its yellow smiley-face mascot, but there is nothing genial about the process by which Wal-Mart gets its suppliers to provide tyres and contact lenses, guns and underarm deodorant at everyday low prices. Wal-Mart is legendary for forcing its suppliers to redesign everything from their packaging to their computer systems. It is also legendary for quite straightforwardly telling them what it will pay for their goods. It also is not unheard of for Wal-Mart to demand to examine the private financial records of a supplier, and to insist that its margins are too high and must be cut.

For many suppliers, though, the only thing worse than doing business with Wal-Mart may be not doing business with Wal-Mart. Last year, 7.5 cents of every dollar spent in any store in the United States (other than auto-parts stores) went to the retailer. That means a contract with Wal-Mart can be critical even for the largest consumer goods companies. Many suppliers cannot grow without finding a way to be successful with Wal-Mart. Many companies admit that supplying Wal-Mart is like getting into the company version of

Wal-Mart stores are not just in the USA

basic training with an implacable Army drill sergeant. The process may be unpleasant but there can be some positive results.

What does the squeeze look like at Wal-Mart? It is usually thoroughly rational, sometimes devastatingly so. Year after year for any product that is the same as that sold last year, Wal-Mart will say,

> 'Here's the price you gave me last year. Here's what I can get a competitor's product for. Here's what I can get a private-label version for. I want to see a better value that I can bring to my shopper this year or else I'm going to use that shelf space differently.'

The Wal-Mart squeeze means vendors have to be as relentless as Wal-Mart at managing their own costs. Perhaps the only way to avoid being trapped in a spiral of growing business and shrinking profits is to innovate. You need to bring Wal-Mart new products which are products that consumers need. Because with those, Wal-Mart doesn't have benchmarks to drive you down in price. They don't have historical data, you don't have competitors, and they haven't bid the products out to private-label makers. That's how you can have higher prices and higher margins.

(Excerpted from *Fast Company,* December 2003, Issue 77, p. 68, downloaded from www.fastcompany. com/homepage/index.html 2 August 2006)

Questions (Suggested answers can be found on the companion website www.thomsonlearning.co.uk/barnes)

1 What are the advantages and disadvantages of supplying to Wal-Mart?

2 To what extent is the relationship between Wal-Mart and its suppliers adversarial and to what extent co-operative?

Building the level of trust required for a successful partnership may well take time and need to be based on mutually beneficial experiences arising from close working relationships. This is likely to be that much more difficult if purchaser and supplier are separated by considerable distances, maybe on the other side of the globe, as is likely to be the case in international purchasing. This can be exacerbated if different time zones, languages and cultures are involved. Consequently, Gattorna (2006) argues that managers need to concentrate much more on improving the psychological ties that bind supply networks together. He maintains that human behaviour is as important as the physical infrastructure of ICT systems, facilities, vehicles, etc.

SINGLE *VS* MULTI-SOURCING

One of the most controversial aspects of partnership sourcing is whether an organization ought to have a single supplier or multiple suppliers for any given purchased good or service.

The advantage of single sourcing is the increased opportunity to build a deep and lasting relationship with the supplier whose commitment to the purchaser should be increased if they have the certainty of receiving orders over an extended period of time. Both parties should also benefit from economies of scale and reduced transaction costs. This should create an environment in which good communications between the two parties can be established. This should then make it easier to work together to solve problems, enhance quality and develop new products and services. A long-term commitment by both sides should also help alleviate any concerns about commercial confidentiality. The disadvantages are that both parties can become too dependent on each other. For the purchaser, this carries with it the risk of disruption in supply. They may also fear price increases if there is no competition. The risk for the supplier is that business will be lost if demand from the purchaser reduces (e.g. due to reduced sales by the purchaser).

WHEN THINGS GO WRONG When lightning strikes

The power of nature to provide the unexpected was vividly illustrated on 17 March 2000 at the Phillips plant in Albuquerque, New Mexico, USA when the furnace was hit by lightning and caught fire. The plant produces the semiconductors used by cell phones manufacturers such as Nokia, Lucent and Ericsson. Despite the fire itself being extinguished in less than ten minutes by the sprinkler system, the plant's clean rooms were totally destroyed. A cleanroom provides the ultra-clean environment necessary for the manufacture of modern electronics; even a small speck of dust can ruin delicate microscopic circuits. The blaze spread smoke throughout the factory thereby contaminating wafers in most stages of production, resulting in the destruction of chips that would have powered some four million mobiles.

Nokia's information systems soon detected a delay in some deliveries of chips from Phillips. Three days after the fire, Phillips called Nokia to explain that as a result there would be a one-week delay. The timing was particularly unfortunate as Nokia was about to launch a new generation of cellphones. These were due to be supplied with chips from the Phillips' plant in Albuquerque. The fire might potentially result in more than 5 per cent of Nokia's annual production being disrupted during what was a boom time in cellphone sales. On hearing the news, Tapio Markki, Nokia's chief component-purchasing manager, decided that he ought to let others within the company know about the situation. His first call was to Pertti Korhonen, Nokia's top troubleshooter. He instigated a thorough investigation and set in place efforts to work with Phillips to recover the situation. Two Nokia engineers were dispatched to Albuquerque to help Phillips. On arrival, they soon realized that it was likely to take two weeks to reinstate the clean rooms to a standard sufficient to resume manufacture.

Mr Korhonen soon recognized that disruption on this scale would require emergency action if Nokia were to avoid significant interruptions to their own production and threatened the company's ability to meet its commitments to its major customers at this important time. A team from Nokia's purchasing department set to work investigating alternative sources of supply for the parts. They were successful in finding suppliers

Lightning can strike – literally out of the blue

for three of the five parts in Japan and the USA. They could offer a million chips each, and, vitally, could ship them within the week. The other two parts were, however, a sole supply from Phillips. This was deemed sufficiently important for Nokia's chairman to call Phillips' CEO directly to demand details about production of these items from other Phillips plants. As a result, the team from Nokia was able to analyze the capacity of all of Phillips' factories and identify opportunities to reroute output to Nokia. Mr Korhonen noted, 'Our goal was simple: For that period, Phillips and Nokia would act as one company regarding those components'. Nokia's actions yielded rewards. A Phillips factory in Eindhoven, Holland, was identified that could provide 10 million chips, while another in Shanghai was able to divert some of its capacity in order to meet Nokia's requirements. The Nokia engineers sent to Albuquerque were able to work with Phillips to find ways of increasing production, thereby manufacturing another two million chips, once production was restored. Taken together, all of these actions resulted in Nokia avoiding any disruptions in its shipments to its customers.

The contrast with some other manufacturers relying on output from the Albuquerque plant is illustrative. Their failure to recognize the seriousness of the problem and take prompt action resulted in significant problems. Ericsson, for example, initially viewed the call from Phillips as a low level discussion between technicians. They seemed content to take the warning of the one-week delay at face value and allow it to run its course. When it became evident that their vital supplies of chips would be subject to much longer delays, the employees involved did not immediately notify their bosses, fearing a reprimand. As a result, news of the fire and its implications did not reach senior mangers until several weeks later. By this time it was too late for Ericsson to do much to rectify the resulting problems. Phillips could not help Ericsson as they had already committed all their spare capacity to Nokia. Ericsson also had extreme difficulty in locating other sources of supply. In the event, Ericsson's production was significantly disrupted as they were short of millions of chips for a key new generation of cellphones. The shortage of chips from Phillips resulted in a shortfall in the production of Ericsson's new high value mobiles, which cost the company dear in terms of lost sales in a highly competitive marketplace. Ericsson recorded a massive loss of US $1.68 billion for its mobile phone division for 2000.

(Source material: 'A Managerial Framework for Reducing the Impact of Disruptions to the Supply Chain' downloaded from Supply Chain Management at http://scm.ncsu.edu/public/risk/risk3.html on 8 August 2006)

Questions (Suggested answers can be found on the companion website www.thomsonlearning.co.uk/barnes)

1 What do the reactions of Nokia and Ericsson tell you about their relationships with Phillips?

2 What lessons can be learnt by Ericsson from this affair?

3 Does Nokia have any lessons to learn?

The advantage in multiple sourcing is that the purchaser can use competitive tendering to exert downward pressure on prices. Having multiple sources also reduces the risk from supply disruption. Using a number of suppliers also widens the knowledge base from which to draw. The disadvantages are associated with the reluctance of a supplier to commit to a relationship with a purchaser that may be short-lived. It is bound to be more difficult to maintain effective communications with a larger number of suppliers. And suppliers may be more tempted to exhibit opportunistic behaviour.

One of the main arguments against single sourcing is that the purchasing organization makes itself completely reliant on that single supplier. Many people think it foolhardy in the extreme to leave your operation vulnerable to any potential disruption in a supply chain that may extend many thousands of miles. Disruptions can happen in many ways, whether due to human error or malevolence, or natural disaster. They can happen to goods in transit, at the supplier's premises, or further back in the supply chain. As the preceding case study 'When lightning strikes' illustrates, it is often the way that organizations react to disruptions that determine their ultimate impact.

SUMMARY OF KEY POINTS

The management of the supply network has become more important as organizations are increasing the proportion of inputs that they purchase. Supply networks are becoming more global in nature.

Managing the supply network involves managing relationships with suppliers individually and collectively.

Supply networks need to be configured with the aim of satisfying the end consumer. The rationalization of a supply network can facilitate improved efficiency and effectiveness.

The basis of the successful co-ordination of a supply network is the integration of the activities of its various components to construct a seamless end to end process.

Outsourcing is a decision with strategic implications. Care must be taken to avoid damaging an organization's core competences.

Global sourcing can offer benefits other than cost reduction, including improved quality, increased capacity, access to technological expertise and broadening the supply base. But global supply networks are much more difficult to manage than domestic ones.

The traditional approach to purchasing is based on an adversarial arm's length relationship between buyer and supplier. In contrast, the partnership approach is based on a close and co-operative relationship between buyer and supplier. The partnership approach is increasingly popular, but relies on mutual trust between buyer and supplier.

There are advantages and disadvantages to single sourcing and multi-sourcing, although the recent trend has been for more single sourcing. However, this can leave the purchaser more vulnerable to disruptions in supply.

WWW.

EXERCISES (Suggested answers can be found on the companion website www.thomsonlearning.co.uk/barnes)

1 Explain why operations managers need to be concerned about their supply networks.

2 Why is supply chain management sometimes referred to as 'virtual integration'?

3 Why has outsourcing proved popular in recent years?

4 Can an organization outsource too many of its activities?

5 Should an organization always outsource to the lowest priced supplier?

6 Why have so many organizations based in advanced economies been attracted to off-shore outsourcing in newly industrializing countries? What are the disadvantages of off-shore outsourcing with suppliers located in newly industrializing countries?

7 What advice would you give to an organization considering off-shoring for the first time?

8 Assess the advantages and disadvantages of the partnership approach (cf. the traditional approach) to supplier relations.

9 Can buyers and suppliers ever really trust one another in commercial relationships?

10 In what circumstances would single sourcing rather than multi-sourcing be more advantageous to a purchaser?

CASE STUDY EXERCISE Coca-Cola HBC

Introduction

Coca-Cola HBC (CCHBC) is one of the largest bottlers of non-alcoholic beverages in Europe. Operating in 28 countries (from the Republic of Ireland to the eastern-most parts of Russia, and from Estonia to Nigeria), it serves approximately 1.5 billion unit cases to customers every year. These unit cases are made up of over 500 flavour and package combinations of carbonated (CSD) and non-carbonated (non-CSD) soft drinks, juices, water, sports and energy drinks, and ready-to-drink beverages such as teas and coffees. This product range is aimed at enabling CCHBC to provide each customer with the right refreshment, at the right price, and in the right place. CCHBC is also one of The Coca-Cola Company's key worldwide bottlers. The company was created in 2000 with the merger of the Athens-based Hellenic Bottling Company SA with Coca-Cola Beverages plc.

The company's strategy focuses on a Four A's credo in order to maintain its constant and growing demand in its markets:

- *Availability:* CCHBC's products reach customers not just within an arm's reach of desire, but also by providing the right package, in the right location, at the right time.

- *Affordability:* provision of affordable choice to customers though a wide variety of desirable, quality products, in an appropriate package for each market, for each occasion and for the right price.

- *Acceptability:* Relentless control, effective customer service, outstanding efficiency, and the best route-to-market, combined with a detailed knowledge of consumer needs, guarantees that CCHBC products are acceptable to consumers across every market.

- *Activation:* Consumer motivation for choosing CCHBC products comes through providing them at the right price for the right brand, in the right location. By placing them in interesting and enticing

Delivering products bearing the brand requires effective supply chain management

point-of-purchase displays, by making them available via precisely placed coolers, or vendors, or racks, or fountains and by making them relevant to the lives of purchasers, CCHBC activates consumer demand.

Supply chain management (SCM)

Effective supply chain configuration and management are critical for achieving the above mentioned four goals and meeting the changing demands of the customers and the marketplace. Supply chain efforts are centred on providing the necessary manufacturing flexibility to support the broadening of the product portfolio while pursuing the most cost effective route-to-market for order taking and delivery to customers.

Technology investments and applications are nowadays key enablers of efficient SCM, and in 2005, CCHBC introduced the single largest and the most successful roll-out of SAP-based Advanced Planning Optimizer (APO) in 16 operations located in seven different Central European countries. This has enabled CCHBC to optimize and co-ordinate operations within its whole network and across borders by consolidating best practices on a single, standard enterprise platform. There are further plans to integrate eight more operations in this platform. The platform facilitates alignment of supply chain and demand planning to achieve sales and operations planning efficiencies. It can create cost saving opportunities and bring CCHBC one step further towards class leadership in the fast moving consumer goods (FMCG) industry. However, the implementation and success of a demand driven SCM is not solely based on the technology infrastructure, but also on the organizational practices that CCHBC initiated with the aim of integrating sales and consumer information into its operations planning. Analytically, information gathered from its SAP platform enables the APO process to take place.

CCHBC believes that the era whereby production planning was based on long-term forecasting has gone. Instead, CCHBC operates on a continuous planning process that is based on achieving a consensus plan amongst all relevant senior managers. In fact, a dedicated Forecasting Manager post has been created, whose responsibility is to use historical sales information and consumer data to produce a demand plan on a weekly basis. This demand planning review is based on the use of scientific methods and data mining tools. Subsequently, the role of the Forecasting Manager is to liaise and communicate his/her findings with the Commercial Manager (in effect the Marketing Manager). The purpose of this process is to cross-check whether scientific demand plans are in agreement or not with the Commercial Manager's sales targets and, if not, to decide on corrective actions at a tactical level (sales promotions, more/less advertising, etc.). The last step concerns the SNOP (Sales and Operations) meeting that takes place once a month between the Chief Financial Officer (CFO), SCM Manager and the Commercial Manager. The aim of all managers involved is to reach a consensus on production and sales targets and then to produce an agreed plan that satisfies the targets and limits of everyone involved. Targets must not exceed the production capacity of the SCM Manager, whilst still achieving the profitability targets set by the CFO and satisfying the Commercial Manager's sales targets. Reaching a consensus plan and a single set of numbers that satisfies everyone is far from an easy task. Internally all the managers have their own individual targets and criteria against which their performance is evaluated, and externally the consensus planning and number setting exercise also needs to satisfy CCHBC's stakeholders. Overall, the success of the continuous planning process heavily depends on the effectiveness, communication and co-operation of the team members.

Moreover, it is not only IT but also the establishment of good relations and partnering with customers, suppliers, retailers and other members of the supply chain that enables CCHBC to save logistics costs whilst addressing and influencing consumer preferences at the point of sale. A number of customer-specific integrated programmes introduced in 2005 illustrate this. For example, in Italy a partnership with the supermarket chain, COOP Italia, was established to pilot a process aimed at achieving a fully integrated business plan. This initiative is supported by Efficient Consumer Response, an industry organization that promotes the alignment of manufacturers and retailers across areas of common business interest such as product identification, traceability and demand/promotional planning. In Switzerland, new trading terms and conditions addressing consumers' requests for clear, simple, fair and business-supported trade agreements were introduced. As a result, customers benefit from a more transparent and efficient system. In the Czech Republic, CCHBC collaborated with a number of retailers for jointly enhancing understanding of consumer shopping behaviour and translating this into a number of profitable common initiatives in the stores.

Overall, CCHBC recognizes that 'better and faster' supply chain execution relies on partnering effectively with its final and intermediate customers in order to identify opportunities for minimizing costs along the entire value chain as well as offering the right product range through tailored packaging innovation. At the same time, CCHBC is developing customized internal systems to further improve SCM efficiency and customer service. A centralized database containing visual marketing material for activating channel specific promotions or consumption occasions was introduced in 2005. This database facilitates the analysis, utilization and sharing of marketing best practice across the entire group and promotes the success of future marketing campaigns.

Working with suppliers

Suppliers to CCHBC range from large international companies to the several thousand local companies that provide ingredients, packaging, equipment and services. Following the company's expansion into Eastern Europe, a number of its international suppliers have also established local production in these countries, allowing CCHBC to source in those countries. For example, the company's Asian resin supplier has created a PET (used to make plastic bottles) plant in Poland, while a key cold drink equipment manufacturer operates production plants in Romania, Poland and Russia from which CCHBC sources coolers and vending machines.

CCHBC procurement specialists strive to build fair and mutually beneficial relationships with suppliers to deliver the best value in terms of quality, cost, service and innovation. As marketplace competition intensifies among retail customers and the cost of raw materials continues to rise, partnership with suppliers is imperative since CCHBC needs to collaborate with them to jointly improve their processes, reduce costs and deliver innovation and efficiencies. For example, CCHBC has worked with packaging suppliers to use less PET resin and glass in lighter weight bottle designs and to use one-piece closures that use less material and are easier to recycle. The new bottling design is 50 per cent stronger, 30 per cent lighter and 30 per cent less expensive compared to conventional bottles. This not only results in lower logistics and packaging costs and waste, but also allows more effective utilization of cooler space. This is important for improving the effectiveness of forward SCM by enabling an increased product range to be presented at the consumption channel.

Relationships with suppliers are managed both at country and Group (i.e. CCHBC) level, with multi-functional teams working with suppliers to ensure quality and enhance efficiency. Ultimate accountability for supplier relationship management rests with the Group's Chief Procurement Officer. With certain key commodities, CCHBC works together with The Coca-Cola Company. All suppliers of ingredients and primary packaging materials (i.e. packaging in contact with beverages or items that bear the trademark) are approved by The Coca-Cola Company. This approval process, in which CCHBC takes part, involves verification of processes, quality and capability.

In addition to expectations of quality and efficiency, CCHBC also requires its suppliers to follow strict standards for business ethics, human rights and labour practices, as well as sound environmental management. These requirements are set out by CCHBC in its Guiding Principles for Suppliers (visit www.coca-colahbc.com), which form part of all its contracts with suppliers. These principles are closely aligned with those of The Coca-Cola Company. Independent auditing of suppliers for compliance with these principles is undertaken by independent third party firms on behalf of The Coca-Cola Company, and a supplier's adherence is required to be verified at least once every two years.

—Marianna Sigala

Questions (Suggested answers can be found on the companion website www.thomsonlearning.co.uk/barnes)

1 How do CCHBC's supply chain management practices help them to achieve their four major strategic aims?

2 How does CCHBC use IT to improve its supply chain management performance?

3 What actions should CCHBC take to improve integration internally and externally within its supply chain?

4 How would you characterize the nature of the relationship between CCHBC and its suppliers?

References

Babbar, S. and Prasad, S. (1998) 'International purchasing, inventory management and logistics research', *International Journal of Operations and Production Management,* 18(1):6–36.

Dornier, P., Ernst, R., Fender, M., and Kouvelis, P. (1998) *Global operations and logistics: text and cases,* New York: John Wiley and Sons.

Forrester, J.W. (1961) *Industrial Dynamics,* Boston, Mass.: MIT Press.

Friedman, T.L. (2006) *The World is Flat: A Brief History of the Twenty-first Century,* London: Penguin Books.

Hagel, J. and Brown, J.S. (2005) *The Only Sustainable Edge: Why Business Strategy Depends on Productive Friction and Dynamic Specialization,* Boston, Mass.: Harvard Business School Press.

Monczka, R.M. and Trent, R.J. (1992) 'Worldwide sourcing: assessment and execution', *International Journal of Purchasing and Materials Management,* 28(4):9–19.

Prahalad, C.K. and Hamel, G. (1990) 'The core competence of the corporation', *Harvard Business Review,* May–June, 71–91.

Trent, R.J. and Monczka, R.M. (2005) 'Achieving excellence in global sourcing', *MIT Sloan Management Review,* 47(1):24–32.

Additional reading

Dornier, P., Ernst, R., Fender, M. and Kouvelis, P. (1998) *Global operations and logistics: text and cases,* New York: John Wiley and Sons.

Gattorna, J. (2006) *Living supply chains,* London: Prentice Hall.

Hagel, J. and Brown, J.S. (2005) *The Only Sustainable Edge: Why Business Strategy Depends on Productive Friction and Dynamic Specialization,* Boston, Mass.: Harvard Business School Press.

Useful websites

WWW.

http://www.cips.org/ The Chartered Institute of Purchasing and Supply (CIPS), an international organization, based in the UK, serving the purchasing and supply profession and dedicated to promoting best practice.

http://www.ism.ws/ The Institute for Supply Management (ISM) is the US based supply management association providing opportunities for the promotion and the expansion of professional skills and knowledge.

http://www.supply-chain.org/ The Supply-Chain Council is a membership organization for supply chain practitioners in a cross section of industries. It has around 1,000 corporate members worldwide.

PART FOUR

INFRASTRUCTURAL ISSUES

PART FOUR

The major strategic decisions in operations can be conveniently divided into the two categories of structure and infrastructure. Infrastructural decisions are concerned with the management of the systems and procedures through which the physical assets are operated. They can be thought of as the software of operations.

Part Four considers the infrastructural decision areas of operations management. (Structural decisions are considered in Part Three.) These issues are also important to an organization, involving the use made of the operating hardware discussed above. It is possible to change aspects of operations infrastructure more quickly and easily than is the case for operations structure. Nonetheless the difficulty of so doing should not be underestimated. Neither should the impact of making inappropriate infrastructural decisions.

The six chapters of Part Four consider the infrastructural decision areas of operations management under six broad headings:

- Chapter 9 – Planning and Control considers the systems used for planning and controlling operations.

- Chapter 10 – Quality considers quality management policies and practices.

- Chapter 11 – Work Organization considers organizational structures, responsibilities and accountabilities in operations.

- Chapter 12 – Human Resources considers recruitment and selection, training and development and management style.

- Chapter 13 – New Product Development considers the systems and procedures used to develop and design new products and services.

- Chapter 14 – Performance Measurement considers financial and non-financial performance management and its linkage to recognition and reward systems.

CHAPTER 9

PLANNING AND CONTROL

INTRODUCTION

This chapter considers one of the most important infrastructural decision areas, namely that of planning and control. Planning and control is concerned with matching supply from the organization's operations with demand from its customers. As such, it lies at the heart of operations management. If demand is greater than supply, some customers may be left dissatisfied. If supply is greater than demand, the organization's operations are unlikely to be making best use of the resources at their disposal. Matching supply and demand is usually a difficult task, as demand typically varies over time, and changing output is usually not a straightforward task.

Planning and control is not itself an international issue. All operations need to be planned and controlled wherever they take place. And, planning and control is a challenging task even when focused on a single location. However, planning and control assumes an international dimension, when, as is increasingly the case, an operation's output is intended to meet demand from different countries and inputs are sourced from yet more countries. This increases the challenge of planning and control. Planning and control becomes even more challenging when its complexity is increased by a requirement to co-ordinate operations that are located in a number of different places, especially where this involves different countries. The increasing internationalization of operations makes planning and control more challenging still.

This chapter discusses the conceptual basis of planning and control in operations, and the principles underlying the different ways of approaching these inter-related tasks. The main approaches that have been developed in planning and control with the aim of matching supply and demand in operations, will be outlined. These include ERP (enterprise resource planning) and JIT (just in time). Closely allied to this is the issue of how organizations approach the issue of planning and control of one of the most important resource inputs, inventory.

THE PRINCIPLES OF PLANNING AND CONTROL

planning
This is concerned with actions taken prior to an event, typically arranging for resources to be provided in order to achieve a desired outcome.

control
This is concerned with remedial action taken in response to things not occurring as planned in order to avoid an undesirable outcome.

control loop
A theoretical model that describes actions taken with the aim of ensuring that the outputs from a transformation process are produced according to plan. This involves measuring the output, comparing it to the plan and, if necessary, taking remedial action upon the process and/or its inputs.

In operations management, planning and control are usually treated together as one subject, as it is difficult to differentiate between these two activities. The main distinguishing feature between them is in relation to timing. Planning is normally concerned with determining the nature and timing of what actions should take place prior to their occurrence. This would typically involve arranging for resources to be provided so that some particular action can be taken in order to achieve a desired outcome. However, as in practice things do not always work out as planned, it may be necessary to take some kind of remedial action as events transpire in order to avoid an undesirable outcome. This is generally termed control. Control is concerned with understanding what is actually happening in the operation, deciding whether there is a significant deviation from what should be happening, and, if necessary, making changes to the operation. However, as most operations are on-going in nature rather than one-off events, planning and control are continuing activities. As such they usually become intertwined and distinguishing between them is practically impossible.

As discussed in Chapter 1, the simple input-output model in which resource inputs are converted to outputs of goods and/or services can be used to describe any operation. This model can be extended to include the actions associated with planning and control. This is termed the control loop and it comprises the following additional elements (see Figure 9.1).

- *A plan:* This would include a statement of what the operation was expected to produce over a given period of time. It would consider the total volume or quantity of outputs along with what mix of different goods or services are intended to be produced. An operating plan would also consider what resources are required to achieve the required level of output. When operating plans are expressed in financial terms, as they frequently are, they are usually termed budgets.

- *Measurement:* The first step in exercising control over the system is to measure its output over the relevant time period. Whilst a number of different measures might be taken, they would certainly include the actual volume or quantity of the output achieved, as well as the mix of different products. It is likely that the quantities of resources used in carrying out the transformation would also be measured.

- *Comparison:* The next stage would be to compare what actually took place with what was planned to happen. This would certainly involve a comparison of actual output with that planned, and probably a comparison of actual resource usage with that planned. It is important to compare like with like when comparing the actual to the plan or budget. Accountants have devised various techniques which help to do this (e.g. standard costing and variance

FIGURE 9.1 The control loop

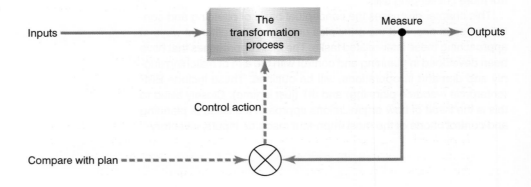

analysis). A thorough analysis of any differences should help provide an understanding of why the plan was not achieved.

- *Control:* The final stage in exercising control is deciding what, if any, action is required and then taking it. This depends on the analysis of any differences between actual and plan. If differences are small, there may be no need for action to be taken. Significant differences between planned and actual would usually prompt some action to try to remedy the situation. However, there are circumstances in which it may also be important not to make too dramatic a response to differences. Overreaction, particularly if the operation system takes some time to respond, may merely aggravate the situation and could cause the system to go out of control. Operations managers need to realize which factors are in their immediate control and over what timescales. These will set limits to their control actions.

There can be many reasons why a plan is not achieved. Customer demand may change. In particular, the total volumes, the mix of goods and services supplied, and their timing may all change with significant impact on costs. Although many of these factors are outside the control of the managers responsible for the operations involved, it is they who must undertake the planning and control of the resources required for the transformation process. As was discussed in Chapter 1, these resources differ in their nature. They usually include the following:

- *People* in the transformation process are either staff or customers. Planning and controlling staff is a vast area of study in its own right, usually covered by the term 'human resource management'. Its application within operations management is addressed in Chapter 12. In practice, most operations managers find that planning and controlling staff occupies most of their time, and is a central concern of their work. It involves recruitment, training, motivation, reward, job design, work organization and all the other activities necessary to manage people. In many service industries, customers are themselves part of the transformation process. Their progression through the process is often compared to processing materials. However, materials do not complain, nor do they take their custom elsewhere if they are kept waiting or not treated properly in the operations process. Some of the issues associated with queuing are addressed in Chapters 6 and 7.

- *Materials* in the transformation process can either be those that are being processed or those that are being consumed in the process. There are few operations that do not involve material resource inputs of one or other of these categories. Although materials do not complain about being stored before or during processing, there are costs involved in storing materials. Most organizations seek ways to minimize those costs, in ways that do not have a detrimental impact on other operations performance objectives. These issues are addressed in more detail later on in this chapter. Another feature of materials is that they usually originate from an external supplier. The management of relationships with suppliers is discussed in Chapter 8, and is considered further in this chapter.

- *Information* is a resource which may be used in the operation or may itself be transformed as part of the process. Recent advances in information and communication technology, particularly associated with the Internet are having a dramatic impact on many operations. These are considered throughout this book, including this chapter.

- *Equipment* and the facilities in which it is housed are usually fixed assets, not being used up immediately but rather over many years. Issues affecting the design and choice of facilities and equipment are discussed in Chapters 5 and 7. As is discussed in Chapter 6, facilities and equipment usually determine the capacity of the operations process and cannot be changed very easily or quickly. Planning and controlling equipment is thus likely to involve much longer timescales than most of the other input resources.

An operations process typically involves a complex interaction of the resources of people, materials, information and equipment. The success of any operation depends on how these resources are managed, both in the short-term and the longer-term. The application of the principles of the control loop can deepen operations managers' understanding of this task. However, they must also consider the different timescales involved in planning and control.

THE ACTIVITIES OF PLANNING AND CONTROL

One of the difficulties in distinguishing between planning and control in operations management is caused by the timescales involved. The longer the timescale involved, the more likely it is to be considered as planning. The shorter the timescale, then the more likely it is to be deemed control. Considering the timescales involved can offer a way of distinguishing between different aspects of planning and control. Although the terminology employed in operations management can often be confusing and ambiguous, a typical classification of planning and control activities would encompass a number of different levels. The overall aim is to move from long-term strategic plans covering perhaps five years or more and develop them in increasing detail, matching operations capacity to customer demand over progressively shorter time periods. The ultimate outcome will be a daily schedule, indicating how the operation will allocate its available resources, determining what is to be done, when, by whom and with what equipment. The various levels of planning and control activities are shown in Table 9.1 and are discussed in more detail below. The timescales associated with these activities must be thought of merely as illustrative. Organizations in different industry sectors may have different planning practices and timescales may also vary depending upon circumstances.

Strategic operations planning

This is concerned with developing long-term plans for an organization's operations. As such, this activity should be part of the organization's corporate strategic planning process, and would normally involve the organization's most senior managers. It would particularly concern the sorts of structural decision areas of operations management discussed in Chapters 5 through to 8. These are typically long-term investment decisions affecting the organization's facilities, equipment and supply network that will determine its operating capacity. Such decisions usually involve large-scale capital expenditure, for example setting up completely new facilities on new sites or

TABLE 9.1 The levels of planning and control activities

PLANNING AND CONTROL ACTIVITIES	TYPICAL TIMESCALES
Strategic operations planning	2–5+ years
Aggregate planning	1–2 years
Master production schedule	3–6 months
Activity scheduling	1–4 weeks
Expediting	Real time

replacing or adding to equipment at existing facilities. It can typically take many months or even years before such investments become available to operate.

Aggregate planning

This level of planning starts to consider in detail how the organization's operations will meet the demand for its products and services over the medium-term. It typically involves attempting to match the total operations capacity of the organization to the demand forecast for the forthcoming 12 or perhaps 24 months. It will usually do this on a month-by-month basis and on a facility-by-facility basis, but is unlikely to go into product mix detail at this stage. Its purpose is to determine whether there is sufficient capacity to meet forecast demand. If not, there may be actions that can be taken to provide additional capacity. Alternatively, it may be possible to take action to manage demand. The other possibility is that there may be insufficient demand for existing capacity, requiring action to be taken to increase demand or reduce capacity. These issues are discussed in Chapter 6.

Master production scheduling

This is a widely used term, originating in manufacturing operations, but it is now used as the generic term to describe the activity of building up a detailed plan to show how sales orders and/or forecasts will be met on a week-by-week and a product-by-product basis. This is expressed as a master production schedule (MPS). Whilst aggregate planning does not usually consider individual products, the master production scheduling does. As such, it works from the details of individual customer orders and sales forecasts by product line. Armed with this information and knowledge of the operations capacity, the scheduler attempts to match available supply with demand, using resources as efficiently as possible to meet customer demand. This is usually a trial and error process via so-called 'rough cut' capacity planning. There are a number of computer models available to help schedulers. These often have to be tailored to the specific circumstances of individual organizations. Through a number of iterations the scheduler will produce a MPS, typically for the next 12 weeks or so. The production of the MPS frequently highlights dilemmas requiring decisions on whether to increase short-term capacity or to permit demand to remain unmet, requiring customers to wait for their orders. This is an on-going activity, in which the schedule will be revised, perhaps on a monthly or even a weekly basis, to take account of changing circumstances, including any backlog of orders.

Activity scheduling

The role of activity scheduling is to develop the MPS into sufficient detail so that work can be assigned on a daily basis to every work centre (i.e. to every work team, individual and machine). The schedule will typically provide details of when individual jobs are required to be started and finished (*sequencing*), their route (if there is a choice) through different stages of the operations process (*routing*), and what task will be assigned to each work centre (*loading*).

    Sequencing is concerned with decisions about how to prioritize the exact order of work at each work centre. The objective is to achieve agreed completion times for each job while minimizing costs. When there are many jobs and many work centres, this can be an exceptionally complex task, and one unlikely to lend itself to an optimum solution in a realistic timescale. To help provide a practical solution to the task, bearing in mind schedulers may do this every week or even every day, a number of sequencing (or dispatch) rules have been developed. These are rules of thumb which

work centre

A collection of resources (people, machines, etc.) assembled together to undertake specific work tasks.

are applied in any given situation to provide an answer to the question, 'What should be done next?' Some alternatives are:

- Shortest processing time – always do the next job available which has the shortest processing time at the work centre concerned. This is aimed at achieving a high rate of work flow and machine utilization.

- Minimum slack time – 'slack time' is the time remaining until the due date less the remaining processing time. Minimizing slack time is aimed at always achieving the due date.

- First come, first served – this is based on a 'fairness' approach to processing queues. If customers are being processed rather than materials or information, this may be the only realistic rule to use.

- Minimum planned start time – using planned start times from existing schedules, always process the job with the minimum planned start time first.

- Minimum due date – always process the job with the earliest due date first.

There are other dispatch rules. Which one is usually used in organizations depends on what criteria are considered most important. Some rules are more likely to achieve higher resource utilization, some lower costs, some greater on-time job completion rates, etc.

Routing is concerned with determining what route or pathway a job will take through the process. In this sense a job can involve the processing of a quantity of materials, information or customers. In operations which are not line or continuous processes, any particular job will have its own unique route through the various stages (i.e. work centres) in the process. The activity of routing maps along this pathway is so that the work requirements for each work centre for each time period can be determined. One of the objectives of routing will be to minimize waiting times for jobs, as it is normally desirable to avoid a build up of work-in-progress. In materials processing operations this is important in order to minimize stockholding costs. In customer processing operations it is important to minimize waiting times so as to avoid queues of potentially irate and dissatisfied customers.

Loading involves determining what work is to be assigned or 'loaded' on to each work centre. Knowing how long each job should take, it is possible to calculate when each job should be completed at each work centre. If capacity is exceeded, waiting times can be calculated. There are two approaches to loading: forward loading or backwards loading. Forward loading starts at the present time and loads jobs forward in time, utilizing the available capacity. Within existing capacity constraints, this will enable jobs to be finished at the earliest possible time. If this is not acceptable (due to customer requirements), decisions can then be made as to whether additional resources can be provided. Backwards loading starts with the due date for each job and works back, assigning the required processing time to the jobs at each work centre, ignoring capacity constraints. This highlights any overloads, forcing the scheduler to take action, by, for example, reallocating work between work centres or providing extra resources.

Activity scheduling involves the often complex allocation of resources to jobs. In most situations it is useful to draw up schedules both for the jobs to be processed and for all of the resources being used in the processing activities. Bar charts (Gantt charts) are often used to display this information. Typical schedules include:

- Job order schedules: These show the sequence of job start and finish times and their constituent processes.

- Human resource schedules: These show the work that each worker will be carrying out during that day or week.

- Equipment schedules: These show how the capacity of each piece of processing equipment will be assigned during the planning period.

- Material schedules: These show what materials will be required. Material control is discussed in more detail later in this chapter.

There will inevitably be constraints on the use of resources which schedulers will need to take into account. These include:

- Equipment: Different machines may have different processing capabilities than others. This may depend upon the task required of them, as will the time needed for change-over and set-up between different tasks. Also, there may be requirements for their maintenance.
- People: Staff may not be available for work for various reasons, including planned holidays, sickness, training, etc. Also, even though it is desirable, it is rare for all workers to be so multi-skilled as to be totally interchangeable.
- Materials: There may be long lead times or other problems for certain materials.

Although often perceived as less than exciting, scheduling is one of the most important and challenging tasks in operations management.

Expediting

This is the term usually used to refer to interventions in day-to-day operations in order to reschedule activities in response to short-term requirements. No matter how well operations planning and activity scheduling are carried out, there will inevitably be reasons why such interventions may be required. A customer makes a change to an order; there is an unexpected material shortage due to problems with a supplier; an important operator suffers a sudden illness; a piece of equipment breaks down, and so on. The intervention required to deal with such unforeseen eventualities is generally referred to as 'expediting'. This activity was traditionally carried out at the supervisory level of management. Expediting is perhaps best considered to be a control, rather than a planning, activity as it is undertaken in order to respond to rapidly changing circumstances. With the complexities of scheduling and the uncertainties of a dynamic external environment, it would be naive in the extreme to believe that such interventions can be completely eliminated or that they necessarily point to a failure in planning. Although it is desirable to limit its use, expediting is an essential part of shop-floor level control, requiring real-time decision-making. If such decisions are not capable of being taken at the time and place required, at best there will be costly delays and at worst inappropriate decisions will be taken, with potentially even more costly consequences.

MEETING CUSTOMER DEMAND

One of the main objectives of planning and control is to meet customer demand. In essence, there are really only two ways in which an operation can respond to customer demand: produce-to-stock or produce-to-order.

Produce-to-stock involves producing in anticipation of receiving an order from a customer. The produce-to-stock approach has the advantage of reducing the risk of not being able to meet customer demands as they arise. This is often necessary in manufacturing operations that supply retail markets. Shoppers will usually only buy items that are on display at the point of sale. In some industries, particularly those supplying seasonal markets, such as fashion clothing, or festivals (e.g. New Year), this can mean having to build up high stock levels, which can prove very costly. It also risks obsolete stock and reduces the possibility of customizing the finished product. Also, where distances between producer and consumer are great (for example when supplying international markets), produce-to-stock may be the only viable strategy due to the time taken to transport the goods. For service operations, a produce-to-stock approach is often not an option, as services can not usually be stored. The underlying challenge in the produce-to-stock approach is that of forecasting future demand. This can be especially problematic in the often turbulent environments that organizations face when operating internationally. Despite improvements in forecasting techniques and computer programming, forecasting demand with any degree of accuracy remains notoriously difficult.

Produce-to-order means waiting until a customer places an order before commencing production. This is often the only available strategy for service providers. In recent years, there has been an increasing trend for more and more manufacturers and retailers to follow service providers in adopting a produce-to-order approach. Despite the risks of a loss of business if customer demand is not fulfilled as required, the reduction in inventory right the way through the supply network is a goal considered well worth pursuing. This approach is based on the JIT (just in time) system of planning and control pioneered by Toyota of Japan, which is discussed in more detail later in this chapter.

The practice of *postponement* has been adopted by many manufacturers as part of a move towards a produce-to-order approach. This involves delaying the final stages of the production process for as long as possible by adopting a produce-to-stock approach to the production of standard parts, sub-assemblies or modules that can be used for a number of different final products. The final product is only produced when there is a definite customer order. This approach reduces inventories and enables some degree of customization to be incorporated once the final order is received. Dell are one of the leading exponents of this approach, with all their computers being produced on an assemble-to-order basis at their factories from standard components (see the case study in Chapter 8 on Dell's Supply Chain Symphony) before shipment direct to the customer.

In produce-to-order, the operation has the necessary resources in place ready to produce once an order has been received. For example, a factory has all the necessary equipment, workers and, possibly, raw material, which can be devoted to a customer's order once received. Similarly, a fast food outlet has all the necessary resources in place to enable it to fulfil a customer's order immediately. An extension of produce-to-order is *resource-to-order,* in which the resources necessary to undertake the work are only put in place once an order had been received. This is typically the case in construction or other project-based operations.

As service providers know, producing to order, especially where customers are not prepared to wait and demand is difficult to predict, presents a constant dilemma for the management of the operation. Providing adequate resource capacity to meet customer demand risks under-utilization of that capacity; on the other hand, providing inadequate resources to meet demand risks dissatisfied customers and consequent loss of business. For organizations involved in international operations this presents a particularly acute dilemma in planning and control. Responsiveness to local customer demand is best achieved through operations being located and managed as close as possible to the customers. However, such an approach risks the loss of economies of scale and scope that might be gained from global operations.

Attempts to solve this dilemma have centred round the use of ICT to enable information to be shared within an organization and across its supply network. Developments in the use of the Internet and the increased processing power of computers have increased opportunities for co-ordinating the planning and control of operations across large geographically dispersed organizations. For many years computer programs have been available to undertake some of the often complex calculations required for the detailed planning and control of operations. The latest generation of these includes Advanced Planner and Optimizer (APO) a set of software applications from the German-based software company SAP. This works by getting real-time

WHEN THINGS GO WRONG Christmas comes but once a year

Predicting demand for the hottest new electronic gadget or the must-have toy for the Christmas holiday season is an annual nightmare for retailers and manufacturers alike. Every year, much-hyped products disappear from the shelves long before most people have done their Christmas shopping, leaving fashion-conscious consumers and frazzled parents wallowing in disappointment and frustration. In 2005 Microsoft's Xbox 360 game console sold out soon after its late November launch in the US and its early December launch in Europe. Its scarcity has been reflected on Ebay, with consoles selling for as much as $1,000 at auction, compared with the official price of about $400. The previous year, it was Robosapiens toys and iPods that failed to appear. Supplies of Sony PlayStations got held up in a supertanker in the Suez Canal and the company had to charter Russian cargo aircraft to make deliveries. Supply disruptions are not confined to toys and consumer goods. UK supermarkets stopped taking orders online for Christmas 2005 grocery deliveries in mid-December this year because of extraordinarily high demand. Even festive specialities can run out because of spikes in demand, as happened when Delia Smith, the celebrity television cook, used cranberries in her *Winter Collection* series. Her chocolate truffle torte also caused a European shortage of liquid glucose.

Forecasting the right quantity of a product and getting it to the right place at the right time is a notorious challenge for businesses, especially when the item is new. The danger in the run-up to Christmas is that non-availability will alienate customers, as well as lose potential sales. Another danger of running out before Christmas, as in the famous 1980s craze for Cabbage Patch dolls, is that when supplies did resume after Christmas, the fad had subsided and the price of the newly abundant dolls dropped.

Yossi Sheffi, director of Massachusetts Institute of Technology's Center for Transportation and Logistics argues that getting it right is not so much about perfecting forecasts as about building flexibility into the supply chain. Where possible, that means broadening the supply base so that production can be stepped

Predicting demand for products like this MP3 music player can be problematic

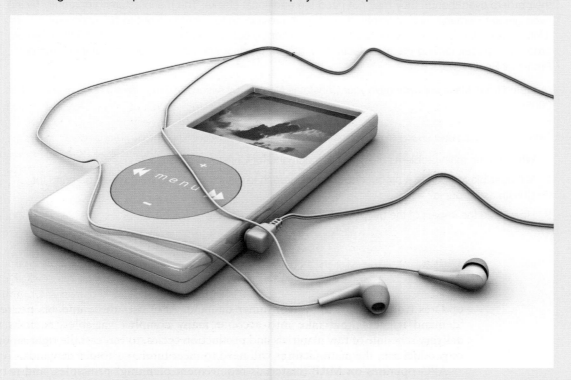

up quickly in different locations, and using components from different sources. 'As soon as you see demand growing, which you can probably judge from pre-orders on the Internet', he says, 'You are prepared to press lots of buttons and expand production massively'.

One example of this kind of multi-sourcing is Hewlett-Packard (HP). HP makes Deskjet printers for North America in plants in Vancouver and Singapore. The former is more flexible and closer to the market, but more costly. So HP assigns stable, high-volume production to Singapore and uses Vancouver to satisfy temporary surges in demand.

Flexible contracts with suppliers are another solution, enabling companies to increase or decrease production rapidly as part of normal service. Jabil Circuit, a US electronics manufacturing services company, requires suppliers to be able to boost deliveries by 25 per cent with a week's notice, and by 100 per cent with four weeks' notice.

Forecasting can be made more accurate by pooling predictions of customer demand across a wide region rather than responding on a store-by-store basis, according to Professor Sheffi. By using common components in different products, companies can also aggregate their forecasts for these products to give a more accurate picture of demand for the parts. A responsive supply chain depends on good communication and co-operation between all its participants. 'It is only as strong as the weakest link. That is why it is so difficult', argues Professor Sheffi. Companies that do it well have an in-built culture of flexibility, with a free flow of information, he says. 'Toyota displays continuous production reports in its plants. Dell updates managers hourly on production. UPS keeps the vast reaches of its network in constant cellphone communication'.

Communication between buyers and sellers can help companies avoid the 'bullwhip effect', whereby minor variations in consumer demand create bigger and bigger fluctuations in orders and inventory levels further up the supply chain. This can be caused, say, when a company does not inform a supplier that an order increase is due to temporary disruption at another supplier. The first supplier assumes customer demand is growing and overreacts by increasing capacity or ordering more from its own suppliers in anticipation.

When new products such as the Xbox 360 are in short supply, a different mechanism can start the bullwhip effect. Aware they may be allocated a fraction of what they ask for, retailers double or triple their orders even though they may not need the additional stocks. The manufacturer, apparently facing even greater demand than anticipated, increases production for what turn out to be 'phantom' orders. 'Unfortunately it is bound to be disappointed when supply catches up with real demand and the phantom orders disappear, leaving the manufacturer with extra product that needs to be sold at lower margins', Professor Sheffi says.

(Adapted from 'Make sure you have your Christmas stock in' by Alison Maitland, www.ft.com 18 December 2005)

Questions (Suggested answers can be found on the companion website www.thomsonlearning.co.uk/barnes)

1 What are the main problems of forecasting demand for Christmas products?

2 Is it possible to operate a produce-to-order approach to planning and control to meet demand for Christmas products?

3 How could the impact of the bullwhip effect be minimized?

updates from retailers about consumer demand. APO uses these updates to create 'demand triggers' that take into account many complex variables, such as the delivery schedule of raw materials and production cycles, to forecast the right amount of product mix the manufacturer will need to meet future customer demands.

APO operates on MRP (materials requirement planning) principles, and is typically integrated within an ERP (enterprise resource planning) system. ERP systems seek to improve planning and control by integrating all information systems within an organization. MRP and ERP are both discussed later in this chapter.

PLANNING AND CONTROL PHILOSOPHIES

There are two basic philosophies to exercising control at shop-floor level in any operating process: supply-push or demand-pull.

Supply-push

This is the approach that has traditionally dominated attitudes to operations control, particularly in Western countries. This approach is based on the assumption that the performance of any system can be optimized by optimizing the performance of the sub-systems that make up the overall system. It aims to do this by controlling the activities of each sub-system through a centralized planning and control system. The exercise of this central control is assumed to be part of the fundamental role of management. In simple situations control might be exercised by a shop-floor manager or supervisor. However, in more complex operations the managers might need to be supported by production planners, controllers, schedulers, etc. This situation is depicted in Figure 9.2a, which shows a number of interconnected work centres, as might be found on a factory-floor. The work to be carried out at each work centre is centrally determined based on a plan aimed at meeting known or forecast customer demand. Instructions are given to each work centre, which it is expected to follow irrespective of what is occurring at the other work centres. Thus, when each work centre has achieved its output for the period it 'pushes' this to the next work centre. The functioning of the system relies on the controller being provided with regular updated information so that instructions can be amended to account for changes in customer orders, the progress of the work, breakdowns, material problems, etc. This can obviously become a highly complex task. Problems will arise if there is any disruption in any one work centre. If this disruption is not spotted and acted upon quickly enough, output from previous processes will continue and result in work-in-progress accumulating. There may, in fact, be an unwillingness to stop work at any given work centre, as its own performance will be seen to have deteriorated. Reward systems, particularly if these involve pay, may even exacerbate this. If such disruption occurs regularly, work centres will wish to build up stocks of input materials just in case of future disruption. Again, their desire will be to optimize their performance. It is asking much of the controller to co-ordinate these activities to achieve optimal total system performance. Exercising central control can be difficult enough within a single operation, but it can become extremely complex and demanding if it extends

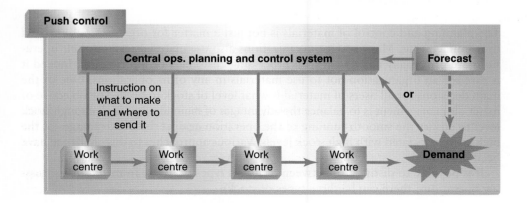

FIGURE 9.2A Push control

FIGURE 9.2B Pull control

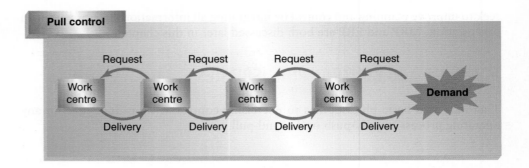

to encompass the wider supply network. In recent years increasingly sophisticated computer software (for example as contained within an ERP system) has become available to aid management in this task.

Demand-pull

An alternative approach to supply-push, originating in Japan, has gained many adherents in recent years. This is demand-pull, which is the basis of the *'kanban'* system of control and of the just-in-time (JIT) approach to planning and control. It aims to optimize the performance of the whole system irrespective of the performance of any one sub-system. The basis of this approach is that each work centre should only produce what is required by the next process in the next time period. Its instructions come directly from the work centre that it supplies. Figure 9.2b illustrates this. If the work is not progressing as planned in any work centre, it adjusts its instructions to the supplying work centre. In this way, work-in-progress stocks are not allowed to build up. If a disruption occurs at any one process, it is quite acceptable for a prior work centre to stop producing until the problem is resolved. Indeed, it is a central tenet of this approach that it is everyone's responsibility to remedy a problem anywhere in the system so that the performance of the whole system can be improved. The role of the central controller is considerably reduced with a demand-pull approach. This use of computer power is not a prerequisite. However, the approach does rely on close co-operation between the different parts of the operating system. If the demand-pull approach is extended to include the wider supply network, then a similar level of co-operation is required from external suppliers. As they have become so closely linked to the operating system, any disruption originating from external suppliers will soon have a detrimental impact on the whole system.

INVENTORY MANAGEMENT

The planning and control of materials is not just a matter for organizations engaged in manufacturing. Many service organizations also use materials even if their operations are principally concerned with processing customers or information. Indeed it is rare for an organization not to use materials in any of its operations. One of the main decisions for all users of material is what level of stock to hold. The objective of materials management is to balance the advantages of maintaining a high enough stock level to ensure the smooth running of the operation against the disadvantages of the high costs associated with high stock levels. Various approaches to this challenge have been developed.

It is possible to distinguish between different types of stock. In materials processing operations, there can be three types of stock:

- *Raw materials,* which are materials that have been received from a supplier and are awaiting processing.
- *Work-in-progress,* which are materials that have undergone at least one stage of processing and are awaiting the next stage.
- *Finished goods,* which are materials that have been fully processed and are awaiting sale to a customer.

Most operations, whether service or manufacturing, are also likely to require items which are used in the operations process but do not themselves form part of the output of the process. These include spares and other maintenance items for equipment, work clothing, consumables, tools, etc. These are often referred to as MRO (maintenance, repair and operating) items.

Raw material inventory

Work-in-progress inventory

(KIRSTY MCLAREN/ALAMY)

(TNT MAGAZINE/ALAMY)

Finished goods inventory

(KEITH VAN-LOEN/ALAMY)

The reasons for holding stock are likely to vary according to the type of stock. For raw materials:

- As a buffer against any uncertainty of supply which may disrupt operations.
- To secure bulk purchase discounts or avoid small order surcharges.
- To buy when prices are low or before a known or anticipated price rise.
- As insurance against anticipated shortages.
- As a buffer against unpredictable demand in operations.

For work-in-progress:

- To disengage the different stages in the operation in order to facilitate flexibility in scheduling different operations and improve utilization rates of individual stages by facilitating longer production runs and fewer change-overs.

For finished goods:

- To make goods available to customers off the shelf.
- As a buffer against variability or uncertainty in supply or operations.
- As a buffer against fluctuations in demand.
- To build up stock to meet anticipated increased sales due to seasonality or marketing activity.

For maintenance, repair and operating (MRO) items:

- As a buffer against uncertain demand for items whose non-availability carries a high risk of disruption to operations.
- As a buffer against uncertain supply.
- In anticipation of extra demand due to planned maintenance.

There is generally some degree of uncertainly about the demand for materials within most operations, due to uncertainty in demand for the final product or service in the marketplaces that the organization serves. However, it is possible to distinguish between two types of demand.

Independent demand is where demand for an item occurs separately from that for any other item. Finished goods typically exhibit independent demand which is normally determined by market forces. Similarly, with many MRO items, demand for which often appears to exhibit a random pattern due to the vagaries of their use by the people and equipment in operations. Approaches to stock control for independent demand items centres on forecasting likely demand and maintaining a suitable level of stock to ensure customers can be supplied on demand. The emphasis is on replenishing the stock as it runs down to ensure it never runs out.

Dependent demand, on the other hand, is demand that is linked to demand for another item. So, for example, a motor car manufacturer will know how many doors, wheels, seats, etc. it needs for each car. Knowing how many cars are intended to be made, it is possible to calculate the demand for every component part that goes into their assembly. The supply of these dependent demand items can then be secured in time for their use.

Understanding whether demand is independent or dependent can help determine what approach to take in managing the inventory of an item.

MANAGING INDEPENDENT DEMAND INVENTORY

The main aim in managing independent demand items is to ensure that stocks do not run out. The main requirements of a stock control system in such circumstances is to determine when and how much to order from suppliers. There are basically two kinds of these so-called order point systems.

- *Reorder level system:* In this system, stock levels are continuously monitored, which requires that records are constantly updated in real-time. With modern computer systems this should not be a problem as long as stock levels are recorded accurately. If the stock level of any item falls to a predetermined level (the reorder level) an order is immediately placed with the supplier for a predetermined quantity of replacement stock (the reorder quantity). The reorder quantity is determined from a review of past usage rates and from knowledge of the lead time for the item (i.e. the time it takes the supplier to fulfil the order). The success of the system relies on the assumption that both the demand for the item and the lead time are fairly constant. The intention is that the replacement stock should arrive just before stocks run out. As a safeguard against any uncertainties in demand or any unreliability in supply, it is usual to hold some safety stock of the item. The *reorder level system* is illustrated in Figure 9.3.

order point systems
Inventory control systems for independent demand items that aim to determine when and how much to order from suppliers to ensure that stocks do not run out.

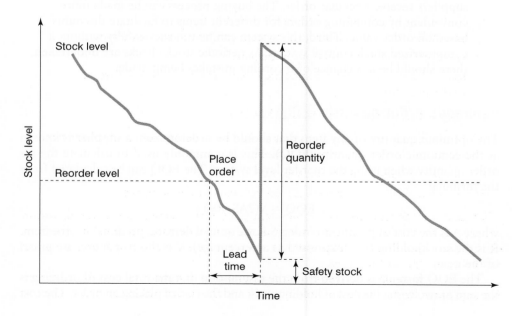

FIGURE 9.3 The reorder level system

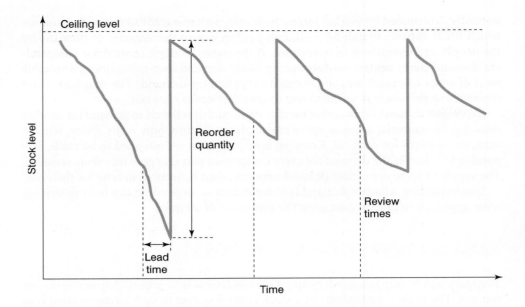

FIGURE 9.4 The cyclical review system

The main advantage of the reorder level system is that order quantities are always the same and so these can be calculated from the economic order quantity (discussed below) or to take advantage of quantity discounts from suppliers.

- *Cyclical review system:* In this system, the stock level is checked at regular intervals (e.g. once a week or every month). An order is then placed with the supplier for a quantity calculated as the difference between a predetermined maximum (or ceiling) level and the current stock level. Thus, the order quantity is likely to vary each time an order is placed. The ceiling level is set to cover demand until the next review time plus the delivery lead time. The *cyclical review system* is illustrated in Figure 9.4.

There are a number of advantages in the continuous review system. First, the system makes it easy to plan the workload of the staff involved. These are fairly simple tasks that can be incorporated into someone's regular routine. However, the impact of the task being neglected may be severe. Second, suppliers receive a regular order. The buying process can be made more convenient by combining orders for different items to facilitate discounts based on order value. Third, this system can be run successfully without a computerized stock control system. As periodic stock checks are undertaken, there should be less chance of recording mistakes being made.

Economic order quantity (EOQ)

The optimum quantity of any item that should be ordered from a supplier is known as the economic order quantity (EOQ). This is commonly used to calculate the re-order quantity when using the reorder level system. The EOQ can be calculated from the formula:

$$EOQ = \sqrt{(2AS/RV)}$$

where A is the cost of placing an order, S is the annual demand (in units) for the item, R is the stockholding cost (expressed as a percentage), V is the cost (purchase price) of the item.

The EOQ formula is derived from the assumption that the total cost of ordering is the sum of two costs: the cost of holding stock and the cost of placing an order. The cost of holding stock rises with the level of stock held. So the bigger the order quantity for a particular item the higher the stockholding cost. The annual cost of placing orders for that item with a supplier (primarily the associated costs of administration) decreases as the order quantity increases because fewer orders will need to be placed. As these two costs pull in opposite directions, it is possible to calculate the order quantity that would minimize the total cost. This is what the EOQ formula does.

The EOQ formula is based on a number of other assumptions:

1 The rate of demand is known and constant. It also assumes the past pattern of demand will hold good into the future.

2 The lead time is known and constant.

3 The unit cost (purchase price) is constant.

4 No stock-outs are allowed.

5 Material is ordered and arrives in one batch (i.e. there are no part deliveries).

6 The item is not dependent on any other product.

These assumptions are highly questionable in practice. They highlight the many problems and shortcomings with the EOQ formula. The main ones are:

1 It is very difficult (if not impossible) to calculate a meaningful figure for A, the cost of placing and processing an individual order in practice. At best, any figure is likely to be an average for all purchasing activities rather than that associated with a specific item.

2 While it is possible to calculate S, the annual demand for the item, from the previous year's figures, this may not hold true during the current year. Also, demand may not be constant over the year. If it fluctuates significantly, then EOQ calculations are likely to give rise to either overstocking or stock-outs.

3 The cost of holding stock, R, is also difficult to calculate in practice. It is likely to be made up of:

   a The cost of capital, which may vary over time as interest rates change.

   b Insurance costs, which may depend on the type of stock being held.

   c Storage costs, which depend on building costs and any special facilities the items may require (e.g. heat, cold, humidity).

   d Obsolescence, which will vary especially if fashion or technology are involved.

   e Deterioration and damage, which again depends on the items.

   f Pilferage or other losses.

4 The cost of the item, V, may vary over time (due to inflation or other market factors) and may also be subject to quantity discounts or small order surcharges.

5 Lead times may vary for many reasons, including the performance of suppliers or their suppliers.

Despite its limitations, EOQ is still widely used in practice and it remains helpful in endeavours to minimize the costs of ordering and holding stocks. However, it is important to recognize its limitations.

The EOQ formula can also be used to calculate the optimum size of a batch (or lot) to be manufactured. In this case the economic batch size (EBS):

$$EBS = \sqrt{(2AS/RV)}$$

where A is the set-up cost for the process (all other symbols are the same as in the EOQ formula).

As well as the shortcomings of the formula discussed above, using it to calculate a production batch size has an additional problem. It takes the set-up cost, A, as a given.

FIGURE 9.5 ABC analysis of
stock

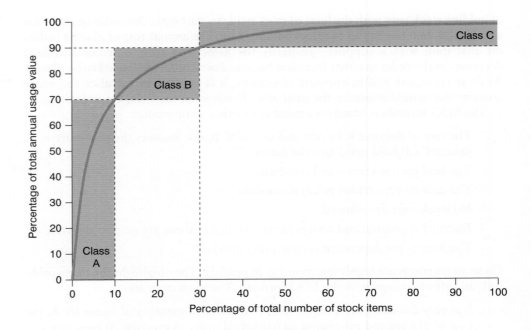

FIGURE 9.5 ABC analysis of
stock

As will be discussed later in this chapter, one of the main aims in many manufacturing processes is to take steps to reduce set-up times. This is particularly the case in the JIT approach to manufacturing, which has led to dramatic reductions in set-up times and costs.

ABC analysis in inventory management

The **80:20 (or Pareto) rule** is a tool of analysis which can be usefully applied to inventory management. An analysis of the annual usage value of stock items (i.e. quantity used × unit cost) allows inventory to be classified into three broad categories:

- Class A: the small proportion (typically 10 per cent) of items which account for the majority of costs (say 70 per cent).
- Class B: a middle group (say the next 20 per cent) of items which account for approximately the next 20 per cent of costs.
- Class C: the large number of items (say 70 per cent) with little value (say 10 per cent of costs).

These figures are treated as rules of thumb rather than applied precisely. However, use of the general principle can enable a classification to be applied in practice. A typical plot of usage value against numbers of stock items is shown in Figure 9.5.

Categorizing stock in this way enables tighter control to be applied to the high value class A items, an intermediate level of control to class B, whilst class C would have the lowest level of control.

MANAGING DEPENDENT DEMAND INVENTORY

As discussed above, dependent demand items are so called because the demand for them depends upon the demand for another item. Dependent demand items are typically the components and raw materials used to manufacture a finished product. So, if there is known, or forecast demand for the finished product, it should be possible to calculate the demand for components and raw materials that go into the product.

Materials requirement planning (MRP) is the name given to the method used to calculate what dependent demand items will be required, and when they will be required, in the manufacturing process. Its aim is to arrange for all the materials required for manufacturing to arrive at the exact times they are required. It is driven from the master production schedule (MPS) for the product. The MPS lists what quantities of the finished product are required in each of the future time periods (usually the next few weeks and months). The MPS can be compiled from known and forecast customer orders. MRP aims to calculate what quantities of materials (raw materials and components) are required when. To do this a detailed list of all the materials that go into the finished product is required, literally down to the last nut and bolt. Such a list is called the bill of materials (BOM). In order to perform the calculations, the MRP system also needs to know the full details of the current inventory status in the organization. This means knowing up-to-date details of stock on hand and materials on order including quoted lead times from suppliers. From this the MRP system can calculate the quantity and timing of orders to be placed with suppliers in order to meet the requirements of the MPS. In most practical situations, the extremely lengthy calculations and large quantities of data involved mean that MRP relies on computer power. Figure 9.6 illustrates the basic concept.

MRP has many advantages over the sorts of traditional order point systems discussed earlier (reorder level, continuous review). These perform quite well in independent demand situations. This is because order point systems are based on the assumption that historical demand patterns will continue into the future, and that demand will be reasonably constant over time. This may not be the case for dependent demand. Indeed, by its very nature dependent demand may be 'lumpy', with a large batch being required at a particular time, but otherwise with demand being zero (i.e. an all or nothing situation). Use of an order point system will either require holding very large stocks of items for long periods when they are not required or risking a stock-out when the items are required. MRP is focused on the future: requirements for all materials are calculated on the basis of known or forecast demand. Thus in theory, MRP should eliminate the need to hold any stocks of raw materials or work-in-progress. Whereas order point systems typically use EOQ calculations to determine order quantities (and these are based on historical data), MRP calculates order quantities on the basis of known demand. Thus, order point systems should work best for finished goods and MRO stocks, and MRP best for raw materials and work-in-progress.

Although the principle of MRP seems quite simple, it must be remembered that in practice it operates under dynamic conditions. In most real life situations, manufacturing takes place in very fast changing environments. There are so many factors that

materials requirement planning (MRP)
A computer-based system of calculating the quantities and timings of materials required for dependent demand items in a manufacturing process.

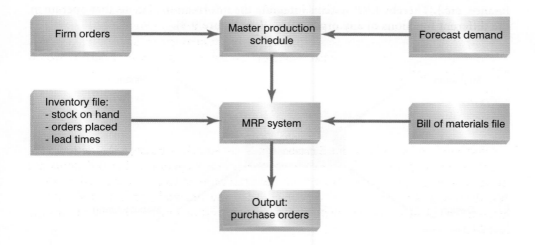

FIGURE 9.6 The basis of an MRP system

can change and affect the progress of orders on the shop-floor. Customers change their orders, designers make modifications, suppliers do not always fulfil their promises, shop-floor workers make mistakes, machines break down, and so on. So the MRP system needs regular and constant updating if it is to keep up with the situation. As with any computer system, the output from an MRP system is only as good as the input given to it. If any of the data on which the MRP calculations are performed is inaccurate or outdated, then the resulting instructions will be inappropriate and misleading. In practice, MRP systems have often failed to deliver the lower inventory levels they promise. Problems seem to arise from the implementation rather than the theory of MRP. It can prove difficult to keep the MRP system up-to-date with the changes that inevitably happen in manufacturing systems. This can lead to a lack of faith in the MRP system. The situation can be further worsened by actions taken, in good faith, to expedite overdue or priority orders, through the use of 'informal' systems outside of the formal MRP system. Thus, suspicion of the fallibility of MRP can become self-fulfilling as people fail to operate the system properly.

The original MRP systems confined their calculations to materials supplied from external sources. Over time, advances in computer processing power made it possible to extend the scope of MRP software to include feedback loops which take account of performance against plan (so called 'closed loop' MRP). They were further extended to include all the other resources required for manufacturing (e.g. staff, equipment) and eventually the other business functions including marketing and finance. This type of software is known as manufacturing resources planning, dubbed MRP2 (or MRP II). They are used to plan and control all aspects of an organization's manufacturing activities and are based upon one integrated database for the whole company (see Figure 9.7).

As with MRP, there have been fairly mixed reports of the success of MRP2 in practice. Proprietary MRP2 software has been available for over 20 years. When used to exercise shop-floor control, MRP2 systems operate on the principle of supply-push control which was discussed earlier in the chapter (see Figure 9.2a). The MRP2 software acts as the central operations planning and control system. However, as with MRP, there still seem to be problems in operating MRP2 systems in practice. These are usually associated with failing to keep the system supplied with up-to-date information to reflect changes occurring in realtime (whether from actions taken on the shop-floor, modifications to designs, amendments to customer orders, etc.).

The latest generation of MRP-based programs, are known as enterprise resource planning (ERP). The best known software supplier is the German company SAP, but there are several others, most notably Oracle. Like its MRP2 predecessors, ERP programs aim to plan, monitor and control all the activities of the organization using a fully integrated computer system. The key component in any ERP system is an integrated database that stores data for the various system modules (operations, HRM, finance, etc.). Thereby ERP systems integrate the information systems that operate in the different functions of any organization (see Figure 9.8).

manufacturing resources planning (MRP2)
A computer-based system of planning and control for manufacturing processes that extends MRP to include all manufacturing resources and links the software for manufacturing planning and control to that for all other functions of the organization via an integrated database.

enterprise resource planning (ERP)
A computer-based system for resource planning and control across an entire organization. ERP is suitable for any type of business, services as well as manufacturing, and not for profit as well as profit seeking organizations.

FIGURE 9.7 The concept of an MRP2 system

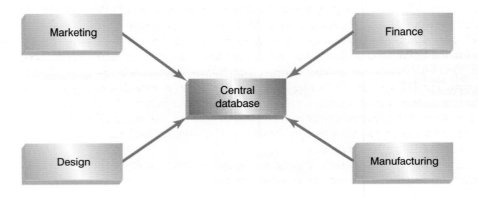

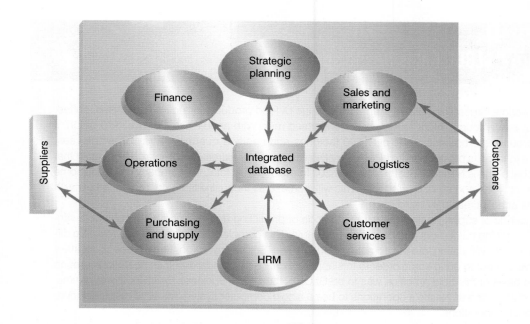

FIGURE 9.8 The concept of an ERP system

ERP systems are suitable for any type of business, services as well as manufacturing, and not for profit as well as profit seeking organizations. Properly used, an ERP system will, for example, track the progress of all materials through the organization, pay invoices to suppliers for goods received, and calculate the efficiency of individual activities carried out within the company's operations. This is an alluring prospect especially for large and complex organizations, especially those operating in international environments. However, ERP systems can be very expensive to install and maintain, with both activities typically requiring the help of outside experts from vendors or management consultants. Some ERP systems are difficult to customize to individual organizational requirements and often require the organization to re-engineer its business processes to meet the needs of the ERP system. This can cause significant disruption and cost to the business. Also, there are often problems associated with the implementation of ERP systems. Extensive staff training is required if the system is to operate to maximum effect. However, as well as functional training, staff may also need to be persuaded of its benefits. Ingrained rivalries between different parts of the organization can lead to a reluctance to share sensitive internal information with other departments. Unless such attitudes are changed, the system will never realize its full potential.

JUST IN TIME (JIT) PLANNING AND CONTROL

The **just in time (JIT)** system of planning and control can be thought of as an alternative to MRP. However, in many respects this is far too restricted a view. JIT encompasses a whole philosophy of manufacturing management, and has become increasingly popular as manufacturing companies the world over have sought to emulate the success of the Japanese motor car manufacturers, particularly Toyota, who originated this approach. The JIT system of planning and control aims to ensure that each stage of a production process produces exactly what is required, 'just in time' for the next stage of the process. JIT seeks to eliminate the need for either raw material stocks from suppliers or work-in-progress by synchronizing the flow of material between each stage of a manufacturing process.

JIT can be thought of as operating at three levels: as a philosophy, as a planning and control system and as an inventory control system.

just in time (JIT)
A manufacturing system that aims to produce only what is required, in the quantity that is required, at the time it is required.

CASE STUDY   GLOBE helps Nestlé span the globe

Nestlé is the world's largest food maker, with a wide range of food products including chocolates, coffee, pasta, mineral water, soups, infant formula and condensed milk. With annual sales of over $70 billion, it operates in around 200 countries, has over 500 factories and nearly a quarter of a million employees. Nestlé's desire to tailor its products to local tastes makes its operations extremely complex. The nearest that it gets to a global brand is Nescafé. But this has over 200 formulations. In total, the company produces some 127,000 different types and sizes of products. This will increase as its business enters more markets with more products at an increasingly rapid pace.

It has thousands of supply chains, scores of methods of predicting demand and an uncountable variety of ways of invoicing customers and collecting payments. This complexity was becoming ever more difficult to manage and was eating into the company's bottom line. So five years ago, Peter Brabeck, Nestlé's Chief Executive, set out to bring some order to this apparent chaos by standardizing its operations around the world. The basis of this bold ambition was to be GLOBE, the Global Business Excellence programme, which is aimed at getting all Nestlé's operations to use a single computer system for all its manufacturing, sales and financial operations.

Nestlé had 14 different enterprise resource planning (ERP) systems from SAP AG of Germany in place in different countries. There was a realization amongst Nestlé's senior executives that a market by market approach to planning and control did not work any more and that they could not continue with the existing systems. They assessed that it would not be possible to integrate them all into one system. They therefore decided to replace them all with a new one, based on new Internet-based software known as mySAP.com. For SAP this would be their biggest ever application of mySAP.com. For Nestlé, too, this would not be an everyday project. GLOBE would cost $2.4 billion, an unheard of amount for a company used to spending $30 million or $40 million when building a factory to make coffee, infant formula, water or noodles. Yet, the company realized that the success of the project would be to treat it as a business initiative, not a technology initiative.

Nestlé headquarters in France

(HEMIS/ALAMY)

The new standardized systems would handle all back office operations, such as taking orders, dealing with suppliers, running factories, calculating demand and paying invoices. A common set of processes, in factory and in administration, backed by a single set of information systems would be used to run its businesses. The objective was to redesign Nestlé's myriad and vast supply chains, for everything from paper to powders to chocolate to water, to eliminate wasteful purchasing practices and to take the best administrative practices and spread them throughout the company's operations. For example, by cutting the number of suppliers from 600,000 to 167,000 it could save $750 million a year.

Brabeck had bet his reputation on the initiative's success. He wanted not just to control spiralling information technology costs, but gain a five or six year lead on Nestlé's key global competitors, such as Unilever and Kraft Foods, in how a global food supplier could operate efficiently. If GLOBE succeeded, Nestlé would have greater operating profits to plow back into innovation, stocking shelves with popular products and satisfying its main multi-national customers, like Wal-Mart Stores and Tesco, the large United Kingdom-based food retailer. The project would make Nestlé the first company to operate in hundreds of countries in the same manner as if it operated as one. That had not been achieved before by any company in the history of global trade, not even the British East India Company at the peak of its tea-trading power.

By 21st August 2006 in an interview with the *Financial Times,* Brabeck was able to claim success for GLOBE. He pointed out that for the first time in history, Nestlé's executives would now be able to hit a button and find real-time data on performance by geography, sales channels and product categories and brands – Nestlé's three key criteria. 'We can give our Wal-Mart global account manager a [profit and loss] responsibility. There's nobody in the world today in consumer goods who's been able to pull all this together', says Brabeck. The GLOBE project had taken more than five years so far, prompting doubts over whether it would ever work. Brabeck reported that it now covered 54 per cent of the business and was expected to cover almost 80 per cent by year end. He pointed out that with GLOBE it would be possible to achieve productivity gains and savings from synergies whilst retaining the benefits of decentralization that enabled local bosses to remain close to their customers. Brabeck said: 'GLOBE is the tool to organize the transformation of this company. It allows us to manage the organizational complexity of our business; to break down this supertanker that we are in to an agile fleet of specialized vessels'.

(Source material: http://www.baselinemag.com/ and www.ft.com)

Questions (Suggested answers can be found on the companion website www.thomsonlearning.co.uk/barnes)

1 How will GLOBE help improve planning and control at Nestlé?

2 Are there any disadvantages from GLOBE for Nestlé?

WWW.

WWW.

JIT as a philosophy

The objective of JIT is to make what is needed, when it is needed and the amount needed. It seeks to do this through the application of three interconnected underpinning principles: eliminating waste, continuous improvement and the involvement of all employees.

Waste is considered to be any activity that consumes resources without creating value for the customer. Taichi Ohno, the Toyota executive credited most with the development of JIT, identified seven sources of waste (or *muda* in Japanese) in production:

- *Overproduction:* producing more than is required for the next stage of the process is wasteful.
- *Waiting time:* any time that materials spend waiting to be processed is wasteful.
- *Transportation:* moving materials around a plant adds only cost and not value and is therefore wasteful.

- *Processes:* some aspects of a process can be wasteful if they are performing work that could be eliminated by better design of either the process or the product.
- *Inventory:* in JIT, holding any stock is considered to be wasteful.
- *Motion:* any unnecessary movement by an operator is considered wasteful.
- *Defective products:* poor quality is wasteful, due not only to wasted work in producing it, but also to the work required to discover and rectify the fault.

Muda (waste) is one of three 'M's (*muda, mura and muri*) that JIT aims to eliminate *Mura* is unevenness in an operation, for example, an uneven work pace in an operation causing operators to hurry and then wait. JIT aims for smoothness in operations. *Muri* is overburdening equipment or operators. JIT aims to make the performance of all work tasks as easy as possible.

Continuous improvement (*kaizen* in Japanese) is the second underpinning principle of JIT. *Kaizen* implies achieving incremental but on-going improvements to all aspects of operations, but especially quality. *Kaizen* also lies at the heart of TQM, discussed in Chapter 10. Because JIT seeks to eliminate inventories, all materials must be flawless and defect-free otherwise production will be disrupted.

The third principle of JIT is the involvement and empowerment of employees. Eliminating the three Ms and the practice of *kaizen* requires the active involvement of all employees. JIT seeks to tap into workers' knowledge of the production processes where they work in order to achieve improvements.

JIT as a planning and control system

JIT planning and control is based on the 'demand-pull' operations control approach described above. In this, demand for material in one operation is signalled to the preceding operation. Thus, a requirement for JIT is that operations are organized in a series of work centres, each carrying out a discrete activity. The method used to control the demand for, and supply of, material from one work centre to another is referred to as '*kanban*' (Japanese for a card or signal). This was the original Toyota method by which instructions were sent from one operation to the next on a card. Only those items and quantities listed on the card are to be produced by the preceding work centre. Parts are normally transported from one work centre to another in a container or bin, typically on wheels. The practice developed of attaching the instruction card to the bin, so that it could be filled with the requested quantity of parts ready for transport to the next work centre. So the bin came to be referred to as a *kanban*.

The simplest form of *kanban* system is illustrated in Figure 9.9. This works as follows. Work Centre 2 have a requirement for parts made at Work Centre 1, so they send a work instruction for the required number of parts via an empty *kanban* (*Kanban* A). On receipt of the *kanban,* Work Centre 1 fulfills the order by placing the parts in the *kanban* (*Kanban* B). When the *kanban* is loaded with the requested number of parts (*Kanban* C), it can be transported to Work Centre 2. Once delivered, the parts are available for Work Centre 2 to use (*Kanban* D).

Use of the kanban system ensures that only the required numbers of parts are produced. The only stock in the system is that in the process of being made, or moved between work centres or from a vendor. Most real life situations are more complex than that shown here (perhaps involving the use of stocking areas as well as different types of *kanban* e.g. *move, produce* or *vendor*), but the principles are the same. Each work centre signals their supplier, whether internal or external when they have a requirement for parts. In order to function smoothly, the system needs to build in some time in order for a work centre to make the required parts. However, the objective is to synchronize production between each work centre on a daily basis. This is made easier if production schedules can be fixed with some degree of stability, ideally one

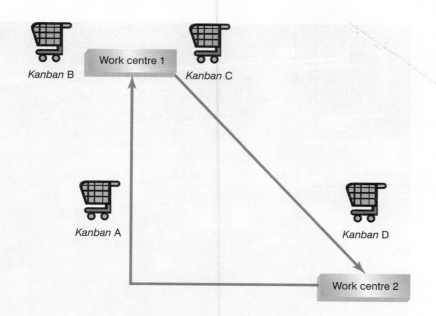

FIGURE 9.9 A simple *kanban* system

to three months in advance. The JIT system works best with reasonably stable levels of production. It finds it difficult to cope with significant fluctuations in demand particularly where this involves a requirement for non-standard items, as these may involve longer lead times from suppliers.

If a work centre is required to produce more than one product type on any one day (and given the need to produce small lot sizes, this is likely), there is likely to be a need for changeovers on machines. JIT requires set-up times to be reduced to an absolute minimum. Similarly, the system finds it difficult to tolerate breakdowns or quality defects. Thus, operating JIT has far-reaching implications, requiring changes in working practices which may involve changes in equipment, physical layout, maintenance, scheduling, skill levels, reward systems, etc.

JIT need not be computer-based, although many practitioners do use computer-based systems. JIT is principally aimed at driving out raw materials and work-in-progress inventories. It can only be used to reduce finished goods stock if there is some certainty of demand from customers. Where this does not exist, finished goods stock will need to be held to protect the manufacturing system against fluctuations in market demand.

JIT as an inventory control system

JIT operates as an inventory control system in that its ultimate objective is zero inventories. In a set of financial accounts inventory is listed as an asset. However under JIT, inventories are viewed as liabilities to be minimized by driving them out of the manufacturing system. The JIT planning and control aims to eliminate work-in-progress inventories within the factory through the use of *kanban*-based pull control. As discussed above, this has significant implications for operations within the factory.

JIT also aims to eliminate raw material inventories. It is sometimes assumed that under JIT, raw material stocks are simply held by suppliers rather than at the factory. This is not the case. Rather the aim is to integrate suppliers into the JIT production process. In effect, suppliers become an extension of the factory which happens to be off site. This means that suppliers also produce exactly what is required JIT for the needs of the factory. Suppliers are typically required to deliver in small quantities several times a day. Operating a JIT system leaves the factory at a very high risk of disruption if suppliers can not meet delivery requirements. Thus, managing relationships

A factory operating lean
production

with suppliers is a major constituent of JIT. This has led practitioners of JIT to reduce their supplier base, usually with a single supplier for each component or item of raw material. This ensures that they can maintain the tightest levels of control and communications with each supplier. Typically, suppliers are also required to be geographically located very close to the production facility, in order to ensure that they can meet the exacting delivery schedules more easily. But above all, JIT inventory control with suppliers needs to be based on the kind of partnership relationship described in Chapter 8, founded on very close long-term relationships built on trust.

Adopting JIT requires a significant shift in thinking about planning and control. Traditional approaches concentrated on achieving a high level of efficiency at each stage of a process, the idea being to maintain high capacity utilization at each stage. This was done, in effect, by de-coupling each stage from the next by allowing work-in-progress inventory to build up. The downside of this is that a build up of inventory is not only costly, but also disruptive. It not only requires space to store it, but it can also hide the presence of any faulty goods; defects can always be replaced from the excess work-in-progress inventory. This means that quality problems are never exposed and so are never tackled and solved. This leads to inefficient working, thereby failing to achieve the original objective. JIT on the other hand considers the production process holistically rather than as a series of independent stages. It believes that concentrating on capacity utilization at each stage of the process only leads to over-production. JIT aims to produce only what is required and will tolerate lower levels of capacity utilization. Having lower levels of inventory in the system exposes any problems, forcing them to be solved. This leads to fewer stoppages and higher levels of efficiency. The major disadvantage of JIT is that it is a high dependency system. Disruption to any part of the system will soon cause the whole system to come to a halt.

Toyota's practices have been well documented. They are widely copied and used throughout the world including in operations well beyond their motor car manufacturing origins. The word 'lean', originally used by Womack and Jones (1996) to describe the philosophy underpinning JIT and its allied practices, has now passed into widespread use; phrases like 'lean production' and 'lean thinking' are now common currency. The benefits of operating in a lean way include increased quality, faster

lean production
An alternative name for just in time.

lean thinking
The application of just in time principles to non-manufacturing organizations.

CASE STUDY It pays to cut out waste: The case of Buck Knives

When Hoyt Buck started making hunting knives in the early years of the twentieth century, his competitors were other Kansas blacksmiths. One hundred years later, Buck Knives is up against companies from across the world, many of them based in countries where labour, utility and other costs are substantially below those in the US. Most companies in these circumstances send their manufacturing offshore. But Hoyt Buck's descendants were reluctant. Instead of exporting jobs to Asia, three years ago they started to import an Asian idea – the 'lean' manufacturing methods pioneered by Toyota.

The story shows, first, that the doctrines of the Toyota production system have spread far beyond the automotive sector. Fifteen years after the publication of *The Machine That Changed the World*, the book that popularized Toyota's management methods, the war against *muda* – Japanese for waste – is being fought across swaths of manufacturing industry and increasingly in services, too. Second, the experience of Buck Knives underlines that lean thinking can be a powerful weapon in the fight to keep manufacturing and other jobs in developed countries.

Lean thinking teaches managers to eradicate anything from the production process that does not add value for customers, including inventory. Instead of stockpiling goods in warehouses and praying that demand forecasts turn out to be accurate – the conventional 'push' model – lean manufacturers aim to produce only in response to firm orders. When an order is placed, raw materials are 'pulled' from the supply chain and down the production line as fast as possible. The result: high speed, no waste, low cost and a happy customer.

Irrespective of whether this ideal is achieved in practice, lean thinkers tend to be sceptical about the supposed benefits of sending jobs to low-wage economies. It is hard to run a low inventory, JIT supply chain when you are sourcing components from across the globe. What if the widgets required for tomorrow's production run are delayed by a typhoon or stuck for three days at the border? Besides, there is nothing lean about shipping steel, shoes or electronic components halfway around the world by container ship. Think of all that *muda* in time, capital and diesel fuel.

Another strand of lean thinking is the notion that frontline workers – whether on the production line or in customer service – are best placed to identify and solve problems. But they can do this only if they are very familiar with the products and can talk directly to the engineers and managers who are likely to be at the root cause of any problem. With this view, sending jobs offshore will result in fewer problems solved and unhappier customers in the long run.

Similarly, lean thinkers tend to be sceptical about the value of outsourcing jobs to contractors, even if the workers stay close by. Overheads may be reduced in the short-term, but learning opportunities are likely to be lost. At Buck Knives you can see these ideas in action. The old production line has been redesigned into a series of circular 'cells' that build knives from start to finish. The new layout minimizes the distance travelled by each product (less *muda*) and encourages communication among employees, allowing them to see the entire manufacturing process. This way of working makes it more likely that production bottlenecks or product defects will be recognized early and dealt with on the spot, says C.J. Buck, Chief Executive and great-grandson of the founder. There is less need for expensive (and sometimes oppressive) supervision.

In true Toyota style, Buck Knives last month staged a symposium for its suppliers to explore ways of improving co-operation. Running a JIT supply chain requires a higher degree of collaboration – and trust – than is usual among manufacturers used to carrying weeks or months of surplus inventory. 'Much of what we are doing today is making the company more like it was when my grandfather was running the business and everything was done on a handshake', says Mr Buck.

To be sure, lean thinking is no panacea. It is hard to learn and even harder to sustain. It has limits. Going lean was not sufficient to get Buck Knives' unit costs down to competitive levels. After more than 50 years in California, where Hoyt Buck moved in 1947, the company last year relocated to Idaho in search of lower overheads. While many of its products still carry a 'Made in the USA' stamp, its less expensive models are now made in Taiwan. And as every Chief Executive knows, a world-class cost structure and commitment to continuous improvement is only table stakes these days.

If Buck Knives wants to be around for another decade – let alone another century – it will have to come up with products that are consistently more desirable than the domestic and international competition. Innovation and inspiration must also be on the cutting edge.

(Excerpted from an article by Simon London, www.ft.com 11 October 2005)

Questions (Suggested answers can be found on the companion website www.thomsonlearning.co.uk/barnes)

1 Buck Knives sells most of its products through retail stores. What problems might this create for its lean manufacturing system?

2 Buck Knives manufactures a large number of different knives (visit http://www.buckknives.com/). What challenges does this present for a lean manufacturing system?

3 What challenges would you envisage that Buck Knives has in ensuring a JIT supply of raw materials?

throughput time, increased flexibility, improved productivity, as well as a dramatic reduction in inventory. The successful application of JIT practices has enabled many manufacturers to adopt more of a produce-to-order approach to planning and control. This requires the operation, and its suppliers, to achieve high levels of quality, speed of response, dependability and flexibility. As such, a competitive advantage is potentially available not only through lower costs, but also through higher quality and being able to provide exactly what customers want when they want it. Retailers have also been adopting similar practices based on lean thinking. Leading supermarkets like Wal-Mart and the UK's Tesco are at the forefront of such approaches, variously termed QR (Quick Response), ECR (Efficient Consumer Response) or similar. JIT is not an easy option or a quick fix. Toyota and its other successful exponents took several decades to develop and perfect its practices. Indeed Toyota would emphasize that their practices continue to evolve as they seek yet more *kaizen*.

SUMMARY OF KEY POINTS

The control loop offers a simple theoretical model for understanding the principles of planning and control for any operation. It involves measuring the output from a transformation process, comparing this to the plan and, if necessary, taking remedial action upon the process and/or its inputs.

Planning and control involves actions at a number of levels, each involving decreasing timescales and increasing detail: strategic operations planning, aggregate planning, master production scheduling activity scheduling and expediting.

There are in essence two ways in which an operation can respond to customer demand: produce-to-stock or produce-to-order.

There are two basic philosophies of control in operations: supply-push and demand-pull.

Inventory control for independent demand items is normally undertaken through an order point system, such as the re-order level or the cyclical review systems.

MRP aims to minimize inventory of dependent demand items by calculating the quantities and timings of their requirements, so that their delivery from suppliers can be arranged accordingly.

MRP2 applies the principles of MRP to the planning and control of all manufacturing resources and integrates the computer systems of all the business's functions. ERP makes the operation of MRP2 suitable for any kind of organization.

JIT is a planning and control system that aims to produce what is required in exactly the required quantities at exactly the time it is required. JIT is based on the underpinning principles of eliminating waste, continuous improvement and the involvement and empowerment of all employees. JIT planning and control uses the *kanban* system for shop-floor control. JIT aims to eliminate inventory and requires close co-operation with suppliers. JIT principles are often referred to as 'lean thinking' and have been applied to many non-manufacturing environments.

EXERCISES (Suggested answers can be found on the companion website www.thomsonlearning.co.uk/barnes)

WWW.

1 What are the advantages and disadvantages of both supply-push and demand-pull as methods of control?

2 What are the major differences between independent and dependent demand?

3 Should inventory be considered to be an asset or a liability?

4 What type of inventory control system would you expect to find in the following operations:
   a Car repair shop
   b Aircraft manufacturing
   c Motor car manufacturing

5 What are the major shortcomings associated with the EOQ formula?

6 Think of at least three examples of customer processing operations, that use sequencing rules other than first come first served.

7 Do you agree with the claim that expediting is merely an indication of poor planning and control?

8 What challenges will a produce-to-order business need to overcome if it is to successfully adopt an MRP system?

9 What are the major problems associated with the implementation of MRP2 and ERP systems?

10 Do you agree with the assertion that every organization should adopt JIT?

11 To what extent can a line of waiting customers in a service operation be considered to be the same as work-in-progress inventory in a manufacturing operation?

12 To what extent does JIT manufacturing preclude the use of international suppliers?

CASE STUDY EXERCISE Tesco's supply chain management practices

Introduction

From humble beginnings, Tesco has grown to become the UK's largest supermarket chain. Over ten years ago, Tesco set its sights on becoming the Toyota of the grocery business. Since then, the company has become renowned for its best practices in supply chain management (SCM), which included lean management and the use of RFID technology. The company has gained an advantage over its competitors by incorporating innovations in its supply chain like point of sale data, continuous replenishment triggered by customer demand, primary distribution, cross dock distribution centres (DC) and use of a single vehicle to serve several stores.

Background

Tesco was founded in 1910 by Jack Cohen, who invested his serviceman's gratuity of £30 in a grocery stall. He opened its first store in 1929. Influenced by the supermarket culture in America, Cohen's maxim for retail was 'Pile it high and sell it cheap'. Tesco opened its first self-service store in 1948 and its first supermarket in 1956. The company continued to expand during the 1960s, and opened its first superstore, with an area of 90,000 square feet, in 1967.

By the 1970s, Tesco's image had become very downmarket at a time when shoppers were becoming more demanding. To arrest the downslide in its fortunes, Tesco overhauled its stores, concentrating on its superstores and refurbishing its remaining smaller stores. Tesco diversified into petrol retailing in 1974. By 1979, the company's turnover had reached £1 billion.

In 1985, Ian MacLaurin became Tesco's first CEO from outside the Cohen family. MacLaurin streamlined Tesco's operations, closing down most of the smaller stores and opening large 30,000 square foot stores in the suburbs. Tesco also introduced a centralized distribution system, added fresh foods and its own label for food products. These were all successful moves.

In the 1990s, the UK supermarket industry faced saturation. Tesco was now the country's second largest supermarket chain with a market share of 16.7 per cent, behind Sainsbury's at 19 per cent. The other major competitors were Asda and Safeway. Several warehouse stores like Costco and discount stores like Aldi, Lidl and Netto also entered the UK. In 1997, Tesco's Marketing Director, Terry Leahy, became the new CEO. He had introduced a new pricing policy of lowering prices to match those of Asda, which resulted in Tesco's prices being 4–5 per cent lower than those at Sainsbury's and Safeway.

Tesco's SCM initiatives

The key period for Tesco's supply chain initiatives was between 1983 and 1996, when the company introduced several systems including point of sale scanning, centralized ordering, centralized distribution, automated warehouse control and electronic data interchange (EDI).

Graham Booth was Tesco's Supply Chain Director from 1985 to 2002. Looking to improve Tesco's supply chain practices, he felt that it was necessary to have a stock replenishment system triggered by customers. Booth approached Dan Jones of Cardiff Business School. Jones, James Womack and Daniel Roos were the authors of *The Machine that Changed the World,* the book that famously explained the concept of 'Lean Production' pioneered by Toyota. The essence of lean is to eliminate waste and remove all activities that do not contribute to the value of products. Using Jones' knowledge of Toyota's manufacturing methods, Tesco set about finding ways in which *'muda'* (waste in all its forms) could be eliminated.

At Jones' suggestion, Booth set up a team of cross functional experts from Tesco and Britvic – a company that supplied cola to Tesco, to analyze the supply chain system for cola. They traced the journey of a cola can backwards from a Tesco checkout counter, to Tesco's regional DC, to the DC of Britvic, the warehouse at Britvic's bottling plant, the filling lines of the cola and ultimately to the can supplier. The team realized that there were several opportunities for making improvements and reducing costs. There was a lot of unnecessary handling while the stock moved from the supplier, to the DC and then to the store. The drinks had 170 touch points[1] and spent 20–40 days in transit at seven different stocking points. The machines were utilizing only 30 to 50 per cent of the time effectively, with the remaining time spent unproductively, either waiting for the next batch to arrive or undergoing repair. Similarly, the trucks were used effectively for only 30 to 50 per cent of the time, the remaining time they were queued up or plying empty.

In order processing, it was found that orders were processed not individually but in batches once a day or once a week, depending on the product and the location of the stores. The processing passed through eight different systems. The projections and the demand that was forecasted by the sales team was amplified, mainly due to long lead times, poor product availability, waiting to obtain full truck loads and different ordering cycles.

Booth felt that a major overhaul was required in the way goods traveled from the suppliers to Tesco's store shelves. Consequently, Tesco decided to introduce a continuous replenishment (CR) system whereby products were replaced immediately, triggered by point of sale data. Multiple replenishments were soon introduced and Tesco's trucks started leaving the DCs every few hours, carrying stocks of items that were close to being sold out.

Within the stores, Tesco worked towards reducing the handling of goods and streamlining their flow. For example, for some goods like soft drinks which needed quick replenishments, shelves were replaced with wheeled dollies.[2] The dollies were rolled from suppliers into the delivery trucks and then to the stores. Once in the stores, the dollies were rolled to the point of sale to take the place of the usual sales racks. This process did away with handling problems and reduced the number of touches, when employees moved products from large pallets[3] to roll cages[4] and then to the stores' shelves. For these products, Tesco achieved availability of 99.8 per cent. The use of dollies reduced the need for handling as they were loaded at the end of the production line and wheeled through till they reached the supermarket. After applying lean solutions, Tesco was able to reduce the touch point for soft drinks from 170 to 20, and the transit time was reduced to one to three days. Table 9.2 details the performance improvements.

Tesco's trucks collected dollies from the DCs to deliver them at different stores under the DC. In each of the stores, the trucks collected empty dollies and returned them to the suppliers, while collecting full dollies and taking them to the DCs. While multiple trips did result in higher carrying costs as the number of miles travelled went up, the increase in the cost of transportation was compensated for by a greater decrease in inventory costs.

In the late-1990s and early-2000s, Tesco entered into agreements with several suppliers including P&G, Unilever and Coca Cola to change the distribution schedules. Weekly deliveries were replaced by daily deliveries, and the suppliers also agreed to place the cans and bottles on wheeled pallets, which could be placed directly into shelf fixtures. Lead times reduced from a maximum of 18 days to three days. Tesco's stock holding reduced from 4.4 weeks to 2.5 weeks. The food range stock keeping units (SKUs) increased from 5,000 to 40,000 and the service levels improved from 92 per cent to 98.5 per cent. The use of lean solutions in its supply chain was one of the factors that helped Tesco double its net profits from £16,452 million in 1998 to £37,070 in 2005 and overtake Sainsbury to become the UK's biggest grocer.

Managing the supply chain

By 2005, Tesco had 2,365 stores across the world (1,780 in the UK) operating on 24.2 million square feet of retail area. In the UK, Tesco operated primarily through four types of stores (see Table 9.3 for Tesco's store format). The company's international operations were spread in 12 countries across the world. The

TABLE 9.2 Tesco before and after lean solution – example of cola

	BEFORE LEAN SOLUTION	AFTER LEAN SOLUTION
Number of storage locations between bottler and consumer	5	2
Order entry points	6	1
Throughput time	20 days	5 days (75% reduction in total inventory)
Service level	98.5% service level (Grocery industry average 92%)	99.5%

TABLE 9.3 Tesco's store formats

Tesco Express	Convenience stores, typically occupying an area of 3,000 square feet. Initially opened as petrol forecourt shops, by 2005 there were around 546 Express stores.
Tesco Metro	City centre stores occupying around 7,000–15,000 square feet. They offer a wide range of products including fresh foods, takeaways and lunchtime items. There were 160 such stores by 2005.
Tesco Superstore	Initially opened during the 1970s, several stores were added during the 1980s and 1990s. By 2005 there were 446 Superstores. They have expanded into several non-food ranges.
Tesco Extra	Typically 50,000 to 100,000 square feet, many Superstores were converted into Extra stores. They provide a wide range of food and non-food items including homeware, clothing, health equipment, beauty products and seasonal furniture.

(WWW.TESCO.COM)

sheer size of Tesco's operations called for high efficiency in the supply chain. Even if the service level was at 99.9 per cent, it still meant six million service failures.

Tesco have continued to look for improvements in its operations under its 'Step Change' program. This identifies processes in the supply chain in need of transformation. The activities are mapped, feasibility assessed and the new process implemented. After a change is implemented, it is measured against the desired output.

Step Change program initiatives include:

- Using hand held scanners in all stores, allowing staff to access product and stock information at the shelf edge.
- Establishing a dedicated clothing distribution centre handling all clothing going into the UK stores, so that suppliers have the option of delivering to just one distribution centre rather than several or to hundreds of stores.
- Use of replaceable shelves to reduce the time used by staff in arranging the items on shelves.
- Self-service checkouts which, by 2005, were used by around 60,000 customers every week, helping to reduce queuing and congestion.

The Step Change program has eliminated several unnecessary processes and has helped Tesco achieve sizeable cost savings (estimated to be £270 million in 2004–2005). The changes have also made routine operations in stores simpler, freeing up more time for staff to attend to customers.

Sourcing

Tesco sources raw materials locally, from several parts in the UK, and from all across the world. A national buying team takes care of sourcing from suppliers in England, while regional buying teams do so for Scotland, Wales and Northern Ireland. Tesco's international sourcing team plays an important role in procuring non-food items. They choose the locations for sourcing, negotiate prices, place orders and check the quality of the products. Tesco established an international sourcing hub in Hong Kong during the 1970s and this works directly with the manufacturers to provide competitive prices. It has several smaller hubs across Asia and Africa. In 1999, Tesco started procuring products like apparel, toys, electrical, household products, homeware, outdoor furniture and sports equipment from Southern China. In 2001, a global buying and sourcing super hub was established in Hong Kong, mainly to take advantage of lower costs in Asian countries like China, Thailand, India, Mauritius, Bangladesh and Sri Lanka.

Logistics and warehousing

Tesco serves its network of stores through its logistics and warehousing arm Tesco Distribution. As of 2004, Tesco had 26 DCs and 18 consolidation centres (CCs) in the UK. There were also three CCs in Spain, one each in Italy and the Netherlands. Through the CCs, smaller loads from suppliers in that region are consolidated, before being shipped to the UK.

Tesco has changed its DCs into cross docking operations. Cross docking is the practice by which products from different suppliers, heading for the same store are unloaded from an incoming truck's trailers and loaded directly into an outbound trailer. This eliminates the need for storage. Inventory holding and order picking have been shifted from Tesco's DCs to manufacturers, enabling Tesco to decrease its inventory holding by one third.

Tesco has also pioneered the primary distribution process, whereby it picks up products from its domestic suppliers through its own trucks, delivering them into its own distribution network. Primary distribution helps Tesco use its distribution fleet to the optimum level through backhauling. As of 2005, more than 65 per cent of the goods from suppliers to Tesco's DCs were carried by the company's own or a contracted fleet. Primary distribution has led to cost savings and has improved on time delivery by 14 per cent and reduced stock holding.

To support primary distribution, Tesco and its suppliers have moved to Collaborative Planning, Forecasting and Replenishment (CPFR) to analyze demand patterns. CPFR involves business partners sharing forecasts and results data through the Internet, in order to reduce inventory costs while at the same time enhancing product availability across the supply chain. The system is used to decide on offline stocking points,[5] to adjust production volumes and the stock to be held.

Tesco is in the process of developing an international supply chain. In Hungary, Tesco had opened a fresh produce DC and an ambient grocery DC in 2002; in 2004 a composite DC and a fresh food DC were opened. In March 2003, Tesco opened a 1.5 million square feet DC in Korea. In 2003, the first DC in Poland was opened in Warsaw. In the same year a 260,000 square feet DC with a capacity of 29,000 pallets was opened in the Czech Republic. In 2004, Tesco opened a 209,000 square feet composite DC in Dublin, to supply products to all the Tesco stores in Ireland.

Continuous replenishment

In the traditional replenishment system, each store decided what products it needed. Their order was centralized and given to the suppliers, who delivered the goods to regional DCs. After all the suppliers delivered their goods at the DC, they were delivered to each store. In the traditional method, sales data were posted at the end of each day and orders made for the next day and delivered the following day (see Figure 9.10 for Tesco's traditional supply chain).

Tesco introduced the CR system in 1999. Tesco's CR system is based on the orders obtained from the checkout counters at different stores. The orders are placed several times a day and the suppliers make several deliveries to the DC. As and when the items arrive, they are assembled and dispatched to the stores. The same system is followed for both food and non-food products. The main aim is to cut costs, reduce lead times, improve product availability and maintain accuracy of orders. (See Figure 9.11 for Tesco's Continuous Replenishment Supply Chain.)

Continuous replenishment is facilitated by Point of Sale (POS) data, which provide real time data about sales as and when they happen. Sales data from the individual stores are routed to the head office. In the CR

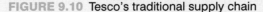

FIGURE 9.10 Tesco's traditional supply chain

| Store order calculation | Central order processing | Production scheduling | Transport to depot, awaiting delivery | Batched delivery to stores once a day |

NOTE: THE REPLENISHMENT REQUIRED ARRIVAL OF ALL THE SUPPLIERS' VEHICLES AT THE DEPOT, AFTER WHICH FINAL DELIVERY TO THE STORES WAS CARRIED OUT

FIGURE 9.11 Tesco – continuous replenishment supply chain

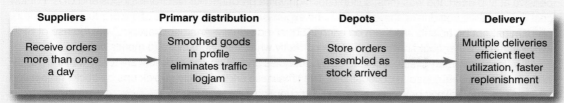

Suppliers	Primary distribution	Depots	Delivery
Receive orders more than once a day	Smoothed goods in profile eliminates traffic logjam	Store orders assembled as stock arrived	Multiple deliveries efficient fleet utilization, faster replenishment

system, there is a continuous flow of data between head office, depots and stores to replenish stocks through an automated order process. Tesco posts data every hour on each of the 40,000 product lines. Multiple deliveries improve the availability, quality and variety of products. Wherever possible, products are cross docked, reducing handling and stock holding. Through this system, Tesco is able to improve availability, maintain optimum stock and offer a wider range of products. The average replenishment time (the time between the order being placed and the order arriving at the distribution) which was previously between 48 to 72 hours was reduced to 24 to 36 hours and the goods reached the stores from DC within 24 hours. Tesco also uses point of sale (POS) data to understand consumer behaviour, project sales and manage stocks at individual stores. Tesco's POS information system has helped it to avoid the 'out of stock' problems which have so bedeviled some of its rivals.

In the UK, sales density is higher than in other markets. Shelves need to be replenished more often as sales are higher; stores that are fully stocked in the morning need to be refilled by noon. Thus, the availability of goods is of prime importance. Tesco has developed an e-procurement program, called The Tesco Information Exchange program[6] (TIE). TIE links all Tesco stores to their suppliers including farmers. Any surge in demand for farm products is directly conveyed to the farmers. Using CR based on TIE, Tesco launched its 'Full and Fresh' program, in which fresh food deliveries are made twice a day. Orders are fed directly to the picking units in the fields, where the required items are packed and dispatched so as to be available on the shelves the next day.

Adopting RFID technology

Tesco started using RFID technology, which it called radio bar codes, on a trial basis in 2003. After the successful completion of a number of pilot programs, Tesco set a deadline of September 2006 for its suppliers to adopt RFID. The main advantage of RFID over bar codes is that it uses microchips to transmit product codes to scanners without human intervention and the products can be tracked throughout the supply chain. RFID provides more information compared to bar codes. RFID has been touted as a system that provides unique identification and security for each package right from the time it is manufactured to the time it is sold.

RFID technology helps in measuring and controlling every aspect of the supply chain. It promotes faster processing of goods, lower costs and higher employee efficiency through improved availability of goods. Other benefits are the option to trace the products from source to consumer, the option to automatically scan the entire shopping trolley resulting in quicker checkout, and reduction in thefts as the scanners at the exit could identify the products that were not paid for.

Looking ahead

The effective use of lean principles has helped Tesco to become the lowest cost retailer in Britain. Consumer demand has become the main driver in store deliveries. Looking ahead, Tesco still has significant challenges in supply chain management. According to some analysts, Tesco was successful in implementing its supply chain strategy, as its stores were located close to one another in the UK and the strategy might not be successful in countries where stores are widely dispersed.

In the East European markets, Tesco's logistics and supply chain are not well developed and rely heavily on deliveries from suppliers. This is a viable proposition for the large stores but not for the smaller ones. As Tesco plans to expand smaller stores in Eastern Europe, developments in the supply chain have become necessary. In Thailand and Korea automated DCs have become operational. For Tesco to gain an edge over other multi-national retailers entering these markets, it is necessary to build viable supply chain solutions.

Industry analysts feel that full-scale implementation of RFID will not be easy. The RFID tag was quite expensive at 50p each and was most suitable for high value products like electronic goods and CDs. For low cost products like soft drinks, they turn out to be expensive relative to the price of the product. Several suppliers might not be able to use them on each product individually. Another challenge with the use of RFID was that the scanner could not read the tags correctly when they were close to metals or liquid.

Also, Tesco's Primary Distribution has many loopholes and, often, the suppliers are ready with the goods, while Tesco is not equipped to collect them. The timeliness and reliability of pick ups by trucks nominated by Tesco was not always better than those of the suppliers.

Notes

1 A touch refers to human effort made in transporting the product.

2 Low mobile platforms that roll on casters, used for transporting heavy loads.

3 A pallet is a flat transport structure made of wood or plastic which can support a variety of goods in a stable fashion while being lifted by any mobile forklift device. The goods are placed on top of the pallet and can be secured to it by straps or stretch-wrapped plastic film.

4 Roll cages are half-pallet sized platforms with four running castors beneath and with a wire cage mounted on the platform to contain goods during transport. Roll cages are used to transport goods within the factory, by lorry to a warehouse or retail store and within the store.

5 Any stock that is in excess of a full truck load is known as offline stock. These stocks are used as a buffer against peaks and troughs in demand and are also used as safety stocks against delivery failures.

6 TIE links Tesco with its suppliers using Electronic Data Interchange. By 1995, 1,300 suppliers were a part of the system. By 1999, TIE received 130,000 hits per month. Using TIE Tesco can share all the sales and stock information with the suppliers. The suppliers are able to deal with orders and invoices online. They have access to the Point of Sale data, which details how their products fared across Tesco's retailing network. The suppliers can respond to the changes in demand quickly and ensure optimum supply.

—Abridged from the case study written by P. Indu and Vivek Gupta
(ICFAI Center for Management Research).

Questions (Suggested answers can be found on the companion website www.thomsonlearning.co.uk/barnes)

1 To what extent can Tesco's supply chain practices be said to follow lean (i.e. just in time) principles? (Consider JIT as a philosophy, a planning and control system, and an inventory system.)

2 What are the main differences between operating JIT in retailing and in manufacturing operations?

3 What challenges does the increased internationalization of both its suppliers and its markets present for supply chain management in Tesco?

References

Womack, J.P. and Jones, D.T. (1996) *Lean Thinking: Banish Waste and Create Wealth in Your Corporation,* New York: Simon and Schuster.

Additional reading

Bicheno, J. (1998) *The Lean Toolbox,* Buckingham: Picsie Books.
Ohno, T. (1995) *Toyota Production System: Beyond large scale production,* New York: Productivity Press.

Schonberger, R.J. (1982) *Japanese Manufacturing Techniques: Nine Hidden Lessons in Simplicity,* New York: Free Press.

Waters, D. (2004) *Inventory control and management,* New York: John Wiley and Sons.

Womack, J., Jones, D. and Roos, D. (1990) *The Machine that Changed the World,* New York: Simon and Schuster.

Womack, J.P. and Jones, D.T. (1996) *Lean Thinking: Banish Waste and Create Wealth in Your Corporation,* New York: Simon and Schuster.

Useful websites

WWW.

http://www.apics.org/ The website of APICS, the US-based Association for Operations Management, which acts as a source of the body of knowledge in operations management, including production, inventory, supply chain, materials management, purchasing and logistics.

http://www.inventoryops.com/ A consultancy website, but one containing a rich source of information on inventory management.

http://www.bpic.co.uk/index.htm The website of BPIC, the business performance improvement consultancy. Contains resources and case studies on MRP2 and ERP implementations.

http://www.toyota.co.jp/en/vision/production_system/index.html The Toyota Production Systems explained by the people that invented it. Toyota Motor Corporation's Global Site has several pages dedicated to explaining the origins and constituents of the world's best known, and most influential, production system.

http://www.lean.org/ The website of the Lean Enterprise Institute, a non-profit education and research organization that aims to promote and advance the principles of lean thinking in every aspect of business and across a wide range of industries.

CHAPTER 10

QUALITY

INTRODUCTION

Quality is perhaps the one thing that everyone is in favour of. In fact, you rarely, if ever, hear anyone speaking against it. Furthermore, quality has been something of a 'hot' topic in management for many years. Huge amounts have been written about it by academics, consultants and practitioners. As such, you would think that there would be no quality problems left to solve. Yet, evidence the world over is that organizations often fail to deliver the level of quality that their customers want. It goes without saying that quality is important to customers. If customers are satisfied or better still, delighted, then they will come back for more and recommend the organization to others. So you would think that all organizations would want to meet or exceed their customers' expectations with regard to quality. Yet, in spite of what you expect to be their best intentions, organizations often fail to delight their customers. Quality is not of itself an inherently international issue. Although there are still some national differences in approaches to managing quality, there is now a high degree of consensus about what is the best quality management model. This chapter will describe the main approaches that have been used in quality management and discuss why so many organizations still seem to find it difficult to convert their good intentions to effective action on quality.

THE EVOLUTION OF QUALITY IDEAS

Quality emerged as an important issue in operations management in Japan during the 1950s and has remained on the agenda ever since. Western interest in quality was spawned by the desire to emulate the performance of many Japanese manufacturing companies who came to enjoy worldwide success built on the perceived high quality of their products. It came as a surprise to many in the West to discover that Japanese quality methods were based on the teachings of Americans, particularly Deming and Juran, whose ideas were rejected in their native land, but accepted in a devastated post-war Japan eager to re-establish its industrial base. (See Box 10.1 for a review of some of the most important quality 'gurus'.) By implementing these ideas, the Japanese were able to change the image of their products from that of cheap, low-grade copies to the situation today where a 'Made in Japan' label is accepted as a guarantee of quality.

The theory and practice of quality has evolved over this period from simple quality inspection, whereby products were checked for defects at the end of a production process, to total quality management (TQM), in which the issue of quality is placed at the heart of all the organization's activities. Dale and Cooper (1992) suggest that it is possible to distinguish four stages in the evolution of quality ideas.

1 Quality inspection
2 Quality control
3 Quality assurance
4 TQM

Each stage builds on the previous one, incorporating its ideas as it expands the content of quality (see Figure 10.1). These four stages are not totally distinguishable from one another, but should be viewed as a continuum.

Quality inspection

This is primarily concerned with the inspection and testing of the outputs from a transformation process. Typically, a dedicated quality inspector examines the output of workers. Finished products are either approved for sale to customers or rejected. Rejects may be downgraded for sale as 'seconds', returned to production for rework, or scrapped. Unless inspection is systematic and rigorous, there is a high risk of faulty goods reaching the customer. Even with 100 per cent inspection, human error by

quality inspection
The inspection and testing of the outputs from a transformation process to determine whether they are of saleable quality or if they should be rejected, reworked or downgraded for sale as 'seconds', normally at a lower price.

total quality management (TQM)
A philosophy for quality improvement based on principles of the elimination of waste, continuous involvement and the involvement of all employees.

FIGURE 10.1 The expanding content of quality

Total quality management

Quality assurance

Quality control

Quality inspection

BOX 10.1

The quality gurus

A small number of people have been very influential in the evolution of quality ideas over the last 50 years. They are often referred to as quality gurus. Amongst the most important of these are:

W. Edwards Deming
Originally a statistician, Deming helped pioneer statistical quality control techniques. He advocated the use of such techniques to drive quality improvements by reducing process variation. He strongly believed in employee participation but was critical of motivational programmes, arguing that everyone doing their best is never likely to be enough. He argued that working smarter is required, not working harder, pointing out that workers cannot 'do it right first time' if they work with materials which are outside the requirements of the process on machines that have not been properly maintained. Deming is revered in Japan, where the Deming Prize is the most sought-after award for quality.

Joseph Juran
Like Deming, Juran was also highly influential in post-war Japan. Juran was the first person to advocate defining quality as 'fitness for use' rather than 'conformance to specification'. Juran advocated the use of statistical methods, but also emphasized the need to organize, communicate and co-ordinate. He argued the need to improve by achieving 'breakthroughs' on a project-by-project basis.

Armand Feigenbaum
Feigenbaum originated the term 'total quality control'. He advocated the need to involve all parts of the organization in a systematic approach to quality. He argued the importance of calculating the cost of non-quality, and stressed the need for a 'right first time' attitude.

Philip Crosby
Crosby was the most charismatic of the quality gurus. He is well-known for the concept of 'zero defects' and his assertion that 'quality is free'. His approach to quality was based on four 'absolutes of quality', i.e. defining quality as 'conformance to requirements', using a quality system to prevent defects, measuring quality as the price of non-conformance, and adopting 'zero defects' as the quality standard.

Genichi Taguchi
Taguchi believed quality improvement requires the reduction of variances in performance. He developed methods to ensure that quality is built into products by integrating the contributions of design and manufacturing staff.

Kaomi Ishikawa
Ishikawa stressed the need to involve everyone in the quality improvement process and advocated the use of simple statistical methods and problem-solving techniques. He is credited with the development of the quality circle as a technique to involve workers in improvement efforts. He is also associated with the use of the 'fishbone' cause and effect diagramming technique as a problem solving tool.

inspectors can still lead to faulty goods being approved for dispatch. In this sort of environment, quality is usually seen as the 'quality department's' problem and not the concern of 'operations'. A reactive and blame-placing attitude to quality is likely to develop, with operations staff seeking to hide quality problems to 'outwit' the quality inspectors who act as a kind of police. There is little or no emphasis on prevention.

Quality control

This builds on the quality inspection stage in a number of ways. Statistical techniques like acceptance sampling may be introduced to make inspection more effective. Data from inspection will be used to identify causes of defects and to take corrective action. The major evolution in quality control is its attempt to control the process itself. A quality manual will be developed, detailing how the process should be operated and stipulating process performance data. Statistical methods like control charts are likely to be deployed to monitor process performance. Some elements of operator self-inspection may be introduced. Despite these advances, the quality control stage may still be characterized by a reactive, blame-seeking approach to quality. The emphasis is on meeting the specification with an acceptable level of defects.

quality control
An extension of quality inspection in that it uses data from inspection to identify causes of defects and to take corrective action.

Quality assurance

This stage moves the concept of quality beyond measurement and feedback control towards a more proactive approach aimed at preventing quality problems occurring in the first place. Quality assurance introduces a comprehensive quality management system (QMS) based on a manual which sets out in detail how the entire operation should be managed. The quality of inputs is assured by buying only from suppliers who themselves practice quality assurance. Acceptance sampling techniques may also be used on inputs. The process itself is likely to be controlled through statistical process control techniques applied by workers. Quality planning techniques like failure mode and effects analysis (FMEA) may be used to try to anticipate problems before they occur and take preventative measures. This is likely to involve design or redesign of products and processes. Techniques such as quality function deployment (QFD), also referred to as the 'house of quality', which seek to ensure that designs meets the needs of the customer might be used (see Chapter 13). The costs of quality are likely to be calculated and used as a basis for preventative action. The whole focus moves towards proactively seeking to solve quality problems, attacking their causes not their effects.

quality assurance
This involves taking a proactive approach towards quality management by seeking to prevent defects ever being produced. This usually involves the adoption of a quality management system.

quality management system (QMS)
A systematic approach to proactively managing quality based on documented standards and operating procedures. The best known QMSs are those based on the ISO9000 series of quality standards.

failure mode and effects analysis (FMEA)
A technique used to identify likely causes of failure and their consequences so that preventative actions can be taken.

Quality function deployment (QFD)
A structured procedure that aims to ensure that the design of products and services meets the needs of the customer. (QFD is sometimes also referred to as *the voice of the customer.*) It does so by forcing designers to match each customer requirement of the product with the way that the design meets that requirement. (QFD is sometimes also referred to as *the house of quality.*)

costs of quality
An expression of an organization's performance in quality in financial terms.

TQM

This seeks to switch the emphasis from merely applying tools and techniques to changing attitudes so that quality becomes part of the beliefs and values of everyone in the organization. It is about changing culture to a state where everyone is concerned not merely to conform to customer requirements but to exceed their expectations. TQM is best thought of as a philosophy rather than the application of any particular set of techniques. Indeed, practitioners of TQM can be found using a wide range of tools and techniques, although the use of statistical quality control is considered particularly important by many Japanese TQM exponents.

TQM sees quality as a source of competitive advantage. It is built on the belief that quality needs to be defined from the customer's point of view and that its pursuit will deliver improvements in corporate performance. As such, quality needs to be managed strategically and that requires organization-wide commitment and a long-term perspective. In TQM, the pursuit of quality is viewed as a never-ending goal, a journey rather than a destination. TQM stresses the importance of involving all organizational members in the achievement of quality in all activities. It emphasizes getting things right first time by building quality into operational processes. It focuses on the cost of quality, especially the cost of quality failures. Most importantly, TQM is based on the philosophy of continuous improvement or *kaizen* (in Japanese). The philosophy of TQM (eliminating waste, continuous involvement and the involvement of all employees) is held in common with that of JIT, and provides the underpinnings for the production systems observed in many Japanese manufacturing companies, most notably Toyota. Such companies would not seek to discriminate between the terms TQM and JIT, viewing them as inseparable aspects of their manufacturing practices. Indeed, the very terms TQM and JIT were devised by visiting Westerners' partial understandings of the holistic nature of the Toyota production system.

The successful adoption of TQM requires taking a systemic view of the production system, outside it as well as within it. TQM puts great store on tapping into ideas for quality improvement from anywhere in the organization, its suppliers or customers. It involves working with suppliers to solve quality problems, and with customers to determine how the organization can better meet their needs. It will almost certainly involve workers performing their own inspection and testing, using techniques like statistical process control charts. The TQM organization will ensure that all employees are trained in the use of appropriate tools and techniques for quality improvement. TQM is management-led, but it seeks to harness the energies, ideas and commitment of all employees. The successful implementation of TQM requires a supportive organizational culture. One that seeks to solve quality problems, rather than apportion blame for their existence. In a culture of quality, everyone takes responsibility for achieving quality improvements. Such a culture is operationalized by the application of techniques such as quality circles. These comprise groups of employees who meet regularly to identify and resolve quality problems in their work areas. A culture of quality can only be built on mutual trust, with a management, as Deming puts it, committed to 'drive out fear'.

TQM requires:

- commitment from top managers
- good relations between management and workforce
- good communications and relationships between different departments
- continuous education at all levels
- good relations with customers
- good relations with suppliers
- shop-floor initiatives to be encouraged and facilitated.

Many Western organizations have tried to undertake TQM initiatives in attempts to emulate the quality performance achieved by many Japanese companies. These have had mixed success, and many such initiatives have faded over time. This is often due to a lack of commitment from top management, who all too often see TQM as a quick fix for quality problems.

Most of the ideas of TQM derive from the application of advice of the various quality gurus (see Box 10.1). However, their writings tend to be both extensive and sometimes divergent. As Oakland (1993) puts it, they are talking the same language, but are using different dialects. As such, there is no one agreed best way to implement TQM.

Quality in service operations

The evolving thinking and practice in quality has been concerned mainly with manufactured goods. Quality in service operations has been something of a neglected area, receiving much less attention. However, it seems as if service organizations are now taking quality management increasingly seriously. As already discussed in Chapter 1, services are different from goods in that they are intangible, cannot be stored, are consumed at the point of production and often involve contact with customers. These factors all make the measurement of quality in services far more difficult than with goods. Similarly, the singular nature of many customer service encounters makes their standardization more difficult, if not undesirable, which makes specifying service outputs much more difficult. Because of the person-to-person interaction in customer services, setting quality standards and measuring quality performance need to take into account both the service provider's and the customer's perceptions of quality. Also, any measurement and control of quality during the process must be carried out so that it does not interfere with the provision of the service. As such, the control of quality in a service operation is likely to be limited to control of the process.

Service providers, no less than manufacturers need to understand exactly how customers evaluate quality. However, consumers of services are likely to use somewhat different criteria than consumers of goods. Berry *et al.* (1985) argue that customers assess service quality in terms of ten factors:

1 *Reliability:* the consistency and dependability of performance. It means that the service provider performs the service right the first time and always honours its promises.

2 *Responsiveness:* the willingness or readiness of employees to provide the service. It also involves the speed and timeliness of service provision.

3 *Competence:* employees possess all the skills and knowledge required to perform the service.

4 *Access:* the ease with which customers can contact the service provider and access the service. The service should be easily accessible whether in person, by phone or on-line, that is waiting times should not be too long, hours of operation and contact points should be convenient for customers.

5 *Courtesy:* contact personnel treat customers politely, respectfully, considerately and in a friendly manner.

6 *Communication:* customers are kept fully informed using language and terminology that they can understand. This may mean that the service provider has to adjust its language and communication style for different consumers. It also means customers are listened to.

7 *Credibility:* the trustworthiness, believability and honesty of the service provider. This involves having the customer's best interests at heart.

8 *Security:* the freedom from danger, risk or doubt when dealing with the service provider. This involves physical safety, financial security and confidentiality.

9 *Understanding the customer:* making the effort to understand the needs of each individual customer.

10 *Tangibles:* the physical evidence of the service, such as its physical facilities and the appearance of staff.

Customers may consider these different factors of greater or lesser importance, depending on the service and their own preferences. It is, therefore, vital for service providers to assess their customers' expectations for specific services.

DEFINING QUALITY

Most organizations normally declare themselves to be convinced of the need to achieve high levels of quality. Quality is generally agreed to be a good and desirable thing. Organizations invariably describe themselves as being 'quality' organizations, and point to the 'quality' of their products and services. If everyone is in favour of quality, why is it that so often customers find that they do not get the quality that they want? One of the biggest problems with word 'quality' is that it can, and frequently is, used to mean quite different things.

In his consideration of this issue, Garvin (1988) usefully comes up with five different bases on which quality can be defined:

1 *Perceived:* This approach is based on a view of quality as innate excellence. Quality is 'something that you know when you see it'. Thus, a Rolls-Royce is thought to be a quality car. Similarly Wedgwood is perceived to be quality pottery, and a Rolex is a regarded as a quality watch. Such superior quality can be identified by its look, its touch, its feel, etc. Where a service is involved, judging quality may rely on even more ethereal criteria, like the atmosphere in a restaurant.

2 *Product-based:* This approach views quality in terms of superior product attributes that can be designed and precisely measured. Quality is seen as a measurable set of characteristics. Thus, the quality of a car can be determined by its performance as measured by its top speed, its acceleration, its fuel consumption, etc.

3 *User-based:* This approach sees quality as fitness for use from the customer's perspective. This is based on the marketing view that customers ultimately decide what quality means and that a quality product or service is one that meets the requirement of the customer. However, particularly in mass markets there can be a danger that an individual customer's view may run counter to the collective view obtained by an aggregation of the views of all customers.

4 *Operations-based:* This approach sees quality in terms of conformance to the specification of the product or service. Thus, a quality product or service is one that has been produced as its designers intended, in conformance with its specification, free from any defects. In this way, quality is achieved if all activities are carried out right first time and error free.

5 *Value-based:* This approach modifies the user-based approach by introducing the notion of cost or price into the consideration of quality. Quality is considered to be the best value for money for a given purpose. Different customers may be prepared be accept a product offered with a lower specification if the price is low. The success of budget airlines, like EasyJet or RyanAir, stems from the fact that many travellers are quite happy to forego the higher levels of service provided by traditional airlines. Being able to afford to travel to their desired destinations is far more important to them than complimentary food and drink, in-flight entertainment, executive lounges, etc.

The key point from this analysis is that there is no single 'correct' view of quality. Each of these five approaches can raise its own problems. The *perceived* approach to quality is particularly difficult to operationalize as it is predicated on principles of excellence. These rely almost exclusively on intangible factors, and on an individual's judgement, which is bound to be highly subjective. The *product-based* approach can lead to an over-concentration on creating what the designers believe to be superior product attributes. There is a danger that the views of the customers may be overlooked and the issue of costs neglected. This can often be the case when designers have a technological rather than a customer focus. Conversely, the *user-based* approach may lead to a desire to try to provide customers with whatever they want, irrespective of cost and whether or not the organization has the capability to consistently deliver it. The *operations-based* approach may lead to an enthusiasm only for achieving conformance to the design specification. Operations staff, especially in manufacturing organizations, may not be in regular contact with customers, and may therefore fail to pick up vital feedback about current organizational performance and ideas for new products and services. The *value-based* approach risks placing too high an emphasis on cost. Staff may come to see the achievement of quality as being at odds with the need to meet cost targets. This can be dangerous if this leads to quality being compromised in the pursuit of cost savings.

The absence of a universally agreed understanding of what is meant by quality can lead to different interpretations in different functional areas in an organization. The marketing department is likely to adopt a user-based approach, whereas the design department may prefer a product-based approach and the operations department take on an operations-based approach. This has the potential for significant misunderstanding within an organization. It is clearly desirable for such differences to be surfaced and if possible, a common standpoint of quality agreed.

However, it seems evident that whatever approach is taken to quality, satisfying the customer must occupy a central place in any consideration of quality. Meeting customer requirements is essential if quality is to be managed successfully and so understanding customer requirements is a necessary pre-requisite if quality is to be managed successfully.

So what criteria are customers likely to use when judging quality? Bank (1992) points to five questions that customers might ask, which equate to different elements of quality.

1 The specification: *'What can I expect when I buy the product?'*
   The purpose of a specification is to communicate the characteristics of the product or service to both customers and providers. It should clarify the attributes of the product and the level of performance (in terms of form, function and benefits) that it has been designed to achieve. The specification should enable potential customers to determine whether the product is likely to be able to meet their needs. As such the specification will set customers' expectations.

2 Conformance to specification: *'Will it do what I expect?'*
   Conformance to specification is concerned with the extent to which the performance of the product or service performs in accordance with its design specification. To that extent, customers' expectations are set by the specification, and any shortfall in performance against that specification is bound to lead to dissatisfaction.

3 Reliability: *'Will it continue to do what I expect?'*
   Reliability is the extent to which the product or service continues to achieve conformance to specification over time. Clearly customers will value a motor car that starts first time, every time, and a hairdresser who always provides that perfect style every time you visit.

4 Delivery: *'When can I have it?'*
   It is important here to distinguish between two aspects of delivery: availability and dependability. Availability is concerned with when the product or service is available for the customer. Dependability is concerned with the adherence to a promised delivery time. For some customers, immediate availability is all important, whereas others might be prepared to wait as long as the product is available at the agreed time. For example, if you want to eat now, your prime concern is for availability. As such, you might be prepared to settle for a table at the nearest restaurant with space, or even opt for a takeaway meal. However, if you can wait, you might be prepared to accept a booking for a table at your favourite restaurant for later on. However you would be dissatisfied if your table was not available at the agreed time. This is a case of the restaurant not being dependable.

5 Price: *'How much do I have to pay?'*
   A purchase can be thought of as an exchange, in which a customer obtains goods or services by offering something of value in return. This is usually a payment in the form of money. However, payment may not always be in the form of money but in time, resources, emotional involvement, etc. For example, a religious organization wants 'membership' and a political pressure

group wants 'idea-acceptance'. The important point is that the customer recognizes the extent to which the product or service meets their requirements by placing a value on them. Customers will be satisfied if the price they pay, whether in money or some other form, equates to the value they place on the goods or service.

Customers use the five elements (specification, conformance, reliability, delivery and price) to judge quality. However, they are likely to emphasize different elements depending on the purchase being made. For example, when making a decision about where to eat at home in England, I may be more concerned with specification when considering eating at a Japanese restaurant – these are not very common in England (what can I expect when I eat there?), with conformance when I eat at my favourite Italian restaurant (is it what I expected?), with reliability when I eat at a McDonald's (is it the same as last time?), with delivery if I order from a pizza delivery service (when can I have it?) and price when I go to my local fish and chip shop (how much will I have to pay?). However in reality my expectations are likely to comprise a mixture of these elements, in different combinations in each case.

To further complicate matters, different customers are likely to have different expectations, even of the same product or service. The provider's difficulties are compounded by the fact that the customers' experience is a perception. Different customers may perceive the same product or service quite differently. Returning to the restaurant example, some customers may see a meal as a bodily necessity, others may see it as a means of enjoyment with family and friends, others may be using it as a business opportunity when entertaining clients. Customers can see a motor car as a means of transport, or an expression of their personality or status. In short, the quality of a product or service is whatever the customer perceives it to be. Thus, it is essential to understand quality from the customer's point of view. In some situations, the customer may not be able to judge the technical aspects of the product or service specification. For example, most people would not be capable of judging the medical quality of the examination and diagnosis that they get from a visit to their doctor. So, they may judge the experience in terms of the manner of the doctor, the attitude of the receptionist, or even whether they had to wait for longer than expected.

THE QUALITY GAPS MODEL

quality gap
Any difference between the customers' expectations of a product or service and their perceptions of their experience of it.

Customers' judgement of quality is largely a matter of how well their perceptions of their experience of a product or service live up to their expectations. Any shortfall between what customers expect and what they perceive they are getting can be thought of as a quality gap, which is likely to lead to customer dissatisfaction. Parasuraman *et al.* (1985) offer a helpful model that categorizes different kinds of quality gaps on the basis of their underlying cause. Although originally devised for service operations, the model can be used to analyze quality problems in any organization (see Figure 10.2).

The model identifies five possible gaps:

- **Gap 1: The gap between customers' expectations and management's perceptions of customers' expectations.** This arises when managers do not understand what customers actually consider to be important in the product or service. For example, the managers of a conference facility might consider the quality of the coffee to be the most important aspect of a coffee break. However the customers – the conference organizers – may look for promptness, sufficient space for the delegates to chat in comfort, availability of suitable toilet facilities, etc. Such a situation demonstrates a failure to understand the benefits sought by the customers.

- **Gap 2: The gap between management's perception of customers' expectations and the product specification.** This arises when designers do not draw up a

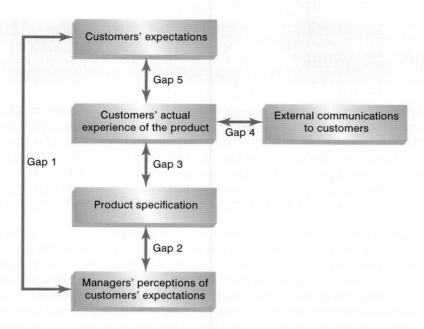

(ADAPTED FROM PARASURAMAN ET AL., 1985)

FIGURE 10.2 The quality gaps model

specification detailed enough to show clearly what they intend the product or service to be. This may leave the employees who deliver the service or make the goods unsure about what is intended. This may also arise because, although the product may be adequately specified, the process used in its production is not. This can be especially problematic in service delivery, where process and product are often inseparable.

- **Gap 3: The gap between the specification and the customers' experience of the product.** This arises when the product is not delivered as specified. There are many potential reasons why this can happen. Perhaps demand has been greater than anticipated, or perhaps resources are constrained. It should be remembered that it is the customers' perception of their experience of the product that is important. This can be affected by many intangible factors, which can be especially important in service delivery.

- **Gap 4: The gap between the customers' experience and the external communications to customers.** This arises when an organization can not deliver what it promises in its advertising or other promotional activity. The lesson here is that organizations would be advised to promise only what they can deliver if they want to have satisfied customers. It is better to under promise and over deliver.

- **Gap 5: The gap between the customers' expectations and the customers' experiences.** Customers' expectations are affected by their own experiences, the recommendations of others and the claims of the supplier. Remember again that customers' experiences are determined by *their* perceptions and not those supplying the product or service. It is essential for suppliers to see things from the customers' standpoint. Parasuraman *et al.* (1988) have developed a standard measuring instrument (SERVQUAL) in the form of a questionnaire, based upon Berry *et al.'s* (1985) criteria for customer service quality (outlined on p. 277), that enables service providers to quantify the quality of the service experienced by customers in terms of Gap 5. SERVQUAL has become a widely used instrument. It can be used by a service provider to track customer service performance over time, for comparing performance at different sites and, if comparative data can be obtained, for benchmarking with competitors or best-in-class practitioners. (The issue of benchmarking is discussed in more detail in Chapter 14.)

WHEN THINGS GO WRONG   Dell and the case of the exploding laptops

On 14 August 2006, the world's biggest computer maker Dell announced the recall of approximately 4.1 million laptops with lithium-ion batteries, made by Sony. Dell said that 'Under rare conditions, it is possible for these batteries to overheat, which could cause a risk of fire'. The recall would be the biggest in Dell's history. The announcement was the first acknowledgement by Dell of a problem that had been pointed out by stories of spontaneously combusting laptops that had been passing around the Internet for some time. The most vivid illustration of the problem was a widely circulated video clip of a laptop exploding into flames at a conference in Japan. Some people claimed Dell had been aware of the overheating problems for at least two years.

Obtaining a suitable power source for laptops has remained a technological challenge for computer manufacturers since their inception. In 1993, Dell was forced to recall an early model and temporarily withdraw from the laptop market after some units overheated. In 2000, Dell also recalled laptops after a manufacturing defect caused overheating that could lead to fires. Dell is far from alone in having battery problems, however, with Compaq, Apple and HP amongst those also affected over the years. Industry experts claim that technological developments in batteries have just not been keeping pace with the demands of the units they power. As one pointed out, 'Faster chips use more power; software makers are introducing more applications; consumers are using bigger displays to watch movies'. Another claimed that 'Lithium-ion batteries have a thermal run-away feature. Although this type of battery is environmentally safer, cheaper and lighter than some alternatives, it is very susceptible to blowing up if the temperature exceeds the specified limits'.

However, Peter Bruce, a lithium-ion expert at St Andrews University in Scotland, said it was important not to exaggerate the risk. 'The worldwide production of lithium-ion batteries exceeded one billion last

Some Dell computers became too hot to handle

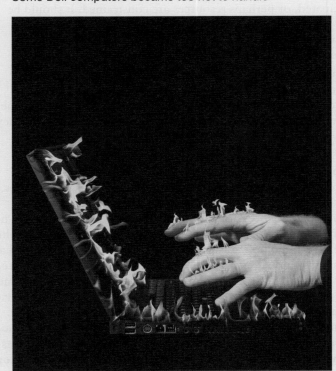

year', he said. 'The proportion of cells causing problems is statistically minute: 99.999 per cent function perfectly well'. Professor Bruce added: 'The problems are more related to quality control and reliability of manufacturing than to any intrinsic defect in lithium-ion technology'. Such views have led some to question Dell's operations. 'These are highly engineered products – there is not a lot of wriggle room in the specification', said Ted Schadler, Vice-President of Forrester Research. 'The pressures of getting computers to market in the quickest possible time and at the lowest possible cost put manufacturers under strain', he added.

Some analysts said that if Dell handled the product recall well, there might be no lasting damage. However, it did come at a sensitive time when the company was under fire for poor customer service and slowing sales growth. Other commentators said that it could be more damaging to Sony, given the Japanese company's reputation for quality in the consumer electronics industry. For as long as anyone can remember, Sony's reputation has been encapsulated in its advertising slogan: 'It's a Sony'. One analyst said, 'Sony's supposed to have a premium brand and they're supposed to have control of their manufacturing', he said. Sony's predicament worsened when a week after the Dell product recall, Apple followed suit, recalling 1.8 million notebooks with Sony batteries.

Despite the damage to both companies' reputations, it looked as if the product recall itself would not be too costly. One analyst estimated that the recall could cost $400m. Sony would contribute towards the costs of a recall. 'Dell will pay some of the costs, Sony will pay some of the costs', Sony announced.

(Source material www.dell.com and www.ft.com)

WWW.

WWW.

Questions (Suggested answers can be found on the companion website www.thomsonlearning.co.uk/barnes)

1 Identify the quality gaps that this case illustrates.

2 What are the likely causes of these gaps?

3 What could Dell do to avoid such quality gaps in the future?

MEASURING QUALITY

It is a fundamental tenet of management that control must be based on measurement. However, measurement presents another problem for quality management as there is no consensus as to what should be measured in order to control quality. There are three possible types of measures that could be used, each of which is used in practice. However, they flow from differing understandings of the term 'quality'.

- *Operations measures:* These tend to be associated with 'conformance to specification' definitions of quality. Such measures are defect or scrap rates, or some other indication of the proportion of non-conforming product. Specifications might include aspects of timeliness, particularly in service industries. Appropriate quality measures here might include, for example, the percentage of deliveries made on time and the percentage of appointments kept on time.

- *Financial measures:* It is argued that in order to gain the attention of senior managers and secure their commitment to quality management, quality should be measured in financial terms. By measuring the cost, its importance can be gauged in terms of its impact on corporate financial performance. The cost of steps to improve quality can then be assessed in terms of their financial impact in the same way as any other expenditure proposal. Some estimates have assessed cost of quality to be as high as 25 per cent of total costs. Figures like that are sure to have the desired attention-grabbing effect.

The costs of quality can be broken down into:

● Appraisal costs
  The costs of inspection and associated activities to check conformance to specification include:
  – Inspection tests and checks on incoming material, operations processes and final goods or services, including any further tests.
  – Inspection equipment.
  – Auditing the operations quality system.
  – Assessing and approving suppliers (vendor rating).
  These are the 'costs of checking it is right'.

● Prevention costs
  The costs associated with designing, implementing and maintaining a quality management system to prevent quality problems occurring include:
  – Determining requirements and setting appropriate specifications for inputs, processes and outputs for each stage of the operation.
  – Planning for quality.
  – Creating and maintaining a quality assurance system.
  – Training operators, supervisors, managers and other staff.
  These are the 'costs of doing it right first time'.

● Internal failure costs
  These are the costs which arise when work fails to achieve the required quality standards. They include:
  – Scrapping defective work, including the wasted materials and the time of people and equipment.
  – Reworking, correcting the defects or repeating the work.
  – Re-inspecting the rectified or repeated work.
  – Downgrading defective products for sale as 'second quality' at a low price.
  – Excess inventory which is often carried to compensate for 'normal' reject rates.
  – Analyzing the reasons for failures.

● External failure costs
  These are the costs which arise when goods or services which do not reach quality standards are actually detected by the customer. They include:
  – Repair or replacement of faulty goods or services.
  – Staff time to handle customer complaints.
  – The handling and investigation of returned faulty goods, including transport costs.
  – Liability claims due to non-conforming goods/services.
  – Financial costs due to delayed payment of invoices.
  – Loss of reputation and lost sales.

Internal and external failures are the 'costs of getting it wrong'. Some of these costs, particularly the less tangible external failure costs, like loss of reputation and lost sales, are difficult to quantify but they are very real nonetheless.

In theory at least, it is possible to calculate the total cost of quality by adding the costs of appraisal and prevention to the costs of internal and external failure. It should be possible to reduce the total cost of quality by putting more effort into quality appraisal and prevention. Increased spending on appraisal and particularly prevention should eventually lead to a reduction in the costs of failure. Prevention should always

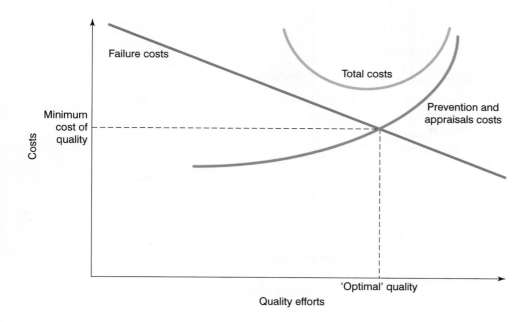

FIGURE 10.3 The traditional view of quality costs

be cheaper than failure because of the costs of correcting mistakes. The traditional view of the costs of quality is that there is a trade-off between appraisal and prevention costs on the one hand and failure costs on the other. This view, as illustrated in Figure 10.3, shows the curve for these two sets of costs, which operate in opposite directions. The total quality cost curve, obtained by adding both sets of costs, is shown on the figure as the top curve.

Viewed in this way it is possible to argue that there is an optimal level of quality effort which will minimize the total cost of cost quality. That is, there is a point at which further spending on prevention will not be recovered in savings in the costs of failure and the total cost of quality will not fall. It can be argued that this point produces an 'acceptable' level of quality. However, it can be seen that at this level of quality effort, quality is less than perfect and the level of defects is greater than zero. This approach to quality is now considered to be dangerous and the concept of an acceptable level of quality is rejected on two main grounds. First, it is difficult, if not impossible, to accurately calculate all the costs of quality, especially the costs of lost opportunities. Second, and probably more importantly, an acceptance of the trade-off concept is an acceptance that defective goods and service will be supplied to customers. In a competitive environment this seems to be very risky if not fool-hardy behaviour.

A more enlightened approach to quality costs rejects the trade-off concept. This view, as shown in Figure 10.4, considers that it is always possible to lower the total cost of quality by extra spending on prevention. No matter how high the level of quality being currently achieved, it is always possible to do better. Whilst these curves are essentially theoretical due to the difficulties of obtaining realistic figures from which to draw them, they do illustrate important philosophical differences in the approach to managing quality. The traditional trade-off approach can lead to a complacent attitude towards quality. The enlightened approach, however, is based on a philosophy of continuous improvement which is the cornerstone of TQM.

Customer measures

These are measures which stem from a user-based 'fitness for use from the customers' perspective' or a value-based view of quality. Typical customer-based measures could be the results of customer satisfaction surveys and the like. These are obviously

FIGURE 10.4 The enlightened view of quality costs

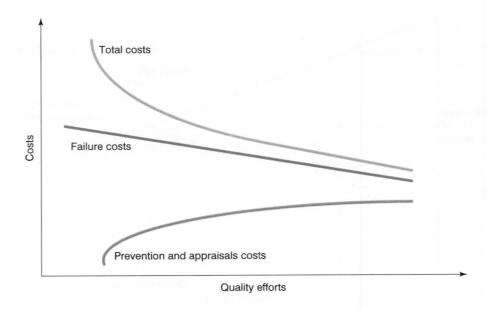

externally focused measures of quality, and tend to be used in organizations where quality is viewed as a strategic issue – a weapon to be employed in the pursuit of increased sales and market share. Customer-based measures are also more prevalent in service industries. Given the intangible nature of most services, this is perhaps both inevitable and desirable. In any case, this approach requires quality to be defined very much from the customers' viewpoint and so will derive from their perceptions. This approach also lends itself to use with internal as well as external customers. The development of customer-based quality measures is still in its infancy but seems to be on the increase. The SERVQUAL instrument, outlined above, represents one attempt to produce a standardized generic questionnaire to measure quality from the customers' perspective in service operations. Many hotels, restaurants, airlines etc. try to assess their service quality by asking customers to fill in evaluation questionnaires.

STATISTICAL QUALITY CONTROL

The use of statistics in quality control is advocated by many of the quality gurus and has been credited as underpinning the improvement in quality achieved by many leading organizations. The basis of the use of statistics is sampling. Where large quantities are involved, it would be costly in the extreme to inspect all the outputs from a process. In some cases, it is impractical or even impossible to undertake a 100 per cent inspection, for example where inspection involves destructive testing. Therefore, a sample, a small number of items, is taken from amongst all the possible items (referred to by statisticians as the 'population') for inspection. Statistical theory can be used to determine the size of sample that is needed in order for the sample to be considered as truly representative of the population under consideration. Statistical theory can also be used to predict the degree of confidence that what is measured in the sample will also apply for those items not in the sample.

A detailed consideration of the statistics underpinning these quality control techniques is outside of the scope of this book, but it is possible to outline the basis of the use of such techniques without going into their detail. Two of the most frequently used statistical quality control techniques are now described, namely acceptance sampling and statistical process control charts.

statistical quality control (SQC)
The application of statistics to the management of quality.

Acceptance sampling

Acceptance sampling is a technique used to determine whether a particular batch of items contains an unacceptably high number of defects. The idea is to check a sample from the batch and then accept or reject the entire batch on the basis of the results from the sample. Acceptance sampling is generally used to check batches of incoming materials intended as inputs in a process or to check the outputs from a process before delivery to a customer.

Acceptance sampling is usually undertaken as part of a commercial agreement between a supplier and a buyer. The supplier will not want good batches to be returned and the customer will not want to accept bad batches. However, as with any sampling scheme, there is a risk that the characteristics of the sample will not be the same as that of the whole batch. The usual procedure is to take a random sample of an agreed number from the batch and test them. If there are no more defective items than the agreed acceptance number, the batch is accepted. If not, then the whole batch is rejected.

Typical numbers might be:

Batch size: 10,000

Sample size: 100

Acceptance number: 2, i.e. the whole batch should be rejected if three or more defective items are found in the sample.

In any sampling scheme, the following must be agreed between supplier and customer:

1 *The acceptance quality level (AQL),* which is the highest percentage of defective items in the batch considered to be acceptable by the customer.

2 *The customer's risk,* which is the chance that a batch which contains more defective items than the AQL will be accepted by the sampling scheme.

3 *The supplier's risk,* which is the chance that a batch which contains fewer defective items than the AQL will be rejected by the sampling scheme.

4 *The lot tolerance percentage of defectives (LTPD),* which is the level of defective items in the batch which both sides agree should always be rejected by the scheme.

Once these are agreed, a sampling scheme can be devised with an agreed sample size and acceptance number per batch to meet their requirements. In practice, it is rare to design a completely new plan as there are many already in existence.

Acceptance sampling offers a cost-effective means of deciding whether to accept or reject a batch of items. It is, however, based on checking quality after the event and cannot, of itself, build quality into a process.

Statistical process control charts

Statistical process control (SPC) charts are used to monitor the performance of a process by checking its output at regular intervals. The results can be used not only to confirm whether the current output is within the permitted range but also to warn of likely problems and hence to prompt preventative action. Thus, SPC charts are a way of building quality into a process. SPC charts are aimed at ensuring that a process is in control by checking that the system is operating within its designated limits. If this is not the case then corrective action can be taken.

The principle underpinning SPC is that any process, no matter how well designed, is bound to produce output that varies to some extent. This is natural variability. This does not necessarily mean that the process is out of control. A process is said to be in control when the variations which do occur are random and within its design range.

FIGURE 10.5 A typical process control chart

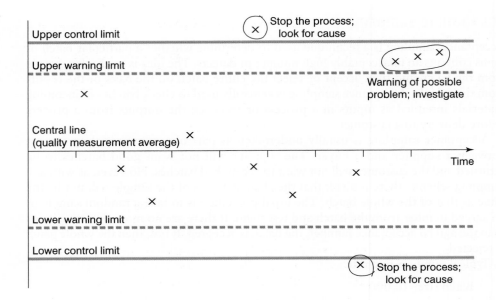

The challenge is to determine whether the variations that do occur have some attributable cause or whether it is random in nature and the process is under control.

SPC charts are constructed by plotting measurements from samples taken from the process at regular intervals. The centre horizontal line of the control chart is set as the mean of the quality measurement being used. The mean can be calculated by measuring a sample from the process. Upper and lower control limits are then set for the process and marked on the chart as horizontal lines above and below the mean line. The upper and lower control limits are normally calculated as ±3 times the standard deviation from the mean. Statistical theory shows that 99.7 per cent of all random variations will be within these control limits. Thus, for most practical situations, if a measurement falls within the upper and lower control limits, the process is in control.

A sample is taken from the process at regular intervals and measured. The result is plotted on the control chart. If the result is within the control limits, no action is taken. If the result is outside the control limits, the process is stopped and the cause of the variation investigated and corrected. Some control charts also set warning limits, typically at ±2 times the standard deviation, which means that 95.5 per cent of all random variations will be within them. Their purpose is to alert the operator that the process may be going out of control. A series of results between the warning and action limits should prompt the operator to reset the machine. Figure 10.5 illustrates a typical process control chart.

The objective of a control chart is to ensure that the process is operating normally, to warn of the likelihood of any potential problems, and to detect when the process is out of control so that corrective action can be taken. The advantage of a control chart, as opposed to acceptance sampling, is that it promotes a proactive approach to quality, seeking to ensure that the process is always producing conforming outputs. Control charts can be particularly powerful when operators actually perform the checks and plot the points on the chart themselves. This provides them with immediate feedback on the quality of the work for which they are responsible.

THE ISO9000 SERIES QUALITY MANAGEMENT SYSTEM

Many quality experts advocate the use of a quality management system (QMS) to underpin what might otherwise remain the good intentions of a TQM approach to managing quality. A QMS offers an ordered and methodical approach to managing quality, as Crosby (1979) puts it 'a systematic way of guaranteeing that organized activities happened the way they are planned'.

Oakland (1993) defines a quality management system as 'an assembly of components, such as organizational structure, responsibilities, procedures, processes, and resources, for implementing quality'. He claims that a good QMS would:

- be a written system
- ensure that the customers' requirements were met
- ensure that the organization's needs were met
- apply to and interact with all the activities of the organization

The ISO9000 series is a set of worldwide standards which offer a framework on which organizations of all kinds can build a quality management system. The standard has its origins as a British Standard, BS5750 first published in 1979. In 1987 this was adopted by the International Organization for Standardization, the body that coordinates the development of technical standards throughout the world, as the international standard for quality. Most countries have their own standards equivalent to (and normally the same as) the ISO9000 series. Some industries have developed their own quality management systems to meet their own more specific requirements based on ISO9000. The motor car industry for example has QS-9000.

In simple terms, ISO9000 requires organizations to 'say what they do, and do what they say'. They 'say what they do' by writing a 'quality manual', a document that details all their operating procedures and practices, and explains how quality is monitored and controlled throughout the organization. They must then demonstrate that they 'do what they say' in the way that they operate the QMS. This usually involves keeping permanent records of all quality checks, tests and other activities so that the quality system can be audited. To be awarded an ISO9000 series certificate, an organization's quality system must be assessed by an ISO approved certification body. Although these are usually based in a single country, many operate internationally, enabling multi-national organizations to operate within the same QMS. The assessors inspect the quality manual and related documentation to ensure it complies with the requirements of ISO9000. They then inspect the organization's operations to ensure that what is written down actually happens in practice. They are likely to make some recommendations, but if no major discrepancies are found, the organization will be issued with a certificate of compliance. Further regular inspection visits will be made to assess continued compliance. If serious faults are found, the certificate can be withdrawn.

The benefits claimed for ISO9000 Series Certification include:

1 *Giving confidence to both buyer and seller:* The advantage of any standard is that it gives both buyer and seller the confidence of knowing exactly what they are agreeing to. Buyers know that an ISO9000 accredited supplier has a quality system of recognized standard in place. This removes the need for buyers to impose their own system, with its attendant costs. Similarly, suppliers are relieved of the cost of having to comply with different systems for different customers. By seeking quotations only from ISO9000 accredited suppliers, buyers can have confidence that all potential suppliers have a common minimum quality capability. This makes direct comparisons between competing suppliers much easier.

2 *Improved efficiency:* By operating to an ISO9000 series standard, the supplier should be operating more efficiently, accruing the cost benefits that flow from improved quality. This should particularly be the case if the supplier has not previously had a systematic approach to managing quality. The ISO9000 series, like any QMS seeks to build in quality at every stage of the organization's activities. As such, it should reduce the costs of quality, especially the costs of failure, by reducing waste, rework and defects. This should also serve to increase customer satisfaction.

3 *Marketing benefits:* Possession of an ISO9000 series certificate offers marketing benefits to the organization. At worst, this might be from the increasing requirement of many purchasers that they will only buy from organizations with ISO9000 series accreditation. It may be simply to nullify the advantage of competitors who have already gained ISO9000 certification. At best, ISO9000 series certification can be used to enhance the organization's image and demonstrate to existing and potential customers that the organization takes quality seriously.

However, the ISO9000 approach to quality does have its critics. Indeed some very large purchasing organizations do not value it and instead impose their own quality systems on their suppliers, believing these to be more appropriate and superior. The main criticisms levelled at ISO9000 are:

1 *It is bureaucratic:* The requirement to document procedures and actions can seem like a huge imposition on organizations that have not previously operated such a system. The process of initial certification does require a lengthy exercise to produce the necessary quality manual and other documentation. However, as there is considerable scope for organizations to design their own procedures within the ISO9000 system, it is possible to minimize the bureaucratic burden. On the other hand, there is a danger, inherent in all bureaucracies, that the system becomes an end in itself, rather than the means of managing quality.

2 *It is costly to implement:* The costs of installing ISO9000 comprise the fees to the certification body and the work of staff and consultants in preparing and assisting on assessment. There are then the on-going costs of running the system, including continuing registration fees. All these costs are not insignificant, especially to smaller organizations. However, the costs need to be seen as an investment. Even though they increase the quality costs of prevention, they should produce a payback by reducing the quality costs of failure, thereby reducing the total costs of quality.

3 *It does not guarantee the quality of the product:* This argument is based on the fact that ISO9000 does not itself require the organization to set any particular standard of quality for the goods or services that it produces. Indeed, the basis of ISO9000 is that the organization can specify any standard it likes. As long as its quality system ensures that it produces to that standard, it can achieve ISO9000 series certification. This has led to apocryphal claims along the lines of it being possible to make lifejackets out of concrete and still gain ISO9000 registration. The counter argument to this is that no organization can be successful if its products and services fail to satisfy customers. Also, in its latest version introduced in 2000, ISO9000 requires organizations to demonstrate how their QMS ensures that its products and services meet customer requirements.

4 *It is not suitable for service organizations:* This criticism arises from the fact that ISO9000 has its origins in quality systems devised for manufacturing environments. As such, the language and concepts used tend to sit more comfortably with those who produce physical goods rather than services. However, the revisions of 2000 endeavored to address this issue and more recent ISO9000 series documentation addresses the requirements of specific service environments such as health series, education and local government.

5 *It is not suitable for small organizations:* Owners and managers of small businesses have been long-term critics of the ISO9000 approach to quality management. They claim that it is complex, unwieldy, and above all costly, especially for very small businesses. ISO has been trying to address this problem by publishing specific guidance for the small business sector. It also has a section of its website dedicated to SMEs.

CASE STUDY: Faultless quality at Dalepak

Mick White began Dalepak as a small packaging company with his wife Sheila in 1991. By 2006, they employed over 80 people across three sites in Northamptonshire, England and serviced some of the country's biggest and best known companies such as the Ford Motor Company, Stanley Tools, One For All (UK) Ltd and acted as a supplier to Woolworth's, Dixon's, Currys, Argos and Index to name but a few.

They now do a great deal more than just contract packing, having expanded their service portfolio to include freight forwarding, customs bonded warehousing, distribution worldwide, client customer care, client sales administration, product quality control, field marketing, in-store merchandising (where it employs 250 part-time in-store merchandisers) and selling clients' products on the Internet, as well as providing consultancy in many fields.

The Ford Motor Company is their biggest customer, accounting for 20 per cent of their business. Dalepak's contract with Ford is essentially an unpacking and repacking operation. Boxes of parts arrive in Northampton having travelled from Ford plants all over the world. The boxes can contain anything from an engine to a car aerial. They then have to be sorted, checked and re-boxed ready to be sent to dealers and garages around the country. They have to be turned around within a day, often within hours. They pack around 200,000 spare parts, ranging from a tiny spring to a van door, every week for the car giant.

ISO9000 can help raise quality standards in any operation

That's about 1 every 1.2 seconds. Great care is needed to get the right things in the right boxes. Dalepak is proud of its quality record with this demanding customer. As of September 2005, in the last 19,213,900 parts that they had packed, they had not made a single error. A real testament to the effort that this small company puts into its quality management.

So how has the company achieved this? Mick White, managing director, gives much of the credit to their decision to adopt the ISO9000 standard in 2001. Since then they have had zero defects in their contract with Ford – not making a single mistake. In 2004 Dalepak received the Beacon Award from British Standards (BSi) for best practice in ISO9000 in small to medium sized business. BSi is the accreditation body for the ISO9000 series in the UK.

'When the stock arrives, the paper work is compared with all the items and they're matched up', explains Operations Supervisor John Paredes. 'They then go down the conveyer to the packing team'. Supervisor Denise Knight admits there is pressure to keep up the 100 per cent record, but they have at least three areas dedicated to checking orders are correct. 'We have special checks on the out door, I check the seals and check the bench sheets to check everything is going through OK, and there's another check in shipping', explains Denise.

Mick says that, 'For us to succeed, it's vital that our employees are able to perform. Our people are our tools'. He adds, 'We learned that it was not the process itself but the results of applying the process that delivered such powerful change'. Stevan Breeze, Chief Executive of the British Standards Institute, says, 'That is the point. It's not about achieving a standard, it's about raising standards by using the system'. Dalepak's record of zero defects is bound to come to an end sooner or later, but for companies like this working in a competitive market, quality control is what they live or die by. Striving for quality has been a key factor in its achievement.

(Source http://www.bbc.co.uk, http://www.telegraph.co.uk and http://www.dalepak.ltd.uk)

Questions (Suggested answers can be found on the companion website www.thomsonlearning.co.uk/barnes)

1 To what extent has ISO9000 accreditation helped Dalepak to raise its standards?

2 To what extent does ISO9000 accreditation give Dalepak a competitive advantage in the marketplace?

6 *It does not improve quality:* In one sense, this is true. The main focus of the ISO9000 QMS is to ensure organizations achieve conformance to specification by demonstrating that they do what they say they will do. As such, it is aimed at achieving a specified standard rather than raising that standard. However, this is a narrow and somewhat theoretical view. As many organizations have no existing QMS, adopting ISO9000 is almost bound to improve the consistency of their operations. Also, the introduction of a formalized approach to the management of quality is bound to sensitize people to the whole issue of quality. It would be a cynical organization that only wanted to use ISO9000 accreditation as a marketing ploy, rather than as a basis for improving its quality. Also, the 2000 revisions to ISO9000 include a requirement to demonstrate how the organization ensures a continual improvement in its products, processes and systems.

ISO9000 AND TQM

TQM and quality management systems such as ISO9000 represent two rather different approaches to managing quality. TQM emphasizes the importance of an appropriate organizational culture, whereas ISO9000 promotes the benefits of a procedural approach to quality management. The differences in the two approaches are highlighted in Table 10.1.

	TQM	ISO9000
Description	A strategy to gain a competitive edge by taking on a culture of continuous quality improvement	A standard to give assurance to customers that the company can give a guaranteed level of quality
Character	People driven	Procedure driven
Goal	A steady improvement in quality: no quality level is good enough – something can always be improved	Achieving and maintaining certification
Culture	Assumption that causes of poor quality have to be discovered and that good suggestions for improvements may come from any level in the organization	The production of good written procedures and adherence to them are all important

TABLE 10.1 TQM and ISO9000 compared

Does this mean that these differences make TQM and ISO9000 incompatible? Some academics do not believe so. Johnston *et al.* (1993) argue that the key to managing quality is people's behaviour. They claim that this is determined by a combination of people's attitudes and the systems that are in place at work. ISO9000 is primarily concerned with putting into place systems designed to ensure behaviour that is aimed at achieving conformance to pre-set quality standards. Without such systems people may not know what actions they must take to ensure that they produce goods and services of the required quality. Without systems there is no requirement on people to work in the most appropriate way. At its worst TQM relies on mere exhortation. By itself this is usually doomed to failure. With appropriate systems in place, attitudes will also be influenced as people see the benefits that can accrue by adhering to those systems. However merely changing the systems themselves is not likely to be enough to achieve the significant and on-going improvements in quality which are required in increasingly competitive markets with rising customer expectations. This is where TQM goes further than a quality management system, like ISO9000. TQM is primarily concerned with changing attitudes. Thus, in concert with ISO9000, TQM can lead to the desired changes in behaviour throughout the organization.

QUALITY AWARDS

Like most other developments in quality, the practice of recognizing outstanding performance in quality management through formal quality awards, started in Japan. The Deming Application Prize for companies was established by the Union of Japanese Scientists and Engineers in the early-1950s. The Malcolm Baldrige National Quality Award (MBNQA) was initiated in the USA in 1987 and the European Quality Award (EQA) was launched in 1992. As well as affording tremendous prestige, not to mention the wonderful promotional opportunities, for the winners, these awards are also aimed at stimulating excellence in quality more widely in their respective countries. Organizations are attracted to enter, not only by the prospect of winning, but also to take advantage of the benefits on offer from subjecting themselves to the rigor of the application process.

BOX 10.2

The Quality Awards

Deming Prize

The Deming Prize is the oldest quality award, dating back to 1951. It is regarded as extremely prestigious in Japan, although entry is now also open to non-Japanese companies. Winners must demonstrate a company wide commitment to quality control based on statistical quality control. Applicants are judged in ten aspects of quality management: policy and objectives, organization and its operation, education and its extension, assembling and dissemination of information, analysis, standardization, control, quality assurance, effects and future plans. Applicants must submit a detailed written submission and short-listed companies are subject to an extensive site visit.

Malcolm Baldrige Award

Inspired by the Deming Prize, the MBNQA was introduced in 1987, and was seen as a means of inspiring quality improvements in American industry more widely. It was named after the Secretary of Commerce who was killed in an accident shortly before the necessary legislation passed through the US Congress. The assessment process is similar to the Deming Prize, but uses nine criteria: leadership, strategic planning, customer and market focus, information and analysis, human resources focus, process management and business results.

The late Dr W. Edwards Deming, founder of the W. Edwards Deming Institute

FIGURE 10.6 The EFQM Business Excellence Model

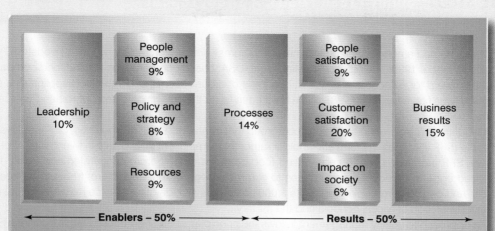

Leadership 10%	People management 9%	Processes 14%	People satisfaction 9%	Business results 15%
	Policy and strategy 8%		Customer satisfaction 20%	
	Resources 9%		Impact on society 6%	

← Enablers – 50% → ← Results – 50% →

European Quality Award

The European Quality Award (EQA) seeks to emulate the MBNQA in Europe. It is administered by the European Foundation for Quality Management (EFQM) and was first awarded in 1992. Winners are expected to demonstrate excellence in the practice of TQM. Assessment for the award is based on the EFQM's *Business Excellence Model,* which has nine elements (see Figure 10.6). Five of these elements (leadership, policy and strategy, people management resources and processes) are classified as 'enablers' which produce organizational 'results' (the elements of customer satisfaction, people satisfaction, impact on society and business results). In additional to the EQA itself, many European countries also have their own individual country awards, usually based on the EFQM Business Excellence Model.

In addition to their role as the basis for the various quality awards, the models underlying the awards are also often used by organizations wanting to asses their quality performance. Both the MBNQA and EFQM's Business Excellence Models are widely used in such self-assessment. Such models enable quantification of an organization's quality practices and performance in a very practical way, helping managers to see the outcomes of what can for many appear to be somewhat ethereal and theoretical aspects of TQM. This can provide a basis for the tracking of quality performance over time or for comparison with the performance of other organizations. (This is discussed in further detail in Chapter 14.)

SIX SIGMA

Six Sigma is an approach to quality improvement pioneered by the US company, Motorola in the 1980s. Since then it has developed into a methodology for quality management, made commercially available though a large consulting community and used by many organizations across the world. Six Sigma is based on, and driven by, the application of the techniques of statistical quality control. It aims to improve the capability of processes to the point at which they can be guaranteed to produce zero defects. Statistically this is achieved when the customer's specification limits for the item being produced is twice that of the natural variation of the process limits. As the section on statistical process control charts earlier in this chapter explained, the natural variation in the output from a process that is in control is ± 3 times the standard

CASE STUDY Sunny Fresh Foods: A sweet repeat

When it was named amongst the 2005 winners of the prestigious MBNQA, Sunny Fresh Foods (SFF) was repeating its feat of 1999. The Monticello, Minnesota, USA, based company was the first food company to receive the award for a second time. Whilst hundreds of organizations have submitted applications since the MBNQA was first awarded in 1987, there have been fewer than 80 winners and only a handful of repeat winners.

A subsidiary of Cargill, an international food group that operates in over 60 countries, SFF employs over 600 people (SFF insists on the term stakeholder rather than employee) in its plants in Minnesota, Michigan and Iowa. SFF produces over 160 egg-based food products ranging from refrigerated and frozen liquid pasteurized eggs to precooked egg entrees to scrambled egg mixes, cholesterol-free and fat-free egg products, and peeled hard-cooked eggs. Its 2,000 customers include quick-service restaurants, business and institutional food services, schools and the military.

SFF's approach to quality management follows the principles of Baldrige-based Cargill Business Excellence Process. These involve maintaining a focus on the company's *Core Purpose* ('to be the supplier of choice to our customers worldwide') and *Core Values* ('Customer Focus, Safety, Quality, Stakeholder Focus, and Ethics'). These tenets are applied to all aspects of the company's daily activities from customer service and stakeholder training to strategic planning and new product development.

SFF senior managers hold annual meetings with stakeholders in small groups throughout the company each year to discuss businesses plans, capture concerns, and answer questions. Internal communication is also fostered through the orientation programme, presentations during Continuous Improvement training, bimonthly Recognition Meetings, and the SFF internal newsletter, *The Eggceptional News*. Stakeholders throughout the organization participate by serving on task forces and cross-functional teams to research and explore opportunities for improvement and innovation. This approach seems to be effective, with more

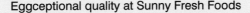

Eggceptional quality at Sunny Fresh Foods

than 90 per cent of stakeholders agreeing with the statements: 'I understand the goals of Sunny Fresh', 'I understand how my job affects the customer', and 'My managers demonstrate and communicate focus on the customer' – a figure that far exceeds the US average for similar stakeholder surveys. SFF treats external communication equally seriously, endeavoring to build long-term business relationships based on trust and understanding with customers, suppliers, local communities, regulatory agencies and others.

SFF's business planning is driven by the continual measurement of key performance indicators. Action plans are devised to drive improvements in performance in line with the company's long-term Strategic Business Plan. Customer needs and expectations are considered paramount to the planning process, whether for the long- or short-term. Sales and marketing data, customer purchasing and consumption patterns, consumer research and dietary trends are all closely monitored.

SFF devotes significant resources to training and to implementing safe and efficient business processes. There is a special focus on both food safety and personal safety. In the former, the company surpasses the US Department of Agriculture's and the Food and Drug Administration's requirements. In the latter, injury frequency rates have dropped from 15 in 2000 to approximately 6.8 in 2004. The plant in Lake Odessa, Michigan, has gone five years without a lost-time accident, the plant in Panora, Iowa, 14 years. SFF has also pioneered a number of innovative production work systems, including 20-minute rotations of stakeholders among workstations, and programmes that ease new stakeholders into physically demanding tasks and partner them with experienced 'buddies'.

SFF has achieved measurable improvements in quality performance. On-time deliveries reached 99.8 per cent in 2005, and customer complaint levels are maintained well below the Six Sigma world-class level. Even as product complexity has increased, customer satisfaction from 2001 to 2005 remained near 100 per cent. For all products, the length of time to resolve customer complaints has declined from 2.8 days in 1997 to 0.8 days in 2005. Resolution satisfaction climbed from 92 per cent in 1997 to 100 per cent in 2002 and has remained there. The amount of rework dropped 15 per cent from 2001 to 2002, 61 per cent from 2002 to 2003, and 75 per cent from 2003 to 2004. SFF can also point to the impact of the MBNQA on its bottom line. Since receiving the 1999 award market share has increased, revenues are up by 93 per cent, and sales and profit per stakeholder have increased by 19 per cent.

(Source material http://www.sunnyfreshfoods.com and http://baldrige.nist.gov)

WWW.

WWW.

Questions (Suggested answers can be found on the companion website www.thomsonlearning.co.uk/barnes)

1   To what extent is SFFs approach to quality management based on the principles of TQM?

2   How does SFF ensure that its quality management efforts are more than mere exhortations?

deviation from the mean. As the Greek letter Sigma 'σ' is used to represent the standard deviation in mathematical notation, the natural variation is usually represented as $\pm 3\sigma$. Thus, a process that has twice this capability is said to be a 'six sigma' process. A six sigma process operates with an exceptionally low level of variation. This can be calculated to be the equivalent of allowing 3.4 defects per million opportunities for error. To all intents and purposes this is the equivalent of zero defects.

If the process is capable of producing to exactly the specification limits for a product, that is to control limits of $\pm 3\sigma$, then 99.73 per cent of the outputs are within $\pm 3\sigma$ of the mean and, therefore, only 0.27 per cent are outside $\pm 3\sigma$ of the mean. Although this is a low figure, it still means that 2.7 parts per thousand produced, or 2,700 parts per million (ppm) may be out of specification, even though the process is deemed to be in control. It may be that a defect rate of 2,700 ppm is considered to be too high. If the process can be improved, then the probability of producing a defect part will be reduced, assuming that the specification limits are kept the same. If the process can be improved to the point where the natural variation ($\pm 3\sigma$) of the process is half the specification limits for the product then the probability of producing a part outside the specification limits will be reduced to about two parts per billion.

Six Sigma uses a variety of tools and techniques to improve process capability by redesigning processes, improving equipment, changing operating methods, training operatives, etc. It applies these in a structured way, assigning specific roles and responsibilities to the organizational members involved in its implementation. For many organizations, Six Sigma provides an unachievable target for the level of defects that their processes can ever hope to achieve. However, using its methods in pursuit of the target offers the means of progressively reducing the permitted variability of whatever measure is being used for the quality of a process. This should lead to a progressive narrowing of the range of the control limits (i.e. the distance between the upper and lower control limits) on the process control chart. Any subsequent variation outside of the control limits would then be investigated and its cause eliminated. In this way, by bringing the process under statistical control with tighter and tighter tolerances, the process capability will be improved.

GLOBAL DIFFERENCES IN QUALITY MANAGEMENT

As was discussed in Chapter 3, powerful forces of globalization are acting to drive the internationalization of operations. For many years, academics and other commentators have argued that one of the principle drivers behind globalization is the convergence of consumer tastes throughout the world (e.g. Levitt, 1983). It might be expected that this would in turn lead to a general convergence of customer expectations about what is considered to be an acceptable level of quality in the goods and services they purchase. Whilst there are always likely to be differences between different groups of consumers around the world, especially in the case of developing countries, it might be expected that national differences would continue to reduce. As common standards for the quality of products and services appear to be emerging across the world, it is not surprising to see organizations adopting similar approaches to managing quality in the operations that provide those goods and services. Most notably these are the adoption of the ISO9000 world wide quality standards for quality management systems, the use of TQM, and the advent of quality awards (e.g. the Deming Prize, the MBNQA and the EQA) all based on similar criteria.

However, the existence of such commonality does not always bear up under closer scrutiny. For example, by studying the influence of national cultures on the application of the constructs underpinning the MBNQA and similar quality awards in different countries, Flynn and Saladin (2006) found that the scores companies made in the different MBNQA quality award criteria (leadership, strategic planning, customer and market focus, information and analysis, human resources focus, process management and business results) tended to vary in line with the characteristics of their national cultures (the researchers used Hofstede's dimensions of national culture to measure this; these are discussed in Chapter 11). Although the research is inevitably limited in scope, being confined to plants in three industries (the manufacture of electronics, machinery and transportation components respectively) in five different countries (Germany, Italy, England, Japan, the US), it does provide strong evidence that national culture does affect the way that organizations manage quality. Flynn and Saladin (2006), therefore argue that there can be no universal model (i.e. 'one best way') for managing quality. They maintain that quality management practices need to be adapted to suit local cultures.

Rungtusanatham *et al.* (2005) also explored the question of whether there can be a universal model of quality management due to the convergence of operations management technologies and practices, or whether these are still influenced by national contexts in which they are applied. Using data from the same study as Flynn and Saladin (2006), they investigated the application of TQM (as defined by Deming) in the same plants in the same countries. They also rejected the idea of a universal model for quality management. However, they found evidence that some TQM practices were more readily accepted irrespective of the national context than others. They also found that national culture alone could not explain differences in the applicability of different aspects of TQM in different countries. They specifically point to the length of time that TQM had been in place as an important indicator of its acceptance in practice, arguing that it can take decades for the ideas of TQM to be internalized by national industries.

Whether or not there is a convergence of approaches to managing quality across the world remains a matter of conjecture. However, it is still possible to observe differences in quality performance. Whilst it is possible to argue that in general quality standards, especially in manufactured goods, have been raised across the world, it seems clear that some organizations consistently achieve much higher quality standards than others. It is difficult to understand why this is the case. It is possible to speculate that many organizations, particularly Western ones, find it difficult to make the long-term commitment to quality improvement so characteristic of their Japanese competitors. This highlights the fact that whilst it is generally easy to transfer technology from one country to another, it is seemingly more difficult to transfer working practices. However, what may be most difficult to transfer are the value systems needed to support high levels of performance in quality. It is perhaps not surprising then that the most successful examples of Japanese style approaches to quality management outside of Japan are found in Japanese owned (and usually managed) plants which have been established on greenfield sites. Making a fresh start unencumbered by the past seems to have enabled them to inculcate appropriate value systems to facilitate the establishment of the necessary working practices.

SUMMARY OF KEY POINTS

Ideas about quality have been evolving for more than 50 years. Initially quality management relied entirely on inspection to detect faulty goods. It grew to incorporate the concepts of quality control, then quality assurance and most recently TQM.

TQM is a philosophy for quality improvement based on principles of the elimination of waste, continuous involvement and the involvement of all employees.

Quality can be defined from a number of different perspectives. However, it is particularly important to understand how customers assess the quality of the products and services they experience.

Quality problems can arise if there are gaps between customers' expectations and perceptions of their experience of products and services.

Quality can be measured using operations, financial or customer measures.

Statistical quality control (SQC) can be used where it is impossible, impractical or costly to measure very large numbers of outputs from a process.

The ISO9000 series is a set of worldwide standards for quality management systems, which are suitable for any organization. ISO9000 is based on principles of 'saying what you do, and doing what you say' when managing quality.

Quality awards such as the Deming Prize (Japan), the MBNQA (USA) and the EQA not only offer a way for organizations to assess their quality performance against world leaders.

Six sigma is a structured methodology for improving quality, based on the application of the techniques of statistical quality control.

Despite the global convergence of operations management technologies and practices there are national differences in the suitability and effectiveness of different aspects of quality management.

WWW.

EXERCISES (Suggested answers can be found on the companion website www.thomsonlearning.co.uk/barnes)

1 How would you answer the criticism that TQM is just a fad whose time has past?

2 Why is managing quality in service organizations so difficult?

3 How should the following organizations define quality in their operations:
   a A motor car manufacturer
   b A clothing manufacturer
   c A supermarket
   d An airline
   e A university

4 What quality gaps might there be in the following operations:
   a A budget airline
   b A traditional full service airline
   c The latest computer game
   d An expensive watch

5 What would be the main costs of quality in the following organizations:
   a A motor car manufacturer
   b A fast food restaurant
   c A hospital
   d A hairdressers

6 What are the advantages of using statistical process control (SPC) charts to manage quality? What are the specific challenges of using SPC charts to manage these aspects of quality in the following operations:
   a The size of a manufactured component
   b The on-time arrival of trains
   c The length of waiting lines in a theme park
   d The time taken to answer the phone at a call centre

7 Should all organizations seek ISO9000 accreditation?

8 What are the advantages and disadvantages to an organization of applying for one of the quality awards, such as the Deming Prize, the MBNQA or the EQA?

9 What are the advantages and disadvantages of the Six Sigma approach to quality improvement?

10 Why have many organizations from Anglo-Saxon cultures (e.g. the US and UK) had difficulty implementing TQM?

CASE STUDY EXERCISE Ritz-Carlton

Introduction

In 1992, the Ritz-Carlton Hotel Company became the first hotel organization to receive a MBNQA. Ritz-Carlton is one of the world's leading hotel companies. It has 63 hotels in 21 countries, 18,475 guest rooms and employs around 32,000 people. Competition in hospitality continually increases, while travelers are becoming more and more demanding, expecting high levels of reliability, care and personalized services. Consequently, the achievement of an internationally recognized quality award provides a real competitive advantage.

The Ritz-Carlton Gold Standards (see Figure 10.7) which focus on customer care and give great emphasis on good human resource management, are one of the major factors that help the company to achieve superior quality. These Gold Standards are reinforced daily in a variety of forums including: lectures on new employee orientation; developmental training; daily line-up meeting; administration of both positive and negative reinforcement; mission statements displayed; distribution of Credo Cards. The Credo is the first topic of internal meetings and peer pressure. Moreover, Ritz-Carlton's quality management system features a strong leadership and strategic commitment in quality, product and process planning, control and continuous improvement that are effectively supported by a good information management system. The major elements of the quality management system are outlined below.

Leadership and cross functional teams

The wants and needs of customers drive Ritz-Carlton's strategic planning. Its goal is to become the first hospitality company with 100 per cent customer retention; all plans must address this goal. However, strong leadership is necessary to integrate quality into the business planning process and to establish the credibility of a total quality strategic focus. Therefore, at each Ritz-Carlton hotel, the senior manager assumes the role of the quality leader with the responsibility to serve as a resource and adviser to teams for developing and implementing plans. Teams at all levels – corporate, management and employee – set objectives and

FIGURE 10.7 The Ritz-Carlton golden standards

THREE STEPS OF SERVICE

1. A warm and sincere greeting. Use the guest's name if and when possible.
2. Anticipation and compliance with guests' needs.
3. Fond farewell. Give them a warm goodbye and use their names if and when possible.

We are Ladies and Gentlemen serving Ladies and Gentlemen

THE EMPLOYEE PROMISE

At the Ritz-Carlton, our Ladies and Gentlemen are the most important resource in our service commitment to our guests.

By applying the principles of trust, honesty, respect, integrity and commitment, we nurture and maximize talent to the benefit of each individual and the company.

The Ritz-Carlton fosters a work environment where diversity is valued, quality of life is enhanced, individual aspirations are fulfilled and the Ritz-Carlton mystique is strengthened.

CREDO

The Ritz-Carlton Hotel is a place where the genuine care and comfort of our guests is our highest mission.

We pledge to provide the finest personal service and facilities for our guests who will always enjoy a warm and relaxed, yet refined, ambience.

The Ritz-Carlton experience enlivens the senses, instils well-being and fulfils even the unexpressed wishes and needs of our guests.

---

devise action plans. At property level, Senior Leaders, Hotel Guidance Teams and every member of staff are provided with high level organizational performance data on a daily basis. This is because each production and support process is assigned an 'executive owner' at the corporate office and a 'working owner' at the hotel level. These owners are responsible for the development and improvement of these processes. They have the authority to define the measurements and determine the resources needed to manage these processes. They involve all concerned in determining what must be done differently to reach the company's objectives. In this way, quality is achieved at all organizational levels through delegation, ownership of responsibility and empowerment.

The Senior Leadership team also spends at least six to seven weeks working with the company staff (using a combination of hands-on behaviour modelling and reinforcement) whenever a new hotel property opens. This includes the President and the Chief Organization Officer (COO) who personally demonstrates the guest/employee interface image and facilitates the first vision statement for each newly formed department. During these formative sessions, which all employees must attend, the President and COO personally interacts with every new employee both individually and in group settings. His in-depth knowledge of hotel operations and enthusiasm for the Gold Standards are an inspiration for everyone. Hotel property leaders are continuously evaluated through the annual employee satisfaction surveys, while their continuous professional development is overseen at the Leadership Centre at corporate headquarters.

However, Ritz-Carlton also recognizes that the hotel product and service is a complex one involving and requiring the shared responsibility of more than one hotel department. In this vein, the hotel has established standards, procedures, and training to ensure cross-functional communication and prevent problems from occurring. For example, customized hotel products and services, such as meetings and banquet events, receive the full attention of local hotel cross-functional teams (marketing, operations, legal teams, etc.), involving all internal and external suppliers, verifying production and delivery capabilities before each event, critiquing samples, and assessing results.

Process management

Good process management, either in the form of variation identification and correction of its root cause or in the form of continuous improvement, is also at the heart of the Ritz-Carlton TQM system. Employees at the lowest level of the organization (who are most familiar with the process) have the responsibilities to identify and resolve process upsets. So, the company has a policy by which the first person who detects a problem is empowered to break away from routine duties, investigate and correct the problem immediately, document the incident and then return to their routine. Employees are also empowered to 'move heaven and earth to satisfy a customer', to enlist the aid of other employees to resolve a problem swiftly, to spend up to $2000 to satisfy a guest, and to speak with anyone in the company regarding any problem.

Ritz-Carlton also has eight mechanisms devoted solely to the improvement of process, product and service quality:

1. *New hotel start-up improvement process:* A cross-sectional team from the entire company gathers to identify and correct problem areas.

2. *Comprehensive performance evaluation process:* Staff empowerment to develop the job procedures and performance standards for their work.

3. *Quality circles:* Employees can propose and advance a good idea through peer approval.

4. *Standing problem-solving team:* A standing work area team that works on any problem they choose.

5. *Quality improvement team:* Ad hoc teams created for solving a problem identified by an employee or leaders.

6. *Strategic quality planning:* Annual area teams that identify their missions, primary action plans, internal objectives, action plans and progress reviews.

7. *Streamlining process:* Annual evaluations aiming to delete processes, products or services that are no longer valuable to the customer.

8. *Process improvement:* Teams of corporate leaders, managers and employees to improve the most critical processes.

Human resource management

The human resource management approaches of Ritz-Carlton heavily underpin its quality system and values. The company uses a highly predictive character trait recruiting instrument for determining a candidates' fitness for each of its 120 job positions. Successful candidates go through a two day mandatory orientation process, which includes classroom-based training on the Gold Standards. Apart from this, training delivery also involves on-the-job training such as: daily line-up meetings and briefing sessions with the shift supervisor; self-study documents; training certification for work areas in which it is required in order to start working; developmental assignments in which people choose to expand their knowledge and experience within and across hotels and functions (this reflects the company's commitment to reward and promote worthy employees). Most training is evaluated through examinations, while other methods include audits, performance reviews and appraisals. Finally, an annual survey of all employees is conducted to determine their levels of satisfaction, well-being, motivation and also their understanding of basic quality standards. Findings are compared to outside world-class service companies and benchmarking results are used for improving company's practices.

Information management

Customer focus and process improvement would not have been feasible without the collection, analysis and use of relevant information. Ritz-Carlton collects data by conducting focus groups, surveying customers and competitors, carrying out sector analysis as well as by monitoring internal processes. Information is clustered under the following categories and the use of information and communication technology is very critical for analyzing, sharing and disseminating the knowledge to relevant employees:

- The 6 P's Concept for understanding customers and their priorities and laying the groundwork for process design: Problem or need of the customer; Product (what is it); Promises (what it can do for the customer); Personal advantage (what the customer can do because of it); Positioning (the benefit of it *vs* the competition); Price/value (what customers must give up in time or money to achieve it).

- Operation of the CLASS database; this is the guest profiling system that gathers guests' preferences and provides it to front-line staff who can use this information for operating the Guest Recognition Program.
- The complaint resolution process.
- Standard performance measurements including advance bookings, service quality indicators, revenue per available room, customer satisfaction determination and the profit and loss account. These measures both precede and lag the operation, so they are both forward looking and reaction-based.

The success and results of Ritz-Carlton's quality management system are widely known. Ritz-Carlton represents the highest scores of internal and external customers' and suppliers' satisfaction relative to its worldwide competitors. Ritz-Carlton also achieves higher gross profit margins relative to its competing luxury hotels since 1996. A recent survey undertaken by the Cornell School of Hotel Administration and McGill University asking 3,400 managers in the lodging industry to identify 'Best Practices' in hotel quality management, has named the Ritz-Carlton as the overall Best Practice Champion.

—*Marianna Sigala*

WWW.

Questions (Suggested answers can be found on the companion website www.thomsonlearning.co.uk/barnes)

1 What are the main constituents of Ritz-Carlton's TQM system?

2 Why are leadership and empowerment both important in TQM? How are they practised in Ritz-Carlton?

3 Why is process improvement required in TQM? How is this achieved by Ritz-Carlton?

4 How does Ritz-Carlton evaluate the results of its quality management system?

References

Bank, J. (1992) *The Essence of Total Quality Management,* Hemel Hempstead: Prentice Hall.

Berry, L.L., Zeithaml, V.A. and Parasuraman, A. (1985) 'Quality counts in services too', *Business Horizons* 28(3):44–52.

Crosby, P.B. (1979) *Quality is Free,* New York: McGraw-Hill.

Dale, B.G. and Cooper, C. (1992) *Total Quality and Human Resources: An Executive Guide,* Oxford: Blackwell.

Flynn, B.B. and Saladin, B. (2006) 'Relevance of Baldrige constructs in an international context: A study of national culture', *Journal of Operations Management* 24(5):583–603.

Garvin, D. (1988) *Managing Quality,* New York: Free Press.

Johnston, R., Chambers, S., Harland, C., Harrison, A. and Slack, N. (1993) *Cases in Operations Management,* London: Pitman.

Levitt, T. (1983) 'The Globalization of Markets', *Harvard Business Review* 61(3):92–102.

Oakland, J.S. (1993) *Total Quality Management,* Oxford: Heinemann.

Parasuraman, A., Zeithaml, V.A. and Berry, L.L. (1985) 'A Conceptual Model of Service Quality and Its Implications for Future Research', *Journal of Marketing* 49(4):41–50.

Parasuraman, A., Zeithaml, V.A. and Berry, L.L. (1988) 'SERVQUAL: A multiple-item scale for measuring consumer perceptions of service quality', *Journal of Retailing* 64(1):12–40.

Rungtusanatham, M., Forza, C., Koka, B.R., Salvador, F. and Nie, W. (2005) 'TQM across multiple countries: Convergence Hypothesis versus National Specificity arguments', *Journal of Operations Management* 23(1):43–63.

Additional reading

Bicheno, J. (1998) *The Quality 60: A Guide for Service and Manufacturing,* Buckingham: Picsie Books.

Deming, W.E. (1986) *Out of the Crisis,* Center for Advanced Engineering Study, Massachusetts Institute of Technology.

Useful websites

http://www.iso.org The website of ISO, the International Organization for Standardization, the body representing over 150 countries, that co-ordinates the development and application of technical standards for products, services and management systems throughout the world.

http://www.iso.org/iso/en/iso9000-14000/understand/index_one.html The ISO's webpage that acts as a portal to their webpages that explain ISO9000 and other standards for management systems.

http://www.efqm.org/ The website of the European Foundation for Quality Management. Information about the Business Excellence Model and the European Quality Award, along with information about the EFQM's activities and publications.

http://www.baldrige.nist.gov/ Details about the Malcolm Baldrige National Quality Award.

http://www.deming.org/ The W. Edwards Deming Institute promotes the ideas of the man many consider to be the father of quality management. Also contains details of the Deming Prize.

http://www.qualitydigest.com/ The website of *Quality Digest,* a practitioner publication with useful articles, information and web links.

http://www.asq.org/ The website of the American Society for Quality, a membership organization devoted to quality, containing useful information knowledge, tools, publications and other resources.

http://www.quality.co.uk/ The Quality Network which is a portal to useful information and resources.

CHAPTER 11

WORK ORGANIZATION

INTRODUCTION

Chapters 11 and 12 are both concerned with an issue of vital importance to the management of operations in all organizations; namely managing people. There can be few, if any, organizations that do not employ people to carry out the work associated with producing the goods and services required by its customers. The way that those people are managed is likely to make a significant difference to the performance of the operation. It is perhaps not surprising that more management attention is devoted to managing people than any other aspect of management, particularly within operations, where most of the organization's employees are typically found. Managing people is an integral part of managing operations and, therefore, it is included as a topic within this book, even though the study of the management of people in organizations more generally is the focus of the academic disciplines of human resource management and organizational behaviour.

As outlined in Chapter 2, the infrastructural decision areas of operations include two which are concerned with managing people, namely work organization and human resource management. Perhaps the best way to distinguish between these topics is to view work organization as being primarily concerned with the way that people are brought together and managed collectively, whereas human resource management is primarily concerned with the way that people are managed as individuals. The distinction is not, however, entirely clear-cut as the two topics inevitably overlap and interact one with another. Nonetheless, they are considered separately: work organization in this chapter and human resource management in the one following, Chapter 12.

Most operations rely on the collaborative efforts of a group of people. Indeed the whole point of business organizations is to bring people together in order to work together. This chapter is concerned with understanding the factors that influence the way that workers are brought together to perform work tasks. Work organization can be thought of as having two related aspects; structure and culture.

structure
The way in which employees are formally divided into groups for co-ordination and control.

culture
'That set of assumptions and beliefs that are taken-for-granted and held in common by members of an organization' (Schein, 1985). Culture can operate at a national as well as an organizational level.

Structure is the formal aspect of work organization. An organization's structure is concerned with the way in which numbers of workers are brought together in groups in order to undertake specific work tasks. It is also concerned with how different groups of workers interrelate with one another and with the managers who are given responsibility for the work undertaken by the various groups. It is also concerned with which managers have authority over other individuals and groups within the organization. Structure can be, and normally is, depicted diagrammatically on any number of organizational charts. These are normally drawn to show a hierarchy of increasing senior managers, culminating with the most senior executive at the top of a pyramid. An organizational structure diagram also depicts the formal reporting and communication channels, and so it also reflects the formal distribution of power within the organization.

Culture on the other hand is the informal aspect of work organization; something very intangible in nature. Often encapsulated in the phrase 'the way we do things around here', culture comprises the attitudes, experiences, beliefs and values of an organization. As such, culture permeates an organization, irrespective of its structure. However, there can be cultural differences between different parts of an organization; certain sub-groups often display differences. For example, those working in sales departments tend to have somewhat different cultures than those working in technology functions such as IT departments. Multinational organizations are also likely to find that national cultural differences affect the behaviour of workers in their operations based in different countries or regions. More and more organizations are operating across national boundaries. Even within a single country, workforces are becoming increasingly diverse, often being composed of people from a number of different countries. In the globalized business world, understanding national culture has become an important issue for operations managers.

In recent years, many organizations have found that in order to meet changing market demands they have had to become more responsive and flexible. In order to achieve this, organizations have realized that it is important to empower their workers by giving them greater discretion and control over the way that they perform their work. This has often been accompanied with a recognition of the increased importance of team working. Devolving more power to lower levels in an organization poses significant challenges for those more used to management styles more suited to achieving control over a workforce rather than for securing the level of commitment needed in this new operating environment. The challenge has been magnified by the greater diversity typically found within workforces in many countries. Operations managers need to address both the structural and cultural aspects of the work organization decision area in response to these changes. This chapter will discuss these issues in more depth.

STRUCTURE

This section will consider the ways in which operations staff can be organized in order to carry out their work. People who work in operations are but one part of an organization, so any discussion of the organizational arrangements for operations needs to be placed in the context of the entire organizational structure.

Structural variables

The structuring of organizations has been studied extensively by researchers for many years, with the overwhelming conclusion that there is no one best way to structure any organization. The renowned Aston Research Programme (Pugh, 1998) concluded that there are three key dimensions of organizational structure that need to be considered:

1 *Centralization:* The extent to which decision-making is concentrated at a single point in the organization. More centralization is likely to lead to tighter

managerial control but also to greater inflexibility due to a lack of worker autonomy.

2 *Formalization:* The extent to which jobs are standardized and governed by rules and procedures. Extensive formalization is one of the main characteristics of a bureaucracy. Greater formalization is likely to improve the efficiency of individual operations but may lead to increased inflexibility as workers may become incapable of performing non-standard tasks.

3 *Specialization:* The extent to which the work carried out by the organization is divided up into separate elements. Greater specialization tends to increase the complexity of organizational structures as there is likely to be greater horizontal differentiation (i.e. more groupings of different types of workers) and greater vertical integration (i.e. more hierarchical layers of management). Greater specialization may also increase spatial differentiation as the organization may have more sites. Greater specialization can lead to more adaptability as workers can adapt to changing requirements more quickly, but may also lead to inflexibility if their area of expertise is very narrow.

The purpose of organizational structure is to enable managers to co-ordinate and control the activities of workers so that tasks can be undertaken in the most efficient and effective manner. The factors that influence the choice of structure include the organization's:

Strategy: An organization needs a structure that suits its strategy. The more elaborate the strategy (e.g. more products, more markets), the more complex the structure is likely to have to be with greater horizontal, vertical integration and spatial differentiation. Thus, the challenge of determining their structure is particularly acute for multi-national corporations. The more countries they operate in and the more diverse their product range, the more complex their structure is likely to have to be.

Size: It seems obvious that organizational size (i.e. the number of people employed) would affect the way that an organization is structured. Increased size is likely to lead to increased formalization and specialization, but it might also be expected to result in decreased centralization. Again, this is usually another complicating factor for multi-national corporations which are invariably large.

Technology: The type of technology used in the organization's operations can be classified in terms of the extent to which it supports routine or non-routine operations. Routine technologies are associated with greater specialization and formalization. Thus, organizations involved in mass production of standardized products or services are likely to find structuring more straightforward than those involved in project or jobbing production or professional services.

Environment: Organizations need to adapt to their environments if they are to survive and prosper in the longer-term. The more dynamic and uncertain the environment, the less centralization and formalization would be expected. For multi-national corporations which typically operate in a number of different countries that can each have quite different business environments, this is yet another complicating factor, and one which tends to favor more decentralized structures.

The dilemma confronted by all organizational structures is the desire on one hand to maximize efficiency and, on the other, to maximize responsiveness to environmental change. This issue was first studied over 40 years ago by Burns and Stalker (1961). They draw a distinction between mechanistic and organic organizations. Mechanistic organizations are characterized by their high level of bureaucracy and hierarchical structures, in which communications pass up and down the corporate hierarchy. This arrangement enables workers to undertake a narrow range of tasks with little variability and under a high degree of managerial control. Mechanistic organizations are thus able to achieve their tasks with a high degree of efficiency and reliability. They are best suited to stable environments. Organic organizations on the other hand have much less bureaucracy and hierarchy. Workers are given much greater autonomy and are able to undertake a much wider range of tasks. The less formal arrangements mean that workers are better able to communicate across departmental lines. Thus, organic organizations are able to be much more innovative, as control is sacrificed for creativity. They are best suited to more dynamic and unstable environments.

Research studies of organizational structures in many different countries tend to show that the basic relationships between the factors that influence structure and the dimensions of structure seem to hold across the world. Thus, it is possible to generalize about what factors need to be taken into account when considering the most appropriate organizational arrangements within operations. The simpler and more repetitive the tasks, and the lower the degree of environmental uncertainty then the greater the degree of centralization, formalization and specialization that is appropriate (i.e. more mechanistic). This is likely to suit mass production operations such as fast food outlets or motor car manufacture. Conversely, the more complex and non-repetitive the tasks and the more uncertain the environment then the lower the degree of centralization, formalization and specialization that will be appropriate (i.e. more organic). This is likely to suit specialist manufacturers, for example like tailoring or specialist services, such as management consultants.

Structural types

Although organizational structures can and do vary tremendously, it is possible to identify a number of basic types as follows.

Simple structures

When organizations are very small, they do not really need a formal structure as such. Very small organizations do not tend to have any identifiable departments or functions. They are likely to produce a limited range of products and services, using a similarly limited process and technology. If tasks are simple, it is likely that they can all be carried out by a number of different people. Most workers are likely to perform multiple tasks. Both formalization and specialization will be minimal. However, there is likely to be extreme centralization centred on one individual or, at the most, very few people. This gives the organization great flexibility to cope with any uncertainty in its environment, but it is likely to be inefficient. However, as organizations grow, tasks are likely to become more complex. The organization is likely to respond by adopting a formal but simple structure in which different individuals start to specialize in particular tasks, applying the principles of the **division of labour**. Individuals who specialize in a narrow range of tasks are likely to be able to do so much more efficiently than those who undertake a greater number of tasks. However, this is usually achieved at the expense of flexibility.

division of labour
The principle that efficiency will be increased by each worker specializing on a single task rather than workers performing a number of different tasks.

Functional structures

As an organization grows further, it is likely to adopt a functional structure in which people performing similar tasks work together in separate departments based on the main business functions such as sales, accounts and operations (see Figure 11.3).

Specialization increases as each department concentrates on a limited range of tasks in order to do so efficiently. A functional structure would typically have an

CASE STUDY Re-structuring R & D at Unilever

On 21 November 2006, Unilever announced its decision to re-structure its European Foods Research and Development operations with the aim to improve its competitiveness.

The changes will see the consumer goods company concentrate its new product development activities for Foods in six 'Centres of Excellence' in Germany, Poland, Italy, the Netherlands, France and the UK. The centres will each be devoted to new product development based on a specific technical capability that can be applied across the categories in Unilever's product portfolio. For example, the Centre of Excellence 'structured emulsions' will work on mayonnaises (e.g. Hellman's), spreads (e.g. Flora) and dressings (e.g. Amora). The design principle behind these capability based development centres is that they will have the critical mass to develop a world-class technical capability which can be applied across categories, for local, regional and global innovations.

Unilever will keep small country R & D teams in each of the 21 countries which will focus on the technical implementation of innovations in that countries. Furthermore, these countries R & D teams will provide input to the Centres of Excellence on the specific needs of that country for new product development. These countries' R & D teams do not develop new products themselves.

The current European Foods R & D organization employs 1,160 people in 64 locations across Europe, with 39 locations involved in new product development. As a result of this reorganization, Unilever will move to 29 Foods R & D locations with six Centres of Excellence doing all the new product development. The changes will see the loss of 240 jobs. Unilever expects to relocate an additional 260 jobs to the consolidated Foods R & D centres across Europe.

The announcement of the re-structuring followed an extensive review of its R & D operations led by Vindi Banga, President of Unilever's Foods Category. Vindi Banga said:

'The review showed that we have great people and strong capabilities. However, it also showed that by organizing ourselves so that we could leverage our scale and play to our strengths we can improve our market competitiveness. By getting the benefits of focus and synergies I am convinced that today's announcement will make a significant difference to our innovation delivery'.

FIGURE 11.1 Unilever Foods R & D Europe new product development

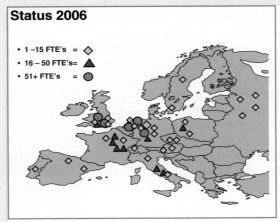
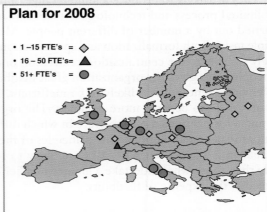

Status 2006

- 1 – 15 FTE's = ◇
- 16 – 50 FTE's = ▲
- 51+ FTE's = ●

- ▪ 39 locations product development
- ▪ Fragmentation over countries and categories

Plan for 2008

- 1 – 15 FTE's = ◇
- 16 – 50 FTE's= ▲
- 51+ FTE's = ●

- ▪ 6 Global Centres of Excellence
- ▪ Differentiating capabilities
- ▪ Global leverage

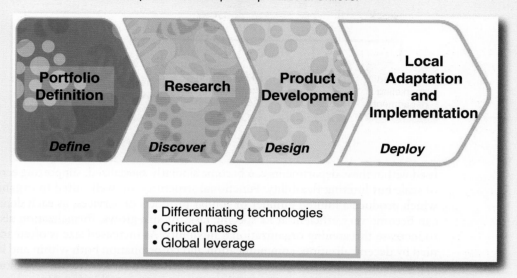

FIGURE 11.2 The new product development process at Unilever

Portfolio Definition — *Define*

Research — *Discover*

Product Development — *Design*

Local Adaptation and Implementation — *Deploy*

- Differentiating technologies
- Critical mass
- Global leverage

Vindi Banga, the President of Unilever Foods, said the centres would help the company deliver 'bigger, better, bolder innovations faster'.

The implementation of the restructuring started in 2007 with the aim to be completed by the end of 2008. The restructuring is part of the more extensive 'One Unilever' restructuring plan, which aims to simplify the Anglo-Dutch company's complicated corporate structure. The final aim, according to Unilever, is to 'increase leverage of its scale, improve its marketplace competitiveness, deliver functional excellence, and create a more competitive cost-structure allowing it to strengthen its focus on its consumers and customers'.

Unilever has around 179,000 employees in almost 100 countries. In 2006 it generated sales of €40 billion and spent €953 million (£644 million) on R & D. Unilever is one of the world's leading suppliers of fast moving consumer goods in the food, hygiene and personal care markets. It has a product portfolio that includes some of the world's best known brands such as Knorr, Hellmann's, Flora, Bertolli, Dove, Lux, Pond's, Lynx, Sunsilk, Persil, Cif and Domestos.

(Source material www.ft.com and www.unilever.com. With special thanks to Unilever for their additional contributions.)

WWW.

Questions (Suggested answers can be found on the companion website www.thomsonlearning.co.uk/barnes)

WWW.

1 Would you expect R & D operations to have a mechanistic or organic structure?

2 Assess the appropriateness of Unilever's new structure for its European Food R & D operations by considering the dimensions of organizational structure (centralization, formalization and specialization) and the contextual variables (strategy, size, technology and environment.)

3 What problems might arise as a result of the new structure?

4 How could this new structure help to deliver 'bigger, better, bolder innovations faster'?

operations department, responsible for producing all its goods and/or service outputs. Such a department would be responsible for all input resources and would be able to develop very specific knowledge and expertise. As an organization grows further, more specialization is possible with additional sub-division amongst the workforce within each function. Thus, within the operations function, separate departments may be dedicated to specific tasks within certain processes or products. The technology

FIGURE 11.3 A function structure

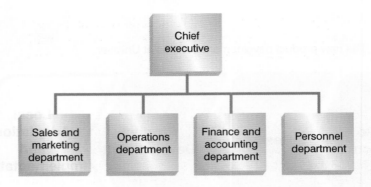

used within these departments can become similarly specialized, supporting economies of scale but limiting flexibility. Functional structures are well suited to organizations which produce a limited number of similar products or services, as each department can become very efficient at its specific task. As size grows, formalization also tends to increase threatening organizational flexibility. As increased size is often accompanied by decentralization, communication and co-ordination both within and between departments can become more difficult. This problem is likely to become more acute the more processes the operations department is responsible for. However, a functional structure is likely to be the best solution within a single site. However, once an organization has operations at a number of different locations, the issue of managerial control and co-ordination becomes more challenging. Where different locations house inter-linked operations that form part of a process producing the same or similar products (i.e. in a vertically integrated supply chain), or where each location houses a similar operation serving similar markets (e.g. a chain of burger bars), then a functional structure is likely to be appropriate. However, as the number of sites increases, co-ordination and control becomes increasingly difficult and other structural solutions might be more appropriate. This is especially so if different sites operate relatively independently of each other, and produce different products and serve different markets.

Multi-divisional structures

Divisional structures are based on the principle of splitting the organization down into smaller more self-contained business units. These units are usually profit centres, (responsible for achieving a required level of profit) and are often termed strategic business units (SBUs) as they are also typically given a high degree of strategic autonomy. Divisions might be formed on the basis of the products that they produce or the market that they serve, or possibly some combination of the two. The structure within a division is likely to be functional, with processes and technology dedicated to a limited number of products or services. However, a number of central services are likely to be provided by the organization's head office. The number, size and importance of these central services can vary. They will typically include corporate level activities such as finance and corporate planning. But there may also be central functional departments (e.g. marketing, personnel and operations) responsible for co-ordinating and perhaps controlling the work of these functions in the various divisions. Figure 11.4 illustrates a very simple example of a divisional structure with two divisions.

In reality, organizations with multi-divisional structures are likely to have a much larger number of divisions. Large global businesses may include divisions with geographic responsibilities, product responsibilities and functional responsibilities. This can make it difficult and costly to co-ordinate and control the organization as a whole due to the inherent tension between the need to centralize and the need to decentralize. Also, the inevitable competition for corporate resources can set up rivalries between the various divisions. All of these factors can combine to reduce the possibility for synergies and economies of scale and scope between divisions.

Matrix structures

Matrix structures offer an alternative to the multi-divisional structure. Matrix structures are based on an acceptance that managers and their work units can have two (or more) reporting lines. These might be functionally, geographically or product-based. Figure 11.5 shows a simple matrix structure with functional and product reporting lines.

Managers and their work units are located at the intersections of the two lines. So that in this example there are four operations managers, one for each of the products A–D. Each operations manager reports both to a product manager and to the head of the operations function. As with the multi-divisional structure, there would probably be a functionally-based support staff at head office. In reality, matrix structures can be much more complex, with many more products and functions. Some can also have more than two reporting lines, perhaps adding a geographic one (e.g. country or region). The idea of a matrix structure is that it seeks to force integration by explicitly acknowledging the tensions between different reports and forcing these to be surfaced and managed. However, they can be costly and difficult to operate in practice due to their complexity.

Network structures

In recent years, many organizations have been faced with more dynamic and unstable environments. In response to this they have sought to become faster, more flexible and more innovative whilst retaining the benefits of size by being able to integrate

FIGURE 11.4 A multi-divisional structure

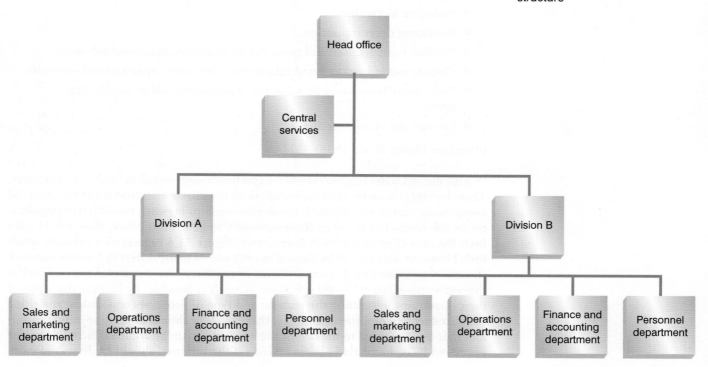

FIGURE 11.5 A matrix structure

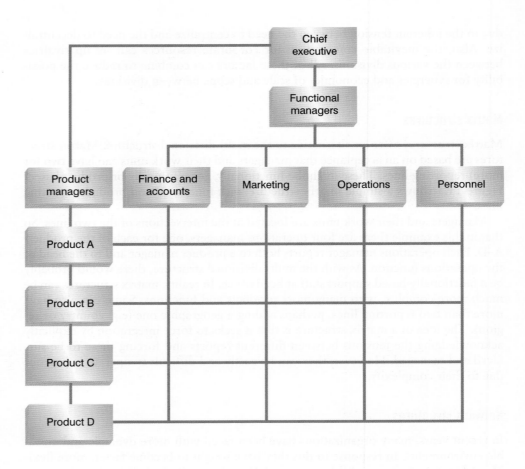

their often disparate activities. There has been a discernible trend in organizational structuring, which can be characterized as:

- Reducing hierarchies.
- Increasing decentralization.
- Smaller, more focused and more autonomous organizational sub-units.
- Greater use of market-based relationships between organizational sub-units.
- More fuzzy boundaries between the organization and its supply chain partners.
- Greater use of outsourcing.

(Based on Mabey *et al.*, 1998)

This has led some organizations to experiment with so-called Network structures. These represent something of the antithesis of organizational structure in the accepted sense, as they are based on much looser relationships between the different organizational sub-units, and between those sub-units and the head office, than would have been the case in more traditional structures. Figure 11.6 represents a network structure. However, this should be viewed as only one of many different possible network structures as these can take many forms in practice. The essence of the network is that each unit within it should specialize as much as possible. By limiting the scope of their operations, restricting the number and type of processes undertaken and using dedicated technology, the intention is that each unit should develop specific capabilities that are accessible to the rest of the network. It can be argued that the advent of improved ICTs, particularly those linked via the Internet, should facilitate the more

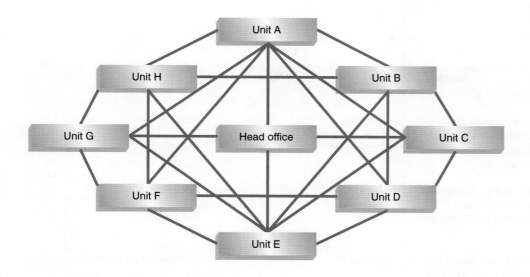

FIGURE 11.6 A network organization

intensive levels of communication and co-ordination necessary to maximize the benefits on offer from a network structure. However, examples of organizations adopting network structures are hard to find in practice.

The role of central operations

In larger and more complex organizational structures, it is usual for there to be some kind of central operations function, typically located at head office. The role played by such a central operations department can vary to reflect:

1 Whether individual business unit operations have the autonomy to determine their own strategy or whether they are required to follow a centrally set operations strategy.

2 Whether the emphasis within individual business unit operations is on achieving a certain level of performance or whether it is on developing their capabilities.

Using these two dimensions, Slack and Lewis (2002) identify four possible roles for central operations; trainer, governor, facilitator and curator (see Table 11.1).

Central operations might be expected to adopt the trainer or governor role in organizations with a high degree of centralization, formalization and specialization in the organization. This would typically be the case in a functional structure. Whereas the facilitator or curator roles would be more likely in matrix or network structures. The role of central operations in multi-divisional structures can vary widely, depending upon the extent to which the business strategies of the various divisions are related to each other. Where strategies are related, it might be expected that central operations would possess the necessary expertise to enable it to act in the trainer or facilitator role. Whereas in more diversified organizations, the role of central operations would be more likely to be that of governor or curator.

Structural choices in international operations

The structure of organizations has been the subject of much debate in managerial literature for many years. Organization theorists from the time of Chandler (1962) onwards have argued that structure should follow strategy. However, as discussed above,

TABLE 11.1 The roles of
central operations

TYPE	OBJECT OF CENTRAL OPERATIONS	CENTRAL OPERATIONS ACTS AS:	BUSINESS UNIT OPERATIONS ACTS AS:
Trainer	Instructs business unit operations in the development and deployment of their capabilities through standardized improvement methods	Teacher Consultant	Pupil Client
Governor	Controls the performance of business unit operations by setting clear priorities and measuring performance against targets	Messenger Judge	Recipient Defendant
Facilitator	Enables business unit operations to develop and deploy their capabilities through shared advice, support and learning	Mentor	Member of a community
Curator	Nurtures the performance of business unit operations by collecting performance data and distributing comparative performance information	Recorder/analyst	Source of, and recipient of information

(BASED ON SLACK AND LEWIS, 2002)

there are many factors that can be relevant when seeking to match organizational structure to strategy. From the operations management perspective, an appropriate organizational structure is one that facilitates co-ordination and communication both within the operations function and between the operations function and the organization's other business functions. The challenge of structuring organizations that have international operations is that much greater than that in those that only operate domestically. An international organization can have operations facilities as well as their customers located in many different countries. Its organizational structure needs to enable it to integrate its different functional activities in different countries and across different products and services, if it produces more than one. As noted in Chapter 4, international operations can be configured in a number of different ways; home operations, multi-domestic operations, regional operations and global co-ordinated operations, each of which represents an increasing challenge for the co-ordination and control of operations.

Examples of different kinds of structures can be found within many international organizations that encompass the full range of structural types discussed in this chapter. Also, given the frequencies with which many organizations undertake re-structuring exercises, it seems clear that the optimal solution has yet to be found in matching organizational strategy to structure.

CULTURE

Organizational culture can be thought of as that set of assumptions and beliefs that are taken-for-granted and held in common by members of an organization (Schein, 1985). It is often thought that a strong organizational culture will benefit an organization. Whilst this might be true if the culture helps the organization to perform well and meet customer expectations. However, a strong culture can also be problematic if it is inappropriate, as it is very difficult to change. The stronger the culture, the more difficult it is to change. Culture is often deeply ingrained in an organization, akin to the heart and soul of the organization. Unlike structure, culture cannot easily be recast by the will of senior managers.

Culture can be thought of as comprising three levels (Schein, 1985).

1 *Artefacts:* The surface culture evidenced through visible representations such as dress, architecture, technology, language, stories, etc. Although these are easy to observe they can still sometimes be interpreted ambiguously and be difficult to decipher by outsiders.

2 *Espoused values:* What people in the organization say about its values. This might be manifest in an organizational mission or vision statement, or other 'official' statements of belief or slogans. This may, however, only reflect the views of organizational leaders, past or present. Perhaps more powerful evidence of espoused values can come from more commonly articulated views by people in the organization. These may more accurately reflect the shared learning on which culture is based.

3 *Basic assumptions:* This is the deepest level of culture, which reflects those beliefs and assumption that are held to be universal truths by the people in the organization. However, these usually remain deep below the surface as they are typically not discussed. They manifest themselves in the unspoken rules of the organization that often exist without people's conscious knowledge, because they have been absorbed through a process of acclimatization and reinforcement over time.

Culture is learnt through socialization within the organization. Thus, the longer people remain in the organization the more deeply ingrained commonly held values and assumptions become, because these are developed and reinforced over time by shared experiences. For new entrants to the organization, confronting organizational culture can be something of a shock, particularly if their previous educational or work background has taken place in a very different cultural context. Many organizations take explicit steps to inculcate organizational values into new recruits through the use of induction training, mentoring schemes, etc.

However, it can be too simplistic to talk about a single organizational culture. In large and complex organization, there may be significant cultural differences between different parts of the organization. This might arise because of different histories and work experiences of different parts of the organization. Working in the organization's factory, for example, is likely to offer a very different experience than working in one of its sales offices. Culture may also develop differently if recruitment and training practices differ in different departments and locations. Differences can be most marked where employees are also part of a profession (e.g. accountants, lawyers, doctors) which have a strong separate culture arising from a distinctive education and on-going association with fellow members of this group. In international organizations, cultural differences between people of different nationalities can be a source of misunderstanding and even conflict that can further dilute or even override the notion of single organizational culture.

The competing values that underpin cultural differences between different parts of an organization can make it difficult either to agree common goals or the means of achieving them. This can make co-operation between different parts of the organization extremely problematic. The general levels of education, training and previous work experience of people in particular departments (whether functionally-based or not) or locations can lead to quite different expectations about how work should be organized and managed. This can be particularly problematic if cross-departmental team working of any kind is required.

Organizational cultural types

A number of different writers have offered models characterizing different cultural types.

Handy (1985) identifies four types of culture, which can be seen as being linked to organizational structure:

- *Power culture:* Power is concentrated in the hands of a few or even a single individual. Control radiates from the centre like a web. There are unlikely to be any rules in a power culture and little bureaucracy. Power cultures are typical of many small entrepreneurial organizations, but can prevail in much larger organizations with a strong autocratic leader (often the founder).

- *Role culture:* This is a very bureaucratic culture, in which people have clearly defined roles. Power derives from a person's position. These organizations are typically very hierarchical with authority delegated to appropriate specialists. Role cultures are prevalent in functionally structured organizations.

- *Task culture:* In this culture the focus is on getting the job done. There is likely to be a prevalence of team working, in which groups of experts are brought together to solve particular problems. Power derives from individual or group expertise. Task cultures are often a feature of matrix structures where multiple reporting lines are the norm.

- *Person culture:* The person culture exists where individuals are more important than the organization. Indeed, the organization may only exist to enable the individuals to function within their industry. There may be little collective effort and so it may be difficult to hold the organization together over time. Many professional organizations (e.g. legal partnerships, or consultancies) can operate as person cultures; each individual brings a particular expertise or clientele to the organization.

Deal and Kennedy (1982) classify organizational culture in terms of the kind of feedback provided to workers about their activities and the degree of risk involved. They identify four cultural types:

1 *The 'tough-guy macho' culture:* Feedback is quick and the risks are high. Such circumstances typically prevail in fast moving financial trading activities such as stock market dealing, but they could also apply to the police or rescue service workers. Work is likely to be individual in nature. This is likely to be a very stressful culture in which to work.

2 *The 'work hard/play hard' culture:* Feedback will be rapid, but few risks are likely to be taken. Such conditions will typically apply to large organizations, which are striving for a high level of customer service. Work is likely to be team-based, with a prevalence of jargon and buzzwords.

3 *The 'bet your company' culture:* In this culture, the risks will be great, but feedback will be slow, perhaps many years before the results are known. Examples of this include R & D or exploration projects (e.g. for oil or minerals), which take years to bear fruit.

4 *The 'process' culture:* This occurs in organizations where there is little or no feedback but risks are low. The focus of people's efforts therefore becomes how work is done, rather than what is achieved. This is typically associated with bureaucracies. Whilst bureaucracies can be criticized for being slow and cautious, their strength is their consistency and reliability, which is often ideal in public services.

As with structure, there is no one ideal culture. Rather it is a question of what culture is most appropriate to the type of work being undertaken. Given that culture is notoriously difficult to change, it may be more sensible to choose to undertake operations for which the organizations' culture is best suited rather than to try to radically change the culture. In particular, it is likely to be better to take account of culture and cultural differences when determining how to organize work groups within an organization, whether within the operations function itself or when assembling cross-functional teams. Whilst it is certainly difficult to successfully undertake wholesale cultural change in organizations, it is possible to educate people to be more aware of organizational culture and to train them to mitigate the worst effects of its consequences.

National culture

As discussed above, an important aspect of the consideration of culture in organizations is that of national culture. Whilst it is important not to resort to the use of national stereotypes, it is obvious to anyone with any experience of working in international organizations that people of different nationalities do seem to exhibit distinctive and identifiable behavioural traits. Different nationalities also seem to demonstrate distinct preferences for organizational arrangements which seem to derive from their national culture.

The work of Hofstede (1980) provides the foundation of the effect of understanding of national culture within organizations. (Hofstede's analysis can be applied to differentiate between regional as well as national cultures.) Hofstede uses four dimensions to analyze these national and regional differences:

1 *Power distance* is the degree to which a society expects there to be differences in the levels of power between different groups of people in organizations. In countries high in power distance there is an acceptance that some individuals wield larger amounts of power than others. So those in authority in organizations will be afforded a high degree of respect, with greater use of titles and other outward signs of power. In societies with low power distance there is a view that power should be equally distributed. So in organizations, signs of power and authority will be downplayed.

2 *Uncertainty avoidance* reflects the extent to which a society accepts uncertainty and risk. In societies with high uncertainty avoidance, there is low tolerance of deviant behaviour and opinion. Organizations are more likely to have many formal rules to govern behaviour. Workers will tend to exhibit low job mobility, often preferring to stay with the same employer for life.

3 *Individualism vs collectivism:* Individualism is extent to which people are expected to look after themselves, whereas collectivism is the extent to which people expect others in the group to which they belong to look after them. This is typically their employer, but it can also be the state in some countries. In cultures high in collectivism, workers tend to offer their employer their loyalty more easily.

4 *Masculinity vs femininity:* Masculinity refers to the traditional male values of competitiveness, assertiveness, ambition and the accumulation of wealth and material possessions. Femininity, on the other hand, refers to the traditional female values of relationships, a concern for others and improving the quality of life.

As an example, the USA is low in power distance and uncertainty avoidance, but high in individualism and masculinity. The USA is of interest, not just because of its importance to the world economy, but also because of its role in developing many of the theories about human behaviour in organizations. Hofstede's analysis should serve to remind us that not all countries are the same as the USA, which might lead us to question the extent to which those theories might apply in other countries. The national culture in Japan, another important economy, for example, whilst similar to the US on masculinity, differs in that it is high on power distance and uncertainty avoidance, but low on individualism.

Subsequent research by Hofstede and other researchers have highlighted other dimensions of culture that vary between different nations (e.g. Hofstede, 1997; Trompenaars and Hampden-Turner, 1997; Schell and Solomon, 1997; Gesteland, 1999). These include:

- *Time horizons:* The importance attached to the future *vs* the past and present. Long-term orientated societies are able to take a long-term view about achieving their goals. They tend to value thrift and perseverance. Short-term orientated societies are much less tolerant and seek much shorter-term gratification. Long-term orientated societies are mostly found in East Asian countries, especially China, Japan, and South Korea. Western nations and the less developed countries tend to have short-term orientations.

- *Time sensitivity:* The importance attached to being on time, adhering to schedules, meeting deadlines, etc. Clockwatching cultures are more prevalent in Northern European countries as well as in Japan and South Korea in Asia.

- *Deal-making vs relationships:* The extent to which work is undertaken on the basis of formal agreements between the people involved and the extent to which it is relies upon the relationships between them. Anglo-Saxon cultures (e.g. USA, UK, Australia) place much greater importance on doing a deal, whereas many Asian countries (e.g. India, Japan, China) place more importance on building relationships between those involved.

- *Formality in social interactions:* The degree of familiarity in social interactions at work. These are manifest in the terms of address used, the form of greetings (e.g. kiss, embrace, handshake, bow), the accepted work attire, etc.

Whilst some national cultures are more homogeneous than others and some are more deeply ingrained than others, these various dimensions can be used to characterize national cultures. From this it is possible to group together countries that have similar national cultures. These following clusters have been identified (Rowan and Shenkar, 1985):

- *Anglo:* Including Australia, Canada, Ireland, New Zealand, South Africa, United Kingdom, United States.
- *Arab:* Including Abu-Dhabi, Bahrain, Kuwait, Oman, Saudi Arabia, United Arab Emirates.
- *Far Eastern:* Including Hong Kong, China, Indonesia, Malaysia, Philippines, Singapore, South Vietnam, Taiwan, Thailand.
- *Germanic:* Including Austria, Germany, Switzerland.
- *Latin American:* Including Argentina, Chile, Colombia, Mexico, Peru, Venezuela.
- *Latin European:* Including Belgium, France, Italy, Portugal, Spain.
- *Near Eastern:* Including Greece, Iran, Turkey.
- *Nordic:* Including Denmark, Finland, Norway, Sweden.
- *Independent:* Some countries do not fall into any of the above clusters. These include Brazil, India, Israel, Japan and South Korea. These countries each have very different national cultures.

The differences between national cultures might therefore be expected to have an impact on work organization. It would seem to be sensible that organizational structures be adopted that best suit an organization's national culture. For example, countries high in Hofstede's power distance and uncertainty avoidance dimensions (e.g. France and Italy) would favor the high centralization and formalization provided by a rigid bureaucracy. Also, in high power distance cultures an autocratic management style would be accepted by workers. However, team working is likely to be seen as desirable in cultures high in Hofstede's femininity dimension, as workers have a high

CASE STUDY GNI: A mini-multinational

GNI, a biotechnology start-up, has fewer than 100 staff. But it has a presence in Tokyo and Fukuoka, Japan; in Shanghai, China; in Cambridge and London in the UK; and in San Jose in California, USA. One of its scientific founders recently moved from the UK to Auckland, New Zealand, to set up a laboratory. From there he will collaborate with his virtual company much as he did before. GNI is proving that it no longer takes much scale to be a multi-national.

GNI was founded in 2001 by Christopher Savoie, a US entrepreneur whose adoption of Japanese citizenship is itself a symbol of international flux. 'We take the best of what is available in each country and put them together', says Mr Savoie. GNI has three main national identities. A Japanese-Chinese partnership, it conducts much of its basic research in the UK, where the regulatory environment and relatively liberal attitudes to scientific use of human tissue make for a good place to perform genetic analysis. Scientists working in collaboration with GNI obtain umbilical cords from the Rosie Maternity Hospital in Cambridge. This provides them with genetic tissue virtually unaffected by the environment, allowing them to analyze the interaction between the genes, whose identities were revealed by the human genome project. Obtaining such material in Japan would be difficult, since Japanese parents traditionally keep their child's umbilical cord.

But if Japan lacks access to experimental tissue, it has two other resources not so readily available in the UK: supercomputers and cash. Much of the data generated in Britain are analyzed in Japan on powerful computers. GNI has also been able to raise about $30 million in Japan since 2001. The country has the world's largest pool of savings; and after regulations on start-ups were recently relaxed, much of it has found its way into biotechnology. Mr Savoie, who studied medicine at Kyushu University and is fluent in Japanese, saw the chance to raise money when rules barring academics from company boards were relaxed. Quickly changing the identity and headquarters of GNI from the US to Japan, he raised enough cash from Japanese investors to keep the company going until 2008, says Kan-Ichiro 'Ken' Suzuki, GNI's chief financial officer.

China is the third node in GNI's network. Here the resource is patients. Many big pharmaceutical companies run clinical trials in China, and patient data from there is starting to be accepted by US and other Western regulators. But GNI thinks it will be the first non-Chinese company to seek Chinese regulatory approval for a drug before applying to regulators in Japan and the West. The pharmaceutical industry concentrates on developing medicines to treat illnesses prevalent in the West. Once a drug is launched in the US and Europe, companies seek approval in Japan and elsewhere in Asia. GNI hopes to turn that model on its head. It is targeting diseases more common in Asia, where, for example, stomach cancer and hepatitis are prevalent. 'Asia has been getting the short end of the stick', says Mr Savoie. For clinical trials, China is a good alternative to Japan. Mr Savoie says trials of a similar quality can be conducted more quickly in China for one-tenth of the cost. It will not be possible to rely entirely on Chinese data to seek regulatory approval elsewhere, Mr Savoie concedes. But it will be easier to justify spending several hundred million dollars on a Japanese or US trial if the medicine has proved effective on Chinese patients.

The Chinese part of GNI's puzzle is completed by Shanghai Genomics, a start-up established by two US-educated Chinese entrepreneurs. GNI merged with Shanghai Genomics last May. Ying Luo, President and Chief Executive of Shanghai Genomics, says collaboration with GNI brings his company better science, more money and an international perspective. He shrugs off any suggestion that tensions between China and Japan, which erupted into riots in Chinese cities last year, could damage the prospects of a Japanese-Chinese venture in the sensitive area of drug testing. He says, 'We are a very good example of how people from different countries can sit down together and solve a common problem'. The merged company is testing two drugs developed by Shanghai Genomics from compounds whose patents had expired. The most advanced is for lung damage that is a side-effect of radiation therapy.

Like the gene networks that GNI studies, the interactions of a virtual company can be complex. Mr Savoie has moved his family from Tokyo to Fukuoka to take advantage of its short flying time to Shanghai. GNI executives have become ardent video-conferencers. Carol Cherkis, Vice-President of business development says meetings are arranged for mornings in some places and evenings in others. But with a company spanning all time zones – she works in San Jose, from where she seeks tie-ups with US-based drug companies – someone has to get up in the middle of the night. 'It's a virtual company', she says, then corrects herself: 'It's a real company. It's just that we're not all in one place'. Mr Savoie says the complexity is simple. 'We have a Chinese cost structure, Japanese supercomputers and, in Cambridge, access to ethical materials [umbilical cords] and top clinical scientists', he says. 'This is a network we can use to take high-level science and turn it into molecules [potential medicine] to compete with the big boys'.

The big boys will not be shaking in their boots. But they might be interested to know that a tiny, unlisted company can now be almost as international as they are.

(Excerpted from 'March of the mini-multinational' by David Pilling, *Financial Times* 3 May 2006)

Questions (Suggested answers can be found on the companion website www.thomsonlearning.co.uk/barnes)

1 What type of organizational structure would you expect to find in GNI?

2 What type of organizational culture would you expect to find in GNI?

3 To what extent would you expect different national cultures to cause problems for GNI's operations?

4 What operational problems might be expected to arise as GNI grows?

concern for relationships at work. Team working, often with little or no direct supervision is also likely to be effective in cultures strong in Hofstede's collectivism dimension, such as Japan. In recent years, organizations in many countries have tried to introduce the kind of Japanese team working approaches typically found in lean manufacturing practices. However, it might be expected that this would be problematic in cultures high in power distance and individualism.

Determining the extent to which they should introduce organizational arrangements which are considered to be best practice in other locations and the extent to which these should be adapted to meet local cultural conditions is a very real dilemma for organizations with international operations. Organizational cultures are typically established within one national culture and are likely to be heavily influenced by that country's culture. There can be a very real risk of culture clashes if organizational arrangements and practices are exported without due consideration for the national culture of the host country.

Organizations that operate in a number of countries would seem to be particularly at risk from clashes of national culture. This is likely to be most acute when close co-operation is required between parts of the organization that are based in different countries, especially when national cultures are from different clusters. Co-operation between countries within the same cluster is likely to be much easier than between those from more than one.

WORK TEAMS

Working in teams has perhaps always been an important feature of work organization. It is very rare for any individual to work in total isolation in any organization. Indeed, one of the main purposes of business organizations is to bring people together so that they can perform work more efficiently and effectively than if they acted alone. Moreover, many work tasks have to be performed by a group of people working collectively; that is the very essence of teamwork. However, teamworking seems to have become increasingly important in operations in recent years. In particular, much of the success of Japanese manufacturing practices, as exemplified by the Toyota Production System has teamworking at its heart. Organizations all around the world have tried to emulate this by introducing more team-based approaches to work. Teamworking practices are based on the belief that when working together effectively, a group of people can make a much greater contribution than would be made by those people working as individuals. A team is more than just a group of people. A team works together on a common task to achieve a specific goal or objective. Teamwork requires cohesion, complimentary skills and leadership. An important issue with regard to team working is the degree of empowerment afforded to the team. Empowerment is the concept that workers are able to take greater control over the work that they do, without reference to higher levels of management. The idea is that workers are given the authority and the resources to take greater control over the decisions that affect their work. If teams are to function effectively, they not only need to understand the extent and limits of the autonomy, but also how decisions which are delegated to them are taken. In particular, it is important to establish the extent to which power resides in the team leader and the extent to which decision-making is exercised collectively.

There are many kinds of teams in organizations. Buchanan and Huczynski (2004) distinguish four types:

Advice (or problem solving) teams are created to make suggestions about how to address a specific work issue or problem. Such teams might be specially convened to address a one-off issue or might be established permanently to tackle on-going problems. Team members need to possess or be trained in problem-solving techniques. In some circumstances advice teams can be given the authority to implement the solutions that they recommend. Perhaps the best known type of advice team is the quality circle. Originating in Japan, a quality circle is a team of workers who come together to solve problems in their own work area. Originally, their remit was to examine quality problems, but in many instances this has now broadened to consider many other issues. Quality circles are one practical manifestation of *kaizen* (the principle of continuous improvement) that forms an integral part of the whole TQM philosophy (discussed in chapter 10). Quality circles can take many forms, but it is generally agreed that it is vitally important that they are given the authority to implement the improvement ideas that they come up with. Failure to do so is likely

empowerment
The concept that workers are given greater control over the work that they do, without reference to higher levels of management.

quality circle
A group of workers who come together to solve quality and other related problems within their work area.

to lead to de-motivation, making it less likely that the team will make the effort to identify further improvements.

Action teams have members with a mix of very specialized skills who come together to undertake a specific task, often of fairly short duration, but one that is repeated under different conditions each time. Examples of this include a hospital surgical team, a symphony orchestra, an aircraft flight crew and a film crew. Action teams are often characterized by the requirement for members to be skilled in the use of specialist equipment or technology. The success of the action team depends on all members performing to peak levels.

Project teams are comprised of members who are brought together to undertake a specific task of fixed duration. Members sometimes join or leave the team throughout the life of the project, depending upon the need for their specialist skills. On completion of the task the team is disbanded. As members often come from different parts of the organization, project teams are often cross-functional teams. Cross-functional teams can often experience difficulties due to the cultural differences that often exist between different functions. Also, the fact that members are in some way representing their home functions means that they may experience divided loyalties. Project teams may also include members drawn from other organizations (e.g. suppliers or customers) and others recruited solely for the duration of the project. The temporary nature of the team and the task can pose specific challenges in team building and co-ordination. Also the unique nature of any project requires members to have creative problem skills as well as their particular technical expertise.

Production teams are responsible for well-defined day-to-day on-going core operations. The expectation is that the production team will remain in place indefinitely and comprises a stable number of members. The technical skills required of team members will vary depending upon the nature of the work. However, there will typically be a requirement for team members to work in close co-operation with each other. Often the team will have to co-ordinate with other teams in the organization. Examples of production teams can be found within factories, customer service operations, retail sales and repairs.

Traditionally, the work of all kinds of teams and especially production teams would be co-ordinated and controlled by a leader (a manager or supervisor) appointed by the organization's more senior managers. However, in recent years many organizations have attempted to give teams greater autonomy, replacing the traditional role of a supervisor with a more collective leadership, by creating self-managed work teams. For example, in a self-managed team, the workers might collectively decide on the planning and controlling of work, the allocation of tasks to team members, the pace of the work, the evaluation of the performance of team members and the recruitment of new members. The idea underpinning the creation of self-managed work teams is that empowering workers provides them with greater motivation and job satisfaction, thereby improving their performance. The idea is to move from a situation where work goals are achieved through the control of employees to one where those goals are achieved through the commitment of employees. However, it is worth noting that increasing empowerment requires employees to possess a greater range of skills and in more depth if self-managed work teams are to successfully cope with their increased responsibilities. Reports of the levels of performance achieved by self-managed work teams are very mixed, suggesting that they may be situationally dependent. One factor that is likely to be significant is national culture. Much of the literature on this subject comes from the USA, an Anglo culture with low power distance and uncertainty avoidance. Americans might therefore be expected to be able to accept the responsibilities and cope with the high levels of ambiguity and uncertainty inherent in self-managed work teams. These factors probably counteract the high levels of individuality in Anglo culture, which might otherwise militate against teamworking. However, it is likely to prove more difficult to use empowerment to achieve high performance in cultures that are high in power distance and uncertainty avoidance.

cross-functional team
A work team comprising members from different functional areas within the organization (e.g. operations, marketing, accounting or human resource management).

self-managed work team
A work team in which workers are empowered to take many of the decisions concerning their work without reference to management.

work team
A group of people who work together on a common task to achieve a specific goal or objective.

Japanese style teamworking

The move towards more autonomous teamworking, based on giving workers more control and greater job satisfaction through participation, was pioneered in a number of American and Scandinavian countries. However, Japanese style teamworking as typified by the Toyota Production System is somewhat different to this. It has a number of distinctive features (Morita, 2001):

1 Multi-skilled workers
2 Continuous development of workers' skills
3 Assignment of tasks to teams rather than individuals
4 Supervisors act as role-models for workers and as a buffer between managers and workers.

The Toyota Production System is based on lean production principles which aim to minimize waste of all kinds including work-in-progress inventories and excess labour. There is little slack within a lean operation. However, highly trained multi-skilled employees operating within the strongly collectivist Japanese culture makes for highly motivated and flexible teams able to deliver maximum output with minimum labour input. The assembly line environment of Toyota makes for jobs that comprise highly standardized repetitive short-cycle work, which can be learnt quickly by new recruits. In contrast to self-managed work teams, the Toyota Production System relies on powerful first-line supervisors for internal control and co-ordination and for external communications. Although Japanese work teams operate as production teams when assembling vehicles, they also operate as advice teams outside of this context. They meet regularly as a quality circle when production is not taking place to develop and implement solutions to quality and other production-related problems. In contrast to their role as a production team, team members have a high degree of autonomy and empowerment when acting in their advice team role.

Virtual teams

Recent advances in ICT have enabled the creation of virtual teams. The operation of virtual teams relies on electronically mediated rather than face-to-face communications. This may be in the form of emails, Internet message boards, groupware, audio or video-conferencing, etc. Such communications can either be synchronous (i.e. in real-time) or asynchronous. Such media allow teams to function when members are separated by both distance and time. This has the advantage of enabling teams to draw upon members who would otherwise be unable to collaborate on the same task. However, communication in virtual teams is considerably impoverished by the absence of non-verbal signals and the lack of opportunity for social interaction. This can lead to misunderstandings which can be amplified if team members are from different national cultures. Members of virtual teams typically have less rapport with each other and are more task orientated. This can lead to a lowering of job satisfaction and motivation. To help alleviate these problems, many proponents and practitioners of virtual teams advocate that members should meet face-to-face at least once when the team is formed and if possible at regular intervals thereafter.

Factors affecting team effectiveness

Not all groups of people achieve the same levels of performance when working under the same conditions. Many factors can influence the effectiveness of a team. These can be brought together under four categories (Robbins, 2003: 264).

● *Work design:* The design of the work task required to be carried out has a major impact on performance. First, there must be a need for people to work

WHEN THINGS GO WRONG All together now: Teambuilding at Toyota NAPCC

Every day, in the Southern California desert city of Ontario, some 242,000 auto parts arrive from Japanese and US suppliers at the Toyota North American Parts Center California (NAPCC). Inside, some 400 workers receive, sort and store the parts in ceiling-high racks, or pick, pack and load them onto trucks for delivery to a dozen regional centres in the US and worldwide. In so doing, NAPCC employees are the crucial link in a supply chain that gets error-free shipments to these centres within five days of an order or, for priority items, within an astounding two hours. Impressive as the operation is, however, what NAPCC does is not nearly as remarkable as how it does it. In most warehouses, workers wait for supervisors to tell them what to do, and supervisors, in turn, don't welcome suggestions from the floor. In contrast, NAPCC is organized into 54 work teams, whose members, or 'warehouse associates', are expected by management to come up with ways to make the work more stimulating – and the workers more productive.

When NAPCC began hiring in 1996, it promised its recruits a distinctly Japanese-influenced warehouse process. They would be working in a team culture, not an authoritarian environment. Work teams are central to Toyota's lean production system. Small groups would be guided by a team leader rather than bossed by a foreman. Teams should help ensure that operational problems and employee conflicts are resolved when and where they occur, by the people who are closest to the issue at hand. For NAPCC job applicants who had spent most of their working lives in command-and-control warehouse environments, the prospect of teamwork was a huge and welcome change.

Reaching new heights through teamwork

However, before the NAPCC new hires could be schooled in a team approach, the demand for parts exploded. NAPCC quickly hired an additional 200 temporary workers to help. Still, the problems mounted. Orders were delayed, for example, because of computer glitches in inventory-tracking. Not surprisingly, customers started to complain. To cope with the crush, NAPCC supervisors adopted a command-and-control style, an understandable reaction under the circumstances. Unfortunately, the 'traditional supervisory structure' culture persisted even after order flow had stabilized. What had been envisioned as an operation comprised of small teams had transmogrified into 13 supervisor-driven 'home positions' that consisted of up to 50 or more workers taking orders from group leaders and assistant group leaders. The associates, however, had not come to NAPCC for old-style management. 'They were telling us in opinion surveys that NAPCC was not delivering on its initial commitment to teams', said Joe Kane, NAPCC's national customer support financial administration manager. 'Our work group structure made it extremely difficult to build strong partnerships with our associates'.

NAPCC managers knew they had to address these important issues. They set up a nine member cross-functional planning team with the goal of restoring workers' trust by creating the team environment that had been promised. They decided to apply the principle that for a team to most effectively meet its objectives, each member's unique personal strengths must be identified and utilized, by the individuals themselves as well as by the team as a whole. To do this they enlisted the help of management consultants from The Gallup Organization, who applied *StrengthsFinder,* Gallup's management tool that identifies an individual's strengths and helps managers match individuals to tasks that play to their strengths, while managing around their weaknesses. Through this strengths-based approach, NAPCC's managers realized that their previous tendency to overlook individual characteristics was one of the root causes of their associates' frustration. This approach helped transform large work groups into motivated and mutually supportive small teams.

NAPCC managers decided to keep the original 13 home positions, but also to break down each position into a series of much smaller teams of seven to ten associates, each with its own autonomy, accountability and team leader. Workers in each position organized themselves into smaller teams. When the re-structuring and training intervention began not everyone was psyched about the renewed emphasis on teams. Many associates responded to the reorganization with cynical disbelief. However, over time, the enthusiasm of those who did take *StrengthsFinder* eventually won over the disaffected associates. That commitment grew with the realization that the overall effort was not just for show.

Within a year of the intervention, Toyota's own productivity measure showed a 6 per cent increase in overall per-person productivity. There were also less quantifiable signs of improvement. Says one team leader, 'If there's a problem, we stop and deal with it'. Also, NAPCC's human resources department reports that it is involved in fewer disciplinary actions because teams handle most of them on their own. Happily, the change for the better does not seem transitory and Toyota can now rely on its NACPP associates for continuous improvement.

(Abridged from 'All Together Now' by Julie Connelly, *The Gallup Management Journal*, 15 March 2002, downloaded from http://gmj.gallup.com on 4 December 2006)

Questions (Suggested answers can be found on the companion website www.thomsonlearning.co.uk/barnes)

1 Why was teamworking at NACPP not a success initially?

2 How was the *StrengthsFinder*-based initiative able to overcome these problems?

together. Thus, the task must be one which is suitable for a group of workers to perform collectively. A group can only truly become a team if it is undertaking a common task. Second, the performance of the team will be increased if members are highly motivated. Motivation has been shown to increase if the team has a high degree of control over the way the work is carried out, if team members have the opportunity to use different skills and if the work consists of a task that is whole and identifiable and has a significant impact on others. (The impact of work design on motivation is discussed in further detail in Chapter 12.)

- *Team composition:* The factors that need to be taken into account when considering the composition of a team include:

  The skills of team members: An effective team must have members who not only have the necessary technical skills but also problem-solving, decision-making and interpersonal skills. It is not necessary for all team members to have all these skills, as long as individuals have complimentary skills that ensure that the team as a whole has the full range.

  The personalities of team members: High performing teams tend to be made up of members who have personalities with high levels of extroversion, agreeableness, conscientiousness and emotional stability. However, unlike skills, it is important that all team members have a minimum level of these personality characteristics. The cohesiveness of the team is likely to be seriously disrupted, if these are lacking in any single member.

  The flexibility of team members: Team performance will be enhanced if members are flexible enough to undertake each other's work. Thus, cross-training to facilitate multi-tasking should yield dividends.

  The preference of team members for team working: Not all workers are team-players. Thus, it is better to recruit team members from amongst people who have a preference for team working.

  The allocation of team roles: Researchers have shown that successful teams need members to play different roles. For example, Belbin (2003) identifies up to nine different roles within three different headings; cerebral, action-orientated and people-orientated. Whilst people can undertake different and even multiple roles, it is better that team members are assigned roles that best suit their preferred style.

  The size of the team: In order to include the range of skills and other attributes necessary to perform the task, the minimum size of a team is probably four or five. The maximum size is probably ten otherwise significant communication and co-ordination problems can emerge.

- *Context:* Four contextual factors appear to influence team performance:

  Resources: Any work group is part of a larger organizational system, therefore it relies on the availability of resources and support from other parts of the organization. Without adequate resources it cannot succeed.

  Leadership: Usually a work group will have a formal leader, with a title such as department or unit manager, supervisor, team leader, etc. Whilst organizational researchers are generally agreed that leadership does make a difference to group performance, they are by no means agreed about how this happens. There is little empirical evidence to suggest that good leaders have to possess particular characteristics or exhibit particular behaviours. This makes it difficult to know what type of person should undertake a leadership role. Most theories of leadership argue that leaders need to have a concern both to achieve the task and for the well-being of the members of the team. Having a leader who is people orientated is likely to make for higher levels of team satisfaction, but it will not guarantee a high level of productivity. Noting that leadership styles can vary along a continuum from highly autocratic at one end to highly participative at the other, a number of theorists have argued that the best approach to leadership will depend upon the situation and particularly upon the characteristics of other team members.

Climate of trust – members of effective teams tend to trust one another. This improves co-operation and bonds the team together. Similarly, effective leadership within a team relies on members having a high degree of trust in the leader.

Performance evaluation and rewards – Evaluating and rewarding employees on an individual basis, as is typically the practice in many Western organizations, is not likely to reinforce the team ethos. On the contrary, team effort and commitment is likely to be damaged if individuals are singled out for special attention and reward. It is particularly challenging for organizations in highly individualistic cultures (e.g. in the Anglo cluster) to adapt their evaluation and reward systems to reinforce group rather than individual performance.

- *Processes:* To be effective, teams need processes that enable members to work together successfully. Factors that support this include:

A common purpose: Effective teams share a common purpose that provides members with an overarching direction, guides their actions and reinforces their commitment to the team.

Specific goals: Effective teams also have specific goals which are measurable, stretching and yet realistic. Such goals energize the team by providing a focus for their efforts. Once achieved, such goals also give the team a great sense of achievement and job satisfaction.

Team efficacy: Effective teams have self-confidence. They succeed because they believe that they will succeed. The development of such a belief depends upon creating the conditions in which a team can achieve initial, albeit small scale, successes. Recognizing and celebrating such successes, builds the self-confidence necessary to achieve longer-lasting and more significant success.

An appropriate level of conflict: On the one hand, a high level of conflict within a team can be destructive and result in dysfunctionality, animosity and conflict. On the other hand, unless there is some conflict, the team can become apathetic, complacent or even arrogant, with the resultant risk of groupthink. Some level of conflict is necessary in order to promote discussion, a critical assessment of team performance and improved decisions.

groupthink
The phenomenon in which the desire for consensus leads a group to make bad or irrational decisions which members might otherwise individually consider to be unwise.

Accountability: In effective teams, members understand that they are individually and collectively accountable for its performance. They therefore have developed mechanisms for ensuring that all team members accept their full responsibility and that no-one can escape the consequence of their actions (or inactions).

Workforce diversity

As discussed previously, much of the success of Japanese manufacturing is based on effective teamworking. Many of the practices found in factories in Japan were developed in the years following the Second World War. At that time, Japan was, and to a large extent still is, a very homogeneous and cohesive society. This is typically not the case in many other countries today. Workforces are typically more diverse in terms of their gender, ethnicity, degree of disability, sexual orientation, religion, language, etc. This can make for significant challenges for the management of work teams. Many, if not most teams benefit from being composed of members with a diverse range of skills, knowledge and attitudes. There is much research evidence that suggests that heterogeneous teams are more successful than those that are more homogeneous, especially if the work calls for the use of creative or cognitive skills. Although increased diversity promotes conflict, this can stimulate creativity which leads to improved decision-making. Thus, having a heterogeneous workforce ought to make it easier to ensure that teams will possess the characteristics required to make them successful. However, increased diversity in a team is likely to make its functioning more difficult. Initially, at least, heterogeneous teams find it more difficulty to learn how to work with each other. However, it is possible to overcome this over time as team members learn how to work through their disagreements and adapt to their different ways of working. This can be helped if team members received diversity training to help them understand the viewpoints of others and if all team members are trained in the application of process techniques for group decision-making and problem-solving.

SUMMARY OF KEY POINTS

Work organization concerns the way that workers are brought together to undertake specific tasks. This is affected by organizational structure and culture.

The key dimensions of organizational structure are centralization, formalization and specialization. The most appropriate structure for any organization depends on its strategy, size, technology and environment.

The basic types of organizational structure are simple, functional, multi-divisional, matrix and network.

Organizational culture can be thought of as 'the way we do things around here'. It comprises three levels: artefacts, espoused values and basic assumptions.

Culture varies at the organizational and national levels.

Most operations are carried out by workers cooperating in a team.

Four factors influence the effectiveness of a work team, namely work design, team composition, context and processes.

Increasingly diverse workforces can be a source of strength for work teams, but training is needed to ensure that they function effectively.

EXERCISES (Suggested answers can be found on the companion website www.thomsonlearning.co.uk/barnes)

1 What factors should organizations take into account when designing their structures?

2 What type of organizational structure is most likely to be suited to the following types of business:
   a A domestic appliance manufacturer primarily serving a large home market.
   b A domestic appliance manufacturer with plants and markets in many countries.
   c A specialist management consultancy serving mostly local businesses.
   d An international management consultancy.

3 What role is more likely to be played by a central operations department in the following type of structure:

a Functional
b Multi-divisional
c Matrix
d Network

4 Using either Handy's or Deal and Kennedy's classifications of organizational culture, assess which types of cultures would be the best and worst environment for self-managed and cross functional teams to operate in.

5 What are the advantages and disadvantages of the following types of teams:

a A self-managed work team
b A cross-functional team
c A virtual team
d A Japanese-style team

6 What advantages do Japanese-style teams have over traditional supervisor-led teams?

7 Why can increasing the diversity of team membership increase its effectiveness? Are there any disadvantages to increasing team diversity?

8 Can virtual teams ever function as effectively as those that rely on face-to-face contact?

9 Use Hofstede's dimensions of national culture to identify the kinds of countries in which self-managed work teams are more likely to succeed and those in which they are more likely to fail.

10 View the websites of a number of different organizations (perhaps visit three or four) for information about:

a Can you find information about their organizational structures?
b What type of organizational culture is suggested by the information on display?
c Assess the extent which the structure and culture of each organization seems to fit.
d Assess the extent to which the organizational culture matches the national culture of each organization.

CASE STUDY EXERCISE Alpha Bank

Introduction

Alpha Bank Group is one of the leading banking and financial services groups in Greece and a major player in South East Europe. It offers a wide range of services, including retail and corporate banking, credit cards, asset management, investment banking, private banking, insurance, brokerage, leasing and factoring. Founded in 1879, the group has around 400 branches in Greece, where it employs over 8,000 people. The group also has an international presence with 176 branches throughout South East Europe (including Cyprus, Romania, Serbia, Bulgaria, Albania, the Former Yugoslav Republic of Macedonia, Jersey (the Channel Islands), London and New York, employing over 3,000 people.

There are many reasons that make the countries of South East Europe very attractive to Alpha Bank. With their growth indices remaining at high levels, structural reforms well under way and infrastructure projects being completed at a rapid pace, these countries have developed a dynamic that renders them highly attractive to foreign investors. Moreover, since the level of development is very low and the margins high in the financial sector, the prospects are very favourable as the demand for financial services is continuously rising. This seems set to continue given the EU accession of Bulgaria and Romania.

Alpha Bank's stated aim is to be the largest regional bank with 1,200 branches by 2010. Indeed, the group aims to carry on the growth of its network's activities, with special emphasis on retail banking, while simultaneously not undermining the continuous productivity improvements of its branches. The ultimate aim is to improve profitability by increasing revenues and effective cost management. To achieve this, it is planned to reduce the average number of staff employed per branch from 18 to at the most 16 through Information Technology applications and investments, re-structuring operations and process reengineering. Thus, beyond the establishment of new branches, the Bank's plans include the application of uniform IT systems in all its units in the wider region, the recruitment of specialized personnel, the equipping of the network's branches with ATMs and the provision of services such as debit and credit cards, web-banking, etc. As a result, the new branches to be established in both Greece and South Eastern Europe will deploy smaller workforces and at the same time be able to serve more customers and improve services.

Operational re-structuring and IT investments

The operational re-structuring plans are based on the Bank's central policy principles of upgrading the quality of the services provided and increasing productivity. The first priority of the plan is to bring similar activities into specialized central units. Specifically, the group's international trading activities and support for mortgage products are now managed centrally within the respective specialist units that have been created to house them. The centralized management of the above services, as in the consumer credit products (cards and consumer loans) relies on the development and operation of a Uniform Document and Application Form Digitalization and Processing Platform. The Bank has centralized the management of activities related to letters of guarantee (a service enabling customers to pursue international trade activities via the Internet) and has developed an IT application for centralized processing of post-dated cheques. The group is also currently developing an upgrade of the Corporate Credit Applications system to support the centralized management of this and related operations.

Alpha Bank have made ATMs widely available throughout SE Europe

Other important IT investments of the group include: the upgrade of the central IT, Accounting and Management Information Systems (MIS) infrastructures; the replacement of the Central Development IT System, and the installation of a fully comprehensive system for responding to catastrophic data loss; the installation of the Windows 2000 operating platform and a parallel upgrade of the hardware, the internal telephone service; and the creation of a centralized card and ATM database. In addition, the process of receiving, checking and executing standing orders has been automated and new systems introduced for Shared Register Management and Payroll applications. The Bank has also completed the adaptation of its operating systems to International Accounting Standards, which is a crucial facilitator for its international expansion.

Group's support for effective IT transfer

The Bank has launched the IT project 'Overseas Network Uniform Technology Base' as part of its strategy of expanding its overseas network. In particular, the central system of its subsidiaries and branches in Cyprus, Albania and Romania have been replaced, while the replacement of the central systems of branches in Serbia, Bulgaria, and FYROM (Former Yugoslavia Republic of Macedonia) are under development. In addition, a project for the centralized management of the SWIFT systems for the Bank's subsidiaries abroad was completed by the incorporation of Serbia, and the upgrade of the telecommunications networks in Cyprus and Albania. (SWIFT is an industry-owned co-operative that supplies secure, standardized messaging services and interface software to financial institutions all around the world.)

Support for developing the Overseas Network also included the planning and implementation of an operational model under a uniform framework of regulations, principles and operational procedures at the Group level. The implementation of this commenced in 2005 with the creation of a framework of principles and models for IT systems and services development, a framework for uniform planning procedures and the development of new or modified existing products and the identification of the actions required to open a new branch. In order to achieve better co-ordination of all the above, the group also created an Overseas' Network Operations and IT Support Unit in early 2006.

Because of the importance of South East Europe to the Bank's revenues, the group also formed an Overseas Retail Banking Division whose aim is to transfer Greek know-how, organization and products to the countries of the region. The objective is to maintain the high annual growth rates of 30–40 per cent in loans and deposits which the group attained in 2005 into the future. Although these rates exceed the market average, it is expected that they will decline as the markets in the region mature. The Bank's total market share in South Eastern Europe stood at 5.7 per cent in 2005. The target is to reach 8 per cent by the end of 2008.

Staff training and re-education are vitally important for ensuring that new IT applications are used and the associated operational re-structurings are effective. Consequently, training programmes over the last few years have focused on meeting the requirements for achieving the operational plan. These have included training for:

- Improving skills in sales.
- Improving customer service techniques.
- Improving managerial skills.
- Reinforcing and complementing employees' knowledge about the Bank's products and services.
- Multi-cultural skills and international business.

Training programmes take place outside of Bank premises, both in Greece and abroad, as well as through long-distance online courses. E-learning provides training opportunities equally available for everybody, irrespective of time and place limitations, thereby making better use of time, improving productivity and speeding the adaptation and absorption of new information.

Aims and impacts of the operational re-structuring and IT investments

All of these activities are part of a comprehensive three year rolling Operational Plan for the Bank that aims to support its strategy of developing a client-centric approach whilst reducing operating expenses. Analysis of the Bank's operations has demonstrated the positive impact of the IT-enabled centralization of its operations within the various specialized units. Gains have included improved efficiency in internal operations and the reduction of operational risks. Standard uniform procedures have been introduced and physical movements of documents and other time-consuming procedures have been eliminated. Customer service has also been shown to have improved, with customers in all branches reporting shorter waiting times and the receipt of enhanced quality, timely and accurate information.

However, the most important benefit is that branches are evolving from units that merely process customers' requests into product sales-centres that are supported by the specialized central units. This repositioning of the Bank's branches and the re-structuring of the group's network also has tremendous implications for the skills required by staff working within the branches. Marketing knowledge and competencies as well as customer service have now become the major criteria for staff recruitment as well as for their development. Consequently, the role of the Overseas' Retail Banking Division is enhanced as it is responsible for the transfer of information and know-how about the Bank's marketing schemes and new product development from the Greek market into the branches in other countries. Furthermore, a centralized Quality Assurance Unit has been formed which aims to upgrade the quality of the services provided by introducing uniform quality award schemes, customer satisfaction ratings, market research questionnaires, etc.

—*Marianna Sigala*

WWW.

Questions (Suggested answers can be found on the companion website www.thomsonlearning.co.uk/barnes)

1 Given the strategy, size, technology and environment of Alpha Bank do you think its move towards more centralization is appropriate?

2 What are the advantages of the greater centralization for the Bank? Are there any disadvantages?

3 What problems might you have expected Alpha Bank to encounter as it implemented its re-structuring plan?

4 What steps did the Bank take to ensure the successful implementation of its new operational structures and systems?

5 Can you identify any possible problems that the Bank does not seem to have addressed?

References

Belbin, R.M. (2003) *Management teams: Why they succeed or fail* (2nd edition), London: Butterworth Heinemann.

Buchanan, D. and Huczynski, A. (2004) *Organizational Behaviour – An Introductory Text* (5th Edition), London: Prentice Hall.

Burns, T. and Stalker, G.M. (1961) *The management of innovation,* London: Tavistock.

Chandler, A.D. (1962) *Strategy and structure,* Boston, MA: MIT Press.

Deal, T.E. and Kennedy, A.A. (1982) *Corporate cultures: The rites and rituals of corporate life,* Harmondsworth: Penguin Books.

Gesteland, R.R. (1999) *Cross-cultural business behavior: negotiating and managing across cultures,* Copenhagen: Copenhagen Business School Press.

Handy, C. (1985) *Understanding organizations* (3rd edition), London: Penguin.

Hofstede, G. (1980) *Culture's consequences: International differences in work-related values,* London: Sage.

Hofstede, G. (1997) *Cultures and organizations: Software of the mind,* New York: McGraw-Hill.

Mabey, C., Salaman, G. and Storey, J. (1998) *Human resource management: A strategic introduction* (2nd edition), Oxford: Blackwell Publishers.

Morita, M. (2001) 'Have the seeds of Japanese teamworking taken root?' *New Technology, Work and Employment* 16(3):178–190.

Pugh, D.S. (1998) *The Aston Programme* (Vols. I, II and III), Classic research in management series, Aldershot: Ashgate.

Robbins, S.P. (2003) *Organizational behavior* (10th Edition), Upper Saddle River, NJ: Prentice Hall.

Rowan, S. and Shenkar, O. (1985). 'Clustering countries on attitudinal dimensions: a review and synthesis', *Academy of Management Review* 10(3):435–454.

Schell, M.S. and Solomon, C.M. (1997) *Capitalizing on the global workforce,* Chicago: Irwin.

Schein, E. (1985) *Organizational culture and leadership,* New York: Jossey-Bass.

Slack, N. and Lewis, M. (2002) *Operations strategy,* Harlow: Pearson Education.

Trompenaars, F. and Hampden-Turner, C. (1997) *Riding the waves of culture,* London: Nicholas Brealey.

Additional reading

Belbin, R.M. (2003) *Team Roles at Work,* London: Butterworth-Heinemann.

Hofstede, G. (1997) *Cultures and organizations: Software of the mind,* New York: McGraw-Hill.

Robbins, S.P. (2003) *Organizational behavior* (10th edition), Upper Saddle River, NJ: Prentice Hall.

Trompenaars, F. and Hampden-Turner, C. (1997) *Riding the waves of culture,* London: Nicholas Brealey.

Useful websites

www.

http://www.geert-hofstede.com A website run by the consultancy ITIM International and dedicated to Geert Hofstede's work and ideas on cultural dimensions. Contains data on these dimensions for many countries.

http://www.belbin.com/ The website of Belbin Associates, a consultancy that promotes and develops Belbin's ideas on teamworking.

CHAPTER 12

HUMAN RESOURCE MANAGEMENT

INTRODUCTION

This chapter and the preceding one (Chapter 11 – Work Organization) both consider the management of people in operations. Whereas Chapter 11 was primarily concerned with the way that people are organized and managed collectively in order to perform work tasks, this chapter will move the focus to the level of the individual worker.

The people who work in an organization are its human resources; one of the transforming resources that form part of the input resources in the transformation process that constitutes any operation. An operation's human resources are invariably one of its most important resources and the way that those resources are managed can make a huge difference to the performance of the operation. This chapter will consider how organizations acquire their human resources (i.e. recruitment and selection) and how, once acquired, they seek to increase their capabilities to undertake their role within the transformation process (i.e. training and development). It will go on to consider how organizations can make best use of their human resources. Getting the most out of people at work can be affected by two issues. First, job design. Historically, designing the work tasks that people are required to perform has been approached in a number of different ways. This chapter will examine these. Second, reward and remuneration. The way that people are evaluated and rewarded, at work, especially with regard to their pay, has been shown to have a big impact on their performance. The chapter will therefore also go on to discuss the issue of reward and remuneration and its relationship with performance. Finally, the way that people are managed in any organization is inevitably influenced by contextual issues that affect the operations in which they are employed. These include a range of economic, cultural and legislative factors, which are typically specific to any given country. International

LEARNING OBJECTIVES

On completion of this chapter, you should be able to:

Describe how organizations recruit and select the people who work in their operations.

Outline different organizational strategies for training and development of workers in operations.

Explain the main approaches to job design.

Understand different approaches to reward and remuneration and the issues associated with attempts to relate pay to performance.

Appreciate national contextual factors that affect the management of human resources in operations.

organizations are affected by these contextual factors both in their country of origin and in other countries in which they employ people. This chapter will also examine some of these issues.

RECRUITMENT AND SELECTION

All organizations need to recruit new workers at some point, either to expand or replace those who have left to work elsewhere, to retire, etc. The traditional approach to recruitment has been to try to get the best possible match between the person and the job that they are hired to do. The approach often adopted to try to do this has been to draw up a detailed job description of the post to be filled and then to devise a person specification for the type of person most likely to be able to perform the job. The person specification would outline the characteristics required by the potential post holder, including any physical attributes (e.g. state of health or speech) attainments (e.g. highest level of education, relevant experience), aptitudes (e.g. verbal reasoning, numerical aptitude), interests (social or sporting activities) personal circumstances (e.g. ability to work shifts, full or part time hours) etc. The person specification could be used both to attract suitable applicants and as the basis for selection of the person to be offered the post after using selection techniques such as tests, exercises and interviews. (More details can be found in any standard Human Resource Management text.) However, in recent years this approach has been criticized for taking a static view of work. In most organizations, the exact nature of any job rarely lasts for long. The changing nature of technology, products and markets typically means that job descriptions change frequently and specific skills quickly become outdated. Therefore, it is argued, recruitment should be undertaken on the basis of a person's aptitude for change and their ability to acquire new knowledge and learn new skills. Recruiting only to fill a specific vacancy also displays a very narrow view of recruitment. The recruitment process offers a strategic opportunity to the organization to ensure that all new employees possess the attitudes and aptitudes that are considered most appropriate in the light of the organization's future strategic direction. Appropriate attitudes might be deemed to be customer-centeredness, flexibility, the ability to work in a team and valuing diversity. Appropriate aptitudes might be the ability to learn, communication skills and the capability of accepting responsibilities for decision-making. The idea is to ensure that employees will not only be able to make an immediate contribution to the organization by performing a specific task, but that they are equipped to cope with whatever challenges they may face in the future. With this approach, recruitment and selection is focused on identifying long-term members of the organization rather then employees hired for a specific job. As such, it is essential that all new employees are fully supportive of organizational values, for example as expressed in a statement of values, mission statement or similar document. Consequently, many employers now assess potential employees using criteria based on more generic skills and attitudes rather than job specific skills. Techniques used to do this include psychometric tests and assessment centres. Psychometric tests are written tests that provide information about a candidate's aptitudes (for example in verbal reasoning and numeracy) and their personality. Assessment centres are used to observe candidates for employment who are required to undertake various tests and activities such as group discussions, group activities and role-playing exercises. The idea is to simulate meaningful activities that can provide information about candidates' actual behaviour, rather than relying on what they might say in an interview.

In international organizations, a key issue in recruitment and selection is the extent to which vacancies in any given location should be filled with locally recruited staff (so called host country nationals (HCN)) and the extent to which it should those from the organization's home country (parent country nationals (PCN)).

job description
This outlines the duties and responsibilities required for a particular job or position.

person specification
A list of the knowledge, experience and skills necessary for a person to be able to perform a particular job.

psychometric tests
Written tests that assess a person's aptitude and personality in a measured and structured way. Such tests are often used by employers as part of their recruitment and selection processes.

assessment centres
Centres used to provide information on candidates for jobs. They typically consist of multiple evaluations including job-related simulations, interviews and psychological tests.

host country national (HCN)
A worker from the country of the subsidiary.

parent country national (PCN)
Also termed an expatriate, an employee sent from an organization to work in a subsidiary based in another country.

HCNs are typically recruited to provide the necessary labour for operations in a foreign subsidiary. Indeed, the whole purpose of establishing operations in a particular location may be to access the local labour market. This is often done because of a plentiful supply of low cost labour, but may also be done because of the availability of specific skills. Also, many foreign direct investments are made to take advantage of financial incentives from the host government made with the express purpose of creating employment for local people. This may place a moral or even legal requirement upon the organization to employ a certain number of HCNs.

PCNs are typically employed when an organization enters a new country. These are often recruited from amongst the organization's existing workforce, particularly for managerial posts. Their main purpose is to enable the parent organization to keep control over, and to establish the organization's operating systems and practices in a newly formed subsidiary. Many MNEs continue to use PCNs as senior managers in foreign subsidiaries over the long-term, primarily to maintain control over operations in that country. PCNs with particular technical or functional skills are also commonly recruited for start-ups, technology transfer projects or new product/service introductions, particularly when the organization is deploying proprietary knowledge or technology. One of their roles may be to develop the expertise of PCNs so that they can become more self-sufficient. PCNs might also be recruited to undertake R & D or new product development work in facilities established in a foreign subsidiary. However, host country government may place restrictions on the number of PCNs that can be employed and may also limit the length of their stay.

A key issue for MNEs is what their policy should be towards HCNs with regard to promotion to more senior positions. PCNs may have readily available specific expertise and also be entirely familiar with the organization's way of working and its culture. However, they may be unfamiliar with local customs and conditions, and can experience personal as well as professional problems in integrating into the local operation. PCNs will also typically cost much more to employ than local staff. Also a continuing preference for PCNs at more senior levels may cause resentment and demotivation in HCNs.

A third alternative as a source of labour to staff subsidiaries is that of recruiting **third country nationals (TCN)**. Some MNEs specifically target labour markets in third countries in order to overcome high labour costs or skill shortages in both the parent and host countries. However, with the increased movement of people around the world, TCNs might also be recruited from the host country or the parent country. The recruitment of TCNs is becoming more popular, not only to address labour shortages but also where a MNE wants to develop a more diverse and multicultural workforce. This later point can be particularly well addressed if TCNs are recruited from amongst the organization's existing workforce in another country. Existing workers also carry the advantage of already being acclimatized to the organization's culture.

TRAINING AND DEVELOPMENT

The purpose of training and development is to increase the capacity and capabilities of the organization's human resources in order to improve performance. When viewed in this way spending on training and development is seen as a necessary investment in the human capital rather than mere expenditure. In operations, workers need to possess suitable knowledge and skills in order to achieve the required performance objectives. Investing in training and development can improve the level of workers' efficiency, accuracy, speed, innovation and responsiveness thereby reducing costs and improving quality, speed, dependability and flexibility. It can be helpful to distinguish between the terms training and development. Training is usually associated with

third country national (TCN)
A worker from a country other than the parent or host country.

human resources
The people that work for an organization.

efforts aimed at equipping workers with the specific skills to undertake a particular task. This can involve on-the-job training, perhaps by more experienced colleagues or dedicated instructors, or by learning away from the workplace. Off-the-job training can be provided by instructors in a classroom or simulated workplace environment, or, if appropriate, through self-study using open learning materials or via computer-based training. Increasingly, computer-based training is being provided via the Internet, when it is often referred to as e-learning.

This usually involves self-study of learning material provided via a website, but often supported by online interaction with an instructor. Online learning can help overcome the constraints of time and distance that might prevent learners from attending class. Another advantage of e-learning is that it can enable learners to communicate with their fellow online classmates, thereby reducing the sense of isolation associated with distance learning. Some organizations (e.g. Hilton Hotels) have created their own virtual universities to co-ordinate their e-learning initiatives. These can be especially helpful for international organizations with widely dispersed workforces, enabling them to provide cost effective training worldwide and foster a sense of community between learners wherever they are situated.

Although aimed at improving the performance of workers, the term development is usually applied to efforts aimed at improving a broader range of individual competencies. These might include personal and interpersonal skills, for example in communication, teamworking and problem-solving. A wide variety of techniques can be used in development. These can include more formal classroom-based learning as well as more active work-based learning through the use of action learning involving individual or group projects, often supported by mentors or coaches. Many organizations also take a broader view of development by assigning individuals wholly or partially to task forces or study groups tackling specific problems in the workplace. Individuals might also be seconded full time to another work group for a specific period of time as a development activity. In some cases this might involve transfer to another of the organization's locations.

International organizations frequently use overseas postings in this way, to enable individuals to gain experience of working in other cultural contexts. If such an approach is used widely enough it can prove an effective means not only of developing a cadre of individuals who have gained cross-cultural sensitivities but also of exposing large numbers of employees to workers from other countries. However, this is not without its risks. Those assigned to other countries can have difficulties not only in adjusting to working in a strange culture but also in readjusting on their return to their own country. Also, those working with the assignees can also become resentful at what they perceive to be the specialist treatment afforded the visitors, whose work they may have to support whilst they are adjusting to life in their new environment.

This touches on an issue important for all MNEs. That is what level of skills is the organization looking to develop in a host country workforce? Does it merely wish its host country workers to achieve the minimal level of skills necessary for current requirements, or does it want to develop a workforce equipped not only to meet the future requirements on that site but also perhaps to enable workers at that location to be able to satisfy their ambitions by taking advantage of opportunities at other locations? If host country workers feel that they have only limited prospects, or worse feel that they are being exploited, then there are likely to be significant ramifications in terms of worker morale, absenteeism and retention. Many organizations prepare workers going on international assignments by providing cultural awareness training to help their entry into an unfamiliar culture. The issue of language is also an important one. Whilst it may not be necessary for assignees to be fluent in the language of a host country, if the organization uses a common business language (often English is the common language even if this is not the language of the parent country), it seems essential that they have some language training for their life outside of business hours.

e-learning
The term used to describe the use of web-based learning.

CASE STUDY Infosys offers a passage to India

Infosys Technologies is undertaking a global hiring spree for IT professionals as part of a drive by the Indian outsourcing company to make its workforce more international. Mohandas Pai, a director of India's second largest computer services company, said Infosys wanted to increase the number of non-Indian staff on its payroll by about 30 per cent a year from the 3,000 current employees with plans to recruit hundreds of Western and Japanese IT professionals. 'As we grow further, we have to make sure our workforce reflects the regions from where we derive revenue', Mr Pai said. There is nothing like having a local face to talk to when you are overhauling something as critical as your IT systems and business processes.

India's big IT outsourcing companies are increasingly hiring more domestic talent in developed countries as one way of improving customer relations. Companies such as Infosys are trying to evolve from the old outsourcing model in which they do basic technical work for their overseas clients, such as writing new software for them or overhauling their IT systems. Indian companies want to begin providing the sort of strategic consultancy services supplied by Western competitors, such as advising clients on trends and how to deal with them. As Chief Executive Nandan Nilekani, puts it: how to 'navigate the twists and turns' and 'win in the turns'. In the quarter ended 30 September 2006, this type of business accounted for about 21 per cent of Infosys' $746m in sales. 'In a sense, our whole endeavour is to go from just being perceived as an outsourcing company to somebody who can be a trusted transformation partner for our clients', Mr Nilekani says.

So far, Tata Consultancy Services, India's biggest computer services company, has led the industry in building a multi-national workforce. More than 8 per cent of its 78,000 staff are non-Indians compared with 3 per cent of Infosys' 66,000 employees. Mr Pai said in the year ending June 2007 the company planned to increase its 1,000-strong workforce in the US by 50-60 per cent, its 350-strong workforce in Australia by 10–15 per cent and in Japan its 150 staff by up to 33 per cent.

As part of this plan, Infosys was hiring 300 graduates directly from US universities through its 'Global Talent Programme'. He rejected suggestions that overseas hiring was aimed at supplementing talent

Infosys – Mysore, India

(BELINDA LAWLEY/ALAMY)

shortages in India or that an increase in foreign staff would damage margins. He said software engineers remained far more plentiful in India than overseas – the bottleneck was in providing company training for them, which was why Infosys was expanding its Mysore training centre in southern India.

In an industry as reliant on engineering talent as computer services, the training centre at Mysore is a vital part of this strategy. The facility currently has capacity for 4,500 trainees at a time but this will be increased to 13,500 in about 12 months. Investment in the 335-acre complex, which also includes offices and software development blocks, will total $300 million.

Running a training centre on this scale poses considerable management challenges. Infosys takes graduates from across the world – with varying strengths, abilities and cultural expectations – and must bring them to a similar level of understanding on complex subjects, while instilling them with a sense of the Infosys culture. The company says it can turn most smart graduates into software engineers regardless of their academic background because it hires people with so-called 'learnability' – Infosys jargon for strong logic skills.

Americans exhibit different learning patterns from their Indian and other Asian counterparts. They prefer to keep lectures short and break them up with exercises. By contrast, Indian students can sit through three hours of lectures while some Chinese ones can last nine hours. The company is not concerned with how the trainees learn, so long as it works. So far, no US trainee has dropped out.

Perhaps the most important difference between the US trainees and their local counterparts is that ultimately the foreigners are being groomed for a return to their home markets. The company is kind to them – allowing them, for instance, to take long weekends to see more of the country – with the aim of creating brand ambassadors who are familiar with both Indian culture and their own.

(Based on the articles 'Programmers' passage to India' and 'Infosys embarks on hiring spree' by Joe Leahy published 27th November 2006 at www.ft.com)

Questions (Suggested answers can be found on the companion website www.thomsonlearning.co.uk/barnes)

1 What approach does Infosys take to recruitment and selection?

2 What are the advantages to Infosys' strategy of recruiting non-Indian staff? Are there any potential disadvantages?

3 Critically assess Infosys' strategy of training its non-Indian staff in Mysore before their return to their home countries.

WWW.

WWW.

Another important issue for MNEs is that of where to carry out any training necessary for workers who are to be employed in host country facilities. One alternative is for workers to attend standard training courses at head office in the parent country. This can help to ensure greater control but can be costly. A variation on that approach is to deliver the same course to workers at the host country location. However, that raises the issues of who should deliver the course and to what extent the course might need to be tailored to address local cultural sensitivities. A further issue is whether each location should become responsible for the training and development of its own staff. The important issue in all training and development activities is that they should enable individuals to learn and grow whilst at the same time developing the skills and attitudes that will improve the performance of the organization in the longer-term.

JOB DESIGN

Job design is the process of specifying the work activities carried out by individuals and groups in an operation. It is concerned with the methods used by people performing work tasks and particularly the way that they interface with the technology they use.

job design
The process of specifying the methods used by people performing work tasks and particularly the way that they interface with the technology they use.

Job design needs to addresses the questions of:

- Who does the work?
- What is the exact nature of the task?
- Where is the work carried out?
- When is the work carried out?
- Why is the work carried out?
- How is the work carried out?

The design of the tasks that people are required to perform is fundamental to the success of the operation. Well designed jobs can enable workers to achieve much higher levels of performance than badly designed ones. Yet all too frequently in job design the technology that is to be used can become the prime focus. However, job design that does not also take account of capabilities and limitations of the jobholder is likely to result in the operation achieving a less than optimal level of performance. The performance of operations that involve people and technology is ultimately determined by the people rather than the technology.

scientific management
A management led approach to job design that seeks to establish the best way of performing any task through a process of disaggregation and routinization, using methods such as work study.

Historically, there have been two radically different approaches to job design, namely scientific management and behaviouralism. These reflect the changes in managerial philosophies over the last 100 years or so. This is often a controversial topic reflecting very different views about what is the best way to design work tasks. The approach taken by an organization towards job design is usually a good indication of its underlying attitude towards its workforce. Most people would agree that workers' jobs should be designed in a way that helps them to achieve the organization's objectives, which are usually to ensure that its operations provide the goods and services that customers want, in the required quantity and quality, at the required time, and at the lowest possible cost. Organizations may also want to design jobs so that its operations can respond flexibly to changing customer needs. However, jobs are performed by people who, as individuals, have their own objectives and needs, such as monetary reward, recognition, a safe and pleasant working environment, etc. These are issues of job satisfaction and the quality of working life. In an ideal world individuals would be able to satisfy their own needs in jobs that have been designed to enable operations to meet organizational objectives. If this does not happen, there is obviously potential for dysfunctionality, which can lead to problems. Both approaches to job design arguably reflect a desire to meet the needs of both the organization and its employees. However, scientific management can be criticized for taking the unitarist perspective that assumes that workers share the same objectives as their employers. This is not always the case. Consequently, scientific management can be seen to ignore the needs of workers. On the other hand, the behaviouralist approach can be criticized for placing too much emphasis on the needs of workers, rather than meeting the objectives of the organization. Both approaches are now examined in more detail.

behaviouralism
An approach to job design that aims to improve motivation hence performance by increasing job satisfaction by satisfying workers' individual and collective social needs.

Scientific management

The origins of this approach, as with origins of operations management as a discipline, lie deep in the Industrial Revolution. Prior to this time the craft tradition, in which individual highly skilled workers carried out all the tasks required to produce a particular good or service, was predominant. Craft workers were usually self-employed, making their living by selling their finished goods or providing their services directly to their customers. The Industrial Revolution changed this arrangement as machines were invented that could carry out many of the tasks previously undertaken by the skilled workers. Because of the high cost of investment, the machines could generally only be afforded by entrepreneurial capitalists, who set up the factories necessary to house them. Workers were employed by the factory owners to provide the necessary labour for the machines. These workers sold their labour rather than a finished product, and therefore had less control over the means of production. The tasks associated with operating these machines were often quite simple, which enabled the factory owners to adopt the principle of the division of labour to ensure maximum efficiency in their operations. This enabled individual workers to become specialized in specific tasks by breaking down jobs into separate activities, each carried out by a different individual. These workers were able to become more proficient at a particular task, often utilizing specially devised tools. This approach also had the benefit from the factory owners' perspective of reducing the power of any individual worker. The advent of professional managers merely interposed managerial control rather than direct control by the factory owner.

The development of scientific management was essentially an extension of this approach. In the early years of the twentieth century, Frederick Taylor, an American industrial engineer, pioneered this approach. He argued that work could be carried out more efficiently if the methods used for each job could be improved. This could only be done by studying the existing method in detail and devising new ways of performing the task.

In essence, scientific management approach involves three steps:

1   Studying the job scientifically. This requires the measurement of working times and output levels, and experimenting to devise improved methods.

2   Selecting and training workers in the new method. Selecting a worker suited to the task is fundamental to the method, as is providing adequate training.

3   Installing the new method. The management of this change requires special attention to encourage a co-operative approach. Time may be needed to adjust to the changed method, which may need to be further modified if required.

Scientific management has been subject to much criticism. The principal criticisms are:

● It produces monotonous jobs for people, condemning them to boredom and frustration at work. This not only fails to capitalize on the creative abilities of workers, but it may lead to negative effects like increases in absenteeism, staff turnover, poor quality of work or even deliberate sabotage.

● It is principally about exploiting workers by making them work harder for little (or even no) extra reward.

● It is more concerned with increasing the quantity than the quality of output.

● The resultant short-cycle repetitive jobs carry the risk of physical injury due to the overuse of a narrow range of body movements. This is known as Repetitive Strain Injury (RSI).

● Job specialization makes it difficult for workers to carry out other tasks. This reduces flexibility, making it difficult for the operation to respond to changes in customer demand.

● Job specialization leads to demarcation problems and reduces overall productivity. It can also lead to problems at one point in the production process causing a complete stoppage of all other areas which rely on the output of that area.

● It concentrates all knowledge, information, power and control in the hands of the management. This can lead to an authoritarian and dictatorial management style to which workers may well react in a negative or destructive way.

These criticisms led to scientific management falling out of fashion by the middle of the last century. Some of these criticisms are perhaps a little unfair to Taylor himself. His objective was not to exploit workers, but rather to increase output without placing increased demands upon individual workers. Also, Taylor advocated a joint approach between management and workers to improvement. He also argued that the resulting increased profits should be reflected in the pay of workers. However, many of the more enlightened ideas of Taylor were often ignored by those who subsequently sought to apply his principles of scientific management. Taylor did argue that improvement was primarily the responsibility of management. Thus, the underlying assumption of scientific management is that only management can achieve improvements. This can lead to creative skills of the workforce being ignored, meaning that a huge potential source of improvement could remain untapped.

The modern-day derivative of the scientific management approach is *work study*. This is the systematic examination of work activities in order to seek improvements. Work study comprises two branches:

- *Method study* is concerned with finding the best way of performing a task. Its approach is to analyze a job in minute detail, studying every movement made in order to divide the job into a series of tasks. Method study is usually described as a six step procedure:

  1 *Select* the job to be studied. In order to benefit from method study a job needs to be repetitive, labour intensive and important; otherwise it is not worthwhile making the heavy investment of time required.

  2 *Record* the activities that comprise the work. This involves observing and documenting all the individual human motions that make up the task. A record of the sequence of every motion made by a worker is often made using a graphical representation system such as process charting. This uses series of standard symbols for actions, delays, transport, storage, etc. Sometimes workers are filmed performing the task, so that their every motion can subsequently be studied in minute detail.

  3 *Examine* the way the job is currently performed. This involves studying every step in the method being used, by analyzing the process charts and other records, with a view to eliminating any unnecessary steps, and looking for opportunities to simplify, combine or rearrange any of the motions.

  4 *Develop* the best alternative method. This involves devising a revised process chart to establish the procedure for the new method. The new method needs to make most efficient use of human body, the equipment being used and the arrangement of the workplace. The procedure should specify the skill required by the operator, the equipment needed and the working conditions needed for the task.

  5 *Install* the new method. This requires installing the new equipment and training the operators who will perform work.

  6 *Maintain* the new method. Conduct regular checks to ensure that the new method is working as intended and achieving the desired performance improvement.

- *Work measurement* is concerned with determining how long a particular task should take. This information can be used for a number of purposes, including establishing a benchmark for output rates, allocating tasks amongst team members, product costing, and determining appropriate pay rates in payment by results schemes. The aim of work measurement is to determine the standard time for a task; that is, the time taken by qualified workers without over-exertion as an average over the working day provided that they are motivated to do the work. A qualified worker is one with the necessary physical attributes, intelligence, skills, education and knowledge to perform the task to satisfactory standards of safety, quality and quantity. There are a number of accepted techniques for establishing standard times, including:

1 *Time study:* This involves observing a qualified worker performing the job under specified conditions. The time taken to perform the task is recorded. Normally the observation and measurement is done a number of times to obtain an average. Each time the job is done, the worker's performance is rated. This is somewhat subjective, but it usually involves ratings of between 80 per cent and 120 per cent. The idea is to establish normal performance as 100 per cent. Suitable allowances are then added to include for any periods of rest and relaxation, or other factors that are necessary given the working conditions. From this a standard time can be established.

2 *Predetermined motion time systems (PMTS):* PMTS provide data on the times needed to perform all the basic human motions that might be involved in a work activity. Thus, in theory, the time taken to perform any new job can be calculated by summing the times taken to perform each constituent task. These can be determined using method study techniques. Suitable allowance must be made for any mitigating circumstances (e.g. a difficult working environment). This technique can be particularly helpful for establishing times for new jobs.

3 *Activity (or work) sampling:* This involves the use of statistical techniques to sample work activity at random intervals over a work period. At each sampling point, a record of what is happening is made. This will note what activity the worker was doing, where she or he was delayed, resting and so on. Thereby, the percentage of a workers' time spent on each activity can be established.

Ergonomics can also be thought of as a development from scientific management. Ergonomics is the study of the physiological aspects of job design; that is, how the human body fits to its work surroundings. Ergonomics focuses on the general working environment and more specifically on the immediate physical aspects of the workplace. General environmental concerns include temperature, humidity, illumination and noise levels. Physical aspects of the workplace include consideration of how to avoid or reduce fatigue, physical strain or injury in performing the work task at the interface of person and equipment. Both these aspects are brought together in the recent concerns about so-called sick buildings, that is offices dominated by computers, with air conditioning and artificial lighting rather than windows providing natural light and fresh air.

Behavioural approaches

The growing dissatisfaction with the results of scientific management that emerged in the middle of the last century led to the development of alternative approaches to job design. Scientific management is, in essence, based purely on an economic model of the relationship between job design and performance. It tends to downplay the impact of people's motivation on their performance in their jobs. At best it is assumed that motivation can only be affected by linking pay to performance. This is a very narrow view and one that was being increasingly challenged by the human relations school of management that was emerging at that time. The human relations movement led by Mayo, Herzberg, McGregor and Maslow amongst others, argued that work was a social activity and that people's relationships at work affected their performance. Whereas scientific management emerged at a time when workers were seen as little more than a factor of production, the human relations movement emerged at a time when there was a growing concern for workers' human rights. In the aftermath of the Second World War, there was an increased expectation that ideas of democracy and individual choice

FIGURE 12.1 Hackmann and Oldham's job design model

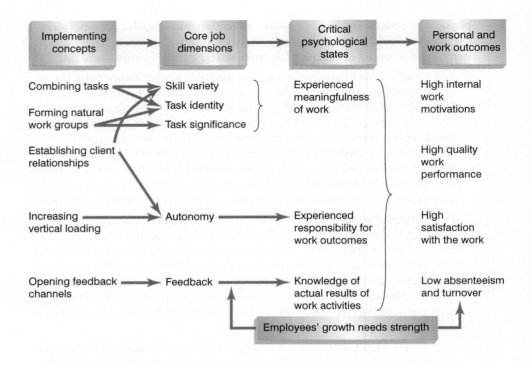

should apply at work as much as other aspects of life. Also, at a time of growing prosperity and labour shortages, organizations were finding it more difficult to attract and retain the workers they needed. Theories of motivation developed by researchers from the human relations movement were based on the notion that workers' motivation was not governed purely by financial considerations. Therefore job design needed to take into account people's innate desire to achieve job satisfaction and to satisfy their individual and collective needs through the social dimension of work.

The job design model devised by Hackmann and Oldham (1975) draws together the main strands of these principles (see Figure 12.1).

The model argues that a person's performance at work is determined by three critical psychological states:

1 *The experienced meaningfulness of work* – the work must be perceived as being important by the worker.

2 *The experienced responsibility for work outcomes* – the worker must be given and accept personal responsibility for the work outcomes.

3 *A knowledge of results* – the worker must receive regular feedback on whether or not the work outcomes are satisfactory.

If these three psychological states are achieved, the worker will experience high internal motivation, leading to high quality work performance and high satisfaction with their work, which will also, in turn, result in low absenteeism and staff turnover.

Hackmann and Oldham maintain that these three critical psychological states are affected by five core dimensions of job design:

1 *Skill variety* – the range of skills needed to perform the work task; increasing the number of skills that need to be used in a job reduces repetition and relieves boredom.

2 *Task identity* – the ability to understand clearly where the job 'fits' into the totality of the activities of the operation.

3 *Task significance* – the extent to which the work is perceived to be valuable and important by the worker.

An increase in any or all of the above three dimensions will lead to an increase in the degree of meaningfulness experienced by the worker.

4 *Autonomy* – the extent of control that can be exercised by the worker over the task. The greater the decision-making authority that workers have, then the greater the degree of responsibility that they will experience in the work.

5 *Feedback* – the more feedback that workers receive about their performance at work, the more knowledge they will have about the results of their work.

Hackmann and Oldham combine these factors in their concept of a motivating potential score (MPS) for any particular job. The higher the MPS, the greater the satisfaction that can be derived from the job. The idea is that jobs should be designed to maximize the MPS. They developed a means of measuring MPS through a questionnaire they entitled the Job Diagnostic Survey.

The Hackmann and Oldham model also incorporates an important moderating factor, based on the assumption that the extent to which a worker can be motivated varies between individuals. The degree to which a person can be motivated by a particular job depends upon their 'growth needs strength'; that is their desire for self-esteem or self-actualization. The higher their growth needs strength, the greater the likelihood they will achieve a high level of the desired personal and work outcomes from the job.

The advantage of the Hackmann and Oldham model is that it suggests a number of steps that can be taken to increase the motivating potential of any job. These are:

- *Combining tasks:* This will avoid the worst excesses of job specialization by designing jobs that require workers to draw on a wider range of skills, thereby increasing skill variety. This can also serve to make the work more meaningful to the worker, increasing task identity.

- *Forming natural work groups:* This will promote the collective ownership of the job by enabling workers to identify how their individual tasks create a meaningful whole. This will improve task identity and task significance.

- *Establishing client relationships:* Enabling workers to communicate directly and establish a relationship with the users of the products or services they produce increases skill variety, autonomy and feedback.

- *Increase vertical loading:* Vertical loading refers to those activities associated with planning and controlling work. These are traditionally seen as being the domain of management. However, the more workers are given responsibility for this aspect of their work, the more it will increase their autonomy.

- *Open feedback channels:* The more feedback that workers receive about their work, the better they are able to understand their performance and whether it is improving or deteriorating. Workers should ideally receive regular direct feedback as they do their job.

Behavioural approaches have led to a number of different job design techniques being developed which attempt to address some of the core job dimensions identified by Hackmann and Oldham. These include:

Job enlargement – This involves giving a worker a larger number of tasks to perform, particularly if the job can be enlarged to provide a more complete job (e.g. producing a complete assembly rather than just one component). As these tasks are likely to be of the same type, this approach is often termed horizontal loading.

Job rotation – This involves rotating workers so that they each perform a number of different jobs over the course of the day or the week. This can be a useful alternative to job enlargement, especially where it is not practical to combine tasks in a meaningful way.

Job enrichment – This aims to increase vertical loading by giving workers greater control and autonomy over their work. This might involve, for example, workers being trained to perform routine maintenance tasks on the machine they operate or perhaps scheduling their own work throughout the day.

Autonomous work groups (or self-managed work teams) – Such groups are given a high degree of self-determination in the management of their day-to-day work, usually including the collective control over the pace of work, assignment of tasks within the group, organization of breaks, etc. Fully autonomous groups will even select their own members and evaluate one another's performance. (This issue is discussed in further detail in Chapter 11.)

Empowerment – This is an extension of the concept of autonomy, whereby staff are given the power and authority to change the way they do their jobs. Empowerment is based on the acceptance that in some circumstances it is impossible and probably undesirable to design every aspect of a job in minute detail. This is particularly the case in many professional and service jobs with a high degree of customer contact. Many service organizations have realized that staff often need to use their discretion when dealing with customers. It is these 'moments of truth', when workers become the embodiment of the organization, that determine the level of customer satisfaction. Empowering workers can make the difference between alienating customers, potentially losing their business forever, or delighting them, thereby securing their future loyalty for many future purchases. Managers can exert little direct control in such situations. However, empowerment does rely on employees being fully committed to the organization's goals and objectives.

Combining scientific management and behaviouralism

At first sight it seems impossible that scientific management and behaviouralism could be used in combination in job design. Although both approaches are aimed at improving performance, they seek to do so using quite different methods. Scientific management is based on establishing managerial control over work through a process of disaggregation and routinization, in order to establish the best way of performing any job. Behavioural approaches, on the other hand, are aimed at improving the performance by achieving a high level of commitment from workers by increasing their involvement and motivation. Scientific management is inherently unattractive to most people in Western democracies as it seems to be based on an autocratic model of management. In terms of McGregor's famous model (McGregor, 1960), it seems firmly grounded in Theory X, which holds that people inherently do not like work and so they must be controlled in order to get them to work effectively. Consequently, the techniques of scientific management became increasingly unpopular and fell from widespread use in the latter years of the twentieth century, particularly in Western organizations. In contrast, behavioural approaches seem aligned with McGregor's Theory Y, which is based on the belief that people are creative, eager to work and strongly desirous of increased responsibility and anxious to participate in the decision-making process. Accordingly, the ideas of behaviouralism have been in the ascendancy in the West for many years.

It perhaps then came as a shock to many Western managers to discover that the ideas of scientific management were very much alive and kicking in many of the most successful Japanese businesses. A striking example of this could be found in the huge reductions in set-up times achieved by Toyota and other Japanese motor car manufacturers. Where it had previously taken many hours to set up the huge presses used to make body parts in motor car manufacture, this could now be done in a few minutes, not only improving productivity but greatly increasing the ability of those manufacturers to respond rapidly to changing customer demand. This was done by the

CASE STUDY Whole Foods Market: Success through people

Founded in 1980 as one small store in Austin, Texas, Whole Foods Market is the world's leading retailer of natural and organic foods, with 189 stores in North America and the United Kingdom. Whole Foods Market business model is based on being highly selective about what it sells, dedication to stringent quality standards and commitment to sustainable agriculture. Its philosophy derives on a belief in a 'virtuous circle entwining the food chain, human beings and Mother Earth: each is reliant upon the others through a beautiful and delicate symbiosis'.

In 2006, the company celebrated its ninth straight year on *Fortune* magazine's annual list of the 100 Best Companies to Work For. The No. 15 spot was its highest ever ranking, and made it one of only 20 companies to be named on the list in all nine years since its inception.

'One of our core values at Whole Foods Market is Team Member happiness and excellence, and we believe our innovative and egalitarian work environment is a major factor in our success as a company', said Walter Robb, Whole Foods Market Co-President and COO.

'Our 39,000 Team Members are passionate and dedicated. They are empowered to make Whole Foods Market not only a great place to shop but also a place to build a career. Our Team Members have a voice and they share in the rewards and success of the company. This has been part of our mission since Whole Foods Market started with a team of 19 people in 1980.'

Whole Foods Market is a highly profitable company, entering the *Fortune* 500 in 2005, ranking 479 among the largest US companies based on sales. The company attributes its success to the involvement of its employees, its 'Team Members', in all aspects of the business. The company says that Team Members have a voice in shaping the direction of the company and their future. Their well-being and happiness is an end in itself, not merely a means to the profits of the business.

John Mackey, the Chairman and one of the co-founders of Whole Foods Market explains that the company's success derives from its belief that 'The customer is our most important constituency, since with no customers, we have no business'. However, he goes on to explain that 'We have empowered our team members to satisfy and delight our customers'.

'New team members are trained to do whatever it takes to satisfy our customers. Happy customers create happy investors. In order to have happy customers we also need to have happy team members because the team members are primarily responsible for creating happy customers. When team members are frustrated, dissatisfied, and unhappy in their work they are unlikely to give the high levels of customer service that the business needs to flourish'.

'Our internal business model within each store is the self-managing team. The teams do their own hiring, work scheduling, and product procurement. They are running their own small business within the store, and they have full responsibility for the business. Each team is empowered on many levels, not only in customer satisfaction'.

'It is absolutely essential to trust team members, and one way to show that trust is through open information. Whole Foods provides open financial information on all levels, since we want to be as transparent an organization as possible without making ourselves overly vulnerable to our competitors. It is essential that the team members have a sense of shared purpose and power. If team members can align around the values and purpose of the business, they are going to have a greater commitment to the business. They will likely unleash greater energy and creativity through that sense of alignment and shared purpose. At Whole Foods, we consciously reject the command and control management style. This top-down, 'Do It My Way' approach is the opposite of team member empowerment. We also teach the importance of 'shared fate', that is the better the company does, the better the customers do, the better the team members do and the better the investors do'.

(Source http://www.wholefoodsmarket.com)

WWW.

WWW.

Questions (Suggested answers can be found on the companion website www.thomsonlearning.co.uk/barnes)

1 How well does Whole Foods Market's approach to human resource management align with the principles of behaviouralism?

2 Use Hackmann and Oldham's job design model to explain some of the success of Whole Foods Market.

3 What job design techniques are in evidence at Whole Foods Market?

rigorous application of work study principles, a key element of scientific management. However, Japanese practice also demonstrated a widespread use of behavioural approaches. Workers are typically organized into teams, which have considerable autonomy and workers are trained to be multi-skilled and expected to be fully flexible, performing whatever tasks are required for the success of the team. Japanese companies also typically seek to draw on the skills and knowledge of the workforce as a means of achieving performance improvements, through suggestion schemes, quality circles and other continuous improvement (*kaizen*) techniques. A key characteristic of the Japanese approach to continuous improvement is the high degree of autonomy given to worker teams to implement their ideas without reference to higher authorities.

Ouchi (1981) coined the term **Theory Z** to describe how the ideas of both scientific management and behaviouralism seem to coalesce in many Japanese practices. Theory Z is based on workers being very participative and capable of performing many varied tasks. Consequently, Theory Z emphasizes job rotation, broadening of skills and continuous training of workers. However, in order to receive the benefits

Theory Z
The termed coined by Ouchi (1981) to describe the management style characteristic of many Japanese companies that combines various aspects of scientific management and behaviouralism. The term Theory Z is an attempt to associate this style with McGregor's Theory X and Theory Y construct.

of this participation and flexibility, managers must be supportive and trusting of their employees. Therefore, Theory Z organizations focus on increasing employee loyalty by providing a job for life and strongly focusing on the well-being of employees, both on and off the job. Although workers must take individual responsibility for their actions, decision-making tends be collective. One way of looking at Theory Z, is that it uses the ideas of behaviouralism to create the conditions under which the ideas of scientific management can be applied in an open and participative fashion with the full support of the workforce.

REWARD AND REMUNERATION

The issue of how people at work are rewarded, usually through financial payment, is often not discussed in operations management textbooks. Yet, for people that work in operations this is invariably an important issue. The amounts that people are paid and how those amounts are determined can have a major impact on their behaviour and hence on the performance of the operations in which they work. Well-constructed pay schemes should be a source of job satisfaction and provide motivation for workers. Yet, badly-constructed pay schemes can provoke widespread dissatisfaction and be very de-motivational. This section will discuss two major issues with regard to reward; the level of remuneration and its linkage to performance.

Levels of pay

The amount that an organization pays its workers for doing a particular job can have a number of purposes. First, the level of pay needs to attract enough suitably qualified people who are prepared to do the job. Thus, pay rates must be competitive within the labour market from which the organization draws its workers. Second, pay must be sufficient to retain existing workers. Whilst people do not just work for money, if pay rates are inadequate they may be tempted to look elsewhere. Third, pay rates must be perceived as equitable by workers. Whilst pay rates must be externally competitive, differences in the rates of pay for different workers must also be seen to be fair within an organization. One aspect of this is to ensure that pay rates adequately recompense workers for difficult or uncomfortable working conditions and for the time that they spend at work, including any unsocial hours (e.g. weekend or shift work). However, a more difficult dilemma is the extent to which the rate of pay is attached to a particular job or to a person. The approach taken in many organizations is to evaluate each job (in terms of the level of skills required, the responsibilities it carries, its complexity, etc.) and assign it to one of a number of pay grades, arranged hierarchically. Each grade has a pay range or band, enabling individuals to be paid more up to the maximum within the band for their job. Progression within a band might be based on length of service or on some kind of individual performance appraisal. Some organizations operate skills (competence or knowledge) based pay schemes within their pay grading structure. Workers who gain extra skills or knowledge are rewarded either by moving up within their existing grade or by moving up to the next grade. Such schemes can be used to ensure pay equity within an organization at a single location, and, where market conditions allow, across different sites. However, organizations that operate internationally may be confronted with vastly different levels of pay in different countries. Indeed, it may be that the organization has deliberately chosen to operate in a particular country because of its low labour costs. This makes it very difficult, if not impossible to address the issue of pay comparability. Whilst some aspects can be justified on the basis of differences in costs of living and the general quality of life, it can cause particular problems when considering pay rates for those posts which could be staffed by either

expatriate
A person temporarily or permanently working in a country other than their home country.

local host country nationals or by the expatriate's parent country or third country nationals. Expatriates may well not be attracted to the post if host country rates of pay are applied. On the other hand, local workers may be de-motivated if expatriates are paid at much higher parent country rates, especially if locals are performing the same work whilst being paid much lower rates. Devising suitable payment schemes for expatriate workers can be highly complex. The most common approach is to enable the worker to maintain parent country living standards whilst providing some kind of financial inducement to accept a foreign assignment. So a package is typically devised that offers a premium to the basic parent country salary for overseas working and makes country specific adjustments for differences in the cost of living, taxation, housing costs, hardship, etc.

Performance related pay

Organizations often seek to link pay to performance. The objective is to motivate workers by offering them the prospect of higher pay for improved performance. The origins of such schemes go back hundreds of years and lie in the concept of piecework, whereby workers were paid for each piece of their output. Variants of this approach still exist today in output linked incentive bonus schemes in which the workers' pay increases the more they produce. Such schemes are often underpinned by the ideas of scientific management and linked to application of its techniques such as work measurement. Whilst output-based payment schemes can increase productivity, this is often achieved at the expense of quality as workers rush to increase their output. They can also increase the stress felt by workers, which can cause ill-health and absenteeism. Also, relationships can be damaged between different groups of workers if schemes are seen to reward people inequitably and between workers and their managers if schemes are not operated openly with objective measures and clear criteria. Consequently, organizations thinking about introducing a performance related pay scheme need to consider carefully what performance measures should be used to trigger extra payments. Aspects of performance other than output volumes might be more appropriate in jobs where other goals are more desirable. Whatever measures are used, the other major consideration in any performance related pay scheme is whether payments should be individually or collectively-based. Individual incentives can be closely related to individual performance and, therefore, highly motivational to the person concerned. However, in many operations, workers need to co-operate with others, typically working in teams. Rewarding the individual rather than the team is likely to be divisive and could lead to a deterioration rather than an improvement in performance. Also, in national cultures that are more collectivist than individualistic, rewarding individual rather then collective performance is unlikely to be perceived as appropriate. If reward is to be collectively-based, the next issue to confront is what group of workers should be used as the basis for any performance related pay. To be effective as a motivational device, the performance measures used as the basis for any reward must be one that is capable of being affected by the behaviour of the group. On the other hand, a very locally based measure may encourage behaviour detrimental to the performance of other groups of workers. Even performance related pay schemes at the level of a single facility could encourage workers to focus purely on the performance of that site, which may prove to be sub-optimal for the organization as a whole. This could be particularly damaging if that facility forms part of a larger supply chain within the organization. Some organizations seek to overcome this problem through the use of bonus schemes based on profit sharing or other organizational level measures. Such schemes have the merit of giving workers a direct stake in the financial performance of their employer. However, they suffer from the problem that workers often can not see a direct link between their performance and any reward they may get.

As a final point in this section it is worth noting that pay is not the only reward sought or achieved by people at work. Behavioural scientists have recognized this for many years. For example Maslow (1943) argued that work can meet a person's need for belonging, self-esteem and even self-fulfilment. Similarly, McCelland (1961) notes how work can satisfy a person's need for achievement. So, for many people having interesting and challenging jobs is as motivational and rewarding as any incentive bonus scheme.

MANAGING EMPLOYEE PERFORMANCE

Most organizations go to great lengths to try to ensure that their operations have the human resources they require. As already discussed in this chapter, this involves trying to recruit and select the right people for the jobs that need to be done; training and developing them so that they have the right knowledge and skills required; designing jobs in such a way that workers can achieve high levels of performance and are motivated to want to do so; devising remuneration schemes that provide adequate levels of financial reward for the work that employees do and will encourage them to do keep doing so in the future; and pay sufficient attention to the non-financial factors that can affect workers attitudes and behaviour at work. Failing in one or more of these matters can lead to poor performance at work. Outward signs of this can invariably be detected in human resource related performance measures such as falling productivity and increasing rates of absenteeism and staff turnover.

High rates of absenteeism are often a sign of poor motivation within a workforce. This can be damaging and disruptive when it affects a small number of workers, but can be completely debilitating for an operation when a large number are involved. A high level of staff turnover is similarly costly. Not only in terms of the resulting disruption to operations, but also in terms of having to repeatedly incur the expenditure associated with the recruitment, selection, induction and training of new employees. People can leave their jobs for many reasons. Sometimes, it is the 'pull' of a new job because of the attraction of better pay, a greater challenge, increased recognition and rewards, etc. However, it is far more likely to be dissatisfaction with their present job that acts to 'push' them away. People typically prefer the stability of their existing position and will often eschew higher pay elsewhere if they are satisfied with their current employer. High turnover in newly hired staff is invariably due to their dissatisfaction with their new employment. This can be due to poor recruitment and selection decisions or because of poorly designed induction programmes.

Most organizations use a performance appraisal system of some kind to assess the individual performance of workers. These usually centre on a performance appraisal interview with an employee's line manager or other more senior manager. At the interview, the employee's work in the preceding period is discussed and reviewed, typically in the light of performance objectives set at the previous appraisal. The reasons for any shortfalls can be discussed and future performance targets agreed. Any training and development needs can be identified, either to address shortcomings or for developmental purposes, and decisions made about how to meet them. A formal record of the decisions reached at the appraisal is normally kept. Some organizations also link decisions about pay to the appraisal process. However, as discussed on p. 352, performance related pay schemes can be something of a two-edged sword in respect to motivating employees in the ways intended. At one level a well-designed and managed performance appraisal system should enable operations managers to improve the motivation of individual employees. However, it can also be invaluable at a second level, namely that of detecting problems that affect larger numbers of workers. This should enable them to address such issues before they seriously affect the performance of the entire operation.

CASE STUDY Spreading the load at Unilever's Purfleet factory

A culture of long working hours and low productivity has long been a feature of British manufacturing industry. Unilever's margarine factory in Purfleet, Essex was just another example of this. (Its main product is Stork brand margarine.) Workers could increase their pay by working extra hours, which were all paid at premium rates of pay. Thus, it was in their financial interest to seek longer hours. However, this reduced productivity and led to increased labour costs, making the plant uncompetitive compared to Unilever's highly efficient Dutch and German factories as well as external competitors, threatening Purfleet's viability. The long working hours also led to high rates of absenteeism, leading to overmanning, further reductions in productivity and higher costs.

Unilever decided to tackle this problem by negotiating the introduction of a flexible working-hours contract with the plant's trades unions. The main elements of the package were:

- Seven-day continuous shift working.
- A system of annualized hours.
- The abolition of overtime pay.

Employees were contracted to work a basic 1779 hours a year. 1700 of those hours were assigned to rostered shifts, leaving 75–80 reserved for training, meetings and other activities. Another 282 paid hours were stored to cover contingencies such as short-term sickness, poor efficiency or plant failure.

The introduction of the scheme led to benefits for both the company and the employees. Operational efficiency increased dramatically – from around 40 to 50 per cent in the first year, climbing to a peak of around 70 per cent. Productivity per head is now higher than in any other Unilever 'spreads' factory. Absenteeism halved to about 2 per cent – below the industry average. While wages increased by about 30–35 per cent, total labour costs did not rise because of huge reductions in overtime pay. Benefits to the employees include higher levels of basic pay, all of which is pensionable, and huge increases in leisure time. Four 12-hour shifts are followed in winter by a five-day break and in summer by a three-day break. There are three rostered holidays, two holidays of 12 days and one holiday of 18 days.

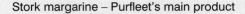

Stork margarine – Purfleet's main product

The main practical problem that arose in introducing the scheme arose from the employees' initial lack of trust in the annualized hours system and how it would affect their leisure time. Many were difficult to contact, which meant the system relied on a committed few who were called in disproportionately. Unilever solved the problem by splitting each shift into three standby groups. Standby times were rostered into shift patterns so people knew when they were likely to be called in.

The factory's HR Manager, Nick Clements, also noted a further benefit from the scheme – a dramatic shift to a more problem-solving, team-working approach. 'People wanted to try to get things operating well, rather than focusing on the next overtime opportunity', he said.

(Source material 'Managing change: practical ways to reduce long hours and reform working practices' Department of Trade and Industry (2005) downloaded from http://www.dti.gov.uk/files/file14239.pdf 20 December 2006)

Questions (Suggested answers can be found on the companion website www.thomsonlearning.co.uk/barnes)

1 How has the new scheme changed workers' motivations with regard to pay?

2 How has the new scheme affected workers' attitudes to work?

3 Why has absenteeism reduced?

4 Use Hackmann and Oldham's job design model to explain the improvements at Unilever Purfleet.

WWW.

WWW.

NATIONAL CONTEXTUAL INFLUENCES ON HRM

The management of people in operations does not take place in a vacuum, rather it is influenced and often constrained by a range of contextual factors. Amongst these are economic, cultural and legislative factors that are specific to the country in which the organization is operating. National contextual factors are important not only in terms of how they affect the actions of the employing organization, but also because they set the expectations and behaviour of employees (and potential employees) in their relationship with the organization. There are, of course, differences in the contextual factors that affect different types of organization in any one country. These can vary depending on industry, organization size, public or private sector, etc. However, differences within a country tend to be much smaller than the differences between different countries. Even where groups of countries are engaged in a formal process of harmonizing aspects of their economic policies and employment legislative, such as within the European Union, there remain significant differences between countries. Differences include:

- *Cultural:* The ways that national culture affects people's attitude and behaviour at work was discussed in some detail in Chapter 11. Operations managers need to take account of this when managing people in different countries. For example, a country's position on Hofstede's individualism-collectivism dimension would be expected to influence the success of self-managed work teams and appropriateness of group-based performance related pay schemes.

- *Employment costs:* The performance of a country's national economy will have a significant influence on rates of pay and the general availability of labour. This can be influenced, certainly over the longer-term, by the policies of the national government. Basic rates of pay are usually set by employers within the context of the national or more local labour markets. However, in some countries, governments play a leading role in determining general rates of pay, for example through minimum wage legislation. Also, government legislation can and does have a significant impact on non-wage costs for employers.

Non-wage costs include employment taxes and social payments for benefits such as pensions and health insurance costs which are statutory requirements in many countries. Also, in many countries, it is normal practice, often supported by legislation, for employers to pay employees for holidays, periods of sickness, maternity and paternity leave; all of which increases the cost of employing workers. Non-wage costs can be very high, approaching 100 per cent of wage costs in some countries. But they do vary dramatically between countries.

- *Workforce skills:* The general levels of education and training of a country's workforce can vary enormously, even between countries that are equally well-developed economically. The UK for example, compares unfavourably with Germany in terms of its ability to provide vocational qualifications for its school-leavers who do not go on to university. This is because of differences in education and training systems, much of which are determined by national government policies. There can also be significant differences in attitudes and policies of employers in different countries, which are also often influenced by national legislation. For example, in some countries, employers are legally required to spend set proportions of their income on training.

- *Conditions of employment legislation:* Labour legislation can affect many aspects of employment and can vary significantly between countries. Examples of this include minimum wage rates, maximum permitted hours of work, requirements for premium rates of pay for overtime working, lengthy consultation periods and compensation pay for termination of employment. In addition to directly affecting labour costs, such legislation can also affect an organization's ability to respond flexibly to changes in demand, for example by varying hours of work, or the numbers of people it employs.

- *Organized labour:* The extent to which organized labour groups, such as trade unions, influence human resource management also varies between countries. Generally, the more developed the country, the more influential organized labour groups are. In many countries, workers have a legal right to join a trade union of their choosing. Although in some countries, trades unions are organizationally specific, rather than truly independent of the employer. In some countries, especially many in the European Union, organizations over a certain size are required by law to have a works council. These comprise elected representatives of the workforce and have a right to be informed and consulted about significant decisions made by the organization, especially those concerning employment.

All these factors influence the way that an organization can conduct its operations in any particular country, since organizations invariably need to employ people within their operations. International organizations are affected by the contextual factors both of their country of origin and of any other countries in which they employ people. This presents a dilemma for all such organizations. That is to what extent should an international organization manage its workforce in line with local conditions and to what extent should it impose corporate standards globally? If the organization follows local human resource management practice too closely it may prove difficult to integrate those operations with others located in other countries. It may also find it difficult to achieve desired levels of efficiency and quality. Local human resource management practices may also raise ethical issues when viewed from the perspective of other countries. On the other hand, if the organization imposes its own corporate practices irrespective of local conditions it risks alienating not only its own local employees but also the wider community in that location. The issue of wage rates is particularly acute. Paying rates in line with those of its parent country would almost certainly result in the loss of the very cost competitiveness sought in a host country. However, failing to pay the host country rates risks accusations of exploitation of host country workers and causing job losses in the parent country.

SUMMARY OF KEY POINTS

The traditional approach to recruitment has been to try to match the person and the job vacancy. A more far sighted approach is to recruit on the basis of a person's attitude, their aptitude for change and their ability to acquire new knowledge and learn new skills.

International organizations face a dilemma of whether to recruit locally from host country nationals or whether to opt for expatriates from parent country or third country nationals.

The purpose of training and development is to improve organizational performance by investing in human capital in order to increase the capacity and capabilities of human resources.

Job design is the process of specifying the methods used by people performing work tasks and particularly the way that they interface with the technology they use.

There are two basic approaches to job design: scientific management and behaviouralism.

Scientific management is a management led approach to job design that seeks to establish the best way of performing any task through a process of disaggregation and routinization, using methods such as work study.

Behavioural approaches to job design aim to improve motivation hence performance by increasing job satisfaction by satisfying workers' individual and collective social needs.

The approaches to job design used in some Japanese manufacturing companies has combined aspects of scientific management and behaviouralism.

Rates of pay must be sufficient to attract and retain sufficient numbers of suitably qualified workers.

Pay differences within an organization must be seen to be justifiable. This poses a particular problem for international organizations paying different rates in different countries for the same work.

Performance related pay schemes aim to motivate workers but can be costly to administer and cause dysfunctional behaviour.

The management of people in operations is influenced and often constrained by economic, cultural and legislative factors specific to a particular country.

EXERCISES (Suggested answers can be found on the companion website www.thomsonlearning.co.uk/barnes)

WWW.

1 What types of recruitment and selection techniques are likely to be most suitable for the following jobs:
   a Assembly line workers for a car manufacturer
   b A production worker for a military aircraft manufacturer
   c A financial services adviser
   d A software designer
   e A management consultant

2 For what types of jobs and under what circumstances would an international organization be more likely to prefer PCNs over HCNs?

3 Should a large multi-national corporation train all its staff at a dedicated training centre at its head office or should each subsidiary train its own employees in their own country?

4 Compare and contrast the benefits and limitations of the scientific management and behavioural approaches to job design in the following different types of processes (see Chapter 7):

    a   Mass production *vs* Jobbing production.

    b   Mass services *vs* Professional services.

5 Find a job that you are able to observe being performed in an organization that you have access to (e.g. as a worker or a customer). Use Hackmann and Oldham's model to assess how likely it is that the current job design will deliver high levels of personal and work outcomes. Suggest ways in which the design of the job could be improved.

6 What factors might limit the applicability of Ouchi's Theory Z in Western countries like the USA and UK.

7 Discuss the claim that 'Organizations should always pay their workers as little as possible'.

8 Discuss the claim that 'People will always work harder for more money'.

9 Do you agree with the assertion that off-shoring work from high to low labour cost countries is exploitation?

10 Discuss the claim that the Japanese human resource management practices that are integral to lean production are little better than discredited Taylorism.

CASE STUDY EXERCISE   Marriott International: Managing diversity

'The diversity of our workforce, owners and suppliers is a key component of our success at Marriott International. Our commitment to diversity is what makes ours one of the most desirable companies to work for and to do business with. It helps us keep our competitive edge as we continue to set the standard for the entire hospitality industry.'

J.W. Marriott, Jr., the Chairman and Chief Executive Officer

Background

Marriott International is a leading worldwide lodging company with over 2,700 properties and approximately 143,000 employees in the United States and 66 other countries. One of the major factors leading to the success and reputation of Marriott has been the core values that the company espouses and has used as the basis of its culture since its foundation in 1927 (see Figure 12.2). The 'Marriott Way' is built on fundamental ideals of service to associates, customers and community. These ideals serve as the cornerstone for all Marriott associates (the term used by Marriott for its employees) fulfilling the 'Spirit to Serve'. Marriott's 'Spirit to Serve' concept includes the following issues:

- Marriott's conviction that their people are the most important asset.
- An environment that supports associate growth and personal development.
- A reputation for employing caring, dependable associates who are ethical and trustworthy.

FIGURE 12.2 Marriott's mission statement and service spirit

Mission Statement Marriott International

Marriott Hotels and Resorts is committed to being the best lodging company in the world by empowering our associates to create extraordinary customer service and shareholder value.

Spirit to serve

Marriott associates are the best in the business. Every day, they serve our guests with skill, enthusiasm and pride, and their hard work makes our success possible. We are dedicated to taking care of our associates by championing diversity and leadership, fostering personal and professional growth, and creating a great workplace.

Marriott Ways – Guarantee of fair treatment

Marriott Corporation policy provides that every employee, regardless of position, be treated with respect and in a fair and just manner at all times. In keeping with its long recognized policy, all persons will be considered for employment, promotion or training on the basis of qualifications without regard to race, colour, creed, sex or national origin.

J.W. Marriott, Jr.
President, Marriott Corporation

- A home-like atmosphere and friendly workplace relationships.
- A performance reward system that recognizes the important contributions of both hourly and management associates.
- Pride in the Marriott name, accomplishments and record of success.

Human resource management

Marriott recognizes that its employees are the prime means by which it can provide high quality service; a source of differentiation in what is a very competitive industry. As such, it is extremely concerned to retain its employees and keep them loyal and dedicated to the company's core mission and values. As such its approach to human resource management is to spend as much effort and money on retaining good associates as on recruiting new ones. Its aim is to create a working environment that changes the corporate mindset from one of 'we take care of our employees' to one of 'we provide opportunities for our employees to take care of themselves'. The human resource practices initiated to achieve this goal include:

New employee orientation: Marriott has replaced the usual practice of requiring newly recruited associates to complete an initial three month probationary period. Instead, new associates now first attend an eight hour training session. They are then assigned a mentor (a 'buddy') to guide them through their first 90 days – thereby drastically reducing initial employee turnover. They then attend a refresher course after the second month. The completion of 90 days is celebrated with an associate recognition banquet.

The 'Partners in career-management' programme: Management level associates attend a workshop called 'partners in career management' to train as 'career coaches'. This enables them to hold more effective dialogues with other associates and help them to examine and manage their careers.

Training and Development: Marriott takes learning and development seriously and offers a wide range of 'off the job' training to all employees, whether managers, team leaders, supervisors or operational staff. The core Marriott International training programmes include Impact Leadership, Business Acumen and Effective Training Skills.

The J. Willard Marriott Award of Excellence: This is seen as a way of motivating associates and encouraging the best possible performance from everyone. Recipients have included a wide cross-section of the Marriott workforce, including dishwashers, chefs and housekeepers.

The Department of Work and Family: This was created to address the issue of how Marriott can help its associates to better balance the demands of home and work.

Staff skills: Marriott's approach to recruitment, training, evaluating and rewarding associates is not to focus so much on skills but rather on attitudes and behaviours. For example, 'Spirit to Serve' training focuses on service excellence, looking at things through the customer's eyes and communication skills.

Positive employee culture

Marriott is widely recognized for its positive employee culture. This is based on the theory that if you 'take care of your employees – they'll take care of your customers, who will return again and again'. As Marriott's guests and many of its local communities (particularly in certain US states) are culturally diverse, the company has realized that by achieving effective diversity management it can transform the differences between its associates into an organizational competence. By trying to match the multicultural profile of guests with the multi-cultural profile of the workforce, Marriott aims to better understand and serve the needs and preferences of all its guests. Moreover, employees with different backgrounds and cultural profiles can also bring new ideas and viewpoints that Marriott can incorporate into best practices for the benefit of its hotels worldwide. Marriott has taken a number of initiatives to encourage the workforce diversity. For example, its use of flexible working arrangements has enabled it to employ students, mothers and retired people, which have helped to create a more flexible capacity to better meet high variations of demand.

Overall, Marriott has recognized that good diversity management is the only way to:

● Attract, develop, and retain the very best talent available.

● Forge the relationships necessary to maintain growth. A positive company culture creates a lasting relationship with employees, so that employees can completely identify with the company they work for. Creating an emotional tie further enhances an employees' willingness to provide the best service.

- Meet the company's responsibilities to associates, customers, partners and stakeholders, thereby enhancing its reputation and social image.

Awards and recognition

For eight consecutive years, Marriott has featured in *Fortune* magazine's '100 Best Companies to Work For' list. It continues to receive numerous awards from the industry in recognition of its commitment to diversity workforce management (see Figure 12.3). More than 16 years ago, Marriott became the first lodging company to establish a diversity programme and continues to set the standard for the industry. Marriott's global diversity commitment encompasses every business unit worldwide and is designed to meet the growth and profit opportunities inherent in ever-changing populations and markets. For example, Marriott hotels in the UK have gained the 'Investors in People' award. Anne Davey, HRM Director at London Heathrow Marriott, argues that 'Investors in People provides the cornerstone for the success of our business'. She believes this helped to recruit the 200 associates in the six months required to open the hotel on time and within budget. The Investors in People award supported its recruitment drive by providing evidence of the company's commitment to the training and development of its staff. Marriott appears to provide an exceptional work environment in London. A recent survey of its associates showed that 88 per cent were happy with how they were employed and trained by the hotel – the top score amongst London hotels and the third highest in the UK. At the same time, customer satisfaction at the hotel was 80 per cent and this translated to revenue £2 million over budget in its first year of operation.

Managing a diverse workforce

Marriott utilizes a mixture of practices in managing its diverse workforce. Its aims are to create:

a Equal employment and career advancement opportunities to everyone.

b A stimulating environment, in which different people are able to work together and to give the best of themselves.

Recognizing that people have different family commitments and personal needs, Marriott aims to create equal opportunities for its associates not only in the workplace, but also in family and social life. Several metrics highlight Marriott's longstanding commitment to diversity: 60 per cent of Marriott associates are minorities and 54 per cent are women. Of new managers hired in 2005, 26 per cent were minorities and 48 per cent were women. Of its college recruits, 30 per cent were minorities and 16 per cent were African American – Marriott's highest number ever. Marriott also supports its employees through an innovative work-life programme – the Marriott Associate Resource Line, which provides confidential advice and referral services for a wide range of personal issues. The toll-free number is staffed by professional social workers, supports more than 100 languages and is available to all Marriott associates.

Marriott has a commitment to increase the diversity of its global workforce by diversifying its suppliers, customers, owners and franchisees. To further support the diversity of its workforce, Marriott also provides multi-cultural training to all its staff through programmes such as its 'Leadership Education Series'. Such programmes teach staff how to lead and build their careers in today's increasingly diverse and complex marketplace. However, Marriott recognizes that some groups of its staff, associates and franchisees may lack specific job-related qualifications and/or more general competencies. Consequently, Marriott has initiated a number of programmes aimed at helping these groups to overcome these deficiencies. The Diversity Ownership Programme is one of these initiatives. It aims to support and encourage minority representation amongst Marriott's franchisees. Assistance mainly consists of providing aspiring minority hotel owners and franchisees with workshops to provide the education, operational and financial support required to run a hotel the 'Marriott Way'. These events not only give aspiring hotel owners an opportunity to learn about the lodging industry, but they also provide a forum for them to meet current owners and franchisees. They help address the needs of prospective minority owners and franchisees,

FIGURE 12.3 Marriott's recent awards for diversity practices

2006 Awards

November – *The Black Collegian,* a career and self-development magazine targeted at African-American students, names Marriott in its 'Top 100 Diversity Employers 2006'. One of only three hospitality companies, Marriott ranked highest on the list.

October – Joe Ryan, outgoing executive vice president and general counsel for Marriott International receives the Matthew J. Whitehead, II Diversity Award from the Association of Corporate Counsel (ACC). The association promotes the common interests of its members, contributes to their continuing education, seeks to improve understanding of the role of in-house attorneys, and encourages advancements in standards of corporate legal practice.

September – *Hispanic Business* magazine ranked Marriott number 11 on the list of the 'Top 50 Companies for Hispanics'.

August – *Latina Style* magazine names Marriott International in its '50 Best Companies for Latinas to Work for in the US' for the eighth year in a row.

July – NABHOOD (National Association of Black Hotel Owners, Operators and Developers) presents Marriott with the organization's first annual 'Champion Award' for diversity leadership, as well as the 'Supplier Diversity Award' for efforts to expand business opportunities to minority suppliers.

July – The NAACP ranks Marriott International the highest of any global lodging company for the seventh time in its annual lodging industry report card.

June – *Black Enterprise* magazine names Marriott International one of the '40 Best Companies for Diversity'. Marriott was recognized in two important categories: 10 Best in Workforce Diversity and 10 Best in Board Diversity.

April – *Diversity Inc.* magazine names Marriott International one of the 'Top 50 Companies for Diversity', for the third consecutive year. At number 22, Marriott is the highest ranking lodging company and the only lodging company to win in two important categories: the Top 10 Companies for Recruitment and Retention and the Top 10 Companies for Executive Women.

April – *The Black Collegian,* a career and self development magazine targeted at African-American students, ranks Marriott in the top 20 in its 'Top Employers for the Class of 2006'.

March – Marriott International receives the 2006 Ronald E. Harrison Award, by the International Franchise Association, for its significant contributions to minorities in franchising.

March – The National Association for Female Executives (NAFE) ranks Marriott on the 'NAFE 2005 30 Best Companies for Executive Women'. Marriott is the only lodging company – and the only Washington, DC area company – on the list.

2005 Awards

December – The Maryland/Washington, D.C. Minority Supplier Development Council recognizes Marriott International as Corporation of the Year for Marriott's supplier diversity efforts and success in growing spending with diverse suppliers in 2005.

August – *Hispanic Business* magazine names Marriott as one of the 'Top 40 Companies for Hispanics'.

August – *Latina Style* magazine names Marriott International on its '50 Best Companies for Latinas to Work for in the US', for the seventh year in a row.

June – *Black Enterprise* magazine names Marriott International as one of the '30 best companies for diversity'.

April – *Diversity Inc.* magazine ranks Marriott International number 12 on its list of 'Top 50 Companies for Diversity'. Marriott is also placed on the top ten lists for Asian Americans, Executive Women and Recruitment and Retention.

January – *Hispanic Trends* selects Marriott as one of the top 50 Corporations for Supplier Diversity. This is a list of large corporations that offer minority firms the best opportunities to become their suppliers.

who often have substantial business experience but limited lodging experience. The Lodging Leader's Outreach programme includes providing minorities and women with additional operations support, as well as flexible application and royalty fee terms, credit enhancement, or other funds used to support the deal or prepare the hotel for opening. Some of Marriott's most recent minority recruitment successes include the establishment of a 'Courtyard by Marriott' hotel with significant minority ownership in Harlem, New York, and the opening of a $43 million 'Residence Inn by Marriott' in Washington DC, co-owned by four Native-American tribes.

Marriott has also initiated several activities for supporting the specific needs of its working mothers, which have been commended by the association, Working Mother. Its 100 Best Companies list is based on the availability and usage of programmes to support working mothers, the accountability of managers to implement programmes and the successful advancement of women into top paying jobs, board positions and management ranks. Marriott has been recognized by Working Mother for the particular support they provide in three areas: flexible scheduling, time off for new parents and childcare options. Maruiel Perkins-Chavis, Vice-President of workforce effectiveness and diversity for Marriott International said that 'Our company is committed to providing all associates with options that help them pursue their career goals while managing their personal lives'. The company's programmes are specifically designed for its broad range of staff, and include financial support through family care spending accounts and flexible work policies. Additional programmes include childcare discounts; education and training; on- or near-site child development centres at ten locations; and referral services for child, elder and family care issues.

—*Marianna Sigala*

Questions (Suggested answers can be found on the companion website www.thomsonlearning.co.uk/barnes)

1 What factors are driving Marriott to seek a more diverse multi-cultural workforce?

2 What benefits does Marriott derive from increasing the diversity in its workforce? Are there any disadvantages?

3 Assess the approaches used by Marriott to increase the diversity of its workforce.

4 What are the most important management practices used by Marriott to manage its diverse workforce? What more could it do?

WWW.

References

Hackmann, J.R. and Oldham, G. (1975) 'A new strategy for job enrichment', *California Management Review* 17(4):57–71.

Maslow, A.H. (1943) 'A Theory of Human Motivation', *Psychological Review* 50:370–396.

McCelland, D. (1961) *The achieving society,* Princeton, NJ: Van Nostrand.

McGregor, D. (1960) *The human side of enterprise,* New York: McGraw-Hill.

Ouchi, W.G. (1981) *Theory Z: How American management can meet the Japanese challenge,* Reading, Ma.: Addison-Wesley.

Additional reading

Beardwell, I., Holden, L. and Claydon, T. (2003) *Human Resource Management: A Contemporary Approach* (4th Edition), Harlow: FT Prentice Hall.

Briscoe, D.S. and Schuler, R.S. (2004) *International Human Resource Management* (2nd Edition), New York: Routledge.

Hall, L., Torrington, D. and Taylor, S. (2004) *Human Resource Management* (6th Edition), Harlow: FT Prentice Hall.

WWW.

Useful websites

http://www.accel-team.com Accel-Team, a UK-based training and development company. Contains some useful articles on team-building, motivation and productivity.

http://www.acas.org.uk ACAS, the UK government backed service that provides information, advice, training and dispute resolution services. The website offers a wide range of (UK specific) information and publications.

http://www.managementhelp.org Free Management Library a US-based website aimed at (US) practitioners offering free access to a range of management resources, especially those related to human resource management issues.

http://www.hr-guide.com HR-Guide, a US-based website containing hundreds of pages of information relating to (US) human resource management issues.

http://www.ilo.org The International Labour Organization is a UN agency that promotes social justice and internationally recognized human and labour rights. A wealth of information about human resource management issues.

http://www.cipd.co.uk The Chartered Institute of Personnel and Development (CIPD) is the UK's professional body for those involved in the management and development of people. Lots of useful information and guides to best HRM practice.

CHAPTER 13

NEW PRODUCT DEVELOPMENT

INTRODUCTION

This chapter will explore how new product development activities are conducted within organizations, particularly those that operate internationally. It is vital for most, if not all organizations, to be able to develop new products and services. There can be very few organizations that can hope to survive, let alone prosper, by continuing to offer the same goods and services to their customers for a long period of time. For any organization, there are normally competitors who will seek to replicate and improve upon its existing products and services; and to do so at lower cost, enabling them to reduce the price to customers. Thus, any competitive advantage gained through product differentiation is likely to be short lived. As such, all organizations need to foster the creativity and innovation needed to ensure that they can develop new goods and services that can be offered to customers. Thus, the new product development (NPD) process is of vital importance to an organization's long-term prospects. The NPD process needs to consider not only what new products should be developed, but also how those products should be made. Products can only be produced successfully if due consideration is given to the processes used to make them. In service operations, the product is often all but indistinguishable from the process. For organizations operating internationally, NPD carries the additional challenges of how to develop products to meet the differing requirements of customers in different countries and how to co-ordinate new product development activity across different locations. This chapter will also consider how NPD can take advantage of the latest advances in technology, both within new products and the processes that produce them. It will also describe a number of the new techniques and tools for NPD that have emerged in recent years.

new product development (NPD)
All those activities directed towards the introduction of new or improved products or services into the market place.

LEARNING OBJECTIVES

On completion of this chapter, you should be able to:

Understand the importance of new product development.

Describe the ways in which new product development activities are conducted.

Appreciate the role of new technology in new product development.

Explain how new techniques can be used to improve the new product development process.

Appreciate the challenges of new product development in international organizations.

THE IMPORTANCE OF NPD

The design and development of its products and services is of vital importance to any organization. The objective of design is to meet the known or anticipated needs and expectations of customers. Designs which fail to satisfy customers will inevitably fail in the marketplace no matter how much they excite their designers. Good design can make an organization's products and services stand out from the crowd, helping to differentiate the organization and possibly enabling it to command higher prices. Good design can also save money. Some studies show that as much as 70 per cent of final costs of a product can be determined by its initial design. Thus, design has a direct impact on the bottom line.

Agreeing what constitutes a good design is likely to prove difficult, but any criteria are likely to include:

- *Aesthetically pleasing.* Beauty is said to be in the eye of the beholder, but well designed products are invariably eye-catching, if not pleasing to the eye of the customer.

- *Satisfying customer needs.* Customers make purchases to satisfy a particular need. As a minimum, the design of the product must hold out the promise that it will meet that need.

- *Meeting customer expectations.* As the quality gaps model (see Chapter 10) points out, any shortfall of performance against expectations is likely to lead to dissatisfaction. Customers' expectations can be set by their previous experiences of the organization's and its competitors products, information from other sources (e.g. word-of-mouth, press reports), as well as by the organization's promotional activities (e.g. advertising).

- *Performing well.* Customers want the product to perform as well as intended. Better still, if the product functions so well as to delight the customer.

- *Reliability.* Customers want the product to perform well every time they use it, not just once or even occasionally.

- *Easy to manufacture and deliver.* This is an issue that is more important to those responsible for the organization's operations than directly for customers. However, a product designed with due consideration for its production will inevitably be better able to achieve conformance to specification more often; a factor which is important to customers. This issue is discussed in more detail later in this chapter.

Design determines what the organization can make available for customers for some time, often many years into the future. Also, the means of producing the product or delivering the service to customers needs to be put in place. That typically requires making large-scale investment in facilities, equipment and people. Once made, these decisions are not easily or cheaply undone. In a rapidly changing world it is usually extremely difficult to predict the future with any certainty, but a future perspective is essential as design decisions usually take some time to implement. Major design decisions are taken only infrequently, reducing the opportunities to learn from previous experience. The decisions associated with new product design are inherently risky. Mistakes can have extremely serious, even catastrophic consequences.

Furthermore, time is often of the essence in new product development. There is invariably pressure to get new products and services to customers as quickly as possible. The benefits of being able to introduce new products quickly include:

- *Increased market share.* Marketers have long argued that the key to long-term profitability is market share. It is always very difficult to take market share from an entrenched competitor. Organizations that have the ability to bring new products to market quickly have a major advantage over slower competitors.

When the market for the product is new with little or no competition, an early market entrant can more easily establish market share. This is especially true for innovative products for which there are no alternatives.

- *Price premiums.* When an organization is the first to bring a new product to market, it has little or no competition. It is therefore likely to be able to charge premium prices, at least until such time as competitors are able to enter the market. The combination of market share and price premiums enables the early entrant to make significant profits, which it can then use to fund further NPD work. As a general rule, the faster a product is introduced into the market ahead of the competition, the more profitable that product will be over its lifecycle.

- *Faster response to competitors.* If an organization has the ability to bring new products to market quickly, it will be better able to respond quickly if it is taken by surprise by a competitor's introduction of a new product. This will minimize the competitive disadvantage that it may suffer by being a latecomer to the market.

- *Setting industry standards.* For revolutionary products, the first to market is often able to set the standards for that industry. This can then act as a significant barrier to entry to competitors, especially if their product is based on an alternative technology. Any attempt to change technologies will be costly, time-consuming and may be doomed to failure.

Developing new products involves a trade-off between the risk of making a costly design mistake and the cost of any delay. The organization will want to launch a new product as soon as possible in order to gain the competitive advantage of being first to market. But it will also want to ensure that it has done all it can to ensure that the design of the product is as good as possible.

In some industries the time to market, that is the time taken from deciding to develop a new product to its market launch, is vital to commercial success. As the case of Sony's PlayStation illustrates, this is particularly true in commercial mass markets with rapidly changing technology.

time to market
The length of time taken to bring a new product to market. It is usually taken as the time from deciding to develop a new product to its market launch.

Although there are many benefits in being the first to market with a new technology, it is not without its problems. As discussed in Chapter 7, a strategy of technology leadership carries with it a number of risks, including:

- The technology may not function as well as expected.
- The anticipated benefits may not be realized as quickly as promised.
- The technology may be unreliable.
- Implementation problems may lead to costly delays and disruptions.
- The market for the new product may not grow as fast as expected.

Consequently, some organizations deliberately opt for a strategy of being a technology follower (i.e. a technology laggard). Waiting for a new technology to become more proven can lower many of the costs associated with the development and introduction of new products, including the capital cost for new equipment.

TYPES OF NEW PRODUCTS

It is possible to categorize three different types of new products on the basis of the degree of innovation associated with them.

1 *Incremental products:* These products involve the least amount of innovation. They are typically derivatives of existing products, which may be enhanced with added features and functionality, or perhaps cut-down in some way to be

WHEN THINGS GO WRONG Sony's PlayStation 3: Virtual reality?

In May 2006, it all looked so promising for computer gaming enthusiasts at the E3 Games Expo in Los Angeles. Sony used the industry's biggest and most important trade show, to unveil their long awaited PlayStation3 (PS3) and announced its launch date and selling price. Sony's PlayStation 2 had hitherto dominated games console sales, having sold more than 100 million units, establishing the Japanese company as the industry's leading brand with a market share of around 70 per cent. However, those looking to move up to PS3 found themselves very disappointed.

In line with ugly industry rumours, the launch date was given as November 2006, rather than as expected in May of that year. The price of PS3 was also felt to be expensive. It would be available in two versions, priced at $499 and $599 in America, €499 ($640) and €599 in Europe, and starting at ¥59,800 ($540) in Japan – although this was later discounted by around 20 per cent to just under ¥50,000 ($428). These would be much higher than the prices of its two rivals, Microsoft's Xbox 360, which had already been on sale for a year, and Nintendo's Wii, which would also be available later in 2006. Like PS3, Wii was also previewed at E3 and had received rave reviews. Nintendo's offering had wowed the crowds with its unorthodox motion-sensing wand-like controller. This enables games-players to wield the controller like a sword or swing it like a tennis racket. 'It's fun!' declared Ankarino Lara of the games website Gamespot. 'The Wii offers games that are accessible for family and friends at low cost'.

PS3, on the other hand received a fairly luke-warm reception. 'It is hard to be over-excited about what Sony has shown', said Margaret Robertson, editor of the games magazine *Edge*. Although PS3 uses a next generation technology called Blu-ray, gamers at the show were less than impressed with what was on display. There was nothing wrong with the games Sony demonstrated, but they looked very much like games on the Xbox 360. The PS3's tilt-sensitive controller was seen as ill-conceived compared with the controller for the Wii. Also, Sony's online service for the PS3, which will link gamers and allow them to download extra content, seemed very similar to Microsoft's Xbox Live service.

Two satisfied customers?

It was clear that Sony would have its work cut out if it was to remain the king of home console gaming. Microsoft's successful early launch of its Xbox 360 had given it a head start over both its rivals. It aimed to consolidate this by launching a raft of new games. Xbox 360 sales had already exceeded 5 million, and Microsoft predicted that that would reach 10 million by November. Many gamers might not be prepared to wait for PS3. On the other hand, those that did wait might be tempted by Nintendo's Wii, which seemed to offer a new way of playing video games.

By September, things had got worse for Sony. The launch of the PS3 had been planned for the lucrative pre-Christmas shopping period. However, Sony was forced to announce that its availability would be seriously hampered in the US and Japan, with the numbers of units halved from 4 million to 2 million. Also, there would be no launch in Europe until March 2007.

Ken Kutaragi, President of Sony Computer Entertainment, blamed the delay on a failure by the Blu-ray Disc Association to agree technical specifications for Blu-ray discs. Blu-ray is locked in a DVD standards war with a rival high-definition disc format, HD-DVD, backed by Toshiba. As the leader of the Blu-ray camp, Sony hopes the PS3 will ensure victory by putting Blu-ray players into millions of homes, thereby encouraging gamers to buy films on Blu-ray discs too.

Industry rumours, however, also suggested that Sony had had technical problems in mass producing the diode for the PS3 Blu-ray disc laser – something of an embarrassment for a company famed for its manufacturing expertise. However, Sony is not the only company that needs blue laser diodes; they are also used in players using the competing HD-DVD standards. The only company other than Sony that can manufacture blue lasers in any numbers is Nichia, also of Japan. Nichia, whose maverick scientist Shuji Nakamura invented the blue laser, said they were struggling with the mass production of the diodes. Some industry analysts think Sony is using the problems with Blu-ray to justify a longer delay to the PS3. The delays would give it time to increase manufacturing, and enable software developers to finish their designs of new games, to ensure that PS3 has a reasonable selection by November. However, Sony is in a precarious position. It has, in effect, bet the company on the success of the PS3 and Blu-ray. Any further delay would mean the company was in very serious trouble.

(Source material www.bbc.co.uk and www.ft.com)

Questions (Suggested answers can be found on the companion website www.thomsonlearning.co.uk/barnes)

1 Why does Sony need to launch PS3 quickly?

2 What problems has Sony had with the development of its PS3?

3 What are the likely causes of these problems?

WWW.

WWW.

offered as low priced versions in more cost sensitive markets. A typical example of an incremental product is the annual model up-grade made by virtually all motor car manufacturers to their vehicles. The advantage of incremental products is that they usually require minimal changes in both the design of the product or service and the processes needed to produce them. Consequently, the resources required for their development are much less than for products involving more radical innovations. As such, incremental products are important to an organization's cashflow as they can enhance or at least protect existing sales income with only minimal additional expenditure. Incremental products also have the advantage that they can be brought to market quickly, enabling the organization to respond to changes in demand or the actions of competitors.

2 *Next generation products:* This category of new product is one in which the whole basis of the product has changed. This is usually driven by changes in technology. An example of this is the change from analogue to digital TV, or the introduction of a completely new model by a motor car manufacturer.

Such a change often provides the basis for a development of a whole family of related products. As such, these types of new products are sometimes called *platform products*. These types of product typically require new production processes and so they require significantly more resources than incremental products. The development of next generation products is essential to an organization's longer-term prosperity, otherwise it risks being left with old fashioned products based on out-of-date technology. Next generation products also provide the basis for the on-going development of incremental products.

3 *Breakthrough products:* These are products that are so significantly different to any existing products that they are able to create a completely new market. They can even provide the basis of whole new industries. Examples of these would be the first personal computer, the first mobile (cellular) phone or the first digital downloading services for recorded music. Breakthrough products usually represent an entirely new product category, often based on revolutionary new technology. They usually require substantial development in both the product design and the processes required to produce them. Hence, they require the commitment of a high level of resources, often over a long period of time. Breakthrough products offer the potential for the greatest reward, but also represent a high risk, as the more radical a product the more likely it is to fail. Breakthrough products can therefore enable the firm to succeed in its current markets, as well as in new markets, that will be created in the more distant future.

SOURCES OF NEW PRODUCT IDEAS

When organizations are looking for ideas about new products and services there are broadly two sources of ideas that they can tap into; the requirements of the market-place and advances in technology. Developing new products from these sources is characterized by two very different mechanisms:

1 *Market-pull:* This approach is based on the premise that organizations should only supply products for which a demand can be identified. The idea is to look to the market to seek out unfilled needs for which new products can be developed (see Figure 13.1). Thus, the NPD process is driven by a pull from the market. Ideas for new products and services come directly from customers or from those close to customers, such as the sales or customer staff. Alternatively, more formal market research can be conducted, perhaps surveying existing and potential customers or seeking to identify emerging needs due to changing demographics, lifestyles, fashion, etc. Many organizations also

FIGURE 13.1 Market sources of new product ideas

monitor the activities of their direct competitors or organizations operating in similar industries in other parts of the world to seek out ideas for new products. This approach relies on the assumption that successful new developments will come by identifying existing or future customer needs which are not being met. On the face of it this seems a very sensible way to proceed. However, it does presuppose that customers know what they want, can articulate their needs and that organizations have the means of recognizing what customers want. This approach also has the drawback that it may not lead to the development of breakthrough products, which would enable an organization to gain an advantage over its competitors. As competitors are likely to have access to the same market research information, it seems unlikely that it can provide a source of significant competitive advantage

2 *Technology-push:* This approach looks to technological advances as the basis for new products. Thus, the NPD process is driven by the push of technology. The idea is to develop new products from activities within the organization, particularly from R & D activities. This approach is prevalent in high-tech organizations. It stems from the view that customers cannot express a desire for things that they do not yet know about. Advocates of this view are likely to argue for high levels of spending on R & D within the organization and often support the idea of governments supporting R & D activities through spending at a national level. This approach offers the prospect of gaining a competitive advantage over competitors by being the first organization to offer new products based on new technology. As discussed above, there are believed to be great rewards for those who can establish market share by being the first to market. However, this approach does involve the high risk associated with new technology failing to perform and customers failing to buy as anticipated. Also, designers who develop new products and services on the basis of their technological excellence can sometimes forget the requirements of customers who may not share their enthusiasm. Customers generally buy products in order to solve specific problems rather than to be wowed by their technological brilliance.

There is conceivably an ideal middle way for NPD, in that products could be designed and developed using technological advances to deliver products that customers will want to buy. This has often proved difficult to achieve in practice. Organizational approaches for achieving such an approach usually rely on promoting co-operation between different departments (R & D, technical, operations, marketing, etc.). This is discussed further later on in this chapter.

THE NPD PROCESS

The NPD process is generally depicted as following a number of discernible stages (see Figure 13.2).

Idea generation

As discussed on p. 370, ideas may come from the market, from technology or from a judicious combination of the two.

Idea selection

It is likely to be impossible to spend time and money in developing all new ideas into products to take to market. Indeed, many of the ideas may well prove not to be such good ideas on closer inspection. Therefore, organizations need to have ways in which

CASE STUDY: Sir Clive rides again

Many people reading this will be too young to remember the Sinclair C5. The C5 was a classic case study that has been used by business studies teachers for many years as an example of how new product development can go drastically wrong. The C5 was a battery powered one-seater tricycle launched in 1985. The rider sat in the vehicle to pedal and was surrounded by a sleek fibreglass shell.

Its British inventor, Sir Clive Sinclair, hoped that the C5 would revolutionize urban transport. Sadly, the C5 failed to take off; it was ridiculed by the press and there were concerns expressed about its safety. One enduring sight was a promotional news item featuring Sir Clive cycling round Piccadilly Circus in London surrounded by large red buses. This image did not give potential users a great deal of confidence in the product.

In the end the C5 was a disaster; it was withdrawn from sale and as is the case with many of these failed products, it has become a collector's item and has achieved something akin to cult status. For Sir Clive it meant financial difficulties and many years spent trying to shake off the stigma that the failure of the C5 brought.

Now, he is back with a new invention – the A-bike. Sir Clive has teamed up with a Chinese firm called Daka (www.daka.com.hk) to develop the bike – it has taken almost 20 years to get to this stage. The bike is called the A-bike because it has the shape of an A when opened out. It is light, weighing in at only 12 lbs, and is likely to be sold for around £200 (US$375). When folded, it is half the size of current folding bikes on the market and is considerably lighter. Sir Clive anticipates marketing the product around the world and points to the fact that 'many thousands' have already been ordered.

The Sinclair C5

At the moment there are some limitations as to who can use the bike. There is a weight limit of 13 stones (180 lbs, 82 kg) and people over six feet four might find the riding experience a little uncomfortable, given the position of the handlebars in relation to leg space. The design of the bike does allow people up to 17 stones (240 lbs, 107 kg) to ride it, but Sir Clive is suggesting that until they have more experience with sales and the use of the bike, the 13 stone limit should apply. It may be that the experience of the C5 has helped Sir Clive and Daka in developing and marketing this product.

Safety seems to be at the heart of the message being put across about the product. Daka has been at pains to point out at the design awards that the bike has been well received so far, as well as citing the fact that the bike has been granted British Standards Approval from the British Standards Institute (BSI). By receiving such an award, the company hopes to convince consumers that the safety and quality of the product is guaranteed. This highlights the importance to companies of getting things like the BSI's kite mark as a badge of quality to help boost the potential success of a product.

Adapted from http://www.bized.ac.uk/cgi-bin/chron/chron.pl?id=2643 13 July 2006, downloaded 20 September 2006

WWW.

Questions (Suggested answers can be found on the companion website www.thomsonlearning.co.uk/barnes)

WWW.

1 What was the underlying cause of the failure of the C5?

2 What steps seem to have been taken in the development of the A-bike to avoid the mistakes of the C5?

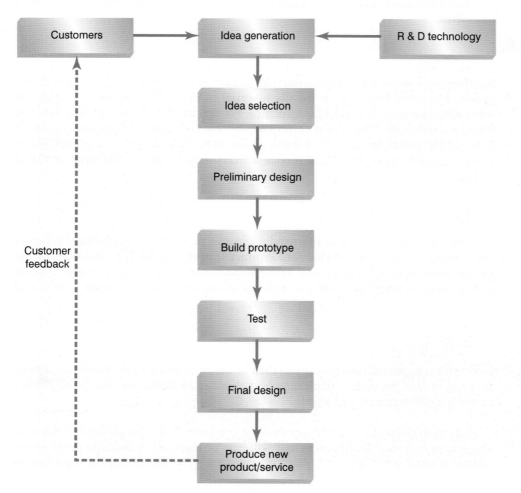

FIGURE 13.2 The new product development process

to determine which ideas to reject at this first stage and which are worthy of further development work. Criteria used in such assessments are likely to include:

Market potential: this would involve discussion with sales and marketing staff or conducting market research with potential customers through interviews, discussion groups, questionnaires, etc. to try to determine whether there is likely to be a market for the product.

Financial feasibility: although information would inevitably be inadequate at this stage, approximate costings are developed, together with estimates of what prices might be attained in the market-place, in order to determine whether acceptable margins are likely to be available.

Operations compatibility: the intention here is to review whether the new product can be produced using existing facilities and equipment, or whether capital investment would be required to provide the necessary means of production. This might involve providing additional capacity or developing new processes, perhaps based on new technology.

Preliminary design

The idea of the preliminary design stage is to take the approved idea and carry out sufficient design work to enable a prototype to be built. Preliminary design needs to be carried out with a fairly clear idea of what market the product or service is seeking to serve, so that an appropriate performance specification can be developed. This will inevitably raise issues involving trade-offs between cost and other performance objectives.

Prototype

Building a prototype will enable further testing of the concept to take place. For goods, a physical prototype is usually essential to evaluate its aesthetic features in three dimensions as well as its performance. For services, the prototype may take the form of a mock-up. The advent of very sophisticated design software packages with enhanced graphics has alleviated much of the need to build physical prototypes in many industries, as products and service delivery systems can be displayed in virtual reality.

Testing

The objective here is to test the product in use to verify its performance before committing to full-scale production. Product testing may be kept in-house or the organization may wish to involve selected customers. Service testing may involve setting up the service operation at a selected site to test market the concept with real customers.

Final design

Information acquired from testing can then be incorporated into the final design prior to a full launch. In reality, there may be a number of alterations involving further prototype development and testing.

After each stage of the process, a decision is taken whether to proceed to the next stage or to halt the NPD process and 'kill' the product. Each decision point in the process is often referred to as a 'gate' or 'stage-gate'. The idea is that the organization will have in place a well-established set of go/no-go criteria that are used as the basis for decision-making at each gate for all new products being developed. The evidence gleaned at each stage of the process can then be considered against the relevant stage-gate criteria in order to decide whether or not to proceed to the next stage. A failure to meet the criteria should lead to a decision to abort, thereby avoiding further spending on what has been adjudged to be a lost cause. Scarce resources can then be concentrated on developing products thought to have the best chances of success. In this respect, the process acts as a kind of multi-stage filter, with progressively more and more new products being rejected as they pass through the stages of the process. The idea of using a structured process, such as this, is to try to improve the chances of success of a new product once it is launched onto the market. Those that make it through should be sufficiently well-developed and tested so as to minimize the risk of costly failure in the marketplace.

There are, however, two significant drawbacks in using such a structured process for NPD. First, there is the risk that good ideas might be rejected. Organizational decision-making is often not the objective rational process it is sometimes depicted. It can be faulty due to inadequate information, a failure to adequately consider the information, individual prejudices and organizational politics. It is not unknown for one organization to reject an idea which is subsequently turned into a commercial success by another. The other problem is in the time taken in following a rigid multi-stage process. The longer it takes to bring a new product to market, the greater the likelihood that a competitor will get there first. Detailed development work, testing and prototyping all takes time. Also, many organizations can be quite slow to take decisions about whether to proceed or not with new products. Bigger organizations are notoriously slow in their decision-making and so can often be outflanked by smaller more entrepreneurial businesses. Although large organizations normally have the resources to develop new products, it is often the case that the most successful new products are initially brought to market by smaller businesses that can operate much more speedily using intuition (i.e. backing a hunch) rather than rationality in their decision-making processes.

PROCESS DESIGN AND NPD

As has already been alluded to above, designing new products and services and the processes that will produce them are inter-related actives. If little or no consideration is given to how a new product will be produced, then difficulties in production are highly likely to arise. This is particularly the case where the products are based on advances in technology, as would be the case with next generation or breakthrough products. However, even relatively small changes in an existing product, as might be the case with incremental products, could have a significant impact on its production. On the other hand, ideas for new products are most likely to gain acceptance and approval if they can easily be produced by the organization's existing processes. Therefore, it seems essential that the NPD process should involve process designers as well as product designers. Involving those with knowledge of the processes through which the products will be produced will help ensure that new processes are designed or existing products modified to best effect for the new product under consideration.

In service operations, the relationship between product and process is even closer, as often the product is synonymous with the process. Consequently, new service development is essentially concerned with process rather than product design. It is possible to view the NPD process as a generic one that is applicable whether the 'product' is a physical good or an intangible service. However, in one respect at least, the development of new services can require an additional consideration to that of products. Front office services involve customer contact. When a new service constitutes a new experience for customers, they may well not know what is expected of them, at least on their initial contact with the service system. Whilst it is commonly understood that new employees need to be trained to deliver a service, the need to train customers to receive the service often remains unrecognized. Customers who do not know how to behave appropriately, or who do not know how to operate self-service technology, are not only likely to have an unsatisfactory experience of the service, but are also likely to diminish the experience of those customers who do possess the relevant knowledge and skills. Identifying customer training needs can be approached in the same way as that for employees. Service designers need to assess the knowledge, skills and attitudes likely to be possessed by likely customers. Where these fall short of those required for the successful operation of the service delivery system, then steps need to be taken to provide customers with the necessary education and training to fill the 'skills gap'. This is likely to involve clear signage and operating instructions in appropriate languages and probably pictures as well. It is also likely to require extra staff being made available to customers, at least in the early stages of their use. It may also be necessary to provide more formal training for customers. In mass consumer markets, this can be quite a challenge as the case of Hong Kong Disneyland demonstrates.

THE IMPACT OF TECHNOLOGICAL INNOVATION ON PRODUCTS AND PROCESSES

New product development often seeks to take advantage of the latest advances in technology. Whilst technological innovation is often the driving force behind the development of new products, the interconnected nature of product and process development means that its impact on process should not be ignored.

The relationship between technological innovations in products and processes was studied for many years by Abernathy and Utterback (Utterback, 1994). They argue that there is a fairly consistent pattern in the respective rates of major innovations in products and the processes used to produce them over the lifetime of the product. Their model is set out in Figure 13.3 (Abernathy and Utterback, 1975).

FIGURE 13.3 Product and process innovation model

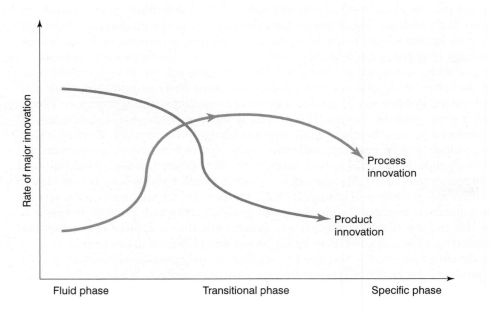

CASE STUDY Hong Kong Disneyland to provide lessons for visitors

Hong Kong Disneyland plans to hold induction programmes in its theme park to educate mainland tourists about Mickey Mouse and Winnie the Pooh after a slow first year. Reporting on its first year of operation, Bill Ernest, managing director, said on 5th September 2006 that a lack of familiarity of Disney characters in China contributed to the park's failure to meet its goal of attracting 5.6 million people in its first year of operation.

'We realized we needed more education materials out in the market place', said Mr Ernest. 'If you haven't grown up with the brand, the characters, the stories or the theme, you are not quite sure what you are walking into', he said. To help Chinese tourists understand the background of Mickey Mouse and the history of the teacup ride, Mr Ernest said the park – the first Disneyland in China – was developing a 'pre-show' to show to its visitors when they arrive at the park. 'When you go in to the park, you will go to an area for 10–15 minutes where we will tell you stories of the lands, the attractions, the characters, how they stand together and what is it that you are about to experience', he said.

Mr Ernest said the movie show, which has never been done in other Disney parks and will be launched in a few months, would allow Chinese tourists 'to learn and catch up' with Disney's history. He also said the company would work on its relationships with Chinese travel agents. Hong Kong Disneyland is majority owned by the territory's government and is trying to win more Chinese tourists as it admitted for the first time that it would not meet its first-year attendance target when it marks its anniversary next Tuesday.

Mr Ernest said that the park had received 'well over' 5 million guests so far, and should be able to hit its 5.6m goal this month or in early October. 'We had a slow start and there were some marketing glitches in the early days', said Mr Ernest. Hong Kong Disneyland has suffered a series of hiccups since its opening last September. During Chinese New Year in February, the park was forced to close due to ticketing

problems, which prompted ticket holders to force their way in by storming through gates and climbing fences. Visitors to the park have also complained about mistreatment, that there are too few attractions and that the park is too small.

'Like all new ventures there have been teething problems and adjustments', said Mr Ernest. But he said the park's attendance had improved significantly in the past six months, thanks to the holiday period and a summer pass programme. In July and August, the park attracted 20,000–30,000 people every day, with half of the visitors coming from China.

(Source www.ft.com 5th September 2006)

Questions (Suggested answers can be found on the companion website www.thomsonlearning.co.uk/barnes)

1   Why does Hong Kong Disneyland find it necessary to train its customers?

2   What are the likely results of having customers who are unfamiliar with the Disneyland 'product'?

3   What else could Hong Kong Disneyland do to better educate and train its customers?

The model characterizes three distinctive phases in the evolution of a technology:

The fluid phase: This is the period in which the product is first developed and introduced to the market. This phase is characterized by a high level of product innovation as producers experiment with the technology and its applications. Much less attention is given to the processes by which the product is made. Considerable experimentation with product design takes place, with particular emphasis on trying to improve the operational features or performance of the product. Typically these product innovations are driven by a better understanding of the needs of users. Sometimes it is the users that provide suggestions for additional innovation and modifications to the product. This phase is characterized by a fairly diverse product line and a high degree of customization. The products tend to be made with standard general purpose equipment. The organizations best placed to compete in the fluid stage are often small, entrepreneurial and dynamic in nature.

The transitional phase: The fluid phase will gradually give way to a transitional phase in which the rate of major product innovation slows down. Product variety reduces and a standard design that has achieved acceptance in the market emerges, perhaps reinforced by industry standards or regulations. This enables much greater attention to be given to the way in which the product is made, and is marked by an increasing rate of process innovation. By this stage, what is termed the 'dominant design' has emerged, which sets the rules of the game for what is often a new industry. This can apply as much to the process as to the product. Towards the end of the transitional phase, the industry is likely to have become much more competitive, with more pressure on costs. Organizations that are unwilling or unable to compete may well leave the scene.

The specific phase: This phase is characterized by an industry that has reached maturity and even decline. The industry focus is firmly on cost reduction and productivity improvements as cost pressures from competitors and customers increase. The product line tends to be highly standardized so that costs can be reduced by mass-production processes utilizing specialized equipment. In the specific phase the rate of major innovation for both product and process starts to reduce markedly. Product and process innovations tend to occur in small incremental steps rather than large step changes. Such conditions tend to favour organizations that can achieve economies of scale. Hence, large well-organized businesses tend to succeed in the specific phase. As the scope for innovation reduces, the industry becomes exposed to attack from newly emerging technologies. These may come from within the industry but often emerge from outsiders and sometimes from unexpected quarters.

The Abernathy and Utterback model provides insights into what can appear to be a confusing scene of constant innovation and change. It shows that technological change does tend to follow a pattern that can offer organizations instructive lessons. It also highlights the need to place NPD within the strategic context of lifecycle of a product and its industry. For example, incremental NPD is unlikely to prove successful in an industry being disrupted by breakthrough innovations.

Christensen (1997) offers insights into how well established organizations are often seemingly caught unawares by disruptive technological innovations. His disruptive innovation model (illustrated in Figure 13.4) depicts the rate of improvement in the performance of the products supplied by an industry over time.

Christensen's argument is quite complex and so is best considered one step at a time. First, he argues that the customers that comprise the market for a product can only utilize or absorb a certain rate of improvement in the performance of that product. This is represented by the dotted line rising slowly upwards. Although, for simplicity's sake, this is depicted as a single line on the diagram, in reality, there will be a distribution of customers around this line, as there will be a range across which different customers can absorb performance improvements. The most demanding high-end customers may never be satisfied with the level of performance on offer, whilst the low-end least demanding customers will be overly satisfied, not being able to utilize the current level of performance. Consequently, the dotted line represents the level of technology that is 'good enough' to serve the market.

Second, he argues that the rate of performance improvement that technological innovations can achieve through new and improved products, almost always outstrips the ability of customers to make use of it. This is shown by the steeply sloping lines in the diagram. The consequence of this is that an organization that aims its products at the current needs of mid-range customers will tend to overshoot what those customers are able to utilize in the near future. This is because organizations tend to direct their innovation efforts at trying to meet the needs of their more demanding

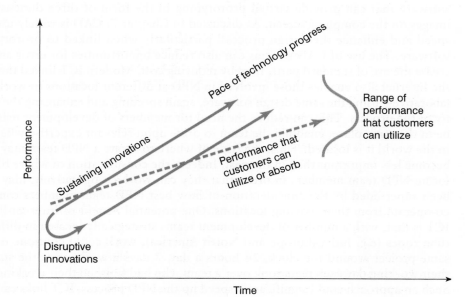

(ADAPTED FROM CHRISTENSEN, 1997)

FIGURE 13.4 Disruptive innovation model

sustaining innovation
An innovation based on the use of
technology whose use is prevalent in
the industry.

disruptive innovation
An innovation based on new technology
that is different from that in prevalent use
in the industry.

customers in order to justify the higher prices needed to achieve the higher profit
margins they require to recoup their spending on NPD.

Third, he distinguishes between sustaining and disruptive innovation. A sustaining
innovation is aimed at providing the more demanding existing customers with products
that have a better performance than those already on offer. Sustaining innovations
can be incremental improvements or more radical in nature. Nonetheless, however
complex the level of technology involved, it is invariably the incumbent players who
excel at sustaining innovations. They are motivated by the knowledge that they can
improve their profit margins if they keep their best customers satisfied. They also
have the resources to enable them to do this.

Disruptive innovations, however, operate in a very different way. They introduce
products and services that are not as good as those currently available. Consequently,
they do not appeal to existing high-end customers. Disruptive technologies tend to
appeal to new or less-demanding customers, as their products are simpler, more
convenient and less expensive. The improvement trajectory of disruptive innovation
is thus different to that of sustaining innovation, with a much lower starting point.
However, once a disruptive product gains a foothold in new or low-end markets, the
disrupters can then initiate a series of improvements. This being a new technology, the
improvements can take place at a rapid pace, enabling it to satisfy more and more
customers. Eventually, the improvements in what was initially a 'not-good-enough'
technology enable it to meet the needs of even the most demanding customers. By this
stage, the disruptors are well on the way to defeating the incumbents. Incumbents
often do not recognize the threat, continuing to perceive it as an inferior technology
until it is too late. In any case, they are locked into a particular way of thinking and
find it politically difficult to acknowledge their growing weakness. They are also
locked into their existing technology, and so may not have the resources or expertise
to enable them to embrace the technology of the disrupters. Thus, whilst existing
industry leaders generally excel at sustaining innovations, successful disruptions are
typically launched by new entrants. Christensen's model carries a particularly important message for industry incumbents with regard to the type of NPD they need to
conduct if they are to avoid being displaced by new entrants. They need to monitor
all forms of emerging technologies and to be prepared to engage with them if they are
to avoid being left behind as technological dinosaurs.

Advances in technology, particularly information processing technologies can
also have an impact on the NPD process itself. As mentioned above, in many industries the need for physical prototypes has been alleviated by the use of sophisticated
software that can provide virtual prototyping in the form of three dimensional
images on the computer screen. As discussed in Chapter 7, CAD is widely used to
speed and enhance the design process, particularly when linked to prototyping
software. The use of CAD systems can also reduce opportunities for error and increase the use of standard parts, thereby reducing cost. Modern ICT linked through
the Internet also enables those involved in NPD at different locations to work col-
laboratively using the same design software, again speeding and enhancing the quality of the process. This can reduce the need for members of development teams to
be in the same place, enabling the team to draw upon relevant expertise wherever
in the world it is located. Thus, the issue of where to locate a NPD team may have
become less important than in the past. Indeed, the consideration of where best to
locate NPD team members in order that they can work co-operatively, may have
been superseded by the consideration of how best NPD team members can best
co-operate from their existing locations. One potential benefit of Internet-linked
ICT is that, with a number of development teams strategically located in different
time zones (e.g. India, Europe and North America), work could continue on the
same project around the clock, 24 hours a day, 7 days a week, as at the start of
their working day each team took over a team who had finished their working day.
Such an approach could significantly speed up the NPD process. ICT links can also

make it easier for development teams to work more closely with suppliers and customers on a global basis.

ADVANCES IN NEW PRODUCT DESIGN PRACTICES

The traditional approach to new product design and development, particularly as practised in large Western corporations, was based on their typically functionally-based structures. That is, work on an NPD project was seen as a series of activities to be carried out by the relevant department. So, typically, responsibility for the work would pass in turn from the Design department who would design the product, to the Operations department, who would produce it, to the Sales department who try to sell it. This approach has been likened to a relay race, in which the project is passed like a baton from one department to another. There are a number of problems with this sequential approach. Each department will have its own specific concerns, which it tends to focus on, often without due regard for the legitimate concern of others in the NPD process. This can lead to products being designed without regard to how they will be manufactured. It can also lead to technological overkill, as designers seek perfectionist solutions without regard for cost or the performance requirements of the marketplace. The development time is lengthened by no department being able to start work until the other is finished. Also, time can be lost in seeking solutions to problems originating from earlier stages in the process, requiring the project to be handed back. Further costs and delays invariably accumulate as people seek to place the blame on other departments.

From the 1980s onwards, many Western manufacturers started to look at the practice of their Japanese competitors who were successfully making inroads into their markets. The Japanese not only seemed to be able to produce better designed products that were easier to manufacture and less prone to failure in use, but they also seemed to be able to bring their products to market much quicker than Westerners. For example, one well regarded study showed that Japanese motor car manufacturers had a time to market of three and a half years on average, whereas for European and US manufacturers it was five years (Clark and Fujimoto, 1991). One of the reasons for this is the way the Japanese companies managed the design process using multi-functional teams. Their approach has been likened to a rugby scrum, with the ball as the project being interchanged between team members to make best use of their skills at appropriate times. A project team is made up of players from the relevant departments (Design, Operations, Sales, etc.). This approach breaks down departmental barriers and the players from the various departments can ensure that their concerns are raised and taken into account; sales people ensuring a customer focus, operations ensuring manufacturability in design, etc. Involving people from other departments also helps ensures that their concerns are raised at an early stage in the development process. Although it can take some time to resolve conflicts arising from the concerns of different departments, it is better to do this as early as possible as decisions taken at this stage are often difficult, costly and time-consuming to undo later on. The other benefit is that work on different aspects of the project can be progressed simultaneously without waiting for full completion of earlier stages. For example, design of tools and dies for manufacture can commence before final product designs are completed.

This approach is sometimes termed 'concurrent' or 'simultaneous' NPD (or 'concurrent' or 'simultaneous' engineering). It is has been widely adopted and is generally considered to represent best practice. A range of different organizational devices can be observed in use by different organizations. Amongst these are matrix structures (where workers remain in their departments but their efforts are co-ordinated by a project manager liaising with their functional manager), task forces (where a dedicated project manager brings together workers from different departments, who are seconded to the project as and when they are needed) and project teams (where

The NPD process: A relay race or a rugby scrum?

the project has its own team of workers and managers, dedicated solely to the work of the project for its duration).

TOOLS AND TECHNIQUES FOR NEW PRODUCT DESIGN

A wide range of tools and techniques have been developed to help improve specific aspects of the new product design and development process. These are often interrelated. This section will briefly outline some of them.

Design for manufacture (DFM)

The objective of DFM is to design the product so that it can be produced most easily and economically. This can best be done by considering process design alongside product design. Type principles adopted with DFM include:

1 Minimize the number of parts and subassemblies.
2 Use standard parts whenever possible
3 Design parts for many uses.
4 Design subassemblies as modules that can be used in multiple ways and in different combinations.
5 Use repeatable well-understood processes.
6 Design for ease of assembly, with minimal handling.
7 Avoid the use of tools, separate fasteners and adjustments.
8 Design products to enable efficient testing and replacement of parts

There is commercially available software to assist with DFM.

Quality function deployment (QFD)

QFD is a structured procedure that aims to ensure that the design meets the needs of the customer. (QFD may also be referred to as *the voice of the customer*.) It does so by forcing designers to match each customer requirement of the product (the 'whats') with the way that the design parameters meet those requirements (the 'hows'). All the whats and hows are brought together in a relationship matrix that forms the centre-piece of a house-shaped diagram. (QFD may also be referred to as *the house of quality*.) The procedure is quite complex, but it involves providing quantitative assessments for customer requirements, the product's performance against competitors' products and the product's technical performance, which are all displayed in different sections of the 'house' (see Figure 13.5). A further section is used to show the relationships between the different design characteristics a series of trade-offs. The analysis provided should serve to crystallize the design options faced by developers. The information from this is then carried forward to develop further QFD matrices for the design of product's component parts, the processes intended to make the product and the operational control system for the processes. The main advantage of QFD is that it forces designers to make explicit considerations that should be present in any design process, but could be missed without this discipline. However, it can be criticized as being rather complex, which if not controlled can become unmanageable.

Taguchi methods

Genichi Taguchi, the Japanese engineer and statistician argues that product failure is mostly caused by poor design. He is credited with developing methods aimed at improving the robustness of designs that is the ability of a product to perform under a variety of operating conditions. The best known of these is Quality Loss Function (QLF). This is a method of calculating the financial loss suffered by the producer and by society at large when there is a variation from the target value in a process. The formula used in the QLF shows that the loss increases quadratically with increasing deviation from the target performance. Adoption of the formula should therefore drive efforts towards reducing variability. Taguchi is also associated with a method called Design of Experiments (DOE) which through the conduct of a series of experiments aims to identify the factors under the control of designers that have most

FIGURE 13.5 A simplified example of a QFD relationship matrix or 'House of Quality'

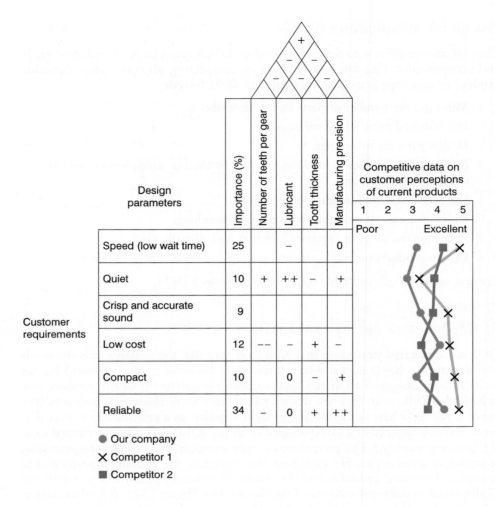

impact on performance. Focusing on these factors will create the greatest improvements in the robustness of the product design.

Complexity reduction

Designers usually strive for simplicity, as complexity invariably increases costs and the likelihood of product failure. There are a number of approaches that are used in pursuit of this aim:

- *Standardization* is an approach that aims to minimize costs by restricting variety in products and services as much as possible. The idea is to offer only those products and services that are valued by a sufficient number of customers to make them profitable. This is assessed by comparing the profit margins and contributions made by each product or service. Wherever possible, unprofitable products should be withdrawn and customers offered alternatives.

- *Commonality* is an approach that seeks to use the same components in as many products as possible. Designing different products with as many common parts as possible reduces operational complexity in supply operations, thereby reducing costs, and also enables lower purchase prices to be negotiated through bulk buying.

- *Modularity* is the principle of commonality applied to sub-assemblies. The idea is to design a finished product or service by bringing together a number of elements that already form part of an existing product. Adopting a modular approach to design across the whole organization can enable a wide range of products to be assembled from existing elements thereby reducing the cost of design as well as achieving lower production costs from economies of scale and scope, and lower input costs from bulk purchasing.

Use of complexity reduction techniques can contribute in efforts aimed at achieving mass customization. This is the term used to describe attempts to combine high volume with high variety in operations, in order to provide customers with customized products at low prices. Whilst this has continued to prove elusive in practice, use of techniques like standardization, commonality and modularity have been adopted by those striving towards this highly desirable outcome.

mass customization
The use of a single process to produce a wide variety of products (or services). It aims to realize unit cost reductions through economies of scope in the same way that mass manufacturing aims to achieve economies of scale.

Failure mode and effect analysis (FMEA)

FMEA is a systematic technique that seeks to identify the cause and effect of product failures. The idea is to list all possible cause of failure, then to calculate a risk priority number (RPN) for each. This is done by calculating the following risk ratings for each risk:

1 The probability that failure will occur.
2 The severity of the consequences of a failure.
3 The probability that the defect causing the failure will be detected before it affects the customer.

The RPN for each risk is calculated by multiplying the three risk rating figures together. Each risk should then be listed in order of descending RPN to form a priority list for preventative actions, with the risk with the highest RPNs being given top priority.

Value engineering and value analysis (VE/VA)

VE is a design technique that seeks to reduce the cost of a product whilst not affecting its value and performance. The term VA is used when the technique is applied to an existing product. To be properly effective, the concept of 'value' needs a broad consideration from the perspective of the customer. Whilst a product's value does have a relationship to the cost of production, for a customer there is also a 'use value' to a product in terms of what it is used for and an 'esteem value' associated with its possession. Perhaps the most common outcome of VE is the decision to use an alternative construction material for the product.

Because most of these techniques are aimed at ensuring that the new product development process better meets the needs of customers, they are often associated with modern approaches to quality management, especially TQM (see Chapter 10).

R & D IN INTERNATIONAL ORGANIZATIONS

One of the most important questions in NPD for organizations that operate internationally is where should they locate their R & D activities. R & D provides a key underpinning for NPD activity and where this takes place has an important impact on the relationship between R & D and the NPD process. It is only in the last decade that there have been significant attempts by multi-nationals to internationalize their R & D activities. Previously, most R & D tended to be carried out in the home country for reasons of security and to take advantage of economies of scale. However, there are increasing pressures to internationalize R & D and NPD activity, due to:

1   *The acceleration of technological progress* – This increases the need for specialization and the international division of labour. This tends to lead to the advent of pockets of innovation in specific technologies in different global locations

2   *Greater technological integration* – More innovation is resulting from the integration of different technologies. This increases the need to collaborate with other organizations, irrespective of their location

3   *The need to reduce time to market* – Firms are under competitive pressure to reduce time to market. This has increased the practice of simultaneous engineering where cross functional teams from, for example R & D, marketing, engineering and operations work together in NPD to better meet specific local customer needs more quickly. This can best be done at a location within the intended market for the product.

Thus, as more organizations internationalize their NPD activities the location of R & D units becomes vitally important. As has already been discussed on pp. 370–371, there are basically two drivers for NPD: market demand and technology. Both of these can influence the consideration of where to locate R & D units. In the case of market demand, an organization might wish to locate an R & D unit near to marketing and operations facilities in order to increase access to key customers and thereby better interpret local requirements. In the case of technology, an R & D unit might be located near to an operations facility that is a centre of excellence within the organization in order to access its specific technological resources, notably suitably qualified staff.

Chiesa (1995) has identified two major categories of factors that organizations need to consider when contemplating where to locate its R &D units.

R & D related factors

These include:

- *Input factor costs:* The costs of R & D staff, equipment and facilities.
- *Internal transfer costs:* The cost of transferring information and knowledge from R & D units to other internal departments like marketing and operations.
- *External transfer costs:* The costs of getting market and technical information from outside sources (e.g. customers, suppliers, research institutes).
- *Organizational costs:* The costs of establishing a new R & D unit, including buildings, recruitment of staff etc.
- *Input resource quality:* The quality of technical staff available from the labour market at a given location.

Non-R & D factors

These include:

- *Existing business locations:* There will be pressure to utilize existing facilities.
- *Local infrastructure:* The existence of transport, communications and other services.

- *Organizational managerial culture:* This influences attitudes to location decisions, for example preferring certain locations.

Chiesa goes on to argue that organizations can be classified as either:

Research orientated: Their strength is their ability to develop technology and to generate streams of innovations from their own research. Or

Development orientated: Their strength is their ability to exploit and apply technology to products and processes.

The two types of organization are likely to adopt quite different approaches to the internationalization of locations for their R & D units. Research orientated organizations tend to keep their research units centralized. However, they might decentralize if necessary in order to access specific resources and recruit technical staff. The critical location decision factor is the input resource quality. Development units, on the other hand, tend to be decentralized in order to minimize internal and external transfer costs. Development units are therefore often located within operations units. The number of such units will depend on the extent to which markets are differentiated. Development orientated organizations tend to have development units centralized close to central operations and marketing, especially if the home market is large and demanding. However, these units may be decentralized to improve learning about markets and key customers. In this case local development units may be used to adapt core products for local markets. If decentralized development units can collaborate it might be possible for them to design products that are suitable for all markets served by the organization. The key issue in considering where to locate is the cost of external transfer. Research units, on the other hand, are likely to be decentralized only in order to monitor technological developments in advanced countries and to carry out joint venture research. Again, the key issue is the cost of external transfer.

CASE STUDY B & B Italia: Winning with design

In the last few years, much of Western Europe's traditional manufacturing has fled east to take advantage of the cheaper labour costs in China, India and Eastern Europe. However, some companies have shown that there are still customers willing to pay more for good design and high quality products.

B & B Italia is one company demonstrating that celebrated Italian design can enable manufacturers to overcome the burden of that country's high labour costs. B & B Italia is one of the most prestigious and innovative names in furniture design. This enables its products to command high prices. For example, its sofas can retail at €10,000 (£7,000, $12,200). Based in Brianza, near Milan – the world's home of design and still the base for 9,000 of Italy's 37,000 furniture and design companies, the company was founded in the 1960s as an innovator in design. Today it likes to think of itself as 'a manufacturer with a high capacity for innovation and technology'. B & B's products sell all round the world. It has over 700 outlets (own stores and concessions in shops) in 54 countries. In 2005 its sales were €150 million, up 10 per cent from 2004.

B & B Italia is, of course, not immune from the cost pressures and had considered re-locating some of its 500-strong workforce outside Italy. However, it decided against it. So, in Brianza B & B workers continue to pour green fireproof plastics into moulds over steel frames. Others scrutinize every centimetre of upholstery from local suppliers for flaws. The company argues that it needs to maintain the integrity of an 'industrial system that links research, manufacturing and marketing'. Maurizio Mazzuchelli, a director of B & B points out that, 'A product made in Italy has an internal value for which people will pay more'. The company,

B & B Italia: A winning design

he says, aims for 'consumer comprehension of the difference'. It is therefore vital for the company to keep control of the manufacturing and distribution of its products in order to develop its brand, which is the basis of its competitive advantage.

A private equity group, Opera, took control of B & B from its founding family in 2002. This has allowed the company to make investments in technology that have enabled it to reduce the number of staff it employs in manufacturing. However, it has increased the number of people in sales and marketing, supporting the brand and, the company hopes, assuring its future.

B & B Italia has also continued to make significant investments, amounting to 3 per cent of its annual sales, in R & D. Its R & D centre in Novedrate, outside Milan, fuels a constant innovation process. 'B & B are very serious in their approach to design', noted one designer, working on the prototype for a 'new interpretation of a sofa'. 'The team have great experience in *imbottito,* or upholstered furniture', he continued. 'We aim to make sure we don't make mistakes in development. That way we will ensure the quality of the final product'.

B & B Italia acknowledges there will always be those who try to imitate and undercut its prices. But it argues that, 'You can not copy a philosophy, a style, or that combination of workmanship and creativity in a product'.

(Sources www.ft.com and www.bebitalia.it)

Questions (Suggested answers can be found on the companion website www.thomsonlearning.co.uk/barnes)

1 Is B & B Italia a *research* or *development* orientated organization?

2 What are the advantages for B & B Italia of continuing to locate all its activities in Italy?

3 Which, if any, of the company's activities should it re-locate to a low-cost country?

SUMMARY OF KEY POINTS

The objective of design is to meet the known or anticipated needs and expectations of customers.

Time is of the essence in NPD. The benefits of speedy NPD include increased market share, price premiums, faster response to competitors and setting industry standards.

NPD can result in incremental products, next generation products or breakthrough products.

New product ideas arise from either market-pull or technology push mechanisms.

A formal NPD process includes stages for idea generation, idea selection, preliminary design, prototyping, testing and final design.

NPD needs to be accompanied by the design of the processes that will produce the products. The design of processes and products should be an inter-related activity.

Technological advances can impact on products, processes and NPD activities.

Concurrent (or simultaneous) design can result in better designs and reduced time to market.

The tools and techniques for NPD include DFM, QFD, Taguchi methods, complexity reduction, FMEA and VE/VA.

The consideration of where international organizations locate their R & D units is influenced by whether they are research orientated or development orientated.

EXERCISES (Suggested answers can be found on the companion website www.thomsonlearning.co.uk/barnes)

WWW.

1 What are the advantages of being the first to market a new product or service?

2 Visit a website that you are familiar with, perhaps one that you use for shopping (e.g. www.amazon.com), or one that provides you with information (www.cnn.com). Does the site represent an example of good design?

WWW.

3 New products can be incremental products, next generation products or breakthrough products. Give three examples of each type.

4 What are the advantages and disadvantages of using a structured multi-stage process for developing new products?

5 Why should new products and the processes that will produce them be developed at the same time?

6 To what extent is the development of new services different from the development of new products?

7 To what extent can digital music downloading from the Internet be seen as a disruptive technology?

8 What are the advantages of concurrent design? What organizational arrangements are most likely to support this approach?

9 Explain how the techniques of DFM, QFD, FMEA and VE can be used to improve NPD.

10 What is the difference between a research orientated and a development orientated organization? How do these differences affect their choice of locations for their R & D activities?

CASE STUDY EXERCISE McDonald's: The Balanced Active Lifestyles menus

Introduction

McDonald's is one of the world's best known brands. Probably the world's leading food service retailer, it has more than 30,000 outlets serving nearly 50 million people in more than 119 countries each day. Its best known menu items are perhaps the Big Mac, Quarter Pounder, Chicken McNuggets, Egg McMuffin and French Fries.

Drivers and results of NPD

The continued long-term financial strength and profitable growth of any business depends heavily on the ability to understand and satisfy the changing needs, wants and lifestyles of current and potential customers. One of the major global trends in the food industry is that more and more people are concerned about food and lifestyle. Healthy, low-fat food and daily exercise are now major issues affecting consumers' decision-making about their food. McDonald's response has been the *Balanced Active Lifestyles* initiative. This international initiative involves the development and promotion of new healthier menu items that are also customized to local tastes and customs.

Outlining McDonald's strategic commitment to this initiative, Mary Dillon (Corporate Executive Vice-President and Global Chief Executive Marketing Officer) declared, 'McDonald's cares about the well-being of each of its guests throughout the world, and by making balanced, active lifestyles an integral part of the brand we aim to make a difference in this area of their lives'.

However, the development of a new menu product aiming to address customers' concerns on well-being issues is not easy. It is a complex process requiring the active involvement of a cross-functional, international team of people from within McDonald's as well as outside experts in the areas of nutrition, wellness and activity. Their challenge is to translate the company's aims into a rich variety of local initiatives. Localization of practices is a must, because if the initiative is to be effective it then has to address the daily realities of people across the globe.

It is difficult to completely isolate the impact of McDonald's balanced, active lifestyles efforts on its business results, but performance statistics from its stores seem to show that the new menu has been well-received by the customers. For example:

- Since its introduction in April 2003, McDonald's USA has sold over 300 million Premium Salads, thereby providing 600 million servings of vegetables.

- Since the introduction of new, fun, youth-inspired packaging for milk jugs, McDonald's USA's sales of milk have doubled.

- McDonald's UK has sold more than 10 million fruit bags, and non-carbonated, no-added-sugar Fruit Shoots drinks made up 23 per cent of all Happy Meal drink sales in 2004. McDonald's Germany is now buying 16,000 tons of salad a year.

- McDonald's USA is the largest buyer of apples in the country according to the US Apple Association.

- McDonald's Canada purchased nearly 175,000 pounds of fresh grape tomatoes for its salads in 2004.

The Balanced Active Lifestyles pillars

The Balanced Active Lifestyles framework has three pillars: **menu choice, physical activity** and **information** (Figure 13.6). Together, these aim to empower individuals to make informed choices about how to maintain the essential balance between energy intake (calories consumed as food) and energy expenditure (calories burned off during physical activity).

Menu choice

McDonald's product range and variety has been increased by adding new product items (e.g. salads, fruits, vegetables and additional sandwich options), developing new product–menu lines and renovating existing

FIGURE 13.6 McDonald's balanced, active lifestyles pillars and motto

McDonald's Balanced, Active Lifestyles

it's what i **eat** and what i **do**

We aim to be a leader in supporting well-being for children and families...everywhere we do business

Menu Choice	**Physical Activity**	**Information**
McDonald's offers a diverse range of menu options at the country level and around the world. The high quality food and beverages come in various portion sizes that can fit into a balanced diet.	McDonald's provides programs and examples in order to inspire physical activity and well-being for families in their daily lives.	McDonald's offers user friendly information on nutrition and additional information to help people balance their lives and achieve their well-being goals.

Brand Leadership • Quality • Safety • Corporate Responsibility

menu options by including healthy food options. Menu developments are also customized to reflect the tastes and customs of local markets.

Examples of localized menu additions include:

- Many McDonald's units in Europe: new Salads Plus menus, including meal-size salad choices, a side salad, fresh fruit bag, and other options.
- McDonald's Canada: a menu of Toasted Deli Sandwiches. Five are available on a whole wheat roll, and the sixth is served on a rye roll.
- McDonald's Hong Kong: a Fresh Choices Menu, with two salads and fruit yogurt.
- In Denmark and Sweden: side order options include carrot slices.
- McDonald's Australia: a QuickStart breakfast menu, including a choice of cereals, juices, reduced fat or non-fat milk, and yogurt.
- McDonald's Taiwan: Toasted rice burger.
- Apples are served whole or with other foods in more than 20 countries around the world.

Examples of local alternatives for Happy Meal choices (sandwich, side order and beverage) include:

- McDonald's UK Happy Meal choices now include semi-skimmed organic milk, non-carbonated no-added-sugar fruit drinks, and fruit bags.
- Happy Meal options in China include a cheese and egg sandwich on a steamed bun, yogurt and milk.
- McDonald's Brazil offers Chambinho – a cream cheese dessert that serves as a rich source of calcium. The nutritional content of the Brazilian Happy Meals has earned the seal of the Sao Paulo State Pediatric Society.
- In France, Germany and Spain, Happy Meal options include Danone® Drinkable Yogurt.
- In Venezuela, customers may substitute fruit juices for soft drinks in Happy Meals.
- Happy Meal beverage choices in Japan include two 100 per cent fruit juices and a fruit-vegetable juice blend, as well as milk, carbonated beverages and oolong tea.
- Happy Meal choices in the USA include 100 per cent low-fat regular and chocolate Milk Jugs, 100 per cent pure apple juice, and Apple Dippers (sliced apples served with an optional low-fat caramel dip).

Physical activity

It is widely accepted that physical activity is a critical component of the energy balance equation. Moreover, adoption and acceptance of McDonald's new menu items would not be successful without customers' willingness to follow and be committed to a balanced lifestyle. To that end, McDonald's aim to find and support ways to inspire and help people find realistic, fun ways to incorporate fitness into their everyday lives. Similar to its menu developments, McDonald's physical activity initiatives are also localized in order to more effectively appeal and reflect peoples' daily lives. Major examples include:

WWW.

- The global *Go Active!* programme (www.goactive.com) that provides online fitness and physical activity resources including: personal fitness assessment tools; a resource library and a wealth of advice to help parents guide their children in safe, healthy eating; fitness activities; an interactive 'virtual trainer' allowing users to generate their own personalized fitness programmes; and a virtual community of users motivating each other by sharing success stories.

- Collaboration with the International Olympic Committee, outstanding athletes and other fitness experts. For example, Bob Greene worked with McDonald's on a multi-dimensional programme to encourage regular walking in Spring 2004, when Greene walked and biked across the US, leading walks and offering balanced, active lifestyles tips to thousands of individuals.

- Sponsorship of global and local sports events (e.g. Olympic Games, FIFA World Cup).

- Promoting walking as an entry point to physical fitness. In 2004, restaurants in the USA, Europe and Latin America offered special adult Happy Meals, including Stepometers™ step-counters motivating users to increase their daily walking.

- Helping children *'Go Active with Ronald McDonald'*. Ronald McDonald has been engaged as the physical activity ambassador. Motivation is a key factor in helping people start and maintain physical activity as a regular part of their lives. The Ronald McDonald Field Program in many parts of the world has been focused on activities and performances that educate and encourage children to walk, move, dance and have fun. Programmes include: the 'Ronald McDonald Sports Zone' in Canada; 'Fitness Fun with Ronald McDonald' in Malaysia; the 'Ronald McDonald Sport and Active Show' in the Netherlands; and the 'Get Moving with Ronald McDonald' show.

Education and information

In order to be able to make smart and appropriate lifestyle and diet choices, customers need relevant, useful, motivational education and information. To that end, McDonald's, have chosen three major distribution media for helping customers access and use information about balanced eating and physical activity: the Internet, tray-liners and brochures. McDonald's multi-faceted education campaign launched in 2005 *'it's what i eat and what i do . . . i'm lovin' it'* is a global initiative communicating the concept of energy balance.

As with the other pillars of the initiative, certain features of the communication programmes are globally the same, but locally relevant content is also being developed for each of these channels in different countries (see Figure 13.7). For example, McDonald's Japan has established special websites that allow customers to access nutrition and allergen information from their cell phones. McDonald's Germany developed an elementary school curriculum on basic nutrition. McDonald's Japan also offers teaching materials for schools including the *Shokuiku no jikan* – Food Education Time.

Communicating important messages effectively is a key priority, so McDonald's continually innovates and develops new, interactive and fun ways for delivering its messages. For example: major local websites include interactive web-based tools, whereby customers may drag menu items onto a virtual tray or into a virtual bag and receive individualized nutrition information on the meal they have built; McDonald's Brazil provides an in-restaurant nutrition guide, with a table that allows customers to calculate nutritional values for their meals. McDonald's Canada provides nutrition information for menu items on posters at the front counter. McDonald's Germany distributes quarterly flyers with questions and answers on food quality, nutrition, and energy balance. McDonald's USA offers wallet cards that show nutritional values and food exchanges.

Implementation of the Balanced Active Lifestyles initiative

The McDonald's Balanced Active Lifestyles approach was initiated at the corporate level in 2003. This was followed by localized actions to reflect and adapt to local habits and preferences. McDonald's efforts to guide and co-ordinate these efforts centre on the following organizational arrangements:

- A cross-functional balanced, active lifestyles team at the corporate level. This has representation from the senior management of relevant departments from around the world. Its aim is to provide strategic direction and facilitate the sharing of best practices across the entire McDonald's system.

- A Global Director of Nutrition, who serves as a resource and key point of contact for all global geographic business units. The Director also co-ordinates dialogue with many of McDonald's key external stakeholders, including government agencies, health professionals and consumers.

McDonald's has recognized that its efforts at new product development needed to involve all parts of the company as well as drawing on the knowledge of external experts. Moreover, as much of the work was aimed at reflecting local needs, many local and regional teams were set up as part of the initiative. For example, McDonald's Australia has partnered UP with The Food Group Australia (FGA) – a team of accredited practicing dietitians who advise the food industry. FGA provides the company with advice and recommendations on childhood nutrition, Happy Meal and other new menu developments, and communications with health professionals.

McDonald's Europe set up a European Nutrition Task Force (ENTF) in July 2002. The ENTF brings together the company's subject area leaders from Quality Assurance, Family Marketing, Menu Management, Communications, Government Relations, Legal and Operations. The ENTF includes a member of the McDonald's Europe Nutritionist Steering Group (NSG) and is lead by the Executive Vice-President of McDonald's Europe. The NSG consists of independent nutritionists from Germany, France and the UK and acts as a sounding board for McDonald's Europe's Balanced Active Lifestyles strategies. This group has

FIGURE 13.7 McDonald's localized information – communication initiatives

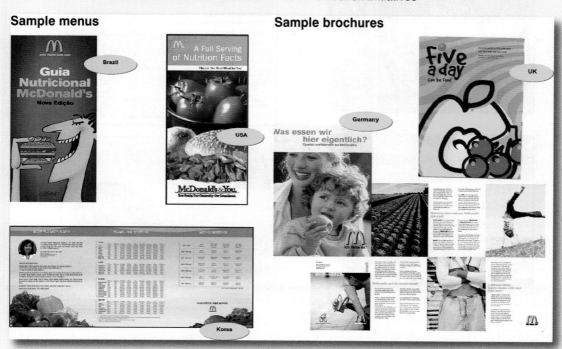

FIGURE 13.7 *(Continued)*

Sample websites

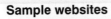

Brazil

Australia

Sample trayliners

France

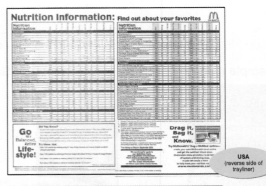

USA
(reverse side of trayliner)

Canada

Australia

devised guidelines based on European recommended daily intakes that will help to inform the future menu development efforts of McDonald's Europe.

At a corporate level, McDonald's has also established:

- A global network of nutrition consultants, including nutritionist teams in place in the US, Europe, Australia and Latin America.

- A 15-member Global Advisory Council on balanced active lifestyles composed of external experts in health, fitness and nutrition from around the world. The Council looks at trends related to balanced, active lifestyles and provides advice and guidance to McDonald's. The Council has encouraged McDonald's to consider initiatives that address:

  - Additional menu choices, including fruit and vegetable options.

  - Promoting physical activity.

  - Focusing on our employees.

  - Setting goals and working to measure the impact of our initiatives.

  - Supporting broader research in the areas of health and nutrition.

—Marianna Sigala

Questions (Suggested answers can be found on the companion website www.thomsonlearning.co.uk/barnes)

1 What were the main drivers for NPD at McDonald's?

2 What were the sources of new product ideas?

3 To what extent has McDonald's approach to NPD followed the stage model of NPD shown in Figure 13.2?

4 Critically assess McDonald's approach to NPD in the *Balanced Active Lifestyles* initiative.

5 Critically assess McDonald's approach to the global co-ordination of its NPD initiative.

WWW.

References

Abernathy, W. J. and Utterback, J. (1975) 'A dynamic model of process and product innovation', *Omega* 3(6):639–657.

Christensen, C.M. (1997) *The Innovator's Dilemma: When New Technologies Cause Great Firms to Fail,* Boston, MA: Harvard Business School Press.

Chiesa, V. (1995) 'Globalising R & D around Centres of Excellence', *Long Range Planning* 28(6):19–28.

Clark, K.B. and T. Fujimoto (1991) *Product Development Performance: Strategy, Organization, and Management in the World Auto Industry,* Boston, MA: Harvard Business School Press.

Utterback, J. (1994) *Mastering the dynamics of innovation,* Boston, MA: Harvard Business School Press.

Additional reading

Bruce, M. and Bessant, J. (2002) *Design in Business: Strategic innovation through design,* London: Pearson Education.

Clark, K.B. and Wheelwright, S.C. (1995) *The Product Development Challenge: Competing Through Speed, Quality, and Creativity,* Boston, MA: Harvard Business School Press.

Fitzsimmons, J.A. and Fitzsimmons, M.J. (2000) *New Service Development: Creating Memorable Experiences,* London: Sage.

www.   ## Useful websites

http://www.design-council.org.uk The website of the UK's Design Council. Lots of
    information and resources on design.
http://www.roundtable.com The website of The Management Roundtable, a US-based
    practitioners' site that provides information and resources for product and technology
    development.
http://www.ideo.com Information about the work of IDEO, one of the leading design and
    innovation consultancies.

CHAPTER 14

PERFORMANCE MEASUREMENT

INTRODUCTION

'How are we doing?' is a question that lies at the heart of operations management. Quite understandably, everyone concerned with any operation wants to know how well it is performing. 'If you can't measure it, you can't manage it' is a phrase that encapsulates the role and importance of **performance measurement** in operations management. The desire to quantify performance is a strong felt need throughout most organizations, especially within the operations function. On first examination, this might seem a fairly straightforward task to undertake. However, a deeper consideration raises a number of questions and issues. These include what aspects of performance to measure, when and how often? This, of course assumes that the aspects of performance that managers are interested in can be quantified. Sometimes this is not easy. Even if quantification is possible, it is important to consider the costs of so doing, because the act of measurement itself has costs associated with it. The more aspects of performance that are measured, the higher the costs are likely to be. So, an associated question is how many measures should be used? The next question to consider is what any performance measurement can tell us about the level of that performance. Answering this invariably requires that there is some comparator against which to assess current performance. So, the question is what should be used as a comparator? International organizations have the additional challenge of determining whether to use national or international benchmarks as comparators for their operations in different countries. The foregoing issues are essentially associated only with keeping score. This is the most basic use for performance measurement. However, for most organizations this is only the start point for performance management. They will usually want to take actions that will improve the level of performance in the light of the measurements taken. This is the other main purpose of performance measurement. The question then becomes one of how best to use performance measurement to drive performance improvement. This chapter will attempt to address these issues.

LEARNING OBJECTIVES

On completion of this chapter, you should be able to:

Explain the importance and purpose of performance measurement in operations.

Understand the basis of performance measurement and performance measurement systems.

Explain how performance standards and benchmarking can be used to assess and improve performance.

Describe the different possible approaches to performance improvement.

Understand the challenges and risks associated with performance improvement initiatives.

performance measurement
The process of quantifying the efficiency and effectiveness of actions.

THE STRATEGIC IMPORTANCE OF PERFORMANCE MEASUREMENT

The strategic importance of performance measurement in operations management lies in its purposes and the consequences, intended and unintended, of the pursuit of those purposes. At its most basic, the purpose of performance measurement is to keep score. This is an essential part of operations management, described by Neely *et al.* (1995) as 'the means of quantifying the efficiency and effectiveness of action [taken to improve performance] . . . an integral element of the planning and control cycle'. Thus, performance measurement plays a central role in operations management. And, as was argued in Chapter 2, operations management is an integral part of strategic management, the means of converting strategic intentions to action. Thus, performance measurement can be seen as the means of linking strategy to action. It can be argued that performance measures can be linked to strategic objectives by the setting of appropriate performance targets. As Neely *et al.* (1995) go on to point out this is a 'somewhat mechanistic view [as] . . . performance measures also have a behavioral impact'. Indeed, much of the purpose of performance measurement is to change behaviour. What is measured in an organization is vitally important because it will influence people's behaviour in one way or another. Their intentions invariably become focused on actions that will improve the chosen measures. Thus, the choice of what to measure becomes a key decision. It immediately signals what the organization considers to be most important and what will inevitably become the focus for management attention. The measures seen to be of most concern to managers will be the measures that people focus on. It could well be said that 'what you measure is what you get!'.

In many organizations this objective is emphasized and reinforced by offering rewards, often monetary, that are based on the achievement of specified performance measurement targets. Performance-related pay, whether for shop-floor workers or for senior executives, remains popular. The whole point of such schemes is to provide direct financial incentives to people to improve whatever performance measures are used as the basis for the scheme. It is important that such measures do promote the kind of behaviour desired by the organization. There is a very real danger that placing too much of an emphasis on certain performance measures can promote the kind of behaviour that is not considered desirable and lead to unintended consequences. It may be that the pursuit of a single performance target leads to other facets of performance being downplayed or neglected.

An example of this can be found within the English public education system. In an effort to drive up educational standards in its secondary schools, the UK government requires every school to publish the performance (in aggregate) of its students' in public examinations at the ages of 16 (GCSE) and 18 (A levels). These are then taken up by the press and published in 'league tables' to identify the best and worse performing schools. This has created a very competitive environment, with those responsible for the management of schools, and the education system more widely, coming under increasing scrutiny. Seen in terms of examination results, English schools have unquestionably improved their performances, with an apparently inexorable rise in the proportion of students achieving better grades each year. However, the annual release of the results invariably prompts another bout of accusations of falling examination standards. Evidence cited to support this includes the fact that top universities say they are no longer able to use A-level results as the basis of offering places to 18 year olds, as so many are now being awarded straight A grades. Whilst increased government spending and a myriad of educational initiatives are claimed by some to be behind the improvements in result, others point to other educational 'performance' figures that give a different picture. Some schools stand accused of boosting their results by only entering students in subjects that they are expected to perform well in.

WHEN THINGS GO WRONG Quality shocks at Toyota

The summer of 2006 saw some unprecedented stories emerge about Toyota, just as the Japanese automaker had overtaken Ford to become the world's second biggest car-maker and was fast closing on General Motors the world's number one. Toyota had relentlessly built its reputation on the superior build quality of its vehicles throughout the 1980s and 1990s, but in the early years of the twenty-first century there were stories of the unthinkable – quality problems at Toyota.

Maybe the signs were there to see in 2002, when Toyota first slipped down the JD Power quality rankings, including the shock news that they had been beaten by General Motors' Buick brand. (The JD Power survey, based on independent research is widely seen as the last word on quality in the auto industry.) It now suffered a further blow to its prestige after being overtaken by South Korea's Hyundai, previously known for low prices rather than high quality. In 2005 Toyota was forced to recall a record 1.4 million cars for repair. Now it was faced with having to recall more than 380,000 Lexus and Toyota Highlander vehicles. Whilst some industry insiders put Toyota's problems down to its rapid expansion, particularly as it was opening factories in ever more countries, few believed Toyota would deliberately sacrifice quality in its quest for even greater capacity. Indeed, the fabled Toyota Production System, developed in Japan is seen by the company as the key safeguard of its quality.

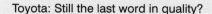

Toyota: Still the last word in quality?

However, perhaps the biggest shock was when Toyota Motors was hit by a criminal investigation over suspicions that officials delayed for eight years a safety recall for a best-selling model that developed a steering fault. The case, brought by Japanese police, was prompted by a car accident that left five people injured, when the steering failed in a Toyota Hilux Surf SUV in August 2004. Toyota said it first discovered the problems in 1996 but they occurred only in 'unusual and extreme' conditions and did not warrant a recall at the time. After additional problems were reported, Toyota carried out another investigation in July 2004 and decided to proceed with the recall of more than 1.5 million vehicles in Japan and other countries in 2004 and 2005. Three Toyota officials who oversee quality control at the automaker have been accused. Toyota said that the officials had not engaged in any wrongdoing and it was co-operating fully with the investigation. Local police in Kumamoto, southern Japan, have sent the Toyota case to the prosecutor's office on suspicion of professional negligence.

The probe has ignited suspicions that renowned Japanese companies have developed a 'culture of concealment' in their quest for perfection amid relentless pressure from top management to meet sales and profit targets. Mitsubishi Motors hid fatal defects in its cars for years and Tokyo Electric Power falsified data related to cracks in its nuclear reactors.

After Japan's transport ministry reprimanded Toyota for failing to act on reports of serious defects in its cars, Masatami Takimoto, Executive Vice-President at Toyota said, 'We would like to deeply apologize for troubling many people concerning the quality and safety of our products'. Akio Toyoda, grandson of the car-maker's founder, has been put in charge of a 'back to basics' campaign to ensure quality takes precedence over cost-cutting or design. Shinichi Sasaki, head of the European operations and a former quality chief, was recalled to Toyota City to support him. JD Power, itself says Toyota remains the industry benchmark and that any drops in quality are not showing up in absolute terms in its survey. Rather it points to the fact that the rest of the industry is slowly narrowing the gap.

(Source material www.ft.com)

Questions (Suggested answers can be found on the companion website www.thomsonlearning.co.uk/barnes)

1 How could Toyota's relentless pursuit of quality have led to the current quality problems?

2 How might a 'culture of concealment' have developed at Toyota?

3 What impact could these events within Toyota's operations have on its business strategy?

One manifestation of this is in some individual students sitting fewer subjects. Another has been the move away from subjects seen as difficult, with entries to science, mathematics and modern languages all experiencing significant falls in recent years. Many educationalists also claim that too much school time is being devoted to training students to be better able to pass assessments, at the expense of encouraging students to be creative, self-organized and able to make connections between different subjects. Meanwhile, employers continue to question the levels of basic numeracy and literacy possessed by the school-leavers that they take on.

An over-zealous pursuit of performance targets can also risk unscrupulous actions by some employees. In extreme cases, it may even be that employees simply falsify records.

PERFORMANCE MEASURES

Determining what to measure is a key issue for performance measurement in operations. The transformation model of operations can be used as one basis for classifying performance measures. Three types of measure can be identified dependent upon the point in the process that they provide information. These are measures of economy, efficiency and effectiveness (see Figure 14.1).

Inputs ──────────────────► The transformation process ──────────────────► Outputs

Economy   Efficiency   Effectiveness

FIGURE 14.1 The three Es of performance measurement

This classification is often referred to as the three Es of performance measurement, as it comprises measures of:

the three Es of performance measurement
Economy, efficiency and effectiveness.

Economy

Measures of economy are concerned with the cost of the goods and services required as inputs for the operations process. It might be thought that the prime objective for those concerned with acquiring inputs would be to achieve the lowest cost possible. However, buying on the basis of price alone is fraught with difficulties. In organizations, it is usually better to consider purchasing decisions on the basis of the so-called five 'rights' of purchasing. These describe the objectives of purchasing activities as the provision of goods and services of the *right quality,* in the *right quantity,* at the *right time,* from the *right supplier,* at the *right price.* Buying on the basis of price alone risks problems in each of these categories:

measures of economy
Measures concerned with the cost of the goods and services required as inputs for the operations process.

Quality: Focusing on price alone risks purchasing goods and services which do not have an adequate specification for their purpose. If suppliers have had to quote very low prices to secure the business, they may be tempted to cut corners to reduce their costs (and thus improve their profit margin) and so endanger quality.

Quantity: It is quite common to be able to negotiate a lower price with suppliers by agreeing to purchase larger quantities. However, purchasing larger quantities than immediately required is likely to involve increased stockholding costs.

Timing: The timing of purchases is vital; too early and stockholding costs will increase, too late and costly delays or disruption may occur in the operations process. Failure to consider this aspect of purchasing risks higher costs.

Supplier: In many respects choosing the right supplier is the most important aspect of purchasing. Failure to consider the reliability, capability and attitude of any supplier risks problems which are likely to increase costs.

In short, a measure that accounts for the *total cost of acquisition* of goods and services, rather than the purchase price alone is likely to provide a much more meaningful measure of economy. However, this is often difficult to establish in practice.

Efficiency

Measures of efficiency are concerned with the performance of the transformation process itself, in terms of its ability to make optimum use of resource inputs in the creation of outputs. As such, measures of efficiency within the three Es framework are expressed in terms of a ratio of outputs to inputs. These are often referred to as measures of productivity and derived from the formula:

measures of efficiency
Measures concerned with the performance of the transformation process itself, in terms of its ability to make optimum use of resource inputs in the creation of outputs.

$$\text{productivity} = \frac{\text{output}}{\text{input}}$$

It is possible to construct a large number of efficiency (or productivity) measures for any given operation. Measures might be based on the totality of outputs, taking into account all products and services produced. Or they might be calculated for individual outputs.

They might be based on output volumes (or quantities) or output value (e.g. numbers of customers served per employee or sales per employee). Similarly, measures might be calculated for a single input factor (e.g. labour) or they might seek to account for all types of inputs (labour, capital, energy, materials and other purchases). Again, they might be based on input volumes (or quantities) or values.

Commonly used measures include:

$$\text{labour productivity} = \frac{\text{output value}}{\text{hours worked}}$$

and

$$\text{total factor productivity} = \frac{\text{output value}}{\text{total value of all resource inputs}}$$

Each measure will be more or less difficult to calculate. Each will have its own particular advantages and disadvantages. What is important is to be clear about the use to which any particular measure will be put.

(N.B. In many texts, efficiency is expressed as a ratio of actual output to the expected output. Expected output is calculated in terms of some standard production rate, which is the output that should be achieved by a fully qualified and experience worker operating under normal conditions. So that,

$$\text{Efficiency} = \frac{\text{Actual output}}{\text{standard production rate}}$$

or

$$\frac{\text{standard time}}{\text{actual time}}$$

Standard production rates and times can be calculated using work study techniques.

Using this approach, efficiency could turn out to be greater than 100 per cent. This is not possible in productivity calculations, as the ratio of output to input can never be greater then 1.)

Effectiveness

measures of effectiveness
Measures concerned with the extent to which the outputs of a process meet the requirements of its customers.

Measures of effectiveness are concerned with the extent to which the outputs of a process meet the requirements of its customers. Thus, measures of effectiveness are focused on outcomes related to customer requirements, and, as such, they are often much more difficult to determine. One approach is to measure levels of customer satisfaction directly, for example through customer satisfaction surveys. It might also be possible to use indirect measures of customer satisfaction, perhaps based on sales figures such as market share. However, these can be affected by external factors such as actions of competitors and the general economic conditions. Some organizations prefer to use internally derived measures that relate more closely to actions being taken within its operations. Being effective means providing what customers want. Thus, it is important to base measures of effectiveness on an understanding of what customers require from the operation. For example, a restaurant might decide to use the number of people served per hour as a measure of its effectiveness. This might be appropriate for a fast food outlet, where customers want to be served as quickly as possible. However, such a measure would be entirely inappropriate in an up-market fine dining restaurant where customers go to savour both the good food and the atmosphere.

DEVELOPMENTS IN PERFORMANCE MEASUREMENT

Modern day performance measurement has its origins in the work of Frederick Taylor in the early years of the twentieth century. His ideas about scientific management (Taylor, 1911) were focused on improving the efficiency of operations by seeking to improve the performance of workers (see Chapter 12). Thus, the focus of performance measurement was primarily on labour productivity, measured in terms of output volumes and labour cost. In an era of labour intensive mass manufacture this made a lot of sense. Scientific management made a significant contribution to the success of Western, and especially US, industry during this period, and so operations management came to be dominated by performance measures that emphasized efficiency and productivity. This continued well into the second half of the twentieth century, when the previously unassailable position of US style management practice was increasingly questioned under the challenge of Japanese manufactured goods. Japanese manufacturers could typically offer a wider variety of goods of higher quality at lower prices than their Western counterparts. To Western eyes, increased variety and improved quality should have led to increased not reduced costs. Western operations managers were therefore forced to reconsider their practices, including their approach to performance measurement. The Japanese success seemed to be due to their pursuit of both efficiency and effectiveness. It seemed clear that the Western tendency to evaluate manufacturing primarily on the basis of cost and efficiency was damaging competitiveness. What was needed was a wider range of more criteria to judge performance. In particular, new measures were required to reflect the new found concern for effectiveness.

The 1980s saw a growing consensus that the traditional performance measures of operations management were inadequate. Neely *et al.* (1995) characterized these shortcomings as:

- Encouraging short-termism
- Lacking strategic focus
- Encouraging local optimization
- Encouraging managers to minimize variance from standard rather than seeking continuous improvement, and
- Failing to provide information on what customers wanted and what their competitors were doing.

The initial response to this was to concentrate on measures of product quality in order to reduce the level of defects. This led, in turn, to a focus on measuring quality within processes and not just at the output stage. This created a growing realization that improved process quality could also improve efficiency much more successfully than the traditional accountancy-based measures that operations managers often had to rely on. The advent of TQM increased the concern to improve effectiveness and responsiveness. This, therefore, saw the introduction of customer based measures. This linked well to the requirements of the increasingly important service operations sector for measures of customer satisfaction. In services, a level of high quality was seen as synonymous with a high level of customer satisfaction.

PERFORMANCE MEASUREMENT SYSTEMS

The dissatisfaction with existing performance measures felt within operations management was reflected more widely in the business world. There was widespread concern that the traditional accounting measures gave only a narrow and backward looking and internally focused perspective of performance. What was required was a more multi-dimensional view of performance. Thus the search began for performance measurement systems that would also encompass non-financial, external and forward looking measures to balance those already in common use. This led to the development of a number of new performance measurement frameworks. The best known of these is 'The Balanced Scorecard' (BSC) of Kaplan and Norton (1992).

The BSC was originally devised as framework for organizing performance measures into four clusters or *perspectives*. These four perspectives (financial, customer,

performance measurement system
A collection of performance measures used by an organization to assess the performance of various aspects of its activities.

The Balanced Scorecard
A performance measurement framework that organizes performance measures into four perspectives (financial, customer, internal processes and learning and development).

internal processes and learning and development) represented, it was argued, the set of measures required by any organization. Examples of the kinds of measures envisaged for each perspective might include:

- *Financial perspective:* return on capital employed, cashflow, profit, value added, turnover per employee.
- *Customer perspective:* customer satisfaction index, market share, percentage sales from new products.
- *Internal business perspective:* quality levels, response time, productivity, inventory turns.
- *Innovation and learning perspective:* time to develop new products, percentage revenue from new services, number of employee suggestions, staff time per new product.

Subsequently, the BSC has been developed to place an increasing importance on its ability to link operational activity to strategic objectives. Consequently, the model is often drawn to show the organization's Vision and Strategy at its centre. (See Figure 14.2).

The BSC can thus become a mechanism to help managers develop a comprehensive organization wide performance measurement system in which an improvement in any individual performance measure should make a contribution to the achievement of organization's vision and strategy. The strength of the BSC is that it enables each organization to develop the details of its own individual performance measurement system. Its use should promote a more strategic consideration of operations, which should lead to performance measures that enable operations to be assessed against a range of performance criteria (e.g. cost, quality, speed, flexibility and dependability), depending upon the strategic objectives set for operations.

As was discussed in Chapter 2, operations management plays a key role in converting strategic intentions to action. The choice of performance measures in operations management is crucial, because their purpose is to drive action. Thus, performance measures can be used as the means of linking operations management to strategic objectives. A number of methods aimed at deriving operations performance measures from business strategy have been developed. Amongst these is a two-stage approach devised by Neely *et al.* (2002). The first stage involves top-level performance measures linked to business objectives for each of the organization's products or services (or families of products or services). In the second stage, these top-level

FIGURE 14.2 The Balanced Scorecard

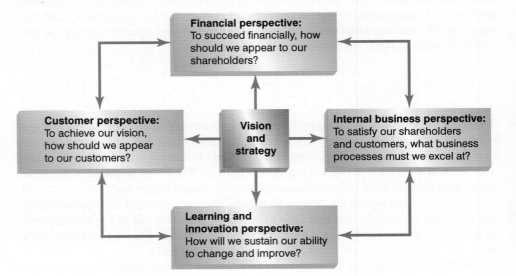

CASE STUDY: Wolseley build a better scorecard

Mel Keeley and his staff at the Build Centre in Romford, to the east of London, have little time for lofty management theories. They are too busy meeting customer demand for bricks and mortar. Being at the front line, however, they are the very employees that Wolseley, the international building products group, had to bring on board when it launched a performance measurement system modelled on the balanced scorecard, which covers a mix of financial and non-financial targets. 'When it was first presented to us, we were a bit sceptical', admits Mr Keeley, whose 15 staff supply local builders and DIY enthusiasts with construction materials, interiors and electrical hire equipment. The group introduced the system in its UK 'heavyside' division to improve performance by binding newer and older businesses together with a common culture and objectives. The balanced scorecard offsets the traditional bias towards purely financial measures by incorporating factors such as customer satisfaction and staff motivation.

Wolseley realized from the start that if it failed to win over those at the sharp end, the project would be pointless. 'We always had in mind that we were going to be delivering this to hard-nosed branch managers', says Adrian Barden, UK managing director, who introduced the programme when he was in charge of the division. 'It had to be meaningful and easy to understand and measure, otherwise they would rubbish it'. Branch managers as well as senior executives were involved in the working party that began designing the programme in late-2001. The team spent several months deciding on the key elements of the business and how to measure them. They settled on 17, from financial indicators such as return on capital employed and sales growth to non-financial measures such as customer satisfaction, branch safety and purchases from preferred suppliers.

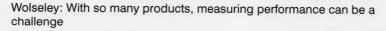

Wolseley: With so many products, measuring performance can be a challenge

To communicate to the branches how they were doing on each measure, the team devised a traffic light system. They discarded references to a 'balanced scorecard' in favour of 'R2G' (red-to-green) – shorthand for the drive to improve performance from unacceptable (red) or acceptable (amber) to excellent (green). Results were sent to the branches each month. 'As the results started to come back and we started to hit green and see what it was doing to our branches, we got more and more enthusiastic about it', says Mr Keeley. 'It keeps you focused on all the major parts of the branch and the business. There are times when you're really busy and you take your eye off a certain aspect of it. This highlights it straightaway'.

Wolseley has done better than most at using a balanced scorecard system to achieve its objectives, according to Andy Neely, professor of operations strategy and performance at Cranfield School of Management. 'Its implementation is one of the most robust and effective that I have ever seen', says Professor Neely, who is completing a study of the scheme. Professor Neely compared 156 Wolseley branches using R2G with a control group of 156 plumbing branches that did not use the system. He picked the nearest plumb branches in each case, on average 4.5km away, controlling for the month, the weather and market demand. Following the launch of R2G, the build branches showed a statistically significant increase in sales and gross profits compared to the plumb branches. Within the build division, however, some branches produced better financial results than others. They were the ones that also performed better on non-financial measures such as customer retention.

In other words, some branches were more enthusiastic than others about wooing customers, suppliers and staff under the scheme, and this produced better financial results. To find out why attitudes to these less tangible aspects of performance varied, Professor Neely interviewed 40 managers. His findings show that most reacted well to the scheme. Some came up with creative ways to boost non-financial performance, for example, by allocating staff to contact builders who had not visited the branch for a while and persuade them to come back. These managers were asked to share their ideas with other branches. A few branch managers remained sceptical about the scheme and one admitted he had 'never taken a blind bit of notice of it'. This was despite bonuses being linked to the scheme's success.

Wolseley's experience demonstrates how a balanced scorecard system can improve financial performance. Mr Barden says the company has similar schemes in other divisions, such as the US lumber business, but only uses it where appropriate.

The emphasis now is on giving branch managers a deeper understanding of how the non-financial elements affect performance.

(Excerpted from 'How to put ideas to work' by Alison Maitland, www.ft.com published 23 May 2006, downloaded 1 November 2006)

Questions (Suggested answers can be found on the companion website www.thomsonlearning.co.uk/barnes)

1 How has Wolseley tried to link operational level performance to the company's business strategy?

2 What steps has Wolseley taken to try to ensure that its performance measurement system gained maximum acceptance within its Build Centres?

measures are cascaded to lower levels by identifying the key drivers of performance. The lower level measures are then designed for the drivers.

Whilst the extended range of performance measures offered by frameworks such as the BSC does provide managers with a more comprehensive picture of their operations, there is a downside to their use in practice. If too many measures are used, managers can become confused as to which to pay most attention to. Different performance measures may provide conflicting indications about what corrective actions are needed. In extreme cases there may just be too many measures to provide the necessary focus for improvement efforts. Also, setting up and operating a performance measurement system can be a costly business. Initiating a new performance measurement system is not only costly but also time-consuming and may also draw managerial attention away from vital day-to-day operations. Many people have also questioned whether the resources required to maintain a comprehensive performance measurement system can ever provide sufficient benefits to justify the on-going costs.

PERFORMANCE STANDARDS

Whatever measures are used to monitor the performance of operations, they can only be useful if there are some comparators against which to assess whether the level of performance achieved is satisfactory or not. This principle is enshrined in the control loop model of operations (see Figure 14.3).

A performance measure can only be useful as a means of determining whether an operation is performing successfully if there is some yardstick against which to compare that performance. What is required is an agreed performance standard which will serve as a comparator for actual performance.

There are a number of possible bases for such a standard:

Internal standards:

    (a) the organization's past performance

    (b) the organization's own targets.

External standards:

    (a) competitors' performance

    (b) best practice

    (c) market requirements.

These are now each discussed in turn.

performance standard
The level of performance deemed suitable for use as the target level of performance against which to compare a particular aspect of performance.

Organization's past performance

The basis of this approach is the use of the organization's own previous performance as a standard against which to judge future performance. Improvement targets can then be set against those standards. This might have the merit of being considered realistic by those involved, but it also runs the risk of generating complacency by an inward focus. It tends to ignore both what the competition is achieving and what the market may be demanding. If the organization carries out a particular operation in more than one location, however, it could use performance measures which compare one location against another to drive improvement up to the standard of the best performing operation. This approach can be particularly useful to organizations operating internationally as it enables them to compare the performance of operations in different countries. The cost of collection and presentation of information in this category should be relatively small.

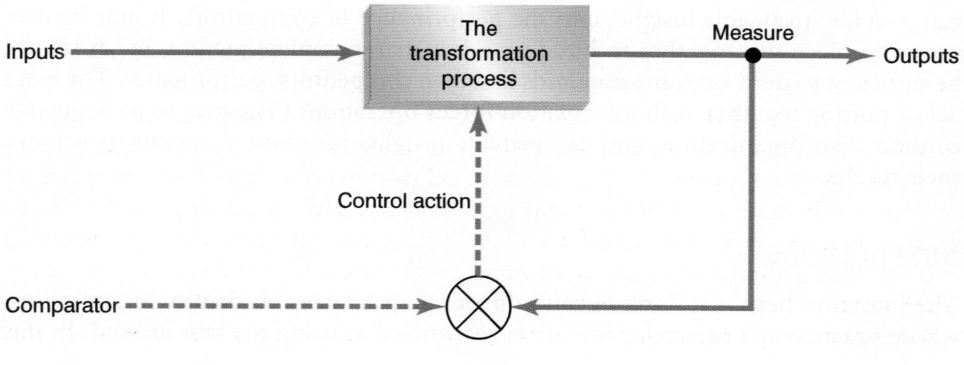

FIGURE 14.3 The control loop

Organization's own targets

Perhaps the most widely used internal performance standard is the annual budget or target. The budget is normally of paramount importance in most organizations. Indeed, the achievement of budget figures often forms the basis of reward (or punishment!) for many managers. The budget specifies directly or indirectly the level of performance required by particular operations. The main problem with budgets is two-fold. First, they are self-determined and therefore internally focused. Like all internal standards, they can ignore the performance of competitors and the requirements of customers. Second, most budgets are based primarily on financial information. This can make for a very narrow information set on which to measure and assess performance. Internally derived performance measures do, of course, have the benefit of being based on information which should be readily available and accessible. The cost of collection and presentation of such information should also be relatively small.

Competitors' performance

In an increasingly competitive environment, it makes sense to adopt performance standards which enable an organization to compare its performance with that of its direct competitors. Whilst it might be possible to do this at an organizational level on the basis of published information, it is usually extremely difficult to access the necessary information to be able to make such a comparison at the level of an individual operation. There are, however, many potential sources of information about competitors at their operations. These include:

1 *Published sources:* Annual reports, press reports, company literature, analysts' reports, government reports, etc.
2 *Secondary sources:*
   - Interviews with analysts, journalists, academics, etc.
   - Direct contact: Plant visits, observations, etc.
   - Indirect contacts: Industry associations, technical seminars, trade associations, chambers of commerce, etc.
3 *Primary market research:* Consumer surveys, trade surveys, industrial market research, etc.
4 *Sales analysis:* For example, by analyzing competitive bids lost and won to identify strengths and weaknesses in comparison to competitors.
5 *Product comparison:* Reverse engineering of products to assess the level of quality and technical sophistication achieved by competitors.
6 *Soft information:* Informal information gathered by word of mouth from own and competitors' employees.

Whilst it can be difficult and time-consuming to gather and analyze, such information can provide invaluable insights into the performance of competitors. It may be necessary to piece this together to build up a less than complete picture, but it should be sufficient to draw up some standards based on competitors' performance. The mere act of putting together such information forces operations managers to look outside of their own organization, and can provide insights into how competitors achieve their results.

Best practice

The intention here is to look beyond direct competitors and identify organizations whose practice in a particular activity is recognized as being the best around. In this respect, at least in theory, an organization could look anywhere in the world for examples of exemplary practices wherever they can be found. The idea is to use the level of performance achieved through the use of best practice as the standard against which to compare current organizational performance in that particular activity. So, for example, if a manufacturing company wanted to establish a standard for the performance of its customer telephone helpline, it might look to an organization with a strong reputation for answering calls quickly such as the emergency services. The major advantage of looking to organizations in different industries is that they are not direct competitors and so are more likely to willingly divulge information.

Market requirements

Whilst looking to the practice of external organizations to set the performance standards is likely to be more difficult than generating ones internally, it is likely to provide more exacting and challenging targets. However, this approach risks ignoring what must be the most important task of any business: namely satisfying customers. If organizations are not meeting customer requirements, then it is difficult to accept that they are performing successfully. Arguably, the objective of any organization's operations is to satisfy customers. Therefore, performance standards should be based upon customer needs and requirements. The task of identifying customer needs is usually considered to be a marketing activity. Various market research techniques have been developed encompassing quantitative and qualitative methods, using both primary and secondary data. However, leaving this task solely to marketers is likely to prove less than satisfactory as the operations function can have much to contribute. People working in operations, particularly service operations, have many contacts with customers and potential customers. They are often well placed to gain an excellent understanding of how well (or badly) the organization's products and services are currently meeting customer needs. They can provide valuable information which can help establish the level of performance required to meet customer requirements. Also, as customer expectations change over time, usually becoming more exacting, organizations need to continually monitor customer needs and requirements and adjust their performance standards accordingly.

BENCHMARKING

The practice of comparing the performance of an operation with that of similar operations in another location is usually termed 'benchmarking'. It is a term that can have a number of different meanings. At its most basic, it merely involves measuring various aspects of performance in the two or more different locations for comparison purposes. As discussed in the preceding section, the idea is to establish a performance standard that can be used as a target for performance improvement. However, the main strength of benchmarking is when it is applied as a springboard to drive performance improvements. The act of measuring particular aspects of performance signals its importance to the organization. When accompanied by challenging performance standards this should galvanize managers into actions designed to achieve progress towards the targeted level of performance. However, an even more potent aspect of benchmarking is when it goes beyond measurement to encompass the study of the practices of the benchmarked organizations. The idea is to compare the organization's own practices and methods with those used in similar operations by organizations that achieve much better levels of performance. Where deficiencies are found, improvements can then be made based on what has been observed in those better performing organizations. When used in this way, benchmarking can offer a powerful mechanism to drive organizational learning.

As with performance measurement benchmarking, practice benchmarking can be undertaken by making comparisons in a number of different ways. There are three main approaches to practice benchmarking:

1 *Internal benchmarking:* This is where practice in one of an organization's locations is compared to that in another. The advantage of this is that information about these operations should be readily available and reliable. It should similarly be fairly easy to gain access to the organization's other facilities in order to study the practices. It may be that different practices have evolved in different locations due to different contextual factors. Organizations that operate internationally can be particularly well placed in this respect and hence in a much better position to learn, than those that only operate in one country. The main disadvantage of internal benchmarking is that even the best level of performance within the organization may be much worse than that achieved elsewhere.

2 *Competitive benchmarking:* This is where organizational practices are compared to those of direct competitors. This is often felt to be the most effective form of benchmarking as competitors are likely to be operating similar processes. Competitors are easy to identify, but they may not be very enthusiastic about allowing a direct competitor to learn from them, and thereby endanger their competitive advantage. One way to overcome this in service businesses is to observe a competitor's front office operations from the perspective of a customer. It is more likely that an organization will allow their operations to be studied by someone in the same industry who is not perceived to be a direct competitor. Consequently, it might be possible to gain access to study an organization that operates in a different country or one that serves a very different market segment.

3 *Best practice benchmarking:* This is where practice in a particular operation within an organization is compared to practice in a similar operation in an organization thought to be exhibiting best practice, preferably world class performance. The idea is to learn from the best performers wherever they are found. It can be particularly instructive to study similar operations carried out in different industries and in different countries, where different practices may have arisen. The advantage of looking to organizations in different industries, and hence those that are not direct competitors, is twofold. First, it can encourage innovative thinking through using different methods. Second, such organizations are likely to be more willing to divulge information. The disadvantage is that it may be difficult to know exactly where best practice for a particular operation is to be found. Also, it may prove difficult in applying their working methods in a very different industry. A well-known, if slightly extreme example of best practice benchmarking is provided by South-West the low cost US airline. They studied the practices of the pit crews at the Indy 500 motor racing circuit in order to help reduce the turnaround time of aircraft between landing and take-off at airports.

The extent to which an organization can benefit from benchmarking will depend on the importance it attaches to the exercise. Voss *et al.* (1998) claim that is possible to identify four different organizational attitudes towards benchmarking, which are revealed by their responses to the receipt of performance data from a benchmarking exercise:

- *Can do* organizations are those that score badly on operational performance practice but use the benchmarking exercise as an opportunity to take action to improve operational performance.
- *Can't do* organizations are those that score badly on operational performance practice but fail to use the benchmarking data to take any action. This can often be due to business pressures.

- *Will do* organizations are high performing organizations that use the results of the benchmarking exercise to take action to further improve operational performance. These are true learning organizations

- *Won't do* organizations are high performing organizations that fail to use the benchmarking exercise to take any further action. These are typically complacent organizations who consider they know all that is needed. The performance of these organizations is under threat in the longer-term.

Organizations that operate internationally may well be much better placed to benefit from benchmarking exercises than purely domestic operators. They not only have direct experience of operating in different contexts, but are also more likely to value the learning obtained from those experiences. As such they are much more likely to be open to ideas from outside of their own domestic environment.

A major problem with all forms of external benchmarking is that of finding organizations that are prepared to grant access to outsiders. There is a natural reluctance to reveal organizational secrets that might ultimately finish up in the hands of competitors and potential competitors, or others who might use such information to the organization's detriment, such as suppliers and customers. One solution to this problem is based on the premise that any organization is likely to want to learn from another. This has led to the setting up of benchmarking clubs. These are networks of organizations that in order to benchmark their operations against others are prepared to grant access to others who want to benchmark them. There are many such benchmarking clubs, organized by neutral bodies such as management consultancies and trade associations. Such bodies are often able to collect a wide range of performance measures from their members, and get their agreement to release them on the condition that they are never revealed on an individual basis, but are instead published as part of industry wide aggregate figures.

PERFORMANCE IMPROVEMENT

One of the most important purposes of performance measurement is in driving performance improvements. If performance improvements are to be made, then decisions are needed in respect of three key issues:

1 The scale and scope of the performance improvement required.
2 The priorities for performance improvement.
3 The approach to making the performance improvement.

Determining the scale and scope of the performance improvement

In theory, determining what aspects of performance need to be improved, and by how much, ought to be a fairly straightforward task. If the current level of performance is measured and compared to the required standard this should highlight any gaps that need to be addressed. However, as already discussed in this chapter, measuring performance and setting appropriate performance standards can often be problematic. A major issue is that of determining what performance measures to use. Schmenner and Vollman (1994) argue that too often organizations tend to fall back on 'the usual suspects' of performance measurement, using the same measures for many years without re-assessing their current worth. Use of inappropriate performance measures gives rise to 'false alarms' in performance monitoring, which can mean actions being taken which may at best achieve little improvement and at worse might even make things worse. Schmenner and Vollman list typical false alarms as labour efficiency, direct cost reduction and machine efficiency. On the other hand failing to measure the right things leads to 'gaps' in performance measurement, meaning that matters which require attention are neglected. Typical gaps are customer satisfaction, new product introduction, employee involvement and integration with customers. However, this research highlights the need for each organization to develop its own specific performance measures.

Determining the 'right' measures will depend upon individual organizational and industry circumstances. In particular, organizations need to ensure that their performance measures are linked to their organizational objectives. Use of a structured performance measurement framework, such as the balanced scorecard, will help avoid false alarms, as measures are more likely to be linked to organizational strategy. It will also help avoid gaps, as a broader range of measures are more likely to be included. The choice of performance measures used within an organization sets the scope of performance improvement being considered. The scale of improvement required will depend upon the choice of performance standard. As already discussed, performance standards can be derived either internally, or by benchmarking against other organizations, or by analyzing customer requirements. Techniques such as product profiling (as proposed by Platts and Gregory) can be useful in comparing an organization's performance with that of competitors. Similarly, Hill's order winners and market qualifiers model can help with respect to assessing performance against customer requirements. (Both of these are discussed in Chapter 2.)

Setting the priorities for performance improvement

Any analysis of current performance is likely to identify a number of areas for improvement whatever performance measures and standards are used. As no organization is likely to be able to tackle all areas at once, what is required is the ability to draw up a priority list for improvement actions. One approach to doing this is Slack's (1994) performance-importance matrix (see Figure 14.4). This requires an assessment of the current level of performance in each of the various factors under consideration and also their importance. Performance is normally compared to that of competitors to determine whether it is better, the same as or worse. Importance to customers can be assessed as either high, medium or low.

FIGURE 14.4 The performance-importance matrix

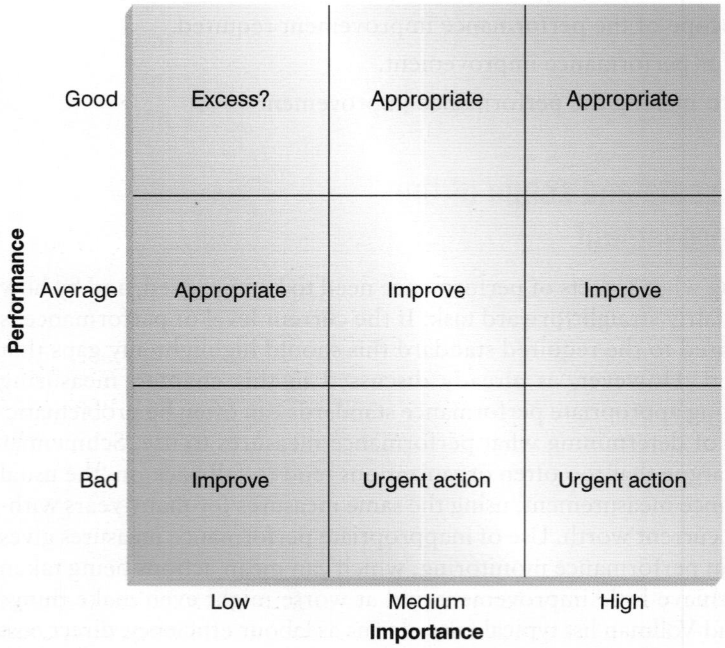

(ADAPTED FROM SLACK, 1994)

Each of the performance factors can then be plotted into one of the squares of a 3×3 matrix, with performance as the vertical axis and importance as the horizontal axis.

As Figure 14.4 shows, the squares are designated as either:

Urgent action: Performance factors in these squares require urgent action to achieve improvement. These factors are important to customers, but the operation's performance falls well below standard and business is probably being lost. Any factors falling in these squares are top priority for immediate improvement action.

Improve: Performance factors in these squares need to be improved, but probably not as a top priority.

Appropriate: Performance factors in these squares are currently at a satisfactory level. However, it would be wise to monitor them in the future to ensure there is no deterioration in performance.

Excess?: Performance factors in this square indicate a level of performance which seems far above that warranted. It may be that resources used to achieve this level of performance would be better directed to factors requiring 'urgent action'.

If the organization's performance measurement system is inadequate, especially with regard to information about competitors' performance and customer requirements, it may be that the assessment of some performance factors will have to rely on the perceptions of the managers involved in the analysis. Nonetheless, the very act of using such a framework forces managers to think through these issues. It maybe that, as Slack argues, they are 'ignorant of their own ignorance' on the subject. In such cases, use of the matrix may prove to be a valuable learning exercise for those involved.

Determining the approach to making the performance improvement

Having identified what needs to be changed and where the priorities for improvement lie, the third issue to consider is what type of approach should be used to try to achieve the required performance improvement. In essence, performance improvements can be undertaken in one of two ways:

1 Step change.
2 Continuous improvement.

Step change

Sometimes also referred to as 'breakthrough' or 'radical' improvement, such a change is designed to achieve a significant one-off improvement in performance. This is represented diagrammatically in Figure 14.5.

A step change approach is likely to be most appropriate when current performance is significantly below that of competitors, and the organization is suffering from a competitive deficit. Such radical change is only likely to be achieved by major innovation in the operation that involves the use of new technology and/or new working methods.

New technology

Technology has always seemed to offer great opportunities for quantum improvements in performance. Recent developments in information and communications

FIGURE 14.5 Step change

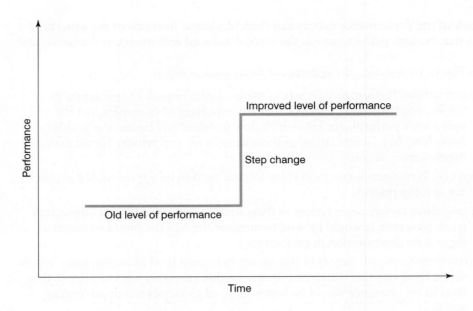

technology, especially those associated with the Internet and mobile technology have further added to such opportunities. As discussed in Chapter 7, examples of this are all around us. Manufacturers have adopted CAD/CAM and CIM systems and increasingly have automated with robotics, AGVs, etc. In the service sector, ICT offers the means of moving virtually limitless amounts of information and money instantaneously with little or no consideration of distance. For organizations, the allure of technology has never been greater. Coupled with the very real fear of being at a competitive disadvantage if they fall behind competitors, most organizations want to capitalize on the latest technological advances. However, many organizations have found themselves disappointed with the level of performance improvements achieved through attempts at step change with new technology.

Reasons for failing to deliver anticipated performance improvements may include:

- *Unrealistic expectations:* It may be that too much was expected from the technology in the first place. Perhaps people were carried away with the enthusiasm of the designers and suppliers of the technology (whether internal or external) eager to extol the benefits of their systems.

- *Technological implementation problems:* This may be particularly acute if the organization is pioneering new technology or its application in a new situation. Yet this is precisely what is often necessary if step change is to be achieved. This type of problem often leads to delays and additional costs in implementing new technology.

- *Design creep:* Because lead times for large technological changes are typically quite long, those specifying the requirements for such systems often change their minds about what is needed. It is common for modification to the original design to be required, which in turn creates more delay and increases costs and complexity.

- *Management change by stealth:* Managers may view the installation of a major new system as an opportune time to make other organizational changes, justifying them by claiming that they are 'because of the new technology' when in reality they are unrelated. If these changes are contentious and unpopular, staff will be unhappy, which is likely to lead to problems in getting acceptance for the new technology.

- *Technology adopted too late:* The alternative to being a technological leader is to be a follower, not adopting technological advances until they are tried and tested. Although this can reduce the risk of delays and unforeseen costs, it increases the risk of losing competitive advantage to those who successfully install new technology.

- *Implementation problems from employees:* It is typical to encounter some reluctance to the adoption of new technology in most organizations. Many people are fearful of the consequences and in extreme cases this can manifest itself in some degree of resistance and even outright hostility. There can be many reasons for this, but uppermost in many employees' minds may be fear of losing their jobs. Most past technological advances have involved the replacement of human labour with machines. Even if this is not the case, insensitive management of the introduction of new technology, particularly if potential users of the technology are not consulted, can engender resentment and lead to a lack of co-operation, which is likely to result in the technology not being used to maximum effect. While many organizations do consult with staff, this can still be done poorly, typically only paying lip service to people's concerns.

Many of the problems associated with the introduction of new technology result from management thinking based on the 'with one bound Jack was free' principle. This occurs when managers naively believe that merely adopting the latest technological advances will solve all their problems. This is unlikely to be the case. The major drawback of the step change approach to performance improvement is that it is 'top-down' in nature. As such, it has to be imposed on, or at best sold to, what may be a reluctant workforce. New technology will thus rely, at least initially, on external 'experts'. There is a risk that the people who will operate the technology in the long-term will feel a sense of alienation from it. This is generally termed the 'not invented here' syndrome. There is no real commitment to use the technology to make it achieve the desired results. New technology will inevitably involve the outlay of capital investment, which may be considerable. With all the potential problems discussed above, it must be recognized that new technology is always a high risk option. Yet, it is often the preferred option of so many managers in many industries.

New working methods

New working methods are often adopted as a result of new technology, although they may sometimes be introduced for use with existing equipment. Typically they can involve changes to:

- The range of tasks that workers perform.
- The way the tasks are carried out.
- The organization of groups of workers.
- The supervision of workers.
- Working hours.
- Payment schemes.
- Other terms and conditions of employment.

Because of the obvious difficulties of introducing such large-scale changes by agreement, managements do not often attempt them without the stimulus of some other major change such as the introduction of new technology, a change of ownership, or an organizational restructuring, often involving redundancies. Nonetheless, the belief that problems can be solved by such major changes remains strong among many managers. 'If only we didn't do it this way' and 'if only we could start again' are common aspirations in those seeking step changes in performance.

Business Process Reengineering (BPR)

As originally conceived, BPR is a technique that uses a step change approach to performance improvement that incorporates both new technology and ways of working. BPR emerged in the 1990s as a response to the difficult economic conditions prevailing at that time that could enable organizations to take advantage of the advances in IT to achieve dramatic improvements in performance. Its originators, US consultants Hammer and Champy (1993), define BPR as:

> 'The fundamental rethinking and radical redesign of business processes to achieve dramatic improvements in critical, contemporary measures of performance such as costs, quality, service and speed'.

This definition highlights the key features of BPR, namely, that it involves:

- *Fundamental rethinking:* the idea is that managers should look completely anew at the way they manage their operations. There should be no assumptions. They should ignore what already exists and instead think about what they would ideally like to put in place if they were starting with a blank canvas.

- *Radical redesign:* managers should look to completely reinvent their organizations not merely to make improvements on what already exists.

- *Dramatic improvements:* The aim of BPR is to achieve significant performance improvements of the order to 100 per cent, rather than incremental improvements of say 10 per cent.

- *Business processes:* BPR is based on a belief that work should be organized around business processes, as these are the means by which value is added for customers.

This latter point is fundamental to BPR. All organizations use the principle of the division of labour as the basis of organizing work activities. Traditionally, this has manifested itself by structural forms based on specialist departments, or functions such as Design, Production, Marketing, Sales, Accounting, etc. Work moves from one function to another, one department to another. BPR on the other hand is based on the process view of organizations. This sees organizations as a series of processes that each transforms resource inputs into outputs of goods and services. BPR argues that it is these processes that add value for the customer. As such, work should be organized around business processes rather than functions. Organizing around functions merely emphasizes the boundaries within organizations, which are often responsible for adding costs and slowing down the progression of work through the organization, rather than adding value for customers. Figure 14.6 compares the functional view with the process view of an organization.

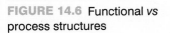
FIGURE 14.6 Functional *vs* process structures

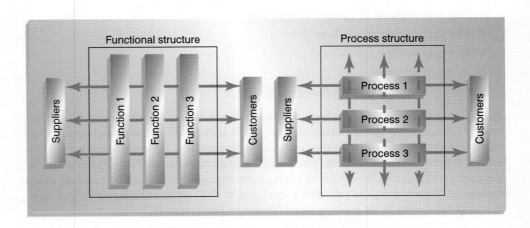

Alongside the new ways of working facilitated by the adoption of a process structure, BPR seeks to capitalize on advances in IT. By allying this to the process perspective, BPR aims to increase the impact of investments in computer power, which have so often failed to achieve the performance improvements envisaged. Proponents of BPR argue that this is because so many applications of IT merely automate existing inefficient processes. BPR aims to avoid this as it is based on the redesign of business processes.

The application of BPR involves:

- *Eliminating* all non-value adding activities.
- *Simplifying* all remaining tasks as much as possible.
- *Integrating* tasks by combining two or more into one.
- *Automating* processes wherever possible through the use of the latest IT.

BPR's popularity peaked in the mid-1990s after which time it became subject to much criticism. For some, it was merely another in a long line of management fads and cure-alls. Others argued that it was a highly risky approach to curing a sick organization; it amounted to the kind of major surgery that might just as easily kill as cure the patient. Also, most BPR initiatives at the time were major cost cutting exercises that resulted in organizational downsizing with significant redundancies within the workforce. Although this was never its prime intention, BPR became synonymous with lay-offs. Indeed many lay-offs were carried out in the name of BPR, even though they were never prompted by the application of BPR principles. Also, as economies around the world moved out of recession into growth, another concern about BPR emerged. Organizations that had undertaken BPR had suffered a double blow; they were left with a demoralized workforce and had little surplus capacity to take advantage of the new growth opportunities. Consequently, the use of BPR, and in particular initiatives making overt use of its title, has considerably diminished. However, its influence remains quite significant, in particular the use of its process perspective, amongst managers looking for step changes in performance.

It is vitally important that organizations do seize opportunities to make step change improvements in performance when they are open to them. For organizations suffering a competitive deficit within their industry, the need can be paramount. However, as discussed above, adopting a step change approach to performance improvement is both risky and difficult. There is, however, a further difficulty in using this approach. Organizations that only attempt to make infrequent step change improvements risk engendering a cynical and defensive attitude to change among their staff. Employees often come to believe that all they have to do is weather this particular storm of change, and then everything will settle down again. This implies that during periods when no major change is happening improvements are not necessary. So often the phrase 'consolidating the changes' comes to mean settling back into complacent ways. The less frequently change occurs, the more dramatic, and indeed traumatic, any such change is likely to be if it is to eliminate a competitive deficit. In this respect infrequent major change can be particularly unproductive, as it prevents the organization thinking of improvement and change as a constant necessity.

Continuous performance improvement

Continuous performance improvement is based on undertaking an on-going series of small incremental improvements.

This is represented diagrammatically in Figure 14.7.

Continuous performance improvement involves a relentless pursuit of improvements, wherever and whenever they can be achieved. In many respects continuous performance improvement is the complete antithesis of step change. Whereas step changes are driven from the top of the organization and are usually technology dominated, continuous performance improvement is driven from the bottom and is

FIGURE 14.7 Continuous
improvement

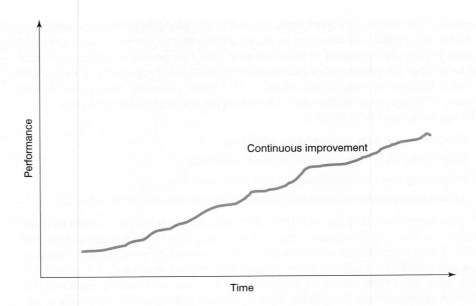

people dominant. Continuous performance improvement seeks to tap the potential for
innovation and creativity within the people that work for the organization. As such it
does not generally require large-scale expenditure, whereas step change usually
requires spending large sums of money.

As discussed in Chapters 9 and 10, continuous performance improvement lies at the
heart of both JIT and TQM. These are themselves the cornerstones of the Toyota
Production System which has been put to such effective use by so many Japanese
manufacturers and extensively copied across the world. Thus, *kaizen* (Japanese for
continuous improvement) has been fundamental to the success of Japanese industry.
Imai (1986) claims that Japan's embrace of *kaizen* betrays a fundamental difference
between Japanese and Western industrial thinking. Westerners tend to believe that in
order to achieve performance improvements money must be spent. If a factory is old,
their first thought is to build a new one. Likewise their instinct is to replace old equipment with the latest technology. The Japanese tend to believe the opposite. Before
they will consider spending on new equipment, they first want to do all they can to
improve the performance of their existing equipment. So they will look to upgrade old
machines and seek new ways of operating them. They will pursue this process of
reform to the limit in order to make the best possible use of existing equipment for
as long as possible. The aim is to get maximum marginal utility out of the existing system. Only when it proves impossible to obtain further improvements out of an existing system will they believe that it is time for more radical action. Their approach is
based on a dictum of 'Do it better; make it better; improve it, even if it isn't broken'.
This is driven by a belief that if you do not do this, you will not be able to compete
with those who do.

Kaizen is essentially a philosophy based on the belief that one should never be
satisfied and always seek to do better. It can only work if it harnesses the creative
energies of all employees. The desire and ability to harness a collective effort for performance improvement seems deeply ingrained in Japanese industry. However, even
in Japan, this does not happen automatically. Techniques are required that will facilitate this. The adoption of quality circles is one obvious way. Quality circles comprise
groups of shop-floor workers who meet regularly to discuss how to solve problems in
their work areas. These are very popular in Japanese factories where they have proved
to be very effective. Importantly, they are empowered to implement any recommendations they come up with. Suggestion schemes are also very actively run in Japan,

CASE STUDY Performance improvement at Ford's Halewood plant

The choice of Ford's Halewood plant near Liverpool, England as the location for the production of Jaguar's new X-type model in 1998, was seen by many as a strange decision. Halewood had been a hotbed of militancy (at one time it held the UK record for the number of car factory strikes) and was making Ford's low-quality Escort model. It seemed more likely to be closed than asked to handle what was acknowledged to be a crucial venture for Jaguar, Ford's luxury car subsidiary.

Yet six years later, Halewood had been transformed to become the plant rated as the best in Ford's global manufacturing network. The company believes it offers a model for how UK manufacturing can compete with low-cost labour from China and Eastern Europe. Its combination of high quality and high productivity is such a success that managers from one of Ford's worst factories are being sent to the Merseyside plant to learn how to listen to their workers. Managers of its underperforming Land Rover factory in Solihull are being told, follow Halewood or face a future with a loss of production, loss of jobs and eventual closure.

So what will happen at Halewood? Certainly a large investment of over £300 million was needed to re-equip the factory with the latest technology to manufacture the 'baby Jag'. But the management team installed by Jaguar faced complex and plentiful challenges. Ford's main emphasis had been on productivity, cost and quality. Jaguar's were the same, but largely in reverse order. Workers were sceptical about management resolve, and were generally adverse to dramatic changes. Meaningful communications between the different layers of the organization were patchy, at best. Six months after the management team's arrival at Halewood, the most important indicators showed the plant was performing even more poorly. They began an intensive dialogue with the unions and set about bridging the communications chasm with the workforce. For the first time in Halewood's history, management oversaw regular quarterly communication sessions with the entire workforce. These involved information sessions regarding important data, quality matrices, developments concerning competitors, etc. Other initiatives included setting up centres of excellence, launching new training initiatives and letting Halewood employees work alongside Jaguar

colleagues elsewhere in the UK. These have over time produced a dramatic improvement in Halewood's performance.

The transformation is illustrated by the willingness of the 3,000 staff to video themselves working to identify improvements. At the height of the plant's militancy, such a suggestion would have prompted workers to walk out for yet another gathering to discuss a strike. This is not to say Halewood has a compliant union, which meekly follows management instructions. Behind the transformation is a reversal of the usual management pyramid; instead of dispensing orders to workers, managers now listen to their ideas. They also share information, something that was anathema to the previous leadership. Managers have had to change as much as workers. 'The attitude has changed completely because everybody is informed', says Cello Ansaldo, a team leader in the press shop. Mr Ansaldo, a Halewood veteran, can examine how well the press shop is performing (productivity is up sharply) and how many accidents there have been (fewer than a third as many as in 2000) on charts posted at the end of his work area. In the past workers were simply told what to do when they turned up each morning, following the practice at the dockyards a few miles down the road. He can also examine plans for a weekend shift due to be introduced in 2007 to cope with extra panels needed to build the new small Land Rover, a replacement for the Freelander. This extra shift, and the extra 1,000 staff who will be taken on to build the next generation Freelander, are the most visible evidence of the success of Halewood.

However, its success means pain elsewhere in the UK. The Land Rover move will result in 1,000 job losses in Solihull, currently the only manufacturing site for the Freelander. Solihull is one of Britain's worst car factories. The offroaders it builds are rated by JD Power as among the least reliable vehicles on sale in the US, at least in part because of poor assembly quality. The intransigence of Solihull's workers was made clear when they rejected a request from the management to stop carrying pens when assembling cars because of the danger of marking the expensive leather seats. That and other changes to working practices, such as not smoking or eating in the new vehicles, have now been accepted – but only after the loss of the Freelander.

Steve Coltate, former plant manager at Halewood, has been made manufacturing director of the Solihill factory, with a brief to push through the same changes that repaired Halewood. These will be familiar to students of Japanese industry: *kaizen,* or continuous improvement; the *andon* system allowing workers to stop the line if they have a problem; JIT delivery of parts to the line and giving teams of workers control of their own assembly process. Toyota's famous system of production has been copied shamelessly.

Yet, none of these quite explains how Halewood managed to be rated by Ford as its best factory. Peter Mircetic, head of Halewood's training centre, says success comes down to a change of ethos. Managers now have 'coaching' role, not just giving instructions. Solihull students at Halewood had better hope they can learn. If they fail, not only their jobs, but many others in Western Europe, could be on the line.

(Based on the article 'Ford's new model shows road ahead' by James Mackintosh, at www.ft.com published 15 April 2004, with additional material from 'Jaguar Comes To Halewood: The Story Of A Turnaround' by Luk Van Wassenhove and Ramina Samii at http://knowledge.insead.edu/abstract.cfm?ct=9690; both downloaded 1 November 2006)

Questions (Suggested answers can be found on the companion website www.thomsonlearning.co.uk/barnes)

1 Is Halewood's performance improvement an example of step change or continuous improvement?

2 How have Ford and Jaguar used benchmarking to drive performance improvements?

3 What performance standards have Ford and Jaguar been using in their operations?

with ideas being evaluated and implemented quickly if approved. In this way workers can see that their contributions are valued and acted upon. This improves motivation and encourages them to make further recommendations.

As discussed in Chapter 9, one of the aims of JIT is to eliminate *miri* (excess: producing more than is required), *muda* (waste: in all its forms) and *mura* (unevenness:

in the flow of materials, parts and goods). Under the principles of *kaizen,* these aims can be translated into a set of 'ultimate' performance standards, namely:

1 *Zero defects:* absolute conformance to specification.
2 *Zero set-up time:* to maximize flexibility, responsiveness and system availability.
3 *Zero handling:* moving materials adds cost, not value, and should be eliminated.
4 *Zero batch size:* to maximize system flexibility.
5 *Zero breakdown:* these waste time and cause inventory to build up.
6 *Zero lead time:* to maximize responsiveness.
7 *Zero surging:* to prevent stock build-up due to fluctuating operating speeds.

These seven zeros provide the drivers for continuous improvement. Although these objectives can never be achieved, they can be used as the basis for setting more realistic targets as short-term goals. Once a specific target has been achieved, a new more exacting target can be set. Targets are set and reset in this way, in an effort to move ever closer to the ultimate performance standards of the seven zeros.

In contrast to infrequent but dramatic step changes, the approach of continuous performance improvement seeks to embed change into the organizational culture. In this way change becomes the norm. Consequently, when major changes are required, they will be less difficult to achieve than in an organization in which change rarely occurs.

Any advocacy of continuous improvement as the means of achieving performance improvement should not be taken as an argument not to undertake step change improvements whenever possible. Organizations that do not seek to benefit from advances in technology and new working methods are almost certainly doomed to see their performance outstripped in the longer-term by competitors that do. There will always be a limit to performance improvement achieved from existing equipment and current working methods. However, as discussed above, relying solely on step change as the means of achieving performance may well result in disappointment. By not seeking continuous improvement in between the step change, the likelihood is that levels of performance will deteriorate during those periods. Consequently, the actual level of performance achieved over time will be less than that planned. Figure 14.8 illustrates this point.

The best results are likely to be achieved by using a combination of step changes and continuous improvement (see Figure 14.9).

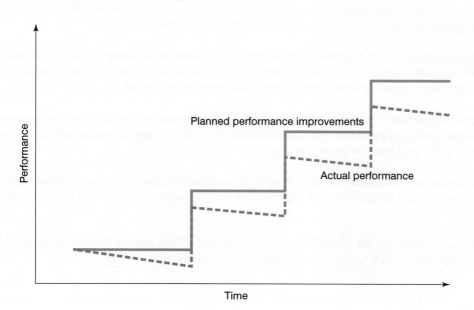

FIGURE 14.8 Planned *vs* actual performance improvement through step changes

FIGURE 14.9 Combining step changes and continuous improvements

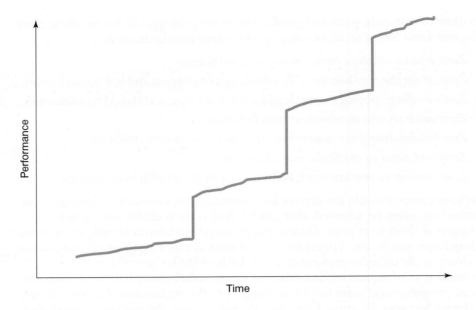

SUMMARY OF KEY POINTS

Performance measurement plays a central role in operations management as it enables the organization to quantify the efficiency and effectiveness of its actions. It is also integral to the planning and control cycle. It is also strategically important as it is part of the means of converting strategic intentions to action.

One of the purposes of performance measurement is to change people's behaviour. Thus, care must be taken to avoid encouraging behaviours that can lead to unintended consequences.

The three Es (economy, efficiency and effectiveness) model classifies performance measures on the basis of the transformation model of operations.

It is generally considered that a performance measurement system needs to have multi-dimensional performance measures comprising financial and non-financial, internal and external and backward and forward looking measures and link operational performance to strategic objectives.

Performance standards provide the means of comparing current levels of performance with those desired. They can be internally derived (based on past performance or internal targets) or externally derived (from an analysis of competitors' performance, best practice or market requirements).

Benchmarking is the practice of comparing the performance of an operation with that of similar operations in another location. There are three main approaches to benchmarking: internal benchmarking, competitive benchmarking and best practice benchmarking.

Performance improvement initiatives need to consider the scale and scope of the performance improvement required, the priorities for performance improvement and the approach to making the performance improvement.

Performance improvements can be undertaken in one of two ways: step change or continuous improvement. The best approach is likely to combine the use of both approaches.

Step change can involve new technology and/or new working methods.

Business Process Reengineering (BPR) is the fundamental rethinking and radical redesign of business processes to achieve dramatic improvements in critical, contemporary measures of performance such as costs, quality, service and speed. It uses a step change approach to performance improvement that incorporates both new technology and new ways of working.

Continuous improvement (*kaizen*) is based on undertaking an on-going series of small incremental improvements.

EXERCISES (Suggested answers can be found on the companion website www.thomsonlearning.co.uk/barnes)

WWW.

1 Why is performance measurement important to operations and strategic management?

2 Explain how a performance measurement system can be used to link operational level activities to an organization's strategic objectives.

3 List as many examples as you can of unanticipated (or even perverse) outcomes that have been the result of organizations changing their performance measures.

4 Why are the measures traditionally used to assess the performance of many operations (e.g. unit costs of production, labour productivity, machine utilization, output volumes) now considered to be inadequate?

5 Suggest suitable measures of economy, efficiency and effectiveness that might be used to assess the performance of the operations in the following organizations:
   a A budget fast food outlet
   b A computer manufacturer
   c A management consultancy
   d A theme park

6 Use the Balanced Scorecard to suggest a set of performance measures for the following types of organization:
   a A manufacturer of domestic appliances
   b A hospital
   c An airline
   d A university

7 What are the benefits and difficulties associated with the different types of benchmarking?

8 Choose a well-known organization (or one that you know well). Which other organizations should they choose for competitive and best practice benchmarking? What performance measures should they use, and why?

9 For a customer service operation that you know well as a customer, construct a performance-importance matrix and identify the aspects of performance that it should concentrate its performance improvement activities on.

10 Compare and contrast BPR and *kaizen* as methods of achieving performance improvements.

CASE STUDY EXERCISE Celine Restaurant

Introduction

Celine Restaurant is a fine dining restaurant located in the centre of Athens. The restaurant is famous for its innovative fusion cuisine and its excellent quality service. However, achieving and maintaining high performance and customer satisfaction is never simple or easy. Mr Argyros, the owner and executive manager of the restaurant, knows well that managing performance needs appropriate measures. However, unlike many in his business, he believes that the calculation of the daily sales to total expenses ratio, used by many restaurants as a key performance metric, is far from adequate. This inputs to outputs ratio is a simple measure of aggregate performance that summarizes restaurant activity. However, it is not capable of providing an understanding of how the results have been achieved or identifying the cause of any problems. That depends on having the performance measures for several sub-systems which contribute to the aggregate performance of the restaurant.

The restaurant performance management system

Mr Argyros conceptualizes his restaurant's operations as three interconnected major sub-systems (Figure 14.10), each one contributing differently to the aggregate restaurant performance. First, the food

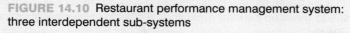

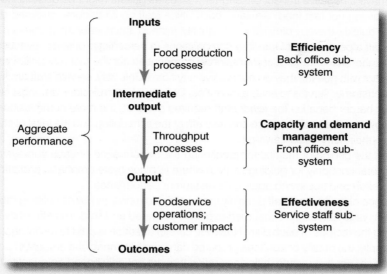

FIGURE 14.10 Restaurant performance management system: three interdependent sub-systems

production sub-system is a back office operation responsible for procuring the food materials and transforming them into dishes. These outputs rely on the capabilities of the kitchen. However, dishes do not represent restaurant revenues unless the next two sub-systems translate them into sales and positive customer experiences. The role of the front office, the second sub-system, is to take guests' reservations or walk-ins, allocate them to utilize the restaurant's table capacity appropriately (for example, ensuring that a table for four is not occupied by a couple for a long time, thereby loosing the opportunity to make higher sales from this table capacity). It is also the role of the front office to promote the dishes of the day and encourage wine orders whilst customers are waiting to be seated in the bar area or when making their orders. The third sub-system comprises the restaurant's service staff, whose role is to manage the guests' experience in an efficient yet effective way, ensuring that customers are satisfied so that they will return and recommend the restaurant to others. Service staff performance is related to the speed and quality of service. The meal experience for customers (taking of order, delivery of first dish, cleaning up, delivery of second dish, etc.) needs to be managed appropriately. Guests will not want to wait too long, but they will also want sufficient time to enjoy their meal. Additionally, the restaurant will want to free up their table so that it can be used for further customers.

Performance metrics in the three sub-systems

Breaking down operations into three sub-systems, has helped the restaurant management better understand how aggregate performance is achieved. Measuring and monitoring intermediate performance can help explain changes in total performance and enable the root causes of problems to be identified so that they can be addressed appropriately. Despite this apparent simplicity, the restaurant management recognizes that the performance and operations of each sub-system are highly interlinked and interdependent. For example, the timely delivery of dishes to guests depends on the production efficiency of back office staff and the effective communication between staff in different sub-systems. Similarly, the ability of front office staff to sell and book a table more than once depends on the efficiency of service staff to manage the meal duration and of production staff to produce the appropriate number of dishes in a timely fashion.

Consequently, although Mr Argyros has to identify different metrics for monitoring the performance of each sub-system, he also appreciates that the use of these intermediate performance metrics for rewarding and motivating staff can be dysfunctional and can have detrimental effects on overall performance. For example, staff bonuses that are based on daily revenues can negatively impact long-term performance, as there would be an incentive to speed up the meal experience in order to serve more guests each day. However, this could have a negative impact on long-term sales as guests might be dissatisfied as their expectation is for fine dining not fast food. Similarly, back office staff could become stressed due to having to prepare food too quickly, thereby diminishing its quality. Instead, the restaurant operates a reward system, which gives all staff a percentage of the daily commissions (a percentage of sales revenues). Kitchen staff are allocated a higher percentage of commission to compensate for the fact that unlike service staff, who are in direct contact with guests, they do not receive any tips. In this way, service staff are further motivated to provide good customer service to ensure more tips. Division of commissions amongst all staff motivates everyone to work harder because the fewer staff required per shift, the more commissions per person. In this way, staff know that their performance can also affect the scheduling and the level of staff, which in turn has an impact on their commission awards.

Consequently, the choice of metrics for monitoring the performance of each sub-system and its staff are critically important not only for guiding staff on where to place more emphasis and efforts, but also for motivating team effort and improving aggregate restaurant performance.

The performance of the kitchen staff is mainly measured and monitored by calculating ratios such as kilos of potatoes, meat, vegetables, etc. consumed to dishes prepared and sold. The efficiency of such ratios is checked by using the recipes of each dish. However, careful attention is paid to the impact of several other factors. For example, the quality of potatoes procured can crucially impact the amount of potatoes required for producing a dish. For this reason, efficiency ratios that are not only based on quantitative metrics (e.g. kilos, litres of oil, etc.) but also on financial metrics (e.g. procurement expenses) are used for benchmarking performance. An assumption is made that better quality potatoes (and so higher procurement prices) can result in higher production efficiency ratios, as less scrap is produced.

Service staff are trained to accept and take full responsibility for the success of the service encounter. Mr Argyros puts a lot of emphasis on the ability of staff to meet customer service requirements, answer queries on the constituencies of dishes, and offer suggestions on selecting dishes and wines, in order to meet sales and service targets. Performance is heavily monitored through several qualitative metrics and guests' comments received through the guests' feedback book, mystery guests' visits and the guests' complaints forms. In addition, quantitative performance metrics are also monitored by tracking the duration of meals. Data are taken from the restaurant's Electronic Point of Sales System (EPOS). This enables all guests' interactions to be recorded, including the time of a guest's order, the time the dish was prepared and then delivered and the time of payment. However, the management does not place too much emphasis on such quantitative data, preferring to consider them mainly in conjunction with customers' feedback, as such data may ignore many mitigating factors such as guests waiting for a friend to arrive, or simply chatting whilst occupying a table. Management intervention has taken place only in one instance when statistical trends in the duration of meals indicated that delays were occurring when a particular dessert was ordered. The back office reported that the cake concerned had to be defrosted and processed in a specific way, so that when many other orders had to be taken care of, oven capacity was insufficient to handle this requirement. Consequently, this cake was taken off the menu.

The occupancy rates and revenues per seat rather than per table are used for monitoring the performance of front office reservation staff. This is because front office staff need to take crucial decisions, sometimes requiring a trade-off between different market segments, when allocating restaurant capacity. Such decisions can crucially affect the performance of the restaurant and, of course, the reward level of all restaurant staff. For example, when deciding whether to accept a group reservation for a specific day, front office staff need to use historical data about sales on that day of the week. For example, for a Friday night they could decide to either:

a not accept the reservation, because the tables could normally be sold easily producing high independent sales, or

b accept the reservation but require a guarantee from the group that their menu choice would compensate for the independent sales lost, or

c try to persuade the group to book at another time on a quieter day of the week.

Mr Argyros has decided that revenue per available seat hour (RevPash) is the best measure that he can use for monitoring the aggregate performance of the restaurant. He also believes that the most appropriate metric for monitoring the utilization of restaurant capacity and increasing revenues is available seat hours. However, achieving high revenue per available seat requires a team effort amongst front office, service and back office staff. Consequently, Mr Argyros operates a reward system based on all staff getting a bonus when the monthly targets for RevPash are achieved.

—Marianna Sigala

Questions (Suggested answers can be found on the companion website www.thomsonlearning.co.uk/barnes)

WWW.

1 What are the advantages and disadvantages of the performance measurement system used by the Celine restaurant?

2 Critically evaluate the behavioural impacts of the Celine Restaurant's performance measurement system.

3 Would you recommend that the restaurant incorporate any additional measures into its performance measurement system?

4 How could Mr Argyros use the restaurant's performance measurement system to improve performance?

References

Hammer, M. and Champy, J. (1993) *Re-engineering the Corporation,* New York: Harper Collins.

Imai, M. (1986) *Kaizen: The key to Japan's competitive success,* New York: McGraw-Hill.

Kaplan, R. and Norton, D. (1992) 'The Balanced Scorecard – Measures that Drive Performance', *Harvard Business Review,* January–February, 71–79.

Kaplan, R. and Norton, D. (1996) 'Using the Balanced Scorecard as a Strategic Management System', *Harvard Business Review,* January–February, 75–86.

Neely, A., Gregory, M. and Platts, K. (1995) 'Performance measurement system design: a literature review and research agenda', *International Journal of Operations and Production Management* 15(4):80–116.

Neely, A., Mills, J., Platts, K., Richards, H. and Bourne, M. (2002) *Getting the measure of your business,* Cambridge: Cambridge University Press.

Schmenner, R.W. and Vollmann, T.E. (1994) 'Performance Measures: Gaps, False Alarms, and the Usual Suspects', *International Journal of Operations and Production Management* 14(12):58–69.

Slack, N. (1994) 'The importance-performance matrix as a determinant of improvement priority', *International Journal of Operations and Production Management* 14(5):59–75.

Taylor, F.W. (1911) *The principles of scientific management,* New York: Harper.

Voss, C.A., Ahlstrom, P. and Blackmon, K. (1998) 'Diagnostic Benchmarking and Manufacturing Improvement', *Proceeding of the 5th European Operations Management Association Conference,* Dublin June 14–17.

Additional reading

De Toni, A. and Tonchia, S. (2001) 'Performance Measurement Systems: Models, Characteristics and Measures', *International Journal of Operations and Production Management,* 21(1/2):46–70.

Kaplan, R. and Norton, D. (1992) 'The Balanced Scorecard – Measures that Drive Performance', *Harvard Business Review,* January–February, 71–79.

Neely, A., Gregory, M. and Platts, K. (1995) 'Performance measurement system design: a literature review and research agenda', *International Journal of Operations and Production Management* 15(4):80–116.

www.

Useful websites

http://www.kaizen-institute.com The Kaizen Institute is an organization that provides consulting services and the website contains useful practical advice.

http://www.benchnet.com The Benchmarking Exchange website, containing useful practitioner advice and information about benchmarking.

http://www.ebenchmarking.com The Benchmarking Network conducts benchmarking training and research. Useful practitioner information on benchmarking.

http://www.balancedscorecard.org The Balanced Scorecard Institute provides training and consulting services in applying best practices in balanced scorecard. Useful practitioner information on the BSC.

http://www.som.cranfield.ac.uk/som/research/centres/cbp/pma The Performance Measurement Association is an academic-practitioner association devoted to advancing knowledge in performance measurement and management.

PART FIVE

THE FUTURE OF OPERATIONS MANAGEMENT

PART FIVE

The final section of this book, Part Five, consists solely of Chapter 15. The purpose of this chapter is to consider what issues are likely to affect operations management in the future. It does this by assessing the implications of current trends in operations management and by identifying emerging issues likely to be of relevance to the future of operations management. It does this in full acceptance that most assessments of the future are more often wrong than right. However, in a fast changing world it is certainly better to give some thought to the future in order to be better prepared for whatever that future may bring.

CHAPTER 15

CURRENT TRENDS AND EMERGING ISSUES

INTRODUCTION

The purpose of this closing chapter is to consider what issues are likely to affect operations management in the future. It will do this in two ways. First, it will draw together some of the strands from previous chapters to review some of the most important issues that continue to affect operations management at the moment. Second, it will speculate about likely future trends by identifying issues that have recently emerged with the potential to have a major impact on operations management. Most visions of the future are usually wrong. Nonetheless, thinking about the future is a worthwhile task as doing so must better prepare us to meet the challenges that we are bound to face. Our view of the future is inevitably framed, and often constrained, by our views of the past and our understanding of the present. The only real certainty is that the world will change in ways that will be difficult to predict.

LEARNING OBJECTIVES

On completion of this chapter, you should be able to:

Assess the implications of current trends in operations management.

Discuss the likely impact of emerging issues on the future of operations management.

AN INTERNATIONAL PERSPECTIVE ON OPERATIONS MANAGEMENT

The driving force behind this book is the conviction that as business organizations around the world become more interconnected, operations management must adopt a more international perspective. Chapter 3 explored some of the major external environmental forces (political, economic, socio-cultural and, especially, technological) that are driving globalization. As Chapter 4 noted, these are providing both market-seeking and resource-seeking opportunities that make it almost inevitable that most organizations have to operate internationally to a greater or lesser extent.

This increasingly international context presents significant new challenges for operations management. One of these key challenges is encapsulated in the often repeated exhortation to globalizers to 'think global and act local'. This phrase neatly captures the dilemma faced by operations managers seeking ways of balancing these apparently contradictory goals. For how can you simultaneously achieve efficiency and effectiveness both globally and locally? There are no simple solutions to this dilemma. Operations managers have to combine and balance the potential actions that they can take in both the structural and infrastructural decision areas of operations management to form a coherent and consistent operations strategy for the unique international context in which their organization operates. Some of the key issues of internationalization affecting these decision areas were discussed in turn in Chapters 5 through 14. For example:

Chapter 5: Facilities considered the issue of where organizations should locate their operations. More and more organizations, service providers as much as manufacturers no longer have to locate their facilities in their country of origin. They often have almost unlimited choice about where in the world some of their operations could be based.

Chapter 6: Capacity noted how the productive capacity of existing facilities should be used to meet customer demand and how and when additional capacity should be added to meet increasing demand. Internationally, this requires an assessment of the country of origin of the demand and from which country supply to meet that demand should be sourced.

Chapter 7: Technology discussed how choices of process technology need to take into account the volume and variety required from a production facility, the existing technology in use at that location and the level of maturity of the technology. Transferring technology into a new location requires an assessment both of the transferability of the technology and the appropriateness of the context in which it will be operated.

Chapter 8: The supply network observed that supply networks have become more important as organizations outsource more of their inputs and more global as organizations increasingly source more of those inputs from outside of their national boundaries. This makes supply chain management increasingly important yet increasingly difficult activity.

Chapter 9: Planning and control noted the different approaches used in order to match supply and demand. This is a challenging task when focused on a single location; especially if the operation's output is intended to meet demand from different countries and inputs are sourced from yet more countries. Planning and control is even more challenging when it also requires the co-ordination of operations located in different countries.

Chapter 10: Quality considered how different approaches to managing quality evolved over time in different countries to form a generally accepted model of quality management. However, despite this, national differences still

CASE STUDY The Santa Ship

When the *Emma Maersk* docked in Felixstowe on the East coast of England on 5 November 2006, many people breathed a huge sigh of relief. Christmas in the UK had not been cancelled. For the vessel dubbed the 'Santa Ship' was offloading 45,000 tonnes of seasonal goods from China.

The *Guardian* newspaper claimed that the 3,000 containers offloaded contained 'mountains of crackers, toys and games as well as decorations, calendars, wrapping paper, food and every imaginable gift'. Its manifest, they said, included electronic dinosaurs, dancing gorillas, radio-controlled cars and motorbikes, electric guitars and drumsticks, soft toys, pinball machines, computers, poker tables, bingo sets, drum kits, electronic toys and pre-school building blocks. Seventeen of its 40 foot containers were full only of sudoku games, nursery rhyme books, jigsaws and soft toys. Christmas decorations amounting to 1,886,000 were loaded in one container; 40,000 rechargeable batteries in another; 12,800 MP3 players in another. Edibles included thousands of frozen chickens, 150 tonnes of New Zealand lamb, pumpkins, 10 tonnes of mussels, 22,280 kg of Vietnamese tea, along with unspecified quantities of swordfish, tuna, noodles, biscuits, jams and 'lunch boxes'. There were potato mashers, slotted spoons and graters to cook with, toothpicks, leather sofas to recline on, new spectacles to watch new televisions by and pyjamas to go to bed in. Pets were not forgotten either, with 138,000 tins of cat food and mountains of dog food!

The *Emma Mearsk*'s safe arrival should have been greeted with cheers of relief from children, parents and retailers throughout the land. If anything had happened to the vessel en route, the British Christmas 2006 would have been much less festive. Being a brand new vessel, the trip to England was part of its maiden voyage, the safety of the vessel should not have been questioned. But then they said the *Titanic* was unsinkable! Measuring 397 metres long, 56 metres wide and 61 metres high, the *Emma Maersk* is the world's largest container vessel. It is able to carry 11,000 containers.

Some see the ship as a symbol of the way that global manufacturing has shifted from Europe and the US to China as that country has benefited massively from the trade that has ensued from its entry into

the World Trade Organization. According to the Department of Trade and Industry, Britain imported a record £16 billion of goods from China in 2006, whilst exporting just over £2.8 billion. The UK accounts for only around 2 per cent of China's trade. China is now the fourth largest economy in the world, and the largest manufacturer and exporter of Christmas goods.

(Source material www.guardian.co.uk, www.maerskline.com and www.ft.com)

Questions (Suggested answers can be found on the companion website www.thomsonlearning.co.uk/barnes)

1 What are the most important challenges for UK and other European retailers if most manufacturing goes off-shore?

2 Is it sensible for UK retailers to rely so heavily on supplies from one source and in one ship?

3 How could UK retailers relying on supplies from the *Emma Maersk* have mitigated the risks to their business operations?

remain between what is the most suitable and effective approach to quality management in different countries.

Chapter 11: Work organization noted the impact of structure and culture on the way that workers are brought together to perform work tasks. National culture is an important facet of organizational culture, and is increasingly important in a globalized business world with more diverse workforces.

Chapter 12: Human resource management considered the various activities involved in managing people in organizations (including recruitment and selection, training and development, job design, reward and remuneration). These are all affected by national differences (in culture, legislation, workforce skills, etc.) which pose particular challenges for international organizations seeking to co-ordinate their human resource management practices and also in their employment of expatriate staff.

Chapter 13: New product development considered the vital activity of developing new products and services. For international organizations this poses the additional challenges of how to develop products to meet the differing requirements of customers in different countries and how to co-ordinate NPD activity across different locations.

Chapter 14: Performance measurement noted different approaches to managing performance in operations. For international organizations this poses particular difficulties in terms of determining appropriate benchmarks for operations in different countries.

However, whatever combination of actions are taken, no operations strategy is likely to prove successful if the operations are thought of as some kind of a 'black box' that can be managed in isolation from the other activities of the organization. Although operations management is often thought of as a mundane activity, it is irrevocably connected to what may be considered to be the more attractive and exciting aspects of business such as marketing, corporate finance or strategy. Yet, no matter how brilliant the marketing campaign, it is only operations that can provide the goods and services which can lead to delighted customers. However creative the financing, it is only through the efforts of operations that adequate financial returns will be achieved. Even if the strategic plan is brilliant, it is only through the actions of operations that a strategy can be implemented. Operations are the heart of any organization as organizational success relies on its activities as they produce the goods and deliver the services required by its customers. Operations must therefore be managed in close collaboration with the other business functions. Thus, operations managers need to understand the issues facing the whole organization so that they can articulate their concerns and develop strategies jointly with managers from other functional areas that will make for organizational success.

CURRENT TRENDS

Recent years have seen a number of changes in the practice of operations management, which has been reflected in the content of operations management as an academic discipline. The most notable of these are the following.

Moving beyond the factory

The roots of operations management lie in manufacturing and for many years the subject focused almost exclusively on what went on within the confines of the factory. This had the benefit of enabling the development of very specific and detailed expertise about the production of physical goods. In particular, it enabled very many mathematically-based tools and techniques to be developed that could help in vitally important factory tasks such as production planning and scheduling, inventory control and quality control. However, restricting operations management to the consideration of factory-based activities alone is increasingly recognized as being ultimately limiting in two ways.

First, the performance of operations is affected by what goes on outside of the factory as much as by what goes on within it. The performance of suppliers and other supply network partners (e.g. intermediaries) can significantly influence the extent to which an organization's operations can satisfy its customers. Thus, supply network relations are increasingly recognized as being vitally important in operations management. (This issue was discussed in detail in Chapter 8 and is considered further on p. 436.) Within the organization, interactions with the other functional areas of business also have a significant impact on the performance of operations. As noted above, customer satisfaction will never be achieved if the marketing department creates expectations that the operations department cannot meet. Similarly, the operations function cannot operate effectively unless the finance department is able to arrange adequate funding and the human resource management department attract and retain workers with the right skills and attitude (discussed in Chapter 12). As discussed in Chapter 2, functional level strategies (for operations, marketing, finance, human resource management, etc.) need to be consistent one with another and with the organization's business strategy if they are to contribute to achieving a competitive advantage. In the past (and perhaps too often today) many organizations consider the prime role of operations as being concerned with cost cutting and the realization of efficiency gains in order to achieve the lowest possible operating costs. However as also discussed in Chapter 2, viewing operations in this way severely constrains its strategic role. As not all organizations compete on the basis of price alone, operations can only be used strategically as a competitive weapon if its performance objectives are aligned with those of the organization's business strategy. These may well require operations to meet customer requirements in other aspects of performance (e.g. quality, flexibility, dependability and speed) and not just cost alone.

Second, the academic study of operations management should not be restricted solely to the production of physical goods because of the decreasing importance of manufacturing to most national economies. As noted in Chapter 1, in most advanced economies manufacturing typically represents less than 20 per cent of GDP. Ignoring the growing importance of service sectors of national economies would increasingly sideline the subject of operations management (and those who teach it) within the business school curriculum.

The growing importance of services

As noted above, service sectors of most national economies have continued to grow in importance. It is invariably the case that as a country develops economically, so the proportion of its GDP from services increases; similarly the numbers employed in services increases. In the USA, the most developed country in the world, around 78 per cent of GDP and 80 per cent of employment in 2005 was from services (BEA, 2007 and CIA, 2007). In other developed countries, services are similarly important to economic activity; with services as a proportion of GDP in 2005, being 76 per cent in the UK, 73 per cent in Japan and 70 per cent in Germany, for example. In developing countries, the services sector is much less important, with for example; services being 54 per cent of GDP in India and 40 per cent in China in 2005 (CIA, 2007). However, in all countries the figure is rising, apparently inexorably. It would be odd indeed if operations management as a subject were to ignore this increasingly important sector of most national economies. Operations management academics have therefore been giving service operations much more attention in recent years. They have done this in two ways. First, by seeking to apply concepts and techniques developed in manufacturing contexts to service environments. Examples of this include the application of lean thinking to services such as hospitals and statistical quality control techniques to monitor performance in sectors such as hospitality and air travel through the use of customer feedback questionnaires. Second, by developing new concepts and techniques that take account of the specific characteristics of service operations. Examples of this include the quality gaps model described in Chapter 10 and queue management techniques discussed in Chapter 7. Both of these trends seem set to continue as services seem set to continue to grow in economic importance. Therefore, it is likely that greater consideration will continue to be given to service issues within the operations management discipline for some time to come.

The increased importance of the supply network

The concept of the supply network was introduced in Chapter 1 and discussed in depth in Chapter 8. For many years there has been a trend for organizations to outsource a greater proportion of their inputs. This seems to have accelerated recently, with more large organizations transferring many of their in-house operations to upstream suppliers and reconfiguring their business models on newly defined core competencies which offer the prospect of greater added value. In particular, many organizations have been making greater use of off-shoring, especially to reduce costs. This looks set to continue with more and more organizations becoming part of international supply networks. The management of supply networks has thus become both more complex and more important. However, the greater use of off-shoring typically causes a physical lengthening of the supply chain. Perversely, this runs counter to much of the lean manufacturing practice developed with such success by Japanese manufacturing companies. Their usual approach is to maximize the use of local sourcing, often requiring their suppliers to site their factory, or at least a warehouse, adjacent to the plant that they serve. Lean supply principles emphasize the importance of integrating suppliers' operations into the organization's own supply network. Doing this when a supplier is located in another country, potentially separated by thousands of miles and operating in a different time zone is bound to pose a significant challenge. It is difficult to see that the management of supply networks will become less important in the foreseeable future. Indeed it seems likely to increase in importance. It is similarly difficult to envisage any diminution of the internationalization of supply networks, so the challenge of integration seems set to remain a specific issue for some time to come.

The increased importance of ICT

As discussed in Chapter 3, the ICT revolution is continuing apace. The processing power of computers continues to increase apparently unabated. This, coupled with the ubiquitous presence of the Internet is shrinking distance, enabling people to communicate and share information very cheaply across the globe. Use of Internet-enabled ICT thus offers a means of overcoming some of the problems arising from the physical separation of organizations within a supply network. Whilst technology mediated communications cannot replace face-to-face human interaction, it does seem to offer the means of addressing some of the challenges of integration discussed immediately above. In particular, unlimited quantities of information can be exchanged instantaneously irrespective of time and place. In the same way, these technologies enable organizations to communicate directly with the end consumers, both organizations and individuals, of their goods and services. This presents both significant customer service challenges and opportunities for producers that are perhaps as yet not fully understood by operations management academics.

The development and use of Internet-based ICTs show every sign of increasing in the foreseeable future. Although the consequences are often unpredictable, a number of consequences of relevance to operations management seem likely:

- *Service operations will become more international:* In the past, most services had a high degree of simultaneity, that is, their outputs were consumed at the point of production. This made them difficult, if not impossible to trade between countries, as providers needed to be physically present at the point of consumption. However, Internet-enabled ICT is changing this, reducing or removing the need for the service provider and consumer to be in physical contact. Similarly, increasingly, many tangible aspects of services can be digitized (e.g. the written word, music, moving images) making it possible to deliver them electronically from a distance. This is prompting two trends. First, operations which were previously thought of as front office, because of the requirement for both customer and service provider to be in the same location, can now be transferred to the back office. It is the information that travels rather than the people. Second, there is now a reduced need for front office and back office operations to be co-located. This means that there are ongoing opportunities to off-shore back office operations to areas of either low cost or high skilled workers. This means that more and more services are capable of being traded internationally. At present only 19 per cent of world trade is in commercial services (WTO, 2006). This looks set to grow over the foreseeable future, meaning that managing operations of all kinds, whether manufacturing or services will become increasingly international in scope.

- *More services will be mass customized:* ICT enables the marginal costs of some activities to fall to almost zero, facilitating more mass service provision. For example the cost of delivering one more copy of a piece of recorded music is much lower (almost zero) compared to transfer on a CD. Greater mass production of services allows more production to take place remote from the customer, and yet at the same time facilitate more direct transactions between provider and consumer. This is opening the way for services to follow manufacturing towards more mass customization (discussed in Chapters 4 and 13). This is particularly the case where those services can be delivered on-line. This provides a challenge to the management of service operations, which have traditionally been seen as having to be either low cost mass production or high cost customized production operations.

- *Services will increasingly be used to differentiate products:* The cost of many manufactured goods has been falling due to off-shoring of manufacturing operations to low labour cost countries. This trend has seen the prices of many mass produced goods continue to fall, making it increasingly difficult for manufacturers to achieve satisfactory levels of profits. More and more suppliers of physical goods are therefore looking to use the provision of accompanying services as the means of differentiating their offerings in order to overcome the effective commoditization of their products. Offering an appropriate package of goods and services gives providers the opportunity to gain a competitive advantage by differentiating their offering from competitors and by customizing their offering to specific customer segments or even individual customers. The Internet enables providers to communicate directly with individual customers, enabling an increasing amount of this service element to be provided at low cost and at a distance.

The use of Internet-based ICTs in business is generally referred to as e-business and was discussed in Chapter 7. New and innovative ways of undertaking e-business are being developed all the time. This trend seems set to continue. Managing operations in the information age is as yet not clearly defined and its challenge only now being addressed. Similarly, the academic study of operations management in e-businesses is as yet under-developed. Much work remains to be done to gain better understandings of the implications of managing operations in the information age.

EMERGING ISSUES

In this final section, a number of apparently emerging issues that are likely to present significant challenges for many organizations are identified and discussed. This is inevitably a somewhat speculative exercise. However, it will be interesting for readers to consider the extent to which these conjectures have impacted operations management in the period subsequent to their inclusion in this book. There are also, perhaps inevitably, likely to be issues not identified here that subsequently do turn out to be important.

Low cost labour

In the last decade or so, arguably the most important issue in operations management has been marked by the increased use of off-shoring to achieve reductions in labour costs. In particular, China, the world's most populous nation, has achieved high levels of economic growth largely on the back of its ability to offer an almost unlimited supply of low cost labour. This has made China the workshop of the world for low cost manufactured goods. To some extent, India has been able to emulate this growth through its ability to mobilize large numbers of workers in the telecommunications and computer services industries. In India's case these are highly educated workers with relevant skills who can be employed for a fraction of the cost of similarly skilled workers in advanced economies. However, the challenge for China, and possibly India, is what happens when living standards and wages rise to such a level as to threaten their competitiveness as low cost labour destinations. This is certainly already starting to happen in the case of China, with some inwards investments starting to move away from the relatively high cost areas in the Shanghai region and the Pearl River Delta (near Hong Kong) to lower cost areas further west. Also, some manufacturing operations are moving from China to lower labour cost destinations in South East Asia. Examples in 2006, cited by the *Economist* (2007), include:

- Intel, the computer chipmaker invested US$1 billion in a new factory in Vietnam, thereby committing as much money to Vietnam in one year as it had to China in the previous ten years.

- Flextronics, the contract electronics manufacturer, chose the Johor region of Malaysia for its latest investment, a M$400 million (US$110 million) factory to make computer printers for HP.

- Yue Yuen, the Hong Kong-based shoemaker, has been diverting production of its trainers and casual footwear (for brands like Nike and Adidas) to Indonesia rather than China and Vietnam.

As discussed in Chapter 7, labour costs are only one consideration in choosing a location for facilities. However, the issue that emerges is that organizations seeking low cost labour are likely to be faced with having to continually move their operations from one location to another. Assuming that new locations with suitably low wage costs can be found, the operations management challenge for such organizations is how to manage such investments. Opening new facilities creates start-up costs, not only in terms of the process technology, but also in terms of workers, who have to be recruited, trained and organized to operate and maintain that technology. Similarly, expertise in planning and controlling, managing quality, and other operations management needs to be developed at any new location. In any new situation, it is likely to take longer to develop the necessary organizational learning skills which can form the basis of future capabilities. Setting up new facilities implies creating new supply arrangements or, at best, disrupting existing arrangements. Any gain from reduced labour costs clearly needs to be off-set against the potential additional costs from the disruption and start-up costs of operating in a new location. In some instances opening new facilities, also implies closing down or downsizing existing facilities. Such activities also bring their own specific challenges. For operations managers in organizations committed to seeking out the lowest possible labour costs, the challenge is to develop ways of managing transferring operations from one location to another, including starting up and closing down operations in the most effective manner.

Population changes

The world is currently witnessing some significant changes in its population. Many advanced economies especially in Europe, Japan and Russia have ageing populations and declining birth rates which will lead to a decline in the overall population in some countries in the longer-term. In the shorter-term, at least, there will be a decline in native populations of working age in some countries. Left unaltered, these demographic trends would be likely to lead to labour shortages and rising rates of pay. However, recent years have seen large-scale movements of people between countries. These human migrations overwhelmingly consist of people of working age. For the most part they are looking to improve their economic and social condition by moving to countries where they can more easily get a job and at rates of pay well above that in their country of origin. The population of the USA has been bolstered by the influx of people, often illegal immigrants from Mexico and other Central and South American countries. The expanded European Union has seen large-scale movements of people both within its borders from east to west, and into the EU from many African and some Asian countries. Much of this has taken place illegally. For the most part these immigrants have mitigated the worst effects of population stagnation and decline in the countries where they have moved. Their existence has certainly expanded the labour market. Immigrant workers are often prepared to meet demand for some hard to fill vacancies and take jobs at lower wage rates than some native workers. Not all immigrant workers are unskilled, but are often unable to find work matching their existing skills due to their qualifications not being recognized or perhaps because of their inability to speak the language of the host country with sufficient proficiency. Immigrant workers thus offer both a challenge and an opportunity for employers. For operations managers, the challenge centres on how to make the best use of these human resources. Immigrant workers may have training or retraining needs different from native workers. It may be necessary to provide language training. In most case their presence increases the diversity of the workforce, necessitating a greater cultural awareness from operations managers in order to integrate them into the organization and avoid conflicts between new arrivals and existing workers. Organizations may also have to give more consideration to their needs outside of the workplace (e.g. their accommodation, health and welfare provision, religion, etc.). As population movements seem set to continue in many parts of the world, the challenge of managing a more diverse workforce seems likely to remain, if not grow, in the near future.

Discontinuities

discontinuity

Any interruption, failure or disruption to operations that causes a loss of intended production.

All operations have to cope with the risk of discontinuity, failure or disruption. It has always been the responsibility of operations managers to manage that risk by trying to avoid any discontinuity in the first place and having plans to cope with and minimize the effects of its consequences should it occur.

Arguably, the risk of a serious discontinuity occurring has increased in recent years. The events of September 11 2001 certainly brought such fears to the forefront of organizational thinking. As well as the on-going threat of terrorist or other deliberately malicious actions to disrupt operations, it seems that there are many other factors that seem to have increased the risks to operations. These can include extreme weather events, fires, disruption to supplies and the illness or death of key employees. Whether or not such threats are greater than in the past is an open question. However, it certainly seems that more operations are more at risk than in the past. Arguably this is due to:

- An increased reliance upon external suppliers.
- More complex supply networks.
- An increased physical separation of the locations in the supply network.
- The adoption of lean production techniques that deliberately set out to reduce the slack in supply networks (e.g. by minimizing buffers of inventory).
- The increased reliance on 'open' ICT networks based on Internet linkages.

All of these factors combine to produce supply networks that typically consist of a large number of highly dependent processes. Each of these could be vulnerable to disruption, which would in turn very quickly disrupt the entire supply network, causing a discontinuity. The increased reliance on the Internet, also makes organizational ICT system more open to external attacks by hackers, or others seeking disruption for whatever reason.

None of these trends are likely to reverse in the near future, so this issue is likely to become even more important than it has in the past. Thus, operations managers need to consider how to minimize their exposure to such risks and to mitigate the worst effects of such discontinuities.

Actions to avoid discontinuities include:

- *Maintenance of equipment:* This involves taking actions to prevent failures in equipment and other physical facilities that might lead to a more serious discontinuity. Actions can include replacing equipment or components that have failed; repairing or replacing equipment or components after a predetermined period of time; repairing or replacing equipment or components when inspection reveals that its condition has deteriorated to a predetermined level.

- *Detecting failures:* the intention here is to detect minor or infrequently occurring failures that have not yet led to major discontinuities. Major discontinuities rarely occur without some kind of prior indication that they might. The key issue is to ensure that systems are in place to detect such weak signals. These might come from employees, customers or other users of the organization's products or services.

- *Assessing the likely cause of discontinuities:* There are a variety of techniques that try to identify and assess likely causes of failure that could lead to discontinuities. Amongst these is failure mode and effect analysis (FMEA) which is a quantitative technique based on assigning probabilities to failures, the severity of the effects of a failure and the likelihood of the failure being detected. Fault tree analysis applies a logic-based approach to identifying all the possible causes of potential failures.

- *Learning from failures:* All operations are bound to experience some kind of failure or more serious discontinuity over time. However, by treating any failure as a learning opportunity, valuable lessons can be learnt that can then be used to try to avoid future failures. There are many approaches and techniques available for such failure analysis. In the case of serious discontinuities or disasters, investigations are usually conducted, often by expert outsiders to determine their causes. Many manufacturers provide traceability for their products by labelling them in order to identify and assess the process that produced them. Many organizations conduct detailed analysis of customer complaints in order to better understand their causes. The critical incident technique can also be particularly useful, in service operations to analyze likely causes of failure.

- *Designing processes for improved reliability:* Analyses of actual and potential discontinuities can provide a wealth of information that can be used to improve the reliability of processes and make them more robust in the face of external threats.

Coping with the consequences of discontinuities is sometimes termed **business continuity planning** or disaster recovery planning. This generally includes:

1 Identifying key business processes, assessing their vulnerabilities and taking action to minimize or eliminate risks.

2 Analyzing the impact on the business of any discontinuity in any of the key business processes.

3 Developing a business continuity plan detailing how to recover from a discontinuity in any of the key business processes. Such plans might involve the identification of replacement or alternative resources, such as facilities and equipment, which would be available in the event of an emergency. It would also assign roles and responsibilities to key staff, including responsibilities for communicating with staff, customers, suppliers and other stakeholders.

4 Communicating the plan to ensure that everyone knows what to do in the event of a discontinuity.

5 Rehearsing the plan to confirm that it would be effective in practice. Use the lessons learnt from the practice to modify the plan if necessary.

business continuity planning
Planning aimed at avoiding discontinuities in operations and taking action to deal with their consequences, including reactivating operations as soon as possible.

Environmentalism

In the wake of increasing scientific evidence of the impact of human activities on the world's natural environment, organizations are coming under increased pressure to modify their operations. There are a wide range of concerns that centre on environmental degradation due to the excessive extraction of water, deforestation, over-fishing, hunting animals to extinction, etc. and pollution of both land, sea and air. However, the number one concern is now generally agreed to be global warming. The overwhelming scientific consensus is that global temperatures are rising and this rise is due to the increased concentration of carbon dioxide, methane and other so-called greenhouse gases. Increases in greenhouse gases are attributed to human

WHEN THINGS GO WRONG   BP: The Texas City explosion

When an explosion in BP's Texas City refinery killed 15 people and injured 170 in March 2005, it was America's worst industrial accident in a decade.

The report investigating the incident, published in January 2007, produced a damning verdict on one of the world's major oil companies. A panel of experts, led by James Baker, the former US secretary of state, said significant process safety culture issues existed at each refinery, not just the Texas City facility. The panel said that whilst BP had an aspirational goal of 'no accidents, no harm to people', it had not provided effective leadership in making certain its management and US refining workforce understand what is expected of them regarding process safety. BP had not provided effective process safety leadership and had not adequately established process safety as a core value.

Responding to the report, Lord Browne, BP's long-standing Chief Executive, denied that cost-cutting was responsible for failings. 'We've never focused on profits above safety', he said. However, the report's findings are likely to be seized on to support civil litigation against BP and could be used as the basis for criminal charges.

The Baker report came to some dismal conclusions about the safety culture at BP's US refineries. The most important of these centred on:

- The lack of connection between the high ideals of BP's board and the day-to-day practice of its operations. There was an absence of effective management accountability for refinery safety in BP's management structure.

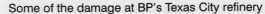

Some of the damage at BP's Texas City refinery

- BP's corporate culture (short-term, decentralized and entrepreneurial) was not appropriate for managing safety.

- The poor relations between workers and managers in BP's refineries. BP had failed to establish a positive, trusting, and open environment.

- The lack of operating discipline, toleration of serious deviations from safe operating practices, and apparent complacency towards serious process safety risks at refineries.

- Poor safety reporting systems that led to a failure to identify and analyze hazards. Incidents and near-misses were probably under-reported and even when spotted their root causes were not correctly identified.

- A failure to provide sufficient resources to sustain a high level of process safety performance.

BP was particularly heavily criticized by the Baker report for its failure to learn from previous safety failings at its Grangemouth refinery in Scotland. In May and June 2000, that plant suffered a power distribution failure, the rupture of a pressurized steam main and a fire that took more than seven hours to put out. Although there were no fatalities or serious injuries, a report by the UK's Health and Safety Executive (HSE) said that was only down to good fortune. BP was subsequently fined £1 million for safety violations. The HSE said that one of the problems at Grangemouth was that management was too focused on safety indicators based on personal injuries and not on the risk of serious incidents. The Baker panel came to exactly the same conclusion at Texas City.

The Baker report made a series of recommendations that were aimed at making BP the industry leader in safety. BP said it would be following all of these but recognized it still has a very long way to go.

Meanwhile, analysts pondered the future of the company in the wake of the Baker verdict. BP's share price was looking low. However, taking the necessary steps to improve its safety and operations performance would take some time; time unlikely to be afforded by investors given their existing negative views of BP following production losses due to corrosion leaks in its pipelines in Prudhoe Bay, Alaska. Although not excessive for a company of BP's size, the financial cost of complying with Baker's recommendations could be up to US$1 billion a year. It was also clear that everything the company now did would be subject to minute scrutiny. Some analysts called for a quick fix, rather than the slow slog of upgrading the company's ageing hardware. There were calls for BP either to get bigger, by merging with another of the oil majors, or smaller, by breaking up into separate refining and extraction companies.

It was clear that BP was in for a troubled time following the Baker report. However, the company would have to face the future with a new Chief Executive. In a surprise announcement a week before the publication of the Baker report, BP said that Lord Browne would now be standing down in July 2007, 18 months earlier than initially announced. Browne has been widely lauded as one of the outstanding business-men of his generation. The Baker report noted that Browne was 'instrumental in shaping BP's corporate culture'.

(Source material www.ft.com 17 and 18 January 2007)

WWW.

Questions (Suggested answers can be found on the companion website www.thomsonlearning.co.uk/barnes)

WWW.

1 What are the consequences of the Texas City disaster?

2 What were the main causes of the disaster?

3 What actions could BP have taken that might have helped to avoid the Texas City disaster?

activity, principally related to the burning of fossil fuels in industrial processes and transportation. Whilst the likely rise in temperature and its impact are the subject of much debate, it is generally accepted that urgent steps need to be taken to reduce greenhouse gas emissions. Pressure is now growing on all organizations to take action to reduce their carbon footprint which is the amount of greenhouse gases they are responsible for. This is usually measured as the quantity of carbon dioxide emitted due to organizational activities. Attempts to reduce carbon emissions look set to become a major issue for all organizations in the next few years. Since the bulk of any organization's activities take place within its operations function, the greatest responsibility for reducing greenhouse gas emissions will fall to operations managers. This will make them the most important people in any organization's efforts to reduce its carbon footprint and move operations onto a more environmentally sustainable basis. The operations function will thus become the focus of organizational efforts to reduce carbon emissions.

Efforts to make operations more environmentally friendly will focus on:

- *Energy efficiency:* In the short-term, the basis for most energy generation and transportation will remain fossil fuel technology. Therefore, there will need to be an increased focus on increasing energy efficiency in processes, buildings and transportation. Increasing the energy of efficiency of processes requires actions to reduce waste and pollution of all kinds, which is likely to require improvements in the design of both processes and products. This is likely to be accompanied by attempts to move away from the use of high carbon emitting fuels such as coal and oil to those that emit less such as natural gas and biofuels.

- *Transportation:* As transportation is a major source of greenhouse gases, organizations need to seek ways of reducing the need for transportation of both people and goods. This will call for a re-examination of supply networks in order to reduce their carbon footprint. This would include sourcing more products locally, using less carbon polluting modes of transport such as road and air transport (and conversely using more water and rail), and using ICT to reduce the need for paperwork and personal travel.

- *Sustainable technologies:* Sustainable technologies are those that are not based on the burning of fossil fuels. These include solar, wind, wave, tidal and, controversially, nuclear for power generation and fuel cells and batteries for transportation. It seems inevitable that there will be greater use of these technologies. This will imply significant changes to both processes and products in many industries, with far reaching effects on many operations.

Social responsibility

Recent years have seen an increased expectation that organizations should behave in a socially responsible manner. There seems to be a renewal of interest in the concept that organizations should be ethical not just towards the environment but in a wider range of issues. This stance is based on the stakeholder view of organizations. The shareholder view of organizations sees the sole purpose of a business as making financial returns for its owners. In contrast the stakeholder view, argues that businesses also have a responsibility to a wider set of interested parties, including customers, employees, suppliers and society at large. From this perspective, organizations are seen to have environmental responsibilities not only to people directly affected by their operations, but, for example, in the case of global warming to generations as yet to come. Other environmental issues include pollution of all kinds, the destruction of natural habitats, genetically modified food products and nuclear energy.

Acting in a socially responsible manner essentially requires that the organization avoids exploitation in its operations. Therefore, organizations need to ensure that all their employees are treated fairly at work, are paid reasonably, are not required to work excessively long hours, have safe and comfortable working conditions, enjoy freedom of association, etc. In particular, children should not be employed. Acting socially responsibly also requires ensuring that these principles are extended to workers of suppliers and all others in the supply network. For organizations operating

CASE STUDY: Carbon neutral at Marks & Spencer

In launching its £200 million 'eco-plan' on 15 January 2007, Marks & Spencer (M & S) set out its ambition to become the UK's greenest retailer. While all the big supermarkets have pledged to reduce their carbon footprint and reduce waste, none has gone as far as M & S. The company joins a handful of British businesses, including HSBC bank and BritishSkyBroadcasting, choosing to become 'carbon neutral', in ensuring their operations do not contribute to climate change.

Chief Executive, Stuart Rose, said that the 100-point plan would impact on every part of M & S's operations over the next five years. Rose said,

'Every business and individual needs to do their bit to tackle the enormous challenges of climate change. Our customers, employees and shareholders now expect us to take bold steps and do business differently and responsibly. We believe a responsible business can be a profitable business. M & S will change beyond recognition the way it operates over the next five years. We will become carbon neutral, only using offsetting as a last resort. This is a deliberately ambitious and, in some areas, difficult plan. We don't have all the answers but doing anything less is not an option'.

The plan will require the company to reduce its greenhouse gas emissions, most of which are likely to arise from the use of energy in its stores and from its transport fleet, by as much as possible. This could be achieved with new equipment, such as low energy lighting, and changes to vehicles, such as running them on electricity or on biofuels derived from plants. M & S said remaining emissions would be offset by investing in projects, such as wind farms or solar energy that reduce emissions in developing countries. The plan also included initiatives such as using only sustainable sources of wood and fish; using recycled plastic rather than oil to make polyester; setting new standards in ethical trade by converting key ranges to

Marks & Spencer's Baker Street store in London

100 per cent Fairtrade cotton; and promoting healthier eating among customers. It will also promote local sourcing and put red airplane labels on foods that have been flown in to the UK. The company will also help its suppliers and customers to change their behaviour. Because of its own-brand, its influence extends to over 2,000 factories, 10,000 farms and 250,000 workers, as well as millions of customers in the UK.

The plan was welcomed by environmentalists. Jonathon Porritt, Founder Director of Forum for the Future, said: 'This plan sets a new benchmark in the way businesses should be tackling critical sustainability challenges. It raises the bar for everyone else'. Blake Lee-Harwood, Campaign Director, Greenpeace UK said: 'We're glad a company like M & S has proposals that begin to match the scale of the challenge of climate change and protecting our oceans and forests'. Robert Napier, Chief Executive, WWF-UK said:

'Research clearly shows us that agricultural activities and other food production and distribution have some of the greatest impacts upon our environment. Such bold aspirations as outlined by Marks & Spencer can only help drive other supermarkets and the retail sector towards supplying products in a way that protects our planet and sustains the natural resources we depend upon'.

(Source material www.marksandspencer.com and www.ft.com)

WWW.

WWW.

Questions (Suggested answers can be found on the companion website www.thomsonlearning.co.uk/barnes)

1 Identify all the aspects of M & S's operations that will be affected by the eco-plan.
2 How can the £200 million investment required by the eco-plan be financially justifiable for the company?
3 Are there any operational advantages in being at the leading edge of developing environmentally friendly operations?
4 Are there any disadvantages?

internationally this can throw up some significant dilemmas arising from differences in rates of pay and working conditions and customs in different countries. Ultimately, organizations need to understand that their operations and those of their suppliers will be judged by the standards of their home country rather then those that might prevail in the country of a subsidiary or a supplier. Acting socially responsibly also implies that organizations treat their suppliers fairly, especially by paying a reasonable price for goods or services. Obviously, this can pose problems when sourcing internationally, as one of the main attractions of purchasing abroad is the lower prices available in many developing countries. Some proponents of corporate social responsibility also argue that organizations should actively source in developing countries in order to support economic development in such countries. However, they would emphasize the need to ensure that fair prices are paid.

Corporate social responsibility requires organizations to afford equal treatment to all individuals (their own employees, those of their suppliers, customers, etc.) and not to discriminate on the basis of gender, race, religion, age, disability, sexual orientation, nationality, political opinion, social or ethnic origin, etc. Again for organizations operating internationally a desire to act socially responsibly can throw up difficult dilemmas. For example, in some Muslim countries, laws and customs dictate that men and women are often treated differently in many aspects of life including work.

Whilst some issues are generally accepted as being integral to corporate social responsibility, some are more controversial. For example, some people believe that organizations should not exploit animals within their operations. Thus, for some any form of animal experimentation is unacceptable. Similarly, genetic engineering applied to animals is unethical to some people. Others believe that genetic modification to all organisms including plants is unacceptable. Some people object to all military activity and so would find any work connected to the armed forces and the arms trade unacceptable.

The views of what different societies consider to be acceptable can change over time. Therefore, organizations need to be sensitive to current views in the different countries in which they operate. The issues that affect the way that organizations manage their operations may well change, but will impact many of the operations management decision areas. Nonetheless many issues relating to corporate social responsibility look set to affect operations for many years to come.

LEARNING TO CHANGE

Although it may be tempting to do so, the activities of operations management cannot be isolated from what often seems to be an increasingly turbulent external environment. To be successful, an organization needs its operations to be able to respond to changes in its environment. Thus, operations managers need to develop the competencies that will better enable their functions to cope with the demands of the world in which it exists. Those competencies can only be built by learning how to interact effectively with other functions and with the wider world outside. For learning is best achieved by exposure to the outside world not by isolation from it.

One of the benefits of operating internationally is the learning opportunity available from exposure to different environments in various parts of the world. The more locations in which an organization operates, the more opportunities it has to learn. It is only through learning that organizations can build the competencies it needs to thrive in an ever changing world. Successful international organizations not only develop their operations as learning centres in each location, but also integrate and co-ordinate learning across their various locations. Various mechanisms are used to achieve this, especially the use of multi-functional, cross-site teams. It is also important to ensure that learning is achieved both from and with others outside of the organization, such as customers, suppliers and even competitors. It is only through sharing knowledge and learning together that the constantly changing international environmental can be better understood.

Organizations operating internationally have more opportunities to learn from best practice and thinking as they are more likely to encounter this at first hand in the various countries in which they operate. This is particularly important for the softer aspects of operations management, those of its infrastructural decision areas.

The hardware of operations management, its structural decision areas, are more easily observed and understood. Technology is generally easy to obtain; it may, for example, be purchased from the same suppliers as a competitor. Often it is easily replicated, either by some form of technology transfer or merely by copying. Consequently, technology, as such, may only provide a transient source of competitive advantage. How that technology is managed and operated is less visible, and so less easily replicable. It has long been a Western (particularly an American) trait, to look primarily to technology for improvement and problem solving. Clearly this is not necessarily a bad thing. However, it may be short-sighted to look to technology as the first and perhaps only way of achieving improvement. Many Japanese organizations have adopted a philosophy of looking to technology as the last way of achieving improvements. Their approach is to endeavour to continually improve the way they use their existing equipment, and only to look to introduce new technology when further improvement with existing technology is impossible. Any organization wishing to emulate such learning practices must not only be actively seeking such improvements, but also be open to external influence as potential sources of solutions to their problems.

Leonard-Barton (1992) argues that a factory (and indeed any operation) can become a 'learning laboratory' by being 'dedicated to knowledge creation, collection and control'. She continues 'In a learning laboratory, tremendous amounts of knowledge and skills are embedded in physical equipment and processes . . . more importantly however are the non-technical aspects, the managerial practices and underlying values that constantly renew and support the knowledge base'. Organizations that operate internationally have unique opportunities for organizational learning, for developing their operational facilities as learning laboratories but they need to create a culture in which those opportunities are seized.

Mathe and Perras (1994) identify three generic learning processes, each of which have been used successfully by service companies expanding their operations globally:

- *Following existing customers and learning from them:* This is the least
  risky option as existing customers will be well known to the organization.
  However exposure to the new environment may be limited and hence less
  learning will occur. Also, the organization is vulnerable to mistakes made by
  the customer.

- *Buying local operations or co-operating with a local service provider:* In this
  approach the choice of acquisition target or local partner is crucial. Making
  the wrong choice, perhaps due to inadequate information, risks poor
  performance in that market.

- *Going it alone and learning from the experience:* This is potentially the most
  rewarding and yet the most risky option. Rewarding because lessons from
  experience are usually deeply imbued. Also the learning is more likely to be
  shared more widely throughout the organization. Risky because it increases
  the likelihood of serious mistakes being made out of ignorance. Learning may
  be slow and painful.

Organizational learning provides the understanding on which the necessary capabilities can be built to enable the operations function to cope with whatever changes the world throws at them. Recent years have seen a growing recognition of the importance of organizational learning and its role in improving performance. The study of organizational learning processes has become known as knowledge management and the ideas associated with it have become increasingly popular.

Knowledge in organizations can be thought of as existing in two forms: explicit or tacit. Explicit knowledge is that which can be easily codified and shared asynchronously. Explicit knowledge includes information and skills that can easily be collected, stored, distributed and shared primarily as electronic or paper documents. This means it is fairly easy to communicate to others. Tacit knowledge, on the other hand, is experiential, intuitive, and communicated most effectively face-to-face. Tacit knowledge is difficult to express in words as it includes cognitive skills such as beliefs, images and mental models as well as technical skills and know-how. Tacit knowledge tends to reside in the collective mindsets of individuals in an organization.

The concept of knowledge management is that, in a fast changing world, the only real basis for competitive advantage is the intellectual capital of a firm. This lies in the minds of the firm's employees in either explicit or tacit form. Organizations therefore need to gather that knowledge and use it to add value in their operations. Some organizations try to capture organizational knowledge through the use of ICT such as document management and knowledge management systems. However, Nonaka and Takeuchi (1995) argue that knowledge management is also a social process, in which knowledge can be created and expanded if there is an interaction between the tacit and explicit forms of knowledge. Their SECI model describes the four processes in which conversions between the two kinds of knowledge take place, namely socialization, externalization, combination and internalization. They depict these processes as occurring in a continuous spiral process that increases in depth with each subsequent iteration (see Figure 15.1). The four processes are:

- *Socialization (tacit to tacit):* This involves the sharing and communication
  of tacit knowledge between people, often without ever producing explicit

knowledge management
The study of how organizations gather and use knowledge in order to add value in their operations and create a competitive advantage.

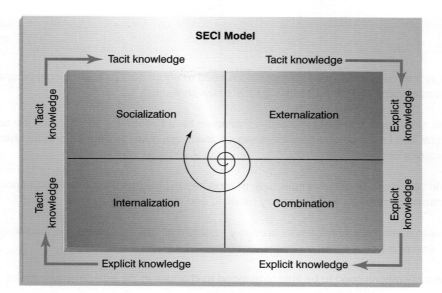

FIGURE 15.1 The four modes of knowledge creation

knowledge. This might involve people sharing their experiences within a team meeting or less formal discussions. It is easier for this to take place where people have a shared culture and language.

- *Externalization (tacit to explicit):* Although tacit knowledge is difficult to convert into explicit knowledge, efforts to do so are often based on individuals allowing their knowledge to be recorded in some way, perhaps via interview questions or story telling. This information can then be stored in some way.

- *Combination: (explicit to explicit):* Explicit knowledge can be shared in meetings, or via documentation. There are now many forms of ICT to enable documents to be managed (classified and stored for searching and retrieval) to make such forms of explicit knowledge widely available within an organization. However, this can also provide an opportunity for knowledge creation, by enriching the information, perhaps by reconfiguring it in some way.

- *Internalization (explicit to tacit):* If individuals are going to act on the basis of explicit knowledge they have to understand and internalize it. This requires them to create their own tacit knowledge. Reading documents from a number of sources can provide an opportunity to create new knowledge by combining their own existing tacit knowledge with the explicit knowledge of others.

Organizations need to create the context that enables these processes to thrive. This can involve the use of appropriate technologies, but also requires an appropriately open and supportive organizational culture. These both represent significant challenges, particularly for organizations operating internationally.

As most organizational activity takes place within its operations, that is where most organizational knowledge is likely to reside. If organizations can continually learn from the experiences of their operations, they will be better able to cope with whatever issues emerge in the future. In a fast changing and increasingly challenging world, all organizations must learn how to adapt their operations if they are to survive and prosper in the future.

SUMMARY OF KEY POINTS

In an increasingly interconnected world, organizations need to adopt a more international perspective in their operations management. This presents significant new challenges.

In order to 'think global and act local', operations managers have to combine and balance the actions in both the structural and infrastructural decision areas of operations management to form a coherent and consistent operations strategy.

Current trends in operations management include moving beyond the factory, the growing importance of services, the increased importance of the supply network, and the increased importance of ICT.

Emerging issues in operations management are likely to centre on low cost labour, population changes, discontinuities, environmentalism and social responsibility.

An organization's operations need to be able to respond to changes in the external environment.

Operating internationally exposes organizations to different environments which can provide significant learning opportunities.

EXERCISES (Suggested answers can be found on the companion website www.thomsonlearning.co.uk/barnes)

1 What aspects of operations management are most affected by increasing internationalization of business?

2 Is it inevitable that in the future all manufacturing operations will be carried out in low labour cost countries?

3 Find at least one example of each of the three Mathe and Perras (1994) generic learning processes for companies expanding their operations globally.

4 What aspects of operations management are most affected by the trends towards more outsourcing?

5 How can manufacturers differentiate their products using services? Find three examples of how this has been done successfully.

6 Identify at least three examples of how organizations are using Internet-based ICT to radically change the way their operations work.

7 What steps could the following type of organization take to (i) reduce the risks of, and (ii) limit the impact of any discontinuities in their operations:
   a An airport
   b A university
   c A chemical manufacturing factory
   d A bank

8 What actions might the following types of organization take to reduce the carbon footprint of their operations:
   a An airline
   b A steel manufacturer
   c A bank
   d A car hire firm

9 What are the most important ethical issues currently affecting the operations of the following types of organizations:

  a Pharmaceutical manufacturers
  b Clothing retailers
  c Fast food retailers
  d Out of town superstores

10 What do you think will be the biggest issues to affect the following types of operations in five years' time:

  a Food manufacturing
  b Healthcare
  c Aircraft manufacture
  d Retail banking

CASE STUDY EXERCISE Infosys: The global delivery model

Introduction

India-based Infosys Technologies (Infosys) is amongst the world leaders in offshore IT application services. Gartner, the highly regarded technology analysts, ranked Infosys as one of the leaders in its 'magic quadrant' for 2006 from 30 leading offshore application service providers. According to Gartner, 'Infosys has strong management capabilities relative to the other pure-play offshore providers. It has a clear vision of the market direction and is building competencies to sustain its leadership position in the market'.

Infosys relies heavily on its Global Delivery Model (GDM). The concept underpinning the GDM is that higher profitability can be achieved by breaking down work into logical components and distributing each component to the location where it can be performed at the highest quality and lowest cost. Its use of GDM enables Infosys to deliver the highest standards by leveraging the skill sets of their manpower in different locations. Its GDM gives Infosys the ability to deploy multi-location, multi-time-zone teams to execute projects efficiently and at low cost.

Background

Infosys was founded in 1981 by a group of seven IT professionals. From the beginning, Infosys relied heavily on overseas projects. One of the founders, Narayana Murthy, stayed in India, while the others went to the US to carry out onsite programming for corporate clients. One of Infosys' first clients was the US-based sports shoe manufacturer Reebok. Infosys hired its first set of employees in 1982 from the Indian Institute of Technology, Chennai. After training, they were sent abroad for onsite projects. At this time, computers were not manufactured in India. Importing a computer required a license – a process that would take several months. Infosys did not have the space to install many computers, so the computers it did purchase were installed in the premises of its customers, where new employees were trained. Proprietary software was then developed at the site. At this time, Infosys focused segments like retailing, finance, distribution and telecommunications.

In its early years Infosys acted as an intermediary for placing Indian software professionals in the US. In the mid-1980s this accounted for around 90 per cent of total revenues. The company's main advantage was its ability to offer high quality manpower at lower cost. By the late-1980s, Infosys started providing on-site services. In order to execute the IT projects, it would station its people at the client's location and they would then develop software to meet their requirements. Local talent, especially in locations in the US was not readily available and was very expensive. For the most part, the company would place Indian employees at the clients' location, which was a costly proposition.

▶

Infosys' success relies on 'knowledge workers' like these

In order to take advantage of the low cost work force in India, Infosys opened a software development centre in Bangalore in 1993. It convinced its clients that their IT projects could be completed in India. Doing projects in India enabled Infosys not only to lower manpower costs but also to develop its technical and managerial skills. Soon, Infosys started obtaining offshore development contracts to write customized software in India to be installed at the client's sites abroad.

By the late-1990s, Infosys had moved from competing on low wages to focus on developing intellectual property. Drawing on the knowledge and experience it obtained by developing software for a variety of clients, Infosys introduced generic products in banking, telecom and retail. Small modifications could be made to these products to meet the needs of particular clients. Infosys started emphasizing the quality of its software in order to differentiate itself from other IT companies. In 1998, Infosys received CMM Level 4 certification, for its software development processes. (The Capability Maturity Model (CMM) is a formalized process that enables an organization to gain control over software development process.) With its growing expertise and focus on quality, Infosys was able to win many big IT projects. Having established itself as a firm with much better capabilities than its competitors, and guaranteeing its clients software products of high quality, the company was able to command higher prices.

By 1999, Infosys had more than 110 customers including multi-national giants like Nestle, Apple and Gap, and had provided mission critical software for clients like Nortel, Reebok and Nordstrom. At this point, Infosys decided to set up development centres, located near to its client's locations, where tasks of strategic importance could be carried out. Initially, two such centres were established close to clients' locations in Fremont, California and Boston, Massachusetts, in October 1999. In January 2000, the first software development centre outside India was set up in Toronto, Canada. In mid-2000, the company opened another centre in London. (See Table 15.1 for details of Infosys milestones.)

In the initial years, the GDM at Infosys was deployed only for application development. With the advancement of technology in communications, the scope of GDM widened to include new services. The growth of services offered under GDM is outlined in Table 15.2. (See Table 15.2 for evolution of GDM in Infosys.)

With new services being added to the GDM every year, the share of new services as a percentage of total revenues kept growing (see Table 15.3 for the details of revenue obtained from new services).

TABLE 15.1 Infosys milestones

YEAR	EVENT
1981	Infosys incorporated
1987	First International office in the US
1993	Completed IPO
1995	Set up development centres across India
1996	Set up first office in Europe in Milton Keynes, UK
1997	Set up office in Toronto
1999	Annual revenues US$ 100 million Listed in NASDAQ Opened offices in Germany, Sweden, Belgium, Australia Set up two development centres in the US
2000	Annual revenues US$ 200 million New office in Hong Kong Global development centres in Canada Three development centres in US
2001	Annual revenue of over US$ 400 million Offices in UAE and Argentina Development centre in Japan
2002	Revenues US$ 0.5 billion Offices in the Netherlands, Singapore and Switzerland
2004	Revenues US$ 1 billion
2006	Revenues US$ 2 billion

(ADAPTED FROM infosys.com)

TABLE 15.2 Evolution of GDM in Infosys

YEAR	ACTIVITIES
Until 1996	Application development and maintenance Software re-engineering
1997–2000	Technology consulting Technology enabled BPR Enterprise solutions
2001–2005	Business process management IT outsourcing Systems integration
2006	Management consulting

(ADAPTED FROM S. GOPALAKRISHNAN, INFOSYS OPERATIONAL HIGHLIGHTS, 2005–2006)

(S. GOPALAKRISHNAN, OPERATIONAL HIGHLIGHTS, 2005–2006)

TABLE 15.3 New services as percentage of revenue

YEAR	NEW SERVICES (%)
2001	22.8
2002	24.9
2003	29.6
2004	35.4
2005	37.7
2006	41.1

The GDM

In the GDM, large scale software development projects were divided into three different categories:

1 Tasks carried out at the location of the client (onsite).

2 Tasks which needed to be carried out closer to the client (near-site).

3 Tasks that could be done in remote locations, where process-driven technology centres with highly skilled manpower were easily available (offshore).

(See Table 15.4 for details of the tasks carried out onsite, near-site and at offshore locations).

TABLE 15.4 Project components – on-site, near-site, offshore

	ON-SITE	NEAR-SITE	OFFSHORE
Strategy and roadmap definition	Client interaction, interviews, reviews, programme leadership, goal setting	Analysis and synthesis	Background research, thought leadership and information support
Development and integration	Architecture requirements, change management and implementation	Requirement analysis, high level design, prototype building, implementation support	Detailed design, code development, testing and integration
Systems integration and package implementation	Client interaction. Process mapping. Solution definition. Architecture change, programme management	Prototype building, high level design, and implementation support	Custom components, integration interfaces and report building
ITO, BPO and AMO	First-level support. Facilities support and programme management	Near-site support centers, service redundancy	Large offshore centres, core service delivery

(www.infosys.com)

The work on projects was carried out 24 hours a day, with teams located at different locations across the world, working around-the-clock. Nandan Nilekani, President, CEO and Managing Director of Infosys, commented, 'The work can be moved depending on where it would be cheaper to do so, or to a place that has unutilized capacity, or special skills'.

Work at different global locations is co-ordinated with support from integrated communication systems and agreed process guidelines. Global development centres (GDCs) carry out activities related to software development. Infosys has two types of GDCs – proximity development centers (PDC) and offshore development centres (ODC).

PDCs or near shore centres, are useful especially for clients, who are reluctant to move their entire project offshore, but at the same time want to reduce the high costs of onsite development. Near-shore facilities are useful for large mission critical projects, which demand round-the-clock responsiveness and local language capabilities. In the near-shore model, some of the risks associated with the offshore model such as lack of control, language and cultural barriers, inadequate infrastructure and geopolitical risks can be avoided. According to S. Gopalakrishnan, Chief Operating Officer and Deputy Managing Director of Infosys, 'The GDM works on the concept of meritocracy of locations. Under this model, near-shore destinations become just another location in the entire global network'.

The ODCs carry out tasks like designing, coding, testing, documentation, maintenance, fixing bugs, warranty support, etc. The ODCs are located mainly in India, with one located in Canada.

Each project team is organized into modules, with each module dealing with one aspect of the project. Instead of carrying out the project sequentially, Infosys deploy the resources and activities simultaneously, with teams interacting so that they are aware of the tasks being carried out by other modules.

Before any project begins, team composition is decided and roles assigned to each team member. Training is provided to fill any competency gaps identified amongst team member. After a project is complete, project teams deliberate on what went right and what went wrong in the course of the project. Every project has a closure report, which details the duration of the project, resources employed, any deviations that occurred and their causes. All employees are required to fill in a worksheet every day to help the project managers to assess the project status. Using the combined database of the team members, the project managers can determine the time and cost required to complete the project.

The success of GDM relies on capturing knowledge on-site so that this can be communicated to the off-site developers. Later the results of their work will need to be reintegrated into the client's system at the on-site location. The major components of GDM are knowledge capture/retrieval, daily handoffs, quality control, continuous improvement, mobilizing and demobilizing staff as required, distribution of staff between onsite and offsite locations, recruiting and training the right kind of people, billing for cross-border teams and connectivity of the locations.

Infosys gives utmost importance to recruitment, training, deploying and retaining the right kind of people. Only candidates with high analytical ability and ability to learn are selected. Other traits deemed necessary were attitude and willingness to work in teams. *Fortune* magazine noted that, 'Securing a position at Infosys is more competitive than gaining admission to Harvard. In 2005, the company had more than 1.3 million applicants for full-time positions and hired only 1 per cent of them' (Harvard College by comparison accepted 9 per cent of applicants).

Infosys has been transforming the knowledge of its individual employees into an organization-wide resource since the early-1990s. Employees' knowledge on topics like technology and software development is incorporated into Bodies of Knowledge (BOK) that can be shared with employees in other countries. In 1996, Infosys launched Sparsh, a corporate intranet to be a repository of all the BOKs. A company-wide knowledge management (KM) program was initiated in 1999, with a centralized portal called KShop.

Infosys has developed a KM tool called People Knowledge Map, which contains the contact information of individuals who are experts in specific areas, enabling them to be contacted as necessary. Infosys also uses CMM to prevent the occurrence of defects, and to quantify and modify its software development process. Project managers thus are able to access this knowledge repository to help solve any problem they are facing.

Infosys benchmarks itself using international quality standards like ISO9000, CMM and the Malcolm Baldrige framework. It also uses Six Sigma to drive improvements. CMM also provides more accurate budgeting and improves the company's ability to meet the goals for schedule, cost, quality, etc.

By 2006, Infosys had 38 global delivery centres as a part of the GDM. About 20 of these are located in different cities in India (including Bangalore, Chennai), with the rest in North America, Asia-Pacific and Europe. Apart from the GDCs, Infosys also had 37 marketing offices located in over 16 different countries (including 14 in the US, 13 in Europe and 5 in India).

GDM – Making The Model Work

For an offshore development project, a team from Infosys visits the client in order to determine their requirements. After agreeing the specifications, some of the team members remain with the client to co-ordinate and manage any changes, while the project managers returned to the GDCs. An on-site co-ordinator remains at the clients' location to communicate with the PDCs and ODCs.

The work is then distributed to PDCs and ODCs. At the GDCs, project managers supervise a large team of IT professionals who developed and implemented solutions as required by the client. Members of the teams visit the client's site as and when required. The three way allocation of manpower among the client site, PDCs and ODCs requires close co-ordination. Every week, client meetings are conducted and a status report prepared to assess progress. The weekly meetings are conducted in real-time meetings, with key personnel from the client and Infosys participating through an audio conference facility. Status reports are derived from the CMM, which provides a strict mechanism using standard templates. Status reports are circulated both to the client and also to all the members involved in the project in the PDCs and ODCs. The clients' systems are linked to the facilities at Infosys in order to carry out simultaneous processing. This enables project managers to retain full control of the project irrespective of location.

To ensure seamless communication between the development centres and the clients, Infosys uses the services of several service providers along with a mix of satellite and fiber optic links with facilities for alternate routing. In India, Infosys uses the services of two telecom carriers to provide high-speed links to connect the GDCs. Internationally, multiple satellite links are used to connect GDCs with network hubs in other parts of the world. In 2005, some top executives were provided with IP phones. Instant messaging is used to communicate across Infosys campuses in India. Video conferencing is used for executive level discussions and training. Infosys established a business continuity and disaster recovery centre in Mauritius. In 2006, 72.3 per cent of the total billed person months originated from GDCs in India; up from 68.1 per cent in 2004.

In order to avoid the risk of predatory pricing by its competitors, Infosys has been trying to move up the value chain by offering high-end services like enterprise solutions and independent testing. In April 2004, it established Infosys Consulting Inc., a wholly owned subsidiary, in Texas, USA, in order to gain greater involvement in its clients' projects and build brand differentiation. This is particularly necessary, in the light of the growing presence of Chinese firms in the IT services industry. According to Michael Guilbault, Senior Analyst, Technology Business Research, 'The combined offering of IT services and consultancy has helped Infosys move up the value chain by increasing its involvement in high-level projects associated with Sarbanes Oxley compliance, the Anti-Money Laundering Act and the Patriot Act'. Infosys, for its part felt that moving into consultancy was a business model innovation, after it had firmly established itself in back-end tasks like code writing and systems integration. According to Nilekani, 'It's like Wal-Mart getting into groceries or Dell getting into printers. We're adding new capabilities at the point of customer contact'.

The Benefits

The GDM is acknowledged to be one of the key factors behind the rapid growth of Infosys' revenues. The company's revenues for 2005–2006 were US$ 2 billion, up four-fold in four years. The company has continued to attract a talented workforce in India and elsewhere. Numbers employed as of March 2006 were 52,700 against 10,700 in 2002.

In 2006, Infosys derived more than 40 per cent of its revenues through new GDM based services. There are several benefits that accrue to clients through the GDM, including cost reductions as high as 35 per cent, 75 per cent reductions in time to market and greater flexibility through customization of its delivery model to meet clients' requirements.

The scope of GDM is not limited to just setting up resource bases across the world. GDM also involves the use of capabilities that have been developed over many years, making the model difficult for others to

(INFOSYS, ANNUAL REPORT, 2005–2006)

TABLE 15.5 Infosys revenues by geographic area

COUNTRIES	2006 (%)	2005 (%)	2004 (%)
North America	64.8	65.2	71.2
Europe	24.5	22.3	19.2
India	1.8	1.9	1.3
Rest of the World	8.9	10.6	8.3

replicate. According to Nilekani, 'The new paradigm of strategic global outsourcing will provide the flexibility to select what to outsource, when to outsource and how to leverage global delivery throughout the value chain'.

The Road Ahead

Realizing the potential of GDM, several other Indian IT companies have also began providing offshore services. Several MNCs like Accenture, IBM Global Services, Electronic Data Systems, have also started operating from India, offering the same offshore rates as Indian companies.

But Infosys remains confident that others can not match their GDM capabilities. They would need to build the model from scratch, by retrenching the manpower in their countries and hiring equally talented employees in other locations with cost advantages. The multi-nationals would need to redesign their operations in order to replicate Infosys' GDM, which would be a very difficult task. According to Nilekani, 'We are adding the garnish to a growing base, and the balance sheet grows to absorb this. The problem for them is the opposite: their revenues decline if they change their model, as they move work from on-site to offshore'.

The entry of multi-nationals in India also puts pressure on Infosys in terms of retaining talented manpower. The multi-nationals have started hiring experienced people from Infosys and other top Indian IT companies by offering them salaries 40 to 50 per cent higher. In order to counter this, Infosys increased salaries during 2003 and also moved to a role-based structure, in which the reward depended on the performance.

Apart from multi-nationals, Infosys also faced stiff competition from other Indian IT companies, such as Wipro Technologies. Industry analysts have expressed fears that Infosys and its GDM is heavily dependent on US-based companies, whose IT spending was decreasing. Additionally outsourcing was being severely criticized within the US. (See Table 15.5 for Infosys' revenues by geographic area.)

Another challenge was growing competition from countries like China and the Philippines, which could offer lower wages and more facilities. According to Clayton Christensen,

'Right now Infosys is at the top of its game. But, in five years, you can bet that Infosys will begin to see some maturity in its core business. At that stage, it will want to find another growth business that is becoming very large. If Infosys wants to have such a business five years from now, it has to start it today'.

(Abridged from the case written by P. Indu and Vivek Gupta (ICFAI Center for Management Research).)

Questions (Suggested answers can be found on the companion website www.thomsonlearning.co.uk/barnes)

WWW.

1 What are the most important factors in the external environment that Infosys has capitalized on?

2 What advantages does its GDM provide for Infosys?

3 Are there any disadvantages in the GDM for Infosys?

4 What are the most significant challenges facing Infosys over the next five years?

5 How well placed is Infosys to meet these challenges?

References

WWW. Bureau of Economic Analysis (2007) *U.S. Economic Accounts* available online at
http://bea.gov/beahome.html.

WWW. Central Intelligence Agency (2007) *The World Factbook* available online at
https://www.cia.gov/cia/publications/factbook/index.html.

Economist (2007) 'The problem with Made in China', 11 January, 68–70.

Leonard-Barton, D. (1992) 'The factory as a learning laboratory', *Sloan Management Review,*
34(1):23–28.

Mathe, H. and Perras, C. (1994) 'Successful global strategies for service companies', *Long
Range Planning* 27(1):36–49.

Nonaka, I. and Takeuchi, H. (1995) *The Knowledge-Creating Company,* Oxford: Oxford
University Press.

WWW. World Trade Organization (2006) *International trade statistics 2006,* available online at
http://www.wto.org/english/res_e/statis_e/its2006_e/its06_toc_e.htm.

Additional reading

Barnes, J.C. (2001) *A guide to business continuity planning,* New York: John Wiley.

Kotler, P. (2005) *Corporate social responsibility,* New York: Wiley.

Starik, M. and Sharma, S. (Eds) (2007) *New horizons in research on sustainable
organisations: emerging ideas, approaches and tools for practitioners and researchers,*
Sheffield: Greenleaf publishing.

Steger, U. (2004) *The business of sustainability,* Basingstoke: Palgrave Macmillan.

Jashapara, A. (2004) *Knowledge Management: An Integrated Approach,* Harlow:
Prentice Hall.

Useful websites

WWW.

http://www.thebci.org The Business Continuity Institute, an organization for business
continuity practitioners which promote the art and science of Business Continuity
Management worldwide. The Institute is UK-based, but working in over 75 countries.

http://www.csr.gov.uk The UK government's website for Corporate Social Responsibility
issues. Provides useful information and acts as a portal to other relevant sites.

http://www.sustainablebusiness.org The Sustainable Business Institute is a non-profit,
organization dedicated to advancing sustainable business practices.

GLOSSARY

80:20 (or Pareto) rule The principle that for many phenomenon, 80 per cent of the consequences stem from 20 per cent of the causes. (Pareto was an Italian economist, who observed that 80 per cent of income in Italy was received by 20 per cent of the population)

Aggregate capacity plan A production plan aimed at meeting the totality of customer demand over the longer-term (i.e. over a period of say one to three years)

Assessment centres Centres used to provide information on candidates for jobs. They typically consist of multiple evaluations including job-related simulations, interviews and psychological tests

B2B (business to business) In e-commerce a transaction that takes place between one business organization and another

B2C (business to consumer) In e-commerce a transaction that takes place between a business organization and an individual consumer (i.e. individual citizens)

Back office The area of an operation in which there is normally no contact with customers

Balanced scorecard Performance measurement framework that organizes performance measures into four perspectives (financial, customer, internal processes and learning and development)

Behaviouralism An approach to job design that aims to improve motivation hence performance by increasing job satisfaction by satisfying workers' individual and collective social needs

Business continuity planning Planning aimed at avoiding discontinuities in operations and taking action to deal with their consequences, including reactivating operations as soon as possible

Business process outsourcing (BPO) Moving certain operations that were previously carried out within an organization to an external supplier. Recently, there has been a trend to outsource support operations as well as core processing operations

Capacity The level of activity or output that an operation (facility or organization) can achieve in a given period of time under normal working conditions

Capacity cushion The amount of excess capacity that an operation has above what is required to meet expected demand

Configuration Decisions about the configuration of operations are concerned with the relationship between operations facilities at different locations

Control This is concerned with remedial action taken in response to things not occurring as planned in order to avoid an undesirable outcome

Control loop A theoretical model that describes actions taken with the aim of ensuring that the outputs from a transformation process are produced according to plan. This involves measuring the output, comparing it to the plan and, if necessary taking remedial action upon the process and/or its inputs

Core competence Something that an organization can do uniquely well. It is a capability that does or can form the basis of a competitive advantage. Core competences are the collective learning of an organization and derive from an ability to co-ordinate diverse production skills and integrate multiple streams of technology

Costs of quality An expression of an organization's performance in quality in financial terms

Cross-functional team A work team comprising members from different functional areas within the organization (e.g. operations, marketing, accounting or human resource management)

Culture Culture can be thought of as 'that set of assumptions and beliefs that are taken-for-granted and held in common by members of an organization' (Schein, 1985). It can operate at a national as well as an organizational level

Degree of automation of technology The extent to which the technology can operate without human involvement

Degree of integration of technology The extent to which separate pieces of technology are connected to each other, within a process or between more than one process

Design capacity The theoretical output that could be achieved by operating continuously throughout a given period at maximum rate

Discontinuity Any interruption, failure or disruption to operations that causes a loss of intended production

Diseconomies of scale Increases in the unit cost of output that occur when production volumes increase too much. Diseconomies of scale may result from the complexity of managing a very large facility, from rising cost of inputs (e.g. due to having to transport raw materials increased distances or from increased labour rates necessary to attract sufficient workers), or from disruptions in production due to operating at very high levels of capacity utilization (e.g. from increased incidents of machine breakdown)

Disintermediation The removal of one or more intermediaries (such as a distributor, wholesaler, broker or agent) in a supply chain. (Known colloquially as 'cutting out the middleman'.) This is a common feature of e-commerce, especially B2C e-commerce

Disruptive innovation An innovation based on new technology that is different from that in prevalent use in the industry

Division of labour The principle that efficiency will be increased by each worker specializing on a single task rather than workers performing a number of different tasks

E – The three Es of performance measurement Economy, efficiency and effectiveness

E-business The sharing of business information, maintaining business relationships and conducting business transactions by means of Internet-based technology

E-commerce The undertaking of business transactions through the medium of Internet-based information and communication technologies (or other computer networks). Sometimes the term electronic business or e-business is used as an alternative to e-commerce. Occasionally the term e-business is used to emphasize the use of ICTs in an organization's own business processes and throughout its entire supply network

E-learning The term used to describe the use of web-based learning

Economies of scale Reductions in unit cost of output due to increasing production volumes. Unit costs savings are achieved by spreading the fixed costs of production over an increased volume and from the increased efficiency available from the division of labour and from using large-scale machinery

Economies of scope Reductions in unit costs available from increasing the number of products produced. Unit costs savings are achieved by spreading certain overhead costs (such as administration, distribution, marketing, etc.) over an increased volume of output, assuming that these costs do not increase as a result of increasing the number of products

EDI (electronic data interchange) The computer-to-computer exchange of structured information via a telecommunication link. EDI has been used by business since the 1970s and there are agreed international standards covering its use. It is still used by many MNEs to automate their purchase of goods and services

Effective capacity The output achievable in a given period after the deduction of output lost due to planned stoppages

Effectiveness A measure of the success of an operation in producing outputs that satisfy customers

Efficiency A measure of the success of an operation in converting inputs to outputs

Empowerment The concept that workers are given greater control over the work that they do, without reference to higher levels of management

Enterprise resource planning (ERP) A computer-based system for resource planning and control across an entire organization. ERP is suitable for any type of business, services as well as manufacturing, and not for profit as well as profit seeking organizations

Expatriate (expat) A person temporarily or permanently working in a country other than their home country

Failure mode and effects analysis (FMEA) A technique used to identify likely causes of failure and their consequences so that preventative actions can be taken

Focused operations Based on Skinner's (1974) idea of a 'focused factory', this is the notion that a facility that concentrates on a single or very narrow range of tasks will outperform one trying to achieve a broader range of tasks. Focus might be achieved by limiting the markets served, the products produced or processes used at a particular facility

Forecasting The act of predicting the future likely level of demand for products and services. Forecasting methods can be either quantitative or qualitative

Front office The area of an operation in which contact with customers normally takes place

Globalization This refers to the increasing integration of economic activity around the world, evidenced by the growth in international trade and the increasing interdependence of national economies. An increase in cross-border social, cultural and technological exchange is also a feature of globalization. Critics of globalization claim it gives too much power to free market economics and multi-national enterprises and has detrimental effects on less developed countries and the environment

Gross domestic product (GDP) A measure of the size of a country's economy. It is defined as the market value of all final goods and services produced within the country

Groupthink The phenomenon in which the desire for consensus leads a group to make bad or irrational decisions which members might otherwise individually consider to be unwise

Host country national (HCN) A worker from the country of the subsidiary

Human resources The people that work for an organization

Internationalization The process of expanding business operations across international boundaries. At first this might only involve exporting or importing goods and/or services. But it might go on to involve the establishment of production facilities in other countries, as well as facilities to support sales, R & D, and other activities in foreign countries

Job description This outlines the duties and responsibilities required for a particular job or position

Job design The process of specifying the methods used by people performing work tasks and particularly the way that they interface with the technology they use

Just in time (or JIT) A manufacturing system that aims to produce only what is required, in the quantity that is required, at the time it is required

Knowledge management The study of how organizations gather and use knowledge in order to add value in their operations and create a competitive advantage

Lean production An alternative name for just in time

Lean thinking The application of just in time principles to non-manufacturing organizations

Less developed country (LDC) A country whose economy is under developed, relying mostly on agriculture (and possibly extractive industries), and whose population has a low standard of living

Manufacturing resources planning (MRP2) A computer-based system of planning and control for manufacturing processes that extends MRP to include all manufacturing resources and links the software for manufacturing planning and control to that for all other functions of the organization via an integrated database

Market access strategy A strategy in which operations are internationalized in order to access and serve markets outside of the home country

Mass customization The use of a single process to produce a wide variety of products (or services). It aims to realize unit cost reductions through economies of scope in the same way that mass manufacturing aims to achieve economies of scale

Materials requirement planning (MRP) A computer-based system of calculating the quantities and timings of materials required for dependent demand items in a manufacturing process

Measures of economy Measures concerned with the cost of the goods and services required as inputs for the operations process

Measures of effectiveness Measures concerned with the extent to which the outputs of a process meet the requirements of its customers

Measures of efficiency Measures concerned with the performance of the transformation process itself, in terms of its ability to make optimum use of resource inputs in the creation of outputs

Multi-national enterprise (MNE) Sometimes also termed a multi-national company (MNC), this is a business organization that has operations in a number of different countries

Network perspective This perspective argues that it is necessary to consider all of an organization's facilities collectively in order to realize their full potential to serve all their customers irrespective of their geographic location

New product development The term used to describe all those activities directed towards the introduction of new or improved products or services into the market place

Newly industrialized economy (NIE) Sometimes also termed a newly industrialized country (NIC), this is a country which has undergone a considerable level of industrialization in the recent past, switching its primary economic activity from agriculture to manufacturing, and possibly services. NIEs are not quite yet at the status of the industrialized nations of the West, but are more advanced than the countries of the third world

Off-shoring Moving certain operations to another county. This could be done either by relocating the affected operations to the organization's own facilities in another country, or by outsourcing the operations to a foreign supplier. The motivation for this is often, but not exclusively, cost saving

Operations facility A collection of resources brought together at one geographic location for the purpose of producing particular goods and/or services

Operations function That part of the organization that has the responsibility for operations management

Operations management This is concerned with the management of the resources and processes required by an organization to produce goods or services for customers

Operations performance objective A criterion against which to evaluate the performance of operations. There are considered to be five possible operations performance objectives: cost, quality, speed, dependability and flexibility

Operations strategy This concerns the pattern of strategic decisions and actions which set the role, objectives and activities of operations (Slack *et al.,* 2004)

Order point systems Inventory control systems for independent demand items that aim to determine when and how much to order from suppliers to ensure that stocks do not run out

Outsourcing One of the terms used to describe the process of obtaining inputs of goods or services from a source outside of the organization

Parent county national (PCN) Also termed an expatriate, an employee sent from an organization to work in a subsidiary based in another country

Performance measurement The process of quantifying the efficiency and effectiveness of actions

Performance measurement system A collection of performance measures used by an organization to assess the performance of various aspects of its activities

Performance standard The level of performance deemed suitable for use as the target level of performance against which to compare a particular aspect of performance

Person specification A list of the knowledge, experience and skills necessary for a person to be able to perform a particular job

Planning This is concerned with actions taken prior to an event, typically arranging for resources to be provided in order to achieve a desired outcome

Process technologies The tools (equipment, machines and other devices) used in operations that transform materials, information or customers

Psychometric tests Written tests that assess a person's aptitude and personality in a measured and structured way. Such tests are often used by employers as part of their recruitment and selection processes

Quality assurance This involves taking a proactive approach towards quality management by seeking to prevent defects ever being produced. This usually involves the adoption of a quality management system

Quality circle A group of workers who come together to solve quality and other related problems within their work area

Quality control An extension of quality inspection in that it uses data from inspection to identify causes of defects and to take corrective action

Quality function deployment (QFD) A structured procedure that aims to ensure that the design of products and services meets the needs of the customer. (QFD is sometimes also referred to as *the voice of the customer.*) It does so by forcing designers to match each customer requirement of the product with the way that the design meets that requirement. (QFD is sometimes also referred to as *the house of quality*)

Quality gap Any difference between customers' expectations of a product or service and their perceptions of their experience of it

Quality inspection The inspection and testing of the outputs from a transformation process to determine whether they are of saleable quality or if they should be rejected, reworked or downgraded for sale as 'seconds', normally at a lower price

Quality management system (QMS) A systematic approach to proactively managing quality based on documented standards and operating procedures. The best known QMSs are those based on the ISO9000 series of quality standards

Queuing theory The mathematical study of waiting lines

Re-intermediation The reintroduction of an intermediary in a supply chain. The growth of e-commerce has prompted the emergence of new kinds of intermediary in many industries

Resource seeking strategy A strategy in which operations are internationalized in order to access and serve markets outside of the home country

Scale Decisions about the scale of operations are concerned with what quantities of goods and services should be produced at any given facility

Scale of technology The processing capacity of a type of technology (rather than its physical size)

Scientific management A management led approach to job design that seeks to establish the best way of performing any task through a process of disaggregation and routinization, using methods such as work study

Scope Decisions about the scope of operations are concerned with what types of goods and services should be produced at any given facility

Self-managed work team Work team in which workers are empowered to take many of the decisions concerning their work without reference to management

Services The intangible outputs from an operation

Statistical quality control (SQC) The application of statistics to the management of quality

Strategy The direction and scope of an organization over the long-term, which achieves advantage in a changing environment through its configuration of resources with the aim of fulfilling stakeholder expectations (Johnson *et al.,* 2005)

Structure The structure of an organization is the way in which employees are formally divided into groups for co-ordination and control

Supply chain Alternative term for a supply network

Supply network The set of interconnected relationships between all the parties that supply inputs to, and receive outputs from an operation (including the suppliers' suppliers and their suppliers etc. And the customers' customers and their customers etc.)

Sustaining innovation An innovation based on the use of technology whose use is prevalent in the industry

Theory Z The term coined by Ouchi (1981) to describe the management style characteristic of many Japanese companies that combines various aspects of scientific management and behaviouralism. The term Theory Z is an attempt to associate this style with McGregor's Theory X and Theory Y construct

Third country national (TCN) A worker from a country other than the parent or host country

Three Es of performance measurement Economy, efficiency and effectiveness

Tier 1 supplier An immediate supplier to an organization, one that supplies directly to the organization. A tier 2 supplier supplies to a tier 1 supplier, and so on. The concept of tiers can also be applied to customers in the supply network. A tier 1 customer is one that is supplied directly from the organization's operations

Time to market The length of time taken to bring a new product to market. It is usually taken as the time from deciding to develop a new product to its market launch

Total quality management (TQM) A philosophy for quality improvement based on principles of the elimination of waste, continuous involvement and the involvement of all employees

Trade-off The concept based on the premise that it is impossible to excel simultaneously at all aspects of operations. This means that an operations strategy can only be successful if it is based upon a single clear goal, determined by a prioritization of operations performance objectives (e.g. cost, quality, speed, dependability and flexibility)

Transformation process The system by which inputs of resources (e.g. people, equipment, materials, energy, information) are converted into outputs of goods and services

Vertical integration The extent to which an organization owns the operations of the suppliers and customers within its supply network

Work centre A collection of resources (people, machines, etc.) assembled together to undertake specific work tasks

Work team A group of people who work together on a common task to achieve a specific goal or objective

Yield management A set of techniques aimed at maximizing income from customer service operations

INDEX